Peterson's

OFFICIAL GUIDE

TO MASTERING

DSST EXAMS

(PART II)

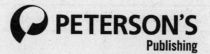

PETERSON'S
Publishing

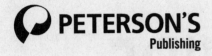

PETERSON'S
Publishing

About Peterson's Publishing

Peterson's Publishing provides the accurate, dependable, high-quality education content and guidance you need to succeed. No matter where you are on your academic or professional path, you can rely on Peterson's print and digital publications for the most up-to-date education exploration data, expert test-prep tools, and top-notch career success resources—everything you need to achieve your goals.

Visit us online at **www.petersonspublishing.com** and let Peterson's help you achieve your goals.

For more information, contact Peterson's, 2000 Lenox Drive, Lawrenceville, NJ 08648; 800-338-3282 Ext. 54229; or find us online at www.petersonspublishing.com.

Peterson's makes every reasonable effort to obtain from reliable sources accurate, complete, and timely information about the tests covered in this book. Nevertheless, changes can be made in the tests or the administration of the tests at any time and Peterson's makes no representation or warranty, either expressed or implied as to the accuracy, timeliness, or completeness of the information contained in this book.

© 2012 Peterson's, a Nelnet company

Facebook® and Facebook logos are registered trademarks of Facebook, Inc. Facebook, Inc. was not involved in the production of this book and makes no endorsement of this product.

Bernadette Webster, Director of Publishing; Mark D. Snider, Editor; Ray Golaszewski, Publishing Operations Manager; Linda M. Williams, Composition Manager; Reyna Eisenstark, Dina Ellsworth, Ph.D., Margaret C. Moran, Nomi J. Waldman, Contributing Writers, Practical Strategies, LLC

ISBN-13: 978-0-7689-3381-9
ISBN-10: 0-7689-3381-1

Printed in the United States of America

10 9 8 7 6 5 4 3 2 1   14 13 12

First Edition

By printing this book on recycled paper (40% post-consumer waste) 78 trees were saved.

Contents

Before You Begin ix
How This Book is Organized ix
Special Study Features xi
You're Well on Your Way to Success xii
Find Us on Facebook xii
Give Us Your Feedback...xii

About the DSST 1
What Is the DSST?..1
Why Take the DSST? 1
DSST Test Centers 4
How to Register for a DSST...4
Preparing for the DSST 4
Test Day 5

1   The Civil War and Reconstruction 7
Diagnostic Test 9
Answer Key and Explanations 12
Causes of the Civil War 15
1861 22
1862 24
1863 29
1864 to May 1865 34
Reconstruction 39
Post-Test...47
Answer Key and Explanations..56
Summing It Up 64

2   Introduction to World Religions 67
Diagnostic Test 69
Answer Key and Explanations...72
Definition and Origins of Religion...75
Indigenous Religions 76
Hinduism 79
Buddhism 81
Confucianism..83
Taoism 85
Judaism...86
Christianity 89
Islam 95
Religious Movements...97

Post-Test...103

Answer Key and Explanations...109

Summing It Up..116

3 Environment and Humanity **119**

Diagnostic Test..121

Answer Key and Explanations...123

Ecological Concepts 126

Environmental Impacts..139

Environmental Management and Conservation 142

Political Processes and the Future...149

Post-Test...153

Answer Key and Explanations...159

Summing It Up..168

4 Personal Finance **171**

Diagnostic Test..172

Answer Key and Explanations...175

Foundations of Personal Finance 178

Credit and Debt 180

Major Purchases...182

Taxes 190

Insurance 193

Investments..199

Retirement and Estate Planning..202

Post-Test...209

Answer Key and Explanations...216

Summing It Up..224

5 Human Resource Management...**227**

Diagnostic Test..229

Answer Key and Explanations...232

An Overview of the Human Resource Management Field 235

Human Resource Planning..237

Staffing..237

Training and Development..240

Performance Appraisals...242

Compensation Issues...243

Safety and Health..246

Employee Rights and Discipline 249

Employment Law..250

Labor Relations..251

International Human Resource Management 252

Current Issues and Trends..253

Post-Test...257

Answer Key and Explanations...265

Summing It Up..272

Contents

6 Organizational Behavior **275**
Diagnostic Test 279
Answer Key and Explanations.. 282
Organizational Behavior Overview 285
Individual Processes and Characteristics............................ 286
Interpersonal and Group Processes and Characteristics.............. 294
Organizational Processes and Characteristics 302
Change and Development Processes................................. 304
Post-Test.. 309
Answer Key and Explanations.. 316
Summing It Up 323

7 Introduction to Business **327**
Diagnostic Test 328
Answer Key and Explanations.. 331
Foundations of Business.. 334
Functions of Business... 341
Contemporary Issues.. 351
Post-Test.. 359
Answer Key and Explanations.. 366
Summing It Up 373

8 Here's to Your Health...**377**
Diagnostic Test 379
Answer Key and Explanations.. 382
Health, Wellness, and Mind/Body Connection 385
Human Development and Relationships 390
Substance Use and Abuse 398
Fitness and Nutrition.. 401
Risk Factors, Diseases, and Disease Prevention 404
Safety, Consumer Awareness, and Environmental Concerns.............. 409
Post-Test.. 415
Answer Key and Explanations.. 421
Summing It Up.. 428

Before You Begin

HOW THIS BOOK IS ORGANIZED

Peterson's Official Guide to Mastering DSST Exams (Part II) provides content outlines of test sections and subsections, diagnostic tests, post-tests, and subject matter reviews for eight different DSST tests. The following table provides a summary of the information covered in each chapter.

Chapter 1: The Civil War and Reconstruction	Background on societal differences between North and South, war campaigns from 1861 to 1865, significance of various battles, homefront and political situation during each phase of the war, costs of the war, federal Reconstruction policies, Southern responses
Chapter 2: Introduction to World Religions	Basic dimensions and approaches of religion; traditions of indigenous religions; the historical development, doctrine, and practice of major world religions; religious movements through history
Chapter 3: Environment and Humanity	Ecological concepts as background such as eco-systems, roles of organisms, population biology, and succession; environmental impacts such as human population growth and physical factors in global climate change; environmental management and conservation policies, including renewable and nonrenewable resources, agriculture, land use, water, wastes, recycling; political processes and ethics
Chapter 4: Personal Finance	Basic terminology and concepts such as setting financial goals and budgeting; consumer credit and bankruptcy; making major purchases; dealing with taxes; buying various types of insurance; saving and investing; planning for retirement and estate planning

Chapter 5: Human Resource Management	Functions and issues, various responsibilities and policies related to staffing, factors affecting training and development, techniques and issues related to performance appraisals, compensation procedures and issues, occupational health and safety issues, employee rights related to discipline and employment law, union procedures and issues, changing patterns in the workforce and workplace
Chapter 6: Organizational Behavior	Basic concepts; individual processes such as perception, personality, attitude, learning, motivation, and work stress; interpersonal and group processes such as group dynamics, group behavior and conflict, leadership, power and politics, and communication; organizational processes such as decision making, structure, and design; change and development processes including basic processes and concepts, and applications and techniques
Chapter 7: Introduction to Business	Basic concepts; functions including management, marketing, finance, accounting, production and operations, management information systems, and human resources; issues including e-commerce, ethics and social responsibility, and the global business environment
Chapter 8: Here's to Your Health	Basic concepts of physical and mental health; human development including reproduction, sexuality, intimacy, healthy aging, and death and bereavement; use and abuse of substances; components of physical fitness; factors and effects of good nutrition; diseases including infectious diseases, cancer, cardiovascular diseases, immune disorders, diabetes, arthritis, genetic-related disorders, and neurological disorders; safety; violence and intentional injuries; consumer and environmental concerns

Each chapter of the book is organized in the same manner:

- Content outline of test sections and subsections, including a comparison of the percentage of questions covered in the diagnostic test and post-test versus the actual exam
- Diagnostic Test—20 questions, followed by an answer key and explanations
- General subject overview and subject review
- Post-Test—60 questions, followed by an answer key and explanations

The content outline at the beginning of each chapter allows you to see the sections and subsection covered on the DSST exams. In each outline, there are three columns that offer helpful information on the number and percentages of questions covered in each section and subsection. The first column lists the percentage of questions covered for each section on the *actual* exam. The second column tells you how many test questions per section and subsection can be found in the chapter. The third column tells you the percent of practice questions per section and subsection in the chapter.

The purpose of the diagnostic test is to help you figure out what you know . . . or don't know. The 20 multiple-choice questions are similar to the ones found on the DSST, and they should provide you with a good idea of what to expect. Once you take the diagnostic test, check your answers to see how you did. Included with each correct answer is a brief explanation regarding why a specific answer is correct, and why other options are incorrect. In most instances, additional information has been added to the answers to increase their usefulness to you. Take note of the questions you miss, so that you can spend more time reviewing that information later. As with any exam, knowing your weak spots greatly improves your chances of success.

Following the diagnostic test in each chapter is a subject matter review. The review summarizes the various topics covered on the DSST exam. Key terms are defined, important concepts are explained, and, when appropriate, examples are provided. As you read the review, some of the information may seem familiar while other information may seem foreign. Again, take note of the unfamiliar because that will most likely cause you problems on the actual DSST. If you need more information about a topic than what the review provides, refer to one of the textbooks recommended for the test.

After studying the subject matter review, you should be ready for the post-test. The post-test for each chapter contains 60 multiple-choice items, and it will serve as a dry run for the real DSST. Take the time to answer all of the questions because they are similar to those found on the specific DSST exam you're studying. As with the diagnostic test, post-test answers and explanations are at the end of each chapter.

SPECIAL STUDY FEATURES

Peterson's Official Guide to Mastering DSST Exams (Part II) is designed to be as user-friendly as it is complete. To this end, it includes two features to make your preparation more efficient.

Overview

Each chapter has a bulleted overview listing the topics covered in the chapter. This will allow you to quickly target the areas in which you are most interested and need to review.

Summing It Up

Each review chapter ends with a point-by-point summary that captures the most important information in the chapter. The summaries offer a convenient way to review key points.

YOU'RE WELL ON YOUR WAY TO SUCCESS

You've made the decision to take the DSST and earn college credit for your life experiences. *Peterson's Official Guide to Mastering DSST Exams (Part II)* will help prepare you for the steps you'll need to achieve your goal—scoring high on the exam!

FIND US ON FACEBOOK

Join the DSST conversation by liking us on Facebook at facebook.com/petersonspublishing. Here you'll find additional test-prep tips and advice. Peterson's resources are available to help you do your best on these important exams—and others in your future.

GIVE US YOUR FEEDBACK

Peterson's publishes a full line of books—test prep, education exploration, financial aid, and career preparation. Peterson's publications can be found at high school guidance offices, college libraries and career centers, and your local bookstore or library. Peterson's books are now also available as eBooks.

We welcome any comments or suggestions you may have about this publication. Your feedback will help us make educational dreams possible for you—and others like you.

About the DSST

OVERVIEW

- What is the DSST?
- Why take the DSST?
- DSST test centers
- How to register for a DSST
- Preparing for the DSST
- Test day

WHAT IS THE DSST?

The DSST is a nationally accepted prior learning assessment program that enables individuals to earn college credit for knowledge they have acquired outside of the traditional university classroom. Experience gained through independent reading, work-related tasks, life experiences, or military training may provide you with the skills and qualifications needed to pass a DSST exam and receive college credit. The American Council of Education (ACE) suggests that colleges award 3 credit hours for passing scores on most DSST exams.

WHY TAKE THE DSST?

DSST exams, previously known as DANTES Subject Standardized Tests, offer a way for you to save both time and money in your quest for a college education. Why enroll in a college course in a subject you already understand? For over thirty years, the DSST program has offered the perfect solution for people who are knowledgeable in a specific subject and who want to save both time and money. A passing score on a DSST exam provides physical evidence to universities of proficiency in a specific subject. Nearly 2,000 accredited and respected colleges and universities across the nation award undergraduate credit for passing scores on DSST exams. With the DSST program, individuals can shave months off the time it takes to earn a degree.

The DSST program offers numerous advantages for people in all stages of their educational development:

- Adult learners
- College students
- Military personnel

1

Adult learners desiring college degrees face unique circumstances—demanding work schedules, family responsibilities, and tight budgets. Yet adult learners also have years of valuable work experience that can be applied toward a degree through the DSST program. For example, adult learners with on-the-job experience in business and management might be able to skip the Business 101 courses if they earn passing marks on DSST exams such as *Introduction to Business* and *Human Resource Management*. Adult learners can put their prior learning into action and move forward with more advanced course work.

Adults who have never enrolled in a college course may feel a little uncertain about their abilities. If this describes your situation, then sign up for a DSST exam and see how you do. A passing score may be the boost you need to realize your dream of earning a degree.

With family and work commitments, adult learners often feel they lack the time to attend college. The DSST program enables adult learners the unique opportunity to work toward college degrees without the time constraints of semester-long course work. DSST exams take 2 hours or less to complete, so in one weekend, you could earn credit for multiple college courses.

The DSST exams also benefit students who are already enrolled in a college or university. With college tuition costs on the rise, most students face financial challenges. The fee for each DSST exam is $80 plus administration fees charged by most testing facilities—significantly less than the average cost of a 3-hour college class, which may be $300 or higher. Maximize tuition assistance by taking DSST exams for introductory or mandatory course work. Once you earn a passing score on a DSST exam, you are free to move on to higher-level course work in that subject matter, take desired electives, or focus on courses in a chosen major.

Not only do students and adult learners profit from DSST exams, but military personnel reap the benefits as well. If you are a member of the armed services at home or abroad, you can initiate your post-military career by taking DSST exams in areas with which you have experience. Military personnel can gain credit anywhere in the world, thanks to the fact that almost all of the tests are available through the Internet at designated testing locations. DSST testing facilities are located at over 500 military installations, so service members on active duty can get a jump-start on a post-military career with the DSST program. As an additional incentive, DANTES provides funding for Internet-based DSST test fees for eligible civilians and members of the military.

Thirty-eight subject matter tests are available in the fields of Math, the Social Sciences, the Humanities, Business, Physical Science, and Technology.

NOTE: DANTES does not fund paper-and-pencil DSST testing at national test centers. Also, DANTES no longer funds retesting on previously funded DSST exam titles.

AVAILABLE DSST EXAMS

Business	Social Sciences
Business Ethics and Society	Art of the Western World
Business Law II	The Civil War and Reconstruction
Business Mathematics	Criminal Justice
Human Resource Management	Foundations of Education
Introduction to Business	Fundamentals of Counseling
Introduction to Computing	General Anthropology
Management Information Systems	A History of the Vietnam War
Money and Banking	Human/Cultural Geography
Organizational Behavior	Introduction to Law Enforcement
Personal Finance	Introduction to the Modern Middle East
Principles of Finance	Lifespan Developmental Psychology
Principles of Financial Accounting	Rise and Fall of the Soviet Union
Principles of Supervision	Substance Abuse
	Western Europe Since 1945
Humanities	*Physical Science*
Ethics in America	Astronomy
Introduction to World Religions	Environment and Humanity
Principles of Public Speaking	Here's to Your Health
	Physical Geology
	Principles of Physical Science I
Math	*Technology*
Fundamentals of College Algebra	Technical Writing
Principles of Statistics	

As you can see from the table, the DSST program covers a wide variety of subjects. However, it is important to ask two questions before registering for a DSST exam.

- Which universities or colleges award credit for passing DSST exams?
- Which DSST exams are the most relevant to my desired degree and my experience?

Knowing which universities offer DSST credit is important information to uncover. In all likelihood, a college in your area awards credit for DSST exams, but find out before taking an exam by contacting the university directly. Second, review the list of DSST exams to determine which ones are most relevant to the degree you are seeking and to your base of knowledge. Schedule an appointment with your college advisor to determine which exams best fit your degree program and which college courses the

DSST exams can replace. Advisors should also be able to tell you the minimum score required on the DSST exam to receive university credit.

DSST TEST CENTERS

You can find DSST testing locations in community colleges and universities across the country. Contact your local college or university to find out if the school administers DSST exams, or check the DSST Web site (www.getcollegecredit.com) for a location near you. Keep in mind that some universities and colleges only administer DSST exams to enrolled students. DSST testing is available to men and women in the armed services at over 500 military installations around the world.

HOW TO REGISTER FOR A DSST

Once you have located a nearby DSST testing facility, you need to contact the testing center to find out the exam administration schedule. Many centers are set up to administer tests via the Internet, while others use printed materials. Almost all DSST exams are available as online tests, but the method used depends on the testing center. Each DSST exam costs $80, and most testing locations charge a fee to cover their costs for administering the tests. Credit cards are the only accepted payment method for taking online DSST exams. Credit card, certified check, and money order are acceptable payment methods for paper-and-pencil tests.

Test-takers are allotted two score reports—one mailed to them and another mailed to a designated college or university if requested. Online tests generate unofficial scores at the end of the test session, where as individuals taking paper tests must wait four to six weeks for score reports.

PREPARING FOR THE DSST

Even though you are knowledgeable in a certain subject matter, you should still prepare for the test to ensure you achieve the highest score possible. The first step in studying for a DSST exam is to find out what will be on the specific test you have chosen. Information regarding test content is located on the DSST fact sheets, which can be downloaded at no cost from www.getcollegecredit.com. Each fact sheet outlines the topics covered on a subject matter test as well as the approximate percentage assigned to each topic. For example, questions on the *Introduction to Business* exam break down in the following way: 25 percent on the foundations of business, 60 percent on the functions of business, and 15 percent on contemporary issues.

In addition to the breakdown of topics on a DSST exam, the fact sheet also lists recommended reference materials. If you do not own the recommended books, then check college bookstores. Avoid paying high prices for new textbooks by looking online for used textbooks. Don't panic if you are unable to locate a specific textbook listed on the fact sheet because the textbooks are merely recommendations. Instead, search for comparable books used in university courses on the specific subject. Current editions are ideal, and it is a good idea to use at least two references when studying for a DSST exam. Of course, the subject matter provided in this book will be a sufficient review for most test-takers. However, if you need additional information, then it is a good idea to have some of the reference materials at your disposal when preparing for the DSST.

Fact sheets include other useful pieces of information besides a list of reference materials and topics. On each fact sheet, you will find a few samples of questions found on the DSST exam in the specific subject matter. The samples provide an idea of the type of questions you can expect on the exam. Test questions are multiple choice with one correct answer and three incorrect choices. The fact sheet also includes information about the number of credit hours that ACE has recommended be awarded by colleges for a passing score on the DSST. However, you should keep in mind that not all universities and colleges adhere to the ACE recommendation for DSST credit hours. Some institutions require DSST exam scores higher than the minimum score recommended by ACE. Once you have acquired appropriate reference materials and you have the outline provided on the fact sheet, you are ready to start studying, which is when this book can help.

TEST DAY

After reviewing the material and taking practice tests, you are finally ready to take the DSST. As with any exam, preparation is the key to a successful test experience. Prepare to do the following four things on the day of the test:

1. **Arrive early.** Be sure to leave enough time to get to the testing site at least fifteen minutes early. In case there's a traffic tie-up, you won't be sitting in your car or on the bus or subway worrying. Being early also ensures you'll have enough time to take care of check-in procedures and settle into your surroundings.

2. **Bring identification.** DSST test facilities require that candidates bring a valid government-issued identification card with a current photo and signature. Acceptable forms of identification include a current driver's license, passport, military identification card, or state-issued identification card. Individuals who fail to bring proper identification to the DSST testing facility will not be allowed to take an exam.

3. **Bring the right supplies.** If you are taking the paper-and-pencil test, you will need to bring several sharpened No. 2 pencils with erasers and a black pen if an essay section is included on the exam. You should also bring a watch since the tests are timed. However, do not bring a watch with a beeping alarm. If you are taking the test online, you will have time to review how the test software works before the timed test begins. Cell phones, books, and papers are not allowed inside the testing center. For some tests, candidates are allowed to use non-programmable calculators, slide rules, and scratch paper, but you should double check with the test administrator when you arrive.

4. **Take the test.** During the exam, take the time to read each question and answer option carefully. Eliminate the choices you know are incorrect to narrow the number of potential answers. If a question completely stumps you, take an educated guess and move on—remember that the DSST is a timed test; you will have 2 hours to take the exam.

With the proper preparation, DSST exams will save you both time and money. So join the thousands of people who have already reaped the benefits of DSST exams and move closer than ever to your college degree.

The Civil War and Reconstruction

The following chart outlines the sections and subsections in The Civil War and Reconstruction test and offers a comparison between the percent of practice questions in this chapter and the actual DSST exam.

CONTENT OUTLINE: SECTIONS AND SUBSECTIONS	PERCENT OF EXAM DEVOTED TO EACH CONTENT AREA	NUMBER OF ITEMS IN THE DIAGNOSTIC TEST AND POST-TEST BY CONTENT AREA	PERCENT OF ITEMS IN THE DIAGNOSTIC TEST AND POST-TEST BY CONTENT AREA
I. Causes of the War	**11%**	**16**	**20%**
A. United States Society in the Mid-Nineteenth Century		2	12.5%
B. Growing Differences Between the North and South		2	12.5%
C. Slavery as a Southern Institution: Importance of Cotton		3	18.75%
D. Abolition Movement: Leaders and Methods		1	6.25%
E. Westward Expansion of Free and Slave Territory		5	31.25%
F. John Brown's Raid on Harper's Ferry		2	12.5%
G. Political Situation in 1860: Republican and Democratic Parties, Abraham Lincoln, and Election Results		1	6.25%
II. 1861	**11%**	**9**	**11.25%**
A. Secession: South Carolina, Confederate Government, and Border States		4	45%
B. Fort Sumter		2	22%
C. Union Army vs. Confederate Army		2	22%
D. First Manassas (Bull Run)		1	11%
III. 1862	**22%**	**14**	**17.5%**
A. Political Situation in the North and South		3	21.5%
B. Army of Potomac Under McClellan		2	14.25%
C. War in the West		1	7%
D. War in the East		2	14.25%
E. Major Battles of 1862		3	21.5%
F. Emancipation Proclamation		3	21.5%
IV. 1863	**21%**	**15**	**18.75%**
A. Casualties		4	26.7%
B. Role of Women in the War		1	6.6%
C. Black Americans and the War: Free Volunteers		3	20%
D. Political Situation		3	20%
E. Major Battles of 1863		4	26.7%

V. 1864 to May 1865	**22%**	**12**	**15%**
A. Political Situation: Northern Demoralization and Presidential Election		1	8.34%
B. War in the West		3	25%
C. War in the East		1	8.34%
D. Sherman's Continued March Through the South: Destruction of the Civilian Base and Logistics		1	8.34%
E. Fall of Richmond and the Flight of Confederate Government		1	8.34%
F. Lee's Surrender		1	8.34%
G. Assassination of Lincoln		1	8.34%
H. End of the Confederacy: Johnston's Surrender		1	8.34%
I. Cost of the War: Human, Economic, and Cultural		2	16.62%
VI. Reconstruction	**13%**	**14**	**17.5%**
A. Presidential Reconstruction Plans		3	21.4%
B. Congressional Reconstruction Plans		4	28.6%
C. Reconstruction in the South: Response to Johnson's Policies		5	35.7%
D. End of Reconstruction: Restoration of White Government		2	14.3%
Grand Total	**100%**	**80**	**100%**

OVERVIEW

- **Diagnostic test**
- **Answer key and explanations**
- **Causes of the Civil War**
- **1861**
- **1862**
- **1863**
- **1864 to May 1865**
- **Reconstruction**
- **Post-test**
- **Answer key and explanations**
- **Summing it up**

DIAGNOSTIC TEST

Directions: Carefully read each of the following 20 questions. Choose the best answer to each question and circle your answer choice. The Answer Key and Explanations can be found following this Diagnostic Test.

1. By about 1860, the South
   - **(A)** had fewer slaves than it had a century earlier.
   - **(B)** supplied nearly three quarters of the cotton for British textile industries.
   - **(C)** was mostly made up of large cotton plantations.
   - **(D)** wanted to make slavery legal in the North.

2. *Uncle Tom's Cabin* was
   - **(A)** a novel that supported the right of Southerners to own slaves.
   - **(B)** a factual account of one man's escape from slavery.
   - **(C)** an antislavery novel meant to convince Northerners to support abolitionism.
   - **(D)** an abolitionist tract written by publisher William Lloyd Garrison.

3. Former Confederate General Joseph E. Johnston is quoted as saying that Lincoln's assassination was "the greatest possible calamity" for the South. He and others felt this way because
   - **(A)** the South would be blamed for the death.
   - **(B)** the Radical Republicans would now be free to exact harsh terms on the South.
   - **(C)** they admired Lincoln.
   - **(D)** they thought former enslaved African Americans would riot in Southern cities.

4. In total, how many battle casualties—wounded and killed—did the North and South have during the Civil War?
   - **(A)** 250,000
   - **(B)** 350,000
   - **(C)** 500,000
   - **(D)** More than 1 million

5. John Brown's goal for his raid on Harpers Ferry was to

   (A) help slaves escape to the North.

   (B) create the independent state of West Virginia.

   (C) overthrow the national government.

   (D) invade the South and abolish slavery.

6. At the start of the Civil War, what was one advantage the South had?

   (A) The South grew most of the country's food and was well-equipped to feed a large army.

   (B) The South had well-trained and experienced officers.

   (C) The South had a much more developed railroad system, which would allow for easier transport of supplies.

   (D) The South had a larger and better-trained navy.

7. What is the significance of First Manassas, also known as Bull Run?

   (A) It was the first Union victory in the Civil War.

   (B) It was the only Civil War battle to take place deep in Northern territory.

   (C) It was the worst defeat of the Confederacy.

   (D) It was the first major battle of the Civil War.

8. What did the Emancipation Proclamation do?

   (A) It freed all slaves in the border states.

   (B) It freed slaves in those Southern states that had seceded from the Union and had not been retaken by Union forces.

   (C) It freed slaves in Southern areas that had been retaken by Union forces.

   (D) It made slavery illegal in the United States.

9. The Copperheads were

   (A) conservative Southern Democrats who regained control of state governments during Reconstruction.

   (B) a group of Northern Democrats who sympathized with the Confederacy.

   (C) Union loyalists in the western portion of Virginia who kept the area from joining the Confederacy.

   (D) another name for Free-Soilers.

10. Who became President in the election of 1876?

    (A) Samuel J. Tilden

    (B) Ulysses S. Grant

    (C) Rutherford B. Hayes

    (D) William T. Sherman

11. After the Civil War, white Southerners

    (A) accepted black voting rights.

    (B) still believed blacks should not be allowed to vote.

    (C) supported the Republican Party.

    (D) accepted political, but not economic rights for blacks.

12. What was the significance of the Union victory at Vicksburg?

    (A) Vicksburg was the last major Confederate stronghold on the Mississippi River.

    (B) Vicksburg forced Lee's Confederate troops to surrender to Grant because their supply lines had been cut.

    (C) Lee was never able to mount another major offensive against the Northern army.

    (D) Sherman burned Vicksburg to the ground, eliminating a major center of commerce for the Confederacy.

13. Which of the following was one of the terms of surrender at the end of the war?

    (A) Confederate soldiers were to be imprisoned until they swore loyalty to the Union.

    (B) Lee's troops would become part of the U.S. army.

    (C) Ordinary soldiers could take their hand guns.

    (D) Confederate soldiers were allowed to go home.

14. Who was the initial commander of the Army of the Potomac?

    (A) Robert E. Lee

    (B) George B. McClellan

    (C) Don Carlos Buell

    (D) Philip Sheridan

15. The Fifteenth Amendment was passed to

    (A) abolish slavery.

    (B) guarantee all citizens equal rights before the law.

    (C) enable freed slaves to exercise the same rights as white citizens.

    (D) guarantee the right of all male citizens to vote regardless of race.

16. By March 1864, General Ulysses S. Grant planned to win the war

    (A) by causing cotton prices to drop.

    (B) by wearing down the Confederate army.

    (C) by sinking Confederate ships.

    (D) with the assistance promised by Great Britain.

17. What was an immediate result of the Confederate attack on Fort Sumter?

    (A) The Southern states organized the Confederate States of America.

    (B) Virginia, North Carolina, Tennessee, and Arkansas seceded from the Union.

    (C) South Carolina became the first state to secede from the Union.

    (D) General George McClellan was appointed commander of the Army of the Potomac.

18. Reconstruction came to an end with

    (A) the success of the Ku Klux Klan.

    (B) the defeat of Grant for President in 1876.

    (C) the Compromise of 1877.

    (D) passage of the Fifteenth Amendment.

19. The major cause of military deaths on both sides in the war was

    (A) disease.

    (B) harsh treatment in prisoner of war camps.

    (C) untended wounds received in battle.

    (D) mortal wounds suffered in battle.

20. What was the *Virginia*?

    (A) A former Union ship that had been repurposed for the Confederate navy

    (B) The first Confederate warship to be sunk in the Civil War

    (C) A battleship that the British had sold to the Confederacy

    (D) A Confederate wooden ship that could not withstand the damage from the ironclad Union ship *Monitor*

ANSWER KEY AND EXPLANATIONS

1. B	5. D	9. B	13. D	17. B
2. C	6. B	10. C	14. B	18. C
3. B	7. D	11. B	15. D	19. A
4. D	8. B	12. A	16. B	20. A

1. **The correct answer is (B).** By about 1860, the South provided 70 percent of the cotton for the British textile industry. The South in 1860 was made up of mostly small plantations and had more slaves than it had in the previous century, so choices (A) and (C) are incorrect. Choice (D) is incorrect because making slavery legal in the North was not an aim of the South. Southerners wanted to be able to extend slavery westward as they moved west.

2. **The correct answer is (C).** *Uncle Tom's Cabin* was written by abolitionist Harriet Beecher Stowe, so choice (D) is incorrect. In addition, it was a novel, not a tract. Her purpose in writing the novel in 1852 was to protest slavery and the Fugitive Slave Act that had been passed two years earlier. Stowe also intended her book to bring more Northerners to the cause of abolition. Choice (A) is incorrect because the novel was written to protest slavery. Choice (B) is incorrect because it was about enslaved people on a plantation.

3. **The correct answer is (B).** A number of Southerners, Johnston among them, feared that with Lincoln dead, no one would be able to keep the Radical Republicans from legislating harsh terms for the readmission of Southern states to the Union. Their fears turned out to be true. Choices (A) and (D) are incorrect. Some Southerners might have respected and even admired Lincoln, choice (C), but this was not the reason for their concern over his assassination.

4. **The correct answer is (D).** Together, the North and South had more than 1 million casualties. The North alone lost 365,000 soldiers and the South, 256,000. In choices (A), (B), and (C), the numbers are too low.

5. **The correct answer is (D).** John Brown's ultimate goal was to abolish slavery, and in 1859, he planned a raid that would eventually spark a violent revolt of slaves across the South. Brown's goal was not to help slaves escape to the North, but to destroy slavery, so choice (A) is incorrect. Choice (B) is incorrect because the western part of Virginia did not split from Virginia until the Civil War. Choice (C), an overthrow of the national government, is incorrect because Brown's goal was to overthrow slavery.

6. **The correct answer is (B).** The Confederate army had a well-trained and experienced set of officers, many of whom—like Robert E. Lee—had attended West Point or other military academies. Choice (A) is incorrect because the major crops of the South were cotton, tobacco, and rice. The South did not have a well-developed railroad system, so choice (C) is incorrect. The South did not have a navy of its own, so choice (D) is incorrect.

7. **The correct answer is (D).** First Manassas (Bull Run), which took place in July 1861, was the first major battle of the Civil War. Fort Donelson, February 1862—quickly followed by the battle to take Fort Henry—was the first Union victory, so choice (A) is incorrect. Choice (B) is incorrect because Gettysburg was the only battle to take place

deep in Northern soil. Choice (C) is incorrect because First Manassas was a decisive victory for the Confederacy.

8. **The correct answer is (B).** The Emancipation Proclamation of 1863 declared free all slaves in states that had seceded from the Union and had not been retaken by federal forces. It did not free slaves in the border states because those states had not seceded from the Union, nor did it abolish slavery, so choices (A) and (D) are incorrect. Choice (C) is incorrect because the Emancipation Proclamation did not free slaves in areas that the Union forces had not as yet retaken.

9. **The correct answer is (B).** Copperheads, also known as Peace Democrats, believed that the Republicans had provoked the South into seceding and wanted a negotiated peace. Choice (A) is incorrect because Southern Democrats who regained control of state governments were self-styled Redeemers. Choice (C) is incorrect because Copperheads were not Union loyalists in western Virginia. Choice (D) is incorrect because Copperheads and Free-Soilers were not the same; the latter were members of the Free-Soil Party who wanted to keep slavery out of new territories.

10. **The correct answer is (C).** Democrat Rutherford B. Hayes was eventually elected President in the election of 1876, even though Samuel J. Tilden, the Democratic Presidential candidate, won the popular vote. Choices (A), (B), and (D) are incorrect. Grant won the Presidency in 1868 and 1872, and Tilden and Sherman were never elected President.

11. **The correct answer is (B).** Southerners in general did not accept the idea of equal rights for African Americans, and some groups tried to prevent them from voting, so choices (A) and (D) are incorrect. Choice (D) is also incorrect because white Southerners in general did not accept economic rights for African Americans either. Choice (C) is incorrect because white Southerners became

Democrats, because Republicans were seen as the party of Lincoln, the end of slavery, and Radical Reconstruction policies.

12. **The correct answer is (A).** With the fall of Vicksburg, the Union had control of the Mississippi. Choice (B) is incorrect because while Lee needed supplies, he surrendered at Appomattox, not Vicksburg, because it was futile to continue fighting in the face of the superior numbers of Union forces and their position. Choice (C) is not true. Choice (D) is incorrect because Sherman burned Atlanta, not Vicksburg.

13. **The correct answer is (D).** One of the terms of surrender was that Confederate soldiers would be allowed to go home. Choice (A) is the opposite of what was true. Choice (B) is incorrect for the same reason. Choice (C) is incorrect because officers could keep their handguns, but not ordinary soldiers who typically had rifles and bayonets.

14. **The correct answer is (B).** McClellan was the initial commander of the Union's Army of the Potomac. Choice (A) is incorrect because Lee commanded the Army of Northern Virginia for the Confederacy. Choice (C) is incorrect because Buell fought in the West as commander of the Army of the Ohio. Choice (D) is incorrect because Sheridan was in charge of the Shenandoah Valley campaign at the end of the war.

15. **The correct answer is (D).** Congress passed the Fifteenth Amendment in response to Southern attempts to prevent African American men from voting. Choice (A) is incorrect because it describes the Thirteenth Amendment. Choice (B) is incorrect because it describes the Fourteenth Amendment. Choice (C) is incorrect because it describes the Civil Rights Act of 1866.

16. **The correct answer is (B).** When Grant took over as commander of all Union armies, his plan was to fight until he wore out the Confederate army. Choices (A) and (C) don't make sense as activities of an army general.

Choice (D) is incorrect because it was the Confederacy that needed help—that never came—from Great Britain.

17. **The correct answer is (B).** After Confederate forces attacked Fort Sumter, forcing a Union retreat, four more states—Virginia, North Carolina, Tennessee, and Arkansas—seceded from the Union. South Carolina had already seceded, so choice (C) is incorrect. Choice (A) is incorrect because the Confederacy was organized on February 4, 1861. Choice (D) is incorrect because McClellan was given command of the Army of the Potomac in July 1861.

18. **The correct answer is (C).** Reconstruction ended with the Compromise of 1877, in which Republican Rutherford B. Hayes was awarded the electoral votes needed to become President in exchange for a promise that all federal troops would be withdrawn from the South. Choice (B) is incorrect because Grant did not run for reelection in 1876. Choice (A) is incorrect because while

powerful in some areas of the South, the Ku Klux Klan was not powerful enough to end Reconstruction, which required a political act. The Fifteenth Amendment, choice (D), is incorrect because it dealt with the voting rights of African Americans, not with Reconstruction.

19. **The correct answer is (A).** More soldiers died of disease in the Civil War than from wounds received in battle, so choices (B), (C), and (D) are incorrect.

20. **The correct answer is (A).** The *Virginia,* a sunken Union ship named the *Merrimac,* had been salvaged by the Confederacy, covered in iron, and used by the Confederates. It fought the Union's *Monitor* to a draw. Choice (B) is incorrect because it wasn't sunk. Choice (C) is incorrect because the ship had belonged to the U.S. Navy, not Great Britain. Choice (D) is incorrect because the two ships fought to a draw; neither ship could sink the other.

CAUSES OF THE CIVIL WAR

The differences between North and South had been evident since the first colonists—gold seekers in Virginia Colony and devout Puritans in Massachusetts Bay—set foot on land. These differences were tempered by the desire of colonists to forge a united front against Great Britain, but as the nineteenth century wore on, the disparity between the regions widened and deepened.

United States Society in the Mid-Nineteenth Century

By the middle of the nineteenth century, about two thirds of the U.S. population lived and worked on farms, but industry was becoming more important as farmers turned from growing crops and raising animals for their own use to commercial agriculture. Mid-century also saw a huge increase in immigration and with it a new cultural diversity.

Sectional differences emerged and hardened during this period. For a variety of reasons, the Northeast became the center of a rapidly developing industrial economy and forged close ties with the new states of the Midwest. These economic and socio-cultural connections underlined and magnified the growing political differences with the South.

Industrialization

At the beginning of the nineteenth century, the United States was a mostly rural and agricultural country. Generally, people lived on farms or in small villages. By the 1820s, however, the U.S. economy began to change as a result of industrialization, first slowly and then rapidly. The development of steamboats, canals, and railroads reduced the cost of shipping goods to market, speeded communication, and increased agricultural and industrial production as demand for goods and food-stuffs grew. At the same time, the number of city dwellers rose from about 7 percent of the nation's population to slightly less than 20 percent by 1860. This was an increase greater than during any other era in U.S. history and was due in part to the increased demand for laborers in urban factories and in part to immigration.

Immigration

During the mid-nineteenth century, immigration also increased sharply. Between 1820 and 1860, some 4.6 million immigrants came to the United States, most after 1840. From a low of about 20,000 in 1820, the numbers jumped to a high of 430,000 in 1854 and tapered off during the rest of the decade. Most immigrants came from Ireland and Germany. The Irish tended to stay in Northeast cities and look for work in factories or as laborers, whereas Germans tended to settle in the Midwest and take up farming.

A variety of push and pull forces specific to ethnic or national groups spurred the rise in immigration. For the Irish, push factors included the potato famine and religious and cultural persecution by British overlords. The growing U.S. economy, which created opportunities for anyone willing to work hard, was the chief pull force.

With immigration came a new religious diversity. Irish immigrants were predominantly Roman Catholic and were especially discriminated against in housing and employment in the mid-nineteenth century because of their religion. Riots against them and church and convent burnings occurred in a few Northern cities during this period. These were carried out by native-born Americans who felt threatened by the immigrants and what they perceived as their alien and potentially dangerous influence on U.S. institutions and values.

Religiosity

By 1860, nearly 80 percent of Americans went to church regularly and religion was influential on secular society. The Southern defense of slavery, for example, was largely formulated by Protestant clergymen and predicated on a supposed biblical validity of the institution. Northern church leaders were instrumental in a variety of reform movements of the day, including abolitionism and temperance. Churches also served as vehicles for social welfare and assistance to the poor.

Standard of Living and Demographics

At the beginning of the nineteenth century, self-employed farmers and artisans made up 90 percent of the free workforce. By mid-century, about 50 percent of white males no longer owned property. They were either factory workers or laborers and belonged to the lower economic class of wage earners or they worked in stores or offices for salaries and belonged to the rising middle class. Professional men such as doctors belonged to the middle class as well. Those who continued to own and work farms in the North or Midwest found their fortunes rising and falling on commodity prices.

In the South, the richest plantation owners lived well, but not as well as wealthy Northern industrialists. These large plantation owners and their families made up a tiny minority of Southerners and as the century wore on, they found themselves in increasing debt. Next came middle-class professionals such as lawyers and doctors and merchants. However, most Southerners worked small farms with five or fewer enslaved workers or with no help other than family members. The latter group scraped by on a subsistence level.

The total U.S. population in 1860 was 31,443,321. This was an increase of over 8 million, or 35.6 percent, from the 1850 Census. About 19.8 percent were urban dwellers and 80.2 percent lived in rural areas.

Of the total population of more than 31 million, 3,950,528, or 13 percent, were enslaved Africans. Most were in Southern states, though slavery was legal in the southern tier of territories. The Census counted 5,155,608 families living in the United States, and of these, 393,975, or 8 percent of the populations, were slave owners.

Growing Differences Between the North and South

By 1860, the economies of the North and the South had radically diverged. The geography of much of the South encouraged the development of large-scale agriculture, first, tobacco, rice, and indigo along the eastern coastal plains and later, cotton in the Deep South and west. The South became dependent on the production of cotton and the use of slave labor. Raw cotton could be processed in greater quantities after Eli Whitney's invention of the cotton gin in the 1790s. That invention plus the use of slave labor spread cotton production across the South and into western areas like Texas. By the mid-1800s, the South grew 60 percent of the world's cotton and provided 70 percent of the raw material for the British textile industry.

At the same time, northern factories manufactured nine tenths of the industrial goods produced in the United States. The North had five times the number of factories as the South and over ten times the number of factory workers. In addition, the North was the center of the nation's finance and commerce. Besides being more industrialized than the South, the North had better transportation systems. By 1860, an extensive railroad system stretched across the Northeast and through the Upper Midwest. In the South, however, disputes between states prevented the construction of major railroad systems across the region. Southern planters and farmers relied on the extensive waterway system, including the Mississippi River, and access to the coast to ship their goods to market.

Perhaps the greatest difference was political and centered on slavery.

Slavery as a Southern Institution: Importance of Cotton

In the South, slavery spread as the economic need for it increased. By 1860, cotton had become the South's most important crop. Cotton exports amounted to more than 50 percent annually of all U.S. exports. Cotton over time depletes the soil of nutrients, so cotton planters moved westward to new land. As more and more Southerners moved west and cleared land to grow cotton, the demand for slaves grew. Most slave labor in the South was used for planting, cultivating, and harvesting single crops on plantations, including rice and tobacco in the Upper South and cotton in the Deep South. Although large slaveholders were few in number, they owned most of the South's enslaved African Americans. Over half of all slaves lived on plantations with 20 or more slaves, and a quarter lived on plantations with more than 50 slaves.

After 1830, white Southerners began to defend slavery as a natural part of society. They argued that it created a beneficial hierarchical institution superior to the democratic society of the North that forced factory workers to find and pay for their own housing, food, and clothing. Many Southerners also defended slavery on racial grounds, claiming that blacks were inferior to whites. By the 1850s, a growing number of Northerners believed that Southerners threatened to subvert basic American ideals of liberty and equality. At the same time, Southerners felt that their interests were not being addressed by the northern-dominated Congress. The threat of ending slavery had the potential to reduce the wealth of many Southerners and also interfered with what they believed were their "property" rights.

Living Conditions of Slaves

On the largest plantations, which were like small villages, some slaves also worked as carpenters, blacksmiths, cabinet makers, and bricklayers. A few worked in the plantation house as cooks and maids or butler and footmen. However, most—both male and female, adults, and children—were field hands. They typically worked ten hours a day, six days a week. The hardest work came during planting and harvesting seasons, when the workday could last 15 hours. Most field hands lived in small one-room cabins in an area called the "slave quarters." Some had small gardens where they grew vegetables to supplement their diets. Generally, slave owners used harsh punishments to control slaves, including whipping, and for those who ran away, branding.

Abolition Movement: Leaders and Methods

In the late 1700s, the Religious Society of Friends, or Quakers, became the first group to organize opposition to slavery. In 1775, Quaker abolitionist Anthony Benezet founded the world's first anti-slavery society. In 1787, it became the Pennsylvania Society for Promoting the Abolition of Slavery. Most abolitionists were white, and the largest number was concentrated in New England. As the movement grew in the 1800s, many women joined.

Early abolitionists adopted the concept of gradualism, believing slavery should be phased out slowly so that the economy of the South would not be disrupted. Gradualists also believed that blacks were inferior to whites. This led to the formation of the American Colonization Society, which proposed to purchase slaves, free them, and send them to a colony in Africa that would be established for this purpose. Abolitionists who believed that free blacks could not easily enter U.S. society saw this as the solution to the problem of what to do with freed blacks if slavery were ended. Although the colony of Liberia was established in 1822 and some African Americans emigrated there, by the late 1820s, it became obvious that colonization was impractical. The Society could not afford to purchase nearly 4 million slaves, and very few African Americans wanted to move to Africa. Many recognized colonization as a way for the United States to rid itself of its black population.

By the 1830s, the U.S. abolitionist movement had changed its focus, mostly because of the leadership of speaker, editor, and publisher William Lloyd Garrison. He demanded immediatism, the immediate end to slavery and establishment of equal rights for all African Americans. Garrison helped found the American Anti-Slavery Society in 1833, and following his lead, hundreds of antislavery societies were created in the North.

In the 1840s, the abolitionist movement split again with Garrison and his followers championing the most radical view. They believed that men should refuse to hold political office, vote, or use the courts until slavery was ended. Any government that upheld slavery by allowing it to continue should be shunned. On the other side were abolitionist leaders who determined to use politics. Some, like members of the Free-Soil Party and the Liberty Party, wanted to prevent slavery from spreading westward rather than to abolish it. Others wanted to use political means to end slavery.

Among those who became powerful speakers against slavery were ex-slaves Sojourner Truth and Frederick Douglass.

Many white women were drawn to the antislavery cause in the 1830s and 1840s because of strong religious or moral principles. Some women joined the movement because, like both enslaved and free blacks, white women were denied many political and economic rights. Among the women who became prominent in antislavery circles were the Southern sisters, Sarah and Angelina Grimké. In 1837, Sarah wrote about the similarities between women and slaves.

Uncle Tom's Cabin

By the late 1850s, the abolitionist movement had reached its peak as an increasing number of Northerners began to oppose slavery. In 1852, abolitionist and author Harriet Beecher Stowe published the novel *Uncle Tom's Cabin*. Stowe's book was written to protest the Fugitive Slave Act of 1850. This law required that all runaway slaves, regardless of where they were found, be returned to their owners. This meant that any formerly enslaved person could be forced back into slavery. Stowe also hoped to bring more Northerners to the cause of abolition through her novel.

With *Uncle Tom's Cabin*, Stowe introduced the brutal reality of slavery to many Americans. Stowe felt that though Northerners were not slave owners, they supported slavery by allowing it to exist. *Uncle Tom's Cabin* became one of the best-selling books of the nineteenth century. Most Southerners, however, were outraged by the book and claimed that it was untrue.

Westward Expansion of Free and Slave Territory

As the United States continued to expand westward, the question of whether to allow slavery to exist in new territories—and ultimately new states—became a topic of much debate in both the North and South.

The Missouri Compromise

In 1803, the United States had purchased a huge tract of land from France, the Louisiana Territory that extended west from the Mississippi River all the way to the Rocky Mountains. Any territory applying to be a new state after this time would tip the balance in Congress toward free states or slave states, depending on whether the territory entered as a free state or a slave state. In 1820, Speaker of the House Henry Clay proposed what became known as the Missouri Compromise, or the Compromise of 1820. All territory north of the southern boundary of Missouri, except Missouri itself, would be free, and all the territory below that line be considered a slave state. At the same time, Missouri could enter the Union as a slave state, if Maine entered as a free state. The Missouri Compromise also stipulated that if fugitive slaves escaped north of the compromise line, they could be caught and returned to their owners.

The Mexican War

Texas was part of the Mexican borderlands and declared its independence from Mexico in 1836. The new republic under President Sam Houston asked the United States to annex it; many Texans were former citizens of the United States who had moved into Mexican territory to farm cotton. One of the reasons for Texans' revolt against Mexico had been Mexico's passage of a law banning the importation of slaves.

The U.S. government declined to annex Texas because it would undoubtedly result in war with Mexico. However, those who supported slavery supported annexation because Texas would enter the Union as a slave state. Conversely, those who opposed slavery opposed annexation. Texas withdrew its annexation in 1838, and the matter might have ended there had it not been for the presidential election of 1844. James K. Polk made annexing Texas the primary goal of his campaign. Polk won and annexed Texas, which entered the Union as a slave state.

However, Mexico refused to recognize the annexation of Texas and in 1846, war broke out between Mexico and the United States. As a result of the Mexican War (1846–1848), the United States acquired a large territory from Mexico, which included parts of present-day Arizona, New Mexico, Wyoming, and Colorado and all of California, Nevada, and Utah.

The Compromise of 1850

Because of the Mexican Cession, the North and South were forced once again to confront the question of whether to extend slavery to new territories. At the same time, Congress debated other issues involving slavery, including whether to allow slavery in Washington, D.C., the nation's capital.

Senator Stephen Douglas of Illinois introduced five separate bills in an effort to gain support from Northerners and Southerners on each issue. The final Compromise of 1850 stated that:

- California could enter the Union as a free state.

- The settlers of the New Mexico and Utah Territories could decide for themselves whether to allow slavery.

- Texas would give up the lands that it claimed in present-day New Mexico, for which it would receive $10 million in compensation.

- The slave trade, but not slavery, would be abolished in the District of Columbia.

- The Fugitive Slave Law set up a commission system to hunt escaped slaves. Commissioners were able to arrest suspected runaways, hold hearings, and return suspected runaways to their owners. Suspected runaways could not testify in their own behalf; commissioners were paid $10 for each slave returned to an owner and $5 if the person was set free.

The Kansas-Nebraska Act

During this time, more Americans were moving west for the rich farmland in the Great Plains. In addition to the argument over the extension of slavery into new territories, Americans were arguing over the route of a proposed transcontinental railroad. Southerners wanted the railroad to follow a southerly route, whereas Northerners wanted a route across the upper Great Plains. Potential settlers also wanted the lands in this region opened to white settlement; it had been closed to whites through a number of treaties with Native American nations.

In 1854, Senator Stephen Douglas proposed a compromise for all three issues. The railroad would follow a central route across the Great Plains, the region would be open to white settlers, and it would be divided into two territories, Kansas and Nebraska. (This original Nebraska Territory went from the northern border of Kansas to Canada; by 1863 Congress had divided the Nebraska Territory into five other states.) Douglas further proposed that the people of Kansas and Nebraska should decide for themselves whether to allow slavery; this was known as "popular sovereignty" and effectively declared the Missouri Compromise "inoperative."

Kansas Wars

Because of Douglas' influence among proslavery Northerners in Congress, the Kansas-Nebraska Act passed in both houses. Douglas had assured Northerners that the region was not suited to plantation agriculture and so would not become slave states. When the election was held, Nebraska voted against slavery as Douglas had predicted.

But in Kansas violence erupted almost immediately. Proslavery and antislavery settlers rushed to the newly created Kansas Territory in an effort to gain control of the soon-to-be-elected territorial government. Financed and armed by antislavery or proslavery groups in the North and South, these rival factions earned Kansas the nickname "Bleeding Kansas." One of the most brutal assaults was on Lawrence, the capital of the antislavery group known as Free-Soilers.

By the end of 1855, there were two competing governments in Kansas, one that was proslavery and one that was run by abolitionists. By 1859, however, antislavery settlers outnumbered proslavery settlers, and two years later, Kansas was admitted to the Union as a free state.

Birth of the Republican Party

Soon after passage of the Kansas-Nebraska Act, meetings were held across the Midwest to discuss the formation of a new political party to oppose it. A meeting in Wisconsin in March 1854 is generally considered the beginning of the Republican Party. Abolitionists, as well as members of the Free-Soil Party, members of the former Whig Party, and antislavery Democrats from the North and West joined the new party.

The Republican Party opposed slavery and supported a strong central government. Southern Democrats believed that Congress had no constitutional right to prohibit slavery in the territories, whereas the Republican Party believed that Congress had the right and ought to exercise it. The Republicans quickly gained supporters in the North.

Dred Scott Decision

In 1857, the Supreme Court added to the conflict over slavery with its decision in the Dred Scott case. Scott sued for his freedom in court, claiming that because he had lived for almost nine years in free territories he was free. A Missouri lower court ruled in his favor, but his owner appealed to the state supreme court, which upheld the owner. The case went to the U.S. Supreme Court.

The Supreme Court ruled against Scott, claiming that because slaves were considered property, the U.S. Constitution protected slaveholders' rights to their property. The court also ruled that Congress had no authority to prohibit slavery in U.S. territories, thus nullifying the Northwest Ordinance and the Missouri Compromise. In addition, the Court ruled that African Americans, enslaved or free, were not and could never become citizens of the United States. Therefore, slaves could not sue to obtain their freedom.

The public reacted strongly to the Dred Scott decision. Southerners felt vindicated, and Northern abolitionists were outraged.

John Brown's Raid on Harper's Ferry

In 1859, abolitionist John Brown, who had participated in the violence that followed the passage of the Kansas-Nebraska Act, planned a violent assault on slavery itself. Brown convinced several wealthy and influential Northern abolitionists of the need for violent action to end slavery. Using financing from these supporters, Brown focused his attention on Harper's Ferry, Virginia (now West Virginia), and the federal arsenal there. To begin the revolt, he planned to capture the arsenal and its weapons and arm the local slave population. Brown and his followers would then travel through the South, gaining strength by freeing and arming slaves along the way.

In the early morning of October 17, 1859, Brown and a small group of men took several hostages and seized control of the arsenal at Harpers Ferry. Unfortunately, Brown's plan failed and his support never materialized. After holding the arsenal for just over one day, he and his surviving men were captured and tried for treason. Though it was unsuccessful, John Brown's raid convinced Southerners that Northerners would resort to violent means in order to stop slavery.

Political Situation in 1860: Republican and Democratic Parties, Abraham Lincoln, and Election Results

With the country divided over slavery, four candidates ran for president in the election of 1860. Former Illinois Congressman Abraham Lincoln ran as a member of the newly formed Republican Party. Lincoln had served one term in Congress beginning in 1846, but his disapproval of the Mexican War made him unpopular and he did not run in 1848. He returned to politics, however, after the passage of the Kansas-Nebraska Act because he feared that slavery would spread to the new western territories. He ran for the Senate in 1858, but lost to Stephen Douglas. Yet Lincoln's great skill in a series of debates with Douglas during the campaign gained him national recognition.

Because of divisions in the Democratic Party over slavery, members could not agree on a candidate. Northern Democrats generally opposed the expansion of slavery, whereas many Southern Democrats believed that slavery should be extended into new territories and states. Ultimately, the party split into two factions: the Northern faction nominated Stephen Douglas of Illinois, and the Southern faction nominated John C. Breckenridge of Kentucky. The Constitutional Union Party, a new party formed by former Whigs, nominated John Bell of Tennessee.

The Republican platform, on the other hand, opposed the spread of slavery into new territories, demanded an end to the internal slave trade, and criticized the Dred Scott decision. It attempted to win the votes of those in the West and Upper Midwest by promising to support passage of the Homestead Act, which would provide cheap land for settlement. Lincoln won the election with almost 40 percent of the popular vote, but the votes were concentrated in the free states. Believing that Lincoln's election would ultimately mean the end of slavery in the United States, many white Southerners threatened to secede from the Union if Lincoln was elected.

1861

When the first shots of the Civil War were fired, no one expected the war to last more than a few months. A series of poor Union commanders, bad military judgments, and the difficulties in fighting the South on its own territory balanced the South's disadvantages such as the lack of banking and financial centers, the need to build a central government, and the lack of a railroad network.

Secession: South Carolina, Confederate Government, and Border States

Six weeks after Lincoln won the presidential race, South Carolina became the first Southern state to secede from the Union. By March 1861, Mississippi, Florida, Alabama, Georgia, Louisiana, Texas, and South Carolina had formed the Confederate States of America in Montgomery, Alabama, and drafted a constitution. Although it was modeled on the U.S. Constitution, the Confederate Constitution specifically guaranteed slavery in the states and territories. As President, the Confederates appointed former U.S. Senator and Secretary of War Jefferson Davis, a graduate of West Point who had served as a regimental commander during the Mexican War.

In his inaugural address, Lincoln announced that he had "no purpose, directly or indirectly, to interfere with the institution of slavery in the States where it exists." He also pledged to enforce the Fugitive Slave Law of 1850, but he warned that he would not permit secession.

Four slave states—(1) Delaware, (2) Maryland, (3) Kentucky, and (4) Missouri—did not join the Confederacy. They were known as "border states" and remained loyal to the Union. It was particularly important that Maryland remain loyal to the Union. Otherwise, Washington, D.C., would be surrounded by the Confederacy. The southwestern section of Virginia refused to support the Confederacy and joined the Union as the state of West Virginia in 1863.

Fort Sumter

When President Lincoln took office, he promised to "hold, occupy, and possess" all federal property in the Southern states. This included the military post of Fort Sumter in Charleston, South Carolina. Angry at Union troops for occupying what they considered Confederate land, the Confederate army fired on Fort Sumter on April 12, 1861. Union troops surrendered the next day. With this first battle, the Civil War had officially begun. Soon after, four more Southern states—(1) Virginia, (2) North Carolina, (3) Tennessee, and (4) Arkansas—seceded from the Union and joined the other seven states of the Confederacy.

Union Army vs. Confederate Army

The South's list of disadvantages was long, but the fact that it was fighting a defensive war was a major advantage.

Leadership

In early 1861, President Lincoln had invited Robert E. Lee, a graduate of West Point who had served in the military for over 30 years, to command the Union Army. Lee declined because, although he disapproved of slavery, his home state of Virginia was seceding from the Union. Instead, Lee assumed command of the Confederate Army of Northern Virginia and proved to be a shrewd military tactician throughout the war.

Major Irvin McDowell of the U.S. Army was given command of the Army of Northeastern Virginia in May 1861, though he had never commanded troops in combat. He was replaced by George McClellan just two months later after the Union defeat at the Battle of Bull Run (First Manassas), the first major battle of the Civil War.

Preparedness

Both the North and South thought the war would be over in months, and both believed they had the advantage. In 1861, the Union states had over 22 million people, compared to just 9 million in the Confederacy, including nearly 4 million slaves. The North also had a navy, which the South lacked; a large railroad system; almost all the supplies of coal, iron, gold, and copper; and almost all of the nation's industry. It also had a strong established government, almost all of the banking and financial centers, and strong trading partners.

The South's advantage was its army of well-trained officers. They had attended West Point or other military academies and had served as officers in the Mexican War. Many Southern young men were used to using firearms and riding horses. In addition, the South reasoned that while the Union had to conquer the territory of the Confederacy, the Confederate army had only to wage a defensive war in response. However, the South had to establish a government; lacked a navy; had little industry, little in the way of natural resources and few railroads; and depended on Great Britain as its major trading partner.

Volunteers and Later Conscription

When the Civil War began, there were fewer than 20,000 soldiers in the federal army, and thousands of them went over to the Confederacy. President Lincoln called for Northern states to send 75,000 volunteers to join the Union Army. At the same time, the Confederacy turned to militia groups to supply soldiers. In the first year of the war, both sides had more volunteers than they could effectively train and equip, forcing the armies to turn away thousands of men. However, as the war progressed and enthusiasm faded, both sides used conscription. The Confederacy passed a draft law in April 1862 for men aged 18 to 35, exempting overseers of slaves and government officials. The U.S. Congress followed in July, authorizing a draft within states that did not have enough volunteers.

First Manassas (Bull Run)

The first goal of the Union army was to march against Richmond, Virginia, the new capital of the Confederacy, which was just 100 miles from Washington, D.C. Northerners believed this would bring an early end to the war. To get to Richmond, the army first had to capture Manassas, a small but important railway junction that led to Richmond, Washington, and the Shenandoah Valley. On July 16, 1861, Union troops set out for Manassas. The two armies met in battle five days later, along the banks of a small stream known as Bull Run. The Confederate troops launched a surprisingly strong counterattack against the inexperienced Union soldiers. One troop of Virginians led by Brigadier General Thomas Jackson stood its ground, earning Jackson the famous nickname "Stonewall Jackson." After ten hours of fighting, the Union troops retreated back to Washington. Almost 5,000 people had been killed, including soldiers from both armies and civilians. Many civilians came out in carriages and on horseback to watch the fighting. The battle convinced both sides that the war would be long and costly.

1862

After Manassas, there were no major battles until 1862. General McClellan was slowly building the Army of the Potomac into a fighting force. At the same time, General Ulysses S. Grant was fighting the Confederacy in western Tennessee.

Political Situation in the North and South

At the same time that the Union and Confederate armies were circling one another, the major political actors were fighting their own skirmishes.

Lincoln's Cabinet

Lincoln's cabinet was made up of important Republican politicians, many of whom Lincoln had not known before taking office. Many cabinet members were better educated than Lincoln, which made some distrust his judgment on various issues. Lincoln had the difficult job of balancing the competing interests of his cabinet while still maintaining strong leadership. William Seward, Secretary of State, became Lincoln's most trusted advisor. He was an abolitionist who was an outspoken foe of slavery, not a belief that all cabinet members shared. Treasury Secretary Salmon P. Chase, who had tried to win the Republican presidential nomination in the 1860 election, often clashed with Lincoln, but was well able to manage the Union's finances during the war.

Davis' Cabinet: Conscription and States' Rights

Many of the problems that occurred in Davis' presidency resulted from state leaders who refused to concede any power to the Confederate government. Davis' Vice President, Alexander Stephens, was such a supporter of states' rights that throughout the war he often supported his home state of Georgia over the central government's interests.

The issue of conscription also caused much dissension among Davis' cabinet. Davis argued that Congress had the power to raise armies, whereas Stephens and other cabinet members argued that only the states had the constitutional power to impose a draft.

A number of cabinet members changed during the course of the war. Dissension within the cabinet over policy and the losing conduct of the war proved to be the greatest challenges to Davis, whose ability to lead faltered as the war progressed.

Southern Hope of European Aid

Jefferson Davis knew that a Union blockade of major southern ports would be very damaging to the Confederacy. He hoped that Great Britain and France, whose industry depended on the South's cotton, would come to the aid of the Confederacy. Britain and France did give the Confederacy several armed warships and allowed their manufacturers to sell weapons and supply them to the Confederacy. Northern diplomats convinced Europeans not to recognize the Confederacy as an independent nation and made it clear that the United States would cut off food shipments to Britain if it did so. Britain and France refused to fight for the South unless the Confederacy could show that it might win the war. The South's losses at Vicksburg and Gettysburg ended all hope of British and French assistance.

Army of Potomac Under McClellan

After the defeat of the Union forces at Bull Run, Lincoln appointed General George McClellan commander of the Army of the Potomac, which was composed of all military forces in the former Departments of Northeastern Virginia, Washington, Baltimore, and the Shenandoah Valley. McClellan had originally been in command of the Army of the Ohio, with responsibility for holding the western area of Virginia. By early 1862, President Lincoln urged McClellan to begin offensive operations. McClellan developed a strategy to defeat the Confederate Army that involved invading Virginia from the sea, seizing Richmond, and then moving on to take the other major Southern cities. However, McClellan was a cautious commander who moved very slowly to execute his strategy.

War in the West

While McClellan was building and training the Army of the Potomac for battle, other generals and their armies were moving into Southern territory in the West and making big gains for the Union.

North's Plan to Control the Mississippi

When Lincoln received news that the Union Army had been defeated at Bull Run, he sought advice from Lieutenant General Winfield Scott. Scott was retired from battle, but was still the Union General-in-Chief at the start of the war. The initial strategy of Scott was known as the Anaconda Plan, after the anaconda snake, which squeezes its prey to death. The plan involved blockading Confederate ports along the Atlantic and Gulf Coasts to cut off cotton exports and prevent manufactured goods from reaching the South. Then the North would take control of the Mississippi River, splitting the South into two parts and blocking the South from using the river to move supplies. Finally, Union troops would invade from both east and west.

Generals Grant, Sherman, and Buell

As a step in gaining control of the Mississippi River, General Ulysses S. Grant and his army invaded western Tennessee in February 1862 and captured Fort Donelson and Fort Henry. Grant then moved farther south and met a large Confederate army at Shiloh. After a disastrous first day of fighting, the Union forces rallied and, with reinforcements, beat back the Confederate army. Grant won a number of decisive battles in the West and was given overall command of Union forces in the Military Division of the Mississippi.

General William Tecumseh Sherman served under Grant in western Tennessee and fought with him at Shiloh. He also led troops at Vicksburg and Chattanooga and at lesser known battles. When Grant was called to take over the Army of the Potomac in 1864, Sherman was given command of the forces in the West.

At the start of the Civil War, General Don Carlos Buell helped organize the Army of the Potomac under McClellan. By December 1861, Buell had become the leader of the Army of the Ohio. During 1862, Buell played an important role in securing Kentucky and Tennessee for the Union. However, he was relieved of command during the fall of that year after a significant loss to the Confederates in Kentucky.

War in the East

While Grant was making headway in the West, McClellan was moving slowly to put the Anaconda Plan into effect in the East.

Peninsular Campaign

In the eastern theater, General McClellan's plan was to use a water route to reach Richmond, thus bypassing the difficult terrain of Virginia. The city of Richmond sat on a narrow peninsula formed by the James and York Rivers. Instead of advancing through northern Virginia, McClellan proposed to send the Army of the Potomac to the tip of the York-James Peninsula by sea, and then travel west by land the shorter distance to Richmond. This so-called Peninsular Campaign began in March 1862, more than seven months after McClellan had taken command.

Union forces fought their way up the Peninsula. They engaged Confederate troops at Yorktown, Williamsburg, and Norfolk, winning each battle. They then met forces under General Joseph E. Johnston at Seven Pines with no side the clear victor. However, Johnston was wounded and General Robert E. Lee replaced him. The armies of McClellan and Lee met in what became known as the

Seven Days' Battle. Although Union forces were better organized, McClellan retreated in the face of Lee's counterattacks. The slaughter of so many soldiers—estimated at 30,000 dead and wounded—had shocked McClellan. This retreat and his failure to act quickly and decisively as a commander cost McClellan his command.

Naval Involvement: Blockade and Blockade Runners

The Anaconda Plan called for a blockade of Southern ports. To evade the blockade, the Confederacy used fast, lightweight ships that were very successful at running the blockade in the early part of the war. Although about 90 percent of these ships broke through the blockade in 1861, a year later this figure had dropped to less than 15 percent. By the end of the war, the Union Navy had captured more than 1,100 Confederate blockade runners.

Naval Involvement: Monitor vs. Merrimac

When the war began, the Union had a small navy and the Confederacy had none. It used private vessels to attack Union merchant ships rather than engage in battle with Union warships. This proved a prudent strategy after the battle between the *CSS Virginia* and the *USS Monitor* in March 1862. The ironclad Confederate warship, the *Virginia,* had previously been a sunken Union ship, the *USS Merrimac*, which the Confederacy had salvaged. The newly refitted and renamed *Virginia* destroyed two Union vessels on the blockade at Hampton Roads, Virginia. The next day, the Union's ironclad, the *Monitor,* engaged in a four-hour battle with the *Virginia*. Though neither was able to sink the other, this combat between two ironclad warships marked a revolution in naval warfare. It also ended any ideas the Confederacy might have had about ending the Union blockade.

Generals Lee and Jackson

Robert E. Lee was offered the position of commander in chief of the Union Army by President Lincoln before Virginia seceded. Instead, Lee joined the Confederate army out of loyalty to Virginia and his family. Although he was the unquestioned military leader of the South, he was not given command of the entire Confederate army until the war's outcome had already been decided. He was a brilliant military strategist, continually outsmarting and defeating opponents whose armies were much larger than his own.

Thomas "Stonewall" Jackson was an intensely religious man. A former teacher at Virginia Military Institute, he believed the Southern cause was sacred. He was fearless in battle. After Jackson won five battles in one month, an aura of invincibility surrounded him. It lasted until his death, in the spring of 1863, during one of his most dramatic victories, the Battle of Chancellorsville.

Major Battles of 1862

Battle	Date	Location	Significance
Shiloh	April 6–7	Tennessee	Confederate forces under Generals Joseph Johnston and Pierre Beauregard launched a surprise attack on General Ulysses S. Grant's troops at Pittsburg Landing, along the Tennessee River. On the first day, the Confederates achieved success, but were defeated on the second day.
Second Manassas	August 28–30	Virginia	The battle was fought on the same ground as the First Manassas, but on a much larger scale. It was a Confederate victory coming at the end of a campaign by Confederate General Robert E. Lee's Army of Northern Virginia against Union General John Pope's Army of Virginia.
Antietam	September 16–18	Maryland	The first major battle in the Civil War to take place on northern soil. General George McClellan confronted Lee's Army of Northern Virginia at Sharpsburg, Maryland. With over 20,000 casualties, it was the bloodiest single day in the war. Lee ultimately withdrew his troops. The result of the battle was inconclusive.
Fredericksburg	December 11–15	Virginia	General Ambrose Burnside, who had replaced McClellan, attacked Lee's army at Fredericksburg on the way to Richmond, but was met with strong resistance. The Union army suffered twice the number of casualties as the Confederate army. It was a major victory for the Confederates.

Emancipation Proclamation

At the beginning of the Civil War, Republicans in Congress demanded that Lincoln end slavery in the United States. But Lincoln refused, explaining that his main goal was to preserve the Union. As the war continued and it became clear that it would not be an easy victory for either side, more Northerners began to demand that Lincoln free the slaves. Some advocates were against slavery because they believed it was morally wrong. Others wanted to punish Southern slave owners and felt that freeing the slaves would seriously disrupt the Southern economy during wartime.

In summer 1862, Lincoln drafted an Emancipation Proclamation to free slaves in those Southern states that had seceded from the Union. Secretary of State William Seward advised Lincoln to wait to issue it until after a Union victory in the war, so that it would not look like a desperate act. After the narrow Union win at the Battle of Antietam, Lincoln felt that the time was right to act. Five days later, he issued the Emancipation Proclamation.

The provisions of the Proclamation went into effect on January 1, 1863. Lincoln did not free all slaves. The Emancipation Proclamation did not free slaves in the border states because these states were not in rebellion against the Union, nor did it free slaves in states or areas in Union hands. It freed slaves only in states or parts of states still under Southern control. However, it was not possible to enforce the order in those areas. The Emancipation Proclamation is, however, considered the turning point of the Civil War.

1863

1863 proved a difficult year for both sides as the war dragged on. A major defeat at Chancellorsville, Virginia, for the Union was balanced by a Confederate defeat at Gettysburg, Pennsylvania, which ended any idea of a Confederate advance on the North.

Casualties

Almost as many soldiers died during the Civil War as in all other U.S. wars combined. Union combat deaths totaled over 100,000, and another nearly 200,000 deaths were caused by disease. Confederate casualties were nearly as high, with approximately 94,000 combat deaths and 140,000 deaths by disease. Nearly twice as many soldiers died from disease as from combat. The causes included poor sanitation, lack of medical knowledge and medical supplies, and contaminated water supplies. Injured soldiers often died from infections, rather than from their wounds.

The Civil War has been called the first modern war because it changed the way wars were fought. New technology made the war more deadly than previous wars. Beginning in 1862, muskets were replaced with rifles that had grooved barrels that enabled soldiers to hit a target a quarter of a mile away. It was also the first war in which soldiers used automated weapons like the Gatling gun, in addition to shrapnel, booby traps, and land mines. Outdated strategies, including massive frontal attacks by rows of soldiers walking in formation, also contributed to the high number of casualties.

The quickest treatment for broken bones or torn blood vessels was to amputate, in order to avoid the inevitable infections that would set in. Any kind of building might be commandeered as a hospital—homes, stores, churches, barns, even wagons in the middle of a battlefield. Portable hospitals, often just tents, were set up near battlefields to take care of sick and injured soldiers.

The U.S. Sanitary Commission, which was founded by volunteers and authorized by the War Department, collected and sent medical supplies, food, and clothing to the sick and wounded. It also sent medical inspectors to army camps and hospitals.

Prisoners of War

Over 400,000 prisoners were taken during the Civil War. At the beginning of the war, because there were no places to detain prisoners, both sides released them on parole. Once they had been formally exchanged for captured enemies of equal rank, these soldiers could take up arms again. In the fall of 1863, the U.S. government suspended prisoner exchanges. Captured soldiers were sent to Union or Confederate prisons, which were overcrowded and unsanitary and ultimately led to the deaths of thousands of soldiers on both sides.

Role of Women in the War

With so many men away at war, women were offered new occupational opportunities. Many women in the North found work in stores and factories that produced weapons and supplies for the war. Many women in the South ran their family businesses, farms, and plantations. Women in both the North and the South organized groups to provide support for the men fighting in the war. Local Ladies Aid Societies knitted socks, rolled bandages, sewed clothing, raised money, and sent food.

A number of women during the Civil War were used as spies, scouts, and smugglers by both sides. Some women disguised themselves in the uniforms of deceased family members and fought alongside the men in both the Union and Confederate armies. It is not certain how many women fought secretly in the war, though the number may be as high as 400. Many were not discovered until they were wounded or killed in battle.

But it was as nurses that women achieved particular distinction during the Civil War. Thousands of women on both sides carried supplies to soldiers and nursed wounded or dying soldiers on the battlefield and in hospitals. Louisa May Alcott, author of *Little Women,* was one such nurse. Dorothea Dix, who championed better care for the mentally ill, was in charge of all Union Army nurses. As result of her experiences, Clara Barton founded the American Red Cross.

Black Americans and the War: Free Volunteers

In July 1862, the Union began to accept black Americans into the army to make up for the high number of casualties among soldiers and the difficulty in recruiting white soldiers. About 186,000 black soldiers served in the Union Army and about 29,000 served in the Navy. African Americans made up about 10 percent of the Union forces. Twenty African Americans were awarded the Congressional Medal of Honor. Three-fifths of all black troops were former slaves. About 38,000 African American military died over the course of the war, mostly from disease.

Because of prejudice against them, African Americans were most often used in support roles in the Union Army—digging trenches, building fortifications, and acting as drivers and hostlers (handling horses). African Americans also served as carpenters, cooks, scouts, and spies. Nevertheless, African American units participated in at least forty-one major battles. The most widely known battle was the assault on Fort Wagner, South Carolina, in 1863, by the 54th Massachusetts Regiment, which consisted of freed blacks recruited in the North. African Americans fought in segregated units, generally under the command of white officers, although between 75 and 100 African Americans became officers.

From 1862 until 1864, when the War Department changed its policy, African Americans were paid a laborer's wage rather than the wage paid to white soldiers, or $10 a month versus $13 a month. In addition, a clothing allowance was deducted from African Americans' pay, whereas the clothing allowance for white soldiers was in addition to their monthly pay.

Slaves in the South

During the war, the Confederates declared that all African American soldiers in the Union army were rebel slaves, regardless of whether they actually were former slaves, and often killed captured African American soldiers. The Confederacy used enslaved people to aid its war effort, but only in support roles, putting them to work in factories, building fortifications, and tending to the sick in hospitals. However, by the middle of the war, some Southerners, including General Lee and Jefferson Davis, had come to the realization that more manpower was needed for the Confederacy to win, and they advanced the idea of using African Americans as soldiers. It was not until 1865 that Davis prevailed and the Confederacy began to recruit African Americans. Initially, Davis had proposed offering enslaved men freedom for themselves and their families, but the final bill passed by the Confederate Congress didn't include a promise of freedom.

Runaway Slaves

The status of runaway slaves depended upon where they were found. The Militia Act of 1862 declared that any slave of an owner who was in territory occupied by Northern troops would be considered free. However, the Fugitive Slave Act of 1850 was still considered legal in the case of slaves who had escaped from owners in the border states. It was not until 1864 that the Fugitive Slave Act was finally repealed, and the pursuit of escaped slaves was no longer a legal concern.

Political Situation

The first two years of the war were difficult for both sides. During 1863, however, the Confederate disadvantages began to take their toll. The lack of financial and banking centers, the dependence on agriculture, the smaller population, and the lack of an organized, stable central government came into play as the Confederate armies began to lose ground to the Union armies.

North: Conscription

Despite the eagerness of early volunteers, it became difficult to recruit white soldiers as the war continued and casualty and death rates mounted. In 1863, Congress authorized the government to enforce conscription for all able-bodied men between 20 and 45. If called for duty, they had to serve—unless they had $300. A man could buy a substitute if he was wealthy enough. Rioting occurred in several states as a result of what was considered the unfairness of the law. Perhaps the most violent were the New York Draft Riots.

North: Copperheads

Although the Democratic Party had broken apart in 1860, some Northern Democrats, particularly in the Midwest, were more tolerant of the South. They had stronger economic and cultural ties with Southerners than did Democrats in the Northeast. Officially called Peace Democrats, they were nicknamed "Copperheads" after a cartoon that showed them as copperhead snakes. They insisted that the Republicans had provoked the South into secession, and they opposed the war and believed there should be a negotiated peace. Some formed secret societies suspected of plotting civil disobedience and even insurrection to support the Confederacy. Their policies became an issue in the election of 1864.

North: Anti-Emancipation Sentiment

Although the Emancipation Proclamation went into effect on January 1, 1863, not all Northerners agreed with it. A majority in fact did not. Slave owners in the border states especially viewed it with suspicion. Irish immigrants who had come in great numbers during the 1840s and 1850s opposed it because they feared competition with free African Americans for work.

North: Profiteering

After a slight economic depression as a result of the uncertain start to the war, the Northern economy boomed. Factories turned out clothes, shoes, ammunition, and weaponry for the Union army. Yet while many companies saw profits rise exponentially, workers' salaries shrank because of inflation. The price of many basic goods doubled during the war, yet salaries rose only half as fast.

Some businessmen turned to profiteering. They sold shoddy goods like leaky tents and tainted meat to the government at high prices. Some also made fortunes smuggling goods in and out of the South. Even legitimate businesses charged the government inflated prices for their goods.

South: Central Government, Inflation, Shortages

The Confederacy, which stressed states' rights above all, faced problems precisely because of its weak central government. State legislatures refused to give the central government the soldiers and money it needed to fight the war because they feared that too much power in Richmond would take power away from the states.

As the North prospered during the war, the South experienced severe financial difficulties. To raise money, the Confederacy imposed a 15 percent tariff on all imports, including goods from the United States. However, because of the Union blockade, many goods were smuggled into the South, and few people paid taxes on them. This ultimately led the Confederacy to print money in order to finance the war, which, in turn, led to high inflation. Over the course of the war, inflation in the South caused prices to rise by 9,000 percent. Many basic foods became too expensive for ordinary families. Food riots broke out in the cities of Mobile, Atlanta, and Richmond.

The Northern blockade made it difficult in the early years of the war and almost impossible in the later years to supply the army with enough clothes, shoes, weapons, and ammunition. Civilians, too, found themselves running short on necessities, including food and clothes. Factory owners found that there weren't always spare parts to repair machinery and no way to buy new machines to replace worn-out ones. Ordinary people who had no hope of or reason for owning slaves began to wonder if the war to "preserve the Southern way of life" was worth fighting.

Major Battles of 1863

Battle	Date	Location	Significance
Stones River (Murfreesboro)	December 31, 1862 to January 2, 1863	Tennessee	Although the battle itself was inconclusive, the Union Army's repulse of two Confederate attacks and the subsequent Confederate withdrawal were a much-needed boost to Union morale after the defeat at the Battle of Fredericksburg, and it dashed Confederate hopes for control of Middle Tennessee.
Chancellorsville	April 30–May 6	Virginia	Union General Joseph Hooker's Army of the Potomac tried to attack Lee's Confederate Army of Northern Virginia. Lee divided his army, which resulted in a significant Confederate victory.
Chickamauga	September 19–20	Tennessee/ Georgia	This battle marked the end of a Union offensive in southeastern Tennessee and northwestern Georgia called the Chickamauga Campaign. The battle was the most significant Union defeat in the Western Theater of the war. After the battle, Union forces retreated to Chattanooga, and the Confederacy maintained control of area.
Chattanooga	November 23–25	Georgia	The Battle of Chattanooga opened the door for the invasion of the Deep South and the capture of Atlanta in 1864. The battle decimated the Confederate Army of Tennessee.

| Vicksburg | May 18–July 4 | Mississippi | Vicksburg was a key city guarding the Mississippi River between Memphis and New Orleans. Grant launched an attack that lasted 48 days. Confederates were forced to surrender because of a lack of supplies. The victory gave the Union full control of the Mississippi River and cut the South in half. |
| Gettysburg | July 1–3 | Pennsylvania | Union General George Meade attacked Lee's troops in Gettysburg. More than 28,000 Confederate soldiers were killed or wounded. This battle is considered the turning point. Lee never again attempted to invade the North. |

By controlling the Mississippi, Grant had effectively removed Texas as a source of supplies to the Confederacy.

1864 TO MAY 1865

A series of battle losses coupled with dwindling resources and general exhaustion from years of fighting a war on its own soil doomed the Confederacy's defensive strategy. The relief that many felt with the end of the Civil War soon turned to disbelief with the assassination of Lincoln by Southern sympathizers. Some Southerners thought that his death would make the rebuilding of the South easier. However, others realized that his death was disastrous for the South. Lincoln had been able to keep the radical members of the Republican Party under control. With his death, they would be free to pursue their idea of justice for the South.

Political Situation: Northern Demoralization and Presidential Election

The outcome of the 1864 presidential election was crucial. It would determine whether the war would end in unconditional surrender or a settlement, which might result in the legal preservation of slavery. Worried about the election's outcome, Republicans and pro-war Democrats formed the National Union Party, which renominated Lincoln and chose Andrew Johnson, a former Democratic Senator from Tennessee, for Vice President. The Democrats nominated General George McClellan who opposed the Emancipation Proclamation and called for an end to the war. Radical Republicans thought Lincoln's plans for readmitting Confederate states to the Union after the war was too lenient, and they nominated General John C. Freemont for President, but he withdrew a month before the election.

Lincoln feared that exhaustion from the long war that was not going well for the Union would lead many Northerners to vote against him. The death toll from the war was steadily mounting. In one month's fighting against the Army of Northern Virginia, the Union had lost 55,000 soldiers. However, General Sherman's successful capture of Atlanta in September 1864 changed the mood in the North. Lincoln won the election easily, receiving 55 percent of the popular vote to 21 percent for McClellan.

War in the West

The end of the war was near if the Union could take Atlanta and Richmond, two major cities in the Confederacy.

Sherman's March Through Georgia

Sherman had fought with Grant in the West, and in 1864, Grant gave Sherman the task of capturing Atlanta. It was part of Grant's final strategy to end the war.

In July, Sherman, now in charge of all Union forces in the West, marched with 100,000 men toward Atlanta, one of the largest cities in the South. In September, Sherman captured and burned Atlanta to the ground. The fall of Atlanta greatly boosted morale in the North—and helped Lincoln in his reelection campaign.

Generals Johnston and Forrest

General Joseph E. Johnston was the original commander of the Confederate army in Virginia, but was badly wounded in the battle of Seven Pines in May 1862 and replaced by Robert E. Lee. Johnston went on to command the Army of Tennessee and attempted to outmaneuver Sherman on the latter's march to take Atlanta. Johnston would dig in to a defensive position ready to fight, but Sherman would swing around Johnston's forces. This went on for two months as Sherman steadily moved toward Atlanta. When Sherman was within striking distance of Atlanta, Davis replaced Johnston with John Bell Hood with disastrous results. Hood fell back to Atlanta, but eventually abandoned the city to save his army.

General Nathan Bedford Forrest was a Confederate cavalry general who began the war as a private and ended it as commander of all cavalry troops in northern Mississippi and western Tennessee. Considered a brilliant tactician, Forrest spent most of 1864 fighting Union forces under Sherman. After the war, he became involved with the Ku Klux Klan, though he later broke with the group.

War in the East

Concerned about the presidential election in the fall and frustrated by continued poor judgment and caution on the battlefield, in March of 1864 Lincoln gave Grant command of all Union armies.

Grant and the Army of the Potomac

Grant devised a plan to end the war that coordinated the activities of all Union forces. The Army of the Potomac and the forces under Sheridan in the Shenandoah Valley and Johnston in western

Tennessee would move simultaneously. In this way, the Confederacy could not move its troops from one place to another to reinforce an army under attack. In addition, Grant planned to move aggressively, striking Confederate forces relentlessly. He wanted to wear out the Confederacy. Ultimately, the plan worked, but it took a year to defeat Lee.

Lee and the Army of Northern Virginia

The Army of the Potomac's campaign against Lee's forces began in early May 1864. Lee and his Army of Northern Virginia remained confident, but in battle after battle, the Confederate army was slowly pushed back toward Richmond. The toll in dead and wounded on both sides was enormous.

Major Battles of 1864

Battle	Date	Location	Significance
Wilderness	May 5–7	Virginia	Grant's and Lee's forces fought in a three-day battle that was ultimately inconclusive. The Union suffered more casualties, but unlike Grant, Lee had no replacements.
Spotsylvania	May 8–21	Virginia	Grant continued to attack Lee's forces. After the inconclusive battle at Spotsylvania Court House, Grant vowed to fight all summer if necessary.
Cold Harbor	May 31–June 12	Virginia	Grant again attacked Confederate forces at Cold Harbor. Although Lee suffered fewer casualties, his army never recovered from these continual attacks. This battle was Lee's last victory of the war.
Shenandoah Valley Campaign	May–October	Virginia	From May to August, Confederate forces under General Jubal A. Early drove Union forces from the Valley. In August, Grant put General Philip Sheridan in charge of the campaign and by October, he had won control of the valley.
Petersburg	June 9, 1864–March 25, 1865	Virginia	Grant hoped to take Petersburg, and then approach Richmond from the south. The attempt failed, which resulted in a nine-month siege.
Atlanta	July 22	Georgia	Union forces commanded by William T. Sherman defeated Confederate forces led by John Hood in Atlanta. The city of Atlanta would ultimately fall to the Union forces in September.

Mobile Bay	August 5	Alabama	A Union fleet attacked a smaller Confederate fleet and three forts that guarded the entrance to Mobile Bay. The capture of this last major Confederate port on the Gulf of Mexico closed the Union blockade east of the Mississippi.

Sherman's Continued March Through the South: Destruction of the Civilian Base and Logistics

After taking Atlanta, Sherman then marched his troops across Georgia toward Savannah. In order to crush Southern morale, Sherman had his men destroy railroad tracks, loot houses, and burn factories along the way. Sherman seized Savannah in December, and then turned northward, capturing Charleston and Columbia, both in South Carolina, and finally heading to Virginia.

Sherman's march had a tremendous impact on many Southerners, who by now had lost their will to fight. Many Confederate soldiers deserted the army and headed home when they heard about Sherman's march through Georgia. What they found at home was a demoralized populous. People were starving because of food shortages, and inflation was rampant. While some were willing to negotiate a peace with the Union, others would agree to nothing less than Southern independence.

Fall of Richmond and the Flight of the Civilian Government

On April 2, 1865, Lee sent a message to Jefferson Davis saying that Richmond could no longer be defended and that he should evacuate the city. That night, Davis and his cabinet set fire to everything of value in Richmond, and then boarded a train to Danville, which was 140 miles to the south. The next day, Union soldiers arrived.

Lee's Surrender

Grant's army had by now cut off Lee's supply lines, forcing Confederate forces to evacuate Petersburg and Richmond. Lee and his men retreated westward, but Grant's troops overtook him about a hundred miles west of Richmond. Recognizing that further resistance would be futile, Lee agreed to surrender. After a series of notes between the two leaders, they agreed to meet on April 9, 1865, in the village of Appomattox Courthouse, Virginia. The meeting lasted approximately two and a half hours. The terms of the surrender were the following:

- Company and regimental commanders would sign a parole for the men of their commands.

- Arms, artillery, and public property were to be turned over to an officer appointed by Grant to receive them.

- Officers were allowed to keep their side arms, personal horses, and baggage.

- Each man was allowed to return to his home, not to be disturbed by federal authorities as long as they observed their paroles.

- Each man could take a horse or mule in order to be able to farm that spring.

Assassination of Lincoln

On April 14, 1865, five days after Grant and Lee agreed to the terms of surrender, President Lincoln was shot by John Wilkes Booth while attending a performance at Ford's Theater in Washington, D.C. Lincoln died early the next morning.

Booth was an actor and Confederate sympathizer, He had initially planned to kidnap President Lincoln, in exchange for Confederate prisoners. Plans were made to carry out the kidnapping on a day when Lincoln was scheduled to attend a function at a Washington hospital. At the last moment, when the President's plans changed, Booth decided on assassination. After firing at Lincoln, Booth escaped the theater, but was found several weeks later by federal soldiers in a barn in Virginia where he was shot and killed. Eight others were arrested and four subsequently hanged for their part.

As in war, the nation was divided over Lincoln's death. Many mourned him. Some Southerners understood that he would have saved them from the harsh penalties that the Radical Republicans were advocating. Others saw a great enemy vanquished.

End of the Confederacy: Johnston's Surrender

In early April 1865, Sherman was pursuing Johnston and his army through North Carolina. When news of Lee's surrender reached Johnston, he sent a message to Sherman asking for a meeting to discuss terms of surrender. On April 18, Sherman offered Johnston terms similar to those that Grant had given to Lee a few weeks earlier. In addition, Sherman would grant all surrendering Confederates U.S. citizenship. Johnston signed the surrender agreement on April 26, 1865. This was the second largest surrender of Confederate soldiers and the end of the war.

Davis' Capture

As Richmond fell, Davis continued south, first hoping to convince Johnston to keep fighting in North Carolina, but Johnston refused. Davis then hoped to get to Texas to establish a new government, but was captured in Georgia on May 10 and imprisoned for two years at Fort Monroe in Virginia. He was indicted for treason in 1866, but was released the next year on a bond signed by newspaper publisher Horace Greeley and other influential Northerners. In 1868, the federal government dropped the case against him.

Cost of the War: Human, Economic, and Cultural

The human cost on both sides was enormous. The North lost 365,000 soldiers; 110,000 of them died in battle. On the Confederate side, 256,000 died, 94,000 in battle. Including the wounded, the two sides together endured over a million casualties.

As a result of the Civil War, a quarter of its white male population of military age in the South either died or was badly wounded. The figure for the Union was one in ten. The high death rate also meant a large number of widows, childless elderly, and fatherless children, as well as women who would never marry.

The Southern economy was in a state of collapse. Southern factories and railroads had been destroyed, and Atlanta, Charleston, Columbia, and Richmond had been burned to the ground. Farmland had been burned by Northern soldiers and untended fields had turned to weeds. Southerners were also faced with collapsed property values, and plantation owners no longer had a cheap source of labor. During the 1860s, the South saw a 60 percent drop in its wealth.

Both the North and the South experienced high rates of inflation, but the South's rate was 80 times higher. Banks and businesses in the South had been shut down during the war. Many planters had no source of capital with which to rebuild their homes or their livelihoods. The Southern "way of life" had ended forever. But the group that benefitted from the war was Northern factory owners who supplied war materiel to the Union.

RECONSTRUCTION

Lincoln's plan for a more humane Reconstruction policy toward the South died with him. The next few years saw a struggle between his successor and Congress over who would dictate the terms of reunification to the South. Those who had seen Lincoln's death as a blow to lenient treatment for the South turned out to be correct.

Presidential Reconstruction Plans

There was no guidance in the Constitution as to whether the President or Congress should direct a national reunification, and there was no agreement in Congress or between Lincoln and Congress over what Reconstruction policy should be. Lincoln had announced his plan for Reconstruction in December 1863 while the Confederacy was still fighting.

Lincoln's Plan

Lincoln's plan had the following provisions:

- A state could be readmitted when 10 percent of a state's citizens eligible to vote in 1860 swore an oath of allegiance to the Union (the Ten Percent Plan).

- Most former Confederates would be granted amnesty once they took the oath of allegiance.

- High-ranking officials in the Confederate government would be required to ask the President for a pardon in order to be granted amnesty.

- States had to guarantee a free education to African Americans.

Once a state had been readmitted, it had to do the following:

- Form a government

- Hold a constitutional convention

- Write a new constitution that included rights for African Americans.

Although the war was not over, certain former Confederate states were completely or in part in Union hands, and Lincoln applied his plan to these states. Tennessee, Arkansas, Virginia, and Louisiana set up new governments before the end of the war.

Johnson's Plan

After Lincoln's death, Vice President Andrew Johnson became President and announced his own plan for Reconstruction, which was similar to Lincoln's.

- Amnesty would be offered to all ex-Confederates except for high-ranking officials and property owners who were worth more than $20,000, a large sum at the time.

- These men could not hold public office or vote unless they asked the President for a pardon.

- The states had to revoke their secession laws.

- War debts that the Confederacy had incurred could not be collected.

- States had to ratify the Thirteenth Amendment, abolishing slavery.

Johnson wanted to readmit the former Confederate states quickly once they accepted the Thirteenth Amendment and pledged loyalty to the Union. Even though a number of former Confederate states failed to fully comply with his provisions for readmission to the Union, President Johnson announced in December 1865 that the Union was restored. By the following year, Johnson had pardoned more than 7,000 high-ranking former Confederates and wealthy Southerners. In addition, Johnson appointed provisional governors in the former Confederate states. Leaders in those states then called constitutional conventions, held elections, and prepared to regain their place in the Union.

Congressional Reconstruction Plans

Many in Congress had disagreed with Lincoln's plan because they believed it was too lenient. They also believed that Reconstruction was the responsibility of Congress, not the President, and some were concerned that Lincoln's plan did not address the rights of former slaves. However, politics also entered into the calculations of some Republican members of Congress who thought that Southern whites, once enfranchised, would become Democrats, and newly elected Democratic members of Congress would then vote against Republican proposals.

Radical Republicans

After the 1860 election, Radical Republicans who supported abolition, distribution of land to former slaves, and equal rights for African Americans became a powerful force in Congress. They disagreed with Lincoln's Reconstruction plan and hoped that Johnson would be more willing to punish the former Confederate states. Believing that Johnson's plan was not harsh enough, they fought to gain control of Reconstruction.

Reconstruction Acts

By 1867, Radical Republicans in Congress had wrested control of Reconstruction from Johnson and began putting into place their own Reconstruction plan. Ratification of the Fourteenth Amendment making African Americans citizens was pivotal to readmitting the former Confederate states to the Union. The Congress' Reconstruction Acts had the following provisions:

- The ten state governments that had not ratified the Fourteenth Amendment (but that Johnson had recognized) were declared illegal. (The exception was Tennessee, which had ratified the amendment.)

- The ten states were divided into five military districts.

- The military districts were overseen by military governors who could use federal troops to protect civil rights and maintain order if needed.

- Each state had to call a convention to write a new constitution.

- Both white and African American adult males were eligible to vote for members of the constitutional conventions.

- Those who had served as officials in the Confederacy could not be members of the constitutional conventions.

- The new state constitutions were to guarantee the vote for African American males.

- The states had to ratify the Fourteenth Amendment.

As a result of these acts, all former Confederate states had returned to the Union by 1870.

Civil Rights Act

In 1865 and 1866, new state governments across the South passed black codes that described the rights and duties of free African Americans. The black codes in general made it unlawful for African Americans to live in certain areas, hold certain jobs, serve on juries, vote, hold public office, own land, and travel without a permit. Some states also set curfews for African Americans. Some laws also made it crime for an African Americans to be unemployed. Those without jobs could be arrested and forced to work to pay their fines.

In 1866, Congress passed the Civil Rights Act, which granted citizenship to African Americans and the "same rights of property and person" as whites. The bill was an attempt to overrule the black codes by affirming the citizenship of newly emancipated African Americans. President Johnson vetoed the bill saying that it violated states' rights. His veto was overturned by a two-thirds majority in both houses of Congress, and the bill became law. Johnson was not the only one who thought the Civil Rights Act was unconstitutional, so Congress passed and the necessary number of states ratified the Fourteenth Amendment to the Constitution.

Fourteenth and Fifteenth Amendments

The Fourteenth Amendment made African Americans citizens of the United States and guaranteed them the same legal rights as whites. The Amendment had the following provisions:

- All persons born in the United States or naturalized were citizens of the United States and the state in which they lived.

- States could not deny citizens their rights without due process.

- Equal protection under the law was afforded to all citizens.

- A state that denied voting rights to any adult male would have its representation in Congress reduced in proportion to the number of citizens whose right to vote had been denied.

- A two-thirds vote of Congress was required to pardon ex-Confederate officials before they could hold federal or state office.

- Confederate debts could not be collected.

- Former slaveholders could not sue for compensation for the loss of slaves.

In 1869, Congress passed the Fifteenth Amendment that guaranteed the right to vote to all adult males regardless of "race, color, or previous condition of servitude." (This included states in the North. In 1868, eleven Northern states did not allow African Americans to vote.) In 1870, the Fifteenth Amendment was ratified.

Impeachment

To prevent the President from obstructing its Reconstruction program, Congress passed several laws restricting presidential powers. One, the Tenure of Office Act, stated that if the President wished to remove an officeholder whose appointment had been confirmed by the Senate, the Senate had to approve. Johnson tested this act in 1868 by dismissing from office Secretary of War Edwin M. Stanton. Stanton supported the Radical Republicans and opposed Johnson's Reconstruction policies. In response, the House of Representatives voted to impeach Johnson. Johnson was saved by one vote in his Senate trial, but his ability to govern was diminished, and he lost his fight to control Reconstruction.

Freedmen's Bureau

In order to help freed African Americans build new lives, Congress created the Freedmen's Bureau in March 1865. The Bureau provided food, clothing, shelter, medical care, and legal help, and set up more than 3,000 schools for newly freed people. Staffed by both military personnel and civilians, the Bureau also helped African Americans find jobs, negotiate wages, and settle disputes between African Americans and white employers.

The act creating the Freedmen's Bureau promised "forty acres and a mule" to freedmen (and white Unionists) who rented and worked the land for three years. At the end of the three years, they could buy the land. Johnson, however, ordered that all land be returned to its original owner, putting an end to the dream of landownership for former slaves.

The Bureau was renewed by Congress in 1866, but was vetoed by Johnson. Johnson believed it was unconstitutional because it continued wartime laws in peacetime. Congress passed the bill over his veto. The Bureau's work ended in 1869.

Reconstruction in the South: Response to Johnson's Policies

Johnson's policies were less harsh than those of the Radical Republicans. However, as a former small farmer from Tennessee, Johnson believed that the future of the South lay with small farmers, not former plantation owners. His policies favored those farmers and alienated the others.

Elected Black Office Holders

Congress required only a majority of those voting to ratify the new state constitutions. As a result, free blacks and white Republicans temporarily gained power in every Confederate state except Virginia. Most African Americans in the South at the time were poor and uneducated, but there were exceptions. Of the African Americans in public office, most were literate, and many were professionals or businessmen. Twenty African Americans were elected to the U.S. House of Representatives and two to the U.S. Senate. The first was Hiram Revels of Mississippi, who was elected to the U.S. Senate in 1870.

Over 600 African Americans served as legislators in Reconstruction governments. However, the only state legislature controlled by African Americans was South Carolina's lower house. No other state legislature was dominated by African Americans.

Scalawags and Carpetbaggers

Though there were a number of African American men in political office in the South, the top positions with the most power were held by white Republicans, who were known derogatorily by white Southern Democrats as "carpetbaggers" and "scalawags." Carpetbaggers were Northerners who had come to the South after the war supposedly with all their belongings packed in carpetbag suitcases in order to seek economic opportunity and power in government. Many of these Northerners were actually businessmen, teachers, and ministers, some employed by the Freedmen's Bureau. The "scalawags," or scoundrels to their opponents, were white Southerners who had opposed secession. Former Confederates accused these Unionists of cooperating with Republicans because they, too, wanted to take advantage of the tenuous political climate in the South.

In truth, corruption was no more widespread in the South than it was in the North during this period. About 80 percent of Southern states' revenues were poured back into the states to rebuild transportation, erect schools, and provide hospitals and orphanages, among other public works.

Secret Terrorist Societies

The new state governments controlled by Northerners angered many Southern whites. New state leaders had raised taxes to pay for new schools and roads, although Southerners couldn't vote until their states had been readmitted to the Union. Many whites were angered to see African Americans voting and holding public office. Some Southerners turned to violence. In 1866, six former Confederate officers formed the Ku Klux Klan to terrorize African Americans. Klan organizations and similar groups like the White Camellias began forming across the South. Klansmen, who wore masks and white sheets, tortured and killed African Americans and sympathetic whites to keep African Americans from voting.

End of Reconstruction: Restoration of White Government

Though Republicans made huge political gains in the South, especially because of the votes of newly enfranchised African Americans, the party still remained unpopular with large segments of Southern voters. In addition to the deep resentment of white Southerners who did not want to accept equality for African Americans, some of the new Republican governments were ineffective. This was in part because many of the region's most experienced government officials had been disqualified because they had served the Confederacy. As a result, Southern governments were often in the hands of inexperienced officials, making it difficult for Republicans to execute their plans for Reconstruction and to enforce the Fourteenth and Fifteenth Amendments.

As resistance and violence continued to spread in the South, Republican power in the region weakened. By 1876, Radical Republican governments had collapsed in all but two of the former Confederate states, and the Democratic Party had taken over. Southern Democrats styled themselves as "Redeemers" saving the South from black Republican rule.

Election of 1876

In the election of 1876, Samuel Tilden, the Democratic presidential candidate, won the popular vote by more than 250,000 over Republican Rutherford B. Hayes. However, Hayes had won 167 electoral votes, and Tilden had won 185. The twenty remaining electoral votes were in dispute. The controversy was prolonged, and the outcome of the 1876 election was not resolved until March 1877, in what became known as the Compromise of 1877.

Compromise of 1877

In return for Southern conservative support for Hayes, a Southern appointment to Hayes' Cabinet, and approval of funding for a Texas and Pacific Railroad, the Republican Party agreed to withdraw all remaining federal troops from the South, officially ending Reconstruction. Only Louisiana, Florida, and South Carolina still had Reconstruction governments by then.

Many white Northerners and even Radical Republicans had tired of intervening in Southern affairs. White Southerners were the winners of this compromise, and Southern African Americans were the losers as black codes and white terrorist societies constricted more and more of their political, economic, and social rights and freedoms.

POST-TEST ANSWER SHEET

1. Ⓐ Ⓑ Ⓒ Ⓓ	13. Ⓐ Ⓑ Ⓒ Ⓓ	25. Ⓐ Ⓑ Ⓒ Ⓓ	37. Ⓐ Ⓑ Ⓒ Ⓓ	49. Ⓐ Ⓑ Ⓒ Ⓓ
2. Ⓐ Ⓑ Ⓒ Ⓓ	14. Ⓐ Ⓑ Ⓒ Ⓓ	26. Ⓐ Ⓑ Ⓒ Ⓓ	38. Ⓐ Ⓑ Ⓒ Ⓓ	50. Ⓐ Ⓑ Ⓒ Ⓓ
3. Ⓐ Ⓑ Ⓒ Ⓓ	15. Ⓐ Ⓑ Ⓒ Ⓓ	27. Ⓐ Ⓑ Ⓒ Ⓓ	39. Ⓐ Ⓑ Ⓒ Ⓓ	51. Ⓐ Ⓑ Ⓒ Ⓓ
4. Ⓐ Ⓑ Ⓒ Ⓓ	16. Ⓐ Ⓑ Ⓒ Ⓓ	28. Ⓐ Ⓑ Ⓒ Ⓓ	40. Ⓐ Ⓑ Ⓒ Ⓓ	52. Ⓐ Ⓑ Ⓒ Ⓓ
5. Ⓐ Ⓑ Ⓒ Ⓓ	17. Ⓐ Ⓑ Ⓒ Ⓓ	29. Ⓐ Ⓑ Ⓒ Ⓓ	41. Ⓐ Ⓑ Ⓒ Ⓓ	53. Ⓐ Ⓑ Ⓒ Ⓓ
6. Ⓐ Ⓑ Ⓒ Ⓓ	18. Ⓐ Ⓑ Ⓒ Ⓓ	30. Ⓐ Ⓑ Ⓒ Ⓓ	42. Ⓐ Ⓑ Ⓒ Ⓓ	54. Ⓐ Ⓑ Ⓒ Ⓓ
7. Ⓐ Ⓑ Ⓒ Ⓓ	19. Ⓐ Ⓑ Ⓒ Ⓓ	31. Ⓐ Ⓑ Ⓒ Ⓓ	43. Ⓐ Ⓑ Ⓒ Ⓓ	55. Ⓐ Ⓑ Ⓒ Ⓓ
8. Ⓐ Ⓑ Ⓒ Ⓓ	20. Ⓐ Ⓑ Ⓒ Ⓓ	32. Ⓐ Ⓑ Ⓒ Ⓓ	44. Ⓐ Ⓑ Ⓒ Ⓓ	56. Ⓐ Ⓑ Ⓒ Ⓓ
9. Ⓐ Ⓑ Ⓒ Ⓓ	21. Ⓐ Ⓑ Ⓒ Ⓓ	33. Ⓐ Ⓑ Ⓒ Ⓓ	45. Ⓐ Ⓑ Ⓒ Ⓓ	57. Ⓐ Ⓑ Ⓒ Ⓓ
10. Ⓐ Ⓑ Ⓒ Ⓓ	22. Ⓐ Ⓑ Ⓒ Ⓓ	34. Ⓐ Ⓑ Ⓒ Ⓓ	46. Ⓐ Ⓑ Ⓒ Ⓓ	58. Ⓐ Ⓑ Ⓒ Ⓓ
11. Ⓐ Ⓑ Ⓒ Ⓓ	23. Ⓐ Ⓑ Ⓒ Ⓓ	35. Ⓐ Ⓑ Ⓒ Ⓓ	47. Ⓐ Ⓑ Ⓒ Ⓓ	59. Ⓐ Ⓑ Ⓒ Ⓓ
12. Ⓐ Ⓑ Ⓒ Ⓓ	24. Ⓐ Ⓑ Ⓒ Ⓓ	36. Ⓐ Ⓑ Ⓒ Ⓓ	48. Ⓐ Ⓑ Ⓒ Ⓓ	60. Ⓐ Ⓑ Ⓒ Ⓓ

answer sheet

POST-TEST

1. During the mid-1800s, immigration to the United States

   (A) decreased as the United States began placing restrictions on European immigrants.

   (B) was much lower than it been the previous century because of European wars.

   (C) increased with the majority of immigrants coming from Eastern Europe.

   (D) increased rapidly with the majority of immigrants coming from Northern Europe.

2. Why was the capture of Fort Sumter important to the Confederacy?

   (A) Its capture held symbolic value.

   (B) It guarded Charleston Harbor, so whoever held it could allow ships into the harbor or keep them from entering.

   (C) If Fort Sumter could be captured, it was hoped that Lincoln would allow the South to go its own way as the Confederate States of America.

   (D) If Fort Sumter could be captured, it would easier to take the other federal forts all across the South.

3. McClellan was replaced as commander of the Army of the Potomac after the Seven Days' Battle because

   (A) the Union forces were poorly organized.

   (B) poor press coverage of McClellan's performance was embarrassing to the President.

   (C) of the huge losses that the Union army suffered.

   (D) he retreated and failed to act quickly and decisively.

4. The Kansas-Nebraska Act had a serious effect on the survival of which political party?

   (A) Republican Party

   (B) Constitutional Union Party

   (C) Democratic Party

   (D) Free-Soil Party

5. Most important public offices in the South during Reconstruction were held by

   (A) African Americans in most areas.

   (B) white Republicans.

   (C) employees of the Freedmen's Bureau.

   (D) men—African American or white— appointed by the military governor the district.

post-test

6. The demise of the Republican Party in the South

   (A) occurred despite the party's strong internal cohesion.

   (B) was accomplished entirely through legitimate political means.

   (C) was largely because of white opposition from outside the party.

   (D) was largely because of white Republicans' refusal to cooperate with blacks.

7. The issuance of the Emancipation Proclamation was significant because it

   (A) guaranteed compensation for slave owners in the border states.

   (B) encouraged slaves to revolt.

   (C) made the Civil War a war to free slaves.

   (D) hardened Southern resolve to win the war.

8. Which of the following is a true statement about the differences that had developed between the North and South by the mid-1800s?

   (A) The North had developed an industrial economy, and the South continued to rely on agriculture as its economic base.

   (B) Immigrants found the South a more tolerant place to settle.

   (C) The North was dependent on foreign trade, whereas the South was more self-sufficient.

   (D) The majority of Southern farmers were large plantation owners.

9. Which of the following was a provision of Lincoln's Reconstruction plan?

   (A) States had to revoke their laws of secession.

   (B) A free education had to be guaranteed to all African Americans.

   (C) Each state had to ratify the Fourteenth Amendment.

   (D) Each state had to ratify the Thirteenth Amendment.

10. Which of the following was NOT part of the Compromise of 1850?

    (A) Slave trade is banned in Washington, D.C.

    (B) California to enter the Union as a free state

    (C) Prohibition of slavery in Washington, D.C.

    (D) A tougher fugitive slave law

11. Which groups made up the new Republican Party founded in 1854?

    (A) Antislavery Southerners and free African Americans

    (B) Abolitionists and members of the former Whig and Free-Soil parties

    (C) Democrats from the South who had split from the party

    (D) Members of the former Whig and Federalist Parties

12. In the Dred Scott decision, the Supreme Court ruled against Scott because

    (A) he had never lived in a free state.

    (B) he was in a free state when his owner died.

    (C) his owner had never freed him.

    (D) it decided that African Americans were not citizens and, therefore, could not sue in court.

13. Which state was the first to secede from the Union in December 1860?

    (A) Virginia

    (B) South Carolina

    (C) Mississippi

    (D) Alabama

14. In the Union Army, African American soldiers were most often used

    (A) in the front lines.

    (B) in rearguard duties such as laborer and driver.

    (C) for spy missions.

    (D) in the cavalry.

15. What was Abraham Lincoln's position on slavery at the start of the Civil War?

    (A) He said that slavery as an institution needed to be abolished in the United States.

    (B) He said that every state should have the right to decide for itself whether or not to allow slavery.

    (C) He said the President had no right to interfere with slavery in the states where it existed.

    (D) He refused to take a position on slavery, fearing it could lead to additional states seceding from the Union.

16. What was the significance of the battle between the *Monitor* and the *Merrimac*?

    (A) It was the first battle between ironclad warships.

    (B) It was the first Confederate victory of the naval war.

    (C) It succeeded in breaking the Union naval blockade.

    (D) It was the last naval battle of the Civil War.

17. What was the first major battle of the Civil War to be fought on northern soil?

    (A) Gettysburg

    (B) First Bull Run

    (C) Cold Harbor

    (D) Antietam

18. The Civil War was different from earlier wars because

    (A) women volunteers were allowed to take care of the wounded and dying.

    (B) it was the first U.S. war to involve naval battles.

    (C) the weaponry that was used was more technologically advanced than in earlier wars.

    (D) both armies used only volunteers.

19. Which of the following battles was important in clearing the way for a march to Atlanta?

    (A) Spotsylvania

    (B) Shenandoah Valley campaign

    (C) Chancellorsville

    (D) Chattanooga

20. What effect did the Union victories at Vicksburg and Gettysburg have on the Confederacy's relations with Great Britain and France?

    (A) The victories convinced Great Britain and France to sever diplomatic relations with the United States.

    (B) The victories convinced Great Britain and France that they could not expect continued exports of cotton from the South.

    (C) The victories convinced Great Britain and France not to recognize the Confederacy as a separate nation.

    (D) The victories convinced Great Britain and France to attempt to negotiate peace between the Union and the Confederacy.

21. The Compromise of 1850
    (A) passed Congress as several individual bills.
    (B) weakened the Fugitive Slave Law.
    (C) abolished slavery in the District of Columbia.
    (D) established New Mexico Territory as a free state.

22. Which of the following statements is true about the South during Reconstruction?
    (A) Corruption in Southern governments was no worse than in the rest of the country.
    (B) Federal troops were able to stop raids by terrorist societies like the Ku Klux Klan.
    (C) Military districts lasted only until all the Southern states were readmitted to the Union in 1868.
    (D) Southern governments initially were controlled by African Americans and Northerners who saw an opportunity to get rich.

23. The Emancipation Proclamation freed slaves in which states?
    (A) Missouri
    (B) Maryland
    (C) West Virginia
    (D) Florida

24. What course did General Sherman follow in 1864?
    (A) He captured Richmond and then cut off access to the Mississippi River.
    (B) He captured Savannah and marched southwest to New Orleans.
    (C) He captured Atlanta, marched southeast to Savannah, and then marched north into South Carolina.
    (D) He captured Charleston, marched south to Savannah, and then burned Atlanta.

25. Which event changed the mood of the election and helped Lincoln win the 1864 election?
    (A) Siege of Petersburg
    (B) Capture of Atlanta
    (C) Shiloh
    (D) Chancellorsville

26. The underlying reason for the impeachment of President Andrew Johnson was
    (A) a power struggle with Congress over Reconstruction.
    (B) his refusal to sign the Fourteenth Amendment.
    (C) his refusal to appoint new justices to the Supreme Court.
    (D) his refusal to make slavery illegal.

27. The biggest problem in trying to create a centralized government for the Confederacy was
    (A) lack of financial support.
    (B) high inflation.
    (C) refusal of states to yield power to the government.
    (D) lack of men with government experience.

28. The surrender of whose command ended the Civil War?
    (A) General Joseph E. Johnston's command
    (B) General Jubal Early's command
    (C) General Thomas "Stonewall" Jackson's command
    (D) General Ambrose Burnside's command

29. Which of the following correctly states the situation in the Confederacy by the end of 1863?

    (A) The deteriorating military situation drew Southerners closer and reaffirmed their determination to win the war.

    (B) African Americans continued to work on plantations, but hoped for a Union victory.

    (C) Because the South had an agrarian economy, it was able to feed its people though the food was plain.

    (D) Ordinary Southerners began to see the war as one being fought to preserve the planter class, not their own interests.

30. The Fourteenth Amendment

    (A) abolished slavery.

    (B) gave the right to vote to African American men.

    (C) made African Americans citizens of the United States.

    (D) banned poll taxes and literacy tests as prerequisites for voting.

31. The Copperheads were

    (A) Northerners who moved South after the Civil War.

    (B) Northern Democrats who opposed the Union war effort.

    (C) white southern Republicans.

    (D) freed slaves who moved to Southern cities.

32. Which of the following was part of Grant's strategy of "total war"?

    (A) Wilderness Campaign

    (B) Anaconda Plan

    (C) Peninsular Campaign

    (D) Sherman's march through Georgia

33. Who commanded the Union forces during the Battle of Fredericksburg?

    (A) Joseph Johnston

    (B) George McClellan

    (C) Robert E. Lee

    (D) Ambrose Burnside

34. Davis proposed in 1865, but the Confederate Congress did not pass, a bill authorizing the use of slaves as

    (A) soldiers for the Confederacy.

    (B) Confederate soldiers in exchange for their freedom.

    (C) Confederate soldiers in exchange for freedom for their families, but not themselves.

    (D) Confederate soldiers in exchange for freedom for themselves and their families.

35. The Battle of Gettysburg was significant because it

    (A) was the longest battle of the Civil War, lasting nine months.

    (B) was the first Civil War battle fought on Northern soil.

    (C) marked a turning point in the war toward the Union side.

    (D) marked the first time that Lee's forces were overwhelmed by Grant's.

36. Why was it important that Maryland NOT join the Confederacy?

    (A) The main routes west ran through Maryland.

    (B) Access to the Ohio River ran through Maryland.

    (C) If Maryland joined the Confederacy, Delaware would be sure to follow.

    (D) If Maryland joined the Confederacy, Washington, D.C., would be surrounded by the Confederacy.

post-test

37. Which statement best explains President Abraham Lincoln's initial justification for the Civil War?

    (A) He believed it was his obligation as President to preserve the Union.

    (B) As an abolitionist, he wanted to end slavery in the United States.

    (C) He wanted to keep the South economically dependent on the industrialized North.

    (D) He wanted to end slavery in order to keep the support of Great Britain and France.

38. Cotton production spurred a westward expansion in the Deep South because

    (A) the slave population was increasing too rapidly for the amount of land available.

    (B) textile mills in Great Britain paid top dollar for American cotton.

    (C) most of the land was already planted in sugar, rice, and indigo.

    (D) cotton agriculture wore out the soil quickly and farmers went west looking for new land to cultivate.

39. Before the Civil War, slavery expanded in the South rather than in the North because

    (A) the South's geography encouraged the development of large-scale agriculture.

    (B) the Constitution outlawed the importation of slaves into the North.

    (C) Congress passed a law forbidding slavery in the North.

    (D) Northern states passed antislavery legislation.

40. What is true about the casualties of the Civil War?

    (A) The South lost the Civil War as a result of their higher number of casualties.

    (B) More soldiers on both sides died from disease than from wounds.

    (C) The Confederacy lost twice as many men as the Union did.

    (D) The Civil War had more casualties than any other war in history.

41. In their plans for Reconstruction, both Presidents Lincoln and Johnson sought to

    (A) punish the South for starting the Civil War.

    (B) force the South to pay reparations to the federal government.

    (C) allow Southern states to reenter the United States as quickly as possible.

    (D) establish the Republican Party as the only party in the South.

42. In what two states were the majority of Civil War battles fought?

    (A) Missouri and Texas

    (B) Georgia and Alabama

    (C) Virginia and Tennessee

    (D) South Carolina and Pennsylvania

43. Following the Civil War, many Southern states enacted black codes to

    (A) restrict the rights of African Americans.

    (B) provide free farmland for African Americans.

    (C) spell out the rights of African Americans.

    (D) support the creation of the Freedmen's Bureau.

44. Which of the following was a moral argument that Southerners used to justify slavery?

    (A) Slavery kept peace among the races.

    (B) Slavery was part of a well-structured hierarchical society and without it, Southern society would collapse.

    (C) Southern slaves were treated more humanely than Northern factory workers.

    (D) Slaves were necessary to the prosperity of the South.

45. Irish immigration sparked a wave of anti-Catholic sentiment, including the founding of which political party?

    (A) Know-Nothing

    (B) Whig

    (C) Southern Democratic

    (D) Liberty

46. How did Ladies Aid Societies aid the war effort?

    (A) They provided medical care to soldiers on the battlefield.

    (B) They acted as spies by taking messages across enemy lines.

    (C) They inspected hospitals and facilities for soldiers recuperating from wounds and illnesses.

    (D) They rolled bandages, sewed clothing for soldiers, and sent food packages to soldiers.

47. One disadvantage the South had at the beginning of the Civil War was

    (A) poor military leadership.

    (B) a lack of industry and financial and banking centers.

    (C) the lack of a deeply held reason worth fighting for.

    (D) a lack of labor to keep the economy going.

48. The capture of Mobile Bay was a significant loss for the Confederacy because

    (A) it was in retaliation for the Confederate capture of Fort Sumter.

    (B) it meant that Sherman could get supplies through the port of Mobile.

    (C) it destroyed the Confederate navy.

    (D) its fall completed the Union blockade of the Confederacy in the Gulf of Mexico east of the Mississippi.

49. Which of the following battles ended in a Union victory?

    (A) First Manassas

    (B) Second Manassas

    (C) Fredericksburg

    (D) Shiloh

50. Who benefited the most financially from the war?

    (A) Northern industrialists who produced war materiel

    (B) Northern workers and labor unions

    (C) British factory owners

    (D) Freed African Americans

51. Which of the following is a true statement about the Confederacy's diplomatic successes?

    (A) Great Britain agreed to sell weapons and supplies only to the Confederacy.

    (B) France and Great Britain agreed to sell weapons and supplies only to the Confederacy.

    (C) France and Great Britain agreed to sell weapons and supplies to the Confederacy as well as to the Union.

    (D) Great Britain declared neutrality and refused to sell weapons and supplies to either combatant.

52. The Union capture of the Mississippi ended the strategic importance of which Confederate state?

    (A) Alabama

    (B) Missouri

    (C) Oklahoma

    (D) Texas

53. How did the Militia Act of 1862 affect enslaved African Americans?

    (A) It didn't; it established conscription for white men in the North.

    (B) It didn't; it set up a system whereby white men could pay someone else to take their place in the Union army.

    (C) It offered freedom to slaves and their families in exchange for the man's service in the Union army.

    (D) It declared slaves of owners in territory occupied by Northern troops to be free.

54. Before John Brown's raid on Harper's Ferry in 1859, what other antislavery activity had he participated in?

    (A) Publication of the newspaper *Liberator*

    (B) The violence in Kansas between antislavery and proslavery supporters

    (C) Establishment of the American Anti-Slavery Society

    (D) Formation of the Free-Soil Party

55. Who was given command of Union forces in the West when Grant took command of the Army of the Potomac?

    (A) General Winfield Scott

    (B) General Don Carlos Buell

    (C) General William Tecumseh Sherman

    (D) General Ambrose Burnside

56. What encouraged Congress to pass the Fifteenth Amendment?

    (A) The fact that African Americans in the North could not vote.

    (B) The fact that African Americans were not considered citizens.

    (C) The fact that all African Americans were not free by the end of the war.

    (D) The fact that the Reconstruction Acts were not being enforced.

57. How were prisoners of war dealt with at the very beginning of the war?

    (A) They were released on parole.

    (B) They were put in overcrowded prison camps.

    (C) They were forced to fight for the opposing army.

    (D) They were usually killed.

58. Why were Southerners suspicious of Northerners who moved South after the war and became part of Reconstruction governments?

    (A) They considered all Northerners to be sympathetic to African Americans who would put the interests of African Americans before those of white Southerners.

    (B) They believed that these Northerners were sent by Congress to break up the Democratic Party.

    (C) They hated anything and anybody that came from the North.

    (D) They believed that these Northerners were there only to take advantage of the South's suffering.

59. When Lee surrendered, Jefferson Davis tried to

(A) deny that Lee had the authority to surrender the Army of Northern Virginia.

(B) board a ship for Great Britain.

(C) get to Texas to set up a new government.

(D) rally troops to defend the capital of Richmond.

60. What was the platform of the new Republican Party?

(A) Opposition to slavery and support of a strong central government

(B) Opposition to slavery and support of states' rights

(C) Support of popular sovereignty, enabling territories to decide whether to be free or slave

(D) Continuation of slavery where it already existed, but no extension of slavery into new territories

post-test

ANSWER KEY AND EXPLANATIONS

1. D	13. B	25. B	37. A	49. D
2. B	14. B	26. A	38. D	50. A
3. D	15. C	27. C	39. A	51. C
4. C	16. A	28. A	40. B	52. D
5. B	17. D	29. D	41. C	53. C
6. C	18. C	30. C	42. C	54. B
7. C	19. D	31. B	43. A	55. C
8. A	20. C	32. D	44. C	56. A
9. B	21. A	33. D	45. A	57. A
10. C	22. A	34. D	46. D	58. D
11. B	23. D	35. C	47. B	59. C
12. D	24. C	36. D	48. D	60. D

1. **The correct answer is (D).** In the mid-1800s, immigrants came in increasing numbers from Ireland and Germany, drawn by the prospects of economic opportunity and political and religious freedom. Choice (A) is incorrect because the United States did not begin placing restrictions on immigration until 1875. Choice (B) is the opposite of what occurred, and wars were one push factor that caused people to emigrate. Most immigrants during mid-1800s came from Northern Europe, so choice (C) is incorrect.

2. **The correct answer is (B).** Seizing Fort Sumter may have had its symbolic value, choice (A), but its real value to the South lay in its position guarding Charleston Harbor. Choice (B) is the better answer. Choice (C) is not true. Choice (D) is incorrect because with the exception of three forts in Florida, all other federal forts across the South were in Confederate hands.

3. **The correct answer is (D).** Choice (A) is incorrect; the Union forces were actually larger and better organized. He lost his command because even with superior forces and organization, he retreated and failed to move quickly and decisively, choice (D). Choice (B) is incorrect, although the press did not treat McClellan's apparent timidity with kindness. Choice (C) is true in that the Seven Days' Battle was indeed bloody. However, that was not the reason for McClellan's removal.

4. **The correct answer is (C).** The Kansas-Nebraska Act had the support of Southern Democrats, but not Northern Democrats, and this split seriously affected the future of the Democratic Party in the elections of 1856 and particularly 1860 because rival Democratic candidates campaigned. Choice (A) is incorrect because the Act helped launch the Republican Party as a haven for those who opposed slavery entirely or simply the extension of slavery into new territories, as well as those who wanted a strong central government to promote business. Choice (B) is incorrect because the Constitutional Union Party was founded and held together

to run John Bell for President in 1860; the party's goal was to avert secession. Choice (D) is incorrect because the Free-Soil Party was not strong enough to win many votes, and members migrated to the Republican Party after its founding.

5. **The correct answer is (B).** Whites dominated Southern politics during Reconstruction and held most public offices. African Americans held a minority of offices, so choice (A) is incorrect. Choice (C) is incorrect; the Freedmen's Bureau was a service agency of the federal government helping freed slaves to find housing, food, clothing, and jobs and provided educational opportunities for them. Choice (D) is incorrect because public offices were filled by elections.

6. **The correct answer is (C).** The Republican Party in the South fell apart mostly because white Southern Democrats opposed it. Choices (A) and (D) are not true. Choice (B) is incorrect because African Americans were kept from voting in many places, and the assumption is that they would have voted for Republican candidates.

7. **The correct answer is (C).** The Emancipation Proclamation turned the Civil War into a war to end slavery. Choice (A) is incorrect because the Emancipation Proclamation did not affect slaves in the border states. Choices (B) and (D) may have been incidental effects of the Emancipation Proclamation, but they were not the reasons behind the document's significance.

8. **The correct answer is (A).** The North and South had developed very different economic interests by the mid-1800s. Choice (B) is not true; the South was not particularly hospitable to immigrants. Choice (C) is incorrect because the South was dependent on exporting cotton, its principal crop. Choice (D) is incorrect for two reasons. The question asks for differences and the answer only deals with one topic, Southern farmers. In addition, the statement is not true. There

were only about 50,000 large plantations and hundreds of thousands of small farms.

9. **The correct answer is (B).** Lincoln wanted a free education for African Americans guaranteed by each state. Choices (A) and (D) were part of Johnson's plan. Choice (C) was part of the Radical Republicans' plan.

10. **The correct answer is (C).** The slave trade, but not slavery was prohibited in Washington, D.C., by the Compromise of 1850. Choices (A), (B), and (D) were all parts of the Compromise of 1850.

11. **The correct answer is (B).** The Republican Party was made up of abolitionists and members of the former Whig and Free-Soil parties. Choice (A) is incorrect; free African Americans could not vote so it would be unlikely that they joined a political party. Choice (C) is incorrect because Democrats who split from the Democratic Party went on to form the Constitutional Union Party. Choice (D) is incorrect because the Federalist Party had collapsed in 1816.

12. **The correct answer is (D).** The Supreme Court ruled that Dred Scott as an African American was not a citizen and, therefore, had no right to sue in court. Choice (A) is incorrect because Scott had lived for nine years in free states. Choice (B) is incorrect because Scott's owner died in Missouri, a slave state. Choice (C) is accurate, but irrelevant.

13. **The correct answer is (B).** South Carolina was the first state to secede following the election of 1860. Choices (C) and (D), Mississippi and Alabama, seceded in January 1861, and Virginia, choice (A), did not secede until after Fort Sumter in April 1861.

14. **The correct answer is (B).** African Americans soldiers—both free and escaped slaves—were discriminated against in the army; they were placed in all-black units, paid less than white soldiers, and given menial jobs. Choice (A) is incorrect although

some units like the 54th Massachusetts did see front line service. Choices (C) and (D) are incorrect.

15. **The correct answer is (C).** In his inaugural address, Lincoln said he believed that he had no right to interfere with slavery in the states where it already existed. Concerned about worsening the situation, he did not propose that slavery should be abolished, so choices (A) and (B) are incorrect. Choice (D) is also incorrect because he did take a position on slavery.

16. **The correct answer is (A).** The battle between the *Monitor* and the *Merrimac* was the first battle between ironclad warships. Choice (B) is incorrect because neither side won. Choice (C) is incorrect because the naval blockade lasted throughout the war and proved increasingly effective. It was the first naval battle of the war, so choice (D) is incorrect.

17. **The correct answer is (D).** The Battle of Antietam in Maryland was the first major battle of the Civil War to take place on northern soil. Choice (A) is incorrect although Gettysburg, Pennsylvania, was the farthest north that the Confederates ventured. Choice (B) is incorrect because Bull Run (Manassas) is south of Washington, D.C., in Virginia. Cold Harbor, choice (C), is also in Virginia.

18. **The correct answer is (C).** The Civil War introduced new weaponry, including the Gatling gun and shrapnel, which were more technologically advanced than weaponry used in previous wars. Choice (A) is incorrect because women had nursed the wounded and died in earlier wars. There have been naval battles since ancient times and both the American Revolution and the War of 1812 had seen naval battles, so choice (B) is incorrect. Choice (D) is incorrect, or there would have been no reason for the draft riots in the North during the war.

19. **The correct answer is (D).** By taking Chattanooga, Grant and Sherman opened the way

to Atlanta. Choices (A), (B), and (C) are all in Virginia and incorrect.

20. **The correct answer is (C).** With Union victories at Vicksburg and Gettysburg, the possibility that the Confederacy would be able to remain independent became extremely remote, so Great Britain and France decided not to offend the United States, an important ally, by recognizing the Confederacy. Choice (A) was never a possibility, so eliminate it. Choice (B) might have been true, but it's not the most significant consequence of the two Union victories and would more likely have been true of the closing of the Union coastal blockade. Choice (D) is incorrect; however, the two victories made any peace negotiations, which some people in both the North and South were pursuing, highly unlikely.

21. **The correct answer is (A).** The Compromise of 1850 was passed as several individual bills in order to get support from Southerners and Northerners, depending on the issue. Choice (B) is incorrect because one of the bills in the package of compromises was the Fugitive Slave Law. Choice (C) is incorrect because the slave trade, but not slavery, was abolished in Washington. Choice (D) is incorrect because according to the compromise, settlers in the New Mexico Territory (and Utah Territory) could decide for themselves whether to allow slavery.

22. **The correct answer is (A).** The 1870s saw a great deal of corruption in the North as well as the South. Choice (B) is incorrect because secret societies continued to terrorize African Americans well after federal troops had been removed from the South. Choice (C) is incorrect because military districts remained in force until the Compromise of 1876. Choice (D) is incorrect because most Southern governments initially were controlled by white Southerners with some African American office holders.

23. **The correct answer is (D).** Florida is the only state in the list that was covered under the Emancipation Proclamation. Slaves in the border states of Missouri and Maryland, choices (A) and (B), were not freed, nor were slaves in West Virginia, which remained in the Union while the rest of Virginia seceded, so choice (C) is incorrect.

24. **The correct answer is (C).** Sherman first captured Atlanta, then marched to Savannah, and finally turned north into South Carolina. Choices (A), (B), and (D) are incorrect.

25. **The correct answer is (B).** A significant event, the capture and burning of Atlanta appeared to be a turning point to many Northerners in the long and costly war, and Lincoln was overwhelmingly reelected. Choice (A) is incorrect because it was one of the battles leading up to Lee's surrender and did not occur until 1865. Choice (C), Shiloh, was a Union victory, but in 1862. Choice (D), Chancellorsville, was a Confederate victory in 1863.

26. **The correct answer is (A).** Congress wanted to take control of Reconstruction away from President Johnson and ultimately used impeachment as a way to gain this control. Choice (B) is incorrect because presidents don't sign Constitutional amendments; Congress passes them and the states ratify them. Choice (C) is not true, and choice (D) is incorrect because the Thirteenth Amendment abolished slavery.

27. **The correct answer is (C).** The biggest problem that Jefferson Davis had in trying to develop a system of central government was states' rights; states jealously guarded their powers. Choices (A) and (B) were problems that the Confederacy faced, but neither was the reason that states didn't obey the central government. Choice (D) is not true.

28. **The correct answer is (A).** Choice (A) is correct. General Johnston surrendered to General Sherman on April 26, seventeen days after Lee had surrendered to Grant.

Choices (B), (C), and (D) are incorrect. Lee had relieved General Early of his command in March 1865 because of a series of losses and his inability to rally troops to fight. General Jackson had been killed at Chancellorsville, and Burnside was a Union general.

29. **The correct answer is (D).** From the draft that favored the wealthy to slave labor to tend their plantations, large landowners were better off during the war than the ordinary Southerner, whether town dweller or yeoman farmer. Choice (A) is incorrect because the situation on the battlefield divided Southerners; some wanted to continue the fight, but many others wanted to negotiate a peace. Choice (B) is incorrect because thousands of African Americans—about 25 percent—abandoned their plantations and fled behind Union lines. Choice (C) is incorrect. The destruction of farms by soldiers from both armies, the effectiveness of the naval blockade, and the destruction of the rail network resulted in widespread hunger across the South.

30. **The correct answer is (C).** The Fourteenth Amendment made African Americans citizens of the United States. The Thirteenth Amendment abolished slavery, so choice (A) is incorrect. The Fifteenth Amendment gave the right to vote to African American men, so choice (B) is incorrect. Poll taxes and literacy tests, choice (D), were inventions of the later 1800s to keep African Americans from voting in the South; the Civil Rights Act of 1965 outlawed them.

31. **The correct answer is (B).** Copperheads were Democrats in the North, particularly the Midwest, who opposed the Union war effort. Choice (A) is incorrect; it was Northern Republicans who moved South after the war and were called carpetbaggers by Southerners. White Southern Republicans were called scalawags by their opponents, so choice (C) is incorrect. Choice (D) is incorrect.

32. **The correct answer is (D).** Sherman's march through Georgia resulted in an estimated $100 million worth of ruined farms and devastated towns. His soldiers lived off the land, burned what they couldn't use, and moved on. Choice (A), the Wilderness Campaign, refers to the three-day battle in northern Virginia. Choice (B), the Anaconda Plan, was General Winfield Scott's plan to defeat the South. The Peninsular Campaign, choice (C), was McClellan's plan to seize Richmond, the capital of the Confederacy, and bring a speedy end to the war. Choices (A), (B), and (C) all occurred before Grant was made commander of Union forces.

33. **The correct answer is (D).** Ambrose Burnside was the commander of Union forces during the Battle of Fredericksburg. Johnston, choice (A), commanded Confederate forces at First Manassas. Choice (B), McClellan, was commander of the Army of the Potomac until the fall of 1862, and Fredericksburg was fought in December. Choice (C), Lee, led the Confederate Army of Northern Virginia.

34. **The correct answer is (D).** Davis proposed offering freedom to slaves who served as Confederate soldiers and their families. However, the final bill called for drafting slaves and did not mention freedom. Choice (A) is incorrect because few African American slaves were drafted as a result of the law. Choices (B) and (C) are incorrect because neither is the complete answer.

35. **The correct answer is (C).** The Battle of Gettysburg was significant because it was the most northerly penetration of Confederate forces, it inflicted a major loss on Lee's army, and he never again attempted to invade the North or to launch a major offensive. Choice (A) is incorrect because the siege of Petersburg lasted nine months; the battle at Gettysburg lasted three days. Choice (B) is incorrect because the Battle of Antietam took place in Maryland. Choice

(D) is incorrect because Lee's army faced the forces of General George Meade.

36. **The correct answer is (D).** Confederate territory would have surrounded Washington if Maryland had seceded. Choice (A) is incorrect because the main routes west went through Missouri. Choice (B) is incorrect because access to the Ohio River lay through Kentucky. Choice (C) is not true; the majority of the state's citizens were Unionists. Only a tiny minority of residents were slave owners.

37. **The correct answer is (A).** President Lincoln initially justified the Civil War because he believed it was his obligation as President to preserve the Union. Choice (B) is incorrect; the abolishment of slavery may have been a long-term goal, but it was not his initial justification for fighting the war. Choice (C) is not true, and neither is choice (D).

38. **The correct answer is (D).** Cotton agriculture quickly depletes the soil of nutrients, so farmers moved west through Alabama and Louisiana and into Texas to grow cotton. Choice (A) is not true. Choice (B) may have been true, but it was not the reason for the migration of cotton planters west. Choice (C) is incorrect; sugar, rice, and indigo were crops of the Upper South, especially around the turn of the nineteenth century.

39. **The correct answer is (A).** Slavery expanded in the South rather than the North because the South's geography encouraged the development of large-scale plantation agriculture. Choice (B) is incorrect because the U.S. Constitution banned the importation of slaves after 1808 in both the North and the South. Choice (C) is incorrect because antislave legislation was left to the states prior to the Thirteenth Amendment. Choice (D) is true, but not the answer to the question.

40. **The correct answer is (B).** More soldiers died from diseases than wounds in the Civil

War. The Civil War had more casualties than any other war in U.S. history, but not of all wars, so choice (D) is incorrect. Choice (A) is incorrect because the Confederacy lost the war by losing battles, although it is true that the number of men that it could field was rapidly dwindling through battle deaths, non-mortal wounds, disease, and at the end, desertions. Choice (C) is the opposite of the truth.

41. **The correct answer is (C).** Both Presidents Lincoln and Johnson wanted to allow Southern states to reenter the Union as quickly as possible after the war. Choices (A), (B), and (D) are untrue.

42. **The correct answer is (C).** The majority of Civil War battles were fought in Virginia and Tennessee. Choices (A), (B), and (D) are incorrect.

43. **The correct answer is (A).** Black codes were established to restrict the rights of African Americans. Choice (C) was the excuse given for passage of the black codes, but was not true. Choices (B) and (D) are not true.

44. **The correct answer is (C).** The question asks for a "moral" argument used by Southerners; only choice (C) is based on a supposed moral consideration. Southerners contrasted the food, shelter, and clothing that slave owners provided their slaves with the capitalist North in which factory workers were paid little for long hours and then had to use their pay to buy food, clothing, and shelter. Choices (A) and (B) are sociological reasons, not moral reasons. Choice (D) is an economic reason.

45. **The correct answer is (A).** "Know-Nothing" was the nickname given to the nativist American Party, which was founded in the 1850s to oppose immigration. Choice (B), the Whig Party, dated back to the mid-1830s and collapsed in the 1850s because of divisions over slavery and national expansion. Choice (C), Southern Democrats, split from Northern Democrats in 1860 over the issue

of slavery, not immigrants. Choice (D), the Liberty Party, was an antislavery party of the 1840s.

46. **The correct answer is (D).** Local Ladies Aid Societies helped the war effort by rolling bandages, sewing clothing for soldiers, and sending food packages to soldiers. Women volunteers in the U.S. Sanitary Commission, not local Ladies Aid Societies, provided nursing care to soldiers on the battlefield, so choice (A) is incorrect. Choice (B) was not the work of Ladies Aid Societies. Choice (C) was also the work of the U.S. Sanitary Commission.

47. **The correct answer is (B).** One disadvantage that the South had at the beginning of the war was a lack of industry and financial and banking centers, which made it difficult to supply the Confederacy and to pay for materials, both military and domestic. Choices (A), (C), and (D) are the opposite of what was true about Southern disadvantages.

48. **The correct answer is (D).** Although the city of Mobile did not fall to the Union until late in the war, the capture of the three forts guarding Mobile Bay and thus the harbor completed the Union blockade of the Gulf of Mexico east of the Mississippi, choice (D). New Orleans had fallen to the Union in 1862. Choice (A) is incorrect; the capture of Mobile Bay was a strategic goal for the Union. Choice (B) is incorrect because Sherman was marching north through Georgia, away from Alabama. Choice (C) is incorrect because though the Confederate navy suffered casualties and damage to its ships, its navy was not destroyed.

49. **The correct answer is (D).** Only the battle of Shiloh, choice (D), was a Union victory. Choices (A), (B), and (C), First and Second Manassas (also known as Bull Run) and Fredericksburg were decisive Confederate victories.

50. **The correct answer is (A).** The Civil War created a boom for Northern industrialists

who supplied war materiel and other supplies such as food rations and uniforms to the army. Choice (B) is incorrect because strikes at factories making war materiel were blocked and labor leaders were imprisoned on Lincoln's orders. Choice (C) is too vague; if the answer said "British textile factory owners," it might have been correct. Choice (D) is incorrect because while former slaves gained their freedom, they were left without the means to earn their living.

51. **The correct answer is (C).** France and Great Britain allowed its citizens to sell weapons and supplies to both the Union and the Confederacy, so choice (C) is correct, and, therefore, choices (A) and (B) are incorrect. Choice (D) is partially true because Great Britain did declare itself neutral, but half a wrong answer is an all-wrong answer.

52. **The correct answer is (D).** Texas was a source of supplies for the Confederacy, and the Union seizure of the Mississippi cut Texas' supply lines to the rest of the Confederacy. Alabama is east of the Mississippi and inland from it, so choice (A) is incorrect. Choice (B) is incorrect because Missouri was a border state and remained loyal to the Union. Choice (C), Oklahoma, was not a state, but the major part of the Indian Territory.

53. **The correct answer is (C).** The Militia Act of 1862 offered freedom to slaves who enlisted in the Union army. The law also gave freedom to the men's families. Choices (A) and (B) both refer to the Draft Law of 1863. Choice (D) refers to a provision of the Emancipation Proclamation.

54. **The correct answer is (B).** John Brown was an active participant in the violence in Kansas, instigating the massacre at Pottawatomie Creek, a proslavery settlement. This was in retaliation for a proslavery attack on the antislavery settlement at Lawrence. Choice (A) was published by William Lloyd Garrison. Choice (C) was founded in 1833 and Garrison, not Brown, was one of its founding members. Choice (D) is also incorrect not only because Brown was not involved, but because the party was willing to allow slavery to continue in the South as long as it didn't expand westward. Both positions were the opposite of Brown's beliefs.

55. **The correct answer is (C).** General Sherman was given command of the army in the West when Grant went east to assume command of the Army of the Potomac in 1864. Choice (A) is incorrect because General Scott was Commander-in-Chief of the Union Army at the beginning of the war, so choice (A) is incorrect. Choice (B) is incorrect because General Buell had been relieved of the command of the Army of the Ohio after significant losses to the Confederates in Kentucky. Choice (D) is incorrect because General Burnside had replaced General George McClellan as commander of the Army of the Potomac in 1862.

56. **The correct answer is (A).** Because eleven Northern states and the border states refused to allow African Americans to vote, Congress passed the Fifteenth Amendment, giving all male citizens the right to vote. Choice (B) is incorrect because the Fourteenth Amendment made all African Americans citizens. Choice (C) is incorrect because the Thirteenth Amendment abolished slavery in all states and territories. Choice (D) is not true.

57. **The correct answer is (A).** At the very beginning of the war, prisoners of war were released back to the opposing side on parole; they were then free to fight again. Later in the war, prisoners were sent to overcrowded and unhealthful prisoner camps where many died, so choice (B) is incorrect. Choice (C) is not true. Choice (D) is partially true in that African American soldiers who were taken prisoner by Confederate soldiers were sometimes killed.

58. **The correct answer is (D).** Southerners were suspicious of Northerners who moved South after the war because they suspected that these people were there only to make their fortunes at the expense of white Southerners. Choices (A), (B), and (C) may have some truth to them, but the overriding reason for Southerners' suspicions according to historians is choice (D).

59. **The correct answer is (C).** Davis fled Richmond and went south looking for an escape route to Texas. However, he was captured in Georgia. Choices (A), (B), and (D) are not true.

60. **The correct answer is (D).** The Republican Platform of 1860 did not go as far as radical abolitionists wished it to. They would have only been happy with a platform that called for the end of slavery, but the party did not go that far while decrying the manipulation of proslavery forces in Kansas and Nebraska. Choice (A) is incorrect because it would more likely have matched the policy of radicals in the party. Choice (B) could describe the policies of Democrats in 1860, so it is incorrect. Choice (C) is incorrect because it is the opposite of what the Republican Platform stated.

SUMMING IT UP

- The differences between the North and South were geographic, economic, and cultural.

- As the nineteenth century wore on, the North was becoming an industrialized economy, whereas the South was becoming more dependent on cotton cultivation, which, in turn, was dependent on the labor of enslaved African Americans. The geography of the Northeast fostered the development of factories and cities, whereas the geography of both the South and Midwest supported larger farms.

- The North, which included the Midwest, was becoming a culturally diverse region because of the influx of European immigrants, especially from Ireland and Germany. The South, on the other hand, was becoming a rigidly stratified society of large-scale planters dependent on slave labor, small slaveowners with a few slaves, yeomen farmers with no slaves, tenant farmers who rented land from larger farmers, poor whites, free blacks, and slaves.

- Southerners defended slavery on religious grounds and as a natural part of society; they argued slavery was more humane than the Northern factory system.

- The first antislavery society was founded in 1775. By the 1830s, the movement had split along philosophical lines. Gradualists called for the slow phasing-out of slavery so that the economy of the South would not be disrupted. William Lloyd Garrison and his followers championed immediatism, the immediate end to slavery and the establishment of equal rights for all African Americans.

- Westward expansion increased tensions between antislavery and proslavery factions: Should slavery be allowed in the new territories? The first attempt to answer the question was the Compromise of 1820, also known as the Missouri Compromise, which divided the Louisiana Territory into slave and free areas. Slavery was prohibited above a certain latitude and allowed below that line with the exception of Missouri, which was allowed to enter the Union as a slave state.

- The annexation of Texas, the acquisition of lands from Mexico at the end of the Mexican War, and the Gadsden Purchase reignited the debate over free versus slave states. The issue was not only about morality, but also of the balance of power in Congress.

- Stephen Douglas proposed the Compromise of 1850 as five separate bills in order to gain enough support among Northern and Southern members of Congress. California would enter the Union as a free state. Settlers in New Mexico and Utah Territories would decide for themselves whether to allow slavery. The slave trade would be ended in Washington, D.C., and the Fugitive Slave Law set up a system to return escaped slaves to their owners.

- In 1854, Douglas again offered a compromise for settling Kansas and Nebraska: settlers would decide for themselves whether to allow slavery in the two territories. Known as popular sovereignty, this compromise led to "bloody Kansas," as proslavery and antislavery forces fought over control of Kansas.

- The Republican Party was founded in 1854 and attracted abolitionists, members of the former Whig Party, members of the Free-Soil Party, and antislavery Democrats from the North and West. The party opposed slavery and supported a strong central government.

- Tensions intensified between North and South because of the Supreme Court's ruling in the Dred Scott decision that African Americans—free and enslaved—were not and could never be citizens and that Congress had no right to ban slavery, thus nullifying the Missouri Compromise.

- John Brown's raid on the federal arsenal at Harper's Ferry, Virginia, added to the tension. He had intended that his raid would ignite a slave revolt across the South, but he was forced to surrender after a day.

- When Abraham Lincoln, the Republican candidate for President in 1860, won the election, South Carolina passed an ordinance of secession in December. By the end of April 1861, after Confederate forces had shelled and captured Fort Sumter in Charleston harbor, ten other states had joined South Carolina in the Confederate States of America.

- The four slave states of Delaware, Maryland, Kentucky, and Missouri remained loyal to the Union and were called "border states."

- Both the North and the South thought the war would be over in a matter of months. The North had many advantages: a larger population, a navy, a large railroad network, financial and banking centers, and an industrialized economy. The South had well-trained and experienced officers and the advantage of fighting a defensive war on its home ground. Southerners also had a common cause that they believed in—the Southern way of life.

- The battle of First Manassas (Bull Run) in July 1861, in which the Confederates routed the Union forces, convinced both sides that the war would be a long one.

- Initial reaction to the war on both sides was enthusiasm with more men volunteering than the armies could handle. As the war dragged on and casualties mounted, it became more and more difficult to recruit soldiers. Both the North and South turned to conscription, and the North allowed African Americans to serve beginning in 1862. However, the Confederate government held out until near the end of the war before allowing African Americans to enlist.

- A major problem that Jefferson Davis had in governing the Confederacy was the lack of cooperation by state governments. They put their states' rights before the need for a central government.

- The North first adopted the Anaconda Plan to blockade Southern ports: seize control of the Mississippi River, thus splitting the Confederacy in two, and invade from east and west.

- General George McClellan moved slowly, methodically, and to Lincoln, timidly. After the devastating Union losses during the Seven Days' Battle, part of the Peninsular Campaign, and his retreat, McClellan was replaced. Lincoln tried several commanders until he placed Ulysses S. Grant, a hero of the campaign in the West, in charge of all Union armies in late 1864.

- Grant's plan was to coordinate the activity of all Union armies and pound the Confederate forces into surrender. Grant accomplished his plan in a series of offensive actions against Lee in Virginia, while Philip Sheridan fought for and won control of the Shenandoah Valley, and William Sherman burned Atlanta and devastated a wide swath of Georgia into South Carolina.

- Lee surrendered his Army of Northern Virginia at Appomattox Courthouse, Virginia, on April 9, 1865. The last Confederate army, that of Joseph Johnston, surrendered on April 26.

- On January 1, 1863, Lincoln issued the Emancipation Proclamation, freeing all enslaved people in areas still under the control of Confederate forces. It did not free slaves in border states or in areas under Union control.

- Lincoln was assassinated on April 14, 1865, by a Southerner.

- Lincoln had proposed a plan for Reconstruction that would have (1) readmitted a state when 10 percent of a state's citizens eligible to vote in 1860 swore an oath of allegiance to the Union (the Ten Percent Plan); (2) granted amnesty to most former Confederates once they took the oath of allegiance; (3) required high-ranking officials in the Confederate government to ask the President for a pardon in order to be granted amnesty; and (4) required the states had to guarantee a free education to African Americans. Once a state had been readmitted, it had to (1) form a government, (2) hold a constitutional convention, and (3) write a new constitution that included rights for African Americans.

- After Lincoln's assassination, Andrew Johnson succeeded to the Presidency and presented his own plan. Much of it was similar to Lincoln's policies, but it also included the following: (1) amnesty would be offered to all ex-Confederates except for high-ranking officials and property owners who were worth more than $20,000, a large sum at the time; (2) these men could not hold public office or vote unless they asked the President for a pardon; (3) the states had to revoke their secession laws; (4) war debts that the Confederacy had incurred could not be collected; and (5) states had to ratify the Thirteenth Amendment, abolishing slavery.

- Radical Republicans who wrestled control of Reconstruction from the President passed a much harsher set of Reconstruction Acts: (1) the ten state governments that had not ratified the Fourteenth Amendment (but that Johnson had recognized) were declared illegal; (2) the ten states were divided into five military districts; (3) the military districts were overseen by military governors who could use federal troops to protect civil rights and maintain order if needed; (4) each state had to call a convention to write a new constitution; (5) both white and African American adult males were eligible to vote for members of the constitutional conventions; (6) those who had served as officials in the Confederacy could not be members of the constitutional conventions; (7) the new state constitutions were to guarantee the vote for African American males; (8) the states had to ratify the Fourteenth Amendment.

- The Thirteenth Amendment, which abolished slavery, had been passed by Congress and ratified by the states in December 1865. Along with the Fourteenth Amendment, which granted citizenship to all African Americans, and the Fifteenth Amendment, which guaranteed the right to vote to African Americans, the three are known as the Reconstruction Amendments.

Introduction to World Religions

The following chart outlines the sections and subsections in the Introduction to World Religions test and offers a comparison between the percent of practice questions in this chapter and the actual DSST exam.

CONTENT OUTLINE: SECTIONS AND SUBSECTIONS	PERCENT OF EXAM DEVOTED TO EACH CONTENT AREA	NUMBER OF ITEMS IN THE DIAGNOSTIC TEST AND POST-TEST BY CONTENT AREA	PERCENT OF ITEMS IN THE DIAGNOSTIC TEST AND POST-TEST BY CONTENT AREA
I. Definition and Origins of Religion	**6%**	**5**	**6.25%**
A. Basic Dimensions of Religion		4	80%
B. Approaches to Religion		1	20%
II. Indigenous Religions	**6%**	**6**	**7.5%**
A. Native North American Traditions		1	16.6%
B. Native South American Traditions		1	16.6%
C. Native West African Traditions		1	16.6%
D. Native Middle Eastern Traditions		1	16.6%
E. Hellenic and Roman Traditions		1	16.6%
F. Shintoism		1	16.6%
III. Hinduism	**10%**	**7**	**8.75%**
A. Historical Development		2	28.5%
B. Doctrine and Practice		5	71.5%
IV. Buddhism	**10%**	**8**	**10%**
A. Historical Development		1	12.5%
B. Major Traditions		1	12.5%
C. Doctrine and Practice		6	75%
V. Confucianism	**6%**	**5**	**6.25%**
A. Historical Development		1	20%
B. Doctrine and Practice		4	80%
VI. Taoism	**4%**	**3**	**3.75%**
A. Historical Development		1	33.3%
B. Doctrine and Practice		2	66.7%
VII. Judaism	**16%**	**13**	**16.25%**
A. Historical Development		3	23%
B. Denominations		4	31%
C. Doctrine and Practice		6	46%

chapter 2

VIII. Christianity	**18%**	**14**	**17.5%**
A. Historical Development		2	14.3%
B. Major Traditions		5	35.7%
C. Doctrine and Practice		7	50%
IX. Islam	**16%**	**13**	**16.25%**
A. Historical Development		2	15.4%
B. Major Traditions		2	15.4%
C. Doctrine and Practice		9	69.2%
X. Religious Movements	**8%**	**6**	**7.5%**
A. Before 1000 C.E.		2	33.3%
B. After 1000 C.E.		4	66.7%
Grand Total	**100%**	**80**	**100%**

OVERVIEW

- Diagnostic test
- Answer key and explanations
- Definition and origins of religion
- Indigenous religions
- Hinduism
- Buddhism
- Confucianism
- Taoism
- Judaism
- Christianity
- Islam
- Religious movements
- Post-test
- Answer key and explanations
- Summing it up

DIAGNOSTIC TEST

Directions: Carefully read each of the following 20 questions. Choose the best answer to each question and circle your answer choice. The Answer Key and Explanations can be found following this Diagnostic Test.

1. Which of the following accurately describes Ramadan?

   (A) It is the Muslim month of fasting.

   (B) It is the Jewish day of atonement.

   (C) It is the forty days before Easter.

   (D) It is the Hindu festival of lights.

2. The Hasidim

   (A) is a modern denomination of Judaism that follows a liberal interpretation of Jewish law.

   (B) are followers of mystical rebbes who live in their own communities separated from the world.

   (C) are descended from Jews who were expelled from Spain and Portugal in the fifteenth century.

   (D) is a twentieth-century denomination that keeps traditional historical Jewish customs.

diagnostic test

3. The purpose of the Second Vatican Council was to

(A) reassert that Confirmation, Penance, the Eucharist, Extreme Unction, Marriage, and Holy Orders as well as Baptism were sacraments.

(B) affirm the basic tenets of the faith by developing what became known as the Nicene Creed.

(C) modernize and revitalize the Catholic Church.

(D) reassert Catholic Church teachings after the Protestant Reformation.

4. The basic sacred text of Hinduism is the

(A) Law of Manu.

(B) Vedas.

(C) Analects.

(D) Bhagavad-Gita.

5. The Pope cannot err in proclaiming a matter of faith and morals when he invokes the doctrine of

(A) encyclicals.

(B) apostolic primacy.

(C) papal infallibility.

(D) papal primacy.

6. Dimensions of basic religions include

   I.   rituals.
   II. taboos.
   III. ancestor worship.
   IV. animism.

(A) I and II only

(B) I and III only

(C) I, II, and IV only

(D) I, II, III, and IV

7. A basic tenet of Confucius' teachings is

(A) the renunciation of all desire in order to enter nirvana.

(B) behaving ethically at all times and in all relationships.

(C) making regular sacrifices to the deities in order to have one's transgressions wiped away.

(D) the balance between dark and light, heaven and earth.

8. In Hinduism, samsara is

(A) the force generated by actions in this life that set up what the next life will be like.

(B) the breaking free of life.

(C) the wandering of the life force from one body and time to another.

(D) a riddle that will help a believer achieve insight.

9. The Second Pillar of Islam is

(A) daily prayer.

(B) almsgiving.

(C) hajj.

(D) fasting.

10. In general, most West African indigenous religions

(A) erect temples for worship.

(B) believe in a central High God.

(C) are monotheistic.

(D) have male and female priests.

11. Which of the following is the body of Islamic law?

(A) Shi'a

(B) Shari'ah

(C) Hadith

(D) Qur'an

12. A practice common to both Protestant denominations in general and the Orthodox Churches is

(A) infant baptism.

(B) married clergy.

(C) belief in the presence of Jesus in the Eucharist.

(D) acceptance of the seven sacraments.

13. The Pentateuch is part of the

(A) Torah.

(B) Talmud.

(C) Haggadah.

(D) Gemara.

14. Right views, right thoughts, and right speech are elements of

(A) the right relationships that Confucius taught.

(B) yin and yang.

(C) Jesus' Sermon on the Mount.

(D) Buddhism's Eight-Fold Path.

15. Liberation theology seeks to

(A) provide life meaning in eastern mysticism.

(B) return Christianity to its original roots.

(C) work for social justice for the poor.

(D) defend Christianity against science and cultural liberalism.

16. Belief that God will send a messiah to save the world from its sins is a tenet of Judaism, Christianity, and

(A) Shintoism.

(B) Buddhism.

(C) Islam.

(D) Hinduism.

17. Passover celebrates the

(A) delivery of the Jews from Egypt.

(B) retaking of the Temple in Jerusalem.

(C) harvest.

(D) delivery of the Jews from Persia.

18. Which of the following men introduced into Protestantism the concept of predestination?

(A) Henry VIII

(B) Martin Luther

(C) John Calvin

(D) John Wesley

19. The Egyptians worshipped

(A) Ahura-Mazda.

(B) Isis and Osiris.

(C) Yahweh.

(D) Shiva.

20. Which of the following are tenets of Hinduism?

  I. Belief in a cycle of rebirth
 II. Multiplicity of deities
III. Caste system
 IV. Adherence to nonviolence

(A) I and II only

(B) I and IV only

(C) I, II, and III only

(D) I, II, III, and IV

ANSWER KEY AND EXPLANATIONS

1. A	5. C	9. A	13. A	17. A
2. B	6. D	10. B	14. D	18. C
3. C	7. B	11. B	15. C	19. B
4. B	8. C	12. B	16. C	20. D

1. **The correct answer is (A).** During Ramadan, Muslims who are physically able and not pregnant must fast from sunrise to sunset from all food and drink. Choice (B) is incorrect because it describes Yom Kippur, a Jewish holy day. Choice (C) is incorrect because the forty days before Easter are known as Lent in the Christian calendar. Choice (D) is incorrect because the Hindu festival of lights is called Diwali.

2. **The correct answer is (B).** Hasidic Judaism was founded in the eighteenth century in Poland and follows a mystical version of Judaism separated from the modern world. Choice (A) is incorrect because it describes Reform Judaism. Choice (C) is incorrect because it describes Sephardic Jews who might be of any denomination today. Choice (D) is incorrect because it describes Reconstructionist Judaism.

3. **The correct answer is (C).** The Second Vatican Council was called by Pope John XXIII in 1962. Its purpose was to modernize and revitalize the Catholic Church. Choice (A) is incorrect because this reaffirmation was one result of the Council of Trent. Choice (D) also describes the Council of Trent, not the Second Vatican Council. Choice (B) is incorrect because the Nicene Creed was promulgated after the First Council of Nicaea in 325.

4. **The correct answer is (B).** Choice (A) is incorrect; the Law of Manu was written after the Vedas and contains ethical and social standards for living, but not all the basic concepts of Hinduism. Choice (C) is incorrect because the Analects collect the teachings of Confucius. Choice (D) is incorrect; the Bhagavad-Gita is an epic poem about deities and heroes.

5. **The correct answer is (C).** The doctrine of papal infallibility, invoked when the Pope speaks "ex cathedra," asserts that the Holy Spirit keeps the Pope from error in proclaiming a doctrine of faith or morals. Choice (A) is incorrect because encyclicals are documents of teachings issued by the Pope, not the doctrines themselves. Choice (B) is incorrect because apostolic primacy refers to the place of the Church of Rome as the first among all Catholic Churches. Choice (D) is incorrect because papal primacy asserts that the Pope as head of the Catholic Church is the supreme priest of the Catholic Church; this doctrine was one of the reasons for the split with eastern Christians.

6. **The correct answer is (D).** All four—(1) ritual, (2) taboos, (3) ancestor worship, and (4) animism—are features of basic religions. Only choice (D) includes all four and so is the correct answer.

7. **The correct answer is (B).** Choice (A) is incorrect; renunciation of desire to enter nirvana is a tenet of Buddhism. Choice (C) is incorrect because Confucius did not teach about deities, sacrifices to them, or forgiveness of sins. Choice (D) refers to the concepts of yin and yang in Taoism.

8. **The correct answer is (C).** Choice (A) is incorrect because the actions in this life that set up what the next life will be like

is called karma. Choice (B) is incorrect because moksha is the breaking free of the life cycle. Choice (D) is incorrect because koan is a riddle used in Zen Buddhism to help a person achieve sudden insight.

9. **The correct answer is (A).** The first pillar of Islam is "There is no God but Allah; Muhammad is the messenger of Allah." Choice (A), daily prayer, is the second pillar. Choice (B), almsgiving, is the third pillar. Choice (D), fasting, is the fourth pillar. Choice (C), the hajj, or pilgrimage to Mecca, is the fifth pillar.

10. **The correct answer is (B).** In general, West African religions typically believe in a central High God who created the world and then withdrew from it. Choice (A) is incorrect because most West African religions do not have temples. Choice (C) is incorrect because typically West African religions are polytheistic. Choice (D) is incorrect because most West African religions do not have priesthoods, male or female; the religions typically have healers (and some have diviners).

11. **The correct answer is (B).** Choice (A) is incorrect because Shi'a is one of the two major branches of Islam; the other is Sunni. Choice (C), the Hadith, is a collection of traditions relating to Muhammad and his companions. Choice (D) is incorrect because the Qur'an is the basic sacred text of Islam.

12. **The correct answer is (B).** Priests may be married in the Orthodox Churches if they are married before ordination. Protestant denominations don't have celibacy requirements for priests and ministers. Choice (A) is incorrect because Protestant churches in general (note this qualifier in the question stem) practice adult baptism, not infant baptism as the Orthodox Churches do. Choice (C) is incorrect because whereas the Orthodox Churches believe in transubstantiation, Protestant denominations accept it. Choice (D) is incorrect because Protestant denomi-

nations do not accept all sevens sacraments, and while Orthodox Churches accept them as major sacraments, they consider other things sacramental as well.

13. **The correct answer is (A).** The Pentateuch is the first five books of the Hebrew Bible and part of the Torah. Choice (B) is incorrect because the Talmud is commentary assembled over the centuries on the Mishnah, a collection of Judaic oral laws compiled in 200 C.E. Together, the Mishnah and the Gemara, choice (D), make up the Talmud. Choice (C) is incorrect because the Haggadah is the order of readings for the Passover Seder.

14. **The correct answer is (D).** The Eight-Fold Path of Buddhism contains a series of steps: right views, right thoughts, right speech, right action, right livelihood, right effort, right mindfulness, and right concentration. Choice (A) is incorrect because the teachings of Confucius on right relationships don't specifically use these terms. Choice (B) is incorrect because yin and yang are elements of Taoism and refer to opposing yet complementary principles of life. Choice (C) is incorrect because Jesus' Sermon on the Mount includes the Beatitudes.

15. **The correct answer is (C).** Choice (A) may seem like a good answer, but it isn't correct. Choice (B) is incorrect because it describes the Church of Jesus Christ of Latter Day Saints, also known as Mormons. Choice (D) is incorrect because it describes the mission of Christian fundamentalism.

16. **The correct answer is (C).** Choice (A) is incorrect because Shinto has no central deity or concept of sin. Practitioners of choices (B) and (D) both believe in personal enlightenment as a way to a personal nirvana.

17. **The correct answer is (A).** Choice (B) is incorrect because Chanukah celebrates the retaking of the Temple in Jerusalem. Choice (C) is incorrect because Sukkoth is a harvest celebration. Choice (D) is incorrect because

Purim celebrates the delivery of the Jews from Persia.

18. **The correct answer is (C).** Choice (A) is incorrect because other than substituting his power for that of the Pope, Henry VIII made few changes in the Catholic Church in England. Choice (B) is incorrect because Martin Luther did not introduce predestination into Protestantism. Choice (D) is incorrect because John Wesley founded Methodism, but he didn't introduce predestination into Protestantism.

19. **The correct answer is (B).** Choice (A) is incorrect because Ahura-Mazda was wor-shipped as the one true god of Zoroastrianism. Choice (C) is incorrect because Jews call their God Yahweh. Choice (D) is incorrect because Shiva, known as the destroyer, is one of the Hindu triad of deities.

20. **The correct answer is (D).** Hinduism includes all four tenets: (I) belief in a cycle of rebirth, (II) worship of a multiplicity of deities, (III) acceptance of the caste system, and (IV) adherence to nonviolence. The only answer choice that contains all four tenets is choice (D).

DEFINITION AND ORIGINS OF RELIGION

Religions—modern and ancient—on the surface appear to be very different, but if you look just a little below the surface, you will find many similarities.

Basic Dimensions of Religion

The Merriam-Webster dictionary defines religion as "the service and worship of God or the supernatural, a commitment or devotion to religious faith or observance, a personalized set or institutionalized system of religious attitudes, beliefs, and practices." Regardless of the religion, all religions, then, have certain characteristics in common: a supernatural aspect, a belief system, and rituals.

In his 1969 work *The Religious Experience of Mankind,* Ninian Smart describes six characteristics of religion in terms of (1) ritual, (2) mythical, (3) doctrinal, (4) ethical, (5) social, and (6) experiential dimensions:

- *Ritual:* Ritual is the practices that members of a religion engage in, such as worship (prayer) and fasting. Ritual includes such rites of passage as baptism and confirmation in Christian churches, bar mitzvah and bat mitzvah in Judaism, and marriage in any given religion.

- *Mythical:* We may call Native American beliefs in how the world started "creation myths," but to Native Americans, they are sacred stories, much as the New Testament is to Christians. Myths are the stories that provide information about the supernatural aspects of a religion as well as its human actors. These stories may be collected as oral tradition or written down as holy scripture.

- *Doctrinal:* Doctrine is the belief system that develops within a religion. Doctrine, or dogma, is a body of teachings that defines the truth, values, rituals, and practices of a religion. Some religions have organized and structured written doctrine, and others do not.

- *Ethical:* A religion's doctrine shapes the code of ethics of a religion, that is, the way that members should behave toward themselves and others based on the religion's teachings.

- *Social:* Religion is social. Religions have members who make up a community and give witness to their faith by their actions.

- *Experiential:* According to Smart, "personal religion normally involves the hope of, or realization of, experience of that [invisible world of the particular religion]." Being "born again" is an example.

Other writers on the subject of a definition of religion use other categories, such as experience as revelation (showing the invisible world of the supernatural to humans in some way) and faith as response to revelation.

Approaches to Religion

Beginning in the nineteenth century, several different approaches to the study of religion have been popular: (1) anthropological, (2) phenomenological, (3) psychological, and (4) sociological. All have their supporters and their critics.

- *Anthropological:* Anthropologists observe and study the religious elements of a culture such as its myths, rituals, and taboos. Taboos are those things that adherents of a religion are forbidden to do, for example, Muslims and Jews may not eat pork.

- *Phenomenological:* Scholars following this school of thought believe that religion is a phenomenon that exists across all cultures and all time. The phenomenological approach has influenced the field of comparative religious studies.

- *Psychological:* The influence of religion on the thoughts and actions of adherents is the subject of this approach.

- *Sociological:* This approach considers religion a social rather than a theological phenomenon.

INDIGENOUS RELIGIONS

Indigenous religions have certain features in common, namely: (1) animism (the elements of nature have spirits), (2) magic (control of nature by manipulation), (3) divination (predicting the future), (4) totem (family or clan identification with animals), (5) ancestor veneration or worship, (6) sacrifice, (7) taboo (certain people, places, and things considered either too holy or too "unclean" to touch), (8) myth, (9) ritual, and (10) rites of passage.

Native North American Traditions

There is no single Native American religion, but there are certain characteristics in common. The religions are generally animistic and polytheistic. Followers of these religions believe that nature is alive with spirits and that people must live in harmony with nature. Some religions also have a central Supreme Being, but unlike the God of Christianity, Judaism, or Islam, this Supreme Being is above the things of Earth. The spirits of nature answer the prayers of the people, not the Supreme Being.

Northern Native American religious traditions include ceremonies, rituals, and taboos. Dance and the use of magic are part of many of these practices. Typically, northern Native Americans did not practice human or animal sacrifice. A rite of passage for the young entering puberty is the vision quest. A young man is sent away from his group to live with no food and little else until his vision appears. Often, the vision includes an animal that becomes the young man's totem. People still go on vision quests, usually when faced with a life-defining decision.

There is no special "priesthood" or hierarchy in northern Native American religions, though there are medicine men and women. They have the power to heal, but they also have the power to cause illness and death.

Native South American Traditions

Major cultures of South America were the Mayan and Aztec, and each had a distinctive religious tradition.

Mayan

The Mayan culture centered on the Yucatan Peninsula. Mainly a farming people, their religion centered on deities related to the harvest and included deities associated with rain, soil, sun, moon, and corn. According to the Mayan creation story, all humans were descended from the Four Fathers who were created from corn. Maize was the name of the corn god. Human sacrifice was practiced.

Aztec

According to Aztec legend, the god Huitzilopochtli, the god of the sun and war, told the Aztec they would be a great people if they did what he said. They were to go in search of land where they could plant corn and beans. When the time was right, that is, when they were strong enough to defeat any opponent, and only then, should they make war. Any captives they took should be sacrificed to the gods. When the wandering Aztec came to an island and saw an eagle sitting on a cactus with a serpent in its beak, the Aztec would know that this was where they should settle.

The Aztec state was a theocracy and a warrior culture, so it is not surprising that Aztec religion was focused on death and the end of the world. The Aztec believed that human sacrifice could forestall the destruction of the world.

Native West African Traditions

Like Native American religions, there is no single African religion, but there are a number of commonalities. African religions are typically polytheistic, but have a central High God who created the world and withdrew from it. This High God is above all the lesser deities, spirits, and ancestors. The spirits are life forces that inhabit nature.

Animism, ancestor veneration, and divination may be aspects of these religious traditions. Similar to northern Native American traditions, spirits in African religions communicate with humans through dreams and signs, and Africans make offerings and sacrifices to the spirits and ancestors. While these are usually simple—such as an offering of food—animal sacrifices on important occasions may also be conducted. Rites of passage, such as ritual circumcision at puberty, are practiced.

Some traditions, especially in West Africa, have male and female priests and temples, but most do not. There are special curers or healers, similar to medicine men and women. Some African religions also have diviners. In some religions, their powers of foretelling the future are important. In others, diviners are called upon to figure out why people are experiencing various problems.

Native Middle Eastern Traditions

Two important religious traditions in the Middle East developed in ancient Egypt and in Persia.

Ancient Egypt

Initially, the sun god Ra was the most important Egyptian deity, but he was supplanted by the god Osiris who, as god of the afterlife, judged the goodness and evil of the dead. Isis who was both his wife and sister was the goddess of magic and familial love. According to the myth, Osiris' brother Set cut Osiris into pieces and scattered him across the earth. Isis brought him back to life. The cult of Isis and Osiris spread across the Middle East and into Greece and the Roman Empire.

Ahmenhotep IV in the 1300s B.C.E. introduced worship of a single god Aton. According to Ahmenhotep, who changed his name to Ikhnaton to honor Aton, Aton was the god of light and truth and had created the world. Ikhnaton became the high priest of the new religion, and worship of Aton became the state religion. After Ikhnaton's death, the worship of Aton ended and Egyptians once again worshipped a variety of deities, including local and regional ones.

One other item of note about ancient Egyptian religion was belief in an afterlife, which was similar to life on earth and for which pharaohs would need food, clothes, drink, and furniture—to make the afterlife as comfortable as this one. They would also need their bodies, which led to the science of mummification. Initially, Egyptians believed that only pharaohs could journey across the river Styx into the afterlife. By the 1500s B.C.E., however, belief in the afterlife had expanded to include all Egyptians.

Zoroastrianism

Unlike the religion of Egypt, Zoroastrianism is still practiced in parts of Iran and India, where adherents are known as Parsis. The religion began sometime between 1600 B.C.E. and 1400 B.C.E, when the creator of goodness and life, Ahura-Mazda, revealed his truths to the prophet Zarathustra, also called Zoroaster. These truths are collected in the Zend-Avesta.

Zoroastrians believe that good and evil are fighting a battle for control of the universe and humanity. One force is Ahura-Mazda—representing good—and the other is Ahriman—the creator of evil and darkness. The battle will end in the final judgment, when the good will receive heaven and immortality and the evil will receive eternal punishment. To fulfill the will of Ahura-Mazda, Zoroastrians follow the threefold path: good thoughts, good words, and good deeds. Their liturgy consists of reciting from the Zend-Avesta and pilgrimages to holy fire-temples.

Hellenic and Roman Traditions

Much of Roman religion was borrowed from the Greeks through cultural diffusion. The Greeks, in turn, appear to have borrowed from Aryans invading from what is now India and from other peoples in the Mediterranean region, namely, the Aegeans and Minoans whom the Greeks conquered.

Hellenic Traditions

The basis of Greek religion was a family of deities who protected and helped the Greeks in their daily lives. The chief deity, Zeus, was the father of all the deities, and his wife Hera was the guardian of women and marriage. Other important deities were Aphrodite, the deity of love and beauty and daughter of Zeus; Poseidon, Zeus' brother and deity of the sea; Pluto, another brother and deity of the underworld where most people went after death; and Apollo, Zeus' son and the guardian of music, poetry, and healing. The most important deities like these six lived on Mount Olympus, an actual mountain in northern Greece. City-states had their own deities as well. For example, Athena who embodied all wisdom was the protector of Athens.

The Greek religion had temples and male and female priests who tended them. The Greeks also practiced divination. They believed that they could ask the deities about the future. Special priests, called oracles, would convey the deities' answers.

A drawback in the eyes of some upper-class Greeks was the lack of an ethical core to the religion of the gods and goddesses. From this discontent and questioning were born several schools of Greek philosophy. In general, the Hellenic philosophies were built on the concepts of balance in human behavior and moderation in all things. Among the important schools were those of Socrates, Aristotle, Plato, and the Stoics.

Roman Traditions

Initially, the Romans were animists. As farmers, they believed that spirits inhabited the natural world. The male head of the family led all religious ceremonies and made sacrifices to the spirits. The lares were the spirits that protected the home and family, and the penates protected the family's storeroom. The spirit of the hearth (fireplace) was Vesta, who came to symbolize not only the individual family, but Roman civilization. The Romans also venerated their ancestors.

In time, the Romans borrowed elements from other religions, most notably the Greeks. The Greek deities became transformed into Roman deities. For example, Zeus became Jupiter, Hera became Juno, and Aphrodite became Venus. The conquest of Egypt brought the Egyptian deity Isis into the Roman pantheon, and the invasion of Asia Minor introduced the Romans to Cybele, the female deity of fertility.

Shintoism

In Shinto teachings, the divine resides in all things in nature from rocks to rainfall. The word "Shinto" means "the way of the kami." The kami are the spirits of the natural world. The influence of the farming culture can be seen in the festivals of Shinto, which celebrate the planting, growing, and harvesting of crops. Two of the important values of Shinto are fertility and family, including ancestor veneration and social cooperation. Worship of ancestors and the deities in nature is called matsuri.

Originally, followers of Shinto did not erect shrines or temples to the divine in nature, but over time, under the influence of Buddhism, people began to erect shrines to house symbols representing the divine in nature. Before entering the shrines, Shintoists perform purification rituals, including washing their hands and rinsing their mouths to cleanse themselves of dirt.

In 1889, the Japanese government established State Shinto to foster nationalism and patriotism among the Japanese. After World War II, State Shinto was ended and the government ceased to support Shinto shrines and priests. However, Sect Shinto, the religious aspects of Shinto, continues today.

HINDUISM

There are an estimated 1 billion Hindus in the world today. The majority live in India and Nepal. They can trace their religion back to the ancient beliefs of the Aryans, a group of nomadic warriors from Central Asia who invaded the Indian subcontinent sometime between 1700 and 1500 B.C.E.

Historical Development

The Aryans worshipped deities that represented beauty and the forces of nature. Among them were Indra, the female deity of the storm; Agni, the female deity of fire; Varna, the female deity of the sky; and Soma, the male deity of the moon who ruled the stars. The Aryans practiced ritual sacrifices of animals to invoke the deities.

Aryans left records of their religious beliefs and practices in writings that developed into the sacred books of Hinduism. The Vedas are collections of hymns, prayers, myths, rituals, and beliefs about the creation and the deities. The Vedas are divided into four collections; the oldest is the Rig Veda and contains more than a thousand hymns. The Upanishads are later writings that were added to the earlier writings and contain advice from Hindu mystics; reincarnation is first mentioned in the Upanishads. In all, there are seven books of sacred writings that make up the basic Vedas.

Also important to Hindus are two epic poems: (1) the Mahabharata and (2) the Ramayana. The former describes two Indian families who are fighting for control of a kingdom in a bloody war. Within the Mahabharata is the poem Bhagavad-Gita, meaning the "Lord's song." In the poem, the god Krishna and Arjuna, a member of one of the warring families, discuss the meaning of duty. The Ramayana tells the story of the wanderings of Prince Rama and his wife Sita who are exiled because of a jealous stepmother.

A later document of importance in the development of Hinduism is the Law of Manu, which describes varna, or the caste system as already in existence in Hindu society. It is possible that the caste system goes back to the Aryan invaders who considered themselves superior to those they conquered. However the caste system began, it came to divide Hindus into a complex and rigid social system of thousands of different castes, or categories, based on hereditary occupations. The dalits, or untouchables, are below the caste system and perform menial manual labor.

Doctrine and Practice

Unlike many religions like Islam, Hinduism had no single founder and no single set of revealed dogma. Hinduism has grown and developed internally and by incorporating outside influences. It is still evolving.

Basic Hindu beliefs involve the following:

- *Nature of Reality:* All reality is one with Brahman, the Ultimate Reality. The individual, or essential, self is called atman and is one with Brahman and everything else in the universe. Everything is simply a representation of Brahman, the formless, nameless, changeless reality.

- *Samsara:* Hindus believe that life is a cycle of birth, life, and death, which they call samsara.

- *Karma:* In what form a person is reborn depends on the law of karma: the actions that an individual performs while living determines future lives. Each reincarnation is the result of previous lives. Do good now and it will be reflected in future lives; do evil and that, too, will be reflected. Good actions raise the status of future lives and evil actions lower future castes.

- *Moksha:* Moksha is release from samsara, which comes with enlightenment. The purpose of the cycle of reincarnations is spiritual progress to reach moksha. Individuals can choose the path of renunciation and find enlightenment or the path of desire and continue the cycle of birth, life, and death.

- *Dharma:* Dharma is the rules and duties for Hindus that provide a guide for living. The goal is to act with detachment, that is, people need to destroy desire if they are to achieve moksha.

- *Stages of Life:* Hinduism sets four stages to progress to enlightenment: (1) student; (2) house-holder; (3) anchorite, a person living in seclusion to meditate and study; and (4) sannyasi, a holy man wandering among the people.

- *Ahimsa:* This is the concept of "do no harm," or acting always in a nonviolent manner.

Hinduism has both a central creator of the world known as Brahma and many other deities. Some are avatars of Brahma. The three major deities, or triad of Hinduism, are (1) Brahma; (2) Vishnu, the preserver; and (3) Shiva, both destroyer and regenerator. Other important deities are (1) Krishna and (2) Rama, both incarnations of Vishnu, and (3) Shakti, also known as Parvati and Kali, among other names, and the wife of Shiva.

Note: Brahman is the Ultimate Reality, Brahma is the creator, and a Brahmin is a member of the priestly caste.

Yoga

The goal of yoga is to free the mind of distractions, so atman can become more open to the Ultimate. There are several schools of yoga, including (1) karma, (2) raja, (3) bhakti, (4) jnana, (5) hatha, and (6) kundalini.

Holy Days

Certain holy days are more prevalent in some areas of India than in others. Major Hindu holy days include:

- *Diwali:* Festival of lights that occurs in autumn and includes a thorough housecleaning to welcome Laksmi, the female deity of wealth

- *Durga Puja:* Celebrates the female deity Durga and the triumph of good over evil; occurs in autumn

- *Krishna Janmashtami:* Celebrates the birth of Krishna and includes fasting for 24 hours; occurs in late summer

- *Ram Navmi:* Celebrates the birth of Rama, an incarnation of Vishnu; occurs in spring

BUDDHISM

Buddhism began as an offshoot of Hinduism. Like Christianity and Islam, Buddhism has a single historical founder.

Historical Development

Buddhism was founded by Siddhartha Gautama who lived in the 500s B.C.E. The son of a wealthy and powerful family, his life changed at the age of 29. Leaving his palace one day, he met an old man, a sick man, a corpse, and a beggar. The misery, sorrow, and decay of life made a great impression on him. In what is known as the Great Renunciation, Gautama gave up his riches and left his family to search for an answer to samsara. He studied with a variety of teachers, but found their teachings unsatisfying. He tried penance and self-mortification, but they, too, seemed lacking to him.

Finally, one night while using yoga and meditation, enlightenment came to him. He realized that the answer was choosing a life that took the middle path between asceticism and indulgence, or desire. That night, Gautama became the Buddha, the fully enlightened one. Gautama Buddha, as he was known from then on, spent the next forty-five years of his life on Earth teaching the middle path.

Buddhism expanded across India over the next 200 years. Monasticism as a way of life developed as some disciples built monasteries and became monks and nuns devoted to prayer and meditation. By the third century B.C.E., Buddhism was spreading outside India to what are today Sri Lanka, Myanmar, Nepal, the nations of Southeast Asia, and eventually to Korea and Japan.

Major Traditions

Buddhism has evolved into several thousand sects. Theravada and Mahayana are the principle sects; Theravada is the more conservative. Unlike Hinduism, Buddhism does not have multiple deities, nor is there a supreme ultimate being.

- *Theravada Buddhism:* This is the path of poverty and celibacy embraced by those men who choose to live as monks. They believe that individuals must achieve enlightenment on their own through meditation and actions, as Gautama Buddha did. When a man achieves enlightenment, he becomes an arhat and is released from samsara at death. However, not all Theravada Buddhists choose monasticism as a way of life. Some men make only a limited commitment to the monastic life. Women may not become monks; however, they can support them with offerings. In this way, they can make merit, that is, influence their karmaic destiny. Theravada Buddhism is practiced today mainly in Thailand, Cambodia, Vietnam, Laos, Myanmar, and Sri Lanka.

- *Mahayana Buddhism:* Most Buddhists belong to this sect. Gautama Buddha's compassion is a central focus. Mahayana Buddhists believe that Gautama Buddha was close to godlike and visited Earth to aid humans. They also believe that he was only one among many Buddhas who are on Earth to help humans. The ideal became bodhisattvas, or Buddhas-in-waiting, who instead of achieving nirvana remain on Earth to help others achieve enlightenment. Unlike Theravada Buddhists who rely on their own efforts, Mahayana Buddhists believe that devotion to Buddhas and bodhisattvas can aid in their efforts to achieve nirvana. Mahayana Buddhism is practiced mainly in China, Tibet, Nepal, Korea, and Japan. Two important forms of Mahayana Buddhism are the following:

  1. *Zen Buddhism:* This sect of Mahayana Buddhism became popular among some Japanese after its introduction from China around 400 C.E. Adherents of Zen believe that the Buddha-nature is all around, and only through meditation will humans be able to discover and understand it and, thus, reach enlightenment. Zen Buddhists use riddles called koans to aid them in finding enlightenment.

  2. *Tibetan Buddhism, also known as Lamaism:* Mahayana Buddhism was originally brought to Tibet in the 600s C.E., but over the centuries, it has evolved in unique ways. While many of the practices of Lamaism are similar to those of other forms of Buddhism, it (1) relies heavily on magic; (2) has a priestly class known as lamas; (3) recites the phrase "Om, the jewel of the lotus, hum" to address the Bodhisattva Avalokiteshvara, the patron of Tibet; and (4) uses a prayer wheel to "say" prayers. The chief lama among lamas is the Dalai Lama, who is not only the spiritual leader of Tibetans, but also considered the temporal ruler.

Doctrine and Practice

Buddhism centers on the Four Noble Truths and the Eight-Fold Path. The Four Noble Truths are:

1. All life is suffering, called dukkha.

2. The source of all suffering is desire, attachment to self.

3. The cessation of desire is the way to end suffering.

4. The path to the cessation of desire is the Eight-Fold Path.

The Eight-Fold Path is (1) right understanding, (2) right thought, (3) right speech, (4) right action, (5) right livelihood, (6) right effort, (7) right mindfulness, and (8) right concentration. People are doomed to samsara because of desire. If people can eliminate desire, they will achieve nirvana, the release from their karma and, thus, from samsara.

Another important concept in Buddhism is compassion for all living things, which is exemplified by Gautama Buddha's life. Buddhists like Hindus practice ahimsa, or nonviolence to all things. While monasticism became important, Buddhism did not reject those who chose to live in the world. It welcomed anyone who was trying to live up to the standards of Buddhist teachings and was also willing to support Buddhist monks and nuns.

Sacred Writings

The two main branches of Buddhism have their own sacred writings. The major works of Theravada Buddhism are the (1) Tripitaka (rules and regulations for Buddhist monasteries, life and teachings of Gautama Buddha, and dictionary and teachings) and (2) Dhammapada (collection of proverbs and adages). Among the major works of Mahayana Buddhism are the (1) Lotus Sutra, (2) Heart Sutras, (3) Tibetan Book of the Dead, and (4) Translation of the Word of the Buddha. "Sutra" in Buddhism means "a collection of the stories and teachings of Gautama Buddha." (In Hindu, "sutra" means "a collection of sayings about Vedic doctrine.")

Holy Days

The various sects have their own holy days and celebrations, but common ones are (1) Buddha Day, April 8, honoring the birth of Buddha; (2) Nirvana Day, February 15, observing his death; and (3) Bodhi Day, December 8, celebrating the day he sat down under the Bodhi tree to achieve enlightenment.

There are also a number of rites of passage in Buddhism, including marriage, pregnancy, birth, adolescence, and, ultimately, death.

CONFUCIANISM

Confucianism is a philosophy—an ethical code of living—rather than a religion. There is no central supreme being who created the world. However, there is a respect for the past, including ancestors; a focus on humane treatment of one another; and a belief in the duty of the government to provide for the well-being of the governed.

Historical Development

Confucianism takes its name from Confucius, who lived from 551 B.C.E. to 479 B.C.E. Around that time, China was undergoing what has come to be called the Warring States Period. A group of independent states was vying for control of China. This lasted until the third century B.C.E. when the Han dynasty consolidated its power and ruled China for 400 years. Over the centuries, Confucian principles came to dominate Chinese government regardless of the dynasty in power; Confucian teachings and their evolution by government bureaucrats provided an orderly structure for society and for governance.

An especially important concept in this development was the Confucian idea of the state as family; family was the basic element of society in Confucian teaching. The emperor was the father of all Chinese and responsible to an impersonal force known as Heaven for the well-being of his people/children. If he did not live up to his role, the people had a mandate from heaven to replace him. In this way, dynasties rose and fell in China for centuries. Claiming that the current emperor was not working in the best interests of the people, a rival would depose him, calling on the mandate of heaven as his authority. In this way, Confucianism was used by various rulers over the centuries to cement their position as supreme earthly rulers.

Another aspect of Confucianism that shaped Chinese society was its influence on the Chinese educational system. In order to advance in the Chinese bureaucracy, a position of prestige and power, a man needed to be educated. Confucianist principles became the focus of this education and centered on learning what constituted right action. The reliance on Confucianism resulted in the development of a conservatism in Chinese society that lasted until the Communist Party came to power in the twentieth century.

Doctrine and Practice

Confucius taught that five relationships exist that involve reciprocal duties and responsibilities, or right action, between:

1. Ruler and subject

2. Father and son

3. Elder brother and younger brother

4. Husband and wife

5. Friend and friend

With the exception of the last relationship, each relationship involves a superior and a subordinate, that is, one person is subject to the other. The subordinate owes loving obedience to the superior, and the superior has a loving responsibility to see to the well-being of the subordinate. Friends owe each other the same responsibility. The correct behavior, or conduct, between the individuals in these relationships is known as li.

In addition to these ethical relationships, Confucius taught the concept of jen, or human-heartedness, also described as sympathy or benevolence, that is, love toward others. It is this quality that makes people social creatures. Unlike many Eastern religions, Confucius did not see the proper role of humans as self-absorbed in meditation and isolated from one another. His goal was to create harmony in society.

Important Works

The Five Classics and the Four Books make up the basic writings of Confucianism. Three books to remember are the (1) Analects of Confucius, one of the Four Books; (2) I Ching, the first of the Five Classics; and (3) Book of Mencius (Meng-Zi). The Analects are stories and sayings of Confucius that his followers collected, the I Ching is a book of divination, and the Book of Mencius is a defense of Confucian teachings by Mencius, a later Confucian scholar. Mencius took the position that human nature is good. Hsun Tzu (Xun-Zi), an even later Confucian scholar, took the opposite position, that human nature is evil.

TAOISM

Taoism developed slightly later in China than Confucianism and is based on a belief in the naturalness of all things. Its spirituality is a complement to the structure and rigid etiquette required in Confucianism rather than a rival belief system.

Historical Development

The beginnings of Taoism date to the 400s and 300s B.C.E. The traditional founder is considered to be Lao-Tzu, who is also credited with writing the Tao Te Ching, the basis of Taoism. The word "Tao" means "the way." It is possible, however, that the Tao Te Ching is actually a collection of writings of earlier ancient scholars. A second important work is the slightly later Chuang-Tzu by a man of the same name; it is a collection of parables and allegories.

Initially, Taoism was a philosophy, but it took on religious elements over the centuries. The huge majority of Chinese were farmers who saw a relationship between nature as described in Taoism and the deities who were part of their daily lives. Taoism was also influenced by Mahayana Buddhism and adapted some of its rituals and the concept of priesthood. Taoism, in turn, influenced Zen Buddhism's focus on nature.

Doctrine and Practice

What is the Tao? According to Taoists, the Tao cannot be defined. It is without measure, shape, or characteristics; it is infinite and unceasing. It simply flows "without motive and without effort." The Tao gives life to all things, but more than life, it gives all things their natures. The Tao is why a human is a human and not a dog or a horse.

The central focus of Taoism is naturalness. Human suffering, pain, and violence are the result of the opposite of naturalness—unnaturalness. At one time, people lived a natural life, unhampered by the conventions and restrictions of society. They had been "in harmony with their nature and with the Tao." This harmony began to change with the introduction by society of social conventions and notions of right and wrong as well as people's growing desire for things outside themselves—whether the possession of material goods or of knowledge. Knowledge is a problem because it leads to ideas that interfere with the spontaneity of oneness with the Tao.

To free themselves, Taoists believe that people must become one with the Tao, and then they will realize that all is one with the Tao. There is no reason or need to seek possessions or knowledge. Instead of right action, Taoists believe in no action, or inaction. Taoists also apply this idea to government. In essence, the government that governs the least, governs best. A ruler who follows the Tao will govern without seeming to govern, ensuring that the people are fed, living in peace, and free of worry.

A basic teaching of Taoism is the concept of yin and yang. The symbol for yin and yang is a circle with two interlocking black and white sections. The white section has a smaller black circle within it, and the black section has a smaller white circle within it. The black represents yin—earth, female, dark, and passive—whereas the white is the yang, the active principle that represents heaven, male, and light.

Meditation is an important vehicle for achieving oneness with the Tao. Unlike Zen Buddhism, which focuses on physical cleansing, Taoism asks adherents to purge their minds of thoughts, thus opening themselves to the Tao.

JUDAISM

The Hebrews, or Israelites, were unique in the history of world religions up to that point in time in basing their national identity on a "single, all-powerful God who made ethical demands and placed responsibilities on them as individuals and as a community," according to the authors of *The Heritage of World Civilizations*. Jews live in and off history.

Historical Development

The Hebrews under the leadership of Abraham probably arrived in the area of Mesopotamia sometime between 1900 and 1600 B.C.E. Some stayed in what was to become known as Palestine, but others moved into Egypt, where they were enslaved. Moses led the Hebrews out of Egypt around the beginning of the thirteenth century B.C.E., and they settled in Canaan, a region of Palestine, which the Bible calls their Promised Land. The Hebrews built a successful kingdom for some 300 years under rulers such as David and Solomon. In the 800s B.C.E., the kingdom split into the kingdoms of Judah, formed by ten tribes, and Israel, formed by two tribes.

Over the next centuries, foreign peoples invaded and conquered the two kingdoms. The northern kingdom of Israel disappeared entirely. The southern kingdom, which included the Temple in Jerusalem, was conquered by the Babylonians in the mid-500s B.C.E. The temple was destroyed and the people taken to Babylon in what is called the Babylonian Captivity. They returned to Judah after the defeat of the Babylonians in 539 B.C.E. and rebuilt the Temple, which the Romans, their new captors, destroyed in 70 C.E. and again in 132 C.E.

The first mention of the Covenant between the Hebrews and Yahweh is in the Hebrew Bible's account of Abraham. The reaffirmation of the Covenant came on Mount Sinai, when Moses received the Ten Commandments. In exchange for obeying these laws, the Jews would receive Yahweh's protection. The troubles—the foreign conquests—were the result of the Jews' failure to abide by their part of the Covenant. The prophets, such as Jeremiah and Ezekiel, were sent to remind the Jews of their Covenant and of the one true God, Yahweh.

Throughout these periods of subjugation, the Jews retained their religion and their sense of being God's chosen people. (1) The synagogue as a local center of worship, (2) the position of rabbi as teacher, (3) kosher food laws, and (4) the Sabbath as day of worship developed during the early period of the Diaspora, which began after the destruction of Israel in 721 B.C.E.

The Diaspora continued after the Jewish revolt of 66 C.E., when the Romans conquered the area, renamed it, and forbid the Jews to enter Jerusalem. Many Jews moved into Western Europe. Over time, they became known as the Sephardim and settled in Spain. Persecuted there during the Inquisition, they fled to Portugal, the Netherlands, North Africa, the Balkans, and the Americas. German Jews became known as Ashkenazi. After persecution there, they moved into Eastern Europe. Ashkenazi and Sephardic Jews have different languages, rituals, and traditions.

Denominations

Modern Judaism has four main divisions, or movements: (1) Orthodox, (2) Conservative, (3) Reform, and (4) Reconstruction. The differences revolve around how strictly each interprets the laws and traditions of Judaism, including the place of women. Although the term may be confusing, Conservative Jews are less conservative than Orthodox Jews. The latter, for example, do not allow women to become rabbis and cantors, whereas Conservative, Reform, and Reconstructionist Jews do. Orthodox Jews also require that the sexes be separated in synagogues. While Orthodox Jews eat kosher at home and outside the home, Conservative Jews typically keep kosher at home, but may eat nonkosher outside the home, and Reform Jews typically do not observe kosher rules. Reconstructionist Jews and Reform Jews have many practices in common, although Reconstructionist Jews tend to follow more of the traditional historical practices of Judaism. Mordecai M. Kaplan is considered the founder of Reconstructionism in the 1930s.

Orthodox Judaism is the largest group within Judaism and is further divided into (1) Modern Orthodox and (2) Hasidic. Hasidic Judaism was founded in the mid-1700s in Poland by Israel ben Eliezer, who came to be known as Baal Shem Tov. He taught a simple faith that included elements of mysticism; he wanted Jews to maintain their identity and traditions and live within their own enclaves separated from non-Jews. Hasidic Judaism attracted many followers in Eastern Europe. The spiritual leader of a group of Hasidic Jews is known as a rebbe, and a rebbe is descended from a line of rebbes.

Another important leader of Judaism was the nineteenth-century German philosopher and writer Moses Mendelssohn. He encouraged Jews to leave their ghettoes and live within the larger society.

Doctrine and Practice

The Hebrews who were surrounded by neighbors worshipping many gods were unique in adopting monotheism, the worship of one God. The basic teachings of Judaism are (1) Yahweh (God) is the supreme creator, (2) Yahweh will send a messiah to redeem the world, and (3) the Jews are God's chosen people. Yahweh formed a covenant with the Jews, who, in return for offering obedience to the Law and worshipping only to Yahweh, would become a great nation. The sense of Judaism as a community of believers is of central importance.

The Ten Commandments are the ethical code of Judaism—the Law—given by Yahweh to the Hebrews as a guide to moral living. A slightly shortened version of the Decalogue is the following:

1. I am the Lord thy God.

2. Thou shall have no other gods before Me.

3. Thou shall not take the name of the Lord thy God in vain.

4. Remember the Sabbath Day.

5. Honor thy father and thy mother.

6. Thou shall not kill.

7. Thou shall not commit adultery.

8. Thou shall not steal.

9. Thou shall not bear false witness against they neighbor.

10. Thou shall not covet thy neighbor's goods.

Moses received these commandments on Mount Sinai during the forty years that the Hebrews wandered in the desert after their exodus from Egypt.

Writings

The Jewish sacred writing are the (1) Hebrew Bible and (2) Talmud. The Bible contains the (1) Pentateuch, (2) Prophets, and (3) writings, or Ketuvim. The Pentateuch is also known as the Torah or the Five Books of Moses; these are the first five books of the Bible. The Prophets contain the writing of the major prophets (Jeremiah, Isaiah, and Ezekiel), as well as the twelve minor prophets. The Ketuvim is a collection of twelve other books, including the Psalms, Song of Songs, and the Book of Ruth.

The Mishnah is the collection of all the disputes and commentary on Jewish law up to the 100s C.E. It was compiled under the direction of Judah. Later, the Gemara was added to the Mishnah to make up the Talmud. The Gemara is additional rabbinic teachings on every aspect of Jewish life. The material in the Talmud is divided into two categories: (1) the Aggadah, which includes parables, sayings, sermons, and stories and is ethical, inspirational, or explanatory in nature and (2) the Halaka, commentary, discussions, and decisions related to Jewish law and practice.

Another work of note is the Sefer Ha'Zohar, commonly referred to as the Zohar. It is one of the books of the Kabbalah, the mystical aspect of Judaism, and focuses on such themes as angels, demons, charms, the coming of the Messiah, and numerology.

Holy Days

Shabbat, or the Sabbath, takes place from sundown on Friday night to sunset on Saturday. There are services Friday night and Saturday morning. Jews are prohibited from engaging in work during this period.

Major holy days include:

- *Rosh Hashanah:* The Jewish New Year celebrated sometime between mid-September and early October

- *Yom Kippur:* The Day of Atonement, which includes fasting and contemplation; comes ten days after Rosh Hashanah

- *Sukkot:* Feast of Booths or Tabernacles, which celebrates the harvest and Yahweh's protection of the Jews during their forty years in the wilderness; nine days between late September and the end of October

- *Chanukah:* Festival of the Lights, also the Festival of Dedication, celebrating the victory of the Maccabees over the Greeks and Syrians in the 100s B.C.E. and the rededication of the Temple in Jerusalem

- *Passover:* Celebrates the deliverance, or exodus, of the Hebrews out of Egypt; seders, special dinners, are held the first two and last two days; comes between March and April for eight days

- *Shavuot:* Celebrates the Yahweh's giving of the Ten Commandments to Moses; comes between late May and early June

The menorah is an important symbol of Chanukah. It holds nine candles, eight for the eight nights of Chanukah and a ninth candle. According to the story of Chanukah, there was only enough oil for one night for the lamps in the Temple, but the oil lasted for eight nights. Each night of Chanukah, an additional candle is lit until all are lit the last night.

Hebrew school teaches Jewish children about their faith. It is typically held on Sundays and one weekday. For older students, it provides preparation for Bar Mitzvah for boys and Bat Mitzvah for girls, their coming-of-age ceremonies.

CHRISTIANITY

The focus of Christians is on the future: the redemptive power in their own lives of Jesus' resurrection. This message has resonated with millions of people since 33 C.E., when Jesus was reported to have died for humankind's sins and risen again. Today, there are over two billion Christians in the world belonging to three branches and more than a dozen denominations. Christianity is a continuation of the promise of the Old Testament, but with a difference.

Historical Development

Jesus of Nazareth is a historical figure; he lived and died in the first century C.E. in Judea. He began preaching around the year 30 and quickly gained a following. His message was one of piety and the abandonment of sin and material things. In the Sermon on the Mount, he laid out a moral code, known as the Beatitudes, for his followers. He was seen as the Messiah promised by Yahweh, the Supreme Being, to the Jews, although they expected a kingdom on earth, whereas Jesus talked about a Day of Judgment when the good would be rewarded and the evil punished. (The word "messiah" translates as "christos" in Greek and Jesus became known as Jesus Christ, that is, Jesus the Messiah.) He proclaimed himself the Son of God. When Jesus attacked the practices of some of the Jewish leaders, and as the crowds following him grew larger, the leaders determined to put a stop to his preaching. They convinced the Roman governor that his preaching was dangerous; the governor arrested Jesus and had him crucified like a common criminal.

After Jesus' death, resurrection, and ascension into heaven, his followers began to preach about Jesus and his mission, initially only among Jews. However, there were two schools of thought about the nature of Christianity: Was it a version of Judaism or a new religion? Some believed that it was a form of Judaism and should be presented only to Jews. Paul of Tarsus was a Jew, but believed that it was a new religion that should be preached to everyone. Once a persecutor of Christians, he had converted in 35 C.E. after a vision and became a zealous missionary among gentiles.

The word of Jesus Christ and his teachings found receptive audiences wherever the new missionaries went, and by the first century C.E., they had attracted the attention of the government. At that time, the emperor was worshipped as a god. Christians mindful of the one God refused to obey and a period of persecution began, which continued more or less until the conversion of the Emperor Constantine to Christianity in 312. By the end of the fourth century, Christianity had become the official religion of the Roman Empire.

In the second century, Christianity had developed a formal organization of bishops and was centered in Rome. Peter had been the first bishop of Rome, and later popes would claim supremacy over the church as successors to Peter, citing Jesus' words: "Thou art Peter, and upon this rock I will build my church." The Eucharist as a celebration of the Lord's Supper had also developed as the central ritual. The title "Catholic" meaning "universal" came to identify the body of teachings of this church and included the Old Testament, the Gospels, and the Epistles of St. Paul.

In addition to adopting Christianity, Constantine established a new capital for the Roman Empire at the ancient site of Byzantium and named it Constantinople. Ultimately, his decision would lead to a schism in the Catholic Church in 1054 when the Western and Eastern branches split over doctrinal issues.

After the collapse of the Roman Empire in 476 and during the Middle Ages, the Catholic Church was often the most stable and unifying force in Western Europe as nomadic peoples moving out of Asia and Vikings from northern Europe invaded. By the sixteenth century, the hierarchy of the Roman Catholic Church in the West had amassed large fortunes, lived less than pious lives, and competed with temporal rulers for power. Into this mix, add disputes over doctrinal issues, and the time was ripe for the Protestant Reformation.

It should be noted that the Catholic Church answered the calls for reform generated by the Protestant Reformation with the Council of Trent that lasted from 1545 to 1563. Among the changes that the Council made were (1) bishops had to live within their dioceses and preach regularly, (2) seminaries to educate priests were to be erected in every diocese, and (3) parish priests were to be better educated and actively minister to their parishioners. However, the Council reaffirmed a number of doctrines that were at the root of the Protestant reformers, namely:

- *The Role of Good Works in Salvation:* Grace, alone, as taught by several Protestant churches, was not enough for salvation

- *The Seven Sacraments:* Not all Protestant churches accept all seven sacraments

- *Transubstantiation:* The changing of bread and wine into the body and blood of Jesus during the act of consecration at Mass

- *Purgatory:* The place where the souls of sinners are purified after death and before entering heaven

- *Clerical Celibacy:* The belief that some or all members of the clergy are required to be unmarried

- *Veneration of the Saints, Relics, and Sacred Images:* Catholics honor and pray to them to intercede with God for them, but do not worship these people and objects

- *Granting of Indulgences:* An indulgence is a remission of the temporal punishment that a priest has given a penitent to perform as a result of sinning. If not performed by the sinner, the sinner would suffer in purgatory. Beginning in the Middle Ages, sinners could give a small amount of money, considered alms, in exchange for an indulgence. By the time of the Reformation, indulgences had been extended to include those who had already died and were presumed to be suffering in purgatory. Indulgences had also become a lucrative way of raising money for the Church and for Church leaders by preying on the fears of the faithful that they or their loved ones would languish in purgatory. It was the actions of a monk named John Tetzel, who was selling indulgences with the proceeds to be split by the Pope who was interested in rebuilding St. Peter's Basilica in Rome, the local Archbishop in debt, and a bank that drew Martin Luther's attention and precipitated the Protestant Reformation.

Major Traditions

Christianity over the centuries has developed three main branches: (1) the Roman Catholic Church, (2) the Eastern Orthodox Church, and (3) more than a dozen Protestant denominations.

Roman Catholic Church

Until the schism in 1054 between the Catholic Church in the West and the East, the history of Christianity was synonymous with the development of the Catholic Church. As noted above, the organizational structure of what became known as the Roman Catholic Church began as early as the first century C.E. with positions of priest and bishop. In time, the structure became increasingly hierarchical. The position of bishop of Rome was elevated to supremacy over all other bishops and was called "Pope." The position of cardinals, who oversaw a number of bishoprics, was added.

At various times and as early as the third century C.E., the Church called councils of bishops and scholars to debate and affirm church doctrine. Among the results were such statements of dogma as the Apostles Creed and the Nicene Creed, which established certain precepts that Catholics had to accept. The Vatican Council of 1870 defined the doctrine of papal infallibility, though the concept had been in practice since the beginning of the Church. According to this principle, the Pope speaks infallibly when he proclaims a doctrine of faith and morals. Not all pronouncements of popes bear this weight. The most recent council was the Second Vatican Council held between 1962 and 1965, which sought to modernize Church practices and doctrines, including allowing Mass to be said in vernacular languages rather than Latin and eliminating the requirement that Catholics abstain from eating meat on Fridays.

Orthodox Church

Even before the schism, there were cultural and linguistic differences that evolved between Christian churches in the two parts of the former Roman Empire. The West spoke Latin and was influenced by

Roman culture, whereas the Eastern part of the Empire had been deeply influenced by the Greeks and spoke Greek. Among the factors that caused the schism were (1) the claim of the supremacy of the Pope of Rome in matters of faith and morals; (2) the doctrine that raised the Holy Spirit equal to God the Father and God the Son; and (3) an eighth-century controversy over the use of icons, highly ornate depictions of Jesus, Mary, and the saints.

There is no single Orthodox Church in that there are several national churches, for example, the Russian Orthodox Church and the Greek Orthodox Church. The Orthodox churches are overseen by a network of patriarchs, and there are a number of commonalities among them, and a number of doctrinal differences and practices that separate these Churches from the Roman Catholic Church:

- The Orthodox Churches do not recognize the primacy of the Pope.

- The Orthodox Churches do not accept the Holy Spirit to be on the same level as God the Father and God the Son, as Catholics do.

- Priests may marry in the Orthodox Churches before ordination, whereas the Roman Catholic Church forbids married priests.

- The Roman Catholic Church does not allow people to receive communion, that is, the Eucharist, before the age of seven, considered the age of reason. The Orthodox Churches allows infants to receive communion.

- The Roman Catholic Mass is said daily, whereas the Orthodox liturgy is not necessarily celebrated daily.

- The Roman Catholic Mass is only sung if it is specifically a High Mass. The Orthodox liturgy is always sung.

- Orthodox churches are highly decorated, especially with icons and gold decorations, whereas the typical Roman Catholic Church is less ornate.

- Orthodox churches accept the seven sacraments as the major sacraments, but believe that whatever the church does is sacramental.

Protestant Denominations

The basic elements that connect the various Protestant denominations are (1) the importance of community and (2) the power of the direct experience of God. In general, Protestants (1) believe that salvation comes through God's gift of grace alone, (2) accept the Bible as revealed and infallible truth, and (3) do not require their priests or ministers to be celibate. Some faiths also (4) accept female and gay clergy, unlike the Catholic Church. (5) Statues and saints are not important and may not even be part of a denomination's theology. (6) The emphasis is on preaching and singing, and (7) services tend not to be daily. Protestant churches also practice (8) adult baptism, unlike the Catholic Church, which has infant baptism.

There are two major doctrinal differences between Protestantism and Roman Catholicism: (1) the Protestant belief on grace alone as the source for salvation and (2) Jesus is present only symbolically in the Eucharist. Catholics believe that salvation comes from a combination of grace and good works and that Jesus through the mystery of transubstantiation is fully present in the Eucharist. (The

Orthodox Churches also believe in transubstantiation and the combination of grace and good works as the path to salvation.)

The major Protestant denominations are:

- *Anglican/Church of England and Episcopalian:* Anglican is the original English church, and the Episcopalian church is the U.S. counterpart. It split from the Roman Catholic Church when the Pope refused to allow King Henry VIII to divorce and remarry. Little changed in hierarchy or practice until the reign of Henry's third child, Elizabeth I. The Anglican Church is still closest in theological doctrine to the Roman Catholic Church.

- *Baptist:* Founded by Separatist John Smyth in Holland; spread to England and then to the American colonies during the First Great Awakening and later to the United States during the Second Great Awakening; agreed-upon theology and practices vary widely.

- *Congregational:* Founded on the ideas of Robert Browne; evolved from the Nonconformist movement in Great Britain that also fostered the Separatist or Puritan reform movement; important in Massachusetts Bay Colony.

- *Lutheran:* Founded by Martin Luther; doctrine of justification, belief that salvation comes through faith alone and the gift of grace, that is, good works are not counted.

- *Methodist:* Founded by John Wesley as a way to reform the Church of England; believes in the Trinity, accepts Baptism and the Eucharist as sacraments.

- *Presbyterian:* Founded on the ideas of John Calvin; emphasizes the doctrine of predestination: belief that God foreordained who would be saved (the elect) and who would not.

- *Seventh-Day Adventist:* Established in the United States in the mid-nineteenth century; observes Saturday as the Sabbath; believes that the Second Coming of Christ is near; accepts the Trinity and the Bible as infallible.

- *Unitarian:* Developed in the late eighteenth century and spread to the United States in the early nineteenth century; rejects the Trinity, original sin, predestination, and the infallibility of the Bible.

See also the Church of Jesus Christ of Latter Day Saints in the section "Religious Movements: After 1000 C.E."

Doctrine and Practice

Christians believe that Jesus was crucified for humankind's sins and rose on the third day. He remained with his disciples, teaching them for forty days, and then ascended into heaven. Jesus is seen as God made Man and, depending on the form of Christianity, as part of the Trinity of the Father, Son, and Holy Spirit. At Pentecost, fifty days after Easter, the Holy Spirit came down upon the Apostles and they began to preach the message of Jesus.

Doctrines such as transubstantiation, the position of Mary, original sin, and infant baptism vary from religion to religion. For example, Catholics believe in original sin; it is the sin that Adam committed, and because of it, all humans are born with this sin on their souls, but baptism removes it. For this reason, Catholics are baptized in infancy. (However, infants who die before they can be baptized are thought to be taken into heaven.) On the other hand, the Orthodox churches reject the concept of inherited guilt associated with original sin. The Orthodox churches also practice infant baptism. Protestant churches generally practice adult baptism, believing that people are saved through God's gift of grace and baptism.

Some denominations support religious, or parochial, school systems, whereas others rely on religious instruction of the young during Sunday School sessions.

Sacred Writings

The Christian Bible is made up of (1) the Hebrew Bible or Old Testament and (2) the New Testament. The latter contains the Gospels of (1) Matthew, (2) Mark, (3) Luke, and (4) John and (5) other writings, including the Acts of the Apostles, the Epistles, and the Book of Revelations, as well as thirteen pieces in the (6) Hebrew Apocrypha. The Epistles are of special importance because they were written by Apostles and others to early Christian communities, discussing their issues and problems.

Depending on the branch or denomination of Christianity, the Bible is either considered to be the exact words of God, or to have been inspired by God.

Holy Days

The major holy days of Christianity, depending on the branch or denomination, are:

- *Christmas:* Celebrates the birth of Jesus, or "God made Man"

- *Epiphany:* Celebrates the visit of the three Magi to the infant Jesus; twelve days after Christmas

- *Lent:* Forty days of fasting and prayer before Easter; begins on Ash Wednesday when Christians are reminded that "thou art dust and unto dust thou shalt return"

- *Palm Sunday:* Beginning of Holy Week; commemorates Jesus' entry into Jerusalem before his crucifixion

- *Holy Week:* Holy Thursday, which recognizes the Last Supper; Good Friday, which commemorates Jesus' death on the cross

- *Ascension Thursday:* Forty days after Easter Sunday; memorializes Jesus' ascent into heaven

- *Pentecost:* Sunday fifty days after Easter; celebrates the descent of the Holy Spirit on the Apostles and the beginning of the Christian church

In addition to these and depending on the branch of Christianity, there are other special days dedicated to the Virgin Mary and to various saints.

ISLAM

Islam is the third monotheistic religion that developed in the Middle East. Muslims believe that Abraham, Jesus, and Muhammad are great prophets, and that Muhammad is the greatest and last prophet, the "Seal of the Prophets," who completes the revelations of God, the Supreme Being, or Allah, to humankind. The word "Islam" means "submission," and "Muslim" means "one who submits." In this case, Muslims submit to Allah.

Historical Development

The historical founder is Muhammad, who lived from around 570 to 632 C.E. in what is today Saudi Arabia. However, Muslims believe that Muhammad was only a vehicle for Allah. Muhammad was born in Mecca, married, and became a wealthy merchant there. In 610 C.E., at about age 40, he received the first of his revelations from Allah through the angel Gabriel. He began to preach the word of the one God, Allah, and to condemn the practice of idolatry among the city's inhabitants. As Muhammad began to gain followers, the authorities of Mecca became concerned and offered him bribes to stop. But Muhammad continued to preach his message of one God and religious piety. Finally, the authorities had had enough and began a campaign of persecution against Muhammad and his followers.

In 622, Muhammad fled Mecca and an assassination plot. His flight is called the Hegira. Muhammad found refuge in Medina, where he was able to bring together warring clans and become the leader of the city. Over the next ten years, his followers grew, and in 632, after years of fighting, they captured Mecca, founding the first Islamic state. Muhammad died shortly after.

After Muhammad's death, Islam continued to grow in numbers and in area, eventually becoming a vast political-religious empire that stretched across much of the Middle East, North Africa, and into Europe. The first four caliphs, as the leaders were known, are called the rightly guided, or orthodox, caliphs. They were relatives of Muhammad or had personally known him and were chosen by other Muslims to lead them. However, in 661, the Umayyad clan seized the caliphate from the fourth caliph, Ali, Muhammad's son-in-law, and shifted the focus of the caliphate to that of a temporal leader rather than a religious leader. The caliphate passed from dynasty to dynasty over the next centuries until the Ottoman Turks seized control of empire in the 1500s. The empire and the title of sultan, which had replaced caliph, ended after World War I.

However, Islam as a religion continued to grow. Today, more than a billion people worldwide consider themselves Muslims. Most belong to the Sunni branch, but Shi'a is the state religion of Iran. Other concentrations of Shi'ites can be found in India, Pakistan, and Iraq. Transcending all divisions is the ummah, the sense of community of believers. Madrasahs are Muslim educational institutions; they range from schools teaching young children to great universities. Their subjects range from the Qur'an to the Hadith to the law.

Major Traditions

Islam is divided into two branches: (1) Sunni and (2) Shi'a. The division goes back to the fourth caliph Ali. Shi'ites believe that Ali should have been the first caliph and that his descendants are the rightful leaders of Islam, whereas the Sunnis believe that no leader was chosen by Muhammad to succeed him. To Sunnis, the four caliphs are the rightful heirs because they were chosen by Muslims themselves. Sunnis, who make up about 85 percent of Muslims, and Shi'ites also have doctrinal differences that divide them.

Sunnis do not have a religious hierarchy, but they do have imams, also called mullahs, who lead the community in prayer. Sunnis look for guidance in their lives to the (1) Hadith, to (2) Shari'ah, which is Islamic law, and to (3) a consensus of interpretation between the Qur'an and Muslim scholars and leaders of the community. The Sunni form of Islam lends itself to interpretations and no one set of interpretations is considered definitive. This flexibility has allowed it to embrace a number of cultures as it spread outward from its original location. Sunnis do believe in a Madhi, or Messiah, whose appearance on earth will signal the beginning of an era of peace that will culminate in the end of the world.

Imams also lead Shi'ites in prayer. However, Shi'ites believe that their imams speak with special authority. They believe that the next Imam after Ali was Zain, Ali's son, who was followed by eleven more Imams. Known as Twelvers, they believe that the Twelfth Imam is still alive and still rules over them—though hidden from them—and that their imams are representatives of this Twelfth Imam. (There is another Shi'ite sect called Seveners who believe that there were seven Imams.) Shi'ites believe that the Madhi will come one day and inaugurate a period of justice before the final end of the world. Shi'ites believe that the Qur'an must be interpreted rather than read literally, because it omits their belief that Muhammad designated Ali as his successor. For Shi'ites, religious and political authority rests not with community, but with the imam. Ayatollahs are experts in Islamic law and religion; a Grand Ayatollah is an expert in religious studies and also a religious leader.

Wahhabism is a conservative movement that began on the Arabian Peninsula in 1744. Its founder Abd-al-Wahhab wanted to reform Islam and return it to what he considered the original, strict interpretation as found in the Qur'an. Wahhabism was adopted by the Sa'ud family that gained control of the kingdom in the early 1800s. Today, Wahhabism is the religion of Saudi Arabia and bound up with Saudi nationalism.

Doctrine and Practice

According to the Qur'an, there are Five Pillars, or duties, that Muslims must perform and these are the foundational principles of Islam. Monotheism, the basic truth of Islam—that Allah is the one God—is revealed in the first pillar.

1. *Repeat the Shahadah, or Confession of Faith:* "There is no God but Allah and Muhammad is the Prophet of God."

2. *Perform Ritual Prayer:* Muslims are called to prayer five times a day and must face Mecca when praying. The five times are before sunrise, at noon, in mid-afternoon, at sunset, and at night before going to sleep.

3. *Fast:* Muslims must fast during the month of Ramadan from sunrise to sunset.

4. *Almsgiving:* Muslims contribute alms, known as Zakat, to the poor, typically 2.5 percent of their wealth.

5. *Pilgrimage, Called the Hajj, to Mecca:* This must be done at least once during one's life. The central focus of Mecca is the Ka'bah, which Muslims must circle seven times, and then they

touch or kiss the Black Stone that it houses. Muslims believe that the black stone was given to Adam by Allah and that Abraham and Ishmael, his son, built the Ka'bah to hold the black stone.

Muslims believe that each person must face Allah at the end and account for the way that he or she lived. While Muslims believe that life is submission, or surrender, to Allah, it is also a test. People have the ability to commit evil and will be held accountable for it. At the time of death, a person's body and soul are separated and on the day of judgment, Resurrection Day, souls and bodies will be reunited and judged by Allah. Those who lived good lives will go to paradise and those who lived evil lives will go to hell.

Shari'ah is the Islamic moral code and religious law.

Sacred Texts

The Qur'an is the major text of Islam; the word "Qur'an" means "reading" or "recitation." Muslims believe that the Qur'an is the exact words of Allah as revealed to Muhammad. There are 114 chapters, or surahs, arranged by length, not topic, and some 6,000 verses.

Hadith is a collection of traditions, analogies, and consensus. The traditions relate to the life and words of Muhammad and that of his companions, and the analogies and consensus are the result of the study of Muslim scholars endeavoring to answer questions, especially ones relating to legal issues and the duties of Muslims. There are thousands of hadith.

Holy Days

The holiest of Muslim celebrations is the month of Ramadan, which occurs in the ninth month of the Muslim calendar (the Muslim calendar has twelve months, but only 354 or 355 days). It honors the giving of the Qur'an to Muhammad. Muslims fast from sunup to sundown each day for the month. Id al-Fitr, the Feast of Breaking the Fast of Ramadan, is celebrated at the end of the month.

Other holy days include:

- *Al-Hijrah:* The Muslim New Year; celebrates Muhammad's journey from Mecca to Medina
- *Mawlid al-Nabi:* Celebrates Muhammad's birthday
- *Laylat al-Qadr:* The Night of Power; occurs on the twenty-fifth day of Ramadan; honors the first revelation to Muhammad

RELIGIOUS MOVEMENTS

A religious movement may be defined as "a movement intended to bring about religious reforms." Using that definition, Buddhism and the Sunni branch of Islam can be considered a religious movement, as can any of the Protestant denominations. A number of such movements developed both before and after the beginning of the second millennium.

Before 1000 C.E.

Three notable religious movements that developed prior to 1000 C.E. were the ancient prophetic movement of the Israelites and Jainism.

Prophetic Movement

The original prophets were similar in some respects to medicine men. For example, they conferred blessings or curses on people, called down rain or sun for a good harvest, and healed the sick. They were also seers to whom Yahweh sent dreams and visions, and they could foretell the future. By around the eleventh century B.C.E., the mission of the prophets changed to one of proclaiming the message of Yahweh. They railed against those who had fallen into idolatry and urged them to return to the worship of the one true God and reaffirm the covenant. The prophets believed that their authority to speak and their message came directly from Yahweh. There were three types of prophets: (1) those who were attached to shrines, (2) those who served as advisors at the court of the kings, and (3) those who were neither cult nor court prophets. Among the best known of the prophets were Samuel, Amos, Hosea, Isaiah, and Micah.

Jainism

Jainism began in the sixth century B.C.E. in India as a reaction to some of the practices of Hinduism. Its traditional founder is Mahavira, who believed that he had found a way to stop the endless cycle of birth, life, and death. Like Hinduism, a person's karma determines his or her future lives, so Jains believe that only a person's own actions can end this cycle. Unlike Hindus, Jains believe that deities are of no help, so there is no reason to pray to them. Individuals must find release from the cycle of reincarnations through their own actions, and those actions should use as little effort as possible. Jainism is an ascetic religion. Those who are able to give up their material lives and become monks are closer to ending their cycle than those who remain "in the world."

The basic tenet of Jainism is that all living things have souls. As a result, Jains practice nonviolence. They also vow to speak truthfully and never take anything that they are not given. Jain monks also vow to be celibate and to renounce all attachments. Jains believe that attachment to material things keeps humans tied to the earthly life.

After 1000 C.E.

Various religions have experienced a number of religious movements over the course of the last thousand years. In addition to those presented here, Lutheranism and other Protestant denominations, the Catholic Counter-Reformation, and Wahhabism all fit the definition of religious movements, but were discussed earlier in the chapter.

Fundamentalism

A major movement that transcends religious boundaries is fundamentalism. Fundamentalists wish to return to the basic, or fundamental, tenets of their religion. In general, the Christian fundamentalists believe that the Bible is the literal word of God and they oppose many trends in modern society, such as abortion, same-sex marriage, and legal protections for women and homosexuals. On the other hand, along with some evangelical Christians, some fundamentalists push for increased environmentalism because they see humans as stewards of God's creation.

Islamic fundamentalists, known as Islamists, wish to strip all modernity from Islamic practices and reinstate theocratic government. The Taliban is an example.

Islamic fundamentalists, known as Islamists, wish to strip all modernity from Islamic practices and reinstate theocratic government. The Taliban is an example.

The Lubavitch, a missionary movement of the Hasidim, is a fundamentalist group within Judaism.

Evangelical Christians

Evangelical Christianity may seem like a modern phenomenon, but it began in Great Britain and was brought to the American colonies. It became the basis of the First Great Awakening, which took place from around 1720 until around 1760, and the Second Great Awakening of 1790s through much of the nineteenth century. Evangelicals stress the need for personal conversion, known as being born again, and, like fundamentalists, place their trust in the authority of the Bible. They also emphasize the saving grace of Jesus' death and resurrection. Evangelical preachers of the Great Awakenings appealed to emotions and found a receptive audience among people for whom the erudite, emotionless sermons of the educated clergy held little appeal and few answers to the dangers and fears of the people. Modern evangelicals fill a similar need for contemporary people beset with fears and concerns about a world moving quickly and in ways that they may not understand or want.

Mormons

The Church of Jesus Christ of Latter Day Saints, known as Mormons, is another Christian movement. Members believe that its founder Joseph Smith was instructed by the angel Moroni where to find golden tablets containing the Book of Mormon, the history and teachings of the Nephite prophets. The Nephites were descended from one of the tribes of Israel that were scattered after the destruction of their kingdom. They had come to the North American continent, and now Moroni was the last prophet. The Mormons have an active mission to convert others to the original, true Christianity.

Ecumenism

The ecumenical movement was an effort of the Roman Catholic, Eastern Orthodox, and some Protestant churches to heal some of the divisions among the Roman Catholic and Eastern Churches, the Roman Catholic Church and Protestant denominations, and among some Protestant denominations. Little progress was actually made, and the ordination of women and the inclusion of gays in the ministry have widened and hardened some divisions and have created new ones within some denominations, for example, the Anglican and Episcopalian churches.

Liberation Theology

In the Roman Catholic Church and in some Protestant circles, liberation theology is a viable way to deal with injustice to the poor. Practiced mainly in Latin America in the latter part of the twentieth century, adherents believe that the gospels support activism, even violence, against oppressive and abusive governments. Because of certain aspects of liberation theology, such as redistribution of wealth from the rich to the poor, which seem close to socialism and communism, the hierarchy of the Catholic Church has reigned in clergy who support liberation theology.

POST-TEST ANSWER SHEET

1. Ⓐ Ⓑ Ⓒ Ⓓ	13. Ⓐ Ⓑ Ⓒ Ⓓ	25. Ⓐ Ⓑ Ⓒ Ⓓ	37. Ⓐ Ⓑ Ⓒ Ⓓ	49. Ⓐ Ⓑ Ⓒ Ⓓ
2. Ⓐ Ⓑ Ⓒ Ⓓ	14. Ⓐ Ⓑ Ⓒ Ⓓ	26. Ⓐ Ⓑ Ⓒ Ⓓ	38. Ⓐ Ⓑ Ⓒ Ⓓ	50. Ⓐ Ⓑ Ⓒ Ⓓ
3. Ⓐ Ⓑ Ⓒ Ⓓ	15. Ⓐ Ⓑ Ⓒ Ⓓ	27. Ⓐ Ⓑ Ⓒ Ⓓ	39. Ⓐ Ⓑ Ⓒ Ⓓ	51. Ⓐ Ⓑ Ⓒ Ⓓ
4. Ⓐ Ⓑ Ⓒ Ⓓ	16. Ⓐ Ⓑ Ⓒ Ⓓ	28. Ⓐ Ⓑ Ⓒ Ⓓ	40. Ⓐ Ⓑ Ⓒ Ⓓ	52. Ⓐ Ⓑ Ⓒ Ⓓ
5. Ⓐ Ⓑ Ⓒ Ⓓ	17. Ⓐ Ⓑ Ⓒ Ⓓ	29. Ⓐ Ⓑ Ⓒ Ⓓ	41. Ⓐ Ⓑ Ⓒ Ⓓ	53. Ⓐ Ⓑ Ⓒ Ⓓ
6. Ⓐ Ⓑ Ⓒ Ⓓ	18. Ⓐ Ⓑ Ⓒ Ⓓ	30. Ⓐ Ⓑ Ⓒ Ⓓ	42. Ⓐ Ⓑ Ⓒ Ⓓ	54. Ⓐ Ⓑ Ⓒ Ⓓ
7. Ⓐ Ⓑ Ⓒ Ⓓ	19. Ⓐ Ⓑ Ⓒ Ⓓ	31. Ⓐ Ⓑ Ⓒ Ⓓ	43. Ⓐ Ⓑ Ⓒ Ⓓ	55. Ⓐ Ⓑ Ⓒ Ⓓ
8. Ⓐ Ⓑ Ⓒ Ⓓ	20. Ⓐ Ⓑ Ⓒ Ⓓ	32. Ⓐ Ⓑ Ⓒ Ⓓ	44. Ⓐ Ⓑ Ⓒ Ⓓ	56. Ⓐ Ⓑ Ⓒ Ⓓ
9. Ⓐ Ⓑ Ⓒ Ⓓ	21. Ⓐ Ⓑ Ⓒ Ⓓ	33. Ⓐ Ⓑ Ⓒ Ⓓ	45. Ⓐ Ⓑ Ⓒ Ⓓ	57. Ⓐ Ⓑ Ⓒ Ⓓ
10. Ⓐ Ⓑ Ⓒ Ⓓ	22. Ⓐ Ⓑ Ⓒ Ⓓ	34. Ⓐ Ⓑ Ⓒ Ⓓ	46. Ⓐ Ⓑ Ⓒ Ⓓ	58. Ⓐ Ⓑ Ⓒ Ⓓ
11. Ⓐ Ⓑ Ⓒ Ⓓ	23. Ⓐ Ⓑ Ⓒ Ⓓ	35. Ⓐ Ⓑ Ⓒ Ⓓ	47. Ⓐ Ⓑ Ⓒ Ⓓ	59. Ⓐ Ⓑ Ⓒ Ⓓ
12. Ⓐ Ⓑ Ⓒ Ⓓ	24. Ⓐ Ⓑ Ⓒ Ⓓ	36. Ⓐ Ⓑ Ⓒ Ⓓ	48. Ⓐ Ⓑ Ⓒ Ⓓ	60. Ⓐ Ⓑ Ⓒ Ⓓ

answer sheet

POST-TEST

Directions: Carefully read each of the following 60 questions. Choose the best answer to each question, and darken its letter on your answer sheet. The Answer Key and Explanations can be found following this Post-Test.

1. Which religion celebrates Diwali, the Festival of Lights?
   - **(A)** Judaism
   - **(B)** Islam
   - **(C)** Mahayana Buddhism
   - **(D)** Hinduism

2. According to Shinto, which of the following are earthly and heavenly spirits?
   - **(A)** Kami
   - **(B)** Koan
   - **(C)** Karma
   - **(D)** Li

3. Paul is important in the history of Christianity because he
   - **(A)** wrote one of the four Gospels.
   - **(B)** was the first bishop of Rome.
   - **(C)** believed that Christianity was more than a Jewish sect.
   - **(D)** converted the Emperor Constantine to Christianity.

4. The break between the Roman Catholic Church and the Eastern Church in 1054 is called a
   - **(A)** heresy.
   - **(B)** schism.
   - **(C)** sect.
   - **(D)** denomination.

5. Which of the following best describes the Tao?
   - **(A)** Fundamental presence in all things
   - **(B)** Harmony with nature
   - **(C)** Self-awareness
   - **(D)** Simplicity

6. Women must sit separately from men in
   - **(A)** Reform synagogues.
   - **(B)** Reconstructionist synagogues.
   - **(C)** Orthodox synagogues.
   - **(D)** Conservative synagogues.

7. Eating pork is considered taboo in
   - **(A)** Islam.
   - **(B)** Hinduism.
   - **(C)** Buddhism.
   - **(D)** Shinto.

8. Which of the following is a characteristic of most religions?
   - **(A)** Asceticism
   - **(B)** Monasticism
   - **(C)** Ceremonies related to rites of passage
   - **(D)** Hierarchical organization

9. Which of the following might a Buddhist do to improve his or her karma?
   - **(A)** Remove shoes before entering a mosque to pray
   - **(B)** Rinse one's mouth and wash one's hands before entering a shrine to pray
   - **(C)** Offer a bowl of food to a monk
   - **(D)** Pray to one's ancestors

10. Which of the following is/are reciprocal relationships described by Confucius?

    I. Father and son

    II. Brother and sister

    III. Ruler and subject

    (A) I only

    (B) I and II only

    (C) II and III only

    (D) I and III only

11. The angel Moroni appeared to

    (A) Moses.

    (B) Joseph Smith.

    (C) Muhammad.

    (D) Abraham.

12. A network of patriarchs is the form of organization in

    (A) Lutheranism.

    (B) Judaism.

    (C) Eastern Orthodox churches.

    (D) the Anglican Church.

13. Jains believe that

    (A) a life devoted to monasticism is not helpful or necessary in finding release from reincarnation.

    (B) praying to the deities will aid humans in their quest for release from reincarnation.

    (C) release from the cycle of reincarnation comes through one's own actions.

    (D) celibacy is unnatural.

14. Why are Catholics baptized?

    (A) As a reminder of Jesus' death and resurrection

    (B) To affirm that they are born again in Christ

    (C) To remove the stain of original sin

    (D) To make amends for the sin of Adam

15. What is the cause of suffering according to Taoism?

    (A) Unnaturalness

    (B) Desire

    (C) Violence

    (D) The innate evil in the world

16. Which of the following best describes a bodhisattva in Mahayana Buddhism?

    (A) A yogi master

    (B) A Buddhist monk

    (C) Anyone working toward enlightenment

    (D) Someone who has achieved nirvana, but remains in life to help others to enlightenment

17. The Aztec practiced human sacrifice to

    (A) ensure a good harvest.

    (B) prevent the end of the world.

    (C) thank the deities for victory in battle.

    (D) instill fear in their enemies.

18. Which of the following describes a way that an anthropologist would study a religion?

    (A) Compare taboos across three religions

    (B) Question subjects on what a worship service means to them

    (C) Observe an initiation rite for an adolescent

    (D) Investigate the impact of a church's outreach to the homeless

19. Dharma is the

    (A) cycle of birth, death, and rebirth in Buddhism.

    (B) release from the cycle of reincarnation in Hinduism.

    (C) religious and moral duties of individuals in Hinduism.

    (D) name given to Buddhas-in-waiting.

20. Which of the following sacraments removes original sin?

    (A) Confirmation

    (B) Baptism

    (C) Eucharist

    (D) Penance, also called Confession

21. At a madrasah, a person would

    (A) study the Talmud.

    (B) make an offering to the kami.

    (C) make an offering to Vishnu.

    (D) study the Qur'an.

22. God as the Creator or Supreme Being is a concept found in

    I.   Christianity.
    II. Judaism.
    III. Native North American religions.
    IV. Islam.

    (A) I and II only

    (B) I and IV only

    (C) I, II, and IV only

    (D) I, II, III, and IV

23. In which of the following would you find icons?

    (A) Russian Orthodox church

    (B) Roman Catholic church

    (C) Mosque

    (D) Buddhist temple

24. What insight about life, death, and rebirth did Gautama receive that "enlightened" him about how to live one's life?

    (A) Monasticism is the proper way to receive enlightenment.

    (B) Life must be lived on a middle path between asceticism and desire.

    (C) Practicing yoga and meditation are the only way to enlightenment.

    (D) All reality is one with Brahman.

25. All of the following are steps in the Eight-Fold Path EXCEPT

    (A) right understanding.

    (B) right speech.

    (C) right action.

    (D) right loyalty.

26. Which of the following statements best describes Islamists?

    (A) They preside over religious courts.

    (B) Their goal is to reestablish theocratic states.

    (C) They are scholars of Islamic law.

    (D) They lead the faithful in prayer services at mosques.

27. Which of the following men urged Jews to leave their ghettoes and live within their larger communities in the nineteenth century?

    (A) Maimonides (Moses ben-Maimon)

    (B) Mordecai Kaplan

    (C) Moses Mendelssohn

    (D) Baal Shem Tov

28. The Jews who settled in Eastern Europe are known as

    (A) Ashkenazi.

    (B) Uzbekistanis.

    (C) Sephardim.

    (D) Sannyasi.

29. The influence of Martin Luther on later Protestant denominations can be seen in their adoption of his doctrine of

    (A) salvation through faith alone.

    (B) baptism as the only sacrament.

    (C) the continuation of the central role of priests/ministers in confession.

    (D) the continuation of Latin for services.

post-test

30. What is the Hindu name for the ultimate reality?

    (A) Yin and yang

    (B) Ahimsa

    (C) Brahman

    (D) Atman

31. The Ka'bah is sacred to Muslims because

    (A) they believe that Abraham and Ishmael built it.

    (B) it is where the angel Gabriel appeared to Muhammad.

    (C) it houses Muhammad's grave.

    (D) it is where Muhammad ascended into heaven.

32. Which of the following believed that human nature is evil?

    (A) Confucius

    (B) Mencius (Meng-Zi)

    (C) Hsun Tzu (Xun-Zi)

    (D) Lao-Tzu

33. The Talmud contains the

    I.   Mishnah
    II. Gemara
    III. Haggadah
    IV. Torah

    (A) I and II only

    (B) I and III only

    (C) I, II, and III only

    (D) I, II, III, and IV

34. Typically, religions have ceremonies honoring which of the following rites of passage?

    I.   Death
    II. Birth
    III. Marriage
    IV. Puberty

    (A) I and II only

    (B) I, II, and III only

    (C) I, II, and IV only

    (D) I, II, III, and IV

35. An Egyptian visiting Rome would have found worship of which of the following familiar?

    (A) Zeus

    (B) Hera

    (C) Isis

    (D) Cybele

36. According to Buddhism, what is the cause of suffering?

    (A) Desire

    (B) Striving after a good reputation

    (C) Material goods

    (D) Human attachments

37. Social virtue, or jen, is a basic concept of

    (A) Islam.

    (B) Shinto.

    (C) Buddhism.

    (D) Confucianism.

38. Kosher laws relate to

    (A) whom Jews may marry.

    (B) what they may and may not do on the Sabbath.

    (C) what Jews may wear.

    (D) what Jews may and may not eat.

39. The division between Sunni and Shi'te Muslims has its origins in

    (A) the dispute over who was the rightful heir of Muhammad.

    (B) how strictly to interpret the Qur'an.

    (C) what the proper role of women is in Islam.

    (D) disagreements over the position of imams in Islam.

40. Jainism developed over dissatisfaction with aspects of

    (A) Buddhism.

    (B) Hinduism.

    (C) Shinto.

    (D) Confucianism.

41. Rosh Hashanah celebrates the

(A) victory of the Maccabees and the rededication of the Temple in Jerusalem.

(B) harvest.

(C) Jewish New Year.

(D) exodus from Egypt.

42. Which of the following is a reason that caused the schism between the Roman Catholic and Eastern Orthodox churches in 1054?

(A) The Eastern Orthodox Church practices adult baptism, and the Roman Catholic Church practices infant baptism.

(B) The Eastern Orthodox Church does not allow any kind of ornamentation, whereas the Roman Catholic Church does.

(C) The Roman Catholic Church claims that the Pope has supremacy over all other churches in matters of faith and morals.

(D) The Orthodox Church's acceptance of married clergy, as long as they were married before ordination.

43. In Islam, ummah is the

(A) niche in the wall of a mosque or a design in a prayer rug pointed in the direction of Mecca during prayer.

(B) call to prayer five times a day.

(C) pilgrimage to Mecca.

(D) community of the faithful.

44. The major divisions of Islam are

(A) Sufi and Shari'ah.

(B) Sunni and Wahhabism.

(C) Shi'a and Sunni.

(D) Twelvers and Shi'a

45. Buddhism differs from Islam in that Buddhism

(A) does not have a historical founder, but Islam does.

(B) practices polytheism, but Islam is monotheistic.

(C) calls its God Buddha and Islam calls its God Allah.

(D) does not have the concept of a single supreme being, but Islam does.

46. All of the following are offshoots of Islam EXCEPT

(A) Sikhism.

(B) Jainism.

(C) Wahhabism.

(D) Sufism.

47. What are Bar Mitzvahs and Bat Mitzvahs?

(A) The name given to twelve books in the Hebrew Bible

(B) Special reading from the Torah to mark Passover

(C) Jewish ceremonies that marks the entrance into manhood for a male and womanhood for a female

(D) A good work or deed

48. Which of the following is a tenet of Confucianism, but NOT Taoism?

(A) Right action

(B) God as creator

(C) Harmony

(D) The less government the better

49. The Hindu caste system is documented in which of the following?

(A) Law of Manu

(B) Rig Veda

(C) Ramayana

(D) Varna

post-test

50. Which of the following best describes the outcome of the Council of Trent?

    (A) It ignored issues raised by the Reformation.

    (B) It reaffirmed Catholic doctrine.

    (C) It made significant changes to Catholic doctrine in a conciliatory gesture that was not reciprocated.

    (D) It was an attempt to modernize the Catholic Church.

51. Which of the following honors the first revelation to Muhammad by the angel Gabriel?

    (A) Id al-Fitr

    (B) Al-Hijrah

    (C) Laylat al-Qadr

    (D) Ramadan

52. Which of the following groups observes the Sabbath most strictly?

    (A) Orthodox Jews

    (B) Reform Jews

    (C) Conservative Jews

    (D) Reconstructionist Jews

53. All of the following developed as a way to preserve Judaism through early centuries of persecution EXCEPT

    (A) synagogues as the center of worship.

    (B) the development of mystical elements in Jewish teaching.

    (C) the rabbi as teacher and explicator.

    (D) designating Saturday as the Sabbath based on the Book of Genesis.

54. Taoism was seen as a complement to, rather than a rival of,

    (A) Hinduism.

    (B) Shinto.

    (C) Theravada Buddhism.

    (D) Confucianism.

55. The basic belief system of Buddhism is the

    (A) Mishnah.

    (B) Four Noble Truths.

    (C) Five Pillars.

    (D) Analects.

56. In indigenous religions, which religious personage foretells the future?

    (A) Animist

    (B) Healer

    (C) Diviner

    (D) Medicine man and woman

57. The triad of Hindu deities is

    (A) Brahma, Krishna, and Shakti.

    (B) Brahma, Vishnu, and Shiva.

    (C) Shiva, Shakti, and Krishna.

    (D) Vishnu, Rama, and Kali.

58. Which of the following is a code of ethics?

    (A) Ten Commandments

    (B) Apostles Creed

    (C) Pentateuch

    (D) I Ching

59. The name of which of the following religions means "submission"?

    (A) Catholicism

    (B) Islam

    (C) Orthodox

    (D) Buddhism

60. Which of the following is the belief that the bread and wine become the body and blood of Jesus at the consecration in the Catholic Mass?

    (A) Predestination

    (B) Justification

    (C) Inclusion

    (D) Transubstantiation

ANSWER KEY AND EXPLANATIONS

1. D	13. C	25. D	37. D	49. A
2. A	14. C	26. B	38. D	50. B
3. C	15. A	27. C	39. A	51. C
4. B	16. D	28. A	40. B	52. A
5. A	17. B	29. A	41. C	53. B
6. C	18. C	30. C	42. C	54. D
7. A	19. C	31. A	43. D	55. B
8. C	20. B	32. C	44. C	56. C
9. C	21. D	33. A	45. D	57. B
10. D	22. D	34. D	46. B	58. A
11. B	23. A	35. C	47. C	59. B
12. C	24. B	36. A	48. A	60. D

1. **The correct answer is (D).** You might be confused by the term "Festival of Lights" because it's also an English translation for the Jewish celebration, Chanukah, but Diwali is the operative word. Choices (B) and (C) are incorrect.

2. **The correct answer is (A).** Choice (B) is incorrect because koan are used in Zen Buddhist to help people reach enlightenment. Choice (C) is incorrect because the law of karma is the determinant in the kind of future lives a person will have, according to Hinduism and Buddhism. Choice (D) is incorrect because li is the principle of correct behavior between individuals in Confucianism.

3. **The correct answer is (C).** Paul was important because he believed that Christianity was a completely new religion. Choice (A) is incorrect because the Gospels were written by Matthew, Mark, Luke, and John. Peter is believed to have been the first bishop of Rome, so choice (B) is incorrect. Choice (D) is incorrect because Paul lived in the first century C.E., and Constantine was converted after a vision in 312 C.E.

4. **The correct answer is (B).** Choice (A) is incorrect because a heresy is a belief in conflict with the orthodox, that is, official, teachings of a church. Choice (C) is incorrect because a sect is a small group that has broken from an established church; the qualifier "small" doesn't fit the size of either the Roman Catholic or Eastern Churches. Choice (D) is incorrect because a denomination is a type of religious body and is larger than a sect.

5. **The correct answer is (A).** The Tao is the fundamental presence or essence of all things. Were you expecting "the way or path" as an answer? The question asks for a description of the Tao, not a definition of the word. Choices (B) and (D) are incorrect although Taoists seek harmony with nature and simplicity in their lives. Choice (C) is incorrect as well.

6. **The correct answer is (C).** Men and women sit together in Reform, Reconstructionist, and Conservative synagogues, so choices (A), (B), and (D) are incorrect.

7. **The correct answer is (A).** Islam prohibits Muslims from eating pork; it is taboo in their religion. (Judaism, which also originated in the Middle East, also prohibits the consumption of pork). Choice (B) is incorrect because pork is not taboo for Hindus, but eating beef is. Choices (C) and (D) are incorrect because pork is not taboo for either Buddhists or adherents of Shinto.

8. **The correct answer is (C).** Religions typically have ceremonies or rituals related to such rites of passage as birth, puberty, marriage, and death. Choice (A) is incorrect because asceticism is the practice of severe self-denial and self-restraint for the purpose uniting with the divine. Most religions don't have members who are ascetics, for example, Protestant denominations. Choice (B) is incorrect because not all religions have monasteries, for example, indigenous religions and Islam. Choice (D) is incorrect because most religions don't have hierarchical organizational structures.

9. **The correct answer is (C).** Actions to improve one's karma are known as making merit. Choice (A) is incorrect because the word "mosque" signals that this is a practice of Muslims, not Buddhists. Choice (B) is incorrect because washing before entering a shrine to pray is a ritual of Shinto. Choice (D) is incorrect because Buddhists do not venerate their ancestors.

10. **The correct answer is (D).** Confucius doesn't mention sisters, so statement II is incorrect. Choices (B) and (C) are, therefore, incorrect because they both include statement II. Choice (A) is incorrect because it omits statement III.

11. **The correct answer is (B).** Moroni appeared to Joseph Smith, gave him the golden tablets that are the sacred writings of the Church of Jesus Christ of Latter Day Saints, and gave him the ability to translate them into English. Choice (A) is incorrect because Yahweh appeared to Moses in the form of a burning bush on Mount Sinai. Choice (C) is incorrect because the angel Gabriel appeared to Muhammad. Choice (D) is incorrect because Yahweh appeared to Abraham.

12. **The correct answer is (C).** Lutheran churches are organized into synods overseen by ministers, so choice (A) is incorrect. Judaism, choice (B), has no organized structure of overseers, so eliminate it. The highest clerical office in choice (D), the Anglican Church, or Church of England, is the Archbishop of Canterbury.

13. **The correct answer is (C).** Choice (A) is incorrect because Jains believe that monks are closer to release than those who live in the world. Choice (B) is the opposite of what Jains believe: Prayer is of no help in attaining release. Choice (D) is incorrect because Jain monks take vows of celibacy.

14. **The correct answer is (C).** Choice (A) may seem like a good answer, but it's incorrect. Choice (B) is incorrect because Catholics believe in infant baptism. This answer hints at being a "born again" Christian, someone who believes in adult baptism. Choice (D) is incorrect because baptism removes the sin inherited from Adam, but doesn't make amends for it.

15. **The correct answer is (A).** According to Taoism, unnaturalness is the cause of suffering, pain, and violence. Violence, choice (C), is one result of unnaturalness so it is not the correct answer. Choice (B) is incorrect; Buddhists believe that desire is the cause of suffering. Choice (D) may seem correct, but it is not.

16. **The correct answer is (D).** In Mahayana Buddhism, a bodhisattva may also be someone who has achieved nirvana, died, and is now prayed to by other Buddhists. Choice (A) is incorrect because yoga in its various

forms is found in Hinduism, not Buddhism. Choice (B) is incorrect because a Buddhist monk is not yet a bodhisattva. Choice (C) is incorrect because a bodhisattva has already achieved nirvana.

17. **The correct answer is (B).** The Aztec believed that by offering human sacrifices to the gods, they could prevent the end of the world. Choices (A), (C), and (D) are plausible, but incorrect.

18. **The correct answer is (C).** Choice (A) describes how a follower of the phenomenologist school of thought would study religion. Choice (B) is incorrect because a psychologist would study how religion influences thoughts and behavior. Choice (D) is incorrect because it is an approach that a sociologist might take.

19. **The correct answer is (C).** Choice (A) is incorrect because the cycle of reincarnation is called samsara in both Hinduism and Buddhism. Choice (B) is incorrect because moksha is the release from the cycle of reincarnation. Choice (D) is incorrect because Buddhas-in-waiting are called bodhisattvas.

20. **The correct answer is (B).** Choice (A) is incorrect because Confirmation is the sacrament that initiates the believer into full and mature participation in the Church. Choice (C) is incorrect because the sacrament of the Eucharist is the body and blood of Jesus. Choice (D) is incorrect because the sacrament of Penance removes the sins that individuals themselves commit.

21. **The correct answer is (D).** A madrasah is an Islamic school, so students would study the Qur'an. Choice (A) is incorrect because a student would study the Jewish Torah at a yeshiva. Choice (B) is incorrect because a person would make an offering to a kami at a Shinto shrine; the names of the shrines vary depending on whom the shrine honors. Choice (C) is incorrect because a Hindu would make an offering to Vishnu at a mandir, a Hindu temple.

22. **The correct answer is (D).** A supreme being or creator of all things—whether known as God, Yahweh, the High God, or Allah—is a concept found in Hinduism, Judaism, Native North American religions, and Islam. Only choice (D) has all four answers.

23. **The correct answer is (A).** Icons decorate Eastern Orthodox churches, so you find icons in Russian Orthodox churches, and choices (B), (C), and (D) are incorrect. Choice (C) is also incorrect for another reason: Muslims believe that representations of Muhammad are blasphemous.

24. **The correct answer is (B).** Buddha's enlightenment led to the Eight-Fold Path and the Four Noble Truths. Choices (A), (C), and (D) are incorrect because these were not what prompted the Buddha's enlightenment. Choice (D) is a tenet of Hinduism.

25. **The correct answer is (D).** Right understanding, right speech, and right action are all aspects of the Eight-Fold Path of Buddhism. Choice (D), right loyalty, is, therefore, the correct answer.

26. **The correct answer is (B).** Islamists are Muslim fundamentalists who want to return Islam to what they consider its original teachings. Choice (A) is incorrect because religious courts are typically presided over by clerics. Choice (C) is incorrect because those who study Islamic law are called mujtahid. Imams lead the faithful in prayer at mosques, so choice (D) is incorrect.

27. **The correct answer is (C).** Moses Mendelssohn encouraged Jews to move out the ghetto and into the modern European world. Baal Shem Tov, choice (D), preached that Jews should maintain their identity and live apart from the secular world. Choice (A) is incorrect because Jewish scholar Maimonides lived in the late twelfth and early thirteenth centuries. Choice (B) is incorrect because Mordecai Kaplan is credited as a founding thinker of Reconstructionist Judaism, which

originated in the United States in the 1920s and 1930s.

28. **The correct answer is (A).** Choice (B) may seem familiar, but this is the name of the people who live in Uzbekistan. Choice (C) may also be familiar, but Sephardic Jews lived in Iberian Peninsula. Choice (D) is incorrect because sannyasi are Hindu ascetics who have renounced all worldly things.

29. **The correct answer is (A).** Even if you weren't sure about the other answers, Luther's concept of justification by faith should have stuck out as the correct answer. It was a monumental change in Christian theology. Choice (B) is incorrect because Luther accepted baptism and the Eucharist as sacraments. Choice (C) is incorrect because Luther didn't accept the rite of confession to a priest. Choice (D) is incorrect because Luther introduced the use of the vernacular, in his case, German, for services and for scripture.

30. **The correct answer is (C).** Choice (A) is incorrect because yin and yang are concepts in Taoism that represent balance. Choice (B) is incorrect because ahimsa is the Hindu and Buddhist principle of nonviolence. Choice (D) is incorrect because atman is the self or soul to Hindus.

31. **The correct answer is (A).** Muslims believe that Abraham and Ishmael built the Ka'bah as a resting place for the Black Stone given to Adam by Allah. Choice (B) is incorrect because Gabriel appeared to Muhammad in various places, but not in the Ka'bah. Choices (C) and (D) are incorrect because Muhammad ascended into heaven, so there is no grave. The site of the ascension was the Dome of the Rock in Jerusalem.

32. **The correct answer is (C).** Hsun Tzu (Xun-Zi) was a later Confucian scholar who believed that human nature was inherently evil, in contrast to choice (B), Mencius (Meng-Zi), who believed that human nature was inherently good. Choice (A), Confucius,

is incorrect because he believed in the natural goodness of people. Choice (D) is incorrect because Lao-Tzu is the traditional founder of Taoism.

33. **The correct answer is (A).** The Talmud includes the Mishnah, a collection of disputes and commentary on Jewish law up to the 100s C.E., and the Gemara, additional rabbinic teachings on Jewish life. Statement III, the Haggadah is the service for seder, and statement IV, the Torah, is the first five books of the Hebrew Bible. Choices (B) and (C) are incorrect because they contain the Haggadah. Choice (D) is incorrect because it contains both the Haggadah and the Torah.

34. **The correct answer is (D).** In general, world religions have ritual ceremonies to celebrate or mark death, birth, marriage, and puberty. Only choice (D) includes all four, so it is the correct answer.

35. **The correct answer is (C).** The cult of Isis and Osiris spread from Egypt across the Middle East and into Greece and Rome. Choice (A) is incorrect because Zeus was the chief Greek deity and Hera, choice (B), was his wife, the guardian of women and marriage. Choice (D) is incorrect because Cybele was a female fertility deity introduced into the Roman Empire from Asia Minor.

36. **The correct answer is (A).** The best answer is always the most complete, and while choice (B), striving after a good reputation; choice (C), material goods; and choice (D), human attachments, are all things that cause suffering, they are specific causes. The best answer for this question is choice (A), desire, which is encompasses the other answers.

37. **The correct answer is (D).** Jen, translated as social virtue and also as human-heartedness, is a basic concept of Confucianism. Choice (A), Islam; choice (B), Shinto; and choice (C), Buddhism are incorrect.

38. **The correct answer is (D).** Kosher laws are dietary laws describing what foods and combinations of foods Jews may and may not eat. There are 620 mitzvah, or commandments, plus commentary in Jewish law that relate to marriage, activities on the Sabbath, and other elements of Jewish life, but they are not kosher laws, so choices (A), (B), and (C) are incorrect.

39. **The correct answer is (A).** Choices (B), (C), and (D) may be differences that have developed between Sunni and Shi'a Muslims, but choice (A) is the origin of any differences that have developed over the centuries.

40. **The correct answer is (B).** Both Jainism and Buddhism developed because of dissatisfaction with aspects of Hinduism. Choice (A) is incorrect because Buddhism itself developed as a reaction to elements of Hinduism. Choices (C) and (D) are incorrect because Jainism is not related to either religion.

41. **The correct answer is (C).** Choice (A) is incorrect because it describes Chanukah, known as the Festival of Lights or the Feast of the Dedication. Choice (B) is incorrect because it describes Sukkot, the Feast of the Tabernacle. Choice (D) is incorrect because it describes Passover.

42. **The correct answer is (C).** Choice (A) is incorrect because both churches practice infant baptism. Choice (B) is a misstatement of the controversy over icons that was one of the reasons that precipitated the schism. The emperor in the East in the early 700s came under the influence of Islam and ordered churches to remove their religious imagery. The Pope condemned this iconoclasm, destruction of icons, or representations, as heresy. In time, the Eastern Church as well returned to the use of icons as symbols. Choice (D) is a difference between the Roman Catholic and Eastern Orthodox Churches, but not a reason that brought about the schism, so it's incorrect.

43. **The correct answer is (D).** Choice (A) is incorrect because the wall niche or rug design pointed in the direction of Mecca is called the mihrab. Choice (B) is incorrect because the call to prayer is the adhan. Hajj is the pilgrimage to Mecca, so choice (C) is incorrect.

44. **The correct answer is (C).** Islam divided into Shi'a and Sunni in a dispute over who was the legitimate successor to Muhammad. Choice (A) is incorrect because Sufism is a mystical branch of Islam, but is not a major division; Shari'ah is Islamic law, not a religious division. Choice (B) is incorrect because while Sunni is correct, Wahhabism is a conservative movement within Islam that originated on the Arabian Peninsula. It is not a major division of Islam. If one part of an answer is incorrect, the entire answer is incorrect. Choice (D) is incorrect because Twelvers are another name given to Shi'ites who believe that there have been Twelve Imams and the Twelfth and last is still alive and is hidden to them.

45. **The correct answer is (D).** There is no ultimate being in Buddhism. Choice (A) is incorrect because both Buddhism and Islam have historical founders, Gautama Buddha and Muhammad, respectively. Choice (B) is incorrect because Buddhism is not polytheistic; however, Islam is monotheistic, worshipping only Allah. Remember that when part of an answer is incorrect, the whole answer is incorrect. Choice (C) is incorrect because although the God of Islam is Allah, Buddha is not the same as a supreme being.

46. **The correct answer is (B).** Even if you weren't sure about Sikhism and Sufism, you should have recognized Jainism as having been founded as a reaction against Hinduism. Choice (A), Sikhism, was founded by Guru Nanak in the late 1400s and early 1500s as a reaction to both Islam and Hinduism. It preaches monotheism and includes the concepts of karma, dharma, and reincarnation. Choice (C) is a very conservative form of

Islam that developed in Saudi Arabia, so eliminate choice (C). Sufism is the mystical tradition within Islam, so it is not the answer to the question either.

47. **The correct answer is (C).** The ceremony for females entering womanhood is called Bat Mitzvah and for males entering manhood is called Bar Mitzvah. Choice (A) is incorrect because this describes the Ketuvim. Choice (B) is incorrect because the service for Passover is called the Haggadah. Choice (D) is incorrect because a good work or deed is called a mitzvah ("mitzvah" also means "commandment"; the plural is mitzvot).

48. **The correct answer is (A).** Confucianism believes in the need for right action, whereas Taoists believe in the need for inaction. Choice (B) is incorrect because neither includes a supreme being who created the world. Choice (C) is incorrect because harmony is a basic principle of Taoism, not Confucianism. Choice (D) is incorrect because the Taoists believed that the less the government governed, the better. Confucianists, on the other hand, believed that people needed a strong, feudal system of government.

49. **The correct answer is (A).** Choice (B) is incorrect because the Rig Veda is a collection of more than a thousand hymns. Choice (C) is incorrect because the Ramayana is an epic poem about Prince Rama and his wife. Choice (D) is incorrect because varna is the name of the caste system.

50. **The correct answer is (B).** The Council of Trent made changes to certain abuses of Church practices, but reaffirmed all issues of dogma. Choice (A) is incorrect because the Council of Trent was convened because of the Reformation and took up issues highlighted by the Reformation. Choice (C) is incorrect because the Council made no changes to doctrine. Choice (D) describes the Second Vatican Council, so it is incorrect.

51. **The correct answer is (C).** Choice (A) is incorrect because Id al-Fitr is known as the Breaking of the Fast of Ramadan. Choice (B) is incorrect because al-Hijrah celebrates Muhammad's journey to Medina from Mecca. Choice (D) is incorrect because Ramadan is the month of fasting.

52. **The correct answer is (A).** Orthodox Jews are the strictest in their observance of Jewish traditions and religious doctrines and practices. Therefore, choices (B), (C), and (D) are incorrect.

53. **The correct answer is (B).** Choice (B) refers to the Kabbalah, a body of mystical teachings that was collected in several volumes and doesn't relate to efforts of the ancient Jews to preserve their identity through centuries of persecution, so it is the correct answer to the question. Choices (A), (C), and (D) are ways that Jews followed to preserve their identity and religion, so they are incorrect answers to the question.

54. **The correct answer is (D).** Taoism was seen as a complement to the rigid etiquette of Confucianism and flourished in China for several centuries. However, as Theravada Buddhism, choice (C), spread in China, a rivalry developed between adherents of the two religions. Over the centuries, rulers influenced by one or the other of the religions persecuted its rival adherents. However, over time, Taoism and Theravada Buddhism along with Confucianism became firmly established as major religions among the Chinese. Choices (A) and (B) are incorrect because neither Hinduism nor Shintoism became forces within Chinese religious life.

55. **The correct answer is (B).** Choice (A) is incorrect because the Mishnah is the collection of all the disputes and commentary on Jewish law up to the second century C.E. It is one part of the Talmud. Choice (C) is incorrect because the Five Pillars are the basic belief system of Islam. Choice (D) is

incorrect because the Analects collect the teachings of Confucius.

56. **The correct answer is (C).** A diviner has the power to see into the future; among the ancient Greeks, the person able to do this was called an oracle. Choice (A) is incorrect because an animist believes that the objects of the natural world, such as rocks, are spiritually alive, but an animist doesn't foretell future events. Choices (B) and (D) are incorrect because these are different terms for people who cure the sick.

57. **The correct answer is (B).** The three major deities, or triad, of Hinduism are Brahma, Vishnu, and Shiva. Choice (A) is incorrect because although Krishna is an incarnation of Vishnu, it's not the same. Shakti is the wife of Shiva, but not one of the triad. Choice (C) is incorrect in part because it contains Shakti and also because Krishna is an incarnation of Vishnu, but not the same. Choice (D) is incorrect because Rama is an incarnation of Vishnu, and Kali is another name for Shakti, the wife of Shiva.

58. **The correct answer is (A).** The Ten Commandments provide a moral guide for Jews

and Christians. Choice (B) is incorrect because even if you couldn't identify the document, the word "creed" tells you that it is a list of beliefs (from the Latin word "credo," meaning "I believe"). Choice (C) is incorrect because the Pentateuch is the first five books of the Bible ("penta" meaning "five"). Choice (D) is incorrect because the I Ching is the Taoist book of divination.

59. **The correct answer is (B).** Choice (A) is incorrect because "Catholic" means "universal." Choice (C) is incorrect because "Orthodox" means "conforming to established beliefs." Choice (D) is incorrect because "Buddhism" is derived from a Sanskrit word meaning "the enlightened one."

60. **The correct answer is (D).** Choice (A) is the belief that God has foreordained some people, known as the elect, for salvation and others for damnation; John Calvin taught this doctrine. Choice (B) is incorrect because justification is the Lutheran doctrine that salvation comes through faith without good works and the gift of God's grace.

SUMMING IT UP

- Shared dimensions of world religions include the (1) ritual, (2) mythical, (3) doctrinal, (4) ethical, (5) social, and (6) experiential.

- Approaches to the study of religion can be classified as (1) anthropological, (2) phenomenological, (3) psychological, and (4) sociological.

- Indigenous religions have certain characteristics in common: (1) animism, (2) magic, (3) divination, (4) totem, (5) ancestor veneration or worship, (6) sacrifice, (7) taboos, (8) myth, (9) ritual, and (10) rites of passage.

- There is no single Native American religion, but there are certain common characteristics. The religions generally are (1) animistic and (2) polytheistic; (3) include a Supreme Being who created Earth and withdrew from it; (4) have ceremonies, rituals, and taboos; (5) do not practice human or animal sacrifice; (6) include rites of passage, such as the vision quest; and (7) have no special "priesthood" or hierarchy.

- Major South American religions with their own distinctive traits were Mayan and Aztec, both of which had priesthoods and practiced human sacrifice.

- There is no single African religion, but there are a number of commonalities; they typically (1) are polytheistic; (2) have a central High God who created the world and withdrew from it; (3) practice animism, (4) ancestor veneration, and (5) divination; (6) make offerings and sacrifices of food, sometimes in the form of animals; (7) have rites of passage; and (8) some have male and female priests and temples.

- An important aspect of Egyptian religion was the cult of Isis and Osiris, which spread across the Middle East and into Greece and the Roman Empire. Ahmenhotep IV introduced monotheism with the worship of Aton, but it did not last past the pharaoh's lifetime.

- According to Zoroastrian theology, the creator of goodness and life, Ahura-Mazda, revealed his truths to the prophet Zarathustra, also called Zoroaster. These truths are collected in the Zend-Avesta. Zoroastrians follow the three-fold path: good thoughts, good words, and good deeds.

- The basis of Greek religion was a family of deities who protected and helped the Greeks in their daily lives. A drawback in the eyes of some upper-class Greeks was the lack of an ethical core to the religion. From this discontent and questioning were born several schools of Greek philosophy, which in general were built on the concepts of balance and moderation in all things.

- Initially, the Romans were animists and also venerated their ancestors. In time, the Romans borrowed elements from other religions, most notably the Greeks, and transformed Greek deities into their own.

- In Shinto teachings, the divine resides in all things in nature; the word "Shinto" means "the way of the kami," meaning the spirits of the natural world. Before entering their shrines, Shintoists perform purification rituals.

- The Aryans, invaders from Central Asia, influenced the development of Hinduism, especially varna, the caste system.

- The oldest sacred writings in Hinduism are the Vedas. Also important are the Mahabharata and the Ramayana, two epic poems, and the Law of Manu.

- Basic Hindu beliefs include belief in (1) Brahman, the Ultimate Reality; (2) samsara; (3) karma; (4) moksha; and (5) the four stages of life on the way to moksha. Hinduism is polytheistic; the major deities are the Triad: Brahma, Vishnu, and Shiva.

- Buddhism's historical founder is Siddhartha Gautama, called the Buddha.

- The major traditions within Buddhism are Theravada Buddhism and Mahayana Buddhism; also important are Zen Buddhism and Tibetan Buddhism.

- Buddhism centers on the Four Noble Truths and the Eight-Fold Path. The Four Noble Truths are (1) all life is suffering, called dukkha; (2) the source of all suffering is desire; (3) the cessation of desire is the way to end suffering; and (4) the path to the cessation of desire is the Eight-Fold Path.

- The Eight-Fold Path is (1) right understanding, (2) right thought, (3) right speech, (4) right action, (5) right livelihood, (6) right effort, (7) right mindfulness, and (8) right concentration.

- The major works of Theravada Buddhism are the (1) Tripitaka and (2) Dhammapada (collection of proverbs and adages). Among the major works of Mahayana Buddhism are the (1) Lotus Sutra, (2) Heart Sutras, (3) Tibetan Book of the Dead, and (4) Translation of the Word of the Buddha.

- Confucianism is a philosophy—an ethical code of living—rather than a religion. Confucius taught that five relationships exist that involve reciprocal duties and responsibilities, or right action: (1) between ruler and subject, (2) between father and son, (3) between elder brother and younger brother, (4) between husband and wife, and (5) between friend and friend. The correct behavior, or conduct, between the individuals in these relationships is known as li.

- In addition to these ethical relationships, Confucius taught the concept of jen, or human-heartedness, also described as sympathy or benevolence, that is, love toward others.

- The Five Classics and the Four Books make up the basic writings of Confucianism. Perhaps the most influential are the (1) Analects of Confucius, one of the Four Books; (2) I Ching, the first of the Five Classics; and (3) Book of Mencius (Meng-Zi).

- The traditional founder of Taoism is considered Lao-Tzu, who is also credited with writing the Tao Te Ching, the basis of Taoism. The word "Tao" means "the way." The Tao is infinite and unceasing. It gives life and their nature to all things.

- The central focus of Taoism is naturalness. Human suffering, pain, and violence are the result of the opposite of naturalness, which is unnaturalness. People must become one with the Tao, and then they will realize that all is one with the Tao. Instead of right action, Taoists believe in no action, or inaction.

- Jews believe that Yahweh made a covenant with them. In exchange for worshipping and obeying Yahweh alone, he will protect them. They believe that Yahweh gave Moses the Ten Commandments, the basic law, on Mount Sinai. The basic teachings of Judaism are (1) Yahweh (God) is the supreme creator, (2) Yahweh will send a messiah to redeem the world, and (3) the Jews are God's chosen people.

- Modern Judaism has four main divisions, or movements: (1) Orthodox, (2) Conservative, (3) Reform, and (4) Reconstruction.

- The Jewish sacred writing are the (1) Hebrew Bible (Pentateuch, Prophets, and Ketuvim) and (2) Talmud. Pentateuch is also known as the Torah or the Five Books of Moses. The Mishnah, the collection of all the disputes and commentary on Jewish law up to the 100s C.E., and the later Gemara make up the Talmud. The Gemara is additional rabbinic teachings on every aspect of Jewish life. The material in the Talmud is divided into two categories: (1) the Aggadah and (2) the Halaka.

- Jesus, worshipped as the Son of God the Father, is the historical founder of Christianity.

- After a schism in 1054, Christianity split into the Roman Catholic Church in Western Europe and the Eastern Orthodox Church. The Protestant Reformation resulted in a further splintering of Roman Catholicism over a number of doctrinal issues.

- The Council of Trent ushered in a Catholic Counter-Reformation that resulted in a reaffirmation of Church doctrine that Protestants disputed, including (1) the role of good works in salvation; (2) the seven sacraments; (3) transubstantiation; (4) purgatory; (5) clerical celibacy; (6) veneration of the saints, relics, and sacred images; and (7) the granting of indulgences.

- A concept central to Protestantism is the justification of faith, that is, faith alone, the gift of God's grace, is sufficient for salvation. Good works are not necessary.

- The Old and New Testaments are the central sacred writings of Christianity.

- Muslims believe that Abraham, Jesus, and Muhammad are great prophets and that Muhammad, the historical founder of Islam, is the greatest and last prophet, the "Seal of the Prophets," who completes the revelations of God, or Allah, to humankind.

- Islam is divided into two branches: (1) Sunni and (2) Shi'a.

- According to the Qur'an, there are Five Pillars, or duties, that Muslims must perform: (1) repeat the shahadah, or confession of faith; (2) perform ritual prayer; (3) fast during the month of Ramadan from sunrise to sunset; (4) give alms; and (5) make a pilgrimage, called the Hajj, to Mecca at least once during one's life.

- The sacred writings of Islam are the Qur'an and the Hadith.

- A number of religious movements have arisen over the centuries to reform existing religions. Among the earliest were the prophetic movement of the Judaism and later ones include Jainism, fundamentalism across a number of religions, evangelical Christianity, the Mormons, ecumenism, and liberation theology.

Environment and Humanity

The following chart outlines the sections and subsections in the Environment and Humanity test and offers a comparison between the percent of practice questions in this chapter and the actual DSST exam.

CONTENT OUTLINE: SECTIONS AND SUBSECTIONS	PERCENT OF EXAM DEVOTED TO EACH CONTENT AREA	NUMBER OF ITEMS IN THE DIAGNOSTIC TEST AND POST-TEST BY CONTENT AREA	PERCENT OF ITEMS IN THE DIAGNOSTIC TEST AND POST-TEST BY CONTENT AREA
I. Ecological Concepts	**30%**	**27**	**33.75%**
A. Ecosystems/Terrestrial & Aquatic		4	14.9%
B. Global Ecology		1	3.7%
C. Atmospheric Structure		1	3.7%
D. Roles of Organisms		2	7.4%
E. Biodiversity & Stability		1	3.7%
F. Energy Flow		1	3.7%
G. Trophic Levels		2	7.4%
H. Food Chains & Webs		1	3.7%
I. Biogeochemical Cycling		2	7.4%
J. Biomes & Productivity		3	11.1%
K. Population Biology		3	11.1%
L. Evolution		3	11.1%
M. Succession		3	11.1%
II. Environmental Impacts	**30%**	**21**	**26.25%**
A. Human Population Growth		2	9.6%
B. Global Climate & Weather		1	4.7%
C. Greenhouse Effect		2	9.6%
D. Ozone Layer		1	4.7%
E. Pollution		8	38.3%
F. Environmental Risk Assessment		1	4.7%
G. Industrial & Agricultural Revolution		2	9.6%
H. Industrial Development in Emerging Nations		1	4.7%
I. Deforestation		1	4.7%
J. Desertification		1	4.7%
K. Eutrophication		1	4.7%
III. Environmental Management & Conservation	**30%**	**24**	**30%**
A. Renewable & Nonrenewable Resources		7	29.1%
B. The Green Revolution		1	4.2%

C. Agricultural Practices		4	16.6%
D. Pesticides & Pest Control		1	4.2%
E. Soil Conservation and Land Use		2	8.3%
F. Air Pollution Control		1	4.2%
G. Drinking Water Quality & Supply		1	4.2%
H. Wastewater Treatment		1	4.2%
I. Solid & Hazardous Waste		2	8.3%
J. Recycling/Resource Recovery		3	12.5%
K. Industrial Ecology		1	4.2%
IV. Political Processes & the Future	**10%**	**8**	**10%**
A. Environmental Laws, Policies, and Ethics		5	62.5%
B. Planning & Decision Making		0	0%
C. International Policy		1	12.5%
D. Differing Cultural/Societal Values		1	12.5%
E. Future Issues		1	12.5%
Grand Total	**100%**	**80**	**100%**

OVERVIEW

- **Diagnostic test**
- **Answer key and explanations**
- **Ecological concepts**
- **Environmental impacts**
- **Environmental management and conservation**
- **Political processes and the future**
- **Post-test**
- **Answer key and explanations**
- **Summing it up**

DIAGNOSTIC TEST

Directions: Carefully read each of the following 20 questions. Choose the best answer to each question and circle your answer choice. The Answer Key and Explanations can be found following this Diagnostic Test.

1. In a temperate deciduous forest, maple trees, birds, and squirrels all live in the same given area. All three species together make up a/an
   - **(A)** ecosystem.
   - **(B)** community.
   - **(C)** population.
   - **(D)** niche.

2. Which process is a method used only in making ocean water suitable for drinking?
   - **(A)** Disinfecting
   - **(B)** Desalination
   - **(C)** Filtering
   - **(D)** Cleansing

3. Which of the following is the best definition of a population?
   - **(A)** A group of interacting organisms
   - **(B)** Organisms that produce offspring
   - **(C)** A group of the same species living in the same location
   - **(D)** A group of organisms in an ecosystem

4. Pollution can be reduced by using renewable energy sources such as
   - **(A)** gas and electricity.
   - **(B)** power and energy.
   - **(C)** coal and oil.
   - **(D)** solar energy and wind power.

5. Which of the following terms describes how water is taken up into the atmosphere from a lake?
   - **(A)** Transpiration
   - **(B)** Evaporation
   - **(C)** Condensation
   - **(D)** Precipitation

6. What is it called when two individuals of the same species have different physical characteristics, and one is able to live long enough to reproduce and the other is not?
   - **(A)** Macroevolution
   - **(B)** Adaptation
   - **(C)** Natural selection
   - **(D)** Coevolution

7. Which of the following occupies the first trophic level?

(A) Consumers

(B) Carnivores

(C) Herbivores

(D) Producers

8. Industrial waste containing dioxins would be considered

(A) medical waste.

(B) hazardous waste.

(C) recyclable waste.

(D) solid waste.

9. The excessive growth of algae in a freshwater ecosystem is called

(A) water pollution.

(B) algalfication.

(C) eutrophication.

(D) deforestation.

10. Which of the following is an example of a species found in a pioneer community?

(A) Lichen

(B) Wildflowers

(C) Fungi

(D) Bacteria

11. The development of agriculture began with the concept of

(A) gathering.

(B) increasing food volume.

(C) manipulating plants and soil.

(D) clearing large plots of land.

12. In 1898, a Swedish scientist predicted that carbon dioxide emissions from excessive burning of fossil fuels could lead to

(A) the greenhouse effect.

(B) the industrial revolution.

(C) air pollution.

(D) global warming.

13. Which type of mining is used if the over-burden material is deep?

(A) Subsurface mining

(B) Strip mining

(C) Hydraulic mining

(D) Coal mining

14. Which process removes large particles from wastewater?

(A) Primary sewage treatment

(B) Secondary sewage treatment

(C) Tertiary sewage treatment

(D) Quaternary sewage treatment

15. The first phase of population growth is often called the

(A) exponential phase.

(B) equilibrium phase.

(C) deceleration phase.

(D) lag phase.

16. Which of the following alternative energy sources does NOT raise environmental issues?

(A) Hydroelectric power

(B) Solar power

(C) Wind power

(D) Geothermal power

17. In the hope of creating a better environmental future, the efficiency revolution aims to

(A) reduce air pollution.

(B) protect all species.

(C) minimize waste of matter and energy.

(D) help people learn to live with less.

18. Which of the following is a type of volatile organic compound?

(A) Lead

(B) Sulfur dioxide

(C) Hydrocarbons

(D) Particulate matter

19. The concept of basing industrial production methods on biological models is called
    (A) Industrial Revolution.
    (B) industrial ecology.
    (C) biological revolution.
    (D) ecological diversity.

20. In 1970, Congress established
    (A) Earth Day.
    (B) the World Health Organization.
    (C) the Environmental Protection Agency.
    (D) Agenda 21.

ANSWER KEY AND EXPLANATIONS

1. B	5. B	9. C	13. A	17. C
2. B	6. C	10. A	14. A	18. C
3. C	7. D	11. C	15. D	19. B
4. D	8. B	12. D	16. B	20. C

1. **The correct answer is (B).** All the different populations living in a certain place make up a community. Choice (A) is incorrect because an ecosystem includes all living and nonliving things in an environment. Choice (C) is incorrect because each of the three species is a separate population. Different species cannot be part of the same population. Choice (D) is incorrect because the role of each organism in a community is its niche.

2. **The correct answer is (B).** The process of desalination is necessary to remove the salts from ocean water so that it can be used as a source of drinking water. Choice (A) is incorrect because all water sources are disinfected with chlorine, UV light, or ozone. Choice (C) is incorrect because filtering is a process that is performed on all drinking water supplies. Choice (D) is incorrect because all water is cleansed before it is safe for drinking.

3. **The correct answer is (C).** A population is defined as a group of the same species living in the same geographical location at the same time. Choice (A) is incorrect because a group of interacting organisms of different types is referred to as a community. Choice (B) is incorrect because a group of organisms that reproduces is a species. Choice (D) is incorrect because a group of organisms in an ecosystem is a community.

4. **The correct answer is (D).** Both solar and water are renewable natural resources. Choice (A) is incorrect because gas is a product of oil, a nonrenewable resource, and electricity can be generated from both renewable and nonrenewable resources. Choice (B) is incorrect because power and energy are not sources of energy. Choice (C) is incorrect because oil and coal are both fossil fuels and are nonrenewable resources.

5. **The correct answer is (B).** Evaporation occurs in bodies of water as water on the surface is changed into water vapor, a gas, and released into the atmosphere. Choice (A) is incorrect because transpiration is the process by which plants lose water through the stomata in their leaves. This results in the release of water into the atmosphere, but through plants, not a body of water. Choice (C) is incorrect because condensation is the change from of a gas to a liquid, and it involves water already in the atmosphere. Choice (D) is incorrect because precipitation comes from water already in the atmosphere that falls to the earth.

6. **The correct answer is (C)**. Natural selection, also referred to as survival of the fittest, occurs when one member of a species is able to survive and reproduce and another dies before reproducing. Choice (A) is incorrect because macroevolution refers to large-scale evolutionary changes over a long period of time. Choice (B) is incorrect because adaptations are changes in an organism or species that don't affect their ability to survive and reproduce. Choice (D) is incorrect because coevolution is when two or more species interact and exert selective pressure on one another, which can lead to adaptations and evolutionary changes in both species.

7. **The correct answer is (D)**. Producers occupy the first trophic level and obtain energy from the sun. This energy is converted and some of it is passed on to other species at higher trophic levels. Choice (A) is incorrect because consumers occupy the second trophic level and above. Choice (B) is incorrect because carnivores occupy either the third or fourth tropic level. Choice (C) is incorrect because herbivores occupy the second tropic level.

8. **The correct answer is (B).** Dioxins are toxic chemicals, and industrial waste containing dioxins is considered to be hazardous waste. Choice (A) is incorrect because dioxins are environmental pollutants and are not considered medical waste or biohazardous material. Choice (C) is incorrect because dioxins are not a recyclable material. Choice (D) is incorrect because dioxins are an organic chemical compound and are considered hazardous waste, not solid waste.

9. **The correct answer is (C)**. The excessive growth of algae and aquatic plants due to added nutrients in the water is called eutrophication. Choice (A) is incorrect because although nutrients can cause water pollution, the excessive growth of algae caused by added nutrients is more specifically called eutrophication. Choice (B) is incorrect because algalfication is not a term used by environmental scientists. The proper term for excessive algae growth is eutrophication. Choice (D) is incorrect because deforestation refers to activities that destroy forest environments, and does not refer to algae growth.

10. **The correct answer is (A).** Lichens are a type of pioneer organism that establish themselves on rocks and contribute to the formation of a thin layer of soil, so other organisms can grow. Choice (B) is incorrect because wildflowers need soil to establish and grow. Choice (C) is incorrect because fungi need to grow on organic material. Choice (D) is incorrect because bacteria are introduced at later stages of succession.

11. **The correct answer is (C).** The origin of agricultural practices began with the concept of manipulating plants and soil to grow desired crops. Choice (A) is incorrect because hunting and gathering of food came before the advent of agricultural practices. Choice (B) is incorrect because increasing food volume was a result of the agricultural revolution, not the beginning of it. Choice (D) is incorrect because clearing large plots of land and manipulating plants and soil were concepts that came after the advent of agriculture.

12. **The correct answer is (D).** During the rise of the Industrial Revolution, Svante August Arrhenius warned that an increase in carbon dioxide could lead to an increase in Earth's temperatures, an effect that we refer to as global warming. Choices (A), (B), and (C) are incorrect because these aren't what Arrhenius warned against.

13. **The correct answer is (A).** Subsurface, or underground, mining is the process of obtaining coal far beneath Earth's surface. A thick overburden means that the coal is buried deep underground. Choice (B) is incorrect because strip mining, or surface mining, involves removing the material on top of the vein of coal to get to the coal. Choice (C) is incorrect because hydraulic mining involves spraying hillsides with high-pressure water jets to dislodge coal

or desired minerals. Choice (D) is incorrect because subsurface mining is a type of coal mining, but there are many different methods of coal mining.

14. **The correct answer is (A).** The removal of large particles from sewage (wastewater) by a process of filtering the water through screens takes place during primary sewage treatment. Choice (B) is incorrect because secondary sewage treatment involves the dissolving away of organic materials with microorganisms. Choice (C) is incorrect because tertiary sewage treatment involves the removal of inorganic nutrients such as nitrogen and phosphorus. Choice (D) is incorrect because there are only three sewage treatment steps, not four.

15. **The correct answer is (D).** The first part of a population growth curve is often referred to as the lag phase because populations grow very slowly at first; the process of reproduction takes some time to get started. Choice (A) is incorrect because the exponential growth phase is the time of a high growth rate of a population. This usually follows the initial lag phase. Choice (B) is incorrect because the equilibrium phase occurs when a population is relatively stable, after the exponential growth phase. Choice (C) is incorrect because the deceleration phase is when the birth and death rates become equal and the population stops growing.

16. **The correct answer is (B).** Solar energy is energy harnessed from the sun and raises no concerns for the environment. Choice (A) is incorrect because the construction of dams and reservoirs necessary to obtain hydroelectric power causes environmental problems in regions downstream of the dam or reservoir. Choice (C) is incorrect because wind generators can harm birds and create annoying noises. Choice (D) is incorrect because geothermal power creates air pollution because of the hydrogen sulfide that is released into the atmosphere.

17. **The correct answer is (C).** As part of the sustainability revolution that aims to promote a more positive environmental future, the efficiency revolution seeks to minimize the wasting of matter and energy resources. Choice (A) is incorrect because the reduction of air pollution is an aim of the pollution prevention revolution. Choice (B) is incorrect because the biodiversity protection revolution is devoted to protecting all life. Choice (D) is incorrect because the sustainability revolution aims to help more affluent countries learn to live more sustainably with less.

18. **The correct answer is (C).** Volatile organic compounds are mostly composed of hydrogen and carbon atoms, and they are, therefore, called hydrocarbons. Choice (A) is incorrect because lead is not an organic compound. Choice (B) is incorrect because sulfur dioxide is not considered a hydrocarbon. Choice (D) is incorrect because particulate matter is a solid form of air pollution, not a volatile gaseous form.

19. **The correct answer is (B).** During the mid-1990s, a concept called industrial ecology emerged. Industrial ecology models methods of industrial production on biological production. Choice (A) is incorrect because the Industrial Revolution marks the advent of the use of coal as a fuel source to power machinery used in the production of goods. Choice (C) is incorrect because there is no such thing as the biological revolution. Choice (D) is incorrect because ecological diversity concerns living organisms and ecosystems, not industrial production.

20. **The correct answer is (C).** The Environmental Protection Agency (EPA) was established by the U.S. Congress in 1970. Choice (A) is incorrect because although the first Earth Day was held in 1970, it is not a government-sponsored organization. Choice (B) is incorrect because the World Health Organization (WHO) is an international organization that was established by the United Nations. Choice (D) is incorrect because Agenda 21 is a statement of principles for the management of global environmental issues.

answers diagnostic test

ECOLOGICAL CONCEPTS

Ecology is the study of how organisms interact with one another and their nonliving surroundings. Ecologists study the ways in which organisms have adapted to their surroundings, how they make use of their surroundings, and how an area is altered by the presence and activities of organisms.

Ecosystems

Even though ecosystems are a complex network of interrelationships between organisms, all ecosystems have two main components:

1. *Abiotic factors* are "non-living" factors such as physical or chemical conditions within an environment. For example, in a salt marsh ecosystem, the abiotic factors would include climate, weather, water temperature, salinity, pH, soil composition, and oxygen content of the water and mud.

2. *Biotic factors* are "living" factors, including all the living organisms within an ecosystem. In a salt marsh ecosystem, the biotic factors would include marsh grass, shrubs, and all plant life; fish, worms, insects, shellfish, crabs, and birds; and microorganisms such as bacteria and plankton.

Biotic factors can be organized into a hierarchy from the lowest level to the highest level:

1. *Organisms:* Individual life forms. For example, in a salt marsh, some organisms are marsh grass, flounder, and fiddler crabs.

2. *Species:* A population of organisms potentially capable of reproducing naturally among themselves to produce offspring that can also reproduce. All members of a species share similar behaviors, genetic structure, and appearance. For example, fiddler crabs are one species that inhabit salt marshes.

3. *Population:* A group of the same species living in the same geographic region at the same time. For example, the fiddler crabs living in a salt marsh in Maryland would be a separate population from fiddler crabs living in a salt marsh in Delaware.

4. *Community:* All of the interacting populations of different species that live in a given area at the same time. In a salt marsh ecosystem, fiddler crabs, fish, birds, and plants all form a community.

Noting the above information, it is easy to see that an ecosystem is a community of different species that interact with one another and with surrounding abiotic factors. The interaction of both biotic and abiotic factors allows an ecosystem to respond to changes in the environment.

Global Ecology

Global ecology is a field of ecology that deals with the relationship of organisms with one another and their environment on a global rather than local scale. Ecologists look at interactions among Earth's ecosystems, land, atmosphere, and oceans in an attempt to understand Earth's systems and predict future changes. All aspects of ecosystems are examined to fully understand global environmental issues. The global environment is very complex, with countless organisms and diverse processes interacting from the microscopic scale to the continental scale. New instruments, models, and theories are continuously developed to address fundamental questions about the way the systems work together.

Role of Organisms

Each species in an ecosystem has a specific role, or job, within the community. Examining the roles of species can help determine how they might interact. The functional role of each species in an ecosystem is its niche. A niche consists of all the physical, chemical, and biological conditions that a particular species requires in order to survive and reproduce within a given ecosystem. A description of an organism's niche always includes all the ways in which it affects other organisms and how it may modify its physical surroundings.

Ecologists have identified three general types of organism-to-organism interactions that take place in all ecosystems:

1. *Predation:* One organism known as the predator kills and eats another organism known as the prey. The predator benefits from this relationship, and the prey is harmed. To succeed, predators have adapted several strategies, such a speed, stealth, or the ability to build a trap for their prey. At the same time, many prey species have adapted characteristics that help them to avoid predation. These characteristics include keen senses, the ability to camouflage, and the ability to remain motionless to avoid detection.

2. *Competition:* Within an ecosystem, many species compete for limited resources such as food, water, sunlight, and territory. Competition is classified as intraspecific if it occurs between members of the same species, and interspecific if it occurs between members of different species. Whichever organism is less harmed by the competition is the winner. One organism may win out over another by one of two ways:

   a. *Interference:* One organism limits the access of another species to a resource.
   b. *Exploitation:* Two or more organisms have equal access to a resource, but one uses it more quickly and efficiently than the other.

   The competitive exclusion principle states that no two species can occupy the same ecological niche in the same place at the same time. The more similar two species are, the fiercer their competition will become.

3. *Symbiosis:* A close, long-lasting physical relationship between two species. The two species are in close physical contact, and at least one of them derives some benefit from the relationship. There are three different categories of symbiotic relationships:

   a. *Parasitism:* A relationship in which one organism, the parasite, lives in or on another organism, the host. The parasite generally derives nourishment from the host, and the host is harmed, or even eventually killed, by the parasite.
   b. *Commensalism:* A relationship between organisms in which one organism benefits and the other is not affected.
   c. *Mutualism:* A relationship between organisms that is beneficial to both organisms. In many cases of mutualism, the species cannot live without each another.

Ecologists divide organisms into four broad categories:

1. *Producers:* Organisms that are able to use sources of energy to make complex, organic molecules from simple inorganic substances in their environment. In almost all ecosystems, energy supplied by the sun is used to carry out photosynthesis in plants, algae, or phytoplankton. All other organisms rely on producers as a food source, either directly or indirectly.

2. *Consumers:* Organisms that require organic matter as a food source. They consume organic matter to obtain energy and organic materials that will help to build and maintain their own bodies. Consumers can be further divided based on what they eat:

   a. *Primary Consumers:* These are organisms that eat producers and are also known as herbivores. Ecosystems generally have a large number of herbivores.

   b. *Secondary Consumers:* These are organisms that eat other consumers and are also known as carnivores. Some carnivores primarily eat herbivores, while others consume carnivores and herbivores.

   c. *Teritairy Consumers*: A carnivore that feeds only on secondary consumers.

3. *Omnivores:* These include both producers (plants) and consumers (animals) in their diet.

4. *Decomposers:* These are organisms that use nonliving organic matter as a source of energy and material to build their bodies. When an organism sheds, excretes waste products, or dies, it provides a source of food for decomposers.

Biodiversity and Stability

"Biodiversity" is a term used to describe the diversity (variations) of genes, species, and ecosystems within a region. "Genetic diversity" is a term used to describe the number of different kinds of genes that are present in a given population. A high genetic diversity means there is a large amount of variation in structure and function among a population, and a low genetic diversity indicates that the population is almost all uniform in its traits. Genetic diversity is dependent on chromosomal mutations, migration of individuals or a population, sexual reproduction, population size, and selective breeding.

Species diversity is a measure of the number of various species within a given area. Some localities have high species diversity (a large number of species) and others have low species diversity. Factors that affect species diversity are the size of the area, human activities, and evolutionary and geological history of an area.

Ecosystem diversity is a measure of the number of different kinds of ecosystems present in a given area. Even if areas appear to have general similarities (for example, all deserts have low rainfall), there are specific organisms that live in each ecosystem that create diversity.

Trophic Levels

All ecosystems are stable, self-regulating units, but they are continually changing. The organisms within an ecosystem are continually growing, reproducing, dying, and decaying. Ecosystems must have a continuous input of energy to remain stable. This energy is usually provided by the sun. Producers obtain energy from a source like the sun, and this energy is then passed through the producers to consumers and decomposers. Each step in the flow of energy through an ecosystem is known as a trophic level.

Producers occupy the first trophic level. Herbivores occupy the second trophic level. The third trophic level consists of carnivores that eat herbivores, and the fourth trophic level consists of carnivores that eat other carnivores.

Omnivores, parasites, and scavengers occupy a different trophic level depending on what they are eating at any given time. For example, if you eat a salad, you occupy the second trophic level, and if you eat a steak, you occupy the third trophic level. Decomposers process food from all trophic levels. The available energy decreases as the trophic level increases.

Food Chains and Food Webs

A food chain describes the relationship of organisms in an ecosystem in terms of who eats whom. Members of a food chain occupy different trophic levels, and energy passes from one organism to another as they are eaten. For example, the leaves on a tree growing beside a lake would take energy from the sun and provide a food source for insects. These insects are a food source for spiders living in the tree. If a spider falls from the tree into the pond, it can then be eaten by a frog. In turn, this frog may be eaten by a bass that is then caught by a fisherman. In the next step of this food chain, the fish is then consumed by humans.

The typical order in a five-step food chain is as follows: producer → primary consumer → secondary consumer → tertiary consumer → decomposers.

Because most consumers eat two or more types of organisms at different trophic levels, multiple food chains can overlap and intersect to form a food web. Complex food webs are more stable than simple food chains, but in this network of interactions, several organisms would be affected if one key organism is reduced in number.

Biogeochemical Cycling

As matter flows through an ecosystem, it gets recycled. Many chemicals that are important to sustain life and the growth of organisms cycle between organisms, the atmosphere, the oceans, and Earth's crust. These chemicals include carbon, nitrogen, oxygen, phosphorus, sulfur, and water. The cycles of these chemicals are called biogeochemical cycles. Biogeochemical cycles involve multiple ecosystems and have global effects.

- *Carbon Cycle:* Carbon is the main element in all living organisms. It is also found in the atmosphere as carbon dioxide and in the oceans and rocks as carbonates. The carbon cycle includes processes and pathways that capture inorganic carbon-based molecules and convert them into organic carbon-based molecules that can be used by organisms. The same carbon atoms are used over and over. Carbon dioxide is fixed into plants and microorganisms through photosynthesis. Carbon passes through the food chains and webs as consumers eat. Fixed carbon in food and waste is broken down through respiration. Carbon from decomposing matter gets released back into soil. Carbon dioxide from the atmosphere moves into oceans. Sediment contains carbonate and compresses over time to form sedimentary rocks. Geological forces such as earthquakes and volcanoes return carbon from rocks back into the atmosphere. Human activity such as burning fossil fuels and raising farm animals like pigs and cattle also releases large quantities of carbon dioxide into the atmosphere.

- *Nitrogen Cycle:* The major source of nitrogen is Earth's atmosphere. It is 78 percent nitrogen gas. Living organisms cannot utilize nitrogen gas, so it must first be converted to another chemical form, such a nitrates or nitrites. The chemical conversions in the nitrogen cycle are made by bacteria and other microorganisms. There are five important steps in the nitrogen cycle:

  1. Nitrogen gas must be made into a chemically usable form by the process known as nitrogen fixation. Nitrogen-fixing bacteria can convert nitrogen gas from the atmosphere into am-

monia, which contains nitrogen, in the soil. Nitrifying bacteria in the soil convert ammonia to nitrates and nitrates. This process is called nitrification.

2. Plants take up nitrates from the soil and incorporate them into amino acids. Animals eat the plants and incorporate the ingested nitrogen from plant amino acids into their own amino acids, proteins, nucleic acids, and other nitrogen-containing organic molecules. This process is called assimilation.

3. After animals and plants die, decomposers convert their nitrogen-containing organic molecules back into ammonia and return it to the soil. This process is called ammonification.

4. The ammonia can be used directly by many types of plants. Nitrifying bacteria in the soil are able to convert ammonia to nitrite and nitrate. Under conditions where oxygen is absent, denitrifying bacteria are able to convert nitrite to nitrogen gas. This process is called denitrification.

5. The nitrogen gas is eventually released back into the atmosphere, where it can then reenter the nitrogen cycle.

• *Phosphorus Cycle:* Phosphorus is another element that is common to living organisms. It is present in many important biological molecules, such as DNA and cell membranes. Phosphorus-containing ATP and ADP are important molecules for storing and utilizing energy in living organisms. Many enzymes require a phosphate group for activation or inactivation. Unlike carbon and nitrogen, phosphorus is not present in the atmosphere, so the phosphorus cycle is limited to soil and water. The major form of phosphorus is the mineral apatite, which is found in rocks and phosphate deposits. The weathering of phosphate rocks leaches phosphate into soil. Then plants take up phosphorus from the soil and incorporate it into their tissue. Animals eat the plants and take up the phosphate. When plants and animals die, decomposers release phosphate back into the soil. Animal excretion also contains phosphate that is released back into the soil.

• *Sulfur Cycle:* Sulfur is important for the production of proteins because the amino acids cysteine and cystine contain sulfur. Sulfur is mainly found in rocks and soil as sulfate minerals. There is also sulfur in the atmosphere in the form of hydrogen sulfide. Weathering exposes sulfates from rocks, which are deposited into soil and aquatic ecosystems. Plants and other photosynthetic organisms take up and assimilate the sulfates into their tissue. Then animals eat plants and assimilate sulfates into their tissue. Death and decomposition of plants and animals convert organic sulfates into inorganic sulfates. Animal excretions also add sulfates to water and soil. Inorganic sulfates are then recycled. During decomposition in both soil and water, sulfates are converted into hydrogen sulfide gas that can escape into the atmosphere, water, soil, and marine sediment. Hydrogen sulfide gas can also come from volcanoes and power plant emissions.

• *Oxygen Cycle:* Molecular oxygen is critical for all living things. It is a by-product of photosynthesis and a necessary reactant for cellular respiration. Biological and chemical processes help to recycle oxygen on Earth. The main supply of oxygen is our atmosphere. Oxygen cycles through the atmosphere, living organisms, and Earth's crust. Oxygen is removed from the atmosphere by chemically reacting with rocks and minerals exposed to weathering. Oxygen is also removed from the atmosphere through respiration of living organisms. Sunlight breaks down water into hydrogen and oxygen, and oxygen is released into the atmosphere. Photosynthesis also breaks down water into hydrogen and oxygen, releasing oxygen into the atmosphere.

- *Hydrologic Cycle:* Water cycles between the atmosphere and Earth's surface and underground, and it exists in three states: (1) solid, (2) liquid, and (3) gas. This cycle is primarily driven by the sun's energy. Water is stored in the atmosphere as water vapor (gas), on Earth's surface as a liquid (lakes, oceans, rivers, streams) or a solid (ice, glaciers), and in the ground as a liquid (groundwater) or a solid (ice in the form of permafrost). Energy from the sun is the source of power that drives the water cycle. Water can move between all these sites in six different ways. (1) Water moves from its liquid or solid state on Earth's surface to the atmosphere into its gaseous state through evaporation and sublimation. (2) Groundwater moves into the atmosphere through plants during the process of transpiration, a part of photosynthesis. (3) Thermal energy from the sun is absorbed by Earth's surface and snow and ice melt into liquid water. This water either flows into lakes, oceans, rivers, or streams or is absorbed as groundwater. (4) Energy released by water vapor in the atmosphere causes precipitation, and liquid water returns to Earth's surface. (5) Once on Earth's surface, water flows through porous surfaces and into liquid groundwater storage. (6) Liquid groundwater can also flow back to Earth's surface and into streams, lakes, rivers, and oceans.

Humans significantly impact the flow of all the biogeochemical cycles through (1) the burning of fossil fuels, (2) the conversions of natural ecosystems to agricultural land, (3) agricultural runoff, and (4) industrialization.

Natural Selection and Evolution

Natural selection is the process that determines which individuals within a species will survive and reproduce, thereby passing their genes on to the next generation. Changes observed over time in the physical appearance or behavior of a species are due to the process of evolution. Individuals in a species who are best adapted to a certain environment will survive best and reproduce more offspring, thus changing the characteristics of a given species over a long period of time. Therefore, natural selection is the mechanism that causes the evolution of a species.

There are several factors involved in the process of natural selection. Individuals within a species have genetic variation; some of the variations are useful, and some are not. Organisms reproduce at such a rate that many more offspring are produced than are needed to replace the parent generation, but most of the offspring die. The excess number of offspring results in a shortage of food supplies and other resources. However, because there is a genetic variation among individuals of a species, some have a greater chance of obtaining the necessary food and resources and, therefore, are more likely to survive and reproduce. Over time, each generation is subjected to the same process of natural selection, so that the percentage of individuals with favorable variations will increase, and the number of individuals with unfavorable variations will decrease.

Therefore, over time, there is a considerable change in the type of species present and their characteristics. Some changes can take place in a few generations, whereas others have taken thousands or millions of years. The process of natural selection plays a key role in evolution, and through the study of fossil records, it is obvious to see that some new species evolve, while others die out.

- *Speciation* is the development of a new species from a previously existing species. In general, speciation occurs as two subpopulations adapt to different conditions and eventually are unable to interbreed because they are so different.

- *Polyploidy* is a condition in plants in which there is an increase in the number of chromosomes in the cells, and this can also lead to the development of a new species that cannot interbreed with the original species.

- *Extinction* is the loss of an entire species and is a common feature in evolutionary history. In general, extinction comes about due to changes in a species' environment or from human intervention.

- *Coevolution* is the idea that two or more species of organisms can influence the evolutionary path of the other. This is a common pattern since all organisms within an ecosystem influence one another.

Succession

Ecosystems respond to environmental challenges through succession. Succession is a series of recognizable and predictable changes over time to maintain the stability of the community. Succession occurs because the activities of a given species cause changes to the environment that make it now suitable for other species. Succession proceeds until a stable climax community is reached. There are two general types of succession:

1. *Primary succession* in new life is colonized in an environment that has a complete lack of life form and minimal water. Primary succession can occur in areas where volcanic activity wipes out life forms in an ecosystem. Primary succession takes a very long time to establish.

2. *Secondary succession* occurs when a portion of an ecosystem is disturbed by an event such as a forest fire. In this case, the area is eventually restored through succession, and it is a much more rapid process than primary succession because soil and water are usually already present.

Regardless of whether succession is primary or secondary, the process occurs in basically the same manner. First, new land is exposed. This land is either devoid of life (primary succession) or disturbed in some way (secondary succession). Next, pioneer species take root. Pioneer species are generally fast-growing plants that can thrive in exposed conditions and have a short-life span. These are usually lichen or mosses, and they begin to modify the ecosystem for the growth of other species. The collection of organisms at this stage is known as the pioneer community. Eventually, as a thin layer of soil is established, longer-lived plants are established.

Each step in the sequence from the pioneer community to the climax community is a successional or seral stage. The entire sequence of stages is known as a sere. At each seral stage, species either replace or coexist with previously existing species, and the ecosystem continues to be further modified at each stage, until the climax community is attained.

In a climax community, long-living plants and animals are sustained by the environment. The difference between a climax community and a successional (seral) community is that climax communities maintain their diversity of species for a long time, and successional communities are temporary. The organisms in a climax community maintain specialized niches, recycle nutrients, and maintain a relatively constant biomass, whereas successional communities do not. The general trend in succession is toward increasing complexity and efficiency.

With respect to aquatic ecosystems, with the exception of the oceans, most aquatic ecosystems are temporary. All aquatic systems receive a continuous input of soil and organic matter, and eventually bodies of water are filled in. This may take thousands of years, but it is a continual process. The successional stages of aquatic ecosystems are often called "wet meadow" stages and mark the transition of an aquatic community to a terrestrial community.

Biomes and Productivity

Biomes are terrestrial climax communities that have a wide geographic distribution. In general, the structure of ecosystems in a biome and the kinds of niches and habitats in those ecosystems are similar. However, it is important to recognize that although the concept of a biome is useful for discussing overall patterns and processes, different communities within a given type of biome show differences in the exact species present.

There are two major nonbiological factors that have an impact on the kind of climax community that develops in a given part of the world: precipitation pattern and temperature range. The aspects of precipitation that are most important are (1) the total amount of precipitation per year, (2) the form of precipitation (rain, snow, sleet), and (3) its seasonal distribution.

Temperature patterns vary greatly throughout regions of the world. Some regions, like tropical areas near the equator or areas near the poles, have a relatively consistent temperature throughout the year, whereas other areas are more evenly divided between cold and warm temperatures. Each type of biome is dependent in large part on precipitation and temperature.

Desert

Deserts are one type of biome in which there are generally less than 25 centimeters of precipitation per year. The form of precipitation varies for each desert. Although deserts are typically thought to be hot and dry (Sahara and the desert of the Southwest United States), there are some desert biomes in which temperatures are quite cool for a major part of the year (Gobi Desert and the deserts of the northwestern United States).

Many species populate a desert biome, but there are usually a low number of individuals of each species. In the past, humans had little impact on desert biomes in part because the hot arid conditions did not allow for agriculture. Hunter-gatherer societies were most common in deserts. However, modern technology allows for water to be transported into deserts, cities have developed in some desert biomes, and there is also limited agriculture.

Grassland

Temperate grassland biomes such as prairies or steppes are widely distributed in temperate regions of Earth. Grasslands generally receive 25–75 centimeters of rain annually. In general, grassland biomes are windy with hot summers and cold winters. In many grassland biomes, fire is an important factor in releasing nutrients from dead plants into the soil and for preventing the invasion of trees.

Between 60 and 90 percent of the vegetation is grass. Primary consumers eat the grasses, and there are often large herds of migratory animals such as bison living in grasslands. Carnivores also inhabit grasslands. Most of the moist grasslands throughout the world have been converted to agriculture. Drier grasslands have been converted to grazing for domestic grazers such as cattle, sheep, and goats. There is very little undisturbed grassland left.

Savanna

Savannas are found in tropical parts of Africa, South America, and Australia. They are characterized by extensive grasslands and occasional patches of trees. These biomes typically have a rainy season in which 50 to 150 centimeters of rain fall, followed by a drought period. Plants and animals time their reproductive activities to coincide with the rainy season, when food and water are more abundant.

Savannas have been heavily impacted by agriculture. Farming is possible in moister regions, and animal grazing is found in drier regions. Irrigation is essential because of the long periods of drought.

Mediterranean Shrublands (Chaparral)

Mediterranean shrublands are located near oceans and are dominated by low shrubs. The climate varies from wet, cool winters to hot, dry summers. Rainfall is 40 to 100 centimeters per year. Vegetation is dominated by woody shrubs, and the types of animals vary widely. Very little shrubland exists that has not been impacted by humans. There are many major cities in this type of biome and also a large amount of agriculture.

Tropical Dry Forest

Tropical dry forests are heavily influenced by seasonal rainfall. This type of biome is found in parts of Central and South America, Australia, Africa, and Asia. Many tropical dry forests have monsoon seasons, and rainfall ranges from 50 to 200 centimeters. There are generally high human populations in tropical dry forests, and wood is harvested from them for fuel and building materials.

Tropical Rain Forest

Tropical rain forests are located near the equator in Central and South America, Africa, Southeast Asia, and some islands in the Caribbean Sea and Pacific Ocean. The temperature is warm and relatively constant, and it rains nearly every day, 200 to 500 centimeters a year. There is extensive vegetation, but soils are generally poor because all of the nutrients are taken up by plants. Tropical rain forests have a greater diversity of species than any other biome. Today, tropical rainforests are under intense pressure from logging and agricultural industries, although agriculture is generally not successful in the long term because of generally poor soil conditions.

Temperate Deciduous Forest

Temperate deciduous forests have changes of seasons, and trees lose their leaves in fall and regrow leaves in spring. This forest is typical in the eastern half of the United States, parts of south central and southeastern Canada, southern Africa, and many areas of Europe and Asia. Winters are generally mild, and plants actively grow for about six months. There are generally 75 to 100 centimeters of precipitation per year distributed evenly. Each region of the world has certain species of trees and other organisms. Most of the temperate deciduous forests have been heavily impacted by human activity. Much has been cleared for agriculture and logging and to develop major population areas.

Taiga, Northern Coniferous Forest, or Boreal Forest

The evergreen coniferous forests found throughout southern Canada, parts of northern Europe, and Russia are known as taiga, northern coniferous forests, or Boreal forests. These biomes have short, cool summers and long, harsh winters, lasting up to six months. There are about 25 to 100 centimeters of precipitation per year, and there is a great deal of snowmelt in spring contributing to humid climates. These regions have many lakes, ponds, and bogs, and conifers are the most common organisms in these biomes. Humans have a less severe impact on these biomes because of low population density. Logging and herding of reindeer are common activities.

Tundra

Tundra is the area north of taiga biomes. It is an extremely cold region with permanently frozen subsoil (permafrost), which means there are no trees. Tundra biomes experience ten months of winter. Less than 25 centimeters of precipitation fall each year, but summer months see generally wet soil conditions due to snow melt. Water is not absorbed into the soil because of the permafrost subsoil layer. Therefore, many shallow ponds and waterlogged areas exist in summer.

Also in summer months, there is a variety of small plants and swarms of insects that are a food source for migratory birds and waterfowl. Tundra is also home to a few hardy mammals such as reindeer and arctic hare. Many species of birds and large mammals migrate during summer months using the scattered patches of small communities known as alpine tundra. Very few people live in tundra biomes, but any damage to this ecosystem is slow to heal because of the very short growing season. Tundra land must be handled with care.

Aquatic Ecosystems

Aquatic ecosystems are shaped by (1) the ability of the sun's energy to penetrate the water, (2) the depth of the water, (3) the nature of the bottom of the body of water, (4) the water temperature, and (5) the amount of salts dissolved in the water. Freshwater ecosystems have little dissolved salt, and marine ecosystems have a high salt content.

Oceans are defined as pelagic marine ecosystems and have many organisms that float or actively swim. Plankton are very small, weak organisms that are carried by currents. Phytoplankton are plankton-like organisms that carry out photosynthesis. Most phytoplankton, such as algae, live in the upper layers of the ocean where the sun's rays penetrate. This region is the euphotic zone. Zooplankton are small, weak swimming animals that feed on phytoplankton. These species swim to the euphotic zone to feed, then are eaten by larger animals such as fish and shrimp at lower depths, which, in turn, are then eaten by larger animals.

- *Bethnic Marine Ecosystems:* Organisms that live on the bottom of oceans are part of bethnic marine ecosystems. The substrate material on the ocean bottom is important in determining which species live in a particular bethnic ecosystem. Temperature also has an impact on bethnic ecosystems. An abyssal ecosystem is a bethnic ecosystem that is situated in great depths of the ocean. No light reaches these ecosystems, so animals must depend on the fall of organic matter from the euphotic zones.

- *Coral Reef Ecosystems:* These are produced by coral animals that build up around themselves cup-shaped external skeletons. The skeletons of corals provide a surface upon which many other species live. Coral reef systems require warm water and are, therefore, found only near the equator.

- *Mangrove Swamp Ecosystems:* These are tropical forest ecosystems found in shallow waters near the shore of marine ecosystems and an adjacent landmass. These ecosystems are dominated by trees that can tolerate the high salt content of the water and excrete salt from their leaves. Seeds of these trees germinate on the tree itself, and then fall into the water and are buried in mud where they take root. These trees have extensive root systems that extend above water to take in oxygen. Mangroves are found in south Florida, the Caribbean, Southeast Asia, and Africa, as well as other parts of the world where there are tropical mudflats.

- *Estuary Ecosystems:* An estuary is an ecosystem consisting of shallow water and a partially enclosed area where fresh water runs into the ocean. The salt content of water in estuaries changes with the tide and the inflow and outflow of the rivers. Organisms in this type of ecosystem have adapted to these changing conditions. An estuary is a productive ecosystem because the shallow regions allow light to penetrate the water, and rich nutrients are dumped from rivers into the basin of an estuary.

- *Freshwater Ecosystems:* These have a much lower salt content than marine ecosystems and have a large range of water temperature. Freshwater ecosystems consist of either relatively stationary water, such as lakes, ponds, or reservoirs, or moving water, such as streams or rivers.

If a lake is deep enough, it has similar characteristics to an ocean ecosystem: There is a euphotic zone at the top, and there are many kinds of phytoplankton and zooplankton. Emergent plants grow near the shores and shallower regions of lakes. They are rooted to the bottom of the lakes and their leaves can float on the surface (water lily) or stick out above the water's surface (cattail). Submerged plants are rooted below the surface, but do not protrude above the surface (Elodea and Chara). The regions of a lake with rooted vegetation are called the littoral zone, and regions where vegetation is not rooted are called the limnetic zone.

The productivity of a lake is dependent upon water temperature and depth. (1) Oligotrophic lakes are deep, clear, cold and have a low nutrient content. There is low productivity in this type of lake. (2) On the other hand, eutrophic lakes are shallow, murky, warm, and nutrient-rich. Productivity is higher in these lakes.

The dissolved oxygen content of water is also important to ecosystems. It determines the kind of organisms that inhabit a lake. When organic molecules enter water, bacteria and fungi break them down. The amount of oxygen used by these decomposers to break down a specific amount of organic matter is known as the biochemical oxygen demand (BOD).

In streams and rivers, water is moving, so organisms like algae attach to rocks. The collection of algae and fungi in streams and rivers is called periphyton. Most streams are shallow, and light can penetrate to the bottom, but because the water is fast-moving, photosynthetic organisms do not accumulate enough essential nutrients for growth. Therefore, most streams are not very productive. Most of the nutrients come from organic matter that falls into streams. In rivers, the water is deeper, and there is less light penetration. Organisms must rely on nutrients flowing in from streams. Rivers tend to be larger than streams with warmer, slower-moving water. Therefore, there is less oxygen in rivers, and different species occupy rivers and streams.

Swamps and marshes delineate the transition from terrestrial ecosystems into freshwater ecosystems. Swamps are wetlands that contain trees that withstand the flooded conditions. Marshes are wetlands dominated by grasses and reeds.

Most freshwater ecosystems have been heavily impacted by human activity. Activity on land affects freshwater systems because there is runoff from land into lakes, rivers, and streams. Agricultural runoff, sewage, and trash affect freshwater ecosystems. Human impact on marine ecosystems comes in the form of overfishing, oil pollution from transportation, oil spills, and trash dumping.

Population Biology

Population biology is a branch of environmental science that is concerned with characterizing the make-up and growth of populations and their impact on the environment and its organisms. A population is a group of individuals of one species that inhabits a given area. Population dynamics focus on the growth and limitations of a population and how that population interacts with its environment with respect to its growth and stability. Population genetics addresses the frequency and distribution of specific genes in a population and how these frequencies might change over time. Population genetics is also concerned with mutation rates within a given population.

Different populations of the same species have different characteristics such as birthrate, mortality, sex ratio, age distribution, growth rate, migration rate, spatial distribution, and density. Demography describes the vital statistics of a given population.

- *Birthrate:* The number of individuals added to a population over a particular time period, through reproduction of the species. Asexual reproduction is the process in which an organism such as bacteria divides to form new individuals. Sexual reproduction is the most common type of reproduction. Most species produce many more offspring than are needed to replace the parent generation. The birthrate in humans is usually described as the number of offspring produced by 1,000 individuals in a given year.

- *Death Rate or Mortality Rate:* The number of deaths in a population over a given time period. For most species, mortality rates are high, but in humans, it is relatively low. One way to study mortality is with a survivorship curve, which shows the proportion of individuals likely to survive at each age. The death rate in humans is referred to as the number of people in 1,000 that die per year. For a population to grow, the birthrate must exceed the death rate in a given year.

- *Sex Ratio:* The relative number of males and females in a given population. The number of females has a bigger effect on the number of offspring produced in a population. However, the typical ratio approximates 1:1.

- *Age Distribution:* The number of individuals in each age range in a population. Age distribution has a large influence on population growth rates. Among humans, different societies see vastly different age distributions, but in general, a large reproductive population will cause future population growth.

- *Population Density:* The number of organisms within a species in a given area. Movement from a densely populated region is called dispersal. Dispersal relieves overcrowding in a given area. The migration of individuals is referred to as emigration. Some organisms may leave their population to become members of a different population. This is called migration, or immigration.

Biological ability to produce offspring is a species' biotic potential. Because most species have a high biotic potential, there is a natural tendency for populations to increase. In general, there is an exponential growth in populations for a given period. There is often a pattern of growth that includes (1) a lag phase in which the population grows more slowly, (2) an exponential growth phase, (3) a declaration phase in which population growth slows due to equal birth and death rates, which leads to (4) a stabile equilibrium phase in which there is a stable population size.

There are several main environmental factors that limit population size. Factors from outside a population are known as (1) extrinsic limiting factors. Factors regulated within a population are called (2) intrinsic limiting factors. As the population increases, (3) density-dependent limiting factors are important. (4) Density-independent limiting factors are influences that control population, but they are not dependent on limiting factors. Limiting factors can be divided into four main categories: (1) availability of raw materials, (2) availability of energy, (3) accumulation of waste products, and (4) interaction between organisms.

The carrying capacity is the maximum population that is able to be sustained in a given area. The carrying capacity is determined by a set of limiting factors. Environmental changes such as forest fires or floods can change the carrying capacity of an area.

A given species has a particular reproduction strategy.

- *K-strategists* are organisms that tend to reach a stable population as the carrying capacity is reached. These species tend to occupy a stable environment and tend to be large organisms that have a long lifespan, produce few offspring, and expend a lot of energy to care for their offspring. These populations tend to be limited by density-dependent limiting factors.

- *R-strategists* tend to be small organisms that have a short lifespan, produce many offspring, do not reach the carrying capacity, and live in unstable environments. These organisms produce many offspring, but do not expend energy to care for them. These species tend to be limited by density-independent limiting factors.

In northern regions of the world, many species follow a population cycle in which periods of large populations are followed by periods of small populations. In general, this occurs because of the nature of ecosystems in this part of the world. Ecosystems are relatively simple with few organisms affecting one another.

Atmospheric Structure

The atmosphere is composed of 78.1 percent nitrogen, 20.9 percent oxygen, and 1 percent of a mixture of other gases, including carbon dioxide, methane, and water vapor. The atmosphere is composed of four layers.

1. *Troposphere:* Extends from Earth's surface to about 10 kilometers above Earth. The actual depth of the troposphere depends on the position of Earth and the season. The temperature of the troposphere decreases by about 6 degrees Celsius for every kilometer above Earth's surface.

2. *Stratosphere:* Extends about 50 kilometers above the top of the troposphere. The stratosphere contains most of the ozone, which is a band between 15 and 30 kilometers above Earth's surface that absorbs sunlight. Since the ozone absorbs sunlight, the upper layers of the stratosphere are warmer than the lower layers.

3. *Mesosphere:* Extends above the stratosphere from 50 to 80 kilometers above Earth's surface with decreasing temperature

4. *Thermosphere:* Extends from 80 to 300 kilometers above Earth's surface and is a layer with increasing temperatures

Gravitational pull keeps air near Earth, but air is not static. As it absorbs heat, it expands and rises, and as air cools, it becomes denser and falls back towards Earth's surface. Therefore, air circulates vertically because of heating and cooling and circulates horizontally because of Earth's rotation. The combination of air movements creates wind and weather patterns.

ENVIRONMENTAL IMPACTS

In order for individuals to survive, they must expend energy. However, some energy sources used by humans in industrialized societies can cause damage to the environment. An ever-growing population must be aware of the impact of population growth and its choice of energy sources on our environment.

Human Population Growth

Human population has been steadily increasing since the modern era, mostly because of the longer life span of populations. Developed countries have an increase in food production and better methods of controlling disease. All of this can be shared with the rest of the world, resulting in an improved quality of life overall. The world population is currently increasing at a rate of 1.2 percent annually. At this rate, the world population is expected to double in about 58 years. Several factors must be taken into consideration to fully understand human population growth. Economic development plays a huge role in population growth. More developed countries have a relatively stable population growth, and less developed countries do not.

Several factors interact to determine the impact of a society's population growth on the resources of a country. These factors include (1) land, (2) natural resources, (3) size of a population, (4) quantity of natural resources consumed, and (5) environmental damage caused by using resources. The relationship of all these factors can be expressed in the equation:

Impact on the Environment = Population × Affluence × Damage Due to Technology ($I = P \times A \times T$)

Population density relates the size of a population to available resources. People in highly developed countries tend to have a greater impact on the environment because of technological development. The ecological footprint of a population is a measure of the land area required to provide resources and absorb waste.

Demography is the study of human populations, their characteristics, and the consequences of growth. Demographers can predict future population growth by looking at biological factors, including the total fertility rate and age distribution. A total fertility rate of 2.1 is a replacement fertility rate whereby parents will be replaced by offspring when they die. If the number of births equals the number of deaths, there is zero population growth.

Social factors that influence population growth are aspects like culture, traditions, and attitudes towards birth control. Political factors also influence human population growth. Developed countries often have low rates of population growth and try to promote more births, whereas countries like China have taken measures to control growth. Immigration also has an impact on the rate of growth in a population. A human population can increase only if populations of other animals and plants decrease. When humans need food, they convert ecosystems into agricultural systems. In some cases, the long-term health of the environment is sacrificed to feed a population.

Countries with the highest standard of living seem to have the lowest rate of population growth, and those with the lowest standard of living have the highest population growth rate. This leads to the demographic transition model that occurs in four stages. (1) Initially, countries have a stable population with a high birthrate and death rate. (2) Improved economic and social conditions cause a decrease in the death rate, so there is a period of rapid population growth. (3) As countries develop an industrial economy, birthrates drop and population growth rates fall. (4) Eventually, birthrates and death rates are balanced again, but this time there is a low birthrate and low death rate.

Pollution

Pollution is any matter or energy that harms the environment, and human actions are the major cause of air pollution. Air pollution is directly related to the population of a given area. There are several categories of air pollutants on Earth. (1) Primary air pollutants are released into the atmosphere in unmodified forms. These pollutants include carbon monoxide, volatile organic compounds (hydrocarbons), particulate matter, sulfur dioxide, and oxides of nitrogen. (2) Secondary air pollutants are primary pollutants that can interact with other compounds in the presence of sunlight to form new compounds such as ozone. (3) The U.S. Environmental Protection Agency (EPA) has a category of air pollutants called criteria air pollutants. These include nitrogen dioxide, ozone, sulfur dioxide, particulate matter, carbon monoxide, and lead.

Water pollution is the result of population growth and industrial growth. (1) A source of water pollution that is readily identifiable because it has a definite point where it enters the water is called a point source. (2) Diffuse pollutants such as those that come from agricultural runoff, urban roadways, and acid rain are nonpoint sources of water pollution. Types of water pollution include municipal, agricultural, industrial, thermal, marine oil, and groundwater pollution.

Ozone Layer

Ozone is a molecule that consists of three oxygen atoms bound to each other. Ground-level ozone is an extremely reactive molecule that can cause irritation to respiratory tissue and damage to lungs. Ozone is a secondary pollutant formed as a component of photochemical smog. However, there is also a necessary layer of ozone in the atmosphere that shields Earth from the harmful effects of ultraviolet (UV) radiation from the Sun. This ozone layer is slowly being depleted as a result of pollutants, especially chlorofluorocarbons (CFC), in the atmosphere. Less ozone in the upper atmosphere results in more UV light reaching Earth's surface. This can lead to increased risks of skin cancer, cataracts, and mutations.

Greenhouse Effect

Energy from the sun enters the atmosphere, but not all of that energy reaches Earth's surface. Clouds and gases high in the atmosphere reflect back about 25 percent of the sun's energy. Another 25 percent are absorbed by gases in the atmosphere, such as ozone, carbon dioxide, methane, and water vapor. Of the 50 percent of the energy that reach Earth's surface, some is reflected back into the atmosphere by rain, snow, ice, and sand. The rest is absorbed by Earth's surface.

As this energy is rereleased into the atmosphere, it is absorbed by gases in the atmosphere known as greenhouse gases. The greenhouse effect actually is necessary to keep the surface of Earth warm enough to sustain life; however, too much of a greenhouse effect due to the accumulation of large quantities of carbon dioxide, chlorofluorocarbons, methane, and nitrous oxide (greenhouse gases) can be harmful to the environment and can lead to global warming and climate change.

Environmental Risk Assessment

Risk to the environment from human activities can be determined through identifying potential hazards and the consequences of these hazards. The magnitude and probability of the consequences also need to be considered when assessing risk. Finally, there needs to be an evaluation of the risk, also known as risk characterization. A concept frequently used in environmental risk assessment is that of source-pathway-receptor. The pathway between a hazard (source) and a receptor (i.e., ecosystem) is investigated. If no pathway exists, then there is no risk to the environment. If a pathway links a source to a receptor, then the consequences need to be assessed.

Industrial and Agricultural Revolutions

The Industrial Revolution, beginning in the mid-1700s, was brought about by the use of coal as a major fuel source in England. It involved the invention of the steam engine and the development of machines to mass produce goods. The steam engine also made large-scale coal mining possible. During the Industrial Revolution and afterwards, energy consumption increased, economies grew, and populations became more prosperous. An increase in coal use also caused an increase in air pollution. Within the span of 200 years, energy consumption increased eightfold, and pollution became a serious problem in some countries.

Early civilizations obtained food by hunting and gathering. The development of agriculture involved manipulating plants and soil to grow desired foods. The increase in yield of food grown allowed for an increase in populations. With the advent of the Industrial Revolution, agriculture was also mechanized. To operate effectively, new machines required large tracts of relatively flat land planted with a single crop, a practice known as monoculture. Although these methods produce abundant crops of food, the clearing of large tracts of land also leads to soil erosion. Because of erosion problems, many farmers now use methods that reduce the time a field is left fallow.

Currently, the most rapid industrial development takes place in emerging nations. This development leads to a disproportionate amount of ecosystem degradation (deforestation, desertification, eutrophication), and loss of biodiversity in those countries. The damage to the environment in these nations can actually increase poverty instead of promoting wealth.

Deforestation

To clear land for agriculture, farmers clear large tracts of forestland, a process called deforestation. Deforestation is mainly used for agricultural purposes, but in some countries, forests are still cleared for wood to be used as a fuel source or for building materials. Removal of trees in tropical regions removes biomass, which contains most of the nutrients in the soil. The soil that is left is poor and not ideal for agriculture. In addition, deforestation leads to erosion of soil.

Deforestation causes carbon dioxide to stay in the atmosphere because there are fewer trees to take it in, which contributes to global warming. Evapotranspiration through the leaves of trees returns water to the atmosphere as part of the hydrologic cycle, but deforestation reduces this process and disrupts the hydrologic cycle. Deforestation also disrupts ecosystems and species that live in forests. (1) Patchwork clear cutting, (2) reforestation, and (3) selective harvesting are methods used to try to avoid deforestation.

Desertification

The conversion of dry arid or semiarid land into desert-like ecosystems is a process called desertification. Desertification is most prevalent in northern Africa and parts of Asia where there is irregular or unpredictable rainfall. In many of these areas, there are populations of nomadic herders or subsistence farmers that are under pressure to provide food for their families, even at a cost to the environment. Overgrazing and over-farming lead to desertification in these areas.

Eutrophication

The excessive growth of algae and other aquatic plants in water with added nutrients is a process called eutrophication. When phosphates or nitrates are added to the surface of a body of water from sources such as organic waste from agriculture or industries, they can act as a fertilizer and cause excessive growth of algae. This undesirable algae growth can interfere with the use of the water. Also, as the algae dies, there is a decrease in oxygen levels in the water, and fish and other aquatic life die.

ENVIRONMENTAL MANAGEMENT AND CONSERVATION

Environmental management and conservation involve a number of highly contentious political issues.

Nonrenewable Resources

Natural resources are those that humans can use for their own purposes, but that they cannot create. Soil, wind, and water are all examples of natural resources. A renewable resource can be formed or regenerated by natural processes, so that it is not used up. However, nonrenewable resources are not replaced by natural processes. Fossil fuels and mountain ranges are nonrenewable on a human time scale.

The energy sources most commonly used by industrialized nations are fossil fuels: oil, coal, and natural gas. They constitute 76 percent of the world's energy sources and are all nonrenewable resources. Nuclear energy accounts for another 6 percent of the energy used. Humans are using up nonrenewable energy sources at a much faster rate than they can be replaced, which eventually will exhaust Earth's supply of these sources.

The mining and processing of fossil fuels takes a toll on the environment as well. (1) Coal can be extracted by surface, or strip, mining, which involves removing the overburden material on top of a vein of coal to get to the coal below the surface. This method is efficient, but it disrupts the landscape. The damage can be minimized by reclaiming the land, but it is rarely restored to its original condition. (2) Underground mining extracts coal that is buried deep beneath Earth's surface. The method poses many safety concerns and health hazards for miners, but it doesn't disturb the above-ground landscape. However, underground mining still raises environmental issues such as subsidence, or sinking of the land, and the accumulation of large waste heaps.

Coal mining and coal transport generates a lot of dust in the atmosphere, and there is also sulfur associated with coal that causes acid mine drainage and air pollution. Burning of coal causes acid deposition in the atmosphere, which is a cause of acid rain. The release of carbon dioxide from coal has become a greater concern with respect to the potential for global warming.

Oil extraction causes less environmental damage, is a more efficient source of energy than coal, and creates less pollution. Liquid oil is more easily transported than solid coal; however, there are major problems associated with oil spills and leaks from oil pipelines. The processing of natural gas is the least disruptive to the environment.

Renewable Resources

Only 18 percent of the world's energy comes from renewable energy sources: 11 percent from biomass, 4.5 percent from hydroelectric power, and only 1.5 percent from a combination of geothermal, wind, and solar energy.

- *Biomass* is the primary source of energy for developing countries. All biomass is produced by green plants that convert sunlight into plant material through photosynthesis. Major types of biomass include wood, municipal and industrial wastes, agricultural crop residue, animal waste, and energy plantations. However, using biomass fuels can create air pollution.

- *Hydroelectric power* relies on water to generate electricity. The construction of reservoirs, however, can cause environmental and social issues. One possible impact is that dams can cause flooding of land around them. Damming a river can prevent the proper flow of water in a river downstream of the dam.

- *Tidal power* can also supply a renewable energy source, but this can result in negative impacts on shorelines.

- *Geothermal power* is linked to geologically active regions where thermal energy from Earth can reach the surface through thin layers of Earth's crust. Geothermal energy creates steam that contains hydrogen sulfide, which causes air pollution.

- *Wind power* is another source of energy, but it is dependent on the variability of winds. Places such as the Dakotas in the United States have the strongest winds, but because they are remote from large energy-using population centers, there would be a loss in electricity as it was transferred to distant areas of the country. The moving blades of wind generators can pose a hazard to birds, depending on where the turbines are located. They can also produce noise that bothers nearby residents.

- *Solar energy* is a renewable energy source that can be collected through means of passive solar or active solar systems.

The Green Revolution

The Green Revolution brought about the introduction of new varieties of plants and farming methods in the 1950s, '60s, and '70s. Both developed and developing countries benefitted from the Green Revolution, and it has caused a significant increase in food production. The Green Revolution came about as a cooperative venture between Western countries to increase productivity and relieve hunger in Mexico and India. High-yield varieties of wheat were developed that were more resistant to pests and diseases. These new crops along with irrigation techniques and chemicals (fertilizers, pesticides, and herbicides) increased food production; however, many farmers in Mexico and India still remained poor.

Over time, more high-yield crops such as rice, sorghum, corn, and beans were introduced. Intensive farming methods to relieve hunger in Latin America and Asia were created. The Green Revolution has not been successful in parts of the world where the climate is arid and irrigation is not possible, such as sub-Saharan Africa. The Green Revolution also made crops more dependent on chemicals, which caused environmental concerns. The crop yield has increased as a result of the Green Revolution, but it has not solved the problems of world hunger.

Agricultural Practices

The basic unit of agriculture is the farm, where farmers must clear land, plant seed, grow crops, and harvest them. Resources like land, water, soil, and seeds must be managed and conserved. There are several different types of agricultural methods practiced throughout the world.

- *Shifting agriculture* is practiced in many areas of the world where soil conditions are poor and human populations are low. It involves the cutting down and burning of trees in small area forests. Once the nutrients in the soil are depleted, the site is abandoned. In some parts of the world with poor soil conditions, such as tropical forests, this method is still used successfully.

- *Labor-intensive agriculture* is practiced in areas of the world with better soil conditions. It is still practiced in much of the world today, and it involves the extensive use of manual labor. This allows for high yields, but low use of fossil fuels. In developing countries, the cost of manual labor is low compared to the cost of mechanized farming equipment.

- *Mechanized agriculture* developed after the beginning of the Industrial Revolution. This type of farming requires large tracts of mostly level land so the machines can operate, and the same crop is planted in large areas to maximize efficiency. In this type of farming, machines and fossil fuels have replaced human labor.

Fertilizers are used to increase crop yields. They can be valuable because they replace nutrients in the soil that are removed by plants. Macronutrients are the three primary soil nutrients: (1) nitrogen, (2) phosphorus, and (3) potassium. Other micronutrients are also present in fertilizers (zinc, boron, manganese). Chemical fertilizers replace inorganic nutrients, but not organic materials in soil. The decomposition of organic matter returns organic nutrients to the soil.

Alternative agriculture methods include sustainable agriculture, which does not deplete soil, water wildlife, or human resources; organic agriculture, which prohibits the use of pesticides and fertilizers; and other alternative agriculture practices that include all nontraditional methods such as hydroponics.

Precision agriculture is a technique of farming that addresses the concerns of conventional agricultural practices, such as fertilizer runoff in water supplies, pesticides accumulating in food chains, and groundwater contaminated by fertilizers. Computer technology allows farmers to vary the amount of fertilizers applied to different places in a crop. Thus, farmers use less chemicals overall more effectively.

Pesticides and Pest Control

In addition to fertilizers, modern mechanized farming practices require other chemicals such as pesticides, insecticides, fungicides, denticides, and herbicides. These chemicals can cause damage to the environment and many species. The use of persistent pesticides, such as DDT, has been mostly banned because of the bioaccumulation and biomagnification effects on species. For example, higher and higher trophic levels feed on lower-level organisms, so the concentration of DDT accumulates and can be up to 2,000 times the original concentration in the highest-trophic-level species.

Another problem with pesticides is that pest populations such as insects, weeds, rodents, and fungi can become resistant to the chemicals. Over 500 species of insects have developed resistance to pesticides. Most pesticides are not specific to a particular organism and end up killing beneficial species as well as harmful ones.

There are also health concerns to humans who either apply pesticides or ingest foods with pesticide residues. For most people, the most critical health problems are related to exposure to small quantities over a long period of time. Many pesticides cause mutations, cancer, and abnormal offspring in experimental animals. Despite this, pesticide use in many countries continues to increase because more food can be produced with the use of pesticides, fewer crops are lost to pests, and less money is lost by farmers.

Soil Conservation and Land Use Practices

Erosion is the wearing away of soil by water, wind, or ice, which is a natural process that has been accelerated by agricultural methods. Soil erosion takes place everywhere in the world, but some areas are more exposed and have a higher degree of erosion than others. Erosion occurs mostly in regions where vegetation has been removed. Deforestation and desertification leave land open to erosion.

In order to maintain the proper soil and nutrients for crop growth, land converted to agricultural use must experience only minimal soil erosion. Therefore, many techniques are used to protect soil from eroding and to minimize the loss of topsoil. Some soil quality management components include (1) enhancement of organic matter, (2) avoidance of excess tillage, (3) efficient management of pests and soil nutrients, (4) prevention of soil compaction, (5) keeping the ground covered so soil is not exposed, and (6) diversifying cropping systems.

Several land use practices can also help to control soil erosion.

- *Contour farming,* or tilling at right angles to the slope of the land, is a simple method of preventing soil erosion and is useful on gentle slopes. Each ridge produced at right angles to the slope acts as a dam to prevent water from running down the slope. Therefore, more water soaks into the soil and less soil is washed away.

- *Strip farming* helps prevent erosion on longer or steeper slopes. Strips of closely sown crops are alternated with strips of row crops. The closely sown crops such as hay or wheat slow down the flow of water, reducing soil erosion.

- *Terracing* is a method of preventing soil erosion on steep land. Terraces are constructed at right angles to the slope.

- *Waterways* are depressions of land on sloped ground where water collects. Instead of allowing the land to remain bare, it should be properly maintained with a sod covering. Then, the speed of water flow is reduced and erosion is decreased.

- *Windbreaks* should be established to stop wind from eroding soil. Windbreaks are plantings of trees or other plants that protect soil from wind.

Methods of tilling the land, such as reduced tillage and conservation tillage, also help to reduce the amount of soil erosion. There are several variations of conservation tillage, including (1) mulch tillage, (2) strip tillage, (3) ridge tillage, and (4) no-farm tilling.

Air Pollution Control

Because humans produce air pollution, it can be controlled by changes in human activity. Motor vehicles are the primary cause of air pollution, including carbon monoxide, volatile organic compounds, and nitrogen oxides. Ozone is a secondary pollutant of motor vehicle use. Even though newer cars emit less nitrogen oxides, the mileage that people drive each year has increased, so NO_x emissions have stayed the same. Almost all other air pollutants have been reduced significantly.

Particulate matter emissions come from industrial activities, mining, farming, and the transfer of grain and coal. Improper land use is also a major source of airborne particulates, as is the burning of fossil fuels and wood. Devices are used by industries to trap particulate matter so it does not escape from smokestacks, but smaller particles that form sulfur dioxide and nitrogen oxides can still escape.

Power plant emissions of sulfur dioxide are also a cause of air pollution. Switching to the use of low-sulfur coal decreases emissions by about 66 percent. Switching to oil, natural gas, or nuclear fuels reduces emissions even more. It is also possible to reduce the sulfur in coal before it is used, but this process is costly and would drive up the cost of electricity.

The accumulation of acid-forming particles on a surface is known as acid deposition. Acid-forming particles are dissolved in rain, sleet, snow, and fog and can also be deposited as dry particles. All forms of precipitation that contain acid-forming particles are known as acid rain. Acid rain is a worldwide problem that stems from natural causes, such as vegetation, volcanoes, and lightening, and human activities, including burning of fossil fuels and the use of the internal combustion engine. The combination of sulfur dioxide or oxides of nitrogen with an oxidizing agent like ozone, hydroxide ions, or hydrogen peroxide, along with water, forms sulfuric and nitric acid in the atmosphere. Acid rain is suspected of causing the death of many forests, and it also causes damage to human-made structures, especially those made of limestone. Sulfuric acid converts limestone to gypsum, which then erodes away. There are also effects of acid rain on aquatic ecosystems, including a progressive loss of organisms as the acidity of the water increases.

Drinking Water Quality and Supply

Drinking water supplies in the United States come mainly from municipal sources. About 37 percent of municipal water comes from wells, and the rest is surface water contained in reservoirs. In rural area, residents obtain water from private wells.

To ensure water quality safety, water is treated by the following processes: (1) raw water is filtered through sand or other substrates to remove particulate matter; (2) chemicals are added to remove dissolved particles; (3) water is disinfected with chlorine, ozone, or UV light to remove organisms. When freshwater is scarce, saltwater can be treated through desalination processes and made suitable for drinking.

Wastewater Treatment

Wastewater consists of storm water runoff, waste from industry, and domestic wastewater. Domestic waste consists primarily of organic matter from food preparation; garbage; washing clothes, dishes, and cars; and human waste. All wastewater must be cleaned before it is released, and, therefore, most municipalities and industries have wastewater treatment facilities.

Sewage treatment is classified as (1) primary, (2) secondary, and (3) tertiary.

- *Primary sewage treatment* is a physical process that removes larger particles by filtering water through large screens and smaller particles by allowing them to settle out of the water as it sits in large tanks or lagoons. Water is removed from above the settled particles and is either released back into the environment or to another treatment stage.

- *Secondary sewage treatment* involves the holding of wastewater until all of the organic matter dissolved in the water is degraded by bacteria and other microorganisms. To promote the growth of microorganisms during this treatment stage, wastewater is mixed with highly oxygenated water, or it is aerated directly with a trickling filter system. Microorganisms eventually settle out of the water in the form of sewage sludge. Water and sludge are separated, and the water is disinfected, usually with chlorine, before it is released.

- *Tertiary treatment* involves techniques to remove inorganic nutrients such as phosphorus and nitrogen in the water that could potentially increase aquatic plant growth.

Solid and Hazardous Waste

Solid waste is made up of objects and particles that accumulate at the site where they are produced or where they are disposed. Solid wastes are produced by agriculture, mining, manufacturing, and municipalities. Nations with high standards of living generally produce more solid waste than less developed nations.

There are several ways that humans dispose of solid waste. Landfills have been the primary means of solid waste disposal. Municipal solid waste landfills are constructed above impermeable clay layers lined with impermeable membranes. Each layer of garbage is covered with fresh soil to keep it from blowing away and to discourage scavengers. Contaminated water is trapped by leachate bottom layers.

Burning refuse in incinerators is another disposal method. Most incinerators are designed to capture thermal energy to make steam that is then used to produce electricity. Organic solid waste can be mulched or composted, and then reused in enriching soils or landscaping. Most municipalities now have composting facilities.

Hazardous wastes are certain by-products of industrial, business, or domestic activities that cannot be disposed of by normal measures. Waste is defined as hazardous if it causes or contributes to an increase in mortality or serious illness, or if it poses a serious threat to human health or the environment. Hazardous waste ranges from waste containing dioxins and heavy metals to organic wastes. Hazardous waste can be liquid or in the form of batteries, computer parts, or CFL light bulbs.

Once a hazardous material has been identified, government agencies such as the Food and Drug Administration (FDA) and Occupational Safety and Health Administration (OSHA) determine acceptable exposure limits to the materials. Hazardous wastes can enter the environment, for example, by evaporating into the atmosphere or leaking through faulty pipes or improper disposal. Industries are now required to report the level of hazardous toxic water released into the atmosphere. Management of hazardous waste materials has become part of industrial processes, but the best way to deal with it is not to produce hazardous waste materials in the first place.

The two most common methods of disposing of hazardous waste are (1) incineration and (2) land disposal, with land disposal being the primary disposal method. Land disposal is carried out in four different ways: (1) deep-well injection, (2) discharge of treated and untreated liquids into sewers or waterways, (3) placement of liquid or sludge in surface pits or lagoons, and (4) storage of solid waste in specially designed landfills. In 1980, Congress developed the Superfund Act to identify hazardous waste sites and clean them up on a priority basis.

Recycling and Resource Recovery

In 2001, recycling efforts, including composting of organic materials, diverted about 30 percent of waste from landfills and incinerators. This was about a twofold increase in waste reduction as compared to 1990. Container laws set in 1972 have provided an economic incentive to recycle. These laws include a two- to five-cent deposit on all recyclable beverage containers. This law reduced beverage container litter by almost 50 percent. Mandatory recycling laws are in effect in many cities and states. Municipalities often provide recycling containers and curbside recycling to assist residents.

Although recycling programs have been successful at reducing waste, there are some economic and technical problems associated with recycling. For example, plastics are recyclable, but each type of plastic requires different recycling methods, and, therefore, all plastics cannot be recycled together. Also, recycling of materials has produced an overabundance of those materials, especially in developing nations. To help reduce waste, people can (1) buy materials that last, (2) have goods repaired instead of discarding them, (3) buy items that are reusable or recyclable, (4) buy beverages in reusable glass containers, (5) use plastic or metal lunchboxes instead of paper bags, (6) use rechargeable batteries, (7) reduce the use of disposable bags, (8) separate recyclables from trash, (9) recycle all recyclable materials, (10) choose items with minimal packaging, (11) compost organic materials, and (12) use electronic sources as opposed to paper sources.

Industrial Ecology

During the mid-1990s, a concept that links industrial production to environmental quality emerged. This concept, called industrial ecology, models methods of industrial production on biological production. It forces industries to manage and account for their waste. Industrial ecology forces industries to view pollution and waste in a new way and ensures that good environmental practices translate to good economics. Businesses have become more environmentally responsible.

POLITICAL PROCESSES AND THE FUTURE

Environmental policy consists of laws, rules, and regulations aimed at preventing or correcting an environmental problem. These policies are developed, implemented, and enforced by government agencies.

Environmental Laws, Policies, and Ethics

The publication of Rachel Carson's *Silent Spring* is considered the beginning of the modern environmental movement. In 1970, with the advent of Earth Day and mounting public concern for the environment, the United States began to address some of the most obvious and pressing environmental problems. Over the last 45 years, important environmental laws, like the Clean Air Acts, Clean Water Acts, Resource Conservation and Recovery Act, Energy Policy Act, Compensation and Liability Act (Superfund), wildlife conservation acts, and land use conservation acts, have helped to protect the environment, wildlife species, and human populations.

Until 1970, most federal agencies acted within their authority without considering the environment, but the National Environmental Policy Act (NEPA) was designed to institutionalize within the federal government a concern for the environment. As a result of NEPA, many states have instituted stronger state environmental policy acts (SEPA). Congress established the Environmental Protection Agency (EPA) in 1970. The EPA helps to shape environmental laws and controls the daily operations of industries and regulates the agencies authorized to protect the environment.

International Policy

Environmental concerns are a growing factor in international relations. Policies related to health, environmental, and natural resource concerns are beginning to enter the mainstream of political policies. There are many international institutions that address the global environment by gathering and evaluating environmental data, helping to develop international treaties, and providing funding and loans to developing countries. Perhaps the most influential organization that has helped shape environmental policy is the United Nations (UN). The UN has 21 agencies that deal with environmental issues. Organizations formed under the UN include the UN Environmental Programme (UNEP), the World Health Organization (WHO), the UN Development Programme (UNDP), and the Food and Agriculture Organization (FAO). However, some agencies fail to make significant progress because they are controlled by members with competing interests. Other institutions don't succeed because they are unable to address issues in their totality. For example, the World Bank can only address issues of air pollution and biodiversity for development projects that rely on funds from the World Bank.

Other organizations that influence environmental decisions are the Global Environment Facility (GEF) and the World Conservation Union (IUNC). All of these and other organization have played a role in the following: (1) expanding the understanding of environmental issues, (2) gathering and evaluating environmental data, (3) developing international environmental treaties, (4) providing funds for sustainable economic development in an attempt to reduce poverty, and (5) helping over 100 nations develop environmental laws and regulations.

The International Organization for Standardization (ISO) was established in 1947 in Geneva to promote the development of voluntary standards for international trade. The ISO is a nongovernmental organization (NGO) that has developed over 10,000 standards that govern products. In the early 1990s, ISO began to work on standards for environmental management. These standards aim to (1) improve the understanding of the environmental impact of activities, (2) have businesses comply with environmental regulations, (3) prevent pollution, (4) audit performance of businesses, and (5) set the standard of disclosing information about a business' environmental policy to the public.

Despite tensions between domestic concerns, international relations, and environmental issues, there have been several successful international conventions and treaties that deal with the environment. In 1987, the Montreal Protocol helped to start a decrease in CFCs in the atmosphere. The Earth Summit in 1992 aimed to develop better integration of national environmental goals with their economic goals. This summit accomplished the following: (1) development of 27 principles to guide the behavior of nations toward better environmentally sustainable patterns, (2) adoption of *Agenda 21,* and (3) a statement of principles for a global consensus on the management, conservation, and sustainable development of all types of forests. Later conferences have been less successful, with the major developing nations of China and India as well as the United States refusing to sign the Kyoto Protocol of 1997.

The European Union also works to maintain strict environmental standards for European countries. By 2000, more than 12 countries had adopted the policy of providing consumers with informational labels that enable them to be "green" consumers.

Differing Cultural and Societal Values

Many people, either within the same culture or in different cultures, differ in their views about the environment. People with widely different worldviews can examine the same data and arrive at different conclusions because they view the problem with different assumptions and values. Some environmental worldviews are human-centered, whereas others are life-centered.

According to the human-centered worldview, humans are the most important species and should manage Earth to their benefit, no matter how it might affect other species. Another human-centered view is the stewardship worldview, in which it is believed that humans have the responsibility to care for and manage the Earth. According to this view, we are borrowing resource from the Earth and have the ethical responsibility to leave the Earth in at least as good a condition as we now enjoy. Those with a life-centered worldview believe we have an ethical responsibility—not just for humans, but for all species—not to degrade Earth's ecosystems, biodiversity, and biosphere.

Future Issues

The message of environmentalism for the future should be one of hope. It calls for a commitment to overcoming today's challenges regarding the environment with respect to world population, pollution, energy sources, and food supplies. The environmental revolution that many environmental scientists hope to achieve in this century has the following components: (1) a biodiversity protection revolution, (2) an efficiency revolution, (3) a sufficiency revolution, (4) an energy revolution, (5) a pollution prevention revolution, (6) a demographic revolution, and (7) an economic and political revolution.

POST-TEST ANSWER SHEET

1. Ⓐ Ⓑ Ⓒ Ⓓ   13. Ⓐ Ⓑ Ⓒ Ⓓ   25. Ⓐ Ⓑ Ⓒ Ⓓ   37. Ⓐ Ⓑ Ⓒ Ⓓ   49. Ⓐ Ⓑ Ⓒ Ⓓ

2. Ⓐ Ⓑ Ⓒ Ⓓ   14. Ⓐ Ⓑ Ⓒ Ⓓ   26. Ⓐ Ⓑ Ⓒ Ⓓ   38. Ⓐ Ⓑ Ⓒ Ⓓ   50. Ⓐ Ⓑ Ⓒ Ⓓ

3. Ⓐ Ⓑ Ⓒ Ⓓ   15. Ⓐ Ⓑ Ⓒ Ⓓ   27. Ⓐ Ⓑ Ⓒ Ⓓ   39. Ⓐ Ⓑ Ⓒ Ⓓ   51. Ⓐ Ⓑ Ⓒ Ⓓ

4. Ⓐ Ⓑ Ⓒ Ⓓ   16. Ⓐ Ⓑ Ⓒ Ⓓ   28. Ⓐ Ⓑ Ⓒ Ⓓ   40. Ⓐ Ⓑ Ⓒ Ⓓ   52. Ⓐ Ⓑ Ⓒ Ⓓ

5. Ⓐ Ⓑ Ⓒ Ⓓ   17. Ⓐ Ⓑ Ⓒ Ⓓ   29. Ⓐ Ⓑ Ⓒ Ⓓ   41. Ⓐ Ⓑ Ⓒ Ⓓ   53. Ⓐ Ⓑ Ⓒ Ⓓ

6. Ⓐ Ⓑ Ⓒ Ⓓ   18. Ⓐ Ⓑ Ⓒ Ⓓ   30. Ⓐ Ⓑ Ⓒ Ⓓ   42. Ⓐ Ⓑ Ⓒ Ⓓ   54. Ⓐ Ⓑ Ⓒ Ⓓ

7. Ⓐ Ⓑ Ⓒ Ⓓ   19. Ⓐ Ⓑ Ⓒ Ⓓ   31. Ⓐ Ⓑ Ⓒ Ⓓ   43. Ⓐ Ⓑ Ⓒ Ⓓ   55. Ⓐ Ⓑ Ⓒ Ⓓ

8. Ⓐ Ⓑ Ⓒ Ⓓ   20. Ⓐ Ⓑ Ⓒ Ⓓ   32. Ⓐ Ⓑ Ⓒ Ⓓ   44. Ⓐ Ⓑ Ⓒ Ⓓ   56. Ⓐ Ⓑ Ⓒ Ⓓ

9. Ⓐ Ⓑ Ⓒ Ⓓ   21. Ⓐ Ⓑ Ⓒ Ⓓ   33. Ⓐ Ⓑ Ⓒ Ⓓ   45. Ⓐ Ⓑ Ⓒ Ⓓ   57. Ⓐ Ⓑ Ⓒ Ⓓ

10. Ⓐ Ⓑ Ⓒ Ⓓ   22. Ⓐ Ⓑ Ⓒ Ⓓ   34. Ⓐ Ⓑ Ⓒ Ⓓ   46. Ⓐ Ⓑ Ⓒ Ⓓ   58. Ⓐ Ⓑ Ⓒ Ⓓ

11. Ⓐ Ⓑ Ⓒ Ⓓ   23. Ⓐ Ⓑ Ⓒ Ⓓ   35. Ⓐ Ⓑ Ⓒ Ⓓ   47. Ⓐ Ⓑ Ⓒ Ⓓ   59. Ⓐ Ⓑ Ⓒ Ⓓ

12. Ⓐ Ⓑ Ⓒ Ⓓ   24. Ⓐ Ⓑ Ⓒ Ⓓ   36. Ⓐ Ⓑ Ⓒ Ⓓ   48. Ⓐ Ⓑ Ⓒ Ⓓ   60. Ⓐ Ⓑ Ⓒ Ⓓ

answer sheet

POST-TEST

Directions: Carefully read each of the following 60 questions. Choose the best answer to each question, and darken its letter on your answer sheet. The Answer Key and Explanations can be found following this Post-Test.

1. Which of the following methods is a way to recycle materials back into different products?
   (A) Downcycling
   (B) Composting
   (C) Closed-loop recycling
   (D) Source separation

2. Which of the following is an essential practice in maintaining good soil quality for farming?
   (A) Keep the ground covered
   (B) Keep crops consistent
   (C) Frequent tilling of land
   (D) Soil compaction

3. Which type of pollution can decimate forests and erode buildings?
   (A) Acid rain
   (B) Ozone
   (C) Carbon monoxide
   (D) Particulate matter

4. One consequence of introducing agricultural technology to a developing country is
   (A) an increased carrying capacity.
   (B) a decreased carrying capacity.
   (C) a steady carrying capacity.
   (D) no effect on carrying capacity.

5. Degradation of ecosystems and loss of bio-diversity in emerging nations is most often due to
   (A) overgrowth of vegetation.
   (B) industrial development.
   (C) flooding.
   (D) poor soil quality.

6. Which of the following gases is thought to be a major contributor to effect of global warming?
   (A) NO_2
   (B) SO_2
   (C) CO_2
   (D) O_3

7. Where is secondary succession likely to occur?
   (A) On a bare rock surface
   (B) Land covered by floods
   (C) Islands created by volcanoes
   (D) A sandy beach

8. The relationship between fungi and plant roots is best described as
   (A) mutualism.
   (B) commensalism.
   (C) parasitism.
   (D) competition.

9. Which of the following fossil fuels has the least impact on the environment?
   (A) Coal
   (B) Oil
   (C) Natural gas
   (D) Geothermal power

10. Which of the following is generally true about soil erosion?

   (A) The amount of topsoil remains relatively constant over long periods of time.

   (B) Soil is eroding faster than it forms.

   (C) There are no effective methods to prevent soil erosion.

   (D) As soil erodes, new soil replaces it.

11. Which of the following is the correct order in a simple five-step food chain?

   (A) producer, tertiary consumer, secondary consumer, primary consumer, decomposer

   (B) decomposer, primary consumer, secondary consumer, tertiary consumer, producer

   (C) producer, primary consumer, secondary consumer, tertiary consumer, decomposer

   (D) decomposer, tertiary consumer, secondary consumer, primary consumer, producer

12. Which of the following is an example of a point source of water pollution?

   (A) Urban street runoff

   (B) Storm drain

   (C) Acid rain

   (D) Fertilizer

13. Which 1976 act regulated the disposal of hazardous waste in the United States?

   (A) Clean Water Act

   (B) Brownfields Program

   (C) Soil and Water Conservation Act

   (D) Resource Conservation and Recovery Act

14. The living components of an ecosystem are called

   (A) biotic factors.

   (B) abiotic factors.

   (C) environmental factors.

   (D) biosphere factors.

15. The ozone layer is a necessary part of the atmosphere protecting Earth's surface from

   (A) meteors.

   (B) air pollution.

   (C) carbon monoxide.

   (D) ultraviolet light.

16. What percent of the world's energy comes from nonrenewable energy sources and nuclear energy?

   (A) 82 percent

   (B) 76 percent

   (C) 18 percent

   (D) 6 percent

17. Which of the following is NOT a factor that determines the carrying capacity of an aquatic ecosystem?

   (A) The salt concentration of the water

   (B) The O_2 levels of the water

   (C) The amount of nutrients in the water

   (D) The food supply

18. Which phenomenon is necessary to keep Earth warm enough to sustain life?

   (A) Biodiversity

   (B) Global warming

   (C) The greenhouse effect

   (D) Depleting ozone layer

19. A primary goal of the Superfund is to

   (A) clean up hazardous waste sites.

   (B) apply certain requirements to storm water discharge.

   (C) prohibit ocean dumping.

   (D) gain control of point source polution.

20. The field of science that aims to understand how all of Earth's ecosystems work together in order to predict future problems is
    (A) ecology.
    (B) biochemistry.
    (C) environmental science.
    (D) global ecology.

21. The total fertility rate of a population is the
    (A) number of births and deaths.
    (B) fertility rate necessary to replace a generation.
    (C) number of children born to each woman in her lifetime.
    (D) number of women of childbearing age.

22. Which of the following is an example of a persistent pesticide?
    (A) DDT
    (B) Diazinon
    (C) Organophosphates
    (D) Carbamates

23. What is one environmental issue that is a result of the Green Revolution?
    (A) Overcrowded farmland
    (B) Increase in labor-intensive agriculture
    (C) Increase in the number of crops grown on a plot of land through multiple cropping
    (D) The use of fertilizer and pesticides

24. Which of the following is NOT a feature of evolution?
    (A) Limiting factors
    (B) Extinction
    (C) Genetic variation
    (D) Natural selection

25. Which biome produces the least biomass?
    (A) Tropical rainforest
    (B) Tundra
    (C) Wetlands
    (D) Desert

26. In 1992, the Earth Summit aimed to develop a better integration of each country's environmental and
    (A) ecological goals.
    (B) biodiversity goals.
    (C) economic goals.
    (D) agricultural goals.

27. Which federal agency regulates the use of pesticides?
    (A) Department of Agriculture
    (B) Environmental Protection Agency
    (C) National Institute of Health
    (D) Food and Drug Administration

28. Which of the following is an example of interspecific competition?
    (A) Moss-tree
    (B) Shark-remora
    (C) Tapeworm-dog
    (D) Hawk-owl

29. Which of the following are among the first organisms that may appear in secondary succession?
    (A) Grasses
    (B) Autotrophs
    (C) Lichen
    (D) Shrubs

30. How does thermal pollution affect fish populations?
    (A) Increases amount of fish
    (B) Decreases amount of fish
    (C) No effect on fish
    (D) Causes mutations in fish

31. Which fuel source can be produced from biomass materials that contain cellulose or starch?

    (A) Carbon dioxide

    (B) Coal

    (C) Ethanol

    (D) Oil

32. Improvements to the combustion engine have decreased which type of air pollution?

    (A) Sulfur dioxide

    (B) Volatile organic compounds

    (C) Oxides of nitrogen

    (D) Carbon monoxide

33. Which of the following is a possible disadvantage of recycling plastics?

    (A) It requires fossil fuels.

    (B) It causes an increase in pollution.

    (C) All types of plastic cannot be recycled by the same methods.

    (D) Most municipalities do not recycle plastic.

34. Which of the following is NOT a source of acid deposition?

    (A) Automobiles

    (B) Trees

    (C) Farm animals

    (D) Factories

35. Which of the following statements most accurately describes the role of nitrifying fixing bacteria in the nitrogen cycle?

    (A) Converts ammonia to nitrites and nitrates

    (B) Converts nitrites to nitrogen gas

    (C) Incorporates nitrates into amino acid

    (D) Converts nitrogen gas into ammonia

36. Which of the following is indicative of a high genetic diversity in a given population?

    (A) Varied structures and abilities

    (B) Uniform structures and abilities

    (C) Highly evolved individuals

    (D) Varied ecosystems

37. The spread of disease in wild fish can be the result of

    (A) fish farming.

    (B) depletion of mangrove swamps.

    (C) decline in the fishing industry.

    (D) heavily populated estuaries.

38. Species that feed at all trophic levels are

    (A) producers.

    (B) carnivores.

    (C) decomposers.

    (D) herbivores.

39. The exploitation of minerals in oceans is controlled by the

    (A) United Nations.

    (B) Clean Water Act.

    (C) Resource Conservation and Recovery Act.

    (D) Law of the Sea.

40. Which of the following processes provides usable energy to producers?

    (A) Photosynthesis

    (B) Cellular respiration

    (C) Digestion

    (D) Osmosis

41. Which process of irrigation conserves the most water?

    (A) Gravity flow irrigation

    (B) Flood irrigation

    (C) Trickle irrigation

    (D) Center-pivot irrigation

42. Which biomes absorb the most CO_2 in the environment?

    (A) Desert and tundra

    (B) Wetlands and forests

    (C) Savannas and chaparrals

    (D) Oceans and grasslands

43. Surface mining regulations require that land damaged from the effects of surface mining must be

    (A) filled with topsoil when the mine is shut down.

    (B) replanted with vegetation.

    (C) converted to an artificial lake.

    (D) cleaned and decontaminated.

44. Which layer of the atmosphere varies in depth dependent upon the season and Earth's relative position?

    (A) Mesosphere

    (B) Stratosphere

    (C) Troposphere

    (D) Thermosphere

45. Which of the following is extracted from shale?

    (A) Oil

    (B) Coal

    (C) Natural gas

    (D) Nuclear energy

46. Which three states have enough wind to power the nation?

    (A) Pennsylvania, New York, Ohio

    (B) Texas, North Dakota, South Dakota

    (C) California, Washington, Oregon

    (D) Florida, Georgia, South Carolina

47. Which of the following is a feature of sustainable agriculture?

    (A) Planting multiple crops in the same field

    (B) Use of fertilizers to increase crop growth

    (C) Only planting in a field every other year

    (D) Practicing monoculture

48. Which of the following converts to an acid in the atmosphere?

    (A) NO_2

    (B) SO_2

    (C) H_2SO_4

    (D) CO

49. Which of the following concepts is frequently used in environmental risk assessment?

    (A) Pollution control

    (B) Damage control

    (C) Source-pathway-receptor

    (D) Source-pathway-control

50. Which best explains why brown beetles survive over green beetles?

    (A) Green beetles taste better to birds.

    (B) Brown beetles are less visible, so birds do not see them.

    (C) Brown beetles reproduce faster than green beetles.

    (D) It happens by chance.

51. The stewardship worldview of environmentalism maintains that

    (A) we must consider our neighbors well-being.

    (B) we must care for all living creatures no matter how small.

    (C) we have a responsibility to care for Earth so it is preserved for future generations.

    (D) we are completely dependent on nature for our survival.

52. The first significant increase in atmospheric CO_2 levels is linked to
    (A) the thinning ozone layer above Antarctica.
    (B) the warming of ocean temperatures.
    (C) an increase in vegetation on Earth.
    (D) the Industrial Revolution.

53. Which scientific practice yields plants with desired traits?
    (A) Mutation
    (B) Genetic crossbreeding
    (C) Chemical enhancement
    (D) Sustainable farming

54. Human populations can best be described as
    (A) r-strategists.
    (B) l-strategists.
    (C) k-strategists.
    (D) survivalists.

55. Which of the following describes the method of contour farming?
    (A) Tilling only in a narrow region that is to receive seeds while all other soil is undisturbed
    (B) Farming at right angles to a slope of land
    (C) Diversifying crops planted in given area
    (D) Leaving a ridge the previous year and planting the new crop in the ridge

56. What is one environmental problem that arose from the Agricultural Revolution?
    (A) Soil erosion
    (B) Air pollution
    (C) Poor crop yield
    (D) Increase in pests

57. Which of the following describes limiting factors?
    (A) A factor that determines the fertility rate of an organism
    (B) Always an intrinsic factor
    (C) An environmental factor that determines size of a population
    (D) Independent of the environment

58. The largest proportion of deforestation is caused by
    (A) acid rain.
    (B) drought.
    (C) agricultural development.
    (D) forest fires.

59. Which energy source can be obtained from a landfill?
    (A) Ethane
    (B) Hydrogen
    (C) Methane
    (D) Steam

60. In which area of the world listed below is desertification most prevalent?
    (A) Western United States
    (B) Northern Africa
    (C) Eastern Europe
    (D) Central America

ANSWER KEY AND EXPLANATIONS

1. A	13. D	25. B	37. A	49. C
2. A	14. A	26. C	38. C	50. B
3. A	15. D	27. B	39. D	51. C
4. A	16. A	28. D	40. A	52. D
5. B	17. A	29. A	41. C	53. B
6. C	18. C	30. B	42. B	54. C
7. B	19. A	31. C	43. B	55. B
8. A	20. D	32. D	44. C	56. A
9. C	21. C	33. C	45. A	57. C
10. B	22. A	34. C	46. B	58. C
11. C	23. D	35. A	47. A	59. C
12. B	24. A	36. A	48. C	60. B

1. **The correct answer is (A).** Downcycling is the recycling of one type of product into different products. Choice (B) is incorrect because composting recycles nutrients from plants and vegetables back into the soil. Choice (C) is incorrect because this involves recycling products into new products of the same type. Choice (D) is incorrect because source separation is the process of separating waste into different recyclable categories.

2. **The correct answer is (A).** Bare soil is susceptible to wind and water erosion, so groundcover protects soil, provides habitats for larger soil organisms like earthworms, and can improve water availability to surrounding areas. Choice (B) is incorrect because the practice of crop rotation, rather than planting the same crop each year, is more beneficial to the soil. Choice (C) is incorrect because frequent tilling is actually damaging to soil and should be avoided. Choice (D) is incorrect because compaction reduces the amount of air, water, and space available to plant roots and soil organisms, so it should be avoided in order to maintain soil quality.

3. **The correct answer is (A).** Acid rain contains sulfuric acid and nitric acid, both of which can kill trees and erode limestone buildings. Choice (B) is incorrect because ozone can destroy chlorophyll in plants, but it is not a major cause of tree decimation and building erosion. Choice (C) is incorrect because although carbon monoxide affects air quality, it doesn't directly kill trees and erode buildings. Choice (D) is incorrect because particulate matter doesn't destroy forests and buildings.

4. **The correct answer is (A).** The carrying capacity within an environment can increase through advances in agricultural technology. Choice (B) is incorrect because the introduction of agricultural technology would increase, not decrease, the carrying capacity. Choice (C) is incorrect because there would be a continual increase in carrying capacity, not a leveling off. Choice (D) is incorrect because agricultural technology would affect the carrying capacity in a positive way.

5. **The correct answer is (B).** Industrial development of emerging nations can lead to loss of biodiversity and ecosystem degradation. Choice (A) is incorrect because an overgrowth of vegetation would lead to potentially greater biodiversity and ecosystem development. Choice (C) is incorrect because flooding is not the major cause of loss of biodiversity or ecosystem degradation in emerging nations. Choice (D) is incorrect because poor soil quality is a possible consequence of industrial development.

6. **The correct answer is (C).** Carbon dioxide (CO_2) is the most abundant of greenhouse gases, and it is thought to be a major contributor to global warming. Choice (A) is incorrect because nitrous oxide, not nitrogen dioxide, is a greenhouse gas. Choice (B) is incorrect because sulfur dioxide is produced when fossil fuels are burned, and it is not a greenhouse gas. Choice (D) is incorrect because ozone is not a greenhouse gas, so it doesn't contribute to global warming.

7. **The correct answer is (B).** Secondary succession begins with the destruction of an existing ecosystem. If land were flooded, existing ecosystems would be destroyed and new ones would form. Choices (A), (C), and (D) are not the best answers because these are all areas where there is likely a lack of organisms and primary succession would occur first.

8. **The correct answer is (A).** The relationship is mutualistic when both species benefit from the relationship. Fungi and plant roots both benefit from the association. The fungus obtains organic materials from the plant roots, and the branched nature of the fungus assists the plant in obtaining nutrients from the soil. Choice (B) is incorrect because in this relationship only one organism benefits, while the other is unaffected. Choice (C) is incorrect because in this relationship, one organism obtains nourishment from a host organism, but in the process it may harm the host. Choice (D) is incorrect because the

relationship doesn't represent a competition between the two species.

9. **The correct answer is (C).** Natural gas is a fossil fuel, but it adds very little to air pollution, and it is the least disruptive to the environment because it produces much less carbon dioxide than other fossil fuels. Choice (A) is incorrect because coal produces a great deal of air pollution. Choice (B) is incorrect because oil produces huge environmental problems if there is an oil spill in the ocean. Choice (D) is incorrect because geothermal energy is a renewable resource, not a fossil fuel.

10. **The correct answer is (B).** Every year, erosion carries away more topsoil than is formed; this occurs mostly because of agricultural practices that often leave soil unprotected from wind and water. Choice (A) is incorrect because some regions of the world lose significant amounts of soil over time. Choice (C) is incorrect because environmental scientists and conservationists work to reduce soil loss through many different soil conservation methods that have been effective in slowing the rate of erosion. Choice (D) is incorrect because soil erodes faster than it is replaced in nature.

11. **The correct answer is (C).** The correct order in a typical five-step food chain is producer, primary consumer (herbivore), secondary consumer (omnivore or carnivore), tertiary consumer (carnivore), and decomposer. Choices (A), (B), and (D) are incorrect because none of them represent the correct order of a typical food chain.

12. **The correct answer is (B).** A storm drain is a point source of water pollution because the source of pollution is readily identified. Choices (A), (C), and (D) are incorrect because these are all examples of nonpoint sources of water pollution.

13. **The correct answer is (D).** In 1976, the U.S. Congress passed the Resource Conservation and Recovery Act to regulate the disposal

of hazardous waste materials. Choice (A) is incorrect because the Clean Water Acts were passed in 1977 and 1987 to help control water pollution. Choice (B) is incorrect because the Brownfields Program cleans up hazardous waste sites, but it doesn't regulate the disposal of hazardous wastes. Choice (C) is incorrect because the Soil and Water Conservation Act was passed in 1977 for the conservation, protection, and enhancement of soil, water, and natural resources.

14. **The correct answer is (A).** Biotic factors are living organisms that interact with the environment. Choice (B) is incorrect because abiotic factors are nonliving components of an ecosystem; they are the matter, energy, and surrounding space that help to shape an environment. Choice (C) is incorrect because an environment encompasses all living and nonliving things interacting together. Choice (D) is incorrect because a biosphere is defined as the life zone of the Earth and includes all living organisms.

15. **The correct answer is (D).** The ozone layer shields Earth from the harmful effects of ultraviolet light radiation. An intact ozone layer absorbs approximately 99 percent of ultraviolet (UV) light and prevents it from reaching Earth's surface. Choice (A) is incorrect because the ozone layer doesn't block meteor showers from reaching Earth. Choice (B) is incorrect because air pollution is found below the ozone layer of the atmosphere. Choice (C) is incorrect because carbon monoxide is a pollutant released into the atmosphere by activities on Earth's surface.

16. **The correct answer is (A).** Nonrenewable fossil fuels and nuclear power provide 82 percent of the world's energy. Choice (B) is incorrect because 76 percent of energy comes from nonrenewable energy sources alone. Choice (C) is incorrect because about 18 percent of the world's energy comes from renewable sources at this time, most of which is produced from biomass, but energy

is also supplied by wind, solar, geothermal, and hydroelectric sources. Choice (D) is incorrect because 6 percent of energy comes from nuclear energy alone.

17. **The correct answer is (A).** The salt concentration doesn't affect the carrying capacity because different species are suited for salt or freshwater ecosystems. Choice (B) is incorrect because the O_2 levels of the water do affect the carrying capacity. Choice (C) is incorrect because the amount of nutrients in the water affects the carrying capacity. Choice (D) is incorrect because the food supply available to organisms affects the carrying capacity.

18. **The correct answer is (C).** The greenhouse effect is necessary to sustain all life on Earth. Choice (A) is incorrect because although biodiversity helps to sustain a variety of life on Earth, it is not necessary to sustain all life. Choice (B) is incorrect because the global warming can be harmful to life on Earth. Choice (D) is incorrect because the depleting ozone layer leads to global warming, not sustained life on Earth.

19. **The correct answer is (A).** A primary goal of the Superfund Act is to clean up hazardous waste sites. Choice (B) is incorrect because it refers to a goal of the Water Quality Act. Choice (C) is incorrect because the prohibition against ocean dumping is a provision of the Marine Protection, Research, and Sanctuaries Act of 1988. Choice (D) is incorrect because it was the Clean Water Act of 1977 that first sought to gain control of point source pollution.

20. **The correct answer is (D).** Global ecology is the study of all of Earth's ecosystems and how organisms interact with one other and their environment. In understanding ecology on a global scale, future problems can be predicted. Choice (A) is incorrect because although ecology is the study of ecosystems and their environment, global ecology is inclusive of all ecological systems. Choice

(B) is incorrect because biochemistry deals with a molecular scale of organisms, not a global scale. Choice (C) is incorrect because environmental science is the study of the environment, not ecological issues.

21. **The correct answer is (C).** The total fertility rate of a population is the number of children born to each woman in her lifetime. Choice (A) is incorrect because the number of births and deaths in a population is not the total fertility rate. Choice (B) is not correct because this describes the replacement fertility rate. Choice (D) is incorrect because the number of women of childbearing age doesn't reflect the total fertility rate.

22. **The correct answer is (A).** DDT is a chlorinated hydrocarbon, which is a type of persistent pesticide. Choice (B) is incorrect because diazinon is a widely used nonpersistent pesticide. Choice (C) is incorrect because organophosphates are nonpersistent insecticides in that they decompose quickly into harmless by-products. Organophospates aren't species-specific and will kill all insects, whether they are harmful or beneficial. Choice (D) is incorrect because carbamates are nonpersistent pesticides that work by interfering with an insect's nervous system.

23. **The correct answer is (D).** One step in the Green Revolution is to produce high yields through the use of large inputs of fertilizer, pesticides, and water, which can lead to fertilizer runoff that affects the environment. Choice (A) is incorrect because the aim of the Green Revolution is to increase global food production by getting higher yields per unit of farmland, which can be done by planting larger, more efficient crops. Choice (B) is incorrect because the Green Revolution did not increase labor-intensive farming. Choice (C) is incorrect because even though one of the main goals of the Green Revolution is to increase the number of crops grown annually on a plot of land through the practice of multiple cropping, this doesn't have an impact on the environment.

24. **The correct answer is (A).** Limiting factors are not a component of evolution. In general, this term refers to factors in an ecosystem that limit its success. Choice (B) is incorrect because extinction is a common feature of evolution. Choice (C) is incorrect because genetic variability is necessary for evolution to occur. Choice (D) is incorrect because natural selection is an important part of evolution. Natural selection is the process in which the individuals of a species best able to survive and reproduce will pass on traits that will continue to be expressed in a species. This process leads to evolution of species.

25. **The correct answer is (B).** Not very many species of plants and animals can survive in the conditions of the tundra, so the biomass in these biomes is very low. Choice (A) is incorrect because a tropical rainforest provides a warm, wet climate that is advantageous to producing multiple species of plants and for sustaining many species of animals, birds, and insects—all of which would create a large biomass. Choice (C) is incorrect because even though wetlands don't produce a large biomass, there are more species living in wetlands than in the tundra. Choice (D) is incorrect because deserts don't have favorable conditions to support a large biomass, but there are more species living in a desert than in a tundra.

26. **The correct answer is (C).** The Earth Summit aimed to integrate environmental and economic goals of countries. Choices (A), (B), and (D) are incorrect because the Earth Summit dealt with integrating economic and environmental concerns.

27. **The correct answer is (B).** The EPA researches and regulates pesticide use. Choices (A), (C), and (D) are incorrect because researching and regulating pesticides is not the function of any of these agencies.

28. **The correct answer is (D).** Hawks and owls are both predators that compete for

the same prey, including mice and rabbits. Because hawks and owls are different species, this is called interspecific competition. Choice (A) is incorrect because moss and trees have a commensal relationship; some moss benefits by growing on the base of a tree, but the tree is not affected. Choice (B) is incorrect because the shark and the remora have a commensal relationship in which the remora benefits and the shark is unaffected. Choice (C) is incorrect because the tapeworm is a parasite to the dog, not a predator.

29. **The correct answer is (A).** Since the damaged area still has intact soil, it would undergo secondary succession, and grass would be one of the first organisms to grow. Choice (B) is incorrect because autotrophic microorganisms would appear in an area where there are no life forms and no intact soil. Choice (C) is incorrect because lichen would be one of the first organisms to appear during primary succession. Choice (D) is incorrect because in secondary succession, shrubs would appear after grasses.

30. **The correct answer is (B).** Fish populations decrease with increasing thermal pollution because the increase in water temperature decreases the oxygen concentration of the water. With less oxygen, fewer fish can survive. Choice (A) is incorrect because thermal pollution kills fish and doesn't increase a fish population. Choice (C) is incorrect because thermal pollution does have an effect on fish populations. Choice (D) is incorrect because thermal pollution decreases the oxygen concentration of the water; it doesn't cause mutations.

31. **The correct answer is (C).** Ethanol is an alcohol used as a fuel source; it is produced by the fermentation of sugar, starch, or cellulose. Choice (A) is incorrect because carbon dioxide is not a fuel source. Choice (B) is incorrect because coal is produced over time and under high pressure from decaying organic matter. Choice (D) is incorrect

because oil is a fuel source produced by oils released from the remains of marine organisms. Like coal, oil forms over a very long period of time.

32. **The correct answer is (D).** Increased fuel efficiency and the use of catalytic converters have reduced carbon monoxide emissions. However, carbon monoxide pollution is still a problem because cars now drive greater distances and there are more cars on the road. Choices (A), (B), and (C) are incorrect because the level of all of these air pollutants is not affected by improvements in the combustion engine and catalytic converter.

33. **The correct answer is (C).** Goods are manufactured using different types of plastic. All of these plastics need to be separated and recycled by different methods, which is not a very cost-effective process. Cheap and plentiful resources such as glass and plastics may cost more to recycle than to dump and manufacture new. Choice (A) is incorrect because recycling doesn't require the use of fossil fuels. Choice (B) is incorrect because recycling can reduce air and water pollution. Choice (D) is incorrect because many municipalities have recycling programs.

34. **The correct answer is (C).** Farm animals don't release any sulfur dioxide or oxides of nitrogen into the atmosphere. Choices (A), (B), and (D) are incorrect because they are all sources of acid deposition.

35. **The correct answer is (A).** Nitrifying bacteria are able to convert ammonia in soil into nitrites and nitrates. Nitrogen-fixing bacteria are able to convert atmospheric nitrogen gas that enters the soil into ammonia that plants can use. Choice (B) is incorrect because denitrifying bacteria convert nitrites into nitrogen gas. Choice (C) is incorrect because the nitrates are taken up by plants and incorporated into amino acids. Choice (D) is incorrect because nitrogen-fixing bacteria are able to convert atmospheric nitrogen

answers post-test

gas that enters the soil into ammonia that plants can use.

36. **The correct answer is (A).** High genetic diversity is a level of biodiversity in which there is a great variation in genetic material within a population; therefore, individuals will have varied structure and abilities. Choice (B) is incorrect because low genetic diversity yields a population that was more uniform in structure and ability. Choice (C) is incorrect because high genetic diversity indicates a variety of genes, but doesn't imply anything about the complexity of the organisms. Choice (D) is incorrect because a high genetic diversity doesn't imply varied ecosystems.

37. **The correct answer is (A).** Fish farmers add nutrients to water in order to produce larger fish in a shorter time period. These added nutrients have led to disease spread from farm-raised fish to wild fish. Choice (B) is incorrect because the depletion of mangrove swamps would disrupt the ecosystem in a negative way, but it doesn't spread disease. Choice (C) is incorrect because the decline of fishing would not spread disease; in fact, there is an increase in the fishing industry, which leads to overfishing and smaller fish populations. Choice (D) is incorrect because estuaries are being depleted of organisms because of the flow of fertilizers, animal wastes, and pesticides down river and into estuaries. Also, estuaries aren't heavily populated.

38. **The correct answer is (C).** Decomposers are organisms that will feed off all other organisms within an ecosystem whenever those organisms shed, excrete waste, or die. Therefore, decomposers feed off organisms at every trophic level. Choice (A) is incorrect because producers are plants and at the first trophic level. Choice (B) is incorrect because carnivores feed and occupy higher trophic levels only. Choice (D) is incorrect because herbivores occupy the second trophic level.

39. **The correct answer is (D).** The Law of the Sea aims to create a legal mechanism for controlling the exploitation of mineral resources in open waters. Choice (A) is incorrect because the United Nations doesn't control the exploitation of minerals. Choice (B), the Clean Water Act, regulates water pollution. Choice (C) is incorrect because the Resource Conservation and Recovery Act controls hazardous waste disposal.

40. **The correct answer is (A).** During photosynthesis, carbon dioxide present in the atmosphere is taken in by plants (respiration) and converted into glucose, an energy source for plants and animals. Choice (B) is incorrect because animals use the process of oxygen respiration to breathe and convert oxygen into carbon dioxide. Choice (C) is not correct because the process of digestion doesn't occur in plants. Choice (D) is incorrect because osmosis doesn't play a role in providing an energy source.

41. **The correct answer is (C).** Trickle irrigation is a very efficient method in which 90 to 95 percent of the water reaches the crops. In this method, small flexible tubing is inserted at or below ground level, and small holes in the tubing deliver water to the plant roots. Choice (A) is incorrect because gravity flow irrigation consists of unlined ditches filled with water; the water flows by gravity to the crops. Choice (B) is incorrect because flood irrigation includes large ditches filled with water similar to gravity flow irrigation. Choice (D) is incorrect because center-pivot irrigation systems use center-pivot sprinklers that move in a circular motion to deliver water to crops, which uses a large amount of water.

42. **The correct answer is (B).** Natural wetlands and forests absorb more CO_2 from the atmosphere than other biomes. Trees and plant life are abundant in these biomes, and so a large amount of CO_2 is absorbed. Choice (A) is incorrect because tundra and deserts don't have a great amount of vegetation.

Choice (C) is incorrect because savannas and chaparral biomes have plant life, but they don't absorb as much CO_2 as forests with large trees and wetlands. Choice (D) is incorrect because oceans don't absorb CO_2.

43. **The correct answer is (B).** The Surface Mining Control and Reclamation Act of 1977 required that all mining companies replant vegetation on land that was strip mined. Choice (A) is incorrect because the land doesn't only need to be covered with topsoil, but to have vegetation planted. Choice (C) is incorrect because there is no regulation specifying that strip-mined land be converted into lakes. Choice (D) is incorrect because the land doesn't need to be decontaminated.

44. **The correct answer is (C).** The depth of the troposphere, the atmospheric layer closest to Earth's surface, is dependent on the position of Earth and the season. Choice (A) is incorrect because the mesosphere depth isn't dependent on Earth's position or the seasons. Choice (B) is incorrect because the stratosphere depth isn't dependent on Earth's position or the seasons. Choice (D) is incorrect because the thermosphere depth isn't dependent on Earth's position or the seasons.

45. **The correct answer is (A).** Sediment rock called shale contains dispersed oil droplets, but this oil is difficult to extract. Choice (B) is incorrect because coal is rock formed from decaying organic matter. Choice (C) is incorrect because natural gas isn't deposited in rock; it is underground above layers of oil and shale. Choice (D) is incorrect because nuclear energy isn't a fossil fuel.

46. **The correct answer is (B).** There is enough wind power in Texas and the Dakotas to power the entire United States. Choices (A), (C), and (D) are incorrect because there is not enough wind power in the states listed to power the whole country.

47. **The correct answer is (A).** In practices of sustainable agriculture, multiple crops are planted on the same plot and harvested at different times. Choice (B) is incorrect because sustainable agriculture doesn't promote the use of fertilizers or chemical pesticides. Choice (C) is incorrect because fields aren't left bare or unplanted. Choice (D) is incorrect because multiple crops are planted in one field.

48. **The correct answer is (C).** When sulfur trioxide enters the atmosphere, it can react with water vapor to form sulfuric acid, H_2SO_4, which is the main component of acid rain. Choice (A) is incorrect because nitrogen dioxide, NO_2, is not a component of acid rain. Choice (B) is incorrect because sulfuric acid is the product formed in the atmosphere from sulfur trioxide. Choice (D) is incorrect because carbon monoxide, CO, is not a component of acid rain.

49. **The correct answer is (C).** A concept frequently used in environmental risk assessment is that of source-pathway-receptor. The pathway between a hazard (source) and a receptor is investigated. If no pathway exists, then there is no risk to the environment. If a pathway links a source to a receptor, then the consequences need to be assessed. Choice (A) is incorrect because pollution control is an action taken to reduce a risk, not assess one. Choice (B) is incorrect because damage control isn't a way to assess environmental risks. Choice (D) is incorrect because control of a hazard isn't a means of assessment, but a means of reducing risk.

50. **The correct answer is (B).** Brown beetles are more camouflaged by soil and dirt, so birds don't notice them as easily as green beetles. Therefore, the brown beetle is less likely to be eaten and more likely to live long enough to reproduce. This process of natural selection favors the brown beetle over the green beetle. Choice (A) is incorrect because the taste of the beetles is no different. Choice (C) is incorrect because

answers post-test

the reproduction rate is no different. Choice (D) is incorrect because the natural selection doesn't happen by chance.

51. **The correct answer is (C).** The stewardship worldview maintains that people have an ethical responsibility to be good stewards of Earth and need to manage it well for future generations. Choice (A) is incorrect because this human-centered worldview focuses on future generations. Choice (B) is incorrect because the stewardship worldview is a human-centered view of the environment. Choice (D) is incorrect because this isn't part of the stewardship worldview.

52. **The correct answer is (D).** A rapid increase of CO_2 in the atmosphere was first observed during the Industrial Revolution when there was a significant increase in the amount of coal burned for energy. Choice (A) is incorrect because the thinning of the ozone layer over Antarctica may be the result of an increase in CO_2, but it is not the cause of an increase in CO_2. Choice (B) is incorrect because warmer ocean temperatures don't increase CO_2. Choice (C) is incorrect because there is less vegetation in many areas, not more.

53. **The correct answer is (B).** Genetic cross-breeding is a method in which scientists cross-pollinate plants with desired traits until they generate seeds that will grow plants with the target desired traits. Choice (A) is incorrect because mutations wouldn't always produce desired traits. Choice (C) is incorrect because chemical enhancement isn't always a safe way to obtain plants with desired traits. Choice (D) is incorrect because sustainable farming is an agricultural practice of farming that doesn't use chemicals.

54. **The correct answer is (C).** Humans can best be described as k-strategists because k-selected species have few offspring and spend a great deal of energy and time ensuring that their offspring survive to reproduc-

tive age. Choice (A) is incorrect because r-selected species have a large number of offspring and don't care for them after they are born. Choice (B) is incorrect because l-strategist is not a term relevant to population biology. Choice (D) is incorrect because survivalist is not a term used to describe human populations.

55. **The correct answer is (B).** Contour farming involves tilling at right angles to the slope of the land. In this method, small ridges are created that help prevent water from running down the slope and eroding the soil. Choice (A) is incorrect because it describes strip tillage, which is a method that involves tilling only in the narrow strip that is to receive the seeds. The rest of the soil and any crop residue from the previous year are left undisturbed. Choice (C) is incorrect because it is describing the method of diversifying cropping systems, which helps supply the soil with a variety of nutrients. Choice (D) is incorrect because the method of leaving a ridge from the previous year is ridge tillage.

56. **The correct answer is (A).** An increase in land developed for agricultural use has caused an increase in soil erosion. Choice (B) is incorrect because air pollution is not caused by agricultural land use. Choice (C) is incorrect because agricultural practices helped to increase crop yields. Choice (D) is incorrect because the Agricultural Revolution didn't cause an increase in pests.

57. **The correct answer is (C).** The limiting factor is a condition of an environment that determines the population size of a given organism. Choice (A) is incorrect because a limiting factor is an environmental influence on the population of an organism, but it doesn't affect fertility rate. Choice (B) is incorrect because a limiting factor is an extrinsic factor. Choice (D) is incorrect because the limiting factor is a condition within the environment.

58. The correct answer is (C). Deforestation worldwide is largely due to the clearing of land for agricultural purposes. Choice (A) is incorrect because acid rain affects some forests, but most forests are cleared by human activity. Choice (B) is incorrect because drought is not a usual cause of deforestation. Choice (D) is incorrect because although forest fires are a cause of deforestation, more forests are cleared for agricultural purposes than affected by forest fires.

59. The correct answer is (C). In a well-designed sanitary landfill, methane gas is trapped as it is released from the decomposing waste. It can then be used as an energy source. Choice (A) is incorrect because methane gas, not ethane, is obtained from landfills. Choice (B) is incorrect because hydrogen is not obtained from a landfill. Choice (D) is incorrect because steam is obtained from geothermal wells, not landfills.

60. The correct answer is (B). Desertification occurs most often in regions like northern Africa because there is irregular and unpredictable rainfall. Choice (A) is incorrect because desertification is more prevalent in northern Africa than the western United States. Choice (C) is incorrect because desertification is not a particular problem in eastern Europe. Choice (D) is incorrect because Central America receives heavy rainfall.

SUMMING IT UP

- Ecosystems are a complex network of interrelationships between abiotic and biotic factors.

- A community consists of all interacting populations of various species living in a given area at the same time.

- There are three types of organisms in organism relationships: (1) predation, (2) competition, and (3) symbiosis. There are three broad categories of organisms: (1) producers, (2) consumers, and (3) decomposers.

- All organisms occupy one or more trophic levels, and available energy decreases as the trophic level increases.

- A food chain or food web describes the relationship of organisms within an ecosystem.

- Biogeochemical cycling is the process by which the most fit and best adapted members of a species survive and reproduce.

- Succession is a series of changes that ecosystems go through in order to maintain the stability of a community.

- Biomes are climax communities that are distributed around the world. In general, the structure of ecosystems within a given type of biome is similar.

- Aquatic ecosystems are shaped by the ability of the sun's energy to reach organisms below the water's surface, the depth to the bottom, the water's temperature, the amount of salts dissolved in the water, and the nature of the body of water.

- Population biology is concerned with the characterization of the make-up, growth, and impact of a population on the environment and its organisms.

- Earth's atmosphere is 78.1 percent nitrogen, 20.9 percent oxygen, and 1 percent other gases, including carbon dioxide, methane, and water vapor.

- There are four layers in Earth's atmosphere: (1) troposphere, (2) stratosphere, (3) mesosphere, and (4) thermosphere.

- Human population growth has a significant impact on the environment and a country's resources. Developed countries tend to have low rates of population growth, and developing countries tend to have higher rates of population growth.

- Pollution is a form of matter or energy that harms the environment.

- The ozone layer is necessary to block harmful UV light, but it is slowly being depleted by human activities.

- The greenhouse effect is necessary to keep Earth's temperature warm enough to sustain life, but too much greenhouse effect can harm the environment.

- The Industrial Revolution brought about the use of coal as a fuel source and the advent of machines, all of which caused a significant increase in pollution.

- The agricultural revolution developed techniques of growing larger quantities of food, especially after the invention of mechanized farm equipment. Agricultural practices can lead to deforestation and desertification, especially in developing countries. Agricultural and industrial runoff can lead to the process of eutrophication in aquatic environments.

- Nonrenewable energy sources constitute 86.5 percent of the world's energy consumption, and only 13.5 percent of our energy comes from renewable sources.

- The Green Revolution introduced new, faster growing and hardier plant varieties and improved farming methods. High yields were achieved through the use of chemical fertilizers, pesticides, and herbicides.

- Agricultural practices are dependent on soil type, land conditions, and economic conditions. Fertilizers increase crop yield, but they cause problems to the environment. Pesticides increase crop yield, but they are harmful to the environment and to human and other species. Alternative agricultural methods aim to preserve the environment by using less or no chemicals.

- Erosion is a natural process, but some land use practices can help to control erosion.

- Human activity produces air pollution, but humans can help to control air pollution by changing activities and practices.

- Water treatment techniques are used to provide safe, clean drinking water and to clean up wastewater before it is released back into the environment. Solid and hazardous waste is disposed of in landfills or incinerated.

- Recycling helps to reduce the amount of solid waste, but there are some technical and economic problems associated with recycling.

- Environmental policy consists of laws, rules, and regulations developed by government organizations to solve environmental problems. International environmental policies are established by the United Nations and other world organizations.

- People either view environmental issues as human-centered or life-centered issues.

- An environmental revolution can address concerns for the environment and Earth's population.

Personal Finance

The following chart outlines the sections and subsections in the Personal Finance test and offers a comparison between the percent of practice questions in this chapter and the actual DSST exam.

CONTENT OUTLINE: SECTIONS AND SUBSECTIONS	PERCENT OF EXAM DEVOTED TO EACH CONTENT AREA	NUMBER OF ITEMS IN THE DIAGNOSTIC TEST AND POST-TEST BY CONTENT AREA	PERCENT OF ITEMS IN THE DIAGNOSTIC TEST AND POST-TEST BY CONTENT AREA
I. Foundations of Personal Finance	**10%**	**11**	**13.75%**
A. Financial Goals, Budgeting, Financial Statements, and Cash Management		6	54.5%
B. Economic Terminology		2	18.2%
C. Institutional Aspects of Financial Planning		1	9.1%
D. Time Value of Money		2	18.2%
II. Credit and Debt	**15%**	**11**	**13.75%**
A. Consumer Credit		9	77.8%
B. Bankruptcy		2	22.2%
III. Major Purchases	**15%**	**11**	**13.75%**
A. Auto		7	63.6%
B. Housing		3	27.3%
C. Other Major Purchases		1	9.1%
IV. Taxes	**15%**	**12**	**15%**
A. Payroll Deductions		4	33.3%
B. Income		5	41.7%
C. Tax Planning/Estimating		3	25%
V. Insurance	**15%**	**12**	**15%**
A. Life Policies		3	25%
B. Property and Liability Policies		5	41.7%
C. Health, Disability, and Long-Term Care Policies		4	33.3%
VI. Investments	**15%**	**12**	**15%**
A. Saving Accounts and Money Markets		4	41.7%
B. Stocks, Bonds, and Mutual Funds		6	50%
C. Sources of Information		2	8.3%
VII. Retirement and Estate Planning	**15%**	**11**	**13.75%**
A. Funding Retirement		5	45.5%
B. Social Security		1	9%
C. Estate Planning		5	45.5%
Grand Total	**100%**	**80**	**100%**

chapter 4

OVERVIEW

- Diagnostic test
- Answer key and explanations
- Foundations of personal finance
- Credit and debt
- Major purchases
- Taxes
- Insurance
- Investments
- Retirement and estate planning
- Post-test
- Answer key and explanations
- Summing it up

DIAGNOSTIC TEST

Directions: Carefully read each of the following 20 questions. Choose the best answer to each question and circle your answer choice. The Answer Key and Explanations can be found following this Diagnostic Test.

1. Who is responsible for paying for debt counseling for debtors filing for bankruptcy?
   - (A) The debtors
   - (B) Federal government through a debt reduction program
   - (C) State government through a debt reduction program
   - (D) Debtors' creditors

2. Which of the following is subtracted from income to arrive at a person's adjusted gross income?
   - (A) Tax credit
   - (B) IRA contribution
   - (C) Real estate taxes
   - (D) Medical expenses

3. Homeowner's insurance typically does NOT cover
   - (A) damage from a lightning strike.
   - (B) equipment used to run a business from home.
   - (C) theft.
   - (D) damage from the weight of snow on a roof.

4. Mary retired after thirty years. She will receive $4,000 a month before taxes in pension benefits from her former employer for the rest of her life. What type of pension plan does her former employer have?
   - (A) Defined-contribution plan
   - (B) Defined-benefit plan
   - (C) Guaranteed plan
   - (D) Simplified employee pension plan

5. The asset that a borrower puts up as repayment for a loan should the borrower default is known as
   - (A) capital.
   - (B) credit.
   - (C) conditions.
   - (D) collateral.

6. Which of the following is taxable income?

   (A) Child support payments

   (B) Interest from municipal bonds

   (C) Tips

   (D) Damages received as a result of a lawsuit against a convicted drunk driver

7. Which of the following types of life insurance has no cash value?

   (A) Variable life

   (B) Universal life

   (C) Whole life

   (D) Term life

8. Using the rule of 72, approximately how long will it take to double $4,000 invested at 3 percent?

   (A) Eight years

   (B) Twelve years

   (C) Eighteen years

   (D) Twenty-four years

9. If a person was concerned about inflation during retirement, that person would be best investing in

   (A) deferred annuity.

   (B) fixed annuity.

   (C) variable annuity.

   (D) life income.

10. A broker lends securities to a client who wishes to sell them now and buy them back later. This is known as a

    (A) margin call.

    (B) market order.

    (C) short position.

    (D) maintenance margin requirement.

11. Which of the following is an example of closed-end credit?

    (A) Buying a pair of shoes at a shoe store

    (B) A mortgage

    (C) Buying a piece of furniture at a department store

    (D) Paying for a doctor's services with a check

12. Which of the following provisions of health insurance policies is the most beneficial for policy holders?

    (A) Internal benefits

    (B) Service benefit

    (C) Fixed dollar benefit

    (D) Assigned benefits

13. A bond has a face value of $10,000 and a bond quote of 95 percent. What is the price of the bond?

    (A) $950

    (B) $5,000

    (C) $9,500

    (D) $10,500

14. Self-employed persons may lower their income tax by deducting which of the following expenses?

    (A) Self-employment tax

    (B) Health insurance

    (C) Contribution to a Roth IRA

    (D) Their state's excise tax

15. When is it better to return a leased vehicle rather than buy it when the lease is up?

    (A) When the market value is less than the residual value

    (B) When the car has reached its capitalized cost

    (C) When the lease rate increases more than 5 percent

    (D) When the end-of-lease payment is higher than the appraisal

16. Which of the following is classified as a long-term financial strategy?

    (A) Saving for a down payment on a house

    (B) Saving for a child's college education

    (C) Buying a new car

    (D) Paying off the $11,000 balance on a credit card

17. Which of the following is considered a high-risk investment?

    (A) Treasury bonds

    (B) Growth stocks

    (C) Blue chip stocks

    (D) Real estate

18. An example of a current liability is a/an

    (A) electric utility bill.

    (B) home mortgage.

    (C) car loan.

    (D) eighteen-month installment loan for a new washer and dryer.

19. The cost of operation of a vehicle includes

    (A) depreciation.

    (B) registration.

    (C) sales tax.

    (D) maintenance.

20. Joint tenancy with right of survivorship is a way to

    (A) avoid paying federal inheritance tax.

    (B) avoid probate.

    (C) ensure that property is not part of an estate for tax purposes.

    (D) divide up an estate equally among all heirs.

ANSWER KEY AND EXPLANATIONS

1. A		5. D		9. C		13. C		17. B
2. B		6. C		10. C		14. B		18. A
3. B		7. D		11. B		15. A		19. D
4. B		8. D		12. B		16. B		20. B

1. **The correct answer is (A).** Under the Bankruptcy Abuse Prevention and Consumer Protection Act of 2005, those who file for bankruptcy must enroll in credit counseling before filing for bankruptcy and in a credit education course after filing for bankruptcy. The debtor pays for both. It's a federal law, but the federal government doesn't pay for the programs, so choice (B) is incorrect, as is choice (C), a state program. Choice (D) is also incorrect.

2. **The correct answer is (B).** Adjusted gross income is income after certain reductions have been subtracted. A contribution to a filer's IRA is one of the items that are used. Choices (C) and (D) are subtracted from adjusted gross income after it has been found. Choice (A), tax credit, is subtracted directly from the amount of tax owed.

3. **The correct answer is (B).** Choice (A), lightning; choice (C), theft; and choice (D), damage from the weight of snow, are typically covered by homeowner's insurance policies. Equipment used in a business operated out of residence is not covered by a homeowner's policy, so choice (B) is the correct answer.

4. **The correct answer is (B).** The scenario describes a defined-benefit plan, choice (B). A defined-contribution plan, choice (A), specifies the contribution of the employer, but not the level of benefits the employee will receive at or during retirement. Choice (C), guaranteed plan, is in essence what a defined-benefit plan is, but that's not the correct term, so it's not the answer. Choice

(D), simplified employee pension plan, known as a SEP, is set up by someone who is self-employed.

5. **The correct answer is (D).** Collateral, choice (D), is an asset that backs a borrower's promise to repay a loan. Choice (A), capital, is the net worth of a borrower. Choice (B), credit, is an agreement under which a person receives money, goods, or services in exchange for a promise to repay the money or pay for the good or service at a later date. Choice (C), conditions, refers to economic conditions that affect a person's ability to repay a loan. Capital, collateral, and conditions along with character and capacity make up what is known as the "five C's of credit."

6. **The correct answer is (C).** Choice (C), tips, is taxable income, but child support, municipal bond interest, and damages from a lawsuit for personal injury or illness, choices (A), (B), and (D), are not taxed.

7. **The correct answer is (D).** Term life insurance has no cash value; it pays only death benefits. Choices (A) and (B) are types of whole life policies, choice (C), and all have cash values; the savings feature is a major advantage of whole life policies. With choice (A), variable life, the cash value as well as the death benefits vary depending on the interest earned in the fund in which it is invested; there is, however, a floor for the death benefits below which they cannot fall. The cash value of universal life, choice (B), also depends on the value of its investments.

8. **The correct answer is (D).** The rule of 72 is: Doubling Time (DT) = 72/interest rate, so 72/3 = 24 years.

9. **The correct answer is (C).** A hedge against inflation is an advantage of variable annuities. Both variable and fixed are investment options of any type of annuity. Variable annuities are invested in equities, which, theoretically at least, increase their returns over time. A fixed annuity, choice (B), is invested in bonds and mortgages; the rate of return is fixed, so increasing inflation will eat into the income. Choices (A) and (D) are types of annuities rather than investment options.

10. **The correct answer is (C).** The question prompt describes taking a short position, choice (C). Choice (A), a margin call, is a call from a broker to a client asking the client to increase the amount of money in his or her account for stock bought on margin; a margin call occurs when the price of the stock falls below the initial margin requirement, or percentage of the stock price invested by the client. The amount of the additional money fulfills the maintenance margin requirement, choice (D). Choice (B), a market order, is an order to buy or sell a stock at the best available price.

11. **The correct answer is (B).** Choices (A), (C), and (D) are all examples of open-end credit, which is a line of credit used for a series of purchases over time and for which the borrower is billed regularly; amounts of repayment vary depending on charges. Closed-end credit is a loan used for a single purchase and must be repaid within a certain period; payments are made regularly and in equal payments.

12. **The correct answer is (B).** A service benefit, choice (B), states the services that the insured will receive, whereas choice (C), fixed dollar benefit, states the amount of money for each service, that is, procedure. A service benefit is better because if a procedure costs more than the fixed dollar amount, the patient has to pay the difference. Choice (A), internal benefits, is a distracter meant to seem like a possibility, but it is nonexistent. Choice (D), assigned benefits, gives the insurance company the authority to pay the doctor, lab, or hospital directly.

13. **The correct answer is (C).** To find the price of a bond, use the formula: Bond Price = Face Value × Bond Quote: $10,000 × 0.95 = $9,500.

14. **The correct answer is (B).** A self-employed person can take a deduction for health insurance. Choice (A) is Social Security. Every worker must pay this tax, and it is not deductible; a self-employed person pays at a rate of 13.3 percent in Social Security and Medicare taxes. A Roth IRA, choice (C), is tax-deferred and has no impact on income tax. Choice (D) is a tax that is paid on certain goods such as gas, tires, and communication services; it is a state and federal tax and is not deductible (like a sales tax is deductible).

15. **The correct answer is (A).** There is no profit to be made on a car that you'll pay more to the dealer to buy than you'll be able to sell in the marketplace, so choice (A) is the best answer. Choice (B) makes no sense because the capitalized cost is the price that the dealer puts on the car to lease it; it is typically 96 percent of the list price. Choice (C) also doesn't make sense because according to the question, the lease is over; also, the lease rate is set when the lease is signed, so it doesn't go up or down over the life of the lease. Choice (D), the end-of-lease payment, has to be paid regardless of whether the lessee buys the car at the end of the lease; this is a provision of an open-end lease, not a closed-end lease.

16. **The correct answer is (B).** Saving for a child's college education, choice (B), is considered a long-term financial strategy. Choice (A), saving for down payment, and possibly choice (D), paying off a large credit

card debt, are medium-term strategies. A medium-term strategy typically takes more than a year, but less than five. Choice (C), buying a new car, is a short-term strategy.

17. **The correct answer is (B).** Growth stocks, choice (B), are high-risk investments compared to the other investments listed. Growth companies are expected to grow more rapidly than the overall economy; therefore, they have a higher rate of return. However, the higher the return, the greater the risk. Treasury bonds, choice (A), are among the most secure investments that a person can make. Blue chip stocks, choice (C), are also safe investments. Choice (D), real estate, entails a moderate amount of risk.

18. **The correct answer is (A).** A current liability is one that must be paid off within a year. Typically, an electric bill, choice (A), must be paid immediately. Choices (B), (C),

and (D) are noncurrent liabilities, though the installment payments due this year for the mortgage, car loan, and new appliances are current liabilities.

19. **The correct answer is (D).** All the answer choices relate to vehicles, but choices (A), (B), and (C)—depreciation, registration, and sales tax—are part of the cost of ownership. Choice (D), maintenance, is part of the cost of operation of a vehicle.

20. **The correct answer is (B).** Property owned as a joint tenancy with right of survivorship passes to the surviving owner or owners without having to pass through probate court. Choice (A) is incorrect because there is no federal inheritance tax, though some states do levy an inheritance tax. Choice (C) describes an irrevocable trust, and choice (D) describes the per capita division of an estate.

FOUNDATIONS OF PERSONAL FINANCE

A person's life typically intertwines nonfinancial and financial goals. In order to achieve nonfinancial goals such as having a satisfying career, a happy marriage, and a family, a person typically needs a certain amount of money. The amount depends on what satisfies a person. One person may only be satisfied with a 20-room mansion, while another may be perfectly happy in a studio apartment. Financial planning is managing one's money in order to achieve economic satisfaction.

Financial Goals

Financial goals involve consumption and savings; consumption may be current or future. What do you need/want now and what will you need/want at some later time? Therefore, financial goals can be categorized as (1) short-term, (2) intermediate, and (3) long-term; they may also be categorized as (1) consumable product, (2) durable product, and (3) intangible purchase. An example of the last is earning a bachelor's degree.

Financial goals change in importance as a person moves through each stage of the life cycle. For example, a couple in their 20s may be saving and investing to get married and buy a house; in their 30s, their financial priority shifts to providing for their growing family, which may include moving to a larger home. However, while the emphasis may have shifted to intermediate priorities, the couple needs to keep their eyes on saving and investing for their retirement. Areas that require people to set financial goals include (1) debt, (2) insurance, (3) investing, (4) retirement, (5) estate, and (6) career.

Budgeting

Once the goals are set, a person needs a plan to achieve them, that is, a budget that allocates money to different items, such as rent or mortgage payments, food, utilities, and savings. The budgeting process is typically done on a monthly basis and includes the following steps: (1) estimating income, (2) allocating for fixed expenses, (3) allocating for variable expenses such as car repairs, (4) allocating for savings, (5) allocating for an emergency fund. The next two steps are ongoing, entering the actual amounts next to the estimated amounts in order to see variances between budgeted and actual, and then analyzing the monthly results to determine how accurate the original budget was and what needs to be changed in order to stay on track to achieve the financial goals.

Financial Statements

Corporations have financial statements, and individuals, couples, and families can have financial statements as well. The first item should be a balance sheet, which lists assets minus liabilities (debt) to show net worth. Assets include (1) liquid assets—cash and anything that can be quickly turned into cash—(2) real estate, (3) personal property, and (4) investments. Liabilities are both short-term, that is, less than one year, and long-term, also called noncurrent liabilities.

The second type of statement is a cash flow statement; it shows inflows and outflows of money, or what came in and what went out. Inflows include salaries, interest, and dividends. A cash flow statement is a useful tool for planning a household budget.

Cash Management

Should savings be kept in a savings account or a CD? Should it be deposited in a commercial bank online or at a credit union? These are questions that are part of deciding a cash management system, a way to have cash, or the equivalent, handy for regular purchases and for emergencies.

The typical places to hold cash are (1) regular checking accounts, (2) interest-bearing checking accounts, (3) savings accounts, (4) money market deposit/demand accounts, (5) money market mutual funds, (6) certificates of deposit (CD), and (7) Series EE and Series I U.S. government savings bonds. The first four have no restrictions on withdrawals. Mutual funds typically have restrictions on the number of checks that may be written each month, and CDs carry a penalty for early withdrawal.

Institutional Aspects of Financial Planning

Deciding on the institutions, that is, financial services organizations and professionals, that a person will need is also part of financial planning. The choices of depository institutions include (1) commercial banks, both bricks-and-mortar and online; (2) savings and loan associations; (3) mutual savings banks; and (4) credit unions. Other companies that provide financial services include (1) life insurance companies, (2) mutual funds, (3) finance companies, (4) mortgage companies, (5) brokerage houses, and (6) financial planners and investment advisors.

Financial planners are licensed and regulated by the Certified Financial Planner Board of Standards, Inc. Not all financial planners who call themselves by this title are licensed, so a person looking for a financial advisor should be aware of this. An investment advisor is a legal term, and investment advisers are regulated by either the Securities and Exchange Commission (SEC) or a state securities regulator, depending on the amount of assets the person manages. Stock and bond brokers are regulated by the Securities and Exchange Commission (SEC). They must register with the SEC and also be members of the Financial Industry Regulatory Authority (FINRA).

There are a number of laws that regulate the securities industry. Some are federal laws such as the (1) Securities Exchange Act of 1934 that resulted from the abuses of the stock market and the crash of 1929; (2) Maloney Act of 1938 that requires that trade associations for the securities industry register with the federal government; (3) Investment Advisers Act of 1940 that requires those advising people about buying and selling securities register with the SEC; (4) Securities Investor Protection Act of 1970 that protects investors from losses caused by actions of their brokers such as failure to warn their clients of impending problems with a company; (5) Sarbanes-Oxley Act of 2002 that deals with corporate financial disclosures; and (6) Dodd-Frank Act of 2010 that resulted from abuses by financial institutions during the first decade of the twenty-first century, which caused the Great Recession.

Time Value of Money

Time value of money is the increase in an amount of money as a result of interest earned on it. It is the future value of money calculated at a certain rate of interest over a certain period of time. Analyzing yield—percentage return on investment—and time period is important in determining where to save and invest. The formula for annual compounding is $FV = PV(1 + i)^n$, where i equals interest and n equals the number of years.

What if a person has a certain goal in mind, such as having $20,000 for a down payment for a condo in four years? To determine how much to invest to achieve a certain amount, the person needs to work backwards to find the present value of money, that is, the current value for a future amount based on a certain rate of interest and certain period of time. The process is called discounting and the formula is $PV = FV/(1 + i)^n$, where i equals interest and n equals the number of years.

Weighing opportunity cost is also part of determining how much to save and invest and where. Opportunity cost is the answer to the question: What will a person give up now in order to have more later? In terms of investments, opportunity cost may also be gauged as amount of risk versus amount of return.

CREDIT AND DEBT

The world—at least the United States—seems to run on credit today. Mailing a package at the post office? Use a credit card. Buying tickets to the movies? Use a debit card. Buying furniture at a department store? Use the store's charge card and be eligible for one-year deferred payment. From paying for a fast-food meal to buying a new car, a person never needs to have cash on hand, just a credit or debit card. With all the ease of using credit, it may take something as disastrous as bankruptcy to bring home the fact that credit comes with a price.

Consumer Credit

Consumer credit is use of credit by individuals, that is, an individual's promise to pay later for the use of a good or service now. The reasons for using credit are many: (1) convenience, (2) the ability to consume more than could be afforded based solely on income, (3) as a hedge against inflation, and (4) for emergencies. The disadvantages of using credit are also many: (1) the temptation to spend more than a person has, (2) the consequences of overspending, (3) the cost of credit, and (4) limitation on future spending power because of the cost of credit for past purchases.

Types of Credit

Closed-end credit is credit used for a specific purchase for a specific period and for a specific amount of money, such as purchasing a vehicle on a three-year loan. Closed-end credit may be in the form of (1) installment sales credit, (2) installment cash credit, and (3) single lump-sum credit. Repayment for the first two is in regular amounts over a period of time.

Open-end credit is a line of credit that enables a consumer to make a series of purchases over a period of time as long as the consumer doesn't go over the amount of the line of credit. The consumer must repay the amount in regular payments, but the payments may be of varying amounts as long as the payments meet the minimum amount stated by the card issuer. This is also known as a revolving credit account. Some stores, such as a cleaner, for example, may offer customers regular charge accounts: the customer charges purchases during the month, and then is sent a bill at the end of the month that is due in full.

Open-end credit instruments include (1) credit/smart cards, (2) a debit card, and (3) a home equity line of credit. A store gift card is similar to a debit card, but it carries a prepaid amount that once exhausted ends the usefulness of the card. A travel and entertainment card must be paid in full each month, unlike credit cards, which can be paid in installments.

Applying for Credit

In qualifying a person for credit, a creditor looks for the five C's of creditworthiness: (1) character, (2) capacity, (3) capital, (4) collateral, and (5) conditions. That last is outside the control of the consumer applying for credit; "conditions" refers to the stability of the person's job and employer.

A creditor checks an applicant's credit score, known as a FICO score, which considers (1) length of credit history, (2) on-time payment history, (3) current amounts owed, (4) types of credit in the credit history, and (5) inquiries from new credit sources. If a person has a low score, there are ways to improve creditworthiness: (1) pay bills on time, (2) don't move debt from one creditor to another, (3) don't open new credit accounts, and (4) reduce credit card balances. It's also important for consumers to check their credit scores annually and correct any mistakes.

Bankruptcy

The Bankruptcy Code was established in 1978 and underwent a major overhaul in 2005. At that time, the Bankruptcy Abuse Prevention and Consumer Protection Act of 2005 was hailed as an important measure to ensure that people do not use bankruptcy court as a revolving door that allows them to spend without a thought to the future, go into overwhelming debt, file for bankruptcy to escape paying off their debts, and then do it all over again.

There are two forms of personal bankruptcy: straight bankruptcy and the wage-earner plan. Straight bankruptcy is filed under Chapter 7 of the Bankruptcy Code, and wage-earner bankruptcy is filed under Chapter 13.

Chapter 7/Straight Bankruptcy

As part of Chapter 7 bankruptcy, a debtor must enumerate for the court his or her assets as well as list creditors with the amounts owed and the debtor's income, property, and monthly expenses. In Chapter 7, the debtor must sell most of his or her assets. Exceptions allow the debtor to keep part of his or her equity in a home or personal property such as a car or truck. In addition, Social Security payments and unemployment compensation may be exempted, as well as equipment used in skilled work.

Most debts are wiped clean, but the price is more than losing many or most of one's assets. Credit reports carry notice of Chapter 7 bankruptcies for ten years. A Chapter 7 bankruptcy can be used only once every eight years.

Chapter 13/Wage-Earner Plan

As part of Chapter 13 bankruptcy, the debtor does not have to sell his or her assets to pay debts. Instead, the debtor works out a plan with court approval to pay off current debts with future earnings over a five-year period. This form of bankruptcy is used only for debtors with a regular income. Credit reports carry Chapter 13 bankruptcies for seven years.

Additional Provisions of the 2005 Act

The 2005 Act puts the following requirements on filers:

- Debtors must undergo credit counseling before filing for bankruptcy.
- Debtors must take a financial education course after entering bankruptcy.

The debtor is required to pay for both. Other costs involved in filing for bankruptcy include court costs, trustees' fees and costs, and attorneys' fees.

In general, certain debts and payments survive a bankruptcy:

- Income taxes
- Alimony payments
- Child support payments
- Student loans
- Any debts deliberately contracted with the idea of filing for bankruptcy
- Court awards, such as restitution of embezzled funds or damages awarded as a result of driving while under the influence of alcohol. Court awards may be discharged in a Chapter 13 filing, but not in Chapter 7.

The Effects of Filing for Personal Bankruptcy

As noted above, the consequences of filing for bankruptcy are far more than losing one's materials assets. Bankruptcy records follow the filer around for seven or ten years. This can affect a person's ability to qualify for credit or a job and to buy insurance.

MAJOR PURCHASES

The largest purchase that consumers typically make is a home. The next largest is a vehicle, but consumer durable goods also have hefty price tags. Comparison shopping involves a trade-off in time versus money, but it is a smart strategy when thousands of dollars are involved. Buying decisions—whether for cars or stocks—involve the same basic steps: gathering information, evaluating alternatives, determining what a person is willing to pay, and paying/financing the purchase.

Auto

As part of gathering information for the purchase of a vehicle, the buyer needs to identify the reasons that he or she wants or needs a car. Is it for recreational driving or is it needed for commuting to work or school or both? Is it for one person, a young couple without children, a growing family, or a family of teenagers with backpacks and sports equipment? The answers to these questions can help answer other questions as well, such as size, options (mechanical, convenience, and aesthetic), and price.

The next big questions to consider are whether to buy or lease a car, and if buying, whether to buy a new or used car. In signing a lease, the lessee agrees to pay a small upfront fee—the security deposit—and monthly payments for use of the vehicle over a period of time. Vehicle leases usually run for three, four, or five years, and at the end of the lease, the lessee may buy the car. Otherwise, the car must be returned to the lessor.

Evaluating Leasing Versus Buying

Leasing a car rather than buying a car on credit reduces the initial outlay and also incurs smaller periodic payments. An additional benefit to leasing a car is intangible. The lessee may be able to lease a car that is more expensive than what the lessee could afford to buy. However, this can be a negative because a more expensive car depreciates more, and finance charges may be higher. A lessee also has no equity in the vehicle. However, the lessee is required to pay for maintenance, mileage over the amount stated in the leasing agreement, some types of repairs, and a penalty for breaking the lease, that is, turning the car in early.

In choosing to lease a car, the buyer has two possibilities: closed-end and open-end. The closed-end lease assumes that the lessee will keep the car in good condition and will drive a predictable number of miles a year, typically 12,000 miles. At the time of the leasing, the lessor estimates a residual value for the car. The residual value is the market value minus depreciation—the decrease in the value of the vehicle in the marketplace based on age, miles driven, and condition. If, when the vehicle is turned in, it is worth less than the estimated resale, or residual, value, the lessor is the loser. Because the risk is on the lessor, monthly payments are usually greater under a closed-end lease than under an open-end lease.

Open-end leasing is more often used by companies than by individuals. With an open-end lease, the risk is on the lessee because the lessee must pay the difference between the residual value and the actual market value of the vehicle at turn-in time. How many miles driven over the contractual amount plus the overall condition of the vehicle affect its resale value. The appraised value—what the vehicle is worth at resale—is also called the realized value. The lessee may be owed a refund if the realized value of the returned vehicle is greater than or the same as the residual value. However, the lessee may have to make an end-of-lease payment if the realized value is less than the residual value. All this should be spelled out in the contract, including a reasonable residual value.

In evaluating leases, a consumer should note (1) the capitalized cost, (2) interest rate, (3) amount of monthly payments, (4) number of monthly payments, (5) the residual value of the vehicle at turn-in time, and (6) the early lease termination fee. The capitalized cost may be listed as the gross capitalized cost, which is the total price of the vehicle plus any other charges included in the cost of the lease, such as finance charges, taxes, and insurance. The adjusted capitalized cost is the gross capitalized cost minus any payments at the time the lease is signed. *Capitalized cost reduction* is the term used for the payments that reduce the gross capitalized cost.

To determine whether to buy or lease, a comparison can be made based on three basic pieces of information: (1) initial costs, (2) monthly payments, and (3) final expenses to pay off the lease. Even considering the time value of money, that is, the interest earned on the difference between the smaller amount of the periodic payments on the lease and the larger amount of payments on the car loan, the buyer typically comes out better.

Determining Purchase Price

If a buyer decides to buy rather than lease, the question becomes whether to get a new or a used vehicle. Some buyers purchase only used cars because of the depreciation factor. The greatest depreciation occurs in the first two or three years of ownership, so these buyers prefer to purchase cars that are two or three years old. The price of a used car is determined by (1) mileage, (2) condition,

(3) features and options, and (4) demand in the marketplace for the make and model. To determine the price that a buyer is willing to pay, he or she may check the prices in car ads and online dealers as well as *Edmund's Used Cars* and *Kelly Blue Book.* On the lot, a buyer should also check the "Buyers Guide" sticker on the car. One item to look for is whether the car is sold "as is" or is still under warranty. Any used car should be checked by the buyer's mechanic to ensure that it is in good working condition.

If the decision is to buy a new car, a buyer should become familiar with the following information:

- *Monroney Sticker Price:* Price that includes the base price, manufacturer's installed options with manufacturer's suggested retail price, transportation charge from the manufacturer to the dealer, fuel economy

- *Base Price:* Price without the options

- *Invoice Price:* Cost to the dealer, which is less than the sticker price

The invoice price is the key item in negotiating for a new car. The difference between the sticker price and the invoice price is the amount available for negotiation.

Financing

In analyzing financing options, a buyer should consider (1) down payment, (2) annual percentage rate (APR), (3) finance charge, and (4) length of the loan. The larger the down payment, the less the risk of paying off a loan on a car that is worth less than what is owed.

Cost of Ownership and Cost of Operation

The cost of ownership includes (1) taxes on the vehicle, (2) vehicle insurance, (3) vehicle registration with the state, (4) depreciation, and (5) the finance charges associated with buying on credit, if the vehicle is not bought for cash.

The cost of operation includes (1) buying gas, (2) doing regular maintenance, and (3) replacing brakes, tires, and other major parts as needed. There may also be other charges, such as renting a garage or space in a parking lot.

Car Warranties

Manufacturers provide warranties on new cars. The warranties are limited by miles driven, number of years, and the parts covered. A typical warranty is 3 years or 36,000 miles. In terms of parts covered, the drive train, engine, and transmission as well as basic parts are covered. Used cars may or may not have warranties, but this information must be stated in the "Buyers Guide."

Housing

Like buying or leasing a vehicle, housing has its own question: rent or buy. Each has its advantages and disadvantages, and each requires identifying needs and wants as well as opportunity costs and trade-offs. Factors that come into play in the decision are assumptions about (1) whether housing prices will increase or decrease; (2) whether returns on financial investments will remain steady, fall, or rise in the future; and (3) what potential tax advantages will be. Because of the costs involved in buying and selling housing, the time that the buyer expects to remain in the home is also a factor.

The Advantages and Disadvantages of Renting

The advantages of renting are (1) mobility, (2) little or no personal or financial responsibility for maintenance or repairs, and (3) the lower initial cost of paying only a security deposit. The disadvantages are (1) inability to derive financial benefits from ownership (tax deductions, increasing equity stake), (2) the likelihood of rent increases over time, and (3) lease restrictions on use of the rental property.

The Advantages and Disadvantages of Home Ownership

Advantages of buying include (1) tax deductions for mortgage interest and property taxes, (2) capital gain that is probably not taxable because of tax adjustments, and (3) fewer restrictions on how the property can be used. Disadvantages are (1) limited mobility, (2) costs associated with maintenance and repairs, (3) high initial costs, and (4) loss of potential interest earned on the money used for the down payment and closing costs. Buying makes better economic sense in the long term, though renting in the short term means lower initial costs.

Types of Housing

Housing that may be rented or purchased falls into several categories. The first category—an apartment—is a rental-only property, whereas the others may be bought as a principal residence or as rental property for an investment.

- *Apartment:* Rental unit in a rental building, though a multifamily dwelling may have a resident owner living in one unit and renting out other units; no financial advantages to the renters

- *Single Family:* A stand-alone dwelling

- *Multifamily:* Multiple housing units within one roofline such as duplex, semidetached housing, or townhouse

- *Condo, or Condominium:* An individually owned unit in a building in which all owners share ownership of common areas such as the lobby and the land under and around the building; owners pay real estate taxes on their units and their shares in the common areas

- *Co-op, or Co-operative:* Ownership of the underlying corporation that entitles the buyer to a lease on a unit; unlike for condos, property taxes are included in the monthly fee

- *Manufactured Home:* Mobile home and prefabricated home; the former may be transported to a site and installed permanently; the latter is partially assembled in a factory and transported to a site where it is permanently installed and assembled completely

In choosing the type of housing to buy, a buyer should consider two sets of factors. One set is the property's (1) size, (2) condition, (3) location, and (4) potential for an increase in value over time. Balanced against these factors are the (1) price, (2) current mortgage rates, (3) amount possible for a down payment, and (4) cost of mortgage payments, insurance, and property taxes on a monthly basis.

The Buying Process

Purchasing a home includes a number of steps, some of which are undertaken simultaneously: (1) determining an amount to spend, (2) determining the down payment, (3) identifying a location in which to begin the housing search, (4) choosing a real estate agent, (5) identifying a property, (6) making an offer and negotiating the price, (7) signing the contract, (8) employing a home inspector, (9) choosing a lender, (10) providing the fee and documentation for a mortgage application, (11) title search by the buyer's attorney, (12) property appraisal by the lender, (13) mortgage approval, (14) choosing title insurance, and (15) the closing.

One issue for buyers in determining the mortgage amount is whether to prepay points, which are a lender's discount on the mortgage. Each point is equal to one percent of the amount of the loan. The more points that are prepaid, the lower the mortgage amount and payments. Prepaying points makes more sense the longer the buyer intends to live in a property.

Types of Mortgages

Longer-term mortgages have smaller monthly payments. Also, larger down payments result in small monthly payments. An overriding factor may be the interest rate. Rates on long-term mortgages such as the 30-year fixed will be higher than a 5/1 adjustable rate mortgage (a fixed rate for 5 years that then adjusts every year). The lender assumes the risk that rates will rise over 30 years and the lender will be out the increase in the value of the money that he or she would otherwise receive from lending at the higher rates.

Depending on the amount of money that the buyer has to put down, the mortgage lender may require that the buyer take out mortgage insurance. Mortgage insurance is a guarantee that the lender will not lose money if the buyer defaults on the loan. The Federal Housing Administration (FHA) and the Veterans' Administration (VA) are government insurers of mortgages. Each has certain requirements in terms of type of housing being purchased, amount of down payment, and income. There are also private mortgage insurance companies. Private mortgage insurance (PMI) is required if a buyer has less than 20 percent to put down on a home. Once the equity reaches 20 percent, the PMI is discontinued.

Most mortgages are referred to as conventional mortgages and the terms typically run 30, 20, or 15 years. The mortgaged property serves as collateral. A conforming conventional mortgage is one that is guaranteed by Freddie Mac or Fannie Mae. A nonconforming mortgage is one that cannot be sold to Freddie or Fannie because it doesn't meet the organization's requirements, for example, it is over the loan threshold. Fannie and Freddie are government-sponsored entities (GSE) that buy mortgages from mortgage lenders in order to return money to the mortgage market and encourage homeownership.

The major formats for mortgages are fixed rate and adjustable, or variable rate, but there are a variety of other types of mortgages as can be seen in the following chart:

Type	Advantage	Disadvantage
Fixed Rate: 30, 20, 15; Conventional	• Same monthly payment over the life of the mortgage • Amount of the payment that goes to the principal increases and the amount paid toward interest decreases over time; known as *amortization* • Ability to prepay the balance in order to refinance	• Locked into a rate when mortgage rates are falling • Costs of refinancing to take advantage of falling rates • May have prepayment penalty
Adjustable Rate: 3/1, 5/1, 7/1; Two-Step; Hybrid	• Fluctuation of monthly payments annually after a set number of years at a fixed rate, though some types of ARMs may reset monthly or semiannually: interest rate adjustment period • Initially lower rate than fixed mortgages • Protection against huge increases in interest rate from one adjustment period to another: rate cap • Limit on increases in monthly payments: payment cap	• Need to rebudget with each rate adjustment • Payment cap: may result in lower monthly payments than needed to repay the loan by the end of the loan term; may require large payment at end of loan term, longer term, or higher monthly payments later: negative amortization • Cost of refinancing if mortgagor chooses to prepay and refinance
Balloon ARM: 3-, 5-, 7-Year Term	• Fluctuation of monthly payments after each interest rate adjustment • Payment of interest only so the payments are lower	• Entire principal owed at the end of the loan term
Interest-Only	• Initial period when interest only is paid on the loan	• Repayment period begins and mortgage is amortized over the new shorter period; increase in monthly payments
Convertible ARM	• Allows conversion of ARM to fixed rate after a certain time • Rate set in original ARM mortgage	• Requires fee • Refinancing may be better deal depending on interest rate and fee
Balloon Loan: 5, 7	• Fixed monthly payments over the life of the loan	• Large payment required at the end of the term of the loan
Graduated Payment Mortgage; Graduated Equity Mortgage	• Fixed rate • GEM: increases applied to principal only • Useful for young homebuyers who expect to see their incomes increase	• Amount of payments increases over time
Shared Equity; Shared Appreciation	• Large personal down payment unnecessary • Part of the down payment is borrowed in return for giving a share in the property to the lender	• At end of term, lender gets a share of the profit on the property in proportion to the amount lent—regardless of whether the borrower sells the house

In reviewing ARMs, it's important to check the rate cap and the payment cap. The annual rate cap limits the amount that a rate may increase, and it may also put a floor on how far a rate may decrease. Typically, an annual cap is no more than 2 percentage points an adjustment period. An aggregate rate cap, or life-of-loan cap, is the limit that a rate may rise during the life of the mortgage. Typically, this is no more than 6 percentage points overall.

Additional Financing Options

There is a variety of financing possibilities in addition to mortgages, such as the buy-down, which is a form of financing that builders of a newly constructed house offer to buyers. The builder pays a percentage of monthly mortgage payments for the first year or two.

When a buyer is also a seller and hasn't closed on the sale of his or her current home, but must close on the new home, the person will use a bridge loan, also called a swing loan or temporary loan.

Many homeowners use the equity in their homes to pay for other large-ticket items such as a new car or a kitchen renovation. These lines of credit are in essence a second mortgage on their homes and add a monthly payment to their budgets.

Reverse mortgages take money out of the equity in a home. They are available only to homeowners over 62 years of age. The money is repaid at the time of the sale of the home.

Over the course of a 30-year mortgage, interest rates may fluctuate wildly depending on the state of the economy. Refinancing may be a good option if a new mortgage can reduce the interest rate by at least 1 percentage point. In calculating whether to refinance, a homeowner should consider the cost of refinancing, which may be $2,500, versus the amount of savings in monthly payments to determine how long it will take to make up the refinancing costs.

Selling a Home

Up to this point, we've been talking about buying housing, but selling housing also requires information gathering and a series of decisions. The first decision, of course, is to sell and the next is at what price. The local government assessment for tax purposes is one indicator, and another is the recent sale prices of comparable homes, known as comps, in your immediate area. A real estate agent can help with the latter. However, depending on the situation in the local market, a seller might hire an independent appraiser to help set the price. The appraiser will consider (1) comps, (2) demand for housing, and (3) current mortgage rates, which may encourage or discourage homebuyers. If the buyer is looking for a mortgage, the potential lender will have the house appraised. The appraisal value for the mortgage must be at or above the asking price or the mortgage will be denied.

Sellers typically use real estate agents, though about 13 percent choose to save the real estate commission and sell their homes themselves. An advantage of using an agent who belongs to the Multiple Listing Service (MLS) is that the property can be shown by a number of different agencies. Using an agent also means that a property will be showcased on the agency's Web site.

There are a variety of agencies for selling real estate. (1) A buyer agency represents buyers only. (2) A dual agency may represent both buyers and sellers. (3) To avoid conflicts of interest in a dual agency, an agent may use a designated agent in the same office to represent either the buyer or seller in the transaction. (4) A transaction brokerage or facilitative brokerage does not represent the interests of either a seller or a buyer, but simply shows properties to a buyer and assists in the general real estate process.

Listing agreements may be of four types. (1) The exclusive right to sell ensures that the broker will receive a commission regardless of who finds a ready, willing, and able buyer. (2) The exclusive agency listing guarantees the broker a commission only if the agent sells the property; if the seller sells it, the broker receives no commission. (3) An open listing gives the right to market a property to a number of realtors. Only the broker who finds the ultimate buyer receives a commission. (4) In a net listing, the broker receives the difference between the final sales price and the price that the seller wants. The type of agency and the type of listing agreement depend on a state's real estate laws.

Other Major Purchases

A vehicle is probably the most expensive single item that a household will buy next to housing. Vehicles are part of a category known as consumer durables that includes such large-ticket items as washers, refrigerators, dishwashers, large-screen TVs, and home surround-sound systems. If these are paid for out of savings, they represent a loss of interest income. If they are paid for on credit, they represent a limitation on future spending. Their operation, maintenance, and repair represent additional expense and ultimately future cost of replacement.

In considering the purchase of a consumer durable, a buyer should consider timing—certain items go on sale at certain times of the year—store, brand, rebates or other deals, and product information such as energy efficiency or safety.

Comparison shopping is an important aspect of getting a good deal on consumer durables. The Internet makes it easy and cost-effective. It is also a convenient way to make purchases—as long as the buyer is dealing with a reputable site. The federal Mail Order Merchandise Rule applies to online merchants as well as catalogue companies and requires that a merchant ship ordered goods within 30 days unless the buyer agrees to a delay. One important issue for consumers to check when considering an online purchase is the site's return policy if the good is unacceptable.

Warranties

A warranty is a guarantee made by the manufacturer or distributor of a good that the good is as represented and will be replaced or repaired if defective. There are implied and express warranties and full and limited warranties.

Goods sold "as is" carry neither an implied nor an express warranty, but all other goods carry an implied warranty and may also carry an express warranty. An implied warranty generally warrants the merchantability and/or fitness for purpose of a good. The former guarantees that the product is of a quality, grade, and value similar to the quality, grade, and value of similar goods, and the latter guarantees that the good is suitable for the ordinary purpose for which the seller sells it and the buyer will use it.

An express warranty is generally in writing and either a full warranty or a limited warranty. A full warranty includes the following provisions:

- If a reasonable number of attempts at resolving the defect have not succeeded, the consumer is eligible for a replacement or a full refund.

- During the period of the warranty, the consumer cannot be charged for parts, labor, or charges to ship the good for repair.

- Whether the registration card was submitted or not does not affect the full warranty.

- The full warranty applies to subsequent owners after the original owner.

- The full warranty in no way affects the scope of the implied warranty.

A limited warranty is any warranty that does not include all these provisions. Extended warranties and service contracts are usually not a good buy.

TAXES

Everyone loves to hate taxes, but they pave the highways, pay air traffic controllers, provide scholarships, repair bridges, fund cancer research, offer seed money to alternative energy companies, provide security at home and abroad, construct a social safety net, and so on. Not only the federal government, but also state and local governments fund their services through direct taxation. The federal government taxes earnings and wealth (and some purchases such as tires and gasoline, for example, through excise taxes); states and many municipalities tax purchases as well as earnings and property; and most states also tax wealth through an estate tax.

Payroll Deductions

Payroll deductions may be mandatory or voluntary. Mandatory deductions include:

- Social Security Taxes, known as FICA (Federal Insurance Contributions Act):
  - o *FICA-O:* Old Age Survivors Benefit
  - o *FICA-M:* Medicare

- Federal income tax

- State income tax if applicable

- County/city wage tax if applicable

- State workers' compensation insurance fund if applicable

Voluntary non-tax deductions may include payment for or contributions to:

- Health insurance

- Dental insurance

- Life insurance

- Long-term care insurance

- 401(k) or 403(b) pension plans

Income Taxes

When you say "income tax," most people think of the federal income tax, but forty-three states tax personal income, and some cities also tax income under a city wage tax provision. The types of income that are taxed are:

- *Earned:* Salary, commissions, tips, bonuses

- *Investment:* Dividends from stock, interest from bonds, rent from properties

- *Passive:* Income from limited partnership or forms of limited participation in a company

Among additional types of income that are taxes are the following:

- Alimony (which is added to the payee's income, but subtracted from the payer's income)

- Capital gains or losses on investments

- Jury duty pay

- Lottery and gambling winnings

- Monetary prizes and awards

- Social Security benefits (partial)

- Pensions

- Rent

- Royalties

- Travel allowance

- Unemployment compensation

While the previous list makes up a person's gross income, there are also certain amounts that are not included in gross income. These include (1) exclusions such as veterans' benefits and military allowances, (2) tax-deferred income such as contributions to traditional IRAs and Keoghs, and (3) tax-exempt income such as the income from state and municipal bonds. These, plus such things as alimony payments, result in a person's adjusted gross income. This is the base amount on which people pay their federal income taxes minus further deductions. The gross adjusted income is the amount used to compute these additional deductions such as mileage for medical visits and contributions to charity.

Deductions

Taxpayers may take the standard deduction if the amount of their deductions is less than the amount of the standard deduction for any given year. The amount of the standard deduction is computed each year by the federal government. If their deductions will be greater than the amount listed as standard for any given year, taxpayers itemize.

The categories of deductions that taxpayers can itemize are:

- State and local taxes (typically income, real estate, and personal property, but taxpayers may deduct their state's sales tax if it is greater than their income tax)

- Interest (investment, mortgage, home equity line of credit)

- Non-reimbursed medical and dental expenses, including mileage to and from appointments

- Charitable contributions

- Non-reimbursed moving expenses related to a job relocation if it is 50 miles from the current location

- Non-reimbursed business expenses such as uniforms

- Losses from casualty and theft

Certain requirements must be met in order to deduct some of these items. For example, to qualify for a medical deduction, the amount of non-reimbursed expenses must be greater than a certain percentage of adjusted gross income; the percentage is reviewed annually by the federal government.

Tax credits may also reduce a person's tax bill. These are subtracted from the taxes owed rather than subtracted from the amount on which taxes are computed. The filer computes the tax owed and then subtracts the full amount of the tax credit.

Withholding

Employees of companies receive a W-2 at the end of the year to verify their earned income and to file their income tax returns. The W-2 indicates the amount of taxes withheld from each paycheck. The amount of the withholding is based on the employee's W-4, which indicates the number of exemptions. Exemptions result in deductions of a certain amount per person from adjusted gross income. The more exemptions, the less tax is withheld. A single person may take more than one exemption if the person expects to have a large tax payment when the return is filed.

Self-employed persons do not fill out W-4s, nor do they receive W-2s. Instead they file and pay estimated taxes each quarter. If they work for a number of other self-employed people or for companies, they receive 1099s at the end of the year from each person or company with the amount of income they received.

Tax Planning/Estimating

In addition to self-employed persons, those who have income other than salaries and wages may also have to file and pay estimated taxes. There are ways to minimize a person's tax bill.

Paying Estimated Taxes

Because the federal government needs revenue to function, it requires that taxpayers with passive income estimate their whole year tax bill and pay it in quarterly installments. These include taxpayers who receive interest on bonds and savings accounts, stock dividends, royalty payments, and retirement or pension plans that are paid out as a lump sum rather than as an annuity. The government allows some leeway in figuring the tax each year. A filer isn't charged a penalty and interest if he or she makes estimated payments that total more than the previous year's tax even though the estimated payments are less than the actual tax for the current year. Also, a taxpayer will not be penalized if he or she pays estimated taxes that are 90 percent or more, but less than 100 percent of the current year's income tax.

Tax Planning

There are a variety of legal ways that can be used to reduce taxes. Among them are the following:

- *Municipal Bond:* Tax-exempt interest under state and federal governments

- *State Bond:* Tax-exempt interest under the federal government and many states (capital gains may be taxed under certain states)

- *Primary Residence:* Tax-deductible property taxes and mortgage interest

- *Home Equity Line of Credit:* Tax-deductible interest on the loan

- *Real Estate as an Investment:* Depreciation

- *Traditional IRA, Keogh, 401(k), Tax-Deferred Annuity:* Tax-deferred investment vehicles for retirement that reduce current adjusted gross income on which taxes are computed

- *529 Savings Plan for Children's Education:* Tax-deferred investment that provides a tax credit

- *Flexible Spending Account for Health Care or Child Care:* Reduction of current adjusted gross income

- *Self-employment:* Advantages in expensing certain costs that owners would otherwise have to pay themselves, such as health insurance premiums and non-reimbursed medical bills

- *Gift Program:* Up to $12,000 per donor per recipient

- *Trust:* Provides income for a beneficiary who is usually at a lower tax rate than the person who used his or her own money to set up the trust

- *Tax Credits:* Variety of such credits, e.g., earned income, child care, home energy

INSURANCE

Insurance is about protecting against possible financial loss. Different kinds of insurance protect against different kinds of financial-related loss such as loss of life, loss of income, and loss of property. Insurance is a way to pool risk over a large number of people so that it becomes predictable. There are four strategies for risk management: (1) risk reduction (taking preventive actions), (2) risk avoidance (eliminating the risk), (3) risk retention (agreeing to have some exposure to a risk), and (4) risk transfer (purchasing insurance).

Life Policies

Buying life insurance has two benefits: it is a way to put aside money in savings and it provides financial security for dependents when the insured dies. In estimating whether a person needs life insurance and if so, how much, it's important to consider the person's life circumstances. A single working person in her mid-twenties probably doesn't need life insurance, whereas a married father in his forties with a wife who doesn't work outside the home and three children needs life insurance.

There are four general ways to determine life insurance needs. (1) The easy method is seven years (the amount of time it is estimated to take for a family's finances to adjust after the death of a breadwinner) times 70 percent of that person's income equals the amount of life insurance required for a typical family. (2) The DINK method estimates life insurance for a "dual income, no kids" couple by including funeral expenses and halving expenses like a mortgage. (3) The nonworking spouse method multiples ten years times $10,000 a year for child-related costs such as child care on the assumption that the nonworking spouse will need to go to work. (4) The family need method itemizes a family's actual costs.

Types of Life Insurance

A life insurance policy may be a term policy, meaning "temporary," or a permanent policy. A term policy is bought for a certain number of years. For beneficiaries to collect, the insured must die within that period; there is no savings buildup with a term policy. There are a variety of permanent policies and each accrues cash: whole life, straight life, ordinary life, and cash value life.

Type	Format	Characteristics
Term: No Savings Buildup	Renewable	• Renewable at the end of the term • Increased premiums as the insured ages
	Multiyear Level/ Straight	• Same premium for the life of the term
	Convertible	• Provision that enables the insured to convert a term to a whole life policy
	Decreasing: Group Mortgage Life and Credit Life	• Same premium for the life of the policy, but decreasing coverage
Permanent: Savings Buildup	Whole Life/ Straight Life/ Ordinary Life/Cash Value	• Same premium for the life of the policy • In comparison to term policies, higher rate in the early years of a whole life policy (term policies increase premiums with each renewal) • Increasing cash and decreasing death benefits over the life of the policy
	Limited Payment Life	• Payment of premiums over a certain period such as twenty years • Insured covered until he or she dies • Payment of death benefits on death of insured • High premium
	Adjustable Life	• Premiums and coverage adjustable as the circumstances of the insured change
	Universal Life	• Flexible premium payments and flexible payment schedule, that is, the insured may pay any amount at any time as well as skip payments • Policyholder receives a report identifying (1) cost of the protection, (2) management costs, and (3) interest on the cash value of the policy (rate of return)
	Variable and Variable-Universal	• Fixed premium • Investment of cash value in a selected portfolio of stocks, bond, money market funds • Cash value may decrease if portfolio loses value • Policyholder receives report similar to universal life • Variable-universal: flexible premiums, investment of cash value in portfolio of stocks, bonds, money market funds
Term	Group Life	• Employer-sponsored life insurance • High premiums

Payment of death benefits may come as a (1) lump-sum payment, (2) limited installment payment, (3) life income option, or (4) payment of interest on the value. For the latter, the insurance company serves as trustee.

Riders or Special Provisions

The face amount of a policy is its amount of death benefits. The policyholder indicates the beneficiary or beneficiaries. Other things a consumer should consider are the (1) cash value, (2) surrender value, (3) premium, and (4) dividend. Special provisions, or riders, can also be added to life insurance policies. These may include accelerated death benefits, accidental death benefits, cost-of-living adjustment, disability waiver of premium, grace period, guaranteed insurability option, settlement option, and survivorship life.

Property and Liability Policies

Property insurance shields people from risks to their homes, vehicles, and personal property such as furniture, electronics, and jewelry. Liability insurance protects people from losses as a result of damage done to other persons or to the property of others. Liability is responsibility under the law for the financial cost of another person's losses or injuries. The cause is usually negligence. Both homeowner's insurance and automobile insurance carry liability coverage.

Homeowner's Insurance

Homeowner's insurance covers:

- The main dwelling and any associated buildings on a property and also typically landscaping

- Additional living expenses for temporary housing should the property be uninhabitable for a period of time due to damage

- Personal property, such as jewelry and electronics, both at home and while the insured is traveling with the items

- Liability for injuries sustained by a guest or for damage done to property by the insured

Personal property insurance typically places a limit on the amount of the replacement value for items. However, a personal property floater can be added to increase replacement limits; the additional coverage increases the premium.

Liability coverage includes payment for medical care for injured parties as well as legal costs for the insured should that person be sued by the injured party or the person's estate.

Typically, losses from natural disasters such as floods and earthquakes are not covered by standard homeowner's insurance, but consumers can buy endorsements to cover these potential risks. Endorsements are changes to the basic policy.

Renters don't buy homeowner's insurance; they purchase renter's insurance, which covers their personal property, additional living expenses, and liability.

In determining how much insurance is needed, a homeowner needs to consider whether to purchase a policy that pays actual cash value or replacement value. The former pays out the current cost of an item minus depreciation, and the latter pays the current cost of an item without factoring in depreciation and is, therefore, more expensive to purchase.

Auto Insurance

All states require drivers to carry some minimum level of auto insurance and more than half of the states have what is called a no-fault insurance system. With no-fault insurance, an injured motorist is paid by his or her own insurance company through a personal injury protection policy regardless of who caused the accident. Payments include medical costs, lost income, and other expenses related to the accident. Depending on the state, a motorist may also need to carry residual bodily liability coverage and property damage coverage.

Three factors affect the cost of auto insurance: (1) make and model of the vehicle; (2) rate base, also known as the rating territory; and (3) driver classification. The newer and more expensive the vehicle, the higher the premium. A person who lives in a city, parks on the street, and drives 50 miles to work every day pays more than a person who lives in the suburbs, parks in her own garage, and only drives around town on the weekends. The risk for theft, damage, or an accident are greater for the first driver than the second one, so the premium is higher. A person's driving record, age, gender, and whether he or she is married or single also affect how much the person pays for car insurance.

Health, Disability, and Long-Term Care Policies

The goal of health, disability, and long-term care insurance is to lessen the financial burdens of providing health care for one's self and family.

Health Insurance

Basic health insurance provides protection for hospital stays, surgery, and medical care. In addition to (1) hospital expense, (2) surgical expense, and (3) physician expense insurance, all of which are typically bought as part of a single insurance policy, a consumer may buy (4) major medical insurance, which pays expenses over and above the basic insurance coverage, typically up to $1 million. Major medical policies have a deductible—an amount that the insured must reach before benefits kick in—and a coinsurance provision through which the insured pays some of the cost of care after the deductible has been reached. Other types of medical coverage include (5) prescription drug coverage and (6) dental and (7) vision insurance.

Health insurance policies typically have the following components:

- *Exclusions:* Those conditions that are not covered under a policy such as pre-existing conditions or pregnancy

- *Guaranteed Renewability:* Renewal year after year as long the premium is paid

- *Internal Limits:* Restricts the amount of payments regardless of the costs

- *Co-payment:* Insurance pays most of the charges, but the insured pays some even after the deductible has been met for the year

- *Benefit Limit:* A ceiling on the amount of costs the insurer will pay

- *Assigned Benefit:* Ability of the insured to sign payment over directly to the doctor or hospital

- *Service Benefit:* Pays by services rather than by cost of services

- *Coordination of Benefits:* Enables the insured to receive benefits from primary and secondary insurance up to the total cost of the procedure or hospital stay, but no more than the total

There are a variety of health insurers: (1) private insurance companies, (2) Blue Cross and Blue Shield, (3) health maintenance organizations (HMOs), and (4) preferred provider organizations (PPOs). The latter may be an exclusive provider organization (EPO) or a point-of-service (POS) organization.

Medicare with its Medigap, Medicare Advantage, and drug prescription plans provides health coverage to those over 65 and people with certain disabilities.

Disability Insurance

Disability insurance provides income for workers who are unable to work because of a disability. What constitutes a disability depends on the insurance policy. Some policies consider a worker to be disabled if the worker cannot perform any type of work, whereas other policies consider a worker disabled if the worker cannot perform the duties of a specific job, and other policies consider a worker disabled if the worker cannot perform work-related duties or duties similar to the work for which the person was trained.

There are several types of disability insurance: (1) group disability policies purchased through an employer, (2) individual disability policies purchased from private insurance companies, (3) Social Security, (4) state workers' compensation funded by employers, (5) disability provisions in employer-sponsored pension plans, and (6) accident, or dismemberment, insurance. To be considered disabled under Social Security guidelines, the disability must last for twelve months and the person must be unable to perform any type of work.

Long-Term Care Insurance

Long-term care insurance is intended to provide custodial care for those who cannot take care of themselves. Typically, policies are sold to those 60 and over who are concerned about becoming ill and disabled as they age. The benefits of a long-term care policy typically kick in when a person cannot perform some of the activities of daily living, which are bathing, dressing, being continent, eating, and being able to get around alone.

Premiums are expensive and become more expensive the older a person is when first purchasing this insurance. If a person is worth more than $1 million or less than $150,000, buying long-term care insurance is probably not a good deal. The wealthier person can buy whatever care is needed, and the poorer person may qualify for government assistance to pay for long-term care.

INVESTMENTS

Every type of investment involves some amount of risk—and hopefully reward. Before beginning an investment program, it's important that a person be aware of his or her risk tolerance—the ability to endure losses in savings and investments during downturns in the economy. The lower one's risk tolerance, the safer the savings and investment vehicles should be. The higher one's risk tolerance, the riskier the savings instruments and investments can be. However, there is a risk-return trade-off. The lower the risk, the lower the returns, and the higher the risk, the greater the returns.

What constitutes risk? Risk factors typically are (1) inflation, (2) changes in interest rates, (3) bankruptcy of a business that a person has invested in—either directly or through stocks and/or bonds, and (4) market risk either because of changes in the economy (systematic risk) or the behavior of investors (unsystematic). Similar risk factors can affect investments made in foreign countries.

As part of developing an investment plan, it's important to consider asset allocation, that is, where to save and invest one's money and diversification within asset classes. The goal of both asset allocation and diversification is to lesson risk. Another important consideration in developing an investment plan is determining goals and where a person is on a timeline to reach those goals. The life-cycle or life stages approach divides a person's life into stages such as young adult or retirement and indicates the type of risk and assets that a person should be acquiring at that point.

Saving Accounts and Money Markets

A savings account is one of the safest places to put money—as long as the account has less than $250,000 and the savings institution is insured by the Federal Deposit Insurance Corporation (FDIC). However, savings accounts and similar savings instruments—certificates of deposit (CD), money market deposit accounts, and money market demand accounts—offer low interest rates because of this safety factor. Interest rates on money market accounts are slightly higher than on savings accounts and about the same as short-term CDs, which are lower than the rates for longer-term CDs.

Bricks-and-mortar and online commercial banks, credit unions, and savings and loans associations offer these savings vehicles. A person may add any amount at any time to both savings accounts and money market accounts and withdraw money at any time by using an ATM or a withdrawal slip. However, a depositor may be limited in the number of checks that can be written in any one month on a money market account. Savings accounts don't have a check-writing feature.

CDs are bought for a certain amount of money for a fixed length of time and generally at a fixed interest rate. A person cannot add to the amount in a CD, and if the CD is redeemed before the specified period, the buyer pays a penalty.

Money market deposit and demand accounts should not be confused with money market funds, which are another form of savings and investing for people with low risk tolerance, but more risk tolerance than those who invest in the other four investment vehicles. Money market funds are sold by securities brokers and mutual fund companies for $1 a share. The funds are not FDIC-insured, but the funds are principal protected, so that the value of a share does not drop below a dollar. Investors make money on the interest that their shares earn. Money market funds are considered safe investments because the companies that manage them buy low-risk, short-term bonds from both the federal government and municipal governments and from well-established corporations. Mutual funds allow check writing, but usually require a minimum amount per check.

Stocks, Bonds, and Mutual Funds

In considering buying and selling stocks, bonds, and mutual funds, a consideration is the amount of capital gains or capital losses that the investor will have. Both will affect the investor's income taxes: losses positively and gains negatively for the investor. The exceptions are tax-exempt federal and municipal bonds.

Stocks and Stock Mutual Funds

A stock is a form of equity, or ownership, in a corporation, and a stock mutual fund is a collection, or portfolio, of stocks from a number of companies. Stocks are classified as common or preferred; both convey voting rights on those who buy them, but preferred stockholders receive their dividends before common stockholders.

The price of a share of stock is the value of the stock. Value can rise and fall as a result of a number of factors including downturns in the economy; natural disasters and hostilities that affect production; changes in government policies, even fear of policy changes; and the financial performance of the individual company. While stocks are a risky investment, they produce higher returns than the previously discussed investment vehicles. However, some stocks are riskier than others, for example, a blue chip company like IBM® that produces quarter after quarter of strong financial results is less risky than a start-up company selling geothermal power or a tablet to compete with Apple®.

When an investor buys shares in a stock mutual fund, the person is buying shares in the company's portfolio of stocks. Buying into a stock mutual fund rather than buying individual stocks diversifies a person's risk because the person has less exposure to any one company. However, the value of the stocks in the portfolio can decline just as the value of individual stocks can decline and, on any given day, may be worth less than the amount spent to buy the shares in the mutual fund. Mutual funds like individual stocks are not government-insured.

Both individual stocks and stock mutual funds may pay dividends. There are two major strategies for buying and selling stocks: long-term and short-term. Long-term investing strategies include (1) buy-and-hold, (2) dollar-cost averaging, (3) dividend reinvestment, and (4) direct investment. Short-term strategies include (1) day trading, (2) buying on margin, (3) selling short, (4) trading in options, and (5) market timing.

In determining what stocks to buy, a person should consider (1) earning per share, (2) price to earnings (P/E) ratio, (3) whether or not there is a dividend, (4) dividend yield, (5) total return, and (6) annualized holding per yield.

Bonds and Bond Mutual Funds

Bonds are investments in debt, not equity, and are sold by corporations and the federal and municipal governments. The company or government entity that issues the bond must pay bondholders annual interest payments for the term of the bond. At its maturity, the face value of the bond must be repaid to bondholders. The annual rate of return on a bond is its yield and is fixed when the bond is sold. Bonds are considered safer investments than stocks, and there are also tax advantages to owning government bonds. U.S. Treasury bonds are exempt from state and local taxes, and municipal bonds are generally exempt from state and local taxes for residents of the state.

Like stocks, the price of bonds may rise or fall, depending on a number of factors similar to those affecting the price of stock. However, the most important factor is the credit quality of the entity that issues the bond. The stronger the company is perceived to be by a bond-rating agency—the more likely that it will make interest payments and repay the face value of the bond—the lower the interest rate. The risk is considered less. The lower the credit rating is, the riskier the investment and the higher the rate. Bond rating agencies like Moody's Investors Services rate the quality of bonds as (1) high-grade, (2) medium-grade, (3) speculative, and (4) default.

A corporate bond may be a (1) mortgage, (2) debenture, (3) subordinated debenture, (4) convertible, or (5) high-yield. A debenture is an unsecured bond, and a mortgage bond is one that is secured by assets of the issuer. A subordinated debenture is unsecured. A convertible bond enables the bondholder to convert the bond into a certain number of shares. A mortgage bond is the least risky and the high-yield is the most risky and, therefore, has the highest rate of return.

Governments—federal, state, local, and agencies—issue bonds to fund operations. Federal issues may be Treasury bills, Treasury bonds, Treasury notes, Treasury STRIPS, and Treasury inflation-indexed bonds. State and local government and agencies, such as transit authorities, secure a common type of municipal bond called a general obligation bond.

Unlike bonds, bond mutual funds don't promise a fixed rate of interest nor is the investor's money repaid. However, buying a bond mutual fund is safer than buying individual bonds because an investor's risk is spread across a number of corporations or government entities. It is also cheaper to buy into a bond fund than to buy individual bonds because they are typically very expensive. Bond mutual funds specialize in a category of bonds: corporate, federal government, or municipal government.

Sources of Information

It's important to become an informed investor and there are many sources that can be consulted for price-to-earnings ratios, past performance, factors that may affect future performance, and similar information:

*   Corporate annual, quarterly, and K-10 reports

*   Investment advisors licensed by the SEC who provide guidance for a fee

*   Business magazines, newspapers, and newsletters

*   Financial news programs on TV and cable

*   Investor subscription services accessed on the Internet

*   Free Internet sites

*   Stock exchange sites

RETIREMENT AND ESTATE PLANNING

Retirement planning involves reviewing assets and living expenses. The increasing average life expectancy, the declining power of the dollar over time because of inflation, and the inadequacy of Social Security and pensions to cover living expenses are three major reasons to begin planning and saving for retirement early. Among the assets to consider in retirement planning are housing and investments, including life insurance and annuities. Downsizing living space and housing expenses has become a goal of many baby-boomers as they move into retirement.

Funding Retirement

There are a variety of ways to fund retirement. A person has no control over some, that is, whether the companies he or she works for during a career have pension plans and what type. There are other methods of retirement funding that a person can choose to invest in, such as a 401(k) plan and an IRA.

Company Pension Plans

Company pension plans are either (1) defined benefit or (2) defined contribution plans. With a defined benefit plan, the company states the monthly benefit that retirees will receive. An amount of money is invested annually for each employee to generate enough dividends and interest to pay the stipulated benefits when the employee retires. The Pension Benefit Guaranty Corporation (PBGC) insures defined benefit plans in case the company goes bankrupt.

With a defined contribution plan, a company does not specify the amount of monthly benefits. The company contributes a certain amount of money into each employee's investment account with a brokerage firm. The amount of benefits depends on how well the investments perform. When employees retire, they can convert the amount in the account to an annuity.

To receive benefits, an employee must vest in the pension plan, that is, work for the company for a certain period of time in order to be eligible for pension benefits. However, under the Employee Retirement Income Security Act (ERISA), an employee is vested in his or her own contributions immediately. The Pension Protection Act of 2006 set up a schedule of vesting for employer contributions. Retirement age for company plans is typically 65; however, employees typically can retire with "55 and 10," that is, at age 55 with 10 years of service.

In addition to monetary benefits, company pension plans may also include medical and disability benefits. Some have a survivorship benefit as well.

Additional Company Retirement Plans

Pension plans are becoming more and more rare. Instead, companies are offering:

- *401(k) for Private Companies, 403(b) for Nonprofits, and 457 for Public Institutions:* Contributions taken from salary/wages; tax-deferred; employers may contribute depending on how the plan is set up

- *Profit-Sharing:* Similar to a defined contribution plan, though the company only contributes in years when there is a profit

- *Employee Stock Option Plan (ESOP):* Employer's contributions in company stock

- *Simplified Employee Pension Plan (SEP):* Immediate vesting; may be set up as a pension plan or a tax-deferred IRA; also used by self-employed persons

- *Savings Incentive Match Plan for Employees (SIMPLE):* Either an IRA or 401(K); company matches employees' contributions

An ESOP is problematic if employees tie up all or most of their retirement funding in their company's stock. If the company's stock value and earnings fall either because of issues with the company or because of a decline in its market sector or in the general economy, retirees can find their income severely curtailed.

Individual Retirement Plans

In addition to company-sponsored retirement plans, there are ways that individuals may save and invest for retirement.

- *Individual Retirement Account (IRA):* Tax deferred until the income is withdrawn; penalties for early withdrawal, that is, prior to age 59½ except for large medical expenses, higher education costs, and first-time homebuyers; certain income and contribution restrictions apply

- *Roth IRA:* Contributions are taxed, but not the income at time of withdrawal as long the account has been in existence for at least five years and the person is 59½; certain contribution restrictions

- *Rollover IRA:* Consolidated contributions from several retirement plans; may occur as a person moves from company to company

- *Spousal IRA:* IRA for a spouse who is a homemaker

- *Keogh (HR-10) Plan:* For contributions from self-employment income only

- *Annuity:* Plan purchased from an insurance company to provide income during retirement; ends only with the person's death

There are several types of annuities: (1) fixed, although the insurance company may change the rate annually, and (2) variable for which the rate of return varies with the performance of the funds in which the insurance company invests. An annuity may also be (3) immediate, which begins to pay income immediately, or (4) deferred, which begins paying at some later date. Income is tax-deferred until an annuity begins to pay it out.

Social Security

Social Security covers almost 100 percent of U.S. workers. Exceptions are federal government employees, survivors of those killed during active duty who are covered under the Department of Veterans Administration, and employees covered under the Railroad Retirement System. To be eligible for Social Security, a worker must work 40 quarters and earn a minimum amount, which is adjusted upward each year to keep pace with increases in wages nationwide. A person's actual amount of benefits is based on the person's actual earnings up to the contribution ceiling for each year.

A person can begin collecting Social Security at age 62, but benefits are reduced by about 25 percent. Beginning with those born between 1943 and 1954, full retirement age is 66. After 1954, full retirement age edges up to 67 for those born in 1960 and later. In addition to the retiree, the person's family may also be eligible to receive Social Security benefits under certain conditions:

(1) a spouse if 62 or older, (2) a spouse if under 62 but taking care of the retiree's child under age 16, (3) a former spouse age 62 or older and children up to age 18, (4) children ages 18 and 19 if they are full-time high school students, and (5) children over 18 with disabilities. Whether a spouse opts to take his or her own benefits or the benefits of the retiree should depend on which spouse will receive the greater benefit.

If a person begins receiving Social Security benefits before full-retirement age and continues to work, benefits are reduced by $1 for every $2 that the person receives over a certain amount. Once a person attains full-retirement age, there is no retirement test of earnings. Up to 85 percent of Social Security benefits can be taxed depending on a recipient's other income. Depending on the rate of inflation, the government calculates an annual cost-of-living adjustment.

Estate Planning

Estate planning isn't just a matter of making sure that a person leaves directions for disposition of his or her assets after death. It's also a matter of building up those assets during one's lifetime. Financial planning is part of a life plan, and planning for the transfer of those assets is part of a death plan.

Wills

Whether a person is part of a married or nontraditional couple or single, everyone needs a written will. Dying without a valid will is called dying intestate. There are various formats for wills, but in some states, a person may be required to leave one half of his or her assets to the spouse:

- *Simple Will:* Leaves everything to a spouse

- *Traditional Marital Share Will:* Leaves half the adjusted gross estate to a spouse and the other half in trust to the spouse or to children or others

- *Exemption Trust Will:* Leaves all but a small amount to a spouse; the remainder is put in trust for the spouse

- *Stated Dollar Amount Will:* Leaves certain amounts to a spouse and to other heirs (leaving a percentage rather than an amount is a safer strategy because the value of an estate may rise or fall depending on economic factors)

Under a simple will, estate taxes are paid at the time of the death of the person whose will is being probated. Under a traditional marital share, half the taxes are paid on the death of the person and half at the death of the spouse. The exemption trust results in almost no tax payment for the estate or at the time of the death of spouse. Taxes may vary under a stated dollar amount depending on how much is left to a spouse.

If there is no requirement to leave half an estate to the spouse or the spouse has predeceased, there are two ways that an estate may be divided: per capita and per stirpes. The former divides the assets into equal shares, and the latter divides everything equally among the branches of a family.

An important part of writing a will is selecting the executor who will see that the terms of the will are carried out and also that all debts are paid and taxes are filed and paid, if required. If a person dies intestate, the court appoints an executor. Those with children or spouses unable to care for themselves or anyone else who is a dependent would also have to name a guardian to handle affairs for the person or persons.

Trusts and Estates

A trust is a legal arrangement by which one party holds the rights to property for the benefit of another party or parties. A testamentary trust is one that comes into existence upon the death of the owner of the property and is typically used for the support of dependent children; minor children cannot inherit property directly. A living trust, formally known as an inter vivos trust, is set up during the lifetime of the owner of the assets and as a result does not require probate. Living trusts are subject to estate taxes, if they are revocable trusts, but not if they are irrevocable. A life insurance trust is a type of living trust that is funded by the proceeds of a person's life insurance upon the person's death.

A trust can also be established by a person for the person's own benefit during his or her lifetime. It is a way to ensure that a person will be taken care of should he or she no longer be able to do so. Trusts can also be set up to (1) provide for the support of a spouse or other dependents, (2) transfer assets without going through probate, (3) reduce estate taxes, and (4) pay estate taxes.

An estate is the sum total of all of a person's assets. How an estate is taxed depends on whether the decedent was married and lived in a community-property state or not. In a community-property state, each spouse owns half of the assets. In a noncommunity-state, individual ownership is recognized, though joint ownership is typical. Joint ownership may be classified as (1) joint ownership with a right of survivorship, (2) tenants in common, and (3) tenancy by entirety. Each has its own tax consequences. Joint ownership with right of survivorship and tenancy by entirety result in no estate tax at the death of the first spouse. Tenants in common also result in no estate tax for a spouse, but if the joint owners are not married, for example, a parent and child, there would be a tax liability.

Life insurance proceeds are not included in an estate if the policy has been assigned to a beneficiary or a trust. Any death benefits from company pensions, profit-sharing, and Keogh plans are not part of a person's taxable estate unless the estate is the payee.

Taxes

The federal government levies a federal estate tax, sometimes called a "death tax," on estates in excess of a certain amount. That amount has varied over the last decade from $1.5 million to $5 million depending on certain temporary tax provisions. Gifting children $12,000 a year ($24,000 for a married couple) is one way to transfer wealth from one generation to the next without incurring taxes. In addition to federal estate taxes, states also levy estate taxes. Rates vary from state to state.

States also levy inheritance taxes on the heirs of a decedent's estate. Tax rates, exemptions, and other provisions vary from state to state. In general, the larger the estate and the greater the distance between decedent and heir, the higher the inheritance tax rate. Gifting during one's lifetime is one way to avoid having an heir pay an inheritance tax. The federal government doesn't levy an inheritance tax.

POST-TEST ANSWER SHEET

1. Ⓐ Ⓑ Ⓒ Ⓓ   13. Ⓐ Ⓑ Ⓒ Ⓓ   25. Ⓐ Ⓑ Ⓒ Ⓓ   37. Ⓐ Ⓑ Ⓒ Ⓓ   49. Ⓐ Ⓑ Ⓒ Ⓓ

2. Ⓐ Ⓑ Ⓒ Ⓓ   14. Ⓐ Ⓑ Ⓒ Ⓓ   26. Ⓐ Ⓑ Ⓒ Ⓓ   38. Ⓐ Ⓑ Ⓒ Ⓓ   50. Ⓐ Ⓑ Ⓒ Ⓓ

3. Ⓐ Ⓑ Ⓒ Ⓓ   15. Ⓐ Ⓑ Ⓒ Ⓓ   27. Ⓐ Ⓑ Ⓒ Ⓓ   39. Ⓐ Ⓑ Ⓒ Ⓓ   51. Ⓐ Ⓑ Ⓒ Ⓓ

4. Ⓐ Ⓑ Ⓒ Ⓓ   16. Ⓐ Ⓑ Ⓒ Ⓓ   28. Ⓐ Ⓑ Ⓒ Ⓓ   40. Ⓐ Ⓑ Ⓒ Ⓓ   52. Ⓐ Ⓑ Ⓒ Ⓓ

5. Ⓐ Ⓑ Ⓒ Ⓓ   17. Ⓐ Ⓑ Ⓒ Ⓓ   29. Ⓐ Ⓑ Ⓒ Ⓓ   41. Ⓐ Ⓑ Ⓒ Ⓓ   53. Ⓐ Ⓑ Ⓒ Ⓓ

6. Ⓐ Ⓑ Ⓒ Ⓓ   18. Ⓐ Ⓑ Ⓒ Ⓓ   30. Ⓐ Ⓑ Ⓒ Ⓓ   42. Ⓐ Ⓑ Ⓒ Ⓓ   54. Ⓐ Ⓑ Ⓒ Ⓓ

7. Ⓐ Ⓑ Ⓒ Ⓓ   19. Ⓐ Ⓑ Ⓒ Ⓓ   31. Ⓐ Ⓑ Ⓒ Ⓓ   43. Ⓐ Ⓑ Ⓒ Ⓓ   55. Ⓐ Ⓑ Ⓒ Ⓓ

8. Ⓐ Ⓑ Ⓒ Ⓓ   20. Ⓐ Ⓑ Ⓒ Ⓓ   32. Ⓐ Ⓑ Ⓒ Ⓓ   44. Ⓐ Ⓑ Ⓒ Ⓓ   56. Ⓐ Ⓑ Ⓒ Ⓓ

9. Ⓐ Ⓑ Ⓒ Ⓓ   21. Ⓐ Ⓑ Ⓒ Ⓓ   33. Ⓐ Ⓑ Ⓒ Ⓓ   45. Ⓐ Ⓑ Ⓒ Ⓓ   57. Ⓐ Ⓑ Ⓒ Ⓓ

10. Ⓐ Ⓑ Ⓒ Ⓓ   22. Ⓐ Ⓑ Ⓒ Ⓓ   34. Ⓐ Ⓑ Ⓒ Ⓓ   46. Ⓐ Ⓑ Ⓒ Ⓓ   58. Ⓐ Ⓑ Ⓒ Ⓓ

11. Ⓐ Ⓑ Ⓒ Ⓓ   23. Ⓐ Ⓑ Ⓒ Ⓓ   35. Ⓐ Ⓑ Ⓒ Ⓓ   47. Ⓐ Ⓑ Ⓒ Ⓓ   59. Ⓐ Ⓑ Ⓒ Ⓓ

12. Ⓐ Ⓑ Ⓒ Ⓓ   24. Ⓐ Ⓑ Ⓒ Ⓓ   36. Ⓐ Ⓑ Ⓒ Ⓓ   48. Ⓐ Ⓑ Ⓒ Ⓓ   60. Ⓐ Ⓑ Ⓒ Ⓓ

answer sheet

POST-TEST

Directions: Carefully read each of the following 60 questions. Choose the best answer to each question, and darken its letter on your answer sheet. The Answer Key and Explanations can be found following this Post-Test.

1. If a homebuyer has less than 20 percent for a down payment, the homebuyer will
   - **(A)** need to buy mortgage insurance.
   - **(B)** have to apply for an FHA mortgage.
   - **(C)** be turned down by the VA.
   - **(D)** need to come up with 5 percent more of the down payment.

2. One difference between CDs and savings accounts and money markets is that
   - **(A)** the interest rate on a CD varies over time, whereas the interest rate on a savings account or a money market does not.
   - **(B)** money cannot be added to a CD over time, whereas money can be added to a savings account or money market.
   - **(C)** a CD is not FDIC-insured, but the other two are.
   - **(D)** a CD is a good savings vehicle for someone with a low tolerance for risk, but the other two are not.

3. The future value of money is
   - **(A)** inflation adjusted.
   - **(B)** the increase in an amount of money including interest earned over time.
   - **(C)** the value of money in today's marketplace.
   - **(D)** money that is received or paid at some later time.

4. How does inflation affect savings?
   - **(A)** The higher the rate of inflation, the less the interest paid on savings will be able to buy.
   - **(B)** The lower the rate of inflation, the higher interest rates rise.

   - **(C)** Inflation has a neutral effect on savings.
   - **(D)** Taxes minimize the impact of inflation on the interest earned in savings accounts.

5. Which of the following does NOT reduce current tax obligations?
   - **(A)** Roth IRA
   - **(B)** Traditional IRA
   - **(C)** Spousal IRA
   - **(D)** SEP

6. A Chapter 13 bankruptcy remains on a person's credit report for
   - **(A)** five years.
   - **(B)** seven years.
   - **(C)** eight years.
   - **(D)** ten years.

7. Jason graduated from college in June. He started a job later that month that is paying him an average salary for a new employee in his field. He's sharing an apartment with three roommates and has $30,000 in student loans to pay off. What should his immediate financial goal be?
   - **(A)** Paying off his student loans as fast possible
   - **(B)** Setting up a retirement plan
   - **(C)** Buying life insurance
   - **(D)** Setting up a six-month emergency fund

8. In calculating income tax, when are tax credits applied in the process?

   (A) Before calculating adjusted gross income

   (B) To gross income

   (C) After calculating the income tax owed

   (D) Before standard deductions and any exemptions are taken

9. It is more desirable for mortgagors to pay their own property taxes and insurance because

   (A) they will know that the payments are made.

   (B) their property taxes will automatically decrease.

   (C) lenders, unless required by law, don't pay interest on escrow accounts.

   (D) they may be able to get a reduction in insurance rates.

10. In terms of benefits, a term life policy provides

    (A) death benefits, can be borrowed against, and cash if it is a policy that pays dividends.

    (B) death benefits and cash if it is a policy that pays dividends.

    (C) death benefits and can be borrowed against.

    (D) death benefits only.

11. A disadvantage for homebuyers to owning any type of housing is the potential

    (A) for disagreements over association rules.

    (B) decline in housing prices.

    (C) lack of privacy.

    (D) assessment fees.

12. The full retirement age for the purpose of receiving Social Security for those born in 1945 is

    (A) 62½.

    (B) 65.

    (C) 66.

    (D) 67.

13. The benefit from a resource that a person gives up in choosing one option over another is called its

    (A) opportunity cost.

    (B) lost opportunity.

    (C) alternative.

    (D) trade-off.

14. In buying a refrigerator, a consumer might consider which of the following?

    (A) Unit pricing

    (B) Features

    (C) Open dating

    (D) Service contract

15. Which of the following is the effective annual rate of return on a savings account taking into account compounding over a 365-day period?

    (A) FICO

    (B) APR

    (C) AGI

    (D) APY

16. Which of the following allows the fastest access to cash with no penalty for emergencies?

    (A) Regular checking account

    (B) Certificate of deposit

    (C) Series EE bond

    (D) Stocks

17. Jake wants to improve his credit score. Which of the following will help him to do this?

    (A) Take out several new credit cards

    (B) Buy several major appliances using store credit

    (C) Open a savings account and make regular deposits each time he is paid

    (D) Check his credit score regularly

18. Cash management involves

    (A) creating an inventory of assets.

    (B) creating a system whereby a person has cash or near cash on hand for purchases and emergencies.

    (C) establishing an emergency fund.

    (D) establishing financial goals.

19. Which of the following is both a health insurer and a health services provider?

    (A) Health maintenance organization

    (B) Preferred provider organization

    (C) Point-of-service plan

    (D) Fee-for-service

20. Which of the following is a typical rider to a life insurance policy?

    (A) Grace period

    (B) Automatic premium clause

    (C) Cost-of-living protection

    (D) Policy loan provision

21. Nadja was comparing credit cards and decided not to take the card from Acme Bank. Which of the following features signaled to Nadja that Acme's card was not a good choice?

    (A) The grace period was 21 days.

    (B) Interest was charged from the day that a purchase was made.

    (C) The card had an annual percentage rate of 8 percent.

    (D) The annual fee was waived because it was a special offer.

22. Reduction of the principal borrowed over the life of a mortgage is called

    (A) RESPA.

    (B) rate cap.

    (C) escrow accounting.

    (D) amortization.

23. Which of the following is an accurate statement about payroll deductions?

    (A) All payroll deductions are mandatory.

    (B) FICA taxes include Old Age Survivors Benefit and Medicare.

    (C) IRA contributions are taken directly as payroll deductions.

    (D) A worker can have the premium for a non-company–sponsored life insurance policy deducted from his or her paycheck.

24. Under which of the following programs, can an employee who has been terminated or laid off continue health insurance for a period of time?

    (A) HIPAA

    (B) Medigap

    (C) COBRA

    (D) COB

25. Any debt that must be paid within a year is a

    (A) current liability.

    (B) noncurrent liability.

    (C) flexible expense.

    (D) dissavings.

26. Which of the following would be the best source to find a corporation's income statement?

    (A) Cable channel focused on business news

    (B) Newspaper's business section

    (C) Corporation's annual reports

    (D) Business magazine

post-test

27. Which of the following is a reason that a person may withdraw money from an IRA before age 59½ without incurring a penalty?

    (A) To buy a car

    (B) To pay for a college education

    (C) To purchase a vacation home

    (D) For a large-scale home renovation

28. An indemnity health insurance policy is NOT ideal because it

    (A) pays only a specified amount regardless of actual costs.

    (B) does not cover preexisting conditions.

    (C) will not pay you directly, only the health-care provider.

    (D) pays only for regular nonsurgical doctors' services.

29. Sal and Joanna decided against taking out an umbrella policy. This was an unwise decision because an umbrella policy

    (A) covers a home office, and Joanna runs a business out of their house.

    (B) protects against flood damage, and they live in a floodplain.

    (C) would have provided minimal health insurance as well as homeowner's and auto insurance.

    (D) extends liability coverage over and above the limits in homeowner's and auto insurance policies.

30. Jim wants to get a car loan, and a friend who works for a finance company told him he could help him. Why isn't a loan from a finance company a good idea?

    (A) A person has to be a member to get a loan.

    (B) Finance companies charge very high interest rates on their loans.

    (C) Finance companies don't show a borrower the APR for their loans.

    (D) Jim wants to buy his car on Saturday and finance companies take as long as a week to process loan applications.

31. After paying bills, the DeLucas generally have about 25 percent of their disposable income left. What is the amount left called?

    (A) Cash inflow

    (B) Disposable income

    (C) Discretionary income

    (D) Liquidity ratio

32. Estimated taxes are paid

    (A) weekly.

    (B) monthly.

    (C) quarterly.

    (D) twice a year.

33. Which of the following has the shortest maturity?

    (A) Treasury Inflation-Protected Security

    (B) Treasury bill

    (C) Treasury note

    (D) Treasury bond

34. Which of the following adjusts the principal according to fluctuations in the Consumer Price Index?

    (A) Treasury Inflation-Protected Security

    (B) Treasury bill

    (C) Treasury note

    (D) Treasury bond

35. Alexis believes that buying used cars makes more financial sense than buying new cars. He bases his belief on the fact that

    (A) most depreciation of new cars occurs in the first two to three years.

    (B) used cars have better warranties than new cars.

    (C) used cars cost less to operate than new cars because they've been broken in.

    (D) registration costs less for older cars than newer cars.

36. What is one disadvantage of a travel and entertainment card?

    (A) The balance must be paid in full.

    (B) A person can withhold payment regardless of the amount of the disputed charge.

    (C) If the store issuing the card goes bankrupt, the cardholder is out the money he or she spent to buy the card.

    (D) If a card is stolen, the person has two days to notify the issuer without penalty.

37. Which of the following may be deducted in calculating personal income taxes?

    (A) Health savings account contributions for the fiscal year

    (B) Life insurance premiums

    (C) Expenses related to moving to assisted living

    (D) Support for an elderly parent

38. Indemnification means that an insurance policyholder

    (A) is held blameless.

    (B) has a waiting period for coverage.

    (C) agrees not to sue the person who caused an auto accident.

    (D) receives approximately the value of the loss, but no more.

39. When are taxes paid on an estate that was left under a traditional marital share will?

    (A) At the time of the death of the spouse whose will is bring probated

    (B) At the time of the death of the spouse who survived

    (C) No taxes required

    (D) Half when the first spouse dies and half when the second spouse dies

40. According to the technical analysis of stock picking,

    (A) the growth in the overall economy should be a factor in valuing a stock.

    (B) movements in the stock market are totally random.

    (C) the value of a stock is the result of supply and demand.

    (D) future earnings predict a stock's current value.

41. Which of the following forms does a worker complete to indicate the number of exemptions he or she has for tax purposes?

    (A) W-2

    (B) W-4

    (C) 1040

    (D) 1099

42. Stan bought a used car "as is." Although there were no express warranties, he has certain protections under

    (A) an extended warranty.

    (B) implied warranties.

    (C) limited warranties.

    (D) judicial warranties.

43. Achieving financial goals depends on how

    (A) much a person earns and saves.

    (B) much a person earns, saves, and invests.

    (C) well the stock market performs.

    (D) well the economy performs.

44. A qualified pension plan is

    (A) a defined contribution plan.

    (B) taxable at the time that contributions are made.

    (C) guaranteed by the Pension Benefit Guaranty Corporation.

    (D) available only to industries with unions.

45. Which of the following is a retirement plan for self-employed persons?

    (A) SEP

    (B) SIMPLE

    (C) 403(b)

    (D) Keogh

46. Which of the following is true about the sale of a residence?

    (A) The loss from the sale of a home can be deducted from income taxes.

    (B) If it is the first home a person is selling, the person may take a first-time homebuyer's credit.

    (C) An increase of $250,000 over the original price of a home can be excluded when computing the capital gains tax on the sale of the home.

    (D) In a foreclosure, a person loses all rights to claim a capital loss.

47. In a no-fault auto insurance plan state, which of the following is typically required?

    (A) Only property damage insurance

    (B) Only insurance to cover medical expenses

    (C) Only insurance to cover damage and medical expenses of the victim(s) of the accident, not the person who caused it

    (D) Uninsured motorist coverage

48. Paul buys the right to purchase from his broker 100 shares of a stock at $43 a share within 30 days. This is known as

    (A) selling short.

    (B) trading in a call option.

    (C) buying on margin.

    (D) day trading.

49. Which of the following is NOT included when calculating debt-to-income ratio?

    (A) Car loan payment

    (B) Student loan payment

    (C) Mortgage payment

    (D) Payments for utilities

50. What is the money factor in a car lease?

    (A) The amount of money being put down on the lease

    (B) The interest rate being charged

    (C) The amount of each payment

    (D) The number of payments

51. A flexible spending account can be used to

    (A) pay for health care.

    (B) pay for adult day care for an elderly relative.

    (C) put aside money to pay estimated taxes.

    (D) be used for retirement expenses.

52. How do high interest rates influence the economic behavior of individuals?

    (A) High interest rates encourage sell offs by investors.

    (B) High interest rates attract investors.

    (C) High interest rates push down prices, so consumer spending increases.

    (D) High interest rates make using credit cheaper, so consumers take on more debt.

53. Which of the following is a difference between a credit card and a debit card?

    (A) The bank will certify that a person has sufficient funds to cover a purchase with a debit card, but not a credit card.

    (B) A debit card is preloaded with a certain amount, whereas the credit card can be used up to the credit limit on the card.

(C) Losses from a stolen credit card are capped at $500, whereas with a debit card, losses are capped at $50.

(D) With a credit card, there is float between the time a person charges a purchase and the person is billed, whereas with a debit card, the amount of the purchase is withdrawn from the account immediately.

54. Which of the following is NOT taxed as part of an estate?

(A) Traditional IRA

(B) Roth IRA

(C) Irrevocable trust

(D) Testamentary trust

55. The original purpose of the alternative minimum tax was to

(A) ensure that people with a large number of deductions and high incomes pay some amount of income tax.

(B) give a tax break to people with low incomes.

(C) consolidate a number of tax credits, such as child care and health accounts.

(D) adjust the tax burden on the elderly living on limited fixed incomes.

56. Which of the following can reduce the premium for auto insurance?

(A) Collision damage waiver

(B) Antilocking brake system

(C) Late model car

(D) A driver in the assigned risk market

57. Sam is buying a new car, trading in his old car. Which of the following will help him figure out how much the new car will cost?

(A) Residual value

(B) Net replacement value

(C) Capitalization cost reduction

(D) Excess value

58. A will that divides an estate per stirpes divides assets

(A) equally among branches of a family.

(B) into equal shares for distribution.

(C) according to stated amounts in the will.

(D) equally between spouse and children.

59. Manjeet invests in a municipal bond fund for its tax benefit. What is the benefit that he derives from this investment?

(A) The fund enables him to evade paying taxes.

(B) The fund provides him with a tax credit.

(C) The interest earned is tax-exempt.

(D) The interest earned is tax-deferred.

60. Which of the following regulates investment advisers?

(A) State securities regulator

(B) Sarbanes-Oxley

(C) Certified Financial Planner Board of Standards, Inc.

(D) FINRA

ANSWER KEY AND EXPLANATIONS

1. A	13. A	25. A	37. A	49. C
2. B	14. B	26. C	38. D	50. B
3. D	15. D	27. B	39. D	51. A
4. A	16. A	28. A	40. C	52. B
5. A	17. C	29. D	41. B	53. D
6. A	18. B	30. B	42. B	54. C
7. D	19. A	31. C	43. B	55. A
8. C	20. C	32. C	44. C	56. B
9. C	21. B	33. B	45. D	57. B
10. D	22. D	34. A	46. C	58. A
11. B	23. B	35. A	47. B	59. C
12. C	24. C	36. A	48. B	60. A

1. **The correct answer is (A).** Choice (B) is incorrect because the Federal Housing Administration (FHA) doesn't offer mortgages; it insures mortgages. Choice (C) is incorrect because, like the FHA, the Department of Veterans Affairs (VA) doesn't offer mortgages; it insures them. In addition, the VA doesn't require mortgage insurance. Choice (D) is incorrect because there is no requirement for a 25 percent down payment related to mortgage insurance.

2. **The correct answer is (B).** CDs are purchased for a specified amount of money at a specified interest rate for a specified period. Choice (A) is incorrect because the interest rate doesn't vary for CDs, but it does vary over time for savings accounts and money market accounts. Choice (C) is incorrect because all three are FDIC-insured as long as they are less than $250,000. Choice (D) is incorrect because all three are good savings vehicles for people with low risk tolerance.

3. **The correct answer is (D).** Choice (A) doesn't make sense. Choice (B) defines time value of money, not future value of money. Choice (C) misstates the definition of the present value of money: the current value for a future amount of money calculated with a specific interest rate for a specific period of time.

4. **The correct answer is (A).** Inflation reduces the buying power of money, so the higher the rate of inflation, the less the interest earned on savings will buy. Choice (B) is incorrect because the lower the rate of inflation, the lower interest rates are. Choice (C) is incorrect because inflation rates impact interest rates either negatively or positively. Choice (D) is incorrect because taxes minimize the amount of interest that a depositor has available for use, not the impact of inflation.

5. **The correct answer is (A).** A person pays taxes on contributions to a Roth IRA, whereas contributions to traditional IRAs, choice (B), and spousal IRAs, choice (C),

are tax-deductible, and the withdrawals are taxed. Contributions to SEPs, choice (D), are made with pretax income, but earnings are taxed when withdrawn.

6. **The correct answer is (A).** A Chapter 13 bankruptcy filing remains on a person's credit report for five years. Choice (B), seven years, is the number of years that information about the regular use of credit, such as taking out a car loan, remains on a credit report. A person may file for Chapter 7 bankruptcy only once in eight years, choice (C), and a record of a Chapter 7 bankruptcy filing remains on a person's credit report for ten years, choice (D).

7. **The correct answer is (D).** Jason needs some cash to fall back on in case he loses his job, has an accident, or is sick for a prolonged period. Choices (A), (B), and (C) are important, but financial planning involves a series of staged goals. However, he should take advantage of any retirement plan that his employer offers because the employer's contribution is in effect "free" money; it doesn't cost Jason.

8. **The correct answer is (C).** Tax credits are applied after the income tax is calculated, which is after the standard deductions and any exemptions are taken, not before, choice (D). Choices (A) and (B) are actually the same answer and are both incorrect; they are the first step in calculating income tax.

9. **The correct answer is (C).** Even if lenders are required to pay interest on escrow accounts, the interest rate is very low—typically lower than the rate on savings accounts or money market accounts. Choice (A) is true, but not the reason and lenders have departments that deal with escrow accounts. Choices (B) and (D) seem to be too good to be true, and they are too good to be true.

10. **The correct answer is (D).** Term life pays death benefits only. Choice (A) is the description of whole life; it would fit the description of universal life if it stated that

the death benefits were flexible. Choices (B) and (C) are incomplete descriptions of whole life.

11. **The correct answer is (B).** Choice (A), association rules, refers to planned unit developments, condominiums, and co-operatives, not stand-alone homes. Choice (C), lack of privacy, may occur in condos and co-ops, but not stand-alone homes. Choice (D), assessment fees, again applies to forms of ownership other than stand-alone homes that are not part of planned unit developments.

12. **The correct answer is (C).** For the purpose of receiving Social Security, full retirement age for those born between 1943 and 1954 is 66. Choice (A), 62½, is the age at which people may begin taking partial Social Security. Choice (B), 65, was full retirement age for those born prior to 1943. Choice (D), 67, is the age at which those born after 1960 may begin receiving full benefits under Social Security.

13. **The correct answer is (A).** The opportunity cost of choosing one thing over another is the loss of the benefit of what was not chosen. Choosing one item over another may be a lost opportunity, choice (B), but that's not an economic concept, so eliminate it. Choice (C), alternative, also is not an economic concept, so eliminate it. Choice (D) is simply the exchange of one thing for another; there is no value placed on the items, so it doesn't match the definition.

14. **The correct answer is (B).** Choice (A), unit pricing, doesn't make sense because consumers typically buy only one refrigerator at a time. Choice (C), open dating, refers to the "use by" labeling on supermarket items. Choice (D), service contract, is usually not a good buy for consumers because products tend to fail within the first year when they are still under warranty.

15. **The correct answer is (D).** Choice (D), annual percentage yield, assumes that the money—principal and interest—will be left

in the account for 365 days. Choice (A), FICO, stands for Fair Isaac Corporation and is a credit reporting company. Choice (B), APR, stands for annual percentage rate and is the actual yearly cost of funds over the term of a loan including fees and any additional costs. Choice (C), AGI, stands for adjusted gross income.

16. **The correct answer is (A).** When a person needs cash, a regular checking account is the fastest way to get cash—whether by ATM or check. There is no penalty involved—assumed there is no overdraft. Choices (B) and (C) are incorrect because there is a penalty for early withdrawal of both CDs and Series EE bonds. The former is typically a month's interest and the latter is three months' interest. A person may be able to sell stocks quickly, choice (D), assuming it's a day when the stock market is open, but there could be a "penalty" if the stock is sold below the price the person paid for it.

17. **The correct answer is (C).** Although checking a credit score, choice (D), is important to ensure that it is accurate, it won't help that credit score if a person doesn't use credit wisely. Choice (C) provides a way to show that a person can be disciplined when it comes to money. Overusing credit doesn't demonstrate that; both choices (A) and (B) can send up red flags to potential creditors. The more inquiries for new credit that show up, the less responsible the person seems.

18. **The correct answer is (B).** A cash management is a system whereby a person has cash or near cash on hand for purchases and emergencies. Choice (A) is a step in creating a balance sheet. Choice (C) is part of budgeting. Choice (D) is an important foundation for personal finance.

19. **The correct answer is (A).** Health maintenance organizations (HMOs) are both insurers and care providers. Choice (B), a preferred provider organization (PPO), is a

provider, not an insurer, as is choice (C), a point-of-service plan (POS). Choice (D), the full name of which is fee-for-service health insurance (FFS), is an insurer only.

20. **The correct answer is (C).** The cost-of-living protection is a rider that is typically added to a life insurance policy because of the effects of inflation in the long term. Choice (A), the grace period; choice (B), the automatic premium clause; and choice (D), policy loan provision are common parts of a life insurance policy. The first provides a window to pay the premium on a policy without incurring a penalty; the second enables the insurance company to pay the premium from the cash value of the policy should the policyholder not pay the premium within the grace period; and the third enables the policyholder to borrow against the cash value of the policy.

21. **The correct answer is (B).** Choices (A) and (B) can't both be correct. Choice (A), a grace period of 21 days, contradicts choice (B), which is a reason not to take a particular card, all else being equal. Choices (A) and (C) are reasons to take a particular card, all else being equal. However, choice (D), while a good deal for the first year, might not be a good deal in the long term if an annual fee is added after the first year. Nadja should keep this in mind and check to see if an annual fee is added at the beginning of the second year.

22. **The correct answer is (D).** Reduction of the principal borrowed over the life of a loan is called amortization. Choice (A) is incorrect because RESPA stands for Real Estate Settlement Procedures Act and refers to closing costs and the closing process for buying a home. Choice (B) is incorrect because a rate cap is the amount by which the interest rate can increase or decrease over the life of an adjustable rate mortgage. Choice (C) seems correct because of the word "escrow," but an escrow account holds money to pay property taxes and sometimes homeowner's

insurance. The lender sets up the account and deposits part of each month's mortgage payment from the homeowner into the account.

23. **The correct answer is (B).** FICA payroll deductions are the Social Security and Medicare contributions that workers make. Choice (A) is incorrect because some payroll deductions are voluntary. Choice (C) confuses IRAs with 401(k) and 403(B) pension plans; deductions for the last two are deducted, but contributions to IRAs are not. Choice (D) is incorrect; an employee can opt into a company-sponsored life insurance program and have the premium deducted, but this is not true for a non-company–sponsored policy.

24. **The correct answer is (C).** COBRA stands for the Consolidated Omnibus Budget Reconciliation Act of 1986. Under this law, many employers are required to offer terminated and laid-off workers the opportunity to continue their health insurance under the employer's plan. Choice (A), HIPAA, stands for Health Insurance Portability and Accountability Act of 1996, which ensures that workers cannot be required to requalify for health insurance when they change jobs or be charged more for health insurance than current employees. Medigap, choice (B), refers to supplemental health insurance for people covered under Medicare. Choice (D), COB, stands for coordination of benefits, a provision of health insurance policies that enables a policyholder to receive reimbursement from several health insurance policies up to 100 percent of allowable medical costs that the person spent.

25. **The correct answer is (A).** A current liability is one that must be paid within a year. A noncurrent liability, choice (B), is one that does not have to be paid within a year. Choice (C), flexible expense, refers to an expense that is controllable, that is, a person can choose to take on the expense or not. Dissavings, choice (D), occurs when

a person's expenses are greater than his or her income, resulting in a decrease in net worth.

26. **The correct answer is (C).** While the other answer choices may provide information about a corporation's sales, profits and losses, and similar information, the primary source for such information is the corporation's own annual reports, which is where choices (A), (B), and (D) pick up the information also.

27. **The correct answer is (B).** A person may withdraw money from a traditional IRA for three reasons, namely, to pay large medical expenses, for higher education, or for a first home, so choice (B) is correct. Choices (A), (C), and (D) are incorrect.

28. **The correct answer is (A).** Indemnity insurance limits payments to a specified amount regardless of actual costs; expense insurance is a better deal. Choice (B) is incorrect because the type of indemnity insurance may or may not cover preexisting conditions; that is not why it is indemnity insurance. Choice (C) is incorrect because indemnity insurance pays the patient directly, not the health-care provider. Choice (D) is incorrect because it describes physicians' expense insurance.

29. **The correct answer is (D).** An umbrella policy adds liability coverage over and above regular homeowner's and auto insurance policies. Choice (A) is incorrect because an umbrella policy would only cover a home office if the underlying homeowner's policy had an endorsement covering it. Choice (B) is incorrect because flood insurance is a separate policy. Choice (C) is incorrect because an umbrella policy doesn't include health insurance, and it doesn't provide homeowner's and auto insurance as such, but increases liability coverage.

30. **The correct answer is (B).** Finance companies typically lend to people with poor or no credit history, so they protect themselves by charging high interest rates. Choice (A)

confuses finance companies with credit unions, which do lend only to members. Choice (C) is incorrect; under the Truth-in-Lending Act of 1968, a lender must give borrowers the APR (annual percentage rate) on loans. Choice (D) confuses finance companies with commercial banks that may take several days for loan processing. Typically, finance companies have quicker turnaround for loan applications.

31. **The correct answer is (C).** The money left after expenses have been paid is called discretionary income. Choice (A), cash inflow, is an individual's or household's income and includes choice (B), salary or wages, and may also include interest and dividend income. Choice (D), liquidity ratio, is a person's or household's liquid assets divided by monthly expenses.

32. **The correct answer is (C).** Estimated tax payments are due quarterly: April 15, June 15, September 15, and the following January 15. Choices (A) and (B) are incorrect, but may be confusing because Social Security—Federal Income Contributions Act tax (FICA)—is paid weekly, every two weeks or monthly, depending on how often a person is paid. Choice (D) is incorrect.

33. **The correct answer is (B).** Treasury bills have the shortest maturities of all Treasury instruments, namely, 4, 13, 26, or 52 weeks. The maturity for choice (A), Treasury Inflation-Protected Security (TIPS), may be 5, 10, or 30 years. Choice (C), Treasury note, has maturities of 2, 3, 5, 7, and 10 years. Choice (D), Treasury bond, has maturities of 30 years.

34. **The correct answer is (A).** The principal in a TIPS is adjusted based on the Consumer Price Index (CPI). If the CPI goes up, the amount of the principal goes up; if it goes down, the amount of the principal decreases. TIPS are a hedge against inflation because the holder is paid the original face value of the TIPS or an inflation-adjusted value, but

never less than the face value. Choices (B), (C), and (D) are incorrect because they don't move with inflation.

35. **The correct answer is (A).** New cars depreciate more rapidly than older cars, so buying a used car can make financial sense. Choice (B) is incorrect; many used cars come with no express warranties. Choice (C) is incorrect because the older a car is, the more maintenance is typically required. Choice (D) confuses registration with insurance. Typically, the older the car, the less reason to have property damage insurance on it.

36. **The correct answer is (A).** The balance on travel and entertainment (T&E) cards like Diners Club® must be paid in full each month. Choice (B) is incorrect because a person can withhold payment on a T&E card only if the amount is over $50. Choice (C) is incorrect because this describes a store gift card. Choice (D) is incorrect because a person is still liable for charges under $50 regardless of the type of credit card.

37. **The correct answer is (A).** Contributions to a health savings account (HSA) is tax-deductible up to certain IRS limits. Choice (B), life insurance premiums, are not deductible, nor are expenses related to moving to assisted living, choice (C). Moving expenses related to a job change are tax-deductible, if the move is more than 50 miles from the current home. Choice (D) is incorrect.

38. **The correct answer is (D).** Indemnification means that a policyholder doesn't have a financial gain from a loss, but receives the approximate value of what was lost. Choice (A) confuses indemnification with no-fault auto insurance. Choice (B) refers to health insurance and not indemnification. Choice (C) confuses indemnification with provisions of no-fault auto insurance.

39. **The correct answer is (D).** Under a traditional marital share will, half the taxes are paid when the first spouse dies and half when the second spouse dies. Choice (A)

describes tax payment under a simple will. Choices (B) and (C) are incorrect.

40. **The correct answer is (C).** According to the technical analysis theory, the forces of supply and demand in the stock market as a whole must be considered in valuing individual stocks. Choice (A) is one factor considered by those who apply the fundamental analysis theory. Choice (B) is part of the thesis of the efficient market hypothesis. Choice (D) is the basis of the fundamental analysis theory of stock valuation that looks at the intrinsic value of stocks.

41. **The correct answer is (B).** The W-4 lists exemptions. The W-2 is an employer's form listing an employee's income for the year, so choice (A) is incorrect. Choice (C), 1040, is the income tax long form. Choice (D), 1099, is the form that self-employed people receive from all the companies that employed them during the year.

42. **The correct answer is (B).** Even though there are no express warranties when a used car is sold "as is," the buyer has some protection because of implied warranties. Choice (A) is incorrect; it is often the term used for a service contract that "extends" the protection of express warranties. Choice (C) is a type of express warranty that limits the categories or costs covered. Choice (D) doesn't exist.

43. **The correct answer is (B).** While it is true that a person will probably do better in a good economy, choice (D), or if the stock market performs well, choice (C)—assuming the person owns stocks or shares in stock funds—the major factors are how much a person earns, saves, and invests. Choice (A) is incorrect because it omits the concept of investing.

44. **The correct answer is (C).** A qualified pension plan is one that meets all the requirements under the Employee Retirement Income Security Act of 1974 (ERISA) and is guaranteed by the Pension Benefit Guaranty Corporation. Choice (A) is incorrect because it is only part of what is true about qualified pension plans; a qualified pension plan may be a defined contribution or a defined benefit plan. Choice (B) is incorrect because in terms of taxation, whether a plan is qualified or not is irrelevant. Taxes are paid at the time that contributions are made if the plan is a Roth IRA, not if it is a 401(k). Taxes on the latter are paid when withdrawals are made. Choice (D) is incorrect because a qualified pension plan is open to any company in any industry.

45. **The correct answer is (D).** Keoghs, also known as HR-10 plans, are retirement plans for self-employed persons. Choice (A), a SEP or Simple Employee Pension Plan, is set up by an employer. A SIMPLE or Savings Incentive Match Plans for Employees, choice (B), was created for small employers to use. Choice (C), 403(b), is an employer-sponsored pension plan for nonprofits, similar to 401(k) plans for for-profit companies.

46. **The correct answer is (C).** Capital gains on investments including real estate must be included in figuring income taxes, but a gain of $250,000 on the sale of a home can be excluded under certain conditions. Choice (A) is incorrect; a loss from the sale of a home is not deductible. For the same reason, choice (D) is incorrect. Choice (B) is incorrect; the first-time homebuyer's credit was an incentive in 2009 and 2010 to get people to buy homes and was used when the home was bought, not sold.

47. **The correct answer is (B).** Personal injury protection (PIP) insurance is required in no-fault insurance states to cover medical expenses and accident-related expenses such as loss of income. No-fault insurance policies typically don't cover damage to property, choice (A); therefore, buying insurance to cover property damage in the event of an accident is important. Choice (C) is incorrect for two reason: (1) property insurance is not required and (2) PIP covers

the policyholder regardless of whether he or she caused the accident. Uninsured motorist coverage, choice (D), is not required under a no-fault insurance system.

48. **The correct answer is (B).** A call option is based on the assumption or wish that the stock will rise in value and the investor will make money on it. Choice (A), selling short, occurs when an investor borrows stock from a broker with the intention of selling it at a higher price and then buying it back when the value decreases, thus making money on the difference between the price sold on the borrowed stock and the price paid to replace the stock. Choice (C), buying on margin, is buying stock in part with borrowed money. Choice (D), day trading, is a method of buying and selling stocks constantly rather than holding them for any period of time.

49. **The correct answer is (C).** In calculating the debt-to-income ratio, the monthly mortgage payment, which is considered a long-term liability, is not included. Choice (A), car loan; choice (B), student loan; and choice (D), utility payments, are included.

50. **The correct answer is (B).** The money factor is the interest rate being charged on the vehicle's capitalized cost, that is, the price of the vehicle. Choice (A) is the down payment, so it is incorrect. Choices (C) and (D) are simply the monthly payments and the number of payments.

51. **The correct answer is (A).** A flexible spending account can be used to pay for health care and for child care. Choice (B) is meant to confuse, but the correct answer would be child care, not adult day care. Choices (C) and (D) are incorrect.

52. **The correct answer is (B).** The answers refer to two forms of interest rates, so you have to figure out which one is the subject of each question: the interest rate that affects the cost of borrowing or the interest rate that is the return on savings and investments. Then you have to figure out if the statement is correct.

Choice (A) refers to return on investment and is the opposite of how investors would react because high interest rates encourage investing, choice (B), which is the correct answer. Choices (C) and (D) refer to the cost of borrowing. High interest rates push up prices, so choice (C) is the opposite of what occurs. Choice (D) is also the opposite of what occurs; the cost of using credit rises, so consumers take on less debt.

53. **The correct answer is (D).** A person using a credit card has time between charging a purchase and when the money for it is due, unlike a person using a debit card, which immediately subtracts the purchase price from the user's bank account. Choice (A) is confusing a certified check with a debit card, so the answer is incorrect. Choice (B) confuses a smart card with a debit card; smart cards are preloaded with an amount. Neither a debit card nor a credit card is preloaded. Choice (C) is incorrect; losses from a stolen credit card are capped at $50, but losses from a stolen debit card are capped at $50 only if the person notifies the bank in less than two days. If it's between two and sixty days before the bank is notified, losses are capped at $500.

54. **The correct answer is (C).** An irrevocable trust is not part of an estate for probate and estate taxation purposes. Choices (A), (B), and (D), traditional and Roth IRAs and testamentary trusts, which are trusts set up by a will, are subject to probate and estate taxes.

55. **The correct answer is (A).** The original purpose of the alternative minimum tax was to ensure that wealthy people who took a large share of special tax credits paid some taxes. However, over time, because the income floor for this tax was never inflation adjusted, the tax has been reaching down into the middle class. Choices (B), (C), and (D) may seem convincing, but are incorrect.

56. The correct answer is (B). An antilocking brake system can reduce the premium for auto insurance. Choice (A), collision damage waiver (CDW), relates to renting a car, not buying auto insurance, and taking this provision when renting a car increases the cost of the rental. When you purchase CDW, the rental company gives up its right to charge you for any damage you cause to the car. Because the company wants to make a profit, it puts a high daily fee on CDWs. Choice (C) is incorrect because the newer the car, the higher the collision coverage that is recommended and, thus, the higher the premium. Choice (D) is incorrect because being in an assigned risk pool means the driver has a bad driving record.

57. The correct answer is (B). Net replacement value is the cost of the replacement (new car) minus the trade-in value of the old car. Choices (A), (C), and (D) all relate to car leases, not outright purchases. Choice (A), residual value, is equal to the original market value of the car minus depreciation over the period of the lease. Choice (C), capitalization cost reduction, is any payment made when the lease is signed and includes cash, a trade-in, and rebates. If a car is appraised at more than the residual value as stated in the lease contract, the additional value is known as excess value, choice (D).

58. The correct answer is (A). Per stirpes means that assets are divided equally among the branches of a family. Choice (B) describes a per capita distribution. Choice (C) refers to a stated dollar amount will. Choice (D) is incorrect.

59. The correct answer is (C). The interest earned on municipal bonds is tax-exempt, choice (C). Choice (A) is incorrect because Manjeet is avoiding paying taxes, which is legal; he is not evading taxes, which is illegal. Choice (B) is incorrect because a tax credit is deducted directly from taxable income and has nothing to do with municipal bonds. Choice (D) is incorrect because he will not have to pay taxes later.

60. The correct answer is (A). Investment advisers may be regulated by their state's securities regulator or by the SEC, depending on the size of the assets the person manages. Choice (B) is incorrect because Sarbanes-Oxley regulates the financial disclosure of corporations. Choice (C) is incorrect because the Certified Financial Planner Board of Standards, Inc. licenses certified financial planners, which is different from an investment adviser. Choice (D) is incorrect because FINRA is a self-policing association of securities firms.

SUMMING IT UP

- Financial goals may be (1) short-term, (2) intermediate, or (3) long-term. They can also be categorized as (1) consumable product, (2) durable product, and (3) intangible purchase. Financial goals change in importance as a person moves through each stage of the life cycle.

- Once financial goals are set, it's important to establish a budget to achieve those goals.

- A cash flow statement shows inflows and outflows of money and is useful in planning a household budget. A balance sheet lists assets minus liabilities to show an individual's or family's net worth.

- Cash management is a way to have cash, or the equivalent, handy for regular purchases and emergencies.

- There are a variety of financial service organizations and professionals who can provide assistance for financial planning and a variety of depository institutions to hold assets.

- The time value of money is the increase in the amount of money as a result of interest earned on it. It is, in other words, the future value of money calculated at a certain rate of interest over a certain period of time.

- Two other important concepts are the present value of money and opportunity cost. The former is the current value of money needed to generate a future amount based on a certain rate of interest and a certain period of time. The latter is what a person gives up in order to gain something else.

- Credit is the promise to pay later for the use of something now. Reasons for using credit include (1) convenience, (2) the ability to consume more than possible based on income, (3) as a hedge against inflation, and (4) for emergencies. The disadvantages of using credit are (1) the temptation to spend more than a person has, (2) the consequences of overspending, (3) the cost of credit, and (4) limitations on future spending power because of the cost of credit for past purchases.

- There are three types of credit: (1) installment sales credit, (2) installment cash credit, and (3) single lump-sum credit. Repayment for the first two is in regular amounts over a period of time.

- The five C's of creditworthiness: (1) character, (2) capacity, (3) capital, (4) collateral, and (5) conditions. A creditor checks an applicant's credit score, known as a FICO score, which considers (1) length of credit history, (2) on-time payment history, (3) current amounts owed, (4) types of credit in the credit history, and (5) inquiries from new credit sources.

- There are two forms of personal bankruptcy: (1) Chapter 7, known as straight bankruptcy, and (2) Chapter 13, known as the wage-earner plan. Filing for bankruptcy stays on a personal financial record for seven or ten years and can affect the ability to qualify for credit or a job and to buy insurance.

- A basic question for many when faced with getting a car is whether to buy or lease. A comparison can be made based on (1) initial costs, (2) monthly payments, and (3) final expenses to pay off the lease.

- A lease may be either closed-end or open-end, though the latter tends to be used more by companies. In evaluating leases, a consumer should note the (1) capitalized cost, (2) interest rate, (3) amount of monthly payments, (4) number of monthly payments, (5) residual value of the vehicle at turn-in time, and (6) early lease termination fee.

- If deciding to buy, a consumer faces the choice: new or used. The price of a used car is determined by (1) mileage, (2) condition, (3) features and options, and (4) demand in the marketplace for the make and model.

- Whether new or used, a car owner must be able to finance costs of ownership and costs of operation.

- The advantages of renting are (1) mobility, (2) little or no personal or financial responsibility for maintenance or repairs, and (3) the lower initial cost of paying only a security deposit. The disadvantages are (1) inability to derive financial benefits from ownership (tax deductions, increasing equity stake), (2) the likelihood of rent increases over time, and (3) lease restrictions on use of the rental property.

- Advantages of buying include (1) tax deductions for mortgage interest and property taxes, (2) capital gain that is probably not taxable because of tax adjustments, and (3) fewer restrictions on how the property can be used. Disadvantages are (1) limited mobility, (2) maintenance and repair costs, (3) high initial costs, and (4) loss of potential interest earned on money used for the down payment and closing costs.

- The larger the down payment on a home, the lower the monthly payments. The longer the term of the mortgage, the higher the interest rate. Depending on the down payment, a lender may require private mortgage insurance.

- Most mortgages are conventional mortgages and are for terms of 30, 20, or 15 years. There are also a variety of other types of mortgage, including adjustable rate mortgages, interest-only, and convertible.

- Payroll deductions may be mandatory or voluntary, depending on whether they are tax or non-tax deductions from wages.

- Taxpayers may take the standard deduction when reporting their income or itemize their deductions if they are higher than the standard deduction in any given year.

- Because the federal government needs revenue to function, it requires that taxpayers with passive income estimate their whole year tax bill and pay it in quarterly installments.

- There are a variety of legal ways to reduce taxes, which is known as tax avoidance.

- Life insurance policies may be term policies or whole life. The latter includes a savings component and has a number of formats. Life insurance policies have a face value, which is the amount of its death benefits.

- Property insurance shields people from risks to their homes, vehicles, and personal property such as furniture, electronics, and jewelry. Liability insurance protects people from losses as a result of damage done to other persons or to the property of others. Both homeowner's and auto insurance may include both components.

- Basic health insurance provides protection for hospital stays, surgery, and medical care. Major medical insurance pays expenses over and above the basic insurance coverage, typically up to $1 million.

- Disability insurance provides income for workers who are unable to work because of a disability. What constitutes a disability depends on the insurance policy.

- Long-term care insurance is intended to provide custodial care for those who cannot take care of themselves. Benefits typically kick in when a person cannot perform some of the activities of daily living: bathing, dressing, being continent, eating, and being able to get around alone.

- Investments involve risk, but the least risky are (1) savings accounts, (2) money market deposit/ money market demand accounts, (3) money market funds, and (4) certificates of deposit. Individual stocks and bonds are more risky than stock mutual funds and bond mutual funds, because with the latter two risk is spread over more companies.

- There are a variety of ways to fund retirement through employer-sponsored plans: (1) company pension plans, which may be defined benefit or defined contribution plans; (2) 401(k), 403 (b), and 457 plans; (3) profit-sharing plan; (4) Employee Stock Option Plan (ESOP); (5) Simplified Employee Pension Plan (SEP); and (6) Savings Incentive Match Plan for Employees (SIMPLE).

- Individuals can also establish retirement plans through: (1) Individual Retirement Account (IRA), (2) Roth IRA, (3) rollover IRA, (4) spousal IRA, (5) Keogh (HR-10) Plan, and (6) annuity, which may be fixed or variable and immediate or deferred.

- Estate planning involves writing a will. Depending on the state, a person may be required to leave at least half of his or her estate to the spouse.

- Trusts may be testamentary or living, also known as inter vivos. A living trust may be revocable or irrevocable.

- The federal government levies a federal estate tax on estates in excess of a certain amount. States also levy estate taxes and some also tax the heirs.

Human Resource Management

The following chart outlines the sections and subsections in the Human Resource Management test and offers a comparison between the percent of practice questions in this chapter and the actual DSST exam.

Please Note: In the third and fourth columns, you will notice that some numbers and percentages are followed by a second number in parentheses. The first number refers to the section as a whole. The number or percentage in parentheses refers to those items that were not able to be placed in a specific subsection, but still belong in the section as a whole.

CONTENT OUTLINE: SECTIONS AND SUBSECTIONS	PERCENT OF EXAM DEVOTED TO EACH CONTENT AREA	NUMBER OF ITEMS IN THE DIAGNOSTIC TEST AND POST-TEST BY CONTENT AREA BY SUBSECTION	PERCENT OF ITEMS IN THE DIAGNOSTIC TEST AND POST-TEST BY CONTENT AREA
I. An Overview of the Human Resource Management Field	4%	4 (1)	5% (25%)
A. Historical Development		2	50%
B. Human Resource Functions		0	0%
C. The Human Resource Manager		1	25%
D. Motivation, Communication, and Leadership		0	0%
E. Ethical Aspects of Human Resource Decision Making		0	0%
II. Human Resource Planning	6%	6	7.5%
A. Strategic Human Resource Issues		3	50%
B. Job Analysis and Job Design		3	50%
III. Staffing	15%	10	12.5%
A. Recruiting		1	10%
B. Selection		2	20%
C. Promotion and Transfers		0	0%
D. Reduction-in-Force		4	40%
E. Voluntary Turnover		3	30%
IV. Training and Development	11%	8	10%
A. Orientation		2	25%
B. Career Planning		0	0%
C. Principles of Learning		2	25%
D. Training Programs and Methods		3	37.5%
E. Development Programs		1	12.5%
V. Performance Appraisals	10%	10 (2)	12.5% (20%)
A. Reasons for Performance Evaluations		2	20%

B. Techniques		4	40%
C. Problems		2	20%
VI. Compensation Issues	**15%**	**13 (1)**	**16.25% (8%)**
A. Job Evaluation		2	15.3%
B. Wage and Salary Administration		2	15.3%
C. Compensation Systems		5	38.4%
D. Benefits: Mandatory and Voluntary		3	23%
VII. Safety and Health	**5%**	**4**	**5%**
A. Occupational Accidents and Illness		4	100%
B. Quality of Work Life		0	0%
C. Workplace Security		0	0%
VIII. Employee Rights and Discipline	**5%**	**4 (4)**	**5% (100%)**
IX. Employee Law	**15%**	**9 (3)**	**11.25% (33.3%)**
A. Equal Employment Laws (e.g., Civil Rights Act Title VII, ADA, ADEA)		2	22.2%
B. Compensation and Benefits (e.g., ERISA, FMLA, FLSA)		1	11.1%
C. Health, Safety, and Employee Rights (e.g., Occupational Safety and Health Act of 1970, WARN)		1	11.1%
D. Union Laws (e.g., NLRA, Taft-Hartley Act, Civil Service Reform Act)		2	22.2%
X. Labor Relations	**6%**	**6 (1)**	**7.5% (17%)**
A. Unions		3	50%
B. Collective Bargaining		2	33%
C. Unionized Versus Nonunionized Work Settings		0	0%
XI. International Human Resource Management	**4%**	**3 (3)**	**3.75% (100%)**
XII. Current Issues and Trends	**4%**	**3**	**3.75%**
A. Workforce Diversity		1	33.3
B. Human Resource Information Systems		1	33.3
C. Changing Patterns of Work Relationships		1	33.3
Grand Total	**100%**	**80**	**100%**

OVERVIEW

- Diagnostic test
- Answer key and explanations
- An overview of the human resource management field
- Human resource planning
- Staffing
- Training and development
- Performance appraisals
- Compensation issues
- Safety and health
- Employee rights and discipline
- Employment law
- Labor relations
- International human resource management
- Current issues and trends
- Post-test
- Answer key and explanations
- Summing it up

DIAGNOSTIC TEST

Directions: Carefully read each of the following 20 questions. Choose the best answer to each question and circle your answer choice. The Answer Key and Explanations can be found following this Diagnostic Test.

1. With what is the field of industrial psychology concerned?

   (A) Training management personnel

   (B) Hiring and firing employees

   (C) Employee testing and assignment

   (D) Trade unions and collective bargaining

2. Which of the following is NOT part of the strategic planning process for HRM?

   (A) Identify employee skills that will enable the organization to attain its goals

   (B) Determine the organization's goals

   (C) Identify employees who exhibit desired skills

   (D) Create policies that will produce the desired employee skills

3. Job evaluations are done by comparing

   (A) salary incentives among employees in different departments.

   (B) evaluations done by supervisory personnel.

   (C) employee responses to exhaustive questionnaires.

   (D) responsibilities and skills required for various jobs.

4. The human resource manager is expected to

   (A) provide personalized and helpful service to customers.

   (B) identify which workers deserve bonuses.

   (C) plan the number of employees that an organization will need.

   (D) give tours to visiting customers.

5. Which of the following is NOT included in employment law?

   (A) Civil Rights Act Title VII

   (B) Americans with Disabilities Act

   (C) Family and Medical Leave Act

   (D) Selective Service Act

6. Ergonomics covers such workplace issues as

   (A) repetitive motion disorders.

   (B) the prevention of food poisoning.

   (C) traffic flow and overcrowding.

   (D) the inhalation of hazardous gases.

7. In a structured job interview, the questioner will

   (A) ask questions as he or she thinks of them.

   (B) be joined by a panel of managers.

   (C) expect certain acceptable responses.

   (D) encourage the applicant to speak spontaneously.

8. Disciplinary action taken against a worker

   (A) should not depend on the worker's seniority.

   (B) may be more lenient with a first offender.

   (C) usually begins with an oral warning.

   (D) is usually administered by the worker's union.

9. Which of the following is true about the Social Security Act of 1935?

   (A) It is a voluntary benefit.

   (B) It is a form of discretionary benefits.

   (C) It is a means of workers' compensation.

   (D) It is a mandatory benefit.

10. What should be the basis for pay, promotion, and retention?

    (A) Employee rankings

    (B) Performance appraisals

    (C) Union membership

    (D) Employee training

11. A recruiter is permitted to take into account an applicant's

    (A) family responsibilities.

    (B) previous work history.

    (C) country of origin.

    (D) posture and dress.

12. What right of workers does the Wagner Act of 1935 protect?

    (A) Working in a closed shop

    (B) Enacting right-to-work laws

    (C) Choosing shop stewards

    (D) Bargaining collectively

13. Which of the following is NOT a requirement of the Worker Adjustment and Retraining Notification Act (WARN)?

    (A) Give 60 days advance notice of the closing of a plant

    (B) Notify the workforce of their right to organize in a union

    (C) Provide workers with retirement benefits

    (D) Close their business for all federal holidays

14. Which of the following describes an apprenticeship program?

    (A) New employees learn how to use simulated versions of the real equipment they will be working on.

    (B) Employers provide informal training through coaching and on-the-job experience.

    (C) New employees learn their jobs through on-the-job training and mentoring.

    (D) New employees learn their jobs through a structured combination of classroom instruction and on-the-job training.

15. Any worker who leaves his or her home country to work in a foreign branch is a/an

   (A) third-country national.

   (B) domestic worker.

   (C) expatriate.

   (D) agent.

16. One way a company can assess how well a worker is doing is by means of

   (A) self-ratings.

   (B) written tests.

   (C) peer reviews.

   (D) a stress test.

17. The passage of the Taft-Hartley Act marked a change from the way

   (A) legislation had favored unions.

   (B) states controlled the growth of unions.

   (C) legislation always favored management.

   (D) businesses bargained with unions.

18. A problem can arise with a performance evaluation if

   (A) the employee being assessed is about to retire.

   (B) the benefits administrator is not involved.

   (C) the supervisor shows bias in favor of some employees.

   (D) there have been multiple complaints about the supervisor.

19. Diversity in the workforce does NOT include being concerned with

   (A) perceived differences.

   (B) race, gender, or marital status.

   (C) varied lifestyles.

   (D) computer skills.

20. Which of the following describes a pay follower?

   (A) A firm that pays less than other companies in the same field

   (B) A firm that hires only the most experienced workers

   (C) A firm that rarely promotes anyone from the outside into management because of the pay differential

   (D) A firm that does not offer incentives to employees

diagnostic test

ANSWER KEY AND EXPLANATIONS

1. C	5. D	9. D	13. A	17. A
2. C	6. A	10. B	14. D	18. C
3. D	7. C	11. B	15. C	19. D
4. C	8. C	12. D	16. C	20. A

1. **The correct answer is (C).** Choice (A) is incorrect because industrial psychology is not concerned with training. Choice (B) is incorrect because this field is not involved with hiring or firing workers. Choice (D) is incorrect because industrial psychology does not encompass trade unions and collective bargaining.

2. **The correct answer is (C).** Identifying employees who already possess the skills and behaviors required to enable an organization to attain its goals is not part of HRM's strategic planning process, so it is the correct answer to the question. Choices (A), (B), and (D) are steps in the strategic planning process.

3. **The correct answer is (D).** Choice (A) is incorrect because incentives are not considered in job evaluations. Choice (B) is incorrect because there is likely to be only one supervisor involved. Choice (C) is incorrect because questionnaires are used for job analysis, not for performance appraisals.

4. **The correct answer is (C).** Choices (A) and (D) are incorrect because a human resource manager does not deal with customers. Choice (D) is also incorrect because that is likely to be done only in consultation with the direct supervisor. Choice (B) is incorrect because bonuses are determined by managers.

5. **The correct answer is (D).** Choices (A), (B), and (C) are incorrect because employment law includes the Title VII of the Civil Rights Act, the Americans with Disabilities Act, and the Family and Medical Leave Act. The Selective Service Act deals with military service.

6. **The correct answer is (A).** Ergonomics involves fitting workplace conditions and job demands to the capabilities of workers. Choice (B) is incorrect because food poisoning is not related to ergonomics. Choice (C) is incorrect because traffic flow and overcrowding are not ergonomic issues. Choice (D) is incorrect because ergonomics does not deal with the inhalation of gases. That would be an OSHA (Occupational Safety and Health Administration) issue.

7. **The correct answer is (C).** Choice (A) is incorrect because asking random questions is not part of a structured interview. Choice (B) is incorrect because a panel of interviewers is not an aspect of a structured job interview. Choice (D) is incorrect because answering spontaneously would defeat the aim of a structured interview, which requires only certain acceptable answers.

8. **The correct answer is (C).** Choice (A) is incorrect because seniority should not influence whether disciplinary action is taken or not, although a long-time employee with a spotless record may be treated more leniently than one with a series of infractions. Choice (B) is incorrect because although leniency for a first offense may be true in some cases, it is not a given. Choice (D) is incorrect because although the union may have set rules on discipline, the union is not involved in administering worker discipline.

9. **The correct answer is (D).** Choice (A) is incorrect because Social Security is not a voluntary benefit, nor is it a discretionary benefit, choice (B). Choice (C) is incorrect because workers' compensation is a separate issue.

10. **The correct answer is (B).** Choice (A) is incorrect because rankings are not part of the evaluation process that affects pay, promotion, and retention. Choice (C) is incorrect because union membership is not a factor in pay, promotion, and retention. Choice (D) is incorrect because it is performance, not training, that affects the employee's evaluation.

11. **The correct answer is (B).** Choices (A) and (C) are incorrect because taking into account family responsibilities and an applicant's country of origin would be a form of bias. Choice (D) is incorrect because considering posture and dress might influence interviewers and would also be a form of bias.

12. **The correct answer is (D).** The Wagner Act, also known as the National Labor Relations Board, protects the rights of workers to organize and bargain collectively. Choice (A) is incorrect because the Wagner Act does not deal with closed shops, which require union membership to work in a company. Choice (B) is incorrect because workers don't enact laws; legislatures do. Right-to-work laws are state laws that make it illegal to refuse to hire someone because he or she doesn't belong to a union. Choice (C) is incorrect because choosing a shop steward is a union membership decision that doesn't involve company management.

13. **The correct answer is (A).** Choices (B), (C), and (D) are covered by WARN. The right to organize is protected under the National Labor Relations Board Act, commonly known as the Wagner Act.

14. **The correct answer is (D).** Apprenticeship programs are formal structured programs that combine classroom learning with on-the-job training. Choice (A) describes vestibule training, not an apprenticeship program. Choices (B) and (C) say essentially the same thing and are both incorrect.

15. **The correct answer is (C).** Choice (A) is incorrect because a third-party national comes neither from the home country of the global business, nor the host country of its branch. Choice (B) is incorrect because a domestic worker would be a citizen of the host country. Choice (D) is incorrect because while an agent may seem like a logical answer, it doesn't fit the description in the question.

16. **The correct answer is (C).** Choice (A) is incorrect because self-ratings are not usually shared with evaluators. Choice (B) is incorrect because employers don't give written tests when assessing a worker's performance. Choice (D) is incorrect because a stress test would test only how well the worker handles stress.

17. **The correct answer is (A).** Choice (B) is incorrect because states did not—and do not—control the growth of unions. Choice (C) is incorrect because the Taft-Hartley Act was a reaction to legislation that favored unions, not management. Choice (D) is incorrect because the Act did not directly affect collective bargaining.

18. **The correct answer is (C).** Choice (A) is incorrect because retirement would not be an issue in an evaluation. Choice (B) is incorrect because the benefits administrator should not be involved in performance evaluations. Choice (D) is incorrect because although there may have been multiple complaints about the supervisor, they would be regarded as a separate issue.

19. **The correct answer is (D).** This question is looking for the answer that doesn't fit. Since choices (A), (B), and (C) are true examples of diversity in the workplace, they are incorrect. Perceived differences, choice (A), is an issue in creating diversity

in the workplace. Similarly, choice (B), race, gender, and marital status, are issues in creating diversity in the workplace. Choice (C) is incorrect because varied lifestyles are also an issue in creating diversity in the workplace. Only choice (D), computer skills, is not a diversity issue.

20. **The correct answer is (A).** Choice (B) is incorrect because hiring the most experienced workers would more likely be true of a pay leader. Choices (C) and (D) are incorrect because although they may seem like possible answers, neither describes a pay follower.

AN OVERVIEW OF THE HUMAN RESOURCE MANAGEMENT FIELD

Human Resource Management (HRM) is concerned with a company's employees, that is, its human resources. The primary goal of HRM is to suggest ways to manage the workplace so that all personnel contribute to the overall success of the company and are appropriately compensated for their contributions.

Historical Development

One of the earliest forms of personnel management was known as industrial welfare. During the Industrial Revolution of the nineteenth century, legislation expanded the responsibilities of those concerned with supervising personnel. For example, new laws regulated the work hours of children and women, and supervisors were required to see that those laws were observed, under penalty of law if they were not.

Other developments further influenced personnel management. Frederick Taylor, a U.S. mechanical engineer, is considered to be the founder of what became known as scientific management. Taylor promoted incentive systems that rewarded workers for meeting or exceeding objectives. He believed that pay should be linked to productivity, thus motivating workers to earn more by being more productive.

Others were also at work on ideas to improve management. During World War I, the new field of industrial psychology was beginning to be applied to the workplace. Industrial psychology is the branch of applied psychology concerned with the effective management of a labor force. For example, testing was introduced to evaluate military personnel so that they would be assigned to appropriate tasks. After the war, employee testing and assignment became a standard procedure in private industry.

In the early part of the twentieth century, many companies began to establish departments whose purpose it was to ensure workers' productivity by increasing job satisfaction, which, in turn, would increase productivity. These departments would eventually evolve into what became known as personnel departments. At first, these departments were concerned mainly with hiring suitable employees, but as their responsibilities became more complex, many personnel departments evolved into the HRM departments of today.

Human Resource Functions

Management functions have gradually expanded to go beyond (1) staffing and (2) training and development. Newer responsibilities include (3) performance appraisals, (4) compensation, (5) safety and health issues, (6) employee rights and discipline, and (7) forecasting staffing needs. A modern HR department may have to deal with many issues, including the following:

- Trade unions and collective bargaining

- Laws guaranteeing civil rights and equal opportunity employment

- Outsourcing

- Globalization

- Information technology

- Pensions and benefits
- The use of part-time and temporary employees
- Mergers and takeovers
- Job sharing
- Federal, state, and local laws
- Flextime and job sharing
- Health-care costs

In many organizations, HRM is considered a strategic partner in developing the business.

The Human Resource Manager

Human resource managers are expected to work in consultation with line managers—those persons with the direct managerial responsibility for employees—before making recommendations about employees. For example, HR managers will seek input from the line managers, and then have those managers review their final written comments. Likewise, HR managers, having determined an organization's training needs, will consult with line managers about the types of training needed and which employees will benefit from that training. Similarly, HR managers may make suggestions regarding performance reviews, promotions, and transfers.

In organizations in which HRM is used strategically, HR managers will also work with senior management in developing strategic goals for the organization and forecasting future employment needs.

Motivation, Communication, and Leadership

HR managers motivate employees by helping them to set personal goals that align with company objectives. Better individual performance is in turn instrumental in helping a company meet its goals. Employees' contributions can then be acknowledged by such incentives as new and challenging assignments, awards, and expressions of appreciation—positive reinforcement that benefits both the individual and the organization. The ability to communicate to workers what their personal goals should be and to recognize their achievements is an example of the kind of leadership ability expected of an effective HR manager.

Ethical Aspects of Human Resource Decision Making

Ethics is a system of moral principles intended to govern a person's or group's behavior. In business, adhering to such a set of principles includes, but is not limited to, following laws and regulations. A major difficulty that the manager faces is the realization that while something may be legal, it is not necessarily moral. Because the goal of the company is to make a profit, the manager must decide whether an action that might be profitable is also morally justified, based on the company's ethical guidelines.

HR managers face ethical decisions every day, and sometimes it may not be easy to make those decisions. In interviewing a prospective employee, for example, the HR manager might have to decide whether to explain a potentially difficult situation the new employee would face, such as taking the place of a highly popular manager who was terminated.

HUMAN RESOURCE PLANNING

The role of the HR department has changed greatly from the days of overseeing hiring and firing. Today's HR department is a strategic partner with upper management in setting goals and executing the company's strategic plan.

Strategic Human Resource Issues

An HR manager is expected to identify the employee skills and behaviors required to meet the company's goals now and in the future. For example, a company may focus on providing customers with personalized and helpful service. To implement this strategy, therefore, the company will seek to hire employees they feel have empathy for others. Training and rewards will center on meeting that goal and should reach every level in the company.

Evaluation of the strategy should be ongoing so that management can make adjustments as needed over time. HRM works closely with company management to carry out and monitor how well employees are achieving the projected goals.

Because of their familiarity with personnel, HRM is especially well suited to anticipating future needs. Because it can assess the strengths and weaknesses of the workforce, HRM should be able to anticipate future needs, such as specialized training programs. HRM can also assist in predicting future staffing needs through the use of (1) trend analysis, (2) ratio analysis, or (3) scatter plots.

Job Analysis and Job Design

Job analysis and job design are part of the process of determining specific tasks to be performed, what methods are used in performing those tasks, and how the job relates to other work in the organization. Through this system, the HRM can identify the skills, duties, and knowledge necessary for performing certain jobs.

This process applies as new jobs are created or old ones are redesigned because of changing requirements or procedures. Job analysis and job design can provide information needed for staffing, training and development, compensation, and safety and health, all of which are crucial to the development of job descriptions. HRM might gather this information by means of (1) observation, (2) questionnaires, (3) interviews, (4) employee logs of their duties, or (5) a combination of methods.

STAFFING

Staffing includes a variety of aspects, such as recruitment and selection in order to ensure that an organization has the right employees in the right jobs to execute the company's strategic plan and achieve its goals.

Recruiting

Recruiting is a process. The first step is deciding, as part of planning and forecasting, what positions to fill. Next, recruiters have to build up a pool of candidates drawn from both (1) internal and (2) external sources. For internal recruiting, HRM consults personnel records to identify employees with the right skills set, and then interviews them for the position. The law requires jobs to also be posted, and workers may respond to job postings when they find a job description that seems to match their skills and experience.

External recruiting may involve using employment agencies. Online recruiting, both through general sites and those sponsored by specific professional associations, are also possibilities. Job fairs, help-wanted ads, and college recruiting and internships allow recruiters to screen candidates for education, attitude, motivation, and communication skills. Well-crafted—and accurate—résumés can also be informative and useful in allowing a recruiter to evaluate applicants.

Selection

How long the actual selection of staff takes can be affected by various factors, including (1) company rules and (2) legal considerations. Company rules on hiring and promotion may depend on the level of the position. For example, someone being considered for an executive position will probably be subject to more scrutiny that an applicant for a job as a word processor.

Legal considerations involve making sure that hiring is not discriminatory in any way and meets all the requirements of legislation governing hiring. Even when the parties involved in the selection process are confident in their final choice, the candidate may be required to undergo a physical exam before being officially hired. Following up on references and checking the accuracy of résumés may also extend the vetting process.

Interviewing—(1) structured or (2) unstructured—makes up a significant part of the selection process. In an unstructured interview, interviewers ask questions as they think of them. For a structured interview, though, the types of questions are predetermined. Even responses that are considered acceptable are delineated in advance.

Some interview questions are intended to explore the applicant's job skills. For example: What courses did you take in college that involved using your organizational skills? Other questions might be more situational, such as asking how the person would react to certain circumstances. Or a question might call on an applicant to describe particular situations in his or her work experience and explain how the candidate handled them.

Applicants may have to submit to several interviews, gradually moving up the levels of management. Some companies conduct panel interviews, with the candidate being interviewed simultaneously by a group of managers or peers who will be working with the candidate or a combination of both.

Promotions and Transfers

When promotions or transfers are considered for company personnel, HRM considers past experience and measurable competence. Still, there is no guarantee that even a high-performing employee will do as well in another position, which suggests that his or her future performance should be monitored in the first few months.

Transfers, which are usually lateral moves, generally mean being responsible for familiar tasks and decisions. Though such moves do not usually mean a higher paycheck, it may be desirable for the employee for other reasons. These might include better working hours, less commuting, or simply the need for a change of environment.

Reduction-in-Force

A reduction-in-force, or RIF, may be the result of such external factors as an economic downturn or a merger or buyout by another company. An RIF that follows a merger or buyout occurs because when the two companies combine, there is a duplication of some staff positions. An internal cause of downsizing might be a company's own plans for reorganizing its work groups or its business.

An RIF is generally permanent. A layoff, on the other hand, is the discharge, often temporary, of workers. Those employees may be rehired once economic conditions improve. To minimize layoffs during a downturn, a company may try reducing everyone's hours and scheduling periodic plant closings or unpaid vacations.

The HR department may be called on to conduct termination interviews in which department personnel break the news to terminated workers and explain their severance packages. A company may also provide outside help in the form of the services of an outplacement firm, which counsels the affected employees by providing instruction on how to strengthen their job-search skills and rewrite their résumés. Outplacement firms may also provide office space and some secretarial help for a period of time for affected employees.

The HR department also needs to deal with the "survivors," the employees who have retained their positions in an RIF situation. An RIF is likely to affect, at least temporarily, the morale of those left behind, challenging their sense of security. The more sensitively the HR department handles the situation, the better the adjustment the remaining staff will make.

Voluntary Turnover

Because of the cost and time involved in recruiting and training new workers, companies remain alert to the rate of employee turnover. So, for example, when personnel from the HR department conduct exit interviews with workers who are resigning voluntarily, they will analyze the workers' responses to certain questions. The aim is to gain insight about why these people are leaving, including their perception of how the company has treated them. Information gathered this way may help the firm in the future to retain high-quality employees.

Retirement is another type of voluntary turnover, at least more so than it has been in the past. Though mandatory retirement age requirements still exist in some companies, there has been a trend in recent years toward phased retirement, which results in retirement being a process rather than an abrupt end to workers' jobs. Phased retirement allows workers to move gradually from full-time work to full retirement. They might begin by reducing the number of hours they work, gradually decreasing those hours over time. This may benefit the company, too, in that it allows management to reduce labor costs without the upheaval of an RIF. The benefit to older workers is that they can keep their benefits while working shorter hours.

Another way a firm may reduce its labor costs without laying off workers is by offering early retirement packages. These offer senior employees benefits that they would not receive if they retired later. However, workers do have the option of turning down such offers. There can also be a disadvantage to the company in making such offers. If it makes the offer to a whole class of workers (for example, senior employees), it risks losing some of its most experienced and able personnel.

TRAINING AND DEVELOPMENT

A large segment of an HR manager's responsibilities involves the training and development of an organization's employees, from top management to hourly workers.

Orientation

First impressions in business are important because it is within the first six months of their employment that many new hires decide whether to stay or leave. Orientation—the initial introduction of employees to their new surroundings—is important for the retention of employees who have just been hired at some expense.

The HR department is likely to be involved in orientation, but other personnel may take part: (1) line managers wishing to establish a productive relationship with a new employee and (2) peers who can anticipate a new employee's interests and concerns. Some employers may institute a buddy system, with a peer becoming a mentor to the new worker. Others may use a team approach, thus providing the newest member with ready access to different knowledge skills.

The orientation process itself may take place over the first few days of a worker's employment. It can also be spread out over a longer period in shorter presentations. In either case, the goal is to acquaint new workers with information such as the firm's history and its core principles, values, and expectations.

Career Planning

How an employee's career develops is important to both that worker and the company itself. Career planning is the ongoing process by which both the individual and the company are involved in that worker's development.

Self-assessment is a vital part of an employee's career planning. It involves recognizing one's interests, skills, and goals. Knowing one's strengths and weaknesses can help a person make the correct career choices and avoid mistakes that lead to job dissatisfaction. For example, if someone accepts a position that is not sufficiently challenging, it can lead to a bored employee making careless mistakes. On the other hand, the challenged worker who can apply his or her skills to a task and feel successful will not only find job satisfaction, but will also contribute to the company's success.

Some companies assist employees in planning their career paths by providing informative materials, personal guidance, and workshops. They might also compensate employees for approved outside courses, including those using e-learning and computer applications.

Principles of Learning

It probably is not logical to expect a single list of the principles of learning to apply to all learning situations. However, the following list recognizes the special requirements of the workplace:

- *Employee Motivation:* This can take many forms. The possibility of promotion, for example, can motivate employees to learn because employees will feel that their ability, training, and experience are likely to be recognized and rewarded.

- *Recognition of Individual Differences:* It is important that workers be rewarded for their particular capabilities by being assigned to learning tasks that recognize and challenge those abilities.

- *Transfer of Learning* (from one position to another): Workers can carry over certain skills from one assignment to another. A management that recognizes and acts on this fact prevents workers from being locked into one career path, especially if it is not a satisfying one.

- *Meaningful Materials:* Print, computer applications, DVDs, online programs, workshops—these are all available for educating workers. To be effective, materials should be up-to-date and directly related to the skills that learners need to master for their jobs. A review by supervisory personnel helps to ensure that the materials are current and appropriate to the company's and the workers' goals.

Management should also recognize that learning can take place both (1) formally and (2) informally. Formal learning may be company-sponsored or the result of individual initiative. It may take place in a classroom, workshop, or online. Informal learning is on-the-job learning, resulting from working and exchanging ideas with colleagues. It is an inexpensive form of learning, and companies are wise to encourage it.

An apprenticeship is another method for learning job-related knowledge and skills. It requires a combination of formal instruction and on-the-job training by a knowledgeable staff member with good communication skills.

Training Programs and Methods

Training includes all those activities designed to provide learners with the knowledge and skills they need to do well in their present jobs. Companies with a reputation for encouraging learning are at an advantage in several ways. For one, training and development programs help in recruiting new workers concerned about how they will advance during their tenure at a company. It is likely, too, that a reputation for learning will attract more highly qualified applicants.

Any training must be done in context—the context being an analysis of the company's actual needs. HRM must ask itself the following types of questions:

- Which workers need to be trained?

- What do they need to learn?

- What do they need to do differently from what they are doing now?

- Will this training help advance the goals of the organization?

Training methods vary from company to company and include (1) instructor-led sessions, (2) online training, (3) virtual classrooms, and (4) case studies. Perhaps the most common one is a class led by an instructor. This method is especially effective with a small group and an instructor who encourages lively discussion. Online, or e-learning, delivered by computer or mobile device has become more and more popular. It not only allows more flexibility in terms of time and distance, but it is also cost-effective once the program is developed. A typical training session ends with a survey to elicit feedback on the effectiveness of the training.

One method often used for management training is the case study. A group leader presents a simulated situation in which a manager is required to analyze the case and then suggest solutions to the problem. The leader must be able to keep the discussion positive and productive. Role-playing and business games similarly involve participants' decision-making skills.

Development Programs

Development programs are also concerned with learning, but center on the skills and knowledge that go beyond the trainee's present job. Development involves individual career planning within the context of organizational development. Human resource development is a major responsibility of the HR department.

Management development seminars and conferences may emphasize such skills as assertiveness training for women, cost accounting, and developing emotional intelligence. While these might not be the types of courses one would find in a college curriculum, they may enhance a management candidate's qualifications for a supervisory position.

As a further stimulus to improving management skills, a company might employ executive coaches from an outside firm. The coach identifies the candidate's strengths and weaknesses, and then helps that executive capitalize on his or her strengths. Coaching, while expensive, has proven to be effective, as shown by assessments from both subordinates and supervisors.

PERFORMANCE APPRAISALS

Pay, promotion, and retention are based on performance appraisals. These evaluations are the way a firm's employees become aware of their standing in the company. Performance appraisals are formal evaluations as opposed to the ongoing assessment of employees' performance that managers should be conducting.

Reasons for Performance Evaluation

Long before the performance appraisals are actually carried out, the process should begin with the supervisor setting the performance standards, or criteria, which employees are expected to meet. These standards should be based on (1) appropriate traits, such as attitude and appearance; (2) appropriate behaviors, such as diligence and organizational skill; (3) competencies, such as business knowledge and interpersonal skills; (4) achievement of goals; and (5) potential for improvement.

Once the appraisals have been conducted, the supervisor works with employees to develop a plan to eliminate any deficiencies. If a worker performs well, he or she will benefit from immediate feedback. Similarly, if worker performance is less than ideal, the sooner the worker receives feedback, the sooner he or she can, in conjunction with the supervisor, take the necessary steps to improve performance.

Techniques

Some companies use a packaged form, either paper or online, that lists the areas on which the employee is to be graded. The types of rankings may vary. For example, the supervisor may have to choose a number from 1 to 7 that he or she believes best represents the employee's progress, with the highest number representing the highest achievement.

Another form might ask the supervisor to judge an employee on the basis of whether listed objectives have been met. As alternatives to having a supervisor make the judgment, there may also be peer reviews, self-ratings, and appraisal by team members or subordinates.

Problems

Performance appraisals are supposed to be based on fair-minded criteria, but they are subjective, and biases and stereotyping can creep in. A manager may be too lenient with one worker and too strict with another. If an employee's view of his or her performance is more positive than the supervisor's evaluation, it can result in a perception of unfair treatment. Also, the evaluation process can be manipulated if the manager wishes to favor one employee or disparage another.

On the other hand, some of the unpleasantness of a poor performance appraisal can be avoided if managers handle problems, such as repeated lateness, as they occur rather than waiting several months to act on issues that need correction. Day-to-day communication and corrective measures can prevent crises from occurring during formal evaluations.

COMPENSATION ISSUES

Compensation is the pay and rewards, such as money bonuses or stock awards, which employees get in exchange for their work. Compensation may be (1) direct or (2) indirect. The former includes salary, wages, commissions, and bonuses, whereas the latter are benefits such as paid vacations, holidays, and medical insurance.

Job Evaluation

Job evaluation is the formal and systematic comparison of a firm's positions. The comparison is designed to determine the value of one job in relation to others. Basically, it attempts to compare the effort, responsibility, and skills required to perform each job. Compensation for each position is then based on this evaluation.

The process begins with the creation of a job analysis for each position. This information is then used to prepare a job description. HRM might then assign rankers to rank the jobs. The rankers must be consistent in the factors they use to make their rankings. Once they have sorted the job descriptions, using the standard of ranking the most difficult job as the highest, the next step may be to assign each rank to a particular pay grade. A pay grade is made up of all jobs that fall within a certain range.

Rankers work independently of one another, but then meet to adjust and average the ratings. When the wages are plotted on a graph, they should reveal a wage curve that can show the relative value of and the average wage for each job.

Of course, most companies do not pay just one rate for all jobs in a particular pay grade. Instead, there may be a number of levels, or steps, within each pay grade. Finally, an employer must account for individual circumstances (such as years of service) before establishing a pay rate for each worker.

Wage and Salary Administration

Clearly, the task of administering wages is complex. The compensation manager in the Human Resources department is responsible for recommending financial compensation by establishing pay rates for various grades. In determining direct financial compensation, the manager must take into account the following factors:

- The company's policies on salaries
- The ability of the company to pay

- Employee job performance

- Employee skills and competencies

- Employee experience

- Employee potential

- Labor union contracts

- Legislation

- Economy

- Cost of living

- Job evaluations

In addition to evaluating these criteria in-house, an administrator has the option of accessing various Internet sites that report on what other firms are paying for comparable jobs. These sites also report on benefits. Besides private, commercial firms, businesses can consult the U.S. Department of Labor's Bureau of Labor Statistics online database of compensation for various industries.

Compensation Systems

The systems that govern decisions on compensation vary from company to company. These compensation policies provide managers with general guidelines for making decisions about compensation. Based on these decisions, a company might fall into one of three categories:

- *Pay Leaders:* Those firms that pay higher compensation than their competitors. Higher-paying companies then logically expect to attract the most highly qualified workers.

- *Market Rate:* Also called the going rate. This is the rate perceived to be the average for similar jobs in the industry.

- *Pay Followers:* Companies that pay less than their competitors. The decision to pay less may be based on the firm's financial condition. It could also reflect the fact that the firm does not believe it requires highly qualified workers.

While these compensation policies indicate a desire to ensure consistency, other factors can alter a policy. For example, there may be pressure to retain high performers through the inducement of a higher salary and/or generous benefits. Other factors that affect such decisions include the following:

- The labor market of potential employees

- Labor unions and their contracts with employers

- The current economy

- Legislation regulating some salaries

The distinction between (1) exempt and (2) non-exempt workers is an example of legislation that affects compensation. By law, companies are expected to adhere to a government policy of classifying workers as either exempt or non-exempt. Exempt workers are those salaried employees categorized as executive, administrative, professional, or outside salespeople. Non-exempt employees, on the

3M SelfCheck™ System

3/10/2013 2:13 PM
MARTINEZ/CLAUDIA M
**************1351
Visa
$4.10
USD
119205
Thank you for using the
3M SelfCheck™ System.

3M SelfCheck™ System

3/10/2013 2:13 PM
MARTINEZ/CLAUDIA M
*********1351

Visa
$4.10
USL
119205
Thank you for using the
3M SelfCheck™ System.

are covered by laws regulating minimum wage, overtime,

ns that, under certain circumstances, give employees addi-
es or hourly pay. Salespeople, for example, may receive a
that meet or surpass a set quota.

ements by awards that may or may not be monetary in nature.
ership plans (ESOP), gift certificates, and merchandise, as
vards.

luntary

ted to administer indirect financial compensation, or ben-
e individual firms initiate others. Examples of mandatory,
ollowing:

Security Act of 1935 was created to provide benefits for
act have since added other kinds of protection for workers.
r workers who are completely disabled.
's survivors—the widow or widower and unmarried chil-

dical insurance for workers over 65.

Although the retirement age for Social Security is gradually rising, that will not affect eligibility for Medicare, which will remain age 65. Employees and employers contribute to the Social Security fund.

- *Unemployment Compensation:* If workers lose their jobs through no fault of their own, they become eligible for unemployment compensation, a joint federal-state program. This insurance program provides temporary benefits payments for a certain number of weeks, typically up to 26 weeks or until the worker finds another job, whichever comes first. It is funded by a payroll tax paid by employers. In times of severe economic downturn, Congress may extend the compensation period as it did during the recession that began in 2007. While the federal government provides guidelines for the program, it is administered by the states. This means that the benefits, including the time period, can vary from one state to another.

- *Workers' Compensation:* If a worker incurs expenses due to a job-related accident or illness, he or she can be reimbursed through this program. Workers' comp, as it is commonly called, also provides some income replacement. Employers purchase the insurance independently through private insurance companies, but the program is subject to federal regulation and is administered by the states.

Discretionary benefits are a form of indirect financial compensation, and individual employers can decide which to offer. The same factors that determine the level of direct compensation—salaries, wages, commissions, and bonuses—influence the types and amount of discretionary benefits employees receive. Some of the most common discretionary benefits include the following:

- Paid vacations

- Sick pay

- Medical benefits

- Life insurance

- Retirement plans

- Stock option plans

- Child care

- Scholarships for dependents

Retirement plans may be one of two types: defined benefits and defined contribution. A defined benefits plan gives retirees a specific amount of income upon retirement. It may be a lump sum or a monthly pension amount and is funded by employers. Under a defined contribution plan, employees don't receive a specific amount of money to fund their retirement. They contribute a portion of their salary toward retirement and employers may or may not also contribute. A 401(k) plan is an example of a defined contribution plan.

Another type of indirect compensation is the voluntary benefit. Voluntary benefits are those offered to employees by a company, but for which employees have to pay because the company feels it cannot afford to do so. However, the company usually pays the administrative costs, and employees benefit because they pay a group rate. These include the following:

- Term life insurance

- Vision insurance

- Long-term care insurance

- Dental insurance

- College savings plans

SAFETY AND HEALTH

U.S. businesses employ more than 130 million workers at 7.2 million domestic workplaces. Workers' safety and health are important to companies because lost time on the job cuts into productivity, raises health-care costs, and could lead to lawsuits, depending on the nature and cause of the injuries. Safety refers to protecting employees from physical injury on the job, and health is the physical and mental well-being of employees.

Occupational Accidents and Illness

The Occupational Safety and Health Act of 1970 was passed specifically to ensure worker safety and health in the United States. It established the Occupational Safety and Health Administration (OSHA) that works with employers to create good working environments. The agency's rules and regulations have helped eliminate many workplace-related fatalities, injuries, and illnesses and reduced the cost to companies of such injuries and illnesses. According to OSHA's Web site, "the rate of reported serious workplace injuries and illnesses has declined from 11 per 100 workers in 1972 to 3.6 per 100 workers in 2009."

If an employee feels endangered by conditions in the workplace, he or she may complain to OSHA, thus possibly initiating an OSHA inspection. The Act protects any employee who requests an inspection, refuses unsafe work, or complains about a dangerous workplace. If the OSHA inspector finds unsafe conditions, this can result in financial penalties for the company. Follow-up inspections check to make sure that the recommendations for improvement have been followed. If conditions have not improved, this results in further penalties. U.S. businesses that do not have safety programs in place or ignore OSHA recommendations contribute to the average $1 billion a week in direct compensation costs to workers for disabling injuries or illnesses.

While it is probably impossible to eliminate every cause of injury or illness on the job, companies can focus on the following areas to reduce hazards and the organization's liability:

- *Unsafe Worker Behavior:* Safety promotion campaigns can improve worker attitudes. It is a fact that workers suffer more injuries when they are new to a job, so placing an emphasis on safety during the first few months of employment can have a significant effect.

- *Unsafe Working Conditions:* A company may find that it must alter working conditions to meet OSHA standards. Though worker safety is the company's responsibility, employees should be encouraged to suggest their own solutions to unsafe conditions. Management must inform all workers of any hazards and take steps to correct them.

- *Job Hazard Analysis (JHA):* JHA requires the assessment of work activities and the workplace to establish whether adequate precautions have been taken to prevent injuries. It involves the systematic identification of potential hazards in the workplace as a step to controlling the possible risks involved. OSHA provides online forms and checklists that employers can download and use to evaluate workplace conditions. Some hazards are obvious, like slippery floors in an area that has a great amount of foot traffic. Others are less so, requiring the kind of expertise a safety engineer can offer. Categories that are analyzed for hazards on such forms are fire prevention, work environment, working/walking surfaces, ergonomics, emergency information (postings), emergency exits, electrical systems, and material storage. The following are examples of OSHA questions relating to fire prevention. Respondents are asked to choose from three possible answers: Yes, No, and N/A (not applicable).

  o Are employees trained on the use of portable fire extinguishers?
  o Is heat-producing equipment used in a well-ventilated area?
  o Are fire alarm pull stations clearly marked and unobstructed?

- *Ergonomics:* Studying people's efficiency in their working environment and then designing the workplace so that employees can function without pain is called ergonomics (from the Greek word *ergon*, "work"). It requires fitting the machine or movements to the worker rather than asking the worker to make the adjustment to such stressful motions as twisting one's whole body. In this way, employers have been able to reduce repetitive motion disorders like carpal tunnel syndrome, bursitis, and tendonitis.

- *Accident Investigation:* It is important that firms investigate any accident; determine the cause; and take steps to prevent other, similar accidents. At the same time, collecting accurate data about accidents over a set period can be valuable, especially if this shows either an increase or a decrease in the frequency and severity of accidents.

Quality of Work Life

Quality of work life can be defined as the extent to which employees can enhance their personal lives through their work environment and experiences. These experiences can include such activities as wellness programs, physical fitness programs, and even substance abuse programs. Prevention of identity theft is of special importance to the HR department, given the amount of personal data in employees' records: Social Security numbers, phone numbers and e-mail addresses, bank account numbers, and so on.

Other policies that can enhance the quality of work life include:

- *Flextime:* Schedule flexibility

- *Compressed Work Week:* Allowing employees to work the same number of hours, but in fewer days

- *Telecommuting:* Working from home

- *Job Sharing:* Two part-time workers splitting one job

- *Part-Time Work:* Giving employees time to take care of personal needs

- A family-friendly workplace with child care

- A generous benefits program

Workplace Security

A feeling of safety in the workplace has come to mean more than just job security. Unfortunately, there have been many cases of workplace violence. Some of the incidents have been carried out by angry workers against fellow employees. The perpetrators are often people who believe that they have not been treated well by management or who have been victims of bullying by the coworkers they are targeting.

Sometimes, violence is carried out by an outsider. Often, the outsider is not targeting the company, but aims to harm someone with whom he has had a personal relationship, such as an estranged wife or girlfriend. Women are the usual victims in these types of attacks. Even dissatisfied customers have been known to react violently to circumstances and attack employees of a company they have a grudge against. Robbery is also a problem for some companies, especially retail establishments.

HRM does have some options for reducing workplace violence, which include the following:

- Keep a minimal amount of cash on hand in retail businesses

- Install a silent alarm system to alert security

- Install surveillance cameras

- Train workers in conflict resolution

- Screen employees for a history of violent behavior, including sexual harassment

- Question unexplained gaps in an applicant's employment

- Check for criminal records involving violence

- Prohibit firearms or other weapons in the facility

Training supervisors to recognize employees who display a tendency to react aggressively to situations, threaten others, or demonstrate antisocial behavior may also prevent a worker from acting violently.

EMPLOYEE RIGHTS AND DISCIPLINE

Most employees are hired and hold their jobs at their employer's discretion. This is known as employment at will, meaning that neither party acknowledges a time limit on that connection. Therefore, either party can terminate the relationship, with due notice. There are, however, some limits on terminating an employee, for example, where legislation or union rules govern such actions. A wrongful termination suit brought by a terminated employee would have to be based on promises or guarantees made by the company, but not adhered to. Then it is up to the claimant to prove that such assurances were made.

Disciplinary Procedures

Prior to termination, there are procedures for dealing with infractions, and it may fall to the HR manager to administer discipline to workers who do not come up to company standards or have failed to follow company rules. The disciplinary action usually occurs only after all other strategies to improve the workers' performance have failed.

Disciplinary actions may take different approaches. It is a given, though, that the action cannot be personal; that is, it should not show either bias or favoritism. Also, the disciplinary action should be taken immediately. It should not be delayed, for example, until the employee's next review, which might be weeks or months away.

Though company rules should be administered consistently, it is realistic to assume that the HR manager might act differently depending on circumstances. For example, if dealing with a first infraction by a new employee, the HR manager might be more lenient in his or her approach. Likewise, if a long-time employee's record has been exemplary until this infraction, the manager might correct the employee's behavior without administering a penalty. Flexibility then becomes a matter of judgment.

Ideally, the manager would apply the minimum penalty to any first offender. The manager would also have to balance the need to avoid damaging employee morale with making sure that all employees understand the need to follow company rules.

The sequence of disciplinary steps begins with an oral warning, followed, if necessary, by a written warning. Beyond that, the HR manager would have to consider whether the situation warrants suspension or termination. Another alternative is demotion, usually with a reduction in pay. In a union situation, this must be handled according to the firm's agreement with the union.

Whatever the resolution, the HR manager should handle any disciplinary action with consideration for the employee's likely emotional reaction as well as that of his or her colleagues. In all cases, the manager's interaction with the employee should be private and never carried out in front of others.

Termination

Termination requires sensitivity and honesty, with the manager explaining what actions warranted the termination. Where there is a union agreement, the manager must follow the rules governing termination with cause. Before it comes to this end, though, it is important that the manager keep in mind that it may be more expensive to hire a replacement than to retain an experienced worker who might only need a period of readjustment.

EMPLOYMENT LAW

As the following table shows, there are a number of laws that govern employee management. There are four categories of employment laws: equal employment; compensation and benefits; health, safety, and employee rights; and union laws. An HR manager needs to be familiar with all of them in order to see that they are administered properly.

EMPLOYMENT LAWS

Equal Employment Laws	
Civil Rights Act Title VII	Makes it unlawful for an employer to discriminate against any individual because of race, color, religion, sex, or national origin
Americans with Disabilities Act (ADA)	Prohibits discrimination against workers with disabilities employed by certain federal contractors and subcontractors
Age Discrimination in Employment Act (ADEA)	Prohibits discrimination against workers within certain age ranges, the ranges changing as the law is amended
Compensation and Benefits	
Employment Retirement Income Security Act (ERISA)	Sets minimum standards for pension programs in private industry to protect employees' contributions
Family and Medical Leave Act (FMLA)	Provides certain employees with up to 12 weeks of unpaid leave under certain circumstances related to family needs
Fair Labor Standards Act (FLSA)	Sets provisions for minimum wage, maximum hours, conditions for overtime pay, equal pay, recordkeeping, and child labor; distinguishes between exempt and non-exempt employees
Health, Safety, and Employee Rights	
Occupational Safety and Health Act of 1970	Requires employers to provide a safe and healthy working environment
Worker Adjustment and Retraining Notification Act (WARN)	Requires 60 days advance notice of a plant closing or mass layoff

Union Laws	
National Labor Relations Act (NLRA)	Supports the right of labor to organize and engage in collective bargaining
Taft-Hartley Act	Prohibits unfair union labor practices, enumerates the rights of employees and employers, allows the U.S. president to bar national emergency strikes
Civil Service Reform Act	Regulates most labor management relations in the federal service

LABOR RELATIONS

A union is an organization of workers who find strength in coming together to deal with their employer. Generally, unions organize because of dissatisfaction with management policies. They strive to improve (1) wages, (2) hours, (3) working conditions, and (4) benefits for their members.

Unions

Although unions, or at least associations of workers, have been around in the United States since the eighteenth century, it was not until the 1930s that unions in the United States began to grow in members and in significance. Until then, lawmakers and court decisions had favored management. But then, during the Great Depression, millions of workers were unemployed, and those who had jobs, especially factory jobs, worked long hours for little pay in unsafe and unhealthful working conditions.

The 1930s saw the passage of several laws that strengthened the rights of workers to organize and of unions to negotiate for their members. Probably the most important of these laws was the National Labor Relations Act of 1935 (also known as the Wagner Act, after Robert F. Wagner, then a U.S. Senator from New York, who sponsored the bill). The NLRA protected the rights of workers to organize and to bargain collectively.

After the passage of the Wagner Act, union membership showed a large increase. However, public attitudes shifted after a number of costly strikes following World War II. Although then-president Harry Truman vetoed the law, Congress overrode his veto to pass the Labor Management Relations Act, also known as the Taft-Hartley Act. The intention of the law was to allow for a more even-handed approach toward labor and management. It placed restrictions on both sides, but probably the most significant one was Section 14b, which allows states to pass right-to-work laws that restrict closed shops. In a closed shop, membership in a union is a condition for being hired and for continued employment.

Collective Bargaining

Beginning with the Wagner Act, both management and labor have been required, by law, to engage in collective bargaining. That is, they must sit down together to negotiate wages, hours, and terms and conditions of employment in good faith. While neither side is forced to accept any demands offered by the people on the other side of the table, it is expected that both sides will negotiate honorably, that is, with sincerity of intention; in other words, "in good faith." Representing the union is the shop steward, a person elected by workers to represent them in these and other dealings with management.

Once the two sides have reached an agreement, the union membership must ratify the agreement. Once management and the union have approved of the deal, it becomes part of the contract between them for the period called for in the contract, usually about three years. A contract generally covers such issues as (1) wages and (2) overtime and such special situations as (3) hazard pay, (4) layoff or severance pay, (5) holidays, (6) vacations, and (7) family care provisions. (8) Grievance procedures, (9) work breaks, (10) strikes, and (11) lockouts as well as (12) management rights are also covered. Items that may not be negotiated are discriminatory treatment of employees, separation of races in the workplace, and a closed shop. The latter requires that a worker join a union in order to be hired. All three are illegal.

Unionized Versus Nonunionized Work Settings

Management in nonunionized work situations probably look at their circumstances as easier than those in a company with a strong union. In a sense, that is the difference between an environment that allows collective bargaining and one that does not have that option. In the first case, bargaining is done by the shop steward on one side and management on the other. Because the shop steward is representing the interests of a whole class of people, the bargaining can be tough. On the other hand, where there is no union, the bargaining must be done on a person-by-person basis.

INTERNATIONAL HUMAN RESOURCE MANAGEMENT

Doing business in a global environment has grown more and more common. It is also complex and challenging. An international HRM office becomes very important to an organization because it is vital that a company's staff be trained for handling the challenges it will face in working globally. Job analysis should identify the specific skills and knowledge base needed to operate successfully in this arena, and the personnel who will be working internationally need to be trained in those skills and knowledge areas. In addition, workers who remain in this country, but interact with global offices also need to receive the training that will enable them to work effectively in an international environment. Among the factors that HRM on the global level must deal with are (1) culture, (2) different legal systems, (3) political risks, and (4) different economic systems.

Companies doing business in the global market may transfer personnel from their domestic offices to work in their satellite firms abroad. These workers are often called expatriates. In addition, U.S. companies typically hire nationals from their host countries or even third-country nationals. For this mixed group of people to work well together, there must be a common language, such as English. For the U.S. workers, having a second language is a plus. In some cases, though, a translator may be necessary. The selection process includes (1) self-selection by employees who see an assignment abroad as a career enhancement and (2) assessing the skills required for the open positions before (3) making a decision and (4) running a background check on the candidate. Once chosen, the employee receives orientation and training before departing for the assignment and online training and development while abroad.

Of primary importance is the fact that management cannot assume that U.S. ways of doing business are universal. Having different cultural and business backgrounds will affect the interactions between the U.S. corporation and personnel from the host country, further reflecting the importance of training in cultural sensitivity. Managers and expatriates also need to be aware that not only are there likely to be cultural differences, but also political, legal, and economic ones. Consideration must also be given to helping the families of the expatriates adjust to their new environment. This may even include, for example, finding jobs for their spouses.

Coordination among offices in multiple countries frequently depends on electronic communication. The Internet can also be useful for training purposes and for responding to calls for assistance. Given the different time zones in which offices of a single corporation may operate, the latter can turn out to be a 24/7 responsibility. In addition, using electronic communication can allow for the creation of teams of workers, even though all team members may never be in the same place together.

If learning about the history, language, and culture of the host company is important before someone relocates, it is also necessary to assist expatriates in reorienting themselves to the U.S. lifestyle before they return to this country.

CURRENT ISSUES AND TRENDS

There are three major trends in HRM today that bear watching: (1) workforce diversity, (2) human resource information systems, and (3) changing patterns of work relationships.

Workforce Diversity

The meaning of the term *diversity in the workforce* has expanded over the years. Originally, its meaning was fairly narrow and mainly concerned with (1) race and (2) gender. Today, it encompasses many perceived differences, such as (3) age, (4) religion, (5) disabilities, (6) country of origin, (7) marital status, (8) family responsibilities, and (9) sexual orientation. The overriding aim is for a diversified workforce that reflects the general population.

Being inclusive requires that employers be open-minded and supportive, so that all employees feel welcome and valued. A cohesive workforce is one in which employees work well together. Prospective employees are drawn to a company with that kind of reputation, and customers benefit from the harmonious environment. As a result, the bottom line benefits.

Human Resource Information Systems

Increasingly sophisticated technology is allowing companies to implement highly useful Human Resource Information Systems (HRIS). An HRIS allows HR to collect and store, in one place, the vast amount of data it needs to research and track information about such things as recruitment and hiring, compliance with legislation and regulations, and the administration of the benefits program. It can identify the costs associated with various activities and present graphs to show inventory levels and disclose profit levels over a set period of time. It allows the production department to fill orders and accounting to bill the right customers in a timely manner. Employees may also have access to information about programs that they can enroll in, insurance coverage, benefits, and retirement plans.

Changing Patterns of Work Relationships

Changes in the workplace are a reflection of the varied lifestyles of the workforce. At one time, employers hired new workers, assigned them a workstation, and expected them to present themselves there at the usual starting time. Of course that still happens, but now there is more flexibility:

(1) the virtual office, (2) contingent workers, (3) unconventional work arrangements, (4) outsourcing, and (5) employee leasing.

For example, with the virtual office, workers may not even have to appear in person, only electronically. A virtual office may be an actual place, but most importantly, it is equipped with telecommunication links that enable workers to connect. However, the office doesn't have to be a fixed place anymore. The computer itself can become the office, and its operator can function just about anywhere.

Contingent workers also have a nontraditional connection with a firm. The "contingency" is that they are subject to chance, that is, to the needs of the employer at a particular time. They may work as part-timers, temporary employees, or independent contractors. Their temporary availability allows the company flexibility and lower expenses than an on-site employee. There are none of the extra costs, such as vacation time or company contributions to medical insurance. The drawback for the employees, though, is that they are readily disposable. Still, companies that utilize contingent workers are going beyond the kind of workers needed only for unskilled jobs. The contingent workers can also be engineers, technicians, and specialists in various fields, including the law.

There are also other unconventional work arrangements. One is the autonomous work group. Under this arrangement, workers are part of a team that decides for itself how the work should be distributed among members of the team.

Outsourcing and employee leasing are other recent options in the business world. Outsourcing involves hiring workers outside the company to do work that was previously done in-house. Employee leasing is perhaps one of the more far-reaching alternatives to standard hiring practice. A company releases its employees, who are then hired by a professional employer organization (PEO). The PEO pays the workers and the expenses normally associated with permanent employees: workers compensation, payroll taxes, and employee benefits.

Will these innovations spread to more and more companies? Time will tell. It may well be that in the future those companies that experiment with such innovative ways of doing business will profit from their willingness to experiment.

POST-TEST ANSWER SHEET

1. Ⓐ Ⓑ Ⓒ Ⓓ	13. Ⓐ Ⓑ Ⓒ Ⓓ	25. Ⓐ Ⓑ Ⓒ Ⓓ	37. Ⓐ Ⓑ Ⓒ Ⓓ	49. Ⓐ Ⓑ Ⓒ Ⓓ
2. Ⓐ Ⓑ Ⓒ Ⓓ	14. Ⓐ Ⓑ Ⓒ Ⓓ	26. Ⓐ Ⓑ Ⓒ Ⓓ	38. Ⓐ Ⓑ Ⓒ Ⓓ	50. Ⓐ Ⓑ Ⓒ Ⓓ
3. Ⓐ Ⓑ Ⓒ Ⓓ	15. Ⓐ Ⓑ Ⓒ Ⓓ	27. Ⓐ Ⓑ Ⓒ Ⓓ	39. Ⓐ Ⓑ Ⓒ Ⓓ	51. Ⓐ Ⓑ Ⓒ Ⓓ
4. Ⓐ Ⓑ Ⓒ Ⓓ	16. Ⓐ Ⓑ Ⓒ Ⓓ	28. Ⓐ Ⓑ Ⓒ Ⓓ	40. Ⓐ Ⓑ Ⓒ Ⓓ	52. Ⓐ Ⓑ Ⓒ Ⓓ
5. Ⓐ Ⓑ Ⓒ Ⓓ	17. Ⓐ Ⓑ Ⓒ Ⓓ	29. Ⓐ Ⓑ Ⓒ Ⓓ	41. Ⓐ Ⓑ Ⓒ Ⓓ	53. Ⓐ Ⓑ Ⓒ Ⓓ
6. Ⓐ Ⓑ Ⓒ Ⓓ	18. Ⓐ Ⓑ Ⓒ Ⓓ	30. Ⓐ Ⓑ Ⓒ Ⓓ	42. Ⓐ Ⓑ Ⓒ Ⓓ	54. Ⓐ Ⓑ Ⓒ Ⓓ
7. Ⓐ Ⓑ Ⓒ Ⓓ	19. Ⓐ Ⓑ Ⓒ Ⓓ	31. Ⓐ Ⓑ Ⓒ Ⓓ	43. Ⓐ Ⓑ Ⓒ Ⓓ	55. Ⓐ Ⓑ Ⓒ Ⓓ
8. Ⓐ Ⓑ Ⓒ Ⓓ	20. Ⓐ Ⓑ Ⓒ Ⓓ	32. Ⓐ Ⓑ Ⓒ Ⓓ	44. Ⓐ Ⓑ Ⓒ Ⓓ	56. Ⓐ Ⓑ Ⓒ Ⓓ
9. Ⓐ Ⓑ Ⓒ Ⓓ	21. Ⓐ Ⓑ Ⓒ Ⓓ	33. Ⓐ Ⓑ Ⓒ Ⓓ	45. Ⓐ Ⓑ Ⓒ Ⓓ	57. Ⓐ Ⓑ Ⓒ Ⓓ
10. Ⓐ Ⓑ Ⓒ Ⓓ	22. Ⓐ Ⓑ Ⓒ Ⓓ	34. Ⓐ Ⓑ Ⓒ Ⓓ	46. Ⓐ Ⓑ Ⓒ Ⓓ	58. Ⓐ Ⓑ Ⓒ Ⓓ
11. Ⓐ Ⓑ Ⓒ Ⓓ	23. Ⓐ Ⓑ Ⓒ Ⓓ	35. Ⓐ Ⓑ Ⓒ Ⓓ	47. Ⓐ Ⓑ Ⓒ Ⓓ	59. Ⓐ Ⓑ Ⓒ Ⓓ
12. Ⓐ Ⓑ Ⓒ Ⓓ	24. Ⓐ Ⓑ Ⓒ Ⓓ	36. Ⓐ Ⓑ Ⓒ Ⓓ	48. Ⓐ Ⓑ Ⓒ Ⓓ	60. Ⓐ Ⓑ Ⓒ Ⓓ

answer sheet

POST-TEST

Directions: Carefully read each of the following 60 questions. Choose the best answer to each question, and darken its letter on your answer sheet. The Answer Key and Explanations can be found following this Post-Test.

1. To provide its customers with personalized service, a firm will
   - **(A)** try to hire workers who feel empathy for others.
   - **(B)** offer generous incentives to its employees.
   - **(C)** interview an applicant's former employers.
   - **(D)** redesign the job to suit the applicant.

2. What must happen before workers have a performance evaluation?
   - **(A)** They must be told what their deficiencies are.
   - **(B)** They must be told what the performance criteria are.
   - **(C)** They must do a self-analysis and share it with the supervisor.
   - **(D)** They must be informed of any raise they will receive.

3. A new employee may benefit from a team approach because
   - **(A)** he or she will have access to different knowledge skills.
   - **(B)** experienced workers usually make good mentors.
   - **(C)** it rules out the need for extensive training.
   - **(D)** he or she can then offer suggestions to improve procedures.

4. Accidents due to unsafe worker behavior often occur
   - **(A)** after an OSHA inspection.
   - **(B)** right after a job hazard analysis.
   - **(C)** during a worker's first few months of employment.
   - **(D)** in a series of accidents.

5. Human resources are a company's
   - **(A)** customers.
   - **(B)** employees.
   - **(C)** supervisors.
   - **(D)** management.

6. A good performance review will depend mainly on whether the worker has
   - **(A)** met all the objectives expected of him or her.
   - **(B)** ever been promoted before.
   - **(C)** been with the firm for twenty or more years.
   - **(D)** a friendly relationship with his or her supervisor.

7. What is the function of a job analysis?
   - **(A)** To determine what skills are needed for certain jobs
   - **(B)** To make employees aware of why they are being terminated
   - **(C)** To develop pay ranges
   - **(D)** To create and maintain up-to-date files on each employee

8. What is the first step in a job evaluation?
   (A) Job analysis
   (B) Job ranking
   (C) Pay grade
   (D) Job description

9. Orientation generally includes
   (A) a test about the company's expectations about new employees' performance.
   (B) a chance for new employees to explain what they expect from their employment in the company.
   (C) six months for new employees to prove their value to the firm.
   (D) information about the firm's history.

10. What is Frederick Taylor known for?
    (A) As an industrial psychologist
    (B) As the founder of scientific management
    (C) As head of the first craft union
    (D) As the originator of personnel departments

11. Alternatives to having a supervisor evaluate an employee include all of the following EXCEPT
    (A) peer reviews.
    (B) written tests.
    (C) evaluation by subordinates.
    (D) appraisal by team members.

12. Which of the following would require that a job design be altered?
    (A) Procedures and requirements for the job change.
    (B) New employees replace more experienced ones.
    (C) Hiring exceeds demand for products or services.
    (D) Weaknesses in the workforce reveal themselves.

13. How can managers avoid accusations of bias in the evaluation process?
    (A) By submitting their critiques in writing to their subordinates
    (B) By ignoring minor deficiencies and concentrating on major problems
    (C) By acting on problems in all workers' performance as they arise
    (D) By having HR sit in all performance appraisals

14. Which of the following describes employment at will?
    (A) An employee may not terminate employment unless the company agrees.
    (B) An employee may or may not choose to sign a contract of employment.
    (C) An employer may terminate an employee for any reason or for no reason.
    (D) An employer may revoke an employee's contract.

15. Which of the following is a political risk that global companies must deal with?
    (A) Emphasis on deference rather than assertiveness
    (B) Potential for government coups in certain regions
    (C) A workplace no-smoking ban
    (D) National 30-hour work week

16. Which of the following is an external source for recruiting?
    (A) Anonymous e-mail inquiries
    (B) Recommendations by employees
    (C) Transfers within the company
    (D) Employment agencies

17. Which of the following statements is NOT true?

    (A) A pay grade is made up of all jobs that fall within a certain range.

    (B) The purpose of a pay curve is to help managers develop a progression between pay grades.

    (C) Most companies pay one rate for all jobs in a pay grade.

    (D) A wage curve shows the relative value of all jobs.

18. A reduction in workforce may occur because of

    (A) a merger with or buyout by another company.

    (B) attrition.

    (C) errors in predicting job needs.

    (D) inadequate training programs to match employees with required skills sets.

19. Generally, unions organize an industry because of dissatisfaction with

    (A) the job market.

    (B) the economy.

    (C) management policies.

    (D) globalization

20. Which of the following is NOT a category of employment law?

    (A) Equal employment

    (B) Health and safety

    (C) Vacations and holidays

    (D) Compensation and benefits

21. The Americans with Disabilities Act applies to discrimination against

    (A) workers employed by certain federal contractors.

    (B) certain age ranges, the ranges changing over time.

    (C) retired workers whose funds have been mismanaged.

    (D) workers reporting hazards to OSHA.

22. Which of the following objectives would be most helpful in evaluating an employee's performance?

    (A) Work efficiently.

    (B) Produce the project on time and on budget.

    (C) Create a new ad campaign by September 15, 2012.

    (D) Develop ten informational fact sheets on Bike X by June 15, 2012.

23. The HR department is able to create a job description by means of

    (A) questionnaires.

    (B) observation.

    (C) interviews of employees in the job.

    (D) a combination of questionnaires, observation, and interviews of employees in the job.

24. What is the primary purpose of a job hazard analysis?

    (A) To teach workers about ergonomics

    (B) To identify work activities that are dangerous

    (C) To encourage workers to apply for disability insurance

    (D) To monitor workers in their first few months on the job

25. In establishing pay rates, the compensation manager must take into account all of the following factors EXCEPT

    (A) the company's policies on salaries.

    (B) the company's ability to pay.

    (C) movement in the stock market in the short term.

    (D) what the company president will receive at retirement.

26. Which of the following describes a defined benefit plan?

    (A) The amount that the retiree receives is fixed at a certain amount for life.

    (B) The amount that the retiree receives depends on how much the company invests for the employee and how well the investment does.

    (C) A defined benefit plan is another name for a 401(k) plan.

    (D) It is a trust that holds company stock and divides the stock among employees based on their earnings.

27. Which of the following statements is NOT true about phased retirement?

    (A) Workers have to retire by age 70.

    (B) Workers can adjust gradually to a new lifestyle while still working.

    (C) Workers can reduce their hours, but keep their benefits while they continue working.

    (D) Employers have a ready-made resource for mentoring younger workers by using phased retirement of experienced workers.

28. In establishing pay rates, when is legislation a factor?

    (A) By law, companies are expected to pay unionized workers more than nonunion workers.

    (B) By law, companies are expected to pay workers more when the economy is growing.

    (C) By law, companies may withhold pay raises when the economy is doing poorly.

    (D) By law, companies are expected to classify workers as either exempt or non-exempt.

29. The right of labor to organize and engage in collective bargaining is covered by which of the following laws?

    (A) Employee Retirement Income Security Act

    (B) National Labor Relations Act

    (C) Age Discrimination in Employment Act

    (D) Taft-Hartley Act

30. Human Resource Information Systems allow for the

    (A) control of Internet communications.

    (B) setting up of virtual offices.

    (C) collection and storage of vast amounts of data.

    (D) monitoring of flexplace and flextime work arrangements.

31. Which of the following describes trend analysis for forecasting staffing needs?

    (A) HRM develops a forecast based on the ratio between factors.

    (B) HRM considers a variety of factors, both current and in the past.

    (C) HRM creates a visual representation of variables, such as the number of departments in an organization and the number of employees in each department.

    (D) HRM looks at staffing needs in an organization's departments over a period of time.

32. In collective bargaining, it is important that

    (A) union members be allowed to sign authorization cards that the union may act for it.

    (B) grievances be settled first.

    (C) both sides be willing to make concessions.

    (D) unions not "salt" the workplace.

33. Where might a person find information on salary ranges in various industries?

    (A) On the Internal Revenue Service's Web site

    (B) From the U.S. Department of Labor's Bureau of Labor Statistics

    (C) In corporations' annual reports

    (D) In various companies' newsletters

34. Which of the following describes an autonomous work group?

    (A) Team of workers deciding for themselves how to handle work assignments

    (B) Third-party contracted work team

    (C) An outsourcing group

    (D) A professional employer organization

35. Which law has been most effective in limiting discrimination in the workplace?

    (A) Fair Labor Standards Act

    (B) Civil Service Reform Act

    (C) National Labor Relations Act

    (D) Civil Rights Act Title VII

36. Outplacement is a company's way of trying to

    (A) reduce the size of its staff through voluntary turnover.

    (B) help terminated workers strengthen their job-search skills.

    (C) learn how workers feel about how the firm treated them.

    (D) gauge how much turnover there has been.

37. Which of the following is a provision of the Taft-Hartley Act?

    (A) Employees could refuse to join a union.

    (B) Unions no longer had to give employers notice of an impending strike.

    (C) The U.S. president was no longer allowed to halt a strike on the basis of a national emergency.

    (D) Employers may not publicize negative opinions about unions among their workers.

38. Which of the following could result in a wrongful termination suit?

    (A) The company did not adhere to guarantees made to the employee when hiring.

    (B) The company found unexplained gaps in an applicant's employment.

    (C) The company does not train workers in conflict management.

    (D) The company does not guarantee worker safety.

39. Surveys presented at the end of a training experience measure

    (A) the need for additional training.

    (B) immediate feedback on the program.

    (C) changes in the participants' behaviors.

    (D) changes in the results that the organization is experiencing because of the training.

40. After a mass layoff, one of a business' concerns is

    (A) what to tell customers.

    (B) the morale of the employees who remain.

    (C) replacing the best salespeople.

    (D) the cost of severance packages.

post-test

41. What does a right-to-work law do?

    (A) Requires employers to hire only union members

    (B) Removes the right to strike from unions

    (C) Removes the requirement that workers in a union shop pay union dues whether they belong to the union or not

    (D) Requires that the union steward negotiate wages for all workers

42. All of the following are important in preparing an employee to work abroad EXCEPT

    (A) information on housing and schools if children will be moving.

    (B) language training.

    (C) cultural sensitivity training.

    (D) repatriation assistance.

43. Worker development is concerned mainly with

    (A) fine-tuning employees' current skills sets.

    (B) employee job satisfaction.

    (C) employees' future career paths.

    (D) improving employee weaknesses.

44. A company that is paying the market rate in salaries is

    (A) paying no more than average.

    (B) paying less than all its competitors.

    (C) paying the highest compensation in the field.

    (D) attracting the most highly qualified workers.

45. What is the purpose of exit interviews of workers who leave an organization voluntarily?

    (A) To gain insight on why they are leaving

    (B) To have them fill out termination paperwork

    (C) To try to persuade them to stay by offering incentives

    (D) To ask them to recommend replacements

46. Which of the following is NOT a category analyzed for hazards under OSHA regulations?

    (A) Walking surfaces

    (B) Emergency exits

    (C) Coin-operated machines

    (D) Electrical systems

47. Which of the following is a true statement about performance appraisals?

    (A) The basis for evaluation at a PA is the set of goals the employee and supervisor set at the last PA.

    (B) The supervisor prepares all paperwork for a PA.

    (C) Supervisors are more likely to schedule PAs with employees who have problems in order to get them over with.

    (D) Rating all employees in a department as average favors all the employees.

48. If an employer uses a performance grading system of 1 to 7, being ranked 6

    (A) suggests the employee has failed to meet the grade.

    (B) suggests a mediocre performance.

    (C) means the employee has exceeded all standards.

    (D) means the employee is considered a high achiever.

49. Of the following, which may NOT be permanent?

    (A) RIF

    (B) Layoff due to economic conditions

    (C) Early retirement

    (D) Resignation

50. What development made the passage of ERISA necessary?

   (A) Compensation and benefits programs became too expensive for most organizations.

   (B) Health, safety, and employee rights were being abused by companies.

   (C) Some retirement funds were mismanaged, and workers lost their retirement benefits.

   (D) Union contracts did not cover members' retirement needs.

51. The principle of transfer of learning means that workers

   (A) are motivated to continually learn new skills.

   (B) learn by asking questions of mentors.

   (C) can avoid being locked into one career path.

   (D) must inform management of their online studies.

52. An agreement between a company and a labor union typically covers

   (A) check card procedures.

   (B) automatic payroll deduction of union dues.

   (C) arbitration procedures.

   (D) closed shop provisions.

53. A major disadvantage of offering early retirement packages is

   (A) having to replace departing workers quickly.

   (B) losing the most experienced workers.

   (C) the strain on the HR department in processing the retirement packages.

   (D) the need to pay for recruiting and training departing workers' replacements.

54. Which situation or condition would most likely attract an OSHA inspector's attention?

   (A) No employees over the age of 40

   (B) Lack of any retirement program

   (C) Foreign-born workers who do not speak English

   (D) The lack of well-marked emergency exits

55. The categories of exempt and non-exempt workers differ in that

   (A) non-exempt employees are covered by laws regulating minimum wage.

   (B) neither category is defined by legislation.

   (C) exempt employees receive an hourly wage and non-exempt employees receive salaries.

   (D) non-exempt employees include outside salespeople and this is not a category of exempt workers.

56. Case studies are useful for management training because

   (A) business games keep managers' attention.

   (B) the manager must analyze a business situation and suggest solutions.

   (C) they stress assertiveness training for women.

   (D) executive coaches take part and are very effective.

57. Employee stock ownership plans are a form of

   (A) monetary compensation.

   (B) gift certificates.

   (C) commissions.

   (D) nonmonetary compensation.

58. In a union situation, demotion as a disciplinary action should

   (A) be avoided to prevent harming employee morale.

   (B) be handled according to the firm's agreement with the union.

   (C) never involve a reduction in pay.

   (D) be delayed until the employee's next review to see if the person has improved.

59. E-learning for employees is popular because

   (A) it is highly flexible.

   (B) it is easy.

   (C) it is not costly to prepare or purchase training materials.

   (D) of its lack of assessments and tests.

60. Which of the following is true about worker's compensation?

   (A) Worker's compensation pays benefits to workers who lose their jobs in a recession.

   (B) It is similar to Social Security payments.

   (C) It is a form of disability insurance.

   (D) It reimburses a worker for expenses incurred in a job-related accident.

ANSWER KEY AND EXPLANATIONS

1. A	13. C	25. C	37. A	49. B
2. B	14. C	26. A	38. A	50. C
3. A	15. B	27. A	39. B	51. C
4. C	16. D	28. D	40. B	52. B
5. B	17. C	29. B	41. C	53. B
6. A	18. A	30. C	42. D	54. D
7. A	19. C	31. D	43. C	55. A
8. A	20. C	32. C	44. A	56. B
9. D	21. A	33. B	45. A	57. D
10. B	22. D	34. A	46. C	58. B
11. B	23. D	35. D	47. A	59. A
12. A	24. B	36. B	48. D	60. D

1. **The correct answer is (A).** Choice (B) is incorrect because offering incentives would not change the character of the applicant. Choice (C) is incorrect because by law, former employers can only verify dates of employment and positions held. Choice (D) is incorrect because redesigning the job would not serve the company's interests.

2. **The correct answer is (B).** Choice (A) is incorrect because discussion of deficiencies happens during a performance appraisal, not before. Choice (C) is incorrect because self-analyses are not shared with supervisors. Choice (D) is incorrect because that happens during or after the evaluation, but not before.

3. **The correct answer is (A).** Choice (B) is incorrect because there is no guarantee that an experienced worker will make a good mentor. Choice (C) is incorrect because the employee may still need training. Choice (D) is incorrect because he or she would not have the on-the-job experience to make suggestions to the team.

4. **The correct answer is (C).** Choice (A) is incorrect because there is no evidence to support a causal relationship between OSHA inspections and accidents, nor between a job hazard analysis, choice (B), and accidents. Choice (D) is incorrect because there is no evidence to support the idea that accidents happen in a series.

5. **The correct answer is (B).** Choice (A) is incorrect because customers are not part of the organization. Choices (C) and (D) are incorrect because while supervisors and management are part of an organization's human resources, they are only parts.

6. **The correct answer is (A).** Choice (B) is incorrect because meeting the current objectives is the most important criterion. Choice (C) is incorrect because length of employment is not important when it comes to assessing current performance. Choice (D) is incorrect because a friendly relationship with the supervisor could result in a subjective performance appraisal by the supervisor.

7. **The correct answer is (A).** Choice (B) is incorrect because a performance evaluation, not a job analysis, would be useful in explaining why an employee is being terminated. Choice (C) is incorrect because a salary survey and a job evaluation are used to help determine pay ranges, not a job analysis. Choice (D) is incorrect because the analysis is independent of any single employee's records.

8. **The correct answer is (A).** Choice (B) is incorrect because job ranking is used in the job evaluation process. Choice (C) is incorrect because pay grades are based on information found through job evaluation. Choice (D) is incorrect because a job description is just that, a description of a job and not a step in the process of job evaluation.

9. **The correct answer is (D).** The purpose of orientation is to provide new employees with information about their employer. Choice (A) is incorrect because orientation is not a testing situation. Choice (B) is incorrect because discussing a new employee's expectations for his or her employment is not part of orientation. Choice (C) is incorrect because proving an employee's value to a company is a matter of working for the company, not learning about it.

10. **The correct answer is (B).** Frederick Taylor is known as the founder of scientific management. Choice (A) is incorrect because he was not an industrial psychologist. Choice (C) is incorrect because he was not involved in the union movement; the first craft unions were founded in Great Britain and the United States in the mid-1800s. The largest in the United States was the American Federation of Labor, which organized a federation of craft unions in 1886. Choice (D) is incorrect because Taylor was not involved in the development of personnel departments, which came much later than Taylor, who died in 1915.

11. **The correct answer is (B).** You're looking for the wrong answer in *except* and *not* questions, and the answer that doesn't fit in this series is choice (B). Written tests are not used as an alternative to having a supervisor evaluate an employee. Choices (A), (C), and (D)—peer review, subordinates' evaluating an employee who reports to a higher-level supervisor, and team member appraisals—are all alternative methods of employee evaluation and so incorrect answers to the question.

12. **The correct answer is (A).** Choice (B) is incorrect because new employees would not affect job design. Choice (C) is incorrect because having too many employees for the amount of work required to meet demand would affect staffing, but not job design. Choice (D) is incorrect because weaknesses in the workforce should not be remedied by changing the job design.

13. **The correct answer is (C).** Choice (A) is incorrect because that would not solve the problem. Choice (B) is incorrect because that would not be helpful to the employee, the supervisor, or the organization. Choice (D) is not a practical solution and doesn't help the manager learn good skills, so eliminate it.

14. **The correct answer is (C).** Employment at will means that there is no written contract between employee and employer that specifies a set period of employment. Either party may terminate employment at any time; the employer may or may not give a reason for termination. Choice (A) is incorrect because employment at will doesn't require the agreement of the employer. Choices (B) and (D) are incorrect because there is no contract involved in employment at will.

15. **The correct answer is (B).** The potential risk of a coup could jeopardize employees' lives and those of their families and do harm to the business. Choice (A) is incorrect because an emphasis on deference is a cultural factor,

not a political risk. Choice (C) is incorrect because a workplace no-smoking ban is a legal factor, not a political one. Choice (D) is both a legal and an economic aspect of doing business in another country.

16. **The correct answer is (D).** Choice (A) is incorrect because an anonymous e-mail would be discounted, if it even got through a company's spam folder. Choices (B) and (C) are incorrect because both are internal sources.

17. **The correct answer is (C).** You want the answer that is *not* true, so eliminate choices (A), (B), and (D) because they are all true statements related to pay grades and wage, or pay, curves. Choice (C) is not true about pay grades and wage curves, so it's the correct answer.

18. **The correct answer is (A).** Choice (B) is incorrect, because attrition is not hiring employees to replace those who leave voluntarily or are terminated for cause. It is a method used as an alternative to an RIF. Choice (C) is incorrect because it is likely that an error in predicting job needs would be corrected by other means, such as choice (B), before an RIF would be necessary. Choice (D) is incorrect because training programs would be revised before employees would be let go.

19. **The correct answer is (C).** Choices (A), (B), and (D) are incorrect because none of these—the job market, the economy, or globalization—would have a direct influence on the decision to organize. They may all, however, have an influence on management policies.

20. **The correct answer is (C).** Vacations and holidays are not a category of employment law, though they are covered under compensation and benefits, which is a category of employment law, so choice (D) is incorrect. Choices (A) and (B) are also categories of employment law, and so are incorrect answers to the question.

21. **The correct answer is (A).** Choice (B) is incorrect because age discrimination is prohibited under the Age Discrimination in Employment Act (ADEA). Choice (C) is incorrect because pensions are guaranteed under the Employment Retirement Income Security Act (ERISA). Choice (D) is incorrect because the Occupational Safety and Health Administration (OSHA) deals with issues of worker safety and health.

22. **The correct answer is (D).** Employee objectives need to be clearly stated and quantifiable. Only choice (D) meets both criteria. Choice (A) can be eliminated because it is vague, as is choice (B). Choice (C) is better, but doesn't indicate what the ad campaign is for.

23. **The correct answer is (D).** Choices (A), (B), and (C) alone are not the best answers. The best answer combines all three: questionnaires, observation, and interviews.

24. **The correct answer is (B).** Choice (A) is incorrect because ergonomics refers to only one issue considered in identifying workplace hazards. Choice (C) is incorrect because disability coverage is provided through workers' comp, which almost all companies must carry by law; some companies also buy additional disability insurance for employees. Choice (D) is incorrect. Although many accidents may occur in a worker's first few months, the primary purpose of job hazard analysis is to protect all workers.

25. **The correct answer is (C).** Movement in the stock market doesn't usually affect company policy on salaries in the short term. Choice (A) is incorrect because a company's policies on salaries are something the compensation manager must take into account. Choice (B) is incorrect because the company's ability to pay is something that does affect salaries. Choice (D) is incorrect because even if the company president's retirement benefits are

expensive, they are not covered under salary policies.

26. **The correct answer is (A).** At one time, the defined benefit plan, which means that the amount the retiree receives is fixed at a certain amount for life, was the typical pension plan for companies that offered pensions to their employees. Today, companies are moving to choice (B), which defines a defined contribution plan. Choice (C) is incorrect because a 401(k) is a form of defined contribution plan, so eliminate it. Choice (D) is incorrect because it describes an employee stock option plan (ESOP).

27. **The correct answer is (A).** Choices (B), (C), and (D) are all true about phased retirement, so they are incorrect answers to the question, whereas choice (A) is not true and the correct answer. There is no set age for retirement; however, age 70 is the age at which people must begin taking their Social Security benefits. Note that although working fewer hours means a reduction in pay, employees keep their benefits.

28. **The correct answer is (D).** Choices (A), (B), and (C) are not a matter of law. Choice (A) is incorrect because if a labor union negotiates a pay raise in its contract, nonunion workers may also receive the raise. Choices (B) and (C) are incorrect because there is no legislation tying salaries to the state of the economy.

29. **The correct answer is (B).** Choice (A) is incorrect because ERISA deals with retirement programs. Choice (C) is incorrect because ADEA deals with discrimination against workers within certain age ranges. Choice (D) is incorrect because the Taft-Hartley Act deals mainly with unfair union labor practices and also enumerates the rights of employees and employers.

30. **The correct answer is (C).** Choice (A) is incorrect because HRIS does not control Internet communications. Choice (B) is incorrect because setting up virtual offices isn't the purpose of HRIS. Choice (D) is incorrect because HRIS does not monitor flexplace and flextime work arrangements, though HRIS may collect data about them.

31. **The correct answer is (D).** Choice (A) is incorrect because it describes a form of forecasting called ratio analysis. Choice (B) is incorrect because HRM would consider only past staffing needs, not a variety of factors. Choice (C) is incorrect because it describes scatter plot analysis.

32. **The correct answer is (C).** Choice (A) is incorrect because authorization cards are used to prove that a large number of a site's workers are interested in joining the union. It is the second step in a unionization effort. Choice (B) is incorrect because dealing with grievances is separate from contract negotiations. Choice (D) is incorrect because "salting" a workplace involves having union members go to work for nonunion companies in an effort to organize the companies.

33. **The correct answer is (B).** Choice (A) is incorrect because the IRS would not give out such information. Choice (C) is incorrect because annual reports provide salary information for upper management, not for all workers in the company, which still isn't the same as salary ranges in an industry. Choice (D) is incorrect for the same reason, and also because such information is not typically published by companies.

34. **The correct answer is (A).** Choices (B) and (C) are both incorrect because they describe outsourcing. Choice (D) is incorrect because a PEO hires employees laid off by a company, pays them and their benefits, and leases their services to companies.

35. **The correct answer is (D).** Choice (A) is incorrect because the FLSA deals mainly with minimum wage, maximum hours, overtime pay, equal pay, recordkeeping, and child labor provisions, as well as distinguishing between exempt and non-exempt employees. Choice (B) is incorrect because

the CSRA is concerned with labor management relations in the federal service. Choice (C) is incorrect because the NLRA supports the right of labor to organize and engage in collective bargaining.

36. **The correct answer is (B).** Choice (A) is incorrect because outplacement is not related to voluntary turnover. Choice (C) is incorrect because learning how terminated employees feel about the company is the purpose of the exit interview. Choice (D) is incorrect because turnover generally relates to voluntary termination, whereas outsourcing is for workers terminated involuntarily. Also, outplacement has nothing to do with monitoring.

37. **The correct answer is (A).** By giving workers the right to not join a union, the Taft-Hartley Act banned the closed shop. Choice (B) is incorrect because unions are required under the law to notify a company 60 days in advance of an impending strike. Choice (C) is incorrect because it is the opposite of what the law says; the U.S. president may intervene and apply for an injunction to halt the strike. Choice (D) is incorrect because the Taft-Hartley Act allows employers to give their side of what unionization may do to the company and to their jobs in the future.

38. **The correct answer is (A).** A wrongful termination suit is brought by a former employee. Choice (B) is incorrect because unexplained gaps should be apparent on a person's resumé and be dealt with during an interview. Also, it is illogical to consider that a former employee would begin a lawsuit because of an omission on his or her part. Choice (C) is incorrect because conflict management training is not a requirement. Choice (D) is incorrect because not guaranteeing worker safety is illegal.

39. **The correct answer is (B).** Choice (A) is incorrect because the need for additional training will be measured on how well

participants learned the information and put it into practice. Choice (C) is incorrect because any possible changes in behavior related to the training have not yet taken place. Choice (D) is incorrect because the employees have not yet had an opportunity to put into practice—or not—what they've learned during the training.

40. **The correct answer is (B).** Choice (A) is incorrect because it is unlikely that management would consider explaining its actions to customers. Choice (C) is incorrect because rehiring the "best salespeople" would be easier and less expensive than replacing them. Choice (D) is incorrect because the costs of severance would be considered before the layoffs, not after.

41. **The correct answer is (C).** Choice (A) is incorrect because employers can hire both union and nonunion workers regardless of whether a state has a right-to-work law. Choice (B) is incorrect because right-to-work laws are state laws, and federal law guarantees the right to strike; federal law takes precedence over state law. Choice (D) is incorrect because the union has a panel of union members that negotiate contract terms, including wages.

42. **The correct answer is (D).** The question asks for the answer that doesn't match the types of training and information that a soon-to-be expatriate would need before he or she goes abroad. Choices (A), (B), and (C) are all the things that the employee will need. Choice (D), repatriation assistance, is given to expatriates as they prepare to come home, not before they leave home.

43. **The correct answer is (C).** Choice (A) is incorrect because development is mainly concerned with future skills, not present skills; improving skills is the work of training programs. Choice (B) is incorrect because worker development is concerned with future positions, not current job satisfaction. Choice (D) is incorrect because although

an employee's weaknesses are of concern, strengthening skills and knowledge would be only one part of the plan for his or her future and would involve training.

44. **The correct answer is (A).** Choice (B) is incorrect because a pay follower pays less than its competitors. Choice (C) is incorrect because paying the highest rate describes a pay leader. Choice (D) is incorrect because it is unlikely that a company paying average compensation would attract the most highly qualified workers.

45. **The correct answer is (A).** Choice (B) is incorrect because while employees may need to fill out paperwork, this is not the purpose of an exit interview. Choice (C) is incorrect because it is not the place of HRM to offer incentives; that would be done by the supervisor, if interested, at the time the employee resigns. Choice (D) is incorrect because while that may occur, it is not the purpose of an exit interview.

46. **The correct answer is (C).** While it is possible that an employee might get his or her hand caught in a vending machine, vending machines are not a category of hazards under OSHA regulations, so choice (C) is the correct answer. Choices (A), (B), and (D) are incorrect answers because they are categories analyzed for hazards.

47. **The correct answer is (A).** Choice (B) is incorrect because the employee completes his or her own evaluation form, which will be used with the supervisor's during the PA interview. Choice (C) is incorrect because human nature being what it is, supervisors who have to deliver unpleasant information tend to put off those PAs. Choice (D) is known as the central tendency error and is incorrect because it favors the underachiever, but not the overachiever.

48. **The correct answer is (D).** Choice (A) is incorrect because the higher the number, the better the grade. Choice (B) is incorrect because it would have to be a lower number

than 6 for an employee to be considered mediocre on a scale of 1 to 7. Choice (C) is incorrect because although it is a good grade, it is does not exceed company standards, which would be more than 7.

49. **The correct answer is (B).** Choice (A) is incorrect because an RIF is intended to be permanent. Choice (C) is incorrect because a retirement, even an early one, is usually permanent. Choice (D) is incorrect because a resignation is likely to be permanent.

50. **The correct answer is (C).** ERISA is the Employment Retirement Income Security Act, which protects retirement funds. Choice (A) is incorrect because the passage of ERISA was separate from the cost of compensation and benefits packages. Choice (B) is incorrect because ERISA deals only with retirement benefits. Choice (D) is incorrect because union contracts usually do cover retirement benefits.

51. **The correct answer is (C).** Choice (A) is incorrect because transfer of skills involves taking what one has learned in one job to a new job. Choice (B) is incorrect because transfer of skills does not refer to passing on information, but to applying it to a new position. Choice (D) is incorrect because transfer of learning has nothing to do with a requirement for employees to inform management when they take courses.

52. **The correct answer is (B).** Choice (A) is incorrect because the check card, or authorization card, is part of the process of organizing a workplace by a union. It is used in place of an election to determine if the workers wish to unionize. Choice (C) is incorrect because any arbitration procedure is set at the time of contract negotiation. Choice (D) is incorrect because a closed shop is illegal and, therefore, could not be part of bargaining agreement.

53. **The correct answer is (B).** Choice (A) is incorrect because it is not likely the firm would be replacing these workers; the pur-

pose of offering early retirement packages is to reduce the workforce. For this reason, choice (D) is also incorrect. Choice (C) is incorrect because while the HR department may have an increased workload temporarily, the major disadvantage to offering early retirement is the loss of experienced employees.

54. **The correct answer is (D).** Choice (A) is incorrect because OSHA is concerned with worker safety, not age discrimination, which is the responsibility of the ADEA. Choice (B) is incorrect because OSHA is concerned with hazardous working conditions, not retirement funds. Choice (C) is incorrect because OSHA is concerned with workplace injuries and illnesses, not foreign-born workers who may or may not be illegal, unless they are affected by those injuries or illnesses.

55. **The correct answer is (A).** Choice (B) is incorrect because the categories are defined by legislation. This answer choice is also wrong because the question asks about the difference between the two categories and this answer choice gives a similarity. Choice (C) is incorrect because the opposite is true; non-exempt employees receive an hourly wage and exempt employees receive salaries. Choice (D) is incorrect because non-exempt employees don't include outside salespeople; they belong in the category of exempt workers.

56. **The correct answer is (B).** While business games may keep managers' attention, they aren't the same as case studies, so choice (A) is incorrect. Choice (C) is incorrect because assertiveness training for women is different from the case study approach to management training, which analyzes business decisions. Choice (D) is incorrect

because executive coaches work one-on-one with managers.

57. **The correct answer is (D).** Choice (A) is incorrect because stock options are not considered monetary compensation. Choice (B) is incorrect because stock options are not in the form of gift certificates. Choice (C) is incorrect because commissions are not the same as stock options.

58. **The correct answer is (B).** Choice (A) is incorrect because a company should not ignore a situation that requires disciplinary action regardless of whether a union is involved. Choice (C) is incorrect because demotion often does involve a reduction in pay. Choice (D) is incorrect because the situation should be dealt with immediately.

59. **The correct answer is (A).** Choice (B) is incorrect because e-learning can be on the level of college courses. Choice (C) is incorrect because preparing or purchasing training materials can be expensive, though over time, e-learning can be cost-effective, if enough employees use the programs. Choice (D) is incorrect because e-learning may have assessments and tests, depending on the type of training involved.

60. **The correct answer is (D).** Worker's compensation is an insurance program in that companies with a certain number of minimum employees must carry to pay medical, death, and income benefits to workers who are injured on the job or contract work-related illnesses. But it is not the same as disability insurance, so choice (C) is incorrect. Choice (A) is incorrect because worker's comp isn't related to job loss from a recession, nor is it related to Social Security payments, so choice (B) is also incorrect.

SUMMING IT UP

- The field of human resource management (HRM) traces its roots back to the Industrial Revolution and a form of personnel management known as industrial welfare. Forerunners of contemporary HRM include the work of Frederick Taylor, industrial psychology, and personnel departments.

- Human resource functions include (1) staffing and (2) training and development. Newer responsibilities include (3) performance appraisals, (4) compensation, (5) safety and health issues, (6) employee rights and discipline, and (7) forecasting staffing.

- HRM works with line managers, employees, and senior management.

- Motivating employees, communicating with workers about their goals and management's expectations, and showing leadership are three important roles of HRM.

- HR departments may be used as a strategic partner with upper management to set goals and execute an organization's strategic plan. HRM assists by predicting future staffing needs through the use of (1) trend analysis, (2) ratio analysis, or (3) scatter plots, as well as forecasting (4) the training needs that will be required.

- Job analysis and job design are part of the process of determining (1) specific tasks to be performed, (2) the methods to be used in performing those tasks, and (3) how the job relates to other work in the organization.

- Staffing involves (1) recruiting, (2) selection, (3) promotions and transfers, (4) reduction-in-force, (5) layoffs, and (6) voluntary turnover. Candidates may come from (1) internal or (2) external sources. Selection of staff can be influenced by (1) company rules and (2) legal considerations. Voluntary turnovers may occur because of (1) resignations and (2) retirements.

- Training includes an orientation program for new employees and training opportunities to build knowledge and improve skill sets for current employees. Principles of learning that need to be recognized in the workplace include (1) the need to motivate employees, (2) recognition of individual differences in learning, (3) the ability of employees to transfer learning, and (4) the need to provide meaningful materials.

- Training methods today can take a variety of forms, including (1) instructor-led sessions, (2) online training, (3) virtual classrooms, and (4) case studies. One-on-one coaching may also be appropriate.

- Development programs center on the skills and knowledge that go beyond the trainee's present job to deal with career planning.

- Pay, promotion, and retention are based on performance appraisals, which are formal evaluations of an employee as opposed to the ongoing assessment of performance that managers should be conducting.

- Job evaluation is the formal and systematic comparison of a firm's positions. It attempts to compare the effort, responsibility, and skills required to perform each job; compensation for each position is based on job evaluation.

- An organization's compensation policies classify it as a (1) pay leader, (2) market rate, or (3) pay follower.

- Employees are either (1) exempt or (2) non-exempt. The latter is governed by legislation regulating minimum wage, overtime, and other rights and worker protections.

- Mandatory benefits include (1) Social Security, (2) unemployment compensation, and (3) workers' compensation. Common discretionary benefits include (1) paid vacations, (2) sick pay, (3) medical benefits, (4) life insurance, (5) retirement plans, (6) stock option plans, (7) child care, and (8) scholarships for dependents. There are also voluntary benefits, such as vision and dental insurance.

- The Occupational Safety and Health Administration (OSHA) is charged with creating safe work environments in U.S. worksites. Areas that companies should focus on to create safe and healthy working conditions are (1) unsafe worker behavior, (2) unsafe working conditions, (3) Job Hazard Analysis to assess worksites, (4) ergonomics, and (5) accident investigation.

- Quality of work life is the extent to which employees can enhance their personal lives through their work environment and experiences.

- Most employees are hired and hold their jobs at will.

- Disciplinary action begins with an oral warning, followed by a written warning, and then possibly suspension, demotion, or termination if the inappropriate behavior is not remedied.

- Employment law is divided into four categories: (1) equal employment, (2) compensation and benefits, (3) health, safety, and employee rights, and (4) unions.

- Labor unions strive to improve (1) wages, (2) hours, (3) working conditions, and (4) benefits for their members. A union contract generally covers such issues as (1) wages and (2) overtime and such special situations as (3) hazard pay, (4) layoff or severance pay, (5) holidays, (6) vacations, and (7) family care provisions.

- HRM assists multinational organizations to recruit, select, assist, and train employees for working abroad. Among the factors that HRM on the global level must deal with are (1) culture, (2) different legal systems, (3) political risks, and (4) different economic systems.

- Important current trends that affect HRM's work are (1) workforce diversity, (2) human resource information systems, and (3) changing work patterns.

Organizational Behavior

The following chart outlines the sections and subsections in the Organizational Behavior test and offers a comparison between the percent of practice questions in this chapter and the actual DSST exam.

CONTENT OUTLINE: SECTIONS AND SUBSECTIONS	PERCENT OF EXAM DEVOTED TO EACH CONTENT AREA	NUMBER OF ITEMS IN THE DIAGNOSTIC TEST AND POST-TEST BY CONTENT AREA	PERCENT OF ITEMS IN THE DIAGNOSTIC TEST AND POST-TEST BY CONTENT AREA
I. Organizational Behavior Overview	6%	5	6.25%
A. The Field of Organizational Behavior		3	60%
1. Definition and framework		0	0%
2. Fundamental concepts		1	33.3%
3. History		2	66.7%
B. The Study of Organizational Behavior		2	40%
1. Scientific approaches		1	50%
2. Research designs		1	50%
3. Data collection methods		0	0%
II. Individual Processes and Characteristics	36%	28	35%
A. Perpetual Processes		5	17.9%
1. Characteristics of the perceptual process		0	0%
2. Barriers to accurate perception of others		2	40%
3. Attributional approaches to perception and behavior		3	60%
B. Personality		6	21.4%
1. Theories of personality		2	33.3%
2. Personality traits and characteristics		2	33.3%
3. Influence of personality on work behavior		2	33.3%
C. Attitudes		3	10.7%
1. Attitude formation		1	33.3%
2. Attitude and values		1	33.3%
3. Key employee attitudes		1	33.3%

chapter 6

D. Learning Processes		6	21.4%
1. Basic models of learning		1	16.7%
2. Major influences on the learning process		1	16.7%
3. Reinforcement theory		4	66.7%
a. Nature of punishment		0	0%
b. Types of reinforcement		2	50%
c. Schedules of reinforcement		2	50%
E. Motivation		8	28.6%
1. Role of motivation in organizations		0	0%
2. Theories of motivation		5	62.5%
a. Process theories (e.g., expectancy, equity, goal-setting)		2	40%
b. Content theories (e.g., Maslow's hierarchy of needs, Herzberg's two-factor theory, Alderfer's ERG theory, relatedness, and growth theory, McClelland's theory of needs)		3	60%
3. Application in organizations		3	37.5%
a. Behavior modification		0	0%
b. Job design		1	33.3%
c. Reward systems		2	66.7%
F. Work Stress and the Individual		0	0%
1. Nature of stress		0	0%
2. Causes and consequences of stress		0	0%
3. Coping with stress: individual and organizational approaches		0	0%
III. Interpersonal and Group Processes and Characteristics	**32%**	**30**	**37.5%**
A. Group Dynamics		5	16.7%
1. Types of groups		1	20%
2. Reasons for group formation		0	0%
3. Stages of group development		3	60%
4. Characteristics of groups		1	20%
B. Group Behavior and Conflict		5	16.7%
1. Levels of conflict		1	20%
2. Consequences of functional and dysfunctional conflict		2	40%
3. Conflict management		2	40%

C. Leadership		10	33.3%
1. Nature of the leadership process		*2*	*20%*
2. Models of leadership		*3*	*30%*
3. Evaluation of models of leadership		*2*	*20%*
4. Implications for managers		*3*	*30%*
D. Power and Politics		5	16.7%
1. Power and influence		*2*	*40%*
2. Interpersonal sources of power		*0*	*0%*
3. Structural and situational sources of power		*1*	*20%*
4. Political behavior in organizations		*2*	*40%*
E. Communication Processes		5	16.7%
1. The communication process		*2*	*40%*
2. Models of interpersonal communication styles		*0*	*0%*
3. Communication networks		*1*	*20%*
4. Barriers to effective communication within organizations		*2*	*40%*
5. Nonverbal communication		*0*	*0%*
IV. Organizational Processes and Characteristics	**19%**	**11**	**13.75%**
A. Organizational Decision Making		3	27.3%
1. Classification and definition of decisions		*0*	*0%*
2. Models of the decision-making process		*1*	*33.3%*
3. Individual versus group decision making		*2*	*66.7%*
B. Organizational Structure		6	54.5%
1. Dimensions of organization structure		*2*	*33.3%*
2. Types of organization structure		*2*	*33.3%*
3. Responsibility and authority		*2*	*33.3%*
C. Organizational Design		2	18.2%
1. Classic approaches		*1*	*50%*
2. Contingency approaches		*1*	*50%*
V. Change and Development Processes	**7%**	**6**	**7.5%**
A. Basic Processes and Concepts of Change		4	66.7%
1. Pressures for change		*0*	*0%*

2. Models and processes for planned organizational change		3	75%
3. Resistance to organizational change		0	0%
4. Corporate culture		1	25%
B. Applications and Techniques of Change and Development		2	33.3%
1. Overview of organization development		1	50%
2. Group and individual change		1	50%
3. Sociotechnological approaches to change		0	0%
4. Structural approaches to change		0	0%
Grand Total	**100%**	**80**	**100%**

OVERVIEW

- Diagnostic test
- Answer key and explanations
- Organizational behavior overview
- Individual processes and characteristics
- Interpersonal and group processes and characteristics
- Organizational processes and characteristics
- Change and development processes
- Post-test
- Answer key and explanations
- Summing it up

DIAGNOSTIC TEST

Directions: Carefully read each of the following 20 questions. Choose the best answer to each question and circle your answer choice. The Answer Key and Explanations can be found following this Diagnostic Test.

1. Jenna regularly attends gatherings at a local restaurant arranged by the professional marketing organization to which she belongs. Jenna hopes to develop contacts with people outside her firm in case she ever needs to find a new job. Which of the following best describes Jenna's activities?

    (A) Illegitimate political behavior

    (B) Legitimate political behavior

    (C) Integrative bargaining

    (D) Risk aversion

2. Which of the following people first identified the ten roles of managers?

    (A) Kurt Lewin

    (B) Henri Fayol

    (C) Henry Mintzberg

    (D) Abraham Maslow

3. Which type of small-group network depends on a central figure to convey the group's communications?

    (A) Single-channel

    (B) All-channel

    (C) Wheel

    (D) Chain

4. The sales manager at Hoffman Car Dealership is concerned because of the dealership's low sales numbers over the last quarter. The sales manager blames the problem on the laziness of his sales team instead of on price incentives offered by competitors. Which of the following best explains the sales manager's beliefs?

    (A) Fundamental attribution error

    (B) Overconfidence bias

    (C) Self-serving bias

    (D) Contrast effect

5. Which of the following involves a sender purposely manipulating information so the receiver will view it favorably?

(A) Selective perceiving

(B) Monitoring

(C) Disseminating

(D) Filtering

6. Which employee personality trait has the most consistent correlation with organizational success?

(A) Openness to new ideas

(B) Conscientiousness

(C) Agreeableness

(D) Extraversion

7. A leader that employees fear is most likely using

(A) coercive power.

(B) expert power.

(C) legitimate power.

(D) referent power.

8. An employee states, "My pay is too low." Which attitude component is the employee most likely expressing?

(A) Emotional

(B) Cognition

(C) Behavior

(D) Affect

9. Which theory is based on the idea that great leaders are born with confidence, integrity, and assertiveness?

(A) Trait theory

(B) Path-goal theory

(C) Expectancy theory

(D) Contingency theory

10. Which model of learning asserts that the consequences of actions shape voluntary behavior?

(A) Observational learning

(B) Classical conditioning

(C) Situational learning

(D) Operant conditioning

11. Which organizational design approach is most likely to generate confusion regarding authority?

(A) Bureaucracy

(B) Matrix

(C) Product

(D) Simple

12. Which of the following represents the highest level of Maslow's hierarchy of needs?

(A) Achievement

(B) Friendship

(C) Security

(D) Shelter

13. Which of the following is the primary benefit of building a strong organizational culture?

(A) Conflict management

(B) Corporate flexibility

(C) Financial stability

(D) Employee loyalty

14. A gainsharing plan is best described as a motivation tool that involves

(A) vertically expanding jobs to enable more worker autonomy.

(B) paying employees a fixed sum for each completed unit of production.

(C) distributing money based on improvements in group productivity.

(D) basing individual promotions on group leadership tasks.

15. At Wilson Manufacturing, the majority of decisions are made by high-level managers. Which of the following terms most likely describes the structure implemented at Wilson Manufacturing?

    (A) Matrix organization

    (B) Centralized organization

    (C) Learning organization

    (D) Decentralized organization

16. In the norming stage of group development, members are more likely to

    (A) accomplish a specific task.

    (B) establish a formal hierarchy.

    (C) form close relationships.

    (D) experience conflict.

17. An organization with a wide span of control will most likely have

    (A) one supervisor managing a few workers.

    (B) many supervisors managing a few workers.

    (C) one supervisor managing many workers.

    (D) many supervisors managing many workers.

18. Which of the following statements best describes the transformational leadership theory?

    (A) Leaders exhibit accuracy in decision making.

    (B) Leaders possess unique risk-taking behaviors.

    (C) Leaders have specific personality traits.

    (D) Leaders provide organizational vision.

19. Lewin's three-step model primarily addresses how organizations can

    (A) minimize conflicts.

    (B) implement changes.

    (C) motivate workers.

    (D) develop leaders.

20. A star quarterback has endorsement contracts with numerous firms, including an electronics manufacturer, a soft drink company, and a sports drink company. Advertisers are most likely hoping that the football star has

    (A) referent power.

    (B) coercive power.

    (C) legitimate power.

    (D) expert power.

ANSWER KEY AND EXPLANATIONS

1. B	5. D	9. A	13. D	17. C
2. C	6. B	10. D	14. C	18. D
3. C	7. A	11. B	15. B	19. B
4. A	8. B	12. A	16. C	20. A

1. **The correct answer is (B).** Legitimate political behavior includes networking, so choice (B) is correct. Choice (A) is incorrect because Jenna is not involved in activities that would harm her employer. Choices (C) and (D) are irrelevant to Jenna's activities.

2. **The correct answer is (C).** Henry Mintzberg is an academic who conducted research on management roles and identified ten of them. Choice (A) is incorrect because Kurt Lewin developed an organizational change model. Choice (B) is incorrect because Henri Fayol identified six functions of management and fourteen principles of management. Choice (D) is incorrect because Abraham Maslow developed the theory of a hierarchy of needs.

3. **The correct answer is (C).** A wheel network depends on one leader to relay information. Choice (A) is not a type of small-group network. Choice (B) is incorrect because all members communicate with one another in an all-channel network. Chain networks follow hierarchies for communication, so choice (D) is incorrect.

4. **The correct answer is (A).** Fundamental attribution error is the tendency to underestimate the power of external factors and overestimate the power of internal factors. Choice (B) is incorrect because overconfidence bias involves being too optimistic. Choice (C) is incorrect because a self-serving bias involves attributing failures to external factors. Contrast effect involves making comparisons between people, so choice (D) is incorrect.

5. **The correct answer is (D).** Filtering occurs when a sender manipulates information, so choice (D) is correct. Selective perception involves hearing what you want to hear, so choice (A) is incorrect. Choice (B) is not a type of communication barrier. Dissemination involves sharing information, but not necessarily manipulating it, so choice (C) is incorrect.

6. **The correct answer is (B).** The most important and consistent trait for both individual and organizational success is conscientiousness, so choice (B) is correct. Openness, agreeableness, and extraversion are not as strongly related to organizational success, so choices (A), (C), and (D) are incorrect.

7. **The correct answer is (A).** Leaders with coercive power use fear tactics and threats to control followers. Expert power refers to a leader's experience, so choice (B) is incorrect. Choice (C) is incorrect because legitimate power is the authority to tell subordinates what to do. A leader with a personality that employees find admirable is using referent power, so choice (D) is incorrect.

8. **The correct answer is (B).** Attitudes develop from three components: cognition, affect, and behavior. The cognitive component is an opinion, such as "My pay is too low." Emotions and feelings are the affective component, so choices (A) and (D) are incorrect. The behavioral component is the individual's intention to behave, so choice (C) is incorrect.

9. **The correct answer is (A).** Trait theory is based on the idea that great leaders are born with characteristics like confidence and aggressiveness. Choices (B) and (D) are leadership theories that do not assert that people are born with leadership qualities. Expectancy theory is a motivation theory, so choice (C) is incorrect.

10. **The correct answer is (D).** The operant conditioning model made famous by B.F. Skinner linked behavior with consequences, so choice (D) is correct. Choice (A) is incorrect because observational learning asserts that people learn by imitating behaviors observed in other people. Choice (B) is incorrect because Pavlov linked associations with responses. Choice (C) is not a model of learning.

11. **The correct answer is (B).** The matrix structure is more likely to cause employees confusion because of its dual line of command. Chain-of-command is clear in a bureaucracy and simple structures, so choices (A) and (D) are incorrect. Departments organized by product are not likely to trigger leadership confusion, so choice (C) is incorrect.

12. **The correct answer is (A).** Choice (A) is correct because achievement falls in the category of ego, which is near the top of Maslow's hierarchy of needs. Choices (B), (C), and (D) are incorrect because all are lower than achievement on Maslow's hierarchy.

13. **The correct answer is (D).** Employees who feel like they belong to a team are more loyal and satisfied, and they are more likely to work hard. Conflict management, corporate flexibility, and financial stability are less likely benefits of a strong corporate culture, so choices (A), (B), and (C) are incorrect.

14. **The correct answer is (C).** Gainsharing is a group incentive plan that distributes money based on improvements in group productivity. Choice (A) describes job sharing. Choice (B) describes a piece-rate pay plan. Gainsharing relates to pay rather than promotions, so choice (D) is incorrect.

15. **The correct answer is (B).** Top executives make the most of the decisions in centralized organizations, so choice (B) is correct. Choice (A) is incorrect because a matrix structure involves two lines of authority. Choice (C) is incorrect because a learning organization excels at problem solving, and authority may or may not be centralized. In decentralized organizations, decision making is dispersed throughout the company, so choice (D) is incorrect.

16. **The correct answer is (C).** During the norming stage, members form close relationships and develop common expectations of member behavior. Choice (A) occurs in the performing stage. A hierarchy forms during the storming stage, so choice (B) is incorrect. Conflict occurs in the storming stage, so choice (D) is incorrect.

17. **The correct answer is (C).** With a wide span of control, many workers report to one supervisor, so choice (C) is correct. A narrow span of control involves a small number of workers reporting to one supervisor, so choice (A) is incorrect. Choices (B) and (D) fail to describe a wide span of control.

18. **The correct answer is (D).** The transformational leadership theory asserts that leaders convey visionary goals to followers. Choices (A) and (B) are not necessarily linked to the transformational leadership theory. Trait theories focus on personal qualities, so choice (C) is incorrect.

19. **The correct answer is (B).** Choice (B) is correct because Lewin's model describes the process of implementing organizational changes. Conflicts, motivation, and leadership are not addressed by Lewin's model, so choices (A), (C), and (D) are incorrect.

20. **The correct answer is (A).** Referent power stems from identifying with a person who has desirable personality traits and resources. Coercive power relies on the fear of negative results, so choice (B) is incorrect. Legitimate power refers to the formal authority to control, so choice (C) is incorrect. Although the star quarterback is a football expert, he is not necessarily an expert on electronics or soda, so choice (D) is incorrect.

ORGANIZATIONAL BEHAVIOR OVERVIEW

Historically, business schools and corporations have focused on developing managers with effective technical skills and have given very little attention to improving the interpersonal skills of managers. However, modern businesses are realizing that managers need people skills on a daily basis to (1) retain high-performing workers, (2) handle employee conflicts, (3) improve workplace productivity, and (4) enhance both worker and firm performance. Organizational behavior addresses these essential managerial skills.

The Field of Organizational Behavior

Organizational behavior is a relatively new field of study that emerged during the 1980s as businesses began to realize the connection between organizational performance and employee behavior. Organizational behavior is a field of study that involves analyzing the effect that individuals, groups, and structure have on an organization's performance.

While the field of organizational behavior only developed within the last three or four decades, the study of management began much earlier. Henri Fayol, an early twentieth-century French businessman, developed the first theory of management. According to Fayol, professional management involved the functions of planning, organizing, commanding, coordinating, and controlling. Fayolism has since been condensed to planning, organizing, leading, and controlling.

In the 1960s, Canadian academic Henry Mintzberg studied five executives for two weeks to determine what they did as managers. Mintzberg identified ten roles that can be categorized as interpersonal, informational, or decisional, but the roles and their associated behaviors are highly interconnected.

MINTZBERG'S MANAGEMENT ROLES

Interpersonal	• *Figurehead:* performs routine duties as symbolic leader • *Leader:* motivates and directs workers • *Liaison:* maintains a network of outside contacts
Informational	• *Monitor:* receives information • *Disseminator:* transmits information to organization members • *Spokesperson:* transmits information to outsiders
Decisional	• *Entrepreneur:* initiates projects and searches for opportunities • *Disturbance Handler:* takes corrective action when problems occur • *Resource Allocator:* makes or approves organizational decisions • *Negotiator:* represents the organization at significant negotiations

The underlying purpose of studying managers has been to improve the performance and effectiveness of an organization, so it was a natural progression that led to the field of organizational behavior. By understanding the impact that individuals, groups, and structures have on organizational performance, firms can function more effectively.

The Study of Organizational Behavior

Although organizational behavior benefits numerous settings, it is primarily intended to help managers handle workplace situations, such as employee motivation, absenteeism, turnover, and productivity. The following table provides an overview of core topics studied at each level of an organization.

TOPICS OF ORGANIZATIONAL BEHAVIOR

Individual	Perceptual processes, personality, attitudes, learning processes, motivation, and work stress
Group	Dynamics, conflict, leadership, power, politics, and communication processes
Structure	Decision-making processes, organizational structure, organizational design, and change processes

Although some managers may have a knack for "reading" people, such attempts at predicting or interpreting behavior often lead to false assumptions. Managers improve their chances of making accurate predictions by balancing personal intuition with research derived from systematic study.

Systematic study involves observing relationships, identifying causes and effects, and drawing conclusions based on evidence. (1) Case studies, (2) field surveys, (3) laboratory experiments, (4) field experiments, and (5) aggregate quantitative reviews are the most commonly used research design methods. (1) Psychology, (2) social psychology, (3) sociology, and (4) anthropology are the fields of study that provide the primary research contributions. Evidence-based management is a growing trend resulting from the vast body of research now available. Rather than relying on hunches and intuition, adherents of evidence-based management rely on the best scientific evidence to make managerial decisions.

INDIVIDUAL PROCESSES AND CHARACTERISTICS

Because individual employees have a significant impact on an organization's performance, understanding individual processes is important in the field of organizational behavior. Perceptions, personalities, attitudes, learning processes, motivations, and stress factors will be discussed in the following sections.

Perceptual Processes

Behavior is based on individual perceptions of the world, so understanding perceptual processes is essential in the study of organizational behavior. Perceptions are how individuals organize and interpret what they experience, which may differ significantly from reality. In the workplace, for example, one employee may perceive a firm's benefits package as exceptional, while another employee may perceive the same compensation as mediocre. In another situation, one coworker may be perceived as loud and obnoxious by some, but perceived as a leader by other individuals.

Three key factors explain why employees frequently have such different perceptions: (1) the perceiver, (2) the target, and (3) the situation. An individual perceiver's (1) attitudes, (2) motives, (3) interests, (4) experiences, and (5) expectations influence personal perceptions. The target or object being perceived has certain distinguishing characteristics that influence perceptions either positively or negatively. For example, a young worker may be perceived as having poor work habits, while a defense attorney may be perceived as unethical. The situation or context also plays a role in perception. A female employee who wears a short skirt to work may be viewed as unprofessional, but if she wears the same skirt to a party, the perceptions would most likely change.

Although perceptions may seem to occur automatically, people are actually employing various techniques when making judgments. These techniques are useful because they speed up the perception process, but they may also act as barriers to accurate perceptions. Understanding the methods and their associated problems will enhance the accuracy of the perception process.

METHODS OF PERCEPTION

Method	Description	Problem
Selective Perception	Interpreting only selected observations of a person based on personal interests, experiences, and attitudes	Quick, narrow interpretations lead to unfounded conclusions.
Halo Effect	Drawing general impressions of a person based on one characteristic	Single traits influence broad conclusions.
Contrast Effects	Evaluating a person's characteristics by making comparisons to another person	Misperceptions occur because individuals are not evaluated in isolation.
Stereotyping	Judging a person based on group association	Generalizations are often unfair and untrue.

The perceptions people develop about one another are known as person perceptions. Scientists have attempted to explain the different ways that judgments are made through attribution theory. According to attribution theory, people try to explain the behavior of others based on internal attributes or external attributes. Behaviors that occur because of internal attributes are under the control of an individual, whereas externally caused behaviors are out of the individual's control. For example, a manager who attributes an employee's tardiness to laziness is making an internal attribution. If the manager attributes the employee's tardiness to bad traffic, she is making an external attribution. Determining whether a person's behavior is caused by internal or external factors depends on the factors of (1) distinctiveness, (2) consensus, and (3) consistency.

- *Distinctiveness:* Does the person behave differently in different situations? If the late employee also fails to complete tasks on time, then the behavior would be judged as an internal attribute. However, if the employee typically performs well, then an external attribution would most likely be made.

- *Consensus:* Does everyone behave similarly when faced with a similar situation? If numerous employees are also late, then the behavior shows consensus and would be attributed to external causes.

- *Consistency:* Does the person behave similarly over a period of time? If the late employee is regularly late, then the behavior would most likely be internally attributed.

Research shows that attributions are often distorted by fundamental attribution errors and self-serving biases. The fundamental attribution error is the tendency to place more value on internal factors than external ones. The tendency of individuals to attribute successes to internal causes and failures to external causes is known as a self-serving bias.

Personality

In the field of organizational behavior, personality refers to an individual's reactions to and interactions with other people. Research indicates that personality traits are determined by a combination of genetic and environmental factors. Characteristics that an individual exhibits in many situations are considered personality traits. Two primary tools are used to identify and classify personality traits: the Myers-Briggs Type Indicator (MBTI) and the Big Five Model.

The MBTI, which consists of 100 questions, is the most frequently used personality-assessment tool. Individuals are identified as one of sixteen personality types based on the following eight factors.

- *Extraverted or Introverted:* Extraverts are outgoing and sociable, while introverts are quiet and shy.

- *Sensing or Intuitive:* Sensing individuals are practical and detail-oriented, whereas intuitive individuals focus on future possibilities.

- *Thinking or Feeling:* Thinking individuals solve problems with logic, whereas feeling individuals depend on emotions.

- *Judging or Perceiving:* Judging individuals prefer control in an orderly world, whereas perceiving individuals are adaptable and spontaneous.

The MBTI is used by many large organizations, and it serves as a useful tool for career guidance. However, the MBTI is based on questionable evidence and is not recommended as a selection assessment.

In contrast, the Big Five Model is supported by a large body of evidence regarding the tool's five personality traits.

- *Extraversion:* Comfort level with relations

- *Agreeableness:* Tendency to defer to others

- *Conscientiousness:* Measure of reliability

- *Emotional stability:* Ability to handle stress

- *Openness to experience:* Range of interests and creativity

Studies have indicated a strong connection between the personality dimensions of the Big Five Model and job performance. The most important and consistent trait for both individual and organizational success is conscientiousness. The following table indicates the link between high scores in each of the five traits and any positive or negative work behaviors.

INFLUENCE OF BIG FIVE TRAITS ON JOB PERFORMANCE

Trait	Significance
Extraversion	• Higher job satisfaction, better interpersonal skills, and higher job performance • More impulsive and more likely to be absent and partake in risky behaviors
Agreeableness	• More compliant, better likeability, and higher job performance • Lower levels of career success and negotiation skills
Conscientiousness	• Better organization, better attention to detail, more persistence, and higher job performance • Lower ability to adapt to change and think creatively
Emotional Stability	• Lower stress levels, higher job satisfaction, and less negative thinking
Openness	• More adaptable to change, more creative, and enhanced leadership • More susceptible to workplace accidents

Attitudes

In the field of organizational behavior, positive or negative evaluations of objects, people, or events are referred to as attitudes. Attitudes develop from three components: (1) cognition, (2) affect, and (3) behavior. The cognitive component is an opinion, such as, "My boss is unfair." The affective component is a feeling, such as, "I'm angry about how much work I have to do on the weekend." The behavioral component is the individual's intention to behave, such as, "I'm going to look for a better job that requires less overtime."

Attitudes are typically connected to values, which are the convictions that a person has about what is right, wrong, or desirable. Values serve as the basis for understanding people's attitudes and motivations. The Rokeach Value Survey, developed by the social psychologist Milton Rokeach, presents a philosophical basis for the association of values with beliefs and attitudes. According to the Rokeach Value Survey, values can be divided into two types: (1) terminal values and (2) instrumental values. Terminal values are goals that an individual would like to accomplish during a lifetime, such as prosperity, equality, family security, happiness, and wisdom. Instrumental values are the means to achieving terminal values, and they are exhibited through behaviors such as hard work, truthfulness, sincerity, dependability, and honesty. Studies indicate that individuals holding similar positions have similar values and vice versa. Such information is important in organizations, as conflicts may arise because executives and hourly workers, for example, have different values.

Although everyone holds many different attitudes, organizational behaviorists primarily focus on (1) job satisfaction, (2) job involvement, (3) organizational commitment, (4) perceived organizational support, and (5) employee engagement.

KEY EMPLOYEE ATTITUDES

Job Satisfaction	Positive or negative feelings about a job based on evaluations of the job's characteristics
Job Involvement	The extent to which employees identify and care about their job
Organizational Commitment	The extent to which employees identify with the goals of an organization and want to continue as members
Perceived Organizational Support	The extent to which employees believe an organization cares for their well-being and values their work
Employee Engagement	An employee's job-related involvement, satisfaction, and enthusiasm

Managers benefit from a strong understanding of employee attitudes, because satisfied and committed workers are more productive and less likely to quit.

Learning Processes

Understanding the basics of the learning process benefits managers, because not all employees will learn information or skills in the same manner. Learning is an active and purposeful process that occurs through experiences and results in permanent behavior changes. Numerous factors influence an individual's learning process, especially in an employment setting, including (1) interest, (2) motivation, (3) experience, (4) memory, (5) ability, (6) context, (7) environment, (8) perception, and (9) maturity.

Psychological studies have led to three basic learning models: (1) classical conditioning, (2) operant conditioning, and (3) observational learning.

MODELS OF LEARNING

Classical Conditioning	A behaviorist model associated with Ivan Pavlov's well-known experiment. Pavlov triggered a dog's salivary response after an association was made between the smell of food and a ringing bell.
Operant Conditioning	A behaviorist model made famous by B.F. Skinner, who linked behavior with consequences. This model asserts that the consequences of actions shape voluntary behavior.
Observational Learning	A social learning theory commonly associated with Albert Bandura's Bobo Doll Experiment. The model asserts that people learn by imitating behaviors observed in other people without the need for direct reinforcement. Observational learning requires (1) attention, (2) motor skills, (3) motivation, and (4) memory.

Reinforcement theory, which stems from B.F. Skinner's work, asserts that consequences influence behavior. In an organization, reinforcement theory is implemented by rewarding desirable employee behavior and punishing unwanted behavior. In psychological terms, a reinforcer, which can be either positive or negative, is anything that increases the probability of a specific response. The following provides a description of the four types of reinforcers and work-related examples.

REINFORCEMENT METHODS

Type of Reinforcer	Description	Example
Positive Reinforcement	Providing a positive response for a desired behavior	Providing a salesperson with a bonus for exceeding a sales quota
Negative Reinforcement	Withholding a negative consequence to increase a desired behavior	Eliminating an undesirable area from a salesperson's territory after the salesperson increases sales in other areas
Punishment	Giving an undesirable consequence to decrease a behavior	Suspending a salesperson for breaking a company policy
Extinction	Removing a reward to decrease a behavior	Eliminating praise for an employee's good work, which may unintentionally lower the desirable behavior

In addition to understanding the different types of reinforcers, effective managers should also understand the schedule of reinforcement. Reinforcers can either be implemented on a (1) continuous schedule or (2) an intermittent schedule. A manager who gives an employee a raise after every successful project is following a continuous schedule. Continuous schedules are either a (1) fixed ratio or a (2) fixed interval. A fixed ratio schedule applies reinforcement after a specific number of behavioral occurrences, whereas a fixed interval schedule applies a reinforcer after a set amount of time.

Intermittent schedules are ones that don't reinforce every instance of desired behavior and are either a (1) variable ratio or a (2) variable interval. Variable ratio schedules apply reinforcers after a variable number of responses, such as giving an employee a bonus after a varying number of desired behaviors occur. Variable interval schedules apply reinforcers after varying periods of time.

According to research, continuous reinforcement is the most effective way to change employee behaviors, but the method is not practical in an organization because not every behavior is observed. Therefore, intermittent schedules are more common in businesses.

Motivation

Surveys have found that most U.S. workers are not enthusiastic about their jobs, so motivation is a serious concern for organizations. Motivation refers to the processes guiding an individual's intensity level, focus, and persistence. Businesses benefit from motivated employees who work hard to accomplish organizational goals, so motivation is a heavily studied topic in the field of organizational behavior. The following table summarizes the most common theories of motivation.

MOTIVATION THEORIES

Maslow's Hierarchy of Needs Theory	Every individual has a hierarchy of five needs: (1) physiological, (2) safety, (3) social, (4) esteem, and (5) self-actualization. The higher-order needs of social, esteem, and self-actualization are satisfied internally, and the lower-order needs of physiological and safety are satisfied externally, such as through salary and tenure.
Herzberg's Two-Factor Theory	Two components on separate continuums motivate employees. Hygiene factors, such as company policies, supervision, work conditions, and salaries, lead to dissatisfaction. Motivators, such as recognition, responsibility, achievement, and advancement, lead to satisfaction.
Alderfer's ERG Theory	Individuals have three needs: (1) existence, (2) relatedness, and (3) growth. Safety and physical comfort are the lowest level of existence needs. Relatedness needs involve a sense of identity in society. Growth needs are the highest level, where individuals feel a sense of accomplishment and fulfillment.
McClelland's Theory of Needs	Employee motivation is influenced by the need for achievement, power, and affiliation.
Goal-Setting Theory	Specific and challenging goals combined with feedback lead to higher levels of employee productivity.
Equity Theory	Employees derive motivation and job satisfaction by comparing their inputs, such as effort, and outcomes, such as income, with those of others. Employees then respond to eliminate any inequities.
Victor Vroom's Expectancy Theory	Employees are motivated to work hard when they believe their efforts will result in desirable outcomes, such as a good performance appraisal leading to a salary increase.

The motivation theories described in the previous table vary in their validity and usefulness. The needs theories of Maslow, Herzberg, Alderfer, and McClelland aren't generally considered valid tools for explaining employee motivation, although some research indicates a connection between achievement and productivity associated with McClelland's theory. Research related to goal-setting theory indicates that employees are motivated by specific and difficult goals, especially when they receive feedback on their progress. However, goal-setting theory fails to address issues of absenteeism, turnover, and job satisfaction. In regards to equity theory, some workers are sensitive to pay inequities while others are tolerant, so it does not provide consistently accurate predictions. Expectancy theory is one of the most supported explanations of employee motivation because of the strong connection between effort, performance, and reward.

Job design is another managerial tool for motivating employees. Studies in job design indicate that how the elements of a job are organized can increase or decrease employee efforts. (1) Job rotation and (2) job enrichment are the two primary methods of redesigning a job. Job rotation involves periodically shifting a worker from one task to another, a technique that reduces boredom in highly routine jobs. Job enrichment increases an employee's responsibility and provides variety through vertical job expansion. For example, instead of having an assembly worker perform one task in the manufacturing process, the worker could assemble an entire unit.

Alternative work arrangements are another tool for motivating employees. (1) Flextime, (2) job sharing, and (3) telecommuting are popular options among firms. Flextime offers flexible work hours for employees, such as 6:00 a.m. until 3:00 p.m. instead of the typical 8:00 a.m. to 5:00 p.m. Job sharing splits one 40-hour job between two or more individuals, which is a popular option for working mothers and retirees. Telecommuting, or working from home at least part of the week, is increasingly popular, especially for employees who spend the bulk of their workday on the computer or the phone.

An increasing number of firms are implementing reward systems through variable-pay programs to motivate workers. The following list describes the different types of variable-pay programs.

- *Piece-Rate Pay:* Workers receive a fixed sum for each unit produced.

- *Merit-Based Pay:* Compensation is based on performance appraisal ratings.

- *Bonuses:* Employees are rewarded for recent rather than historical performance.

- *Skill-Based Pay:* Pay levels are based on the number of skills an employee has or the number of jobs an employee can perform.

- *Profit-Sharing Plan:* An organization-wide plan, rather than an individual pay plan, which distributes cash or stock options based on a firm's profitability.

- *Gainsharing Plan:* A group incentive plan that distributes money based on improvements in group productivity.

- *Employee Stock Ownership Plan:* A benefits plan that enables employees to obtain company stock.

Research indicates that variable-pay programs are effective tools for motivating employees and improving productivity levels. Profit-sharing plans are linked to higher levels of profitability, while gainsharing plans typically improve both worker productivity and attitude. Piece-rate plans have also been found to increase employee productivity.

Motivation theories have a number of implications for managers. Effective managers are sensitive to the individual differences of employees, so they establish individual goals, rewards, and punishments. Allowing employees to participate in setting work goals and solving productivity problems is more likely to generate motivation than dictating goals and solutions. In addition, rewards should be linked to performance, and workers should clearly understand the connection. A weak relationship between rewards and performance leads to job dissatisfaction, turnover, and absenteeism.

Work Stress and the Individual

Stress occurs when an individual faces a real or perceived mental, physical, or social demand associated with an important and uncertain outcome. Although stress typically has negative connotations, in certain situations it can be a positive condition that increases performance levels. Two types of stressors are associated with employment: (1) challenge stressors and (2) hindrance stressors. Challenge stressors are linked to workload, deadlines, and pressure to complete tasks. Hindrance stressors prevent individuals from reaching their goal, such as bureaucracy and office politics.

The primary causes of stress can be divided into three categories: (1) environmental factors, (2) organizational factors, and (3) personal factors. Environmental factors include economic uncertainty and changes in technology. Task and role demands are examples of organizational factors, whereas family problems are personal factors influencing stress. Individuals handle stress differently based on their perceptions, job experience, and social support network. Common consequences of work stress include headaches, high blood pressure, anxiety, depression, decreased job satisfaction, absenteeism, and lower productivity.

So how can employees and organizations minimize work stress? Individuals can (1) exercise regularly, (2) manage their time more effectively, and (3) talk to friends, family, and coworkers about their problems. Organization-wide strategies for reducing employee stress include (1) improved job placement methods, (2) effective training programs, (3) realistic goal setting, (4) improved communication systems, and (5) corporate wellness programs.

INTERPERSONAL AND GROUP PROCESSES AND CHARACTERISTICS

Given that working with other people is an essential and frequent activity for managers, understanding both interpersonal and group processes is beneficial. The following section addresses group dynamics, group behavior, leadership, power, politics, and the communication process.

Group Dynamics

A group consists of at least two individuals who interact to achieve certain objectives. Security, status, self-esteem, affiliation, power, and goal achievement are common reasons that people join groups. (1) Formal groups are designated by an organization to complete specific tasks or projects, such as a sales team. (2) Informal groups develop naturally in the workplace for the purpose of social interaction, such as workers from different departments who gather for lunch regularly.

In addition to being designated as formal or informal, groups can be classified as (1) command, (2) task, (3) interest, or (4) friendship groups. Both command and task groups are formal, while interest and friendship groups are informal. Members of a command group report to the same manager. Each member of a task group plays a different role in completing a specific task for the organization. Interest groups develop when workers share a common concern, such as improving worker safety. Friendship groups are social alliances that form at work and often continue outside of the workplace.

Groups typically develop in the same manner. The following table describes each stage of the group development process.

GROUP DEVELOPMENT STAGES

Stage 1: Forming	Uncertainty among members about acceptable behaviors and group structure. Stage is complete when members feel a part of the group.
Stage 2: Storming	Characterized by intragroup conflict regarding constraints on individuality and group leadership. Stage ends with clarified hierarchy.
Stage 3: Norming	Members form close relationships and develop common expectations of member behavior.
Stage 4: Performing	Working to achieve a specific task. It's the final stage for permanent work groups.
Stage 5: Adjourning	Preparing to disband and complete tasks if group is temporary.

Just as most groups form in the same manner, groups also have common characteristics that influence member behaviors. (1) Roles, (2) norms, (3) status, (4) size, and (5) cohesiveness are the key properties found in groups. Group members have specific roles or expected behavior patterns based on their position in a group. For example, a manager is expected to provide leadership, whereas an employee is expected to follow directions. Norms are the acceptable behavior standards shared by group members. Performance norms indicate how hard group members should work, while appearance norms provide cues about appropriate work attire. Status refers to a group member's rank and is primarily determined by (1) power, (2) degree of contribution, and (3) personal characteristics.

Group performance is significantly influenced by the group's size. Research indicates that smaller groups complete tasks more quickly than larger groups and that employees work more effectively in smaller groups. Cohesiveness refers to how well members work together and how motivated they are to remain in the group. Because cohesiveness influences productivity, managers should strive to (1) form smaller groups, (2) encourage goal agreement, (3) stimulate competition with other groups, and (4) provide rewards to the group rather than to individual members.

Group Behavior and Conflict

No matter how cohesive and productive a group or an organization may be, conflicts are bound to occur. Over the years, the attitudes about workplace conflicts have changed. During the 1930s and 1940s, advocates of the traditional view of conflict asserted that conflict must be avoided because it is harmful. However, conflict can't always be avoided, which led to the interactionist view of conflict. The interactionist school views conflict as a positive activity in some cases that should be encouraged to improve group performance.

The interactionist view realizes that not all conflicts are beneficial, and it separates conflict into two main categories: (1) functional and (2) dysfunctional. Functional conflicts benefit group goals, whereas dysfunctional conflicts obstruct group performance. Functional and dysfunctional conflicts are distinguished by conflict type: (1) task, (2) process, and (3) relationship. Task conflicts are associated with work goals, and process conflicts stem from how work is accomplished. Low degrees of task and process conflicts can be productive if they stimulate new ideas and solutions. Relationship conflicts stem from personality clashes between group members, and such conflicts are nearly always dysfunctional.

Conflicts typically follow a five-stage process as indicated in the following table.

CONFLICT PROCESS

Stage 1: Potential opposition or incompatibility	Conditions create opportunities for conflicts to occur. Conditions include (1) communication problems, (2) task structure, and (3) personal variables.
Stage 2: Cognition and personalization	Conflict issues are defined and parties determine what a conflict is about. Emotions play a role in shaping conflict perceptions.
Stage 3: Intentions	Decisions are made to act in a certain way. The main intentions for handling conflict are (1) competing, (2) collaborating, (3) avoiding, (4) accommodating, and (5) compromising.
Stage 4: Behavior	Conflict becomes visible through (1) statements, (2) actions, and (3) reactions by both parties.

| Stage 5: Outcomes | Consequences result from the actions and reactions of the parties involved. Functional outcomes improve group performance. Dysfunctional outcomes harm group performance. |

The fourth stage of the conflict process is the step for conflict management. Conflict management involves using (1) resolution and (2) stimulation methods to manage conflict levels. Conflict-resolution methods include (1) problem-solving sessions, (2) expanding resources, (3) compromising, and (4) withdrawing from the conflict. Conflict-stimulation methods include (1) realigning work groups and (2) changing rules.

Leadership

All groups require a leader to (1) create plans, (2) inspire members, (3) establish organizational structures, and (4) achieve goals and visions. Firms benefit from understanding what makes a good leader because such knowledge improves individual, group, and organizational performance. The following table provides an overview of the various models of leadership that have been developed to identify leadership skills:

MODELS OF LEADERSHIP

Trait Theories	Personal qualities and characteristics of leaders differ from those of non-leaders.
Behavioral Theories	Behaviors of effective leaders differ from behaviors of ineffective leaders.
Contingency Theories	Situational variables determine whether specific leader traits and behaviors are effective or not according to the Fiedler contingency model.
Leader-Member Exchange Theory (LMX)	Leaders develop personal relationships with some members of a group, but not others. In-group subordinates exhibit better performance and job satisfaction.
Charismatic Leadership Theory	Effective leaders inspire subordinates by (1) articulating a vision, (2) taking risks, and (3) perceiving the needs of others.
Transformational Leadership Theory	Leaders inspire followers by (1) providing vision, (2) communicating high expectations, (3) solving problems, and (4) giving personal attention.

Although early trait theory studies failed to isolate specific leadership traits, later research was more successful when traits were categorized alongside the Big Five personality framework. (1) Extraversion, (2) conscientiousness, and (3) openness to experience are traits that have been strongly linked to effective leadership.

Behavioral theories, which suggest that leaders can be developed, focus primarily on two aspects of leadership: (1) initiating structure and (2) consideration. Initiating structure refers to the extent that leaders define their roles and the roles of employees. For example, a leader with a high degree of initiating structure assigns subordinates to specific tasks and stresses the importance of deadlines. Consideration relates to job relationships and the extent to which a leader helps group members, treats subordinates fairly, and shows appreciation. Studies indicate that leaders with high consideration receive more respect, and leaders with high levels of initiating structure experience high levels of group productivity.

Studies indicate that aspects of the Fiedler contingency model are valid. The Fiedler model includes eight categories, but only three categories are supported by evidence. Critics of the contingency model find the questionnaire and variables confusing and participants' scores unreliable. The Fiedler model is the most well-known contingency theory, but others include the situational leadership theory, path-goal theory, and leader-participation theory.

- *Situational leadership theory* asserts that the best action of a leader depends on the degree that followers are willing and able to complete a task.

- *Path-goal theory* asserts that it is the job of the leader to help followers accomplish goals by providing the necessary information, support, and resources. Leadership style is determined by subordinate preference and task structure.

- *Leader-participation theory* asserts that the way in which leaders make decisions is equally important to the decision itself. The decision tree for this model includes a set of twelve contingency variables, eight problem types, and five leadership styles, which can be too cumbersome for real-world managers.

The leader-member exchange theory is relatively supported by research. Studies show that leaders and followers are clearly different, with differences that are not random. Research also verifies that in-group members perform better and experience greater job satisfaction than out-group members, which is not necessarily surprising. Studies have also shown that the relationship between leaders and followers is even stronger when employees have higher levels of autonomy and control over their job performance.

Many experts believe that charismatic and transformational leadership styles are virtually the same or have only minor differences. In most cases, charismatic and transformational leadership theories are supported with evidence. Such leaders are more effective in some situations and settings than others. Charismatic or transformational leaders are most effective when interacting closely with employees, so such leaders may be more effective in small firms rather than large organizations.

While the extensive amount of leadership research may be overwhelming, managers can take the most relevant information and apply it in a business setting. The following list provides an overview of leadership implications for managers:

- Traits such as extraversion, conscientiousness, and openness to experience are typically associated with strong leaders.

- Consider the situation before assigning a leader as some leaders are task-oriented and others are people-oriented.

- Leaders who show they believe in group members by investing time and resources will most likely be rewarded with productive and satisfied employees.

- Leaders with vision, charisma, and clear communication skills are the most effective.

- Effective leaders develop relationships with group members and show that they can be trusted.

Power and Politics

Power refers to the ability that one person has to influence the behavior of another person, and in organizations, power and politics are natural and unavoidable. Effective managers understand how power functions in an organization. Power in an organization is either (1) personal or (2) formal.

Personal power stems from the characteristics of an individual. The two sources of personal power are (1) expertise and (2) the respect of others. Formal power is derived from an individual's position in an organization. Sources of formal power are (1) the ability to coerce, (2) the ability to reward, and (3) the formal authority to control. The following table provides an overview of the different sources of power:

SOURCES OF POWER

Source	Type	Description
Expert Power	Personal	Based on expertise, special skills, or knowledge. Physicians, tax accountants, economists, and computer specialists have power due to their expertise.
Referent Power	Personal	Based on identification with an individual who possesses desirable resources or traits, such as charisma, beauty, and likability. Individuals who are admired have power over those who want to be like them. Celebrities have referent power, which is why they are commonly used to endorse products.
Coercive Power	Formal	Based on an individual's fear of negative consequences for failing to obey. In the workplace, an individual who wields coercive power may have the ability to suspend, dismiss, or demote an employee. More subtle forms of coercive power involve embarrassing an individual or withholding valuable data or information.
Reward Power	Formal	Based on an individual's ability to bestow valuable rewards or benefits, such as bonuses, raises, promotions, work assignments, sales territories, and work shifts.
Legitimate Power	Formal	Based on an individual's position in an organization's hierarchy. Considered the most common source of power in the workplace, given its broad scope. Individuals comply with those who hold a higher rank in an organization.

Research indicates that personal sources of power are more effective than formal sources of power. Managers who exhibit expert and referent power are more likely to have satisfied employees who are committed to an organization. Coercive power has been shown to have the opposite effect: Employees are dissatisfied with their jobs and lack commitment if their manager uses negative consequences as a control method.

Although political behavior is not a formal job requirement, office politics is a reality that cannot be avoided in most organizations. Individuals with effective political skills are able to use their power sources to influence outcomes in the workplace. Within organizations, political behavior is either (1) legitimate or (2) illegitimate. Legitimate actions involve complaining to a supervisor, developing business contacts through networking, and bypassing the chain-of-command. Illegitimate actions exceed normal organizational behavior by violating implied rules of business conduct. Sabotage and whistle-blowing are examples of illegitimate political behavior. Most organizational political behavior is categorized as legitimate.

According to researchers, a number of factors, both individual and organizational, determine the political environment in an organization. The following factors characterize individuals who are more likely to engage in political behaviors:

- Expect to succeed

- Perceive job alternatives because of skills, reputation, or job market

- Believe they can control their environment

- Show sensitivity to social cues and conformity

- Exhibit Machiavellian personality (manipulative and power hungry)

Organizational factors play an even greater role than individual factors in the degree to which political behaviors occur. Some organizational cultures foster politicking more than others, especially if a firm is experiencing financial difficulties or significant changes. An organizational culture characterized by minimal trust, unclear roles, and ambiguous performance evaluation systems will typically experience a high degree of political activity. A culture with low levels of trust has a higher level of political behavior and a greater likelihood of experiencing illegitimate political behavior. The following list includes the organizational factors that influence political behavior:

- Low trust

- Unclear employee roles

- Subjective performance appraisal systems

- Pressures for high performance

- Political senior managers

For many people, organizational politics are a negative aspect of the job, especially if they don't understand the dynamics of political behavior. Employees who are threatened by organizational politics experience (1) decreased job satisfaction, (2) increased stress, (3) increased turnover rates, and (4) lower performance ratings. However, politically astute individuals are more likely to view politics as an opportunity, and they are more likely to receive (1) higher performance evaluations, (2) more raises, and (3) better promotions than those lacking political skills.

Communication Processes

Clear communication, defined as the transfer and understanding of meaning, is an essential element to organizational success and serves four key functions: (1) controlling behavior, (2) fostering motivation, (3) expressing emotion, and (4) providing information.

Communication is a process that requires (1) a message, (2) a sender, and (3) a receiver as depicted below.

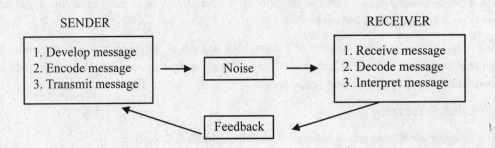

Senders initiate messages by encoding an idea through speaking, writing, gesturing, or making a facial expression. The message passes through a channel determined by the sender. Formal channels are established by an organization to transmit messages and usually follow a chain-of-command, while informal channels occur spontaneously. The message is directed at the receiver who must decode and interpret the message. Communication barriers in the form of noise stand between the sender and receiver and can distort message clarity. (1) Comprehension difficulties, (2) cultural differences, and (3) information overload are common noise problems. The feedback loop is the final aspect of the communication process. Feedback serves to determine whether the receiver understood the message.

Group members in an organization use oral, written, and nonverbal communication to transfer meaning.

INTERPERSONAL COMMUNICATION METHODS

Oral	The vast majority of organizational communication occurs orally through such activities as speeches, one-on-one conversations, and group discussions. Quickness and immediate feedback are the advantages. Message distortions may occur if a message passes between multiple people.
Written	Memos, letters, e-mails, instant messages, and newsletters are used by organizations to convey written messages. Written communication provides both parties with a record of the message for future reference. Typically, they are more logical and clear because the sender is required to consider the message in advance. Disadvantages include the time-consuming nature of written communication and the lack of immediate feedback.
Nonverbal	Oral messages include nonverbal messages, such as (1) body movement, (2) tone of voice, (3) facial expression, and (4) physical distance between sender and receiver. Such communications provide additional meaning to a message.

Nonverbal communication involves various activities, and each one conveys a different meaning. Body language expresses how much individuals like each other and the status between the sender and receiver. For example, a sender and receiver that like and respect each other are more likely to stand close to each other. Senders that feel their status is higher than the receiver's may appear more casual, or if they feel their status is lower, they may act more formal to show deference. The most appropriate physical distance between sender and receiver often depends on cultural norms.

In addition to understanding aspects of interpersonal communication, managers should be aware that communication networks, both formal and informal, exist within organizations. The three primary types of formal small-group networks include the chain, wheel, and all-channel networks.

1. *Chain networks* follow a formal chain-of-command and are characterized by high accuracy, moderate speed, and member satisfaction.

2. *Wheel networks* depend on a central individual or leader to convey information and are characterized by high accuracy and speed, but low member satisfaction.

3. *All-channel networks* allow all members to participate in communication with no single individual taking a leadership position. These networks are characterized by high speed, high member satisfaction, and moderate accuracy.

The grapevine is an informal communication network that involves word-of-mouth message conveyance. Research indicates that nearly 75 percent of all employees in a firm first learn about information through the grapevine. Studies also show that approximately 75 percent of the information flowing through a grapevine is accurate. Organizational grapevines typically have the following three key characteristics:

• Management does not control communications in the grapevine.

• Most employees find grapevine messages more believable than messages conveyed by upper management.

• Grapevines benefit those within the network.

Although managers cannot eliminate rumors that spread through the grapevine, they can reduce negative consequences by (1) providing information to employees, (2) explaining decisions, and (3) maintaining open communication channels.

Effective communication is often distorted in an organization by a variety of barriers. The following table provides an overview of barriers:

COMMUNICATION BARRIERS

Filtering	Sender manipulates information so the receiver will view it more positively, such as telling someone what he or she wants to hear rather than the truth.
Selective Perception	This is the tendency to process messages based on personal interests, experiences, and attitudes.
Information Overload	Receivers select, ignore, or forget information when individuals receive more messages than they can process.
Emotions	Receivers experiencing extreme emotions, such as anger or excitement, may not interpret messages objectively.
Language	Word meanings can vary depending on the context of the communication and the experiences of the sender and receiver. Lack of language uniformity can hinder communication.
Silence	Withholding communication is a common problem in organizations. Employees fail to report operational problems, misconduct, and harassment, which prevent management from correcting problems.
Communication Apprehension	Tension and social anxiety about communicating orally and/or in writing affects 5 to 20 percent of individuals.
Gender Differences	Men and women often communicate differently and for different purposes. Many men communicate to establish status and power, whereas many women communicate to provide support and connections.
Politically Correct Communication	Concerns about being inoffensive can prevent meaningful and accurate communication.

ORGANIZATIONAL PROCESSES AND CHARACTERISTICS

As with individuals and groups, organizations have unique processes and characteristics. The following section discusses decision making, organizational structure, and organizational design.

Organizational Decision Making

When faced with two or more alternatives, organizations, groups, and individuals must make decisions. Building new facilities, expanding services, and downsizing are examples of decisions faced by organizations. Making a decision involves interpreting information and evaluating the strengths and weaknesses of the various alternatives, which can be accomplished through three methods: (1) rational decision making, (2) bounded rationality, and (3) intuitive decision making.

The rational decision-making model assumes that decision makers (1) have all the available information, (2) can identify the relevant options, and (3) can choose the most logical and sensible option. The model involves the following six steps:

1. Define the problem.

2. Identify the decision criteria.

3. Allocate weights to the criteria.

4. Develop the alternatives.

5. Evaluate the alternatives.

6. Select the best alternative.

The rational decision-making model may involve too many assumptions that aren't viable in the real world. Bounded rationality accounts for some of these realities. Economist Herbert Simon first presented the theory of bounded rationality in 1982. According to Simon, individuals are faced with the following three inescapable limitations when making decisions:

1. Only limited information about possible alternatives is available.

2. Individuals have a limited capacity to evaluate available information.

3. Only a limited amount of time is available for making decisions.

As a result, most decision makers search for solutions that are sufficient rather than ideal.

Making a decision based on a hunch exemplifies the intuitive decision-making model. Intuitive decisions occur quickly and typically rely on emotion and experience rather than quantifiable evidence. Current studies suggest that intuition can enhance rational decision making, but it should not necessarily replace rational evaluations, especially on an organization-wide level where numerous intuitive perspectives would be unlikely to agree.

Within organizations, decisions are made by both individuals and groups. Managers benefit from knowing when it is more or less advantageous to have a decision made by a group or an individual. Groups offer a diversity of viewpoints, knowledge, and creativity that benefits the decision-making process. Moreover, decisions made by a group are more likely to be accepted and implemented by group members. However, group decision making is a time-consuming process that involves (1) conformity pressures, (2) conflicts, and (3) ambiguous responsibilities. In contrast, individuals make decisions quickly and efficiently with clear accountability for the final results.

Organizational Structure

In organizations, tasks must be divided, grouped, and coordinated for the greatest efficiency, which is the purpose of having an organizational structure. Organizational structure involves six essential elements: (1) work specialization, (2) departmentalization, (3) chain-of-command, (4) span of control, (5) centralization and decentralization, and (6) formalization. Each of these elements is discussed in the following table:

ELEMENTS OF ORGANIZATIONAL STRUCTURE

Work Specialization	The division of labor established by Henry Ford. Activities are divided into separate jobs and steps with individuals specializing in one task instead of the entire process, which can improve productivity in some industries, but decrease employee satisfaction in others.
Departmentalization	Departmentalization is grouping jobs to coordinate common tasks. Activities are grouped by function, product, service, geography, process, and/or customer.
Chain-of-Command	Chain-of-command is an unbroken line of authority that reaches from the highest to the lowest levels of an organization for the purpose of clarifying authority and responsibility.
Span of Control	Span of control refers to the number of employees that a manager can effectively and efficiently oversee, so it determines the number of levels and managers in an organization. A narrow span of control allows for close supervision, but wider spans are more cost-effective and efficient.
Centralization/ Decentralization	Centralization/decentralization refers to the degree that decision making is concentrated at the top of an organization's hierarchy. Top managers in centralized organizations make most decisions that are implemented by lower-level managers. Decentralized organizations assign decision-making authority to lower-level managers. Decentralization quickens problem solving, lessens employee alienation, and allows for greater employee input.
Formalization	Formalization is the extent to which jobs are governed by rules and procedures. For examples, sales representatives may have more flexibility to perform their tasks than assembly-line workers who must follow specific guidelines.

Organizational Design

Organizational design primarily consists of three classic structures; however, additional designs have been developed in recent years to account for changes in the business world. The simple structure, the bureaucracy, and the matrix structure are the most commonly implemented designs, while the virtual organization and the boundaryless organization designs are relatively new options.

ORGANIZATIONAL DESIGNS

Design Type	Characteristics
Simple Structure	• Considered a flat structure with only 2 to 3 vertical levels, minimal departmentalization, wide spans of control, centralized authority, and minimal formalization • Most commonly used in small businesses run by owner-managers who employ fewer than 50 people
Bureaucracy	• Relies on standardized work processes, specialization, highly formalized rules, centralized authority, narrow spans of control, minimal innovation, chain-of-command decision making
Matrix Structure	• Establishes a dual chain-of-command and combines functional and product departmentalization • Can cause confusion and power struggles, but can maximize activity coordination, improve the flow of information, and achieve economies of scale • Commonly used in advertising agencies, hospitals, universities, construction firms, and government agencies
Virtual Organization	• Major business functions are outsourced by a small, core organization; highly centralized with minimal if any departmentalization; minimizes bureaucratic costs and long-term risks and maximizes flexibility • Limited by unclear responsibilities, slow response time, and intermittent communication • Common in the film industry
Boundaryless Organization	• Idea spurred by former GE chairman Jack Welch, who wanted to eliminate hierarchies, replace functional departments with multidisciplinary teams, and implement limitless spans of control • Used to some degree at 3M, Hewlett-Packard, and AT&T

CHANGE AND DEVELOPMENT PROCESSES

The following section addresses organizational change and organizational development and the forces and processes involved with change.

Basic Processes and Concepts of Change

Given the unstable nature of economies, consumers, competitors, and markets, successful organizations must be willing to make changes when necessary. The (1) changing workforce, (2) technology advancements, (3) major economic shifts, (4) competition, (5) social trends, and (6) global politics pressure organizations into making changes and being flexible.

Organizations making plans to change typically turn to one of four approaches: (1) Kurt Lewin's three-step model, (2) John Kotter's eight-step plan, (3) action research, and (4) organizational development.

PROCESSES OF CHANGE

Lewin's Three-Step Model	1. *Unfreeze:* Ensure that employees are ready for change. 2. *Change:* Implement the desired change. 3. *Refreeze:* Ensure that changes are permanent.
Kotter's Eight-Step Plan	1. Establish a sense of urgency for change. 2. Create a guiding coalition. 3. Develop a vision and strategy. 4. Convey the vision. 5. Empower and encourage others to act on the vision. 6. Plan for, create, and reward advances toward vision. 7. Reassess changes and make necessary adjustments. 8. Reinforce changes by linking them to success.
Action Research	Changes based on systematically collected and analyzed data. The five steps are: 1. Diagnosis 2. Analysis 3. Feedback 4. Action 5. Evaluation
Organizational Development	Systematic effort to improve an organization's effectiveness and adaptability by changing the attitudes, beliefs, and values of employees through long-term training programs.

Change threatens both individuals and the organization. Resistance to organizational changes can be especially harmful at a time when an organization critically needs the support and loyalty of employees. Common sources of resistance among individuals include (1) having to change habits, (2) worrying about security, and (3) fearing economic changes and the unknown. In addition, individuals often process only selected information by ignoring information that challenges the security of their environment. Organization-wide resistance occurs through (1) regulations, (2) processes, (3) restrictive group norms, and (4) threats to specialized groups and power relationships.

Organizational culture plays a significant role in the change and development process. Organizations can overcome resistance by (1) stimulating a culture of innovation, (2) encouraging experimentation, and (3) promoting training and development opportunities for employees. Moreover, (4) a strong corporate culture fosters employee loyalty, which is necessary during times of major upheaval.

Applications and Techniques of Change and Development

Organizational development refers to making planned changes by improving the effectiveness of an organization through research, technology, and training. The primary values underlying organizational development methods include (1) respecting individuals, (2) establishing a trusting and supportive environment, (3) de-emphasizing hierarchical control and authority, (4) openly confronting problems, and (5) encouraging participation in decision making. The following list describes organizational development methods and approaches to implementing change.

- Sensitivity training or T-groups attempt to change behavior through unstructured group interactions. Early attempts were chaotic and have been replaced by alternative methods such as diversity training, executive coaching, and team-building exercises, which are more structured.

- Survey feedback assesses attitudes and perceptions of organizational members. Data is analyzed for discrepancies, and members then gather for discussions and problem solving.

- Process consultation involves hiring an outside consultant to help managers identify processes that need improvement, such as work flow and communication.

- Team building involves interactive group activities to improve trust and communication among team members.

- Intergroup development attempts to alter the attitudes, stereotypes, and perceptions that group members may have towards one another. Most intergroup development sessions focus on differences between departments and occupations, such as between manufacturing and financial divisions in a firm.

- Appreciative inquiry involves the identification of unique strengths in an organization and building on these qualities to improve performance.

- The sociotechnical or structural approach to redesigning organizations focuses on meeting the needs of a changing external environment. Sociotechnical refers to the relationship between people and structure in an organization.

POST-TEST ANSWER SHEET

1. Ⓐ Ⓑ Ⓒ Ⓓ	13. Ⓐ Ⓑ Ⓒ Ⓓ	25. Ⓐ Ⓑ Ⓒ Ⓓ	37. Ⓐ Ⓑ Ⓒ Ⓓ	49. Ⓐ Ⓑ Ⓒ Ⓓ
2. Ⓐ Ⓑ Ⓒ Ⓓ	14. Ⓐ Ⓑ Ⓒ Ⓓ	26. Ⓐ Ⓑ Ⓒ Ⓓ	38. Ⓐ Ⓑ Ⓒ Ⓓ	50. Ⓐ Ⓑ Ⓒ Ⓓ
3. Ⓐ Ⓑ Ⓒ Ⓓ	15. Ⓐ Ⓑ Ⓒ Ⓓ	27. Ⓐ Ⓑ Ⓒ Ⓓ	39. Ⓐ Ⓑ Ⓒ Ⓓ	51. Ⓐ Ⓑ Ⓒ Ⓓ
4. Ⓐ Ⓑ Ⓒ Ⓓ	16. Ⓐ Ⓑ Ⓒ Ⓓ	28. Ⓐ Ⓑ Ⓒ Ⓓ	40. Ⓐ Ⓑ Ⓒ Ⓓ	52. Ⓐ Ⓑ Ⓒ Ⓓ
5. Ⓐ Ⓑ Ⓒ Ⓓ	17. Ⓐ Ⓑ Ⓒ Ⓓ	29. Ⓐ Ⓑ Ⓒ Ⓓ	41. Ⓐ Ⓑ Ⓒ Ⓓ	53. Ⓐ Ⓑ Ⓒ Ⓓ
6. Ⓐ Ⓑ Ⓒ Ⓓ	18. Ⓐ Ⓑ Ⓒ Ⓓ	30. Ⓐ Ⓑ Ⓒ Ⓓ	42. Ⓐ Ⓑ Ⓒ Ⓓ	54. Ⓐ Ⓑ Ⓒ Ⓓ
7. Ⓐ Ⓑ Ⓒ Ⓓ	19. Ⓐ Ⓑ Ⓒ Ⓓ	31. Ⓐ Ⓑ Ⓒ Ⓓ	43. Ⓐ Ⓑ Ⓒ Ⓓ	55. Ⓐ Ⓑ Ⓒ Ⓓ
8. Ⓐ Ⓑ Ⓒ Ⓓ	20. Ⓐ Ⓑ Ⓒ Ⓓ	32. Ⓐ Ⓑ Ⓒ Ⓓ	44. Ⓐ Ⓑ Ⓒ Ⓓ	56. Ⓐ Ⓑ Ⓒ Ⓓ
9. Ⓐ Ⓑ Ⓒ Ⓓ	21. Ⓐ Ⓑ Ⓒ Ⓓ	33. Ⓐ Ⓑ Ⓒ Ⓓ	45. Ⓐ Ⓑ Ⓒ Ⓓ	57. Ⓐ Ⓑ Ⓒ Ⓓ
10. Ⓐ Ⓑ Ⓒ Ⓓ	22. Ⓐ Ⓑ Ⓒ Ⓓ	34. Ⓐ Ⓑ Ⓒ Ⓓ	46. Ⓐ Ⓑ Ⓒ Ⓓ	58. Ⓐ Ⓑ Ⓒ Ⓓ
11. Ⓐ Ⓑ Ⓒ Ⓓ	23. Ⓐ Ⓑ Ⓒ Ⓓ	35. Ⓐ Ⓑ Ⓒ Ⓓ	47. Ⓐ Ⓑ Ⓒ Ⓓ	59. Ⓐ Ⓑ Ⓒ Ⓓ
12. Ⓐ Ⓑ Ⓒ Ⓓ	24. Ⓐ Ⓑ Ⓒ Ⓓ	36. Ⓐ Ⓑ Ⓒ Ⓓ	48. Ⓐ Ⓑ Ⓒ Ⓓ	60. Ⓐ Ⓑ Ⓒ Ⓓ

answer sheet

POST-TEST

Directions: Carefully read each of the following 60 questions. Choose the best answer to each question, and darken its letter on your answer sheet. The Answer Key and Explanations can be found following this Post-Test.

1. Juanita, a new employee, wears stylish clothes and always looks polished. Her coworkers assume she is frivolous and unintelligent, even though they have not spoken to her yet. Which of the following most likely describes the perception method used by Juanita's coworkers?

    (A) Selective perception

    (B) Contrast effect

    (C) Stereotyping

    (D) Halo effect

2. Which of the following statements best summarizes goal-setting theory?

    (A) Establish simple goals to improve employee job satisfaction.

    (B) Address employee goals for self-identity by giving them autonomy.

    (C) Set challenging goals for employees and provide them with feedback.

    (D) Allow employees to set their own goals and eliminate performance appraisals.

3. The first theory of management was developed by

    (A) John Kotter.

    (B) Henri Fayol.

    (C) Kurt Lewin.

    (D) Henry Mintzberg.

4. What is the final stage of group development for a permanent work group?

    (A) Norming

    (B) Storming

    (C) Adjourning

    (D) Performing

5. Catherine, a pharmaceutical sales representative, dramatically increased her sales numbers in two out of her three assigned sales territories. Catherine's manager responds by assigning the third territory, which is considered undesirable, to another sales representative and giving another territory to Catherine. Which of the following methods is most likely being used by Catherine's manager?

    (A) Negative reinforcement

    (B) Positive reinforcement

    (C) Punishment

    (D) Extinction

6. What is the most common type of reinforcement schedule used by businesses?

    (A) Continuous schedule

    (B) Fixed ratio schedule

    (C) Intermittent schedule

    (D) Fixed interval schedule

7. Which of the following is a type of personal power?

    (A) Expert power

    (B) Reward power

    (C) Coercive power

    (D) Legitimate power

8. Which theory asserts that employees are motivated to work hard when they believe they will be rewarded?

    (A) ERG theory

    (B) Expectancy theory

    (C) Goal-setting theory

    (D) Path-goal theory

9. What is the most common source of power in the workplace?

    (A) Expert power

    (B) Reward power

    (C) Coercive power

    (D) Legitimate power

10. Which of the following is most critical to action research?

    (A) Employee attitudes

    (B) Organizational culture

    (C) Data analysis

    (D) Training

11. Which of the following is most likely to encourage a high degree of political behavior within an organization?

    (A) Pressures to excel

    (B) Union involvement in Human Resources

    (C) Over-structured employee roles

    (D) Objective performance appraisal systems

12. Greg, a sales manager, reaches a deal with his firm's CEO to implement flexible scheduling for the sales department. Greg is most likely acting as a

    (A) liaison.

    (B) negotiator.

    (C) figurehead.

    (D) disseminator.

13. Members of a command group are more likely to

    (A) work in different departments.

    (B) belong to the same union.

    (C) share the same manager.

    (D) interact socially.

14. Which of the following has been successfully used in recent years to categorize leadership traits?

    (A) Myers-Biggs Type Indicator

    (B) Fiedler Model

    (C) LMX Theory

    (D) Big Five Model

15. According to the path-goal theory, leadership style is determined by

    (A) leader characteristics.

    (B) reward immediacy.

    (C) group relationships.

    (D) task structure.

16. According to LMX theory research, the relationship between managers and employees grows stronger when

    (A) employees have greater autonomy.

    (B) managers are open to new experiences.

    (C) employees are assigned challenging tasks.

    (D) managers have charisma and long-term vision.

17. What is an advantage of oral communication?

    (A) Expresses emotions clearly

    (B) Provides immediate feedback

    (C) Minimizes common noise problems

    (D) Allows for logical message formation

18. Group hierarchy is most likely established during which stage of group development?

    (A) Norming

    (B) Forming

    (C) Storming

    (D) Performing

19. Which of the following is NOT a personality trait assessed by the Big Five Model?
    (A) Perception
    (B) Extraversion
    (C) Agreeableness
    (D) Conscientiousness

20. What is the primary criticism of the Fiedler model?
    (A) Vague connections between leader behaviors and traits
    (B) Confusion regarding the questionnaire and variables
    (C) Inadequate support from psychological assessments
    (D) Failure to isolate specific leadership characteristics

21. A manager should most likely initiate conflict management strategies when
    (A) conflict first becomes clearly defined.
    (B) both parties determine that a conflict exists.
    (C) problematic conditions create conflict opportunities.
    (D) conflicts become visible through statements and actions.

22. Which decision-making method assumes that individuals face limitations on information and time when making decisions?
    (A) Intuitive decision making
    (B) Rational decision making
    (C) Bounded rationality
    (D) Work specialization

23. Which of the following is NOT a primary need according to David McClelland?
    (A) Power
    (B) Growth
    (C) Affiliation
    (D) Achievement

24. Performance norms primarily indicate
    (A) the way that group members should communicate.
    (B) how group members are expected to behave.
    (C) how hard group members should work.
    (D) the roles that group members should play.

25. A firm that groups jobs by product is most likely using which element of organizational structure?
    (A) Formalization
    (B) Departmentalization
    (C) Work specialization
    (D) Centralization

26. Which of the following is the most commonly used personality-assessment tool?
    (A) Myers-Briggs Type Indicator
    (B) Sentence completion test
    (C) Thematic apperception test
    (D) Big Five Model

27. Which aspect of organizational structure was first established by Henry Ford?
    (A) Departmentalization
    (B) Span of control
    (C) Work specialization
    (D) Formalization

28. According to behavioral theories, a manager who emphasizes deadlines and systematically assigns tasks to employees would most likely exhibit a
    (A) high level of initiating structure.
    (B) high level of consideration.
    (C) low level of initiating structure.
    (D) low level of consideration.

post-test

29. Which of the following statements best summarizes Mintzberg's study?

    (A) Some management roles are more important than others.

    (B) The leadership role is most directly connected to success.

    (C) Most management roles are decision-oriented.

    (D) All roles of management are interrelated.

30. Which of the following is a major feature of a bureaucratic organization?

    (A) Dual chains-of-command

    (B) Standardized work processes

    (C) Minimal departmentalization

    (D) Decentralized authority

31. Which of the following activities is least likely to occur at a firm implementing an organizational development strategy?

    (A) Distributing surveys to work units

    (B) Hiring an outside process consultant

    (C) Developing new job specifications

    (D) Planning team-building activities

32. According to the interactionist view of conflict, which of the following is most likely a dysfunctional conflict?

    (A) Personality clashes

    (B) Different work objectives

    (C) Communication breakdowns

    (D) Unclear work assignment procedures

33. Which organizational design would most likely be used by a small business that employs thirty people?

    (A) Boundaryless organization

    (B) Virtual organization

    (C) Matrix structure

    (D) Simple structure

34. Which term refers to the extent to which employees care about their jobs?

    (A) Job satisfaction

    (B) Job involvement

    (C) Employee engagement

    (D) Employee commitment

35. During the cognition stage of the conflict process, which of the following statements describes what is most likely to occur?

    (A) Conditions create conflict opportunities.

    (B) Emotions shape conflict perceptions.

    (C) Conflicts are actively avoided.

    (D) Conflicts become visible.

36. Multidisciplinary teams are primarily characteristic of

    (A) matrix structures.

    (B) virtual organizations.

    (C) boundaryless organizations.

    (D) bureaucratic organizations.

37. Which of the following involves basing managerial decisions on a systematic study of the best available research?

    (A) Evidence-based management

    (B) Analytical management

    (C) Strategic management

    (D) Rational management

38. Which element of organizational structure determines the number of hierarchical levels and managers in an organization?

    (A) Centralization

    (B) Chain-of-command

    (C) Decentralization

    (D) Span of control

39. John, a sales manager, is interviewing job candidates. The first three applicants are clearly unqualified for the position. He offers the position to the last interviewee, who lacks sales experience, but has a better personality

for the job than the other candidates. Which of the following has most likely occurred?

(A) Halo effect

(B) Stereotyping

(C) Contrast effect

(D) Selective perception

40. Which term refers to identifying and building on an organization's unique strengths during the process of organizational change?

(A) Process consultation

(B) Appreciative inquiry

(C) Intergroup development

(D) SWOT analysis

41. A firm that distributes money based on improvements in a group's productivity is most likely using which type of reward system?

(A) Piece-rate pay

(B) Profit-sharing

(C) Gainsharing

(D) Merit-based pay

42. Which of the following is a major feature of a decentralized organization?

(A) Employees specialize in one task.

(B) Jobs are strictly governed by rules and procedures.

(C) Employees are supervised closely by multiple managers.

(D) Lower-level managers have the authority to make decisions.

43. Which of the following is a conflict-stimulation method?

(A) Realigning work groups

(B) Holding problem-solving sessions

(C) Developing joint compromises

(D) Expanding group resources

44. All of the following factors help determine whether a person's behavior is caused by internal or external issues EXCEPT

(A) consensus.

(B) personality.

(C) consistency.

(D) distinctiveness.

45. The transformational leadership theory is most similar to which of the following?

(A) LMX theory

(B) Contingency theory

(C) Behavioral theory

(D) Charismatic leadership theory

46 Which of the following is asserted by the interactionist school of thought?

(A) Conflict can improve group performance.

(B) Conflict always harms group productivity.

(C) Conflict can be minimized by strong leadership.

(D) Conflict benefits small groups but not large ones.

47. According to Herzberg's theory, job satisfaction factors are

(A) linked to challenging goals.

(B) referred to as hygiene factors.

(C) different from job dissatisfaction factors.

(D) based on higher-order existence needs.

48. Feeling anxious about making an oral presentation at work is an example of a/an

(A) illegitimate job behavior.

(B) communication barrier.

(C) nonverbal cue.

(D) chain network.

post-test

49. Raj has been especially helpful to his manager over the last few weeks by working long hours to complete an important project. However, Raj's manager has not exhibited any appreciation for Raj's hard work, and Raj's motivation has diminished. Which type of reinforcement method has most likely been used by Raj's manager?

    (A) Positive reinforcement

    (B) Negative reinforcement

    (C) Punishment

    (D) Extinction

50. Which of the following is NOT a key function of communication in an organization?

    (A) Increasing performance

    (B) Controlling behavior

    (C) Expressing emotion

    (D) Fostering motivation

51. According to the Big Five Model, a worker with which personality trait is more likely to have a workplace accident?

    (A) Extraversion

    (B) Agreeableness

    (C) Emotional stability

    (D) Openness to experience

52. Contingency theories assert that leader effectiveness is primarily determined by

    (A) personal characteristics.

    (B) behavioral differences.

    (C) situational variables.

    (D) personal relationships.

53. Which of the following is most likely a true statement about groups?

    (A) Competition within a group is detrimental to productivity.

    (B) Small groups complete tasks more quickly than large groups.

    (C) Employers stimulate productivity by rewarding individuals rather than entire groups.

    (D) Employees work more productively and cohesively in large groups than in small groups.

54. Which of the following attempts to determine whether an employee's behavior is caused by internal or external factors?

    (A) Selective perception theory

    (B) Contingency theory

    (C) Expectancy theory

    (D) Attribution theory

55. Ludi received a bonus after six months of working at ION Electronics. She received an additional bonus seven months later and another bonus twelve months later. Assuming that Ludi's bonuses don't correspond to specific accomplishments, which type of reinforcement schedule is most likely being used by Ludi's employer?

    (A) Continuous schedule

    (B) Variable interval schedule

    (C) Fixed ratio schedule

    (D) Variable ratio schedule

56. The purpose of the third step in Kurt Lewin's model is to

    (A) ensure that organizational change is permanent.

    (B) prepare employees for organizational changes.

    (C) implement desired organizational changes.

    (D) develop an organizational change plan.

57. Which theory asserts that group maintenance behaviors can lead to the development of personal relationships with group members?

(A) McClelland's theory

(B) ERG theory

(C) Vroom's theory

(D) LMX theory

58. An employee with a high degree of agreeableness is most likely to have

(A) lower levels of job performance.

(B) better negotiation skills.

(C) lower levels of career success.

(D) more detail-oriented skills.

59. What is the primary benefit of job rotation?

(A) Expanding work teams

(B) Minimizing employee boredom

(C) Appealing to working mothers

(D) Increasing an employee's responsibilities

60. Which of the following is a terminal value according to the Rokeach Value Survey?

(A) Honesty

(B) Sincerity

(C) Equality

(D) Dependability

post-test

ANSWER KEY AND EXPLANATIONS

1. D	13. C	25. B	37. A	49. D
2. C	14. D	26. A	38. D	50. A
3. B	15. D	27. C	39. C	51. D
4. D	16. A	28. A	40. B	52. C
5. A	17. B	29. D	41. C	53. B
6. C	18. C	30. B	42. D	54. D
7. A	19. A	31. C	43. A	55. B
8. B	20. B	32. A	44. B	56. A
9. D	21. D	33. D	45. D	57. D
10. C	22. C	34. B	46. A	58. C
11. A	23. B	35. B	47. C	59. B
12. B	24. C	36. C	48. B	60. C

1. **The correct answer is (D).** Drawing general impressions of a person based on one characteristic, such as appearance, suggests the Halo effect. Selective interpretation occurs when people perceive only what interests them, so choice (A) is incorrect. Contrast effect involves making comparisons, so choice (B) is incorrect. Stereotyping is judging based on group association, such as an ethnic group, so choice (C) is incorrect.

2. **The correct answer is (C).** Research related to goal-setting theory indicates that employees are motivated by specific and difficult goals, especially when they receive feedback on their progress. Choice (A) is incorrect because goals should be challenging. Choices (B) and (D) are not relevant to goal-setting theory.

3. **The correct answer is (B).** Fayol established the first theory of management, so choice (B) is correct. Choices (A) and (C) are incorrect because Kotter and Lewin developed organizational change theories. Mintzberg followed Fayol by identifying ten roles of managers, so choice (D) is incorrect.

4. **The correct answer is (D).** Performing is the final stage of development for a permanent work group. Norming and storming occur before performing, so choices (A) and (B) are incorrect. For temporary groups, adjourning is the last stage, so choice (C) is incorrect.

5. **The correct answer is (A).** Negative reinforcement involves withholding a negative consequence—the undesirable territory—to increase a desired behavior, Catherine's high sales. A bonus is a type of positive reinforcement, so choice (B) is incorrect. A suspension is an example of punishment, so choice (C) is incorrect. Extinction removes a reward to decrease behavior, so choice (D) is incorrect.

6. **The correct answer is (C).** Intermittent schedules are most common in businesses. Continuous reinforcement is the most effective way to change employee behaviors, but it is impractical, so choice (A) is incorrect.

Fixed ratio and fixed interval are types of continuous reinforcement, so choices (B) and (D) are incorrect.

7. **The correct answer is (A).** Expert power is a personal power that is based on an individual's expertise or knowledge. Choice (B), reward power; choice (C), coercive power; and choice (D), legitimate power, are formal powers that stem from an individual's position in an organization.

8. **The correct answer is (B).** Expectancy theory is one of the most supported explanations of employee motivation because of the strong connection between effort, performance, and reward. ERG theory asserts that individuals need existence, relatedness, and growth, so choice (A) is incorrect. Goal-setting theory doesn't link effort with rewards, so choice (C) is incorrect. Choice (D), path-goal theory, is a leadership theory.

9. **The correct answer is (D).** Legitimate power stems from an individual's position in a firm and is the most common source of power because of its broad scope. Expert power, choice (A); reward power, choice (B); and coercive power, choice (C), are less common in work environments.

10. **The correct answer is (C).** With action research, organizational changes are based on systematically collected and analyzed data. Employee attitudes, organizational culture, and training are less relevant, so choices (A), (B), and (D) are incorrect.

11. **The correct answer is (A).** A culture that pressures employees to excel is more likely to foster political behaviors. Union involvement in HR is irrelevant, so choice (B) is incorrect. Unclear employee roles and subjective performance appraisal systems encourage political behavior among workers, so choices (C) and (D), which are the opposite of these, are incorrect.

12. **The correct answer is (B).** The negotiator role involves bargaining with others to obtain advantages, so choice (B) is correct. The liaison and figurehead are both interpersonal roles that involve developing and maintaining good relationships with people, so choices (A) and (C) are incorrect. The disseminator role relates to providing information to subordinates, so choice (D) is incorrect.

13. **The correct answer is (C).** Members of a command group report to the same manager, so choice (C) is correct. Task group members are more likely to work in different departments, so choice (A) is incorrect. Command group members may or may not belong to a union, so choice (B) is incorrect. Friendship group members interact outside of work, so choice (D) is incorrect.

14. **The correct answer is (D).** Although early trait theory studies failed to isolate specific leadership traits, later research was more successful when traits were categorized alongside the Big Five personality framework. Choice (A) is another type of personality assessment, but it hasn't been used to categorize leadership traits. Choices (B) and (C), Fiedler Model and LMX Theory, are leadership models.

15. **The correct answer is (D).** Leadership style is determined by subordinate preference and task structure, according to the path-goal theory. Leader characteristics, personal rewards, and group relationships are not relevant to path-goal theory, so choices (A), (B), and (C) are incorrect.

16. **The correct answer is (A).** Leader-member exchange studies have shown that the relationship between leaders and followers is even stronger when employees have higher levels of autonomy and control over their job performance. Leaders who are open to experiences are typically strong, but this is not linked to LMX theory, which means choice (B) is incorrect. Choices (C) and (D) aren't necessarily associated with LMX theory.

17. The correct answer is (B). Immediate feedback and speed are the main advantages of oral communication. Emotions are not necessarily expressed clearly through oral communication, so choice (A) is incorrect. Noise problems remain with oral communication, so choice (C) is incorrect. Written communication is typically more logical because people have time to consider what they want to communicate, so choice (D) is incorrect.

18. The correct answer is (C). The storming stage is characterized by intragroup conflict regarding group leadership, and it ends with a clarified hierarchy. Hierarchy is typically not established during the norming, forming, or performing stages of group development, choices (A), (B), and (D).

19. The correct answer is (A). The Big Five Model assesses five personality traits: extraversion, agreeableness, conscientiousness, emotional stability, and openness to experience. Perception is an element of the Myers-Briggs test, so choice (A) is the correct answer.

20. The correct answer is (B). Critics of the Fiedler model find the questionnaire and variables confusing and participants' scores unreliable. Choices (A), (C), and (D) are criticisms, but not necessarily associated with Fiedler's contingency theory.

21. The correct answer is (D). The fourth stage of the conflict process, which involves visible behavior, is where conflict management can be enlisted. Conflict management is less necessary in earlier stages of the conflict process, so choices (A), (B), and (C) are incorrect.

22. The correct answer is (C). Bounded rationality assumes that individuals face limitations when making decisions: limited information, limited capacity, and limited time. Choices (A) and (B) are decision-making models that don't account for such limitations. Choice (D) is not related to the decision-making process.

23. The correct answer is (B). According to McClelland, people's three main needs are power, affiliation, and achievement, so choices (A), (C), and (D) are part of McClelland's theory, so they are incorrect answers to the question. Growth is a need according to Alderfer's theory, so the best answer is choice (B).

24. The correct answer is (C). Performance norms indicate how hard group members should work, so choice (C) is correct. Communication, behavior, and roles are less likely to be indicated by performance norms, so choices (A), (B), and (D) are incorrect.

25. The correct answer is (B). Departmentalization involves grouping jobs by product, function, or geography for the purpose of coordinating tasks. Formalization is the degree to which rules govern jobs, so choice (A) is incorrect. Work specialization divides labor into separate jobs to improve productivity, so choice (C) is incorrect. Centralized organizations rely on top managers to make decisions, so choice (D) is incorrect.

26. The correct answer is (A). The MBTI is the most frequently used personality-assessment tool. Choices (B), (C), and (D) are less popular tools for assessing personality.

27. The correct answer is (C). The division of labor, or work specialization, was established by Henry Ford. Ford is not credited for establishing departmentalization, span of control, or formalization, so choices (A), (B), and (D) are incorrect. Span of control, choice (B), originated in the military.

28. The correct answer is (A). Initiating structure refers to the extent that leaders define their roles and the roles of employees, and a manager who stresses deadlines most likely has a high degree of initiating structure. This makes choice (A) correct, and choice (C) incorrect. Consideration relates to job relationships, so choices (B) and (D) are incorrect.

29. **The correct answer is (D).** Each management role is connected to another, so choice (D) is correct. Mintzberg's study doesn't suggest that some roles are more important or more related to success, so choices (A) and (B) are incorrect. Roles are equally distributed between interpersonal, information, and decisional, so choice (C) is incorrect.

30. **The correct answer is (B).** Bureaucracies are characterized by standardization, departmentalization, and centralized authority, making choice (B) correct and choices (C) and (D) incorrect. Dual chains-of-command are an element of the matrix structure, so choice (A) is also incorrect.

31. **The correct answer is (C).** Changing job specifications is least likely to occur during the process of organizational development, so it is the correct answer. A firm is more likely to collect survey feedback about perceptions, hire an outside consultant to assess processes, and implement team building activities. So, choices (A), (B), and (D) are things that an organization would do in implementing an organizational development strategy, and thus incorrect answers to the question.

32. **The correct answer is (A).** Relationship conflicts stem from personality clashes between group members, and such conflicts are nearly always dysfunctional. Task conflicts and process conflicts are functional conflicts that can enhance group performance, so choices (B), (C), and (D) are incorrect.

33. **The correct answer is (D).** A simple structure usually consists of only two to three vertical levels and is most commonly used in small businesses run by owner-managers who employ fewer than fifty people. Choices (A), (B), and (C) are organizational designs more appropriate for larger organizations.

34. **The correct answer is (B).** The extent to which employees identify with and care about their jobs is termed job involvement. Job satisfaction refers to an employee's positive or negative feelings about a job, so choice (A) is incorrect. Employee engagement relates to enthusiasm, so choice (C) is incorrect. Choice (D) is not an organizational behavior term.

35. **The correct answer is (B).** In the cognition and personalization stage, parties determine what a conflict is about, and emotions play a role in shaping conflict perceptions. Conditions create conflict opportunities earlier in the process, so choice (A) is incorrect. Choices (C) and (D) occur later in the process.

36. **The correct answer is (C).** Replacing functional departments with multidisciplinary teams is a feature of boundaryless organizations. Matrix structures combine functional and product departmentalization, so choice (A) is incorrect. Multifunctional teams are not necessarily an aspect of virtual organizations or bureaucracies, so choices (B) and (D) are incorrect.

37. **The correct answer is (A).** Evidence-based management calls for managers to base decisions on the best available scientific evidence rather than feelings and intuitions. Choice (B), analytical management, uses mathematical models to develop solutions to business problems. Choice (C), strategic management, is the process for designing and implementing competitive steps to enhance the performance of an organization. Choice (D), rational management, seems like a good answer, but is meant to distract from the correct answer.

38. **The correct answer is (D).** Span of control refers to the number of levels and managers in an organization. A narrow span of control allows for close supervision, but wider spans are more cost-effective and efficient. Choices (A), (B), and (C) are elements of

organizational structure that don't determine the number of managers in a firm.

39. **The correct answer is (C).** Contrast effect occurs when a person is evaluated based on comparisons to another person. Halo effect involves making a general impression based on one characteristic, so choice (A) is incorrect. Choice (B) is incorrect because John hasn't based his judgments on group associations. Selective perception is a problem associated with narrow interpretations, so choice (D) is incorrect.

40. **The correct answer is (B).** Appreciative inquiry involves the identification of unique strengths in an organization and building on these qualities to improve performance. Process consultation and intergroup development are other organizational methods, so choices (A) and (C) are incorrect. A SWOT (Strengths, Weaknesses, Opportunities, Threats) analysis is used for marketing purposes, so choice (D) is incorrect.

41. **The correct answer is (C).** Gainsharing is a group incentive plan that distributes money based on improvements in group productivity. Piece-rate pay and merit-based pay are both compensation systems for individuals rather than for groups, so choices (A) and (D) are incorrect. Profit-sharing rewards all members of an organization, so choice (B) is incorrect.

42. **The correct answer is (D).** Decentralized organizations assign decision-making authority to lower-level managers. Choice (A) refers to work specialization. Choice (B) describes an organization's level of formalization. Span of control addresses the number of managers and levels in an organization, so choice (C) is incorrect.

43. **The correct answer is (A).** Conflict-stimulation methods include realigning work groups and changing rules. Conflict-resolution, not conflict-stimulation, methods include problem-solving sessions, compro-

mising, and expanding resources, so choices (B), (C), and (D) are incorrect.

44. **The correct answer is (B).** According to attribution theory, consensus, consistency, and distinctiveness are the primary factors that determine whether a person's behavior is internally or externally caused, so choices (A), (C), and (D) are incorrect. Personality is not a factor, which means choice (B) is correct.

45. **The correct answer is (D).** Transformational leadership theory and charismatic leadership theory both suggest that leaders articulate a vision and are inspirational. Choices (A), (B), and (C) are less similar to transformational leadership theory. Choice (A), LMX theory, is about the relationship between leaders and followers and indicates that the more autonomy employees have, the stronger the relationship. Choice (B), contingency theory, posits that situational variables determine whether specific leadership traits and behaviors are effective. According to choice (C), behavioral theory, effective leaders have different behaviors than ineffective leaders.

46. **The correct answer is (A).** The interactionist school of thought views conflict as a positive activity in some cases and should be encouraged in those situations in order to improve group performance. However, interactionists believe that some conflict is harmful, so choice (B) is incorrect; be careful of universal qualifiers like "always" and "everyone." Leadership and group size are not an issue, so choices (C) and (D) are incorrect.

47. **The correct answer is (C).** Two components on separate continuums motivate employees according to Herzberg, so choice (C) is correct. Choices (A) and (D) refer to other motivation theories. Hygiene factors lead to dissatisfaction, and motivators lead to satisfaction, which means choice (B) is incorrect.

48. **The correct answer is (B).** Communication apprehension occurs when a person feels tense about communicating orally, and it is a type of communication barrier that affects nearly 20 percent of all workers. Choices (A), (C), and (D) are not related to communication anxiety.

49. **The correct answer is (D).** Failing to show appreciation for help or failing to compliment employees for working hard are examples of extinction. Negative reinforcement involves removing an undesirable consequence, so choice (B) is incorrect. Choices (A) and (C) are incorrect because Raj has not been rewarded or punished by his manager.

50. **The correct answer is (A).** The four functions of communication in an organization are controlling behavior, choice (B); expressing emotion, choice (C); fostering motivation, choice (D); and providing information. Increased performance may result from clear communication, but it isn't a primary function, which means choice (A) is the best answer.

51. **The correct answer is (D).** Individuals who score high on openness to experience are more creative, but more susceptible to workplace accidents. Extraversion, agreeableness, and emotional stability are not necessarily associated with risky behavior at work, so choices (A), (B), and (C) are incorrect.

52. **The correct answer is (C).** Situational variables determine whether specific leader traits and behaviors are effective or not, so choice (C) is correct. Trait theories assert that personal characteristics are important, so choice (A) is incorrect. Behavioral theories rely on the importance of leader behaviors, so choice (B) is incorrect. Leader-Member Exchange Theory (LMX) focuses on personal relationships between leaders and followers, so choice (D) is incorrect.

53. **The correct answer is (B).** Research indicates that smaller groups complete tasks more quickly than larger groups and that employees work more effectively in smaller rather than larger groups. So, choice (B) is correct and choice (D) is incorrect. A manager benefits from encouraging competition and rewarding groups rather than individuals, so choices (A) and (C) are incorrect.

54. **The correct answer is (D).** According to attribution theory, people try to explain the behavior of others based on internal attributes or external attributes. Selective perception is the tendency to interpret what is important to an individual, so choice (A) is incorrect. Contingency theories relate to leadership, so choice (B) is incorrect. Expectancy theory is a motivation theory, so choice (C) is incorrect.

55. **The correct answer is (B).** Variable interval schedules apply reinforcers after varying periods of time. Choices (A) and (C) are incorrect because Ludi didn't receive bonuses after every success. Variable ratio schedules apply reinforcers after a variable number of responses, which isn't suggested by the information, so choice (D) is incorrect.

56. **The correct answer is (A).** The purpose of the third and final step of Lewin's model is to ensure that organizational changes are permanent. Employees are prepared and a plan is made in the first step, so choices (B) and (D) are incorrect. Plans are implemented in the second, so choice (C) is incorrect.

57. **The correct answer is (D).** The Leader-Member Exchange (LMX) theory asserts that group maintenance behaviors, such as trust, mutual respect, mutual loyalty, and open communication lead to the development of personal relationships with group members. Choices (A), (B), and (C) are incorrect because they relate to motivation rather than leadership and group dynamics.

58. **The correct answer is (C).** Agreeableness is associated with high job performance, low levels of career success, and poor negotiation skills, so choice (C) is correct and choices (A) and (B) are incorrect. Conscientiousness implies better attention to detail, so choice (D) is incorrect.

59. **The correct answer is (B).** Job rotation involves periodically shifting a worker from one task to another, a technique that reduces boredom in highly routine jobs. Choices (A) and (C) are not related to job rotation. Job enrichment expands an employee's responsibilities, so choice (D) is incorrect.

60. **The correct answer is (C).** According to the Rokeach Value Survey, values can be divided into two types: (1) terminal values and (2) instrumental values. Equality is a terminal value, so choice (C) is correct. Honesty, sincerity, and dependability are instrumental values, so choices (A), (B), and (D) are incorrect.

SUMMING IT UP

- In addition to having effective technical skills, managers need to develop people skills in order to (1) retain high-performing workers, (2) handle employee conflicts, (3) improve workplace productivity, and (4) enhance both worker and firm performance. The study of organizational behavior provides the basis for these essential managerial skills.

- Early important theorists in the study of management are (1) Henri Fayol, who developed the first management theory identifying five (now condensed to four) functions of managers and (2) Henry Mintzberg, who identified ten roles of managers categorized as interpersonal, informational, and decisional.

- Evidence-based management relies on (1) observing relationships, (2) identifying causes and effects, and (3) drawing conclusions based on evident.

- Perceptions are how individuals organize and interpret what they experience, which may differ significantly from reality and one another's perceptions.

- Three key factors explain why employees frequently have such different perceptions: (1) the perceiver, (2) the target, and (3) the situation. An individual perceiver's (1) attitudes, (2) motives, (3) interests, (4) experiences, and (5) expectations influence personal perceptions. The target or object being perceived has certain distinguishing characteristics that influence perceptions either positively or negatively.

- The methods of perceptions are (1) selective perception, (2) halo effect, (3) contract effects, and (4) stereotyping.

- According to attribution theory, people try to explain the behavior of others based on internal attributes or external attributes. Behaviors because of internal attributes are under the control of an individual, whereas externally caused behaviors are out of the individual's control. Determining whether behavior is caused by internal or external factors depends on the factors of (1) distinctiveness, (2) consensus, and (3) consistency.

- The Big Five Model is supported by a large body of evidence to support the tool's five personality traits (extraversion, agreeableness, conscientiousness, emotional stability, openness to experiences) and their connection to job performance.

- Attitudes develop from three components: (1) cognition, (2) affect, and (3) behavior. Organizational behaviorists primarily focus on (1) job satisfaction, (2) job involvement, (3) organizational commitment, (4) perceived organizational support, and (5) employee engagement.

- According to the Rokeach Value Survey, values can be divided into (1) terminal values and (2) instrumental values.

- Learning is an active and purposeful process that occurs through experiences and results in permanent behavior changes. The models of learning are (1) classical conditioning, (2) operant conditioning, and (3) observational conditioning.

- Reinforcement methods of learning that operate in the workplace are (1) positive reinforcement, (2) negative reinforcement, (3) punishment, and (4) extinction.

- Reinforcers can either be implemented on a (1) continuous schedule or (2) an intermittent schedule. Continuous schedules are either a (1) fixed ratio or a (2) fixed interval. A fixed ratio schedule applies reinforcement after a specific number of behavioral occurrences, whereas a fixed interval schedule applies a reinforcer after a set amount of time.

- Intermittent schedules are ones that don't reinforce every instance of desired behavior and are either a (1) variable ratio or a (2) variable interval. Variable ratio schedules apply reinforcers after a variable number of responses. Variable interval schedules apply reinforcers after varying periods of time.

- The most common motivation theories are (1) Maslow's hierarchy of needs, (2) Herzberg's two-factor theory, (3) Alderfer's ERG theory, (4) McClelland's theory of needs, (5) goal-setting, (6) equity, and (7) Victor Vroom's Expectancy. Of these, the first four aren't considered valid for employee motivation, but the other three have some merit, especially the expectancy theory.

- Job design (job rotation and job enrichment) as well as alternative work arrangements (flextime, job sharing, and telecommuting) are motivational tools used by companies. Variable-pay programs (piece-rate, merit-based, bonuses, skill-based, profit-sharing, gainsharing, and employee stock ownership) are also popular ways to motivate employees.

- Two types of stressors are associated with employment: (1) challenge stressors and (2) hindrance stressors. The primary causes of stress can be divided into three categories: (1) environmental factors, (2) organizational factors, and (3) personal factors.

- Groups are (1) formal or (2) informal and (1) command, (2) task, (3) interest, or (4) friendship. Groups typically develop in the same way: (1) forming, (2) storming, (3) norming, (4) performing, and (5) adjourning, if temporary.

- Groups have common characteristics that influence member behaviors and those key properties are (1) roles, (2) norms, (3) status, (4) size, and (5) cohesiveness. Research indicates that smaller groups complete tasks more quickly than larger groups and that employees work more effectively in smaller rather than in larger groups.

- Interactionists believe that, in some cases, conflict can be beneficial to the group. Conflict may be (1) functional or (2) dysfunctional. Functional and dysfunctional conflicts are distinguished by conflict type: (1) task, (2) process, and (3) relationship.

- The conflict process has five stages: (1) potential opposition or incompatibility, (2) cognition and personalization, (3) intentions, (4) behavior, and (5) outcomes. The fourth stage is the time for conflict resolution or conflict stimulation.

- Research into leadership styles has produced six major models or theories that identify leadership skills: (1) trait, (2) behavioral, (3) contingency, (4) leader-member exchange (LMX), (5) charismatic, and (6) transformational.

- Power in an organization is either (1) personal or (2) formal. The sources of personal power are (1) expert power and (2) referent power. The sources of formal power are (1) coercive power, (2) reward power, and (3) legitimate power. Political power in an organization may be either (1) legitimate or (2) illegitimate.

- Clear communication—the transfer and understanding of meaning—is an essential element to organizational success and serves four key functions: (1) controlling behavior, (2) fostering motivation, (3) expressing emotion, and (4) providing information.

- Communication is a process that requires (1) a message, (2) a sender, and (3) a receiver.

- Barriers to effective communication include (1) filtering, (2) selective perception, (3) information overload, (4) emotions, (5) language, (6) silence, (7) communication apprehension, (8) gender differences, and (9) politically correct communication.

- Making a decision involves interpreting information and evaluating the strengths and weaknesses of the various alternatives, which can be accomplished through three methods: (1) rational decision making, (2) bounded rationality, and (3) intuitive decision making.

- Organizational structure involves six essential elements: (1) work specialization, (2) departmentalization, (3) chain-of-command, (4) span of control, (5) centralization and decentralization, and (6) formalization.

- Organizational design may be (1) simple, (2) bureaucracy, (3) matrix, (4) virtual, or (5) boundaryless.

- Organizations making plans to change typically turn to one of four approaches: (1) Kurt Lewin's three-step model, (2) John Kotter's eight-step plan, (3) action research, and (4) organizational development.

- Common sources of resistance among individuals include (1) having to change habits, (2) worrying about security, and (3) fearing economic changes and the unknown. Organization-wide resistance occurs through (1) regulations, (2) processes, (3) restrictive group norms, and (4) threats to specialized groups and power relationships.

- The primary values underlying organizational development methods include (1) respecting individuals, (2) establishing a trusting and supportive environment, (3) de-emphasizing hierarchical control and authority, (4) openly confronting problems, and (5) encouraging participation in decision making.

Introduction to Business

The following chart outlines the sections and subsections in the Introduction to Business test and offers a comparison between the percent of practice questions in this chapter and the actual DSST exam.

CONTENT OUTLINE: SECTIONS AND SUBSECTIONS	PERCENT OF EXAM DEVOTED TO EACH CONTENT AREA	NUMBER OF ITEMS IN THE DIAGNOSTIC TEST AND POST-TEST BY CONTENT AREA	PERCENT OF ITEMS IN THE DIAGNOSTIC TEST AND POST-TEST BY CONTENT AREA
I. Foundations of Business	25%	16	20%
A. Forms of Business Ownership		2	12.5%
B. Government and Business		1	6.25%
C. Entrepreneurship		3	18.75%
D. Economics of Business		10	62.5%
II. Functions of Business	60%	49	61.25%
A. Management		9	18.4%
B. Marketing		14	28.6%
C. Finance		4	8.2%
D. Accounting		6	12.2%
E. Production and Operations		6	12.2%
F. Management Information Systems		4	8.2%
G. Human Resources		6	12.2%
III. Contemporary Issues	15%	15	18.75%
A. Role of E-commerce		3	20%
B. Business Ethics and Social Responsibility		4	26.7%
C. Global Business Environment		8	53.3%
Grand Total	100%	80	100%

OVERVIEW

- Diagnostic test
- Answer key and explanations
- Foundations of business
- Functions of business
- Contemporary issues
- Post-test
- Answer key and explanations
- Summing it up

DIAGNOSTIC TEST

Directions: Carefully read each of the following 20 questions. Choose the best answer to each question and circle your answer choice. The Answer Key and Explanations can be found following this Diagnostic Test.

1. What does SWOT stand for?

   (A) Sweat equity, weaknesses, opportunities, threats

   (B) Strengths, weaknesses, opportunities, threats

   (C) Standards, wariness, optimism, threats

   (D) Software, web, opportunities, technology

2. The targeted market segment for the magazine *Popular Science* is probably based on

   (A) geographic region.

   (B) age.

   (C) interest.

   (D) income level.

3. Which of the following describes a drop shipper?

   (A) It inventories goods, sets up displays in stores, and bills for goods that are sold.

   (B) It passes orders on to a manufacturer or another wholesaler and receives a commission.

   (C) It inventories goods and sells directly to retailers.

   (D) It inventories, sells, and delivers goods.

4. Which of the following is an example of public relations?

   (A) Thirty-second ad on a TV show

   (B) Personal appearance by an actor to promote a movie

   (C) Press release about a new product

   (D) Fan Web site for a TV show

5. Which of the following describes the time value of money concept?

   (A) The time value of money is a reason to invest in certificates of deposit.

   (B) The value of money increases or decreases depending on inflation.

   (C) Through investing, money will grow over time by earning interest.

   (D) It is better to pay off debts with future money than with current money because inflation cheapens the value of money over time.

6. Insider trading directly violates ethical conduct toward

   (A) other employees of the company.

   (B) investors in the company.

   (C) the company's customers.

   (D) the company's creditors.

7. Which of the following is the most common form of business ownership in the United States?

   (A) Sole proprietorship

   (B) Partnership

   (C) Limited liability partnership

   (D) Corporation

8. Which of the following systems adds value to all businesses involved in producing goods from raw materials to finished product?

   (A) Distribution channel

   (B) Quality improvement team

   (C) Supply chain management

   (D) Organizational analysis

9. The second step in effective decision making is to

   (A) evaluate alternative solutions.

   (B) choose one solution and execute it.

   (C) generate alternative solutions.

   (D) evaluate how well the solution is working.

10. Which of the following measures the market value of goods and services produced within a country during a year?

    (A) GDP

    (B) GNP

    (C) CPI

    (D) PPI

11. A U.S. tech company hires a company in Ireland to handle its help line. The U.S. company is

    (A) not focused on customer care as a goal.

    (B) entering into a partnership with the Irish company.

    (C) outsourcing work.

    (D) offshoring a part of its business.

12. A cafeteria benefits plan provides employees with

    (A) an incentive to work harder.

    (B) a set dollar amount to be used to select from a variety of benefits.

    (C) reduced price lunches.

    (D) the option of either selecting a profit-sharing plan or a merit salary plan.

13. eBay® is an example of what type of e-commerce?

    (A) Business to business

    (B) Consumer to business

    (C) Business to consumer

    (D) Consumer to consumer

14. An example of direct marketing is a/an

    (A) department store.

    (B) electronic storefront.

    (C) Tupperware® party.

    (D) manufacturer's representative calling on a chain store buyer.

15. Which of the following affect the demand for a product?

    I. Changes in consumer preferences

    II. The price of substitute goods

    III. Decrease in the number of suppliers for the raw materials in the product

    (A) I only

    (B) I and II only

    (C) II and III only

    (D) I, II, and III

16. A major risk to companies that shift manufacturing to other countries is

    (A) the shuttering of their factories domestically.

    (B) home country import quotas.

    (C) the risk of political instability in host countries.

    (D) the high price of foreign labor.

17. A company's extranet is available to

    (A) anyone trolling the Internet.

    (B) employees, customers, and vendors.

    (C) employees and customers.

    (D) employees only.

18. Among other traits, an affiliative leadership style

    (A) uses top-down management.

    (B) inspires employees.

    (C) is collaborative.

    (D) encourages goodwill and harmony among employees.

19. Buying a smartphone because everyone in your group has one illustrates what type of influence on consumer behavior?

    (A) Personal

    (B) Sociocultural

    (C) Psychological

    (D) Demographic

20. Unemployment that is caused by a lack of demand for workers because of conditions in the economy is

    (A) seasonal unemployment.

    (B) cyclical unemployment.

    (C) structural unemployment.

    (D) frictional unemployment.

ANSWER KEY AND EXPLANATIONS

1. B	5. C	9. C	13. D	17. B
2. C	6. B	10. A	14. B	18. D
3. B	7. A	11. C	15. B	19. B
4. A	8. C	12. B	16. C	20. B

1. **The correct answer is (B).** SWOT stands for strengths, weaknesses, opportunities, threats. Choices (A), (C), and (D) are incorrect.

2. **The correct answer is (C).** The market segment for *Popular Science* is probably based on an interest in things scientific. Choice (A), geographic region; choice (B), age; and choice (D), income level, are not likely to be influences on a purchase that doesn't depend on living in a certain region, being in a certain age range, or having a certain income level.

3. **The correct answer is (B).** A drop shipper doesn't inventory the goods that it sells; it passes the orders that it takes on to the manufacturer or another wholesaler and receives a commission. Choice (A) is incorrect because it describes a rack jobber. Choice (C) is incorrect because it describes a cash-and-carry wholesaler. Choice (D) is incorrect because it describes a truck wholesaler.

4. **The correct answer is (A).** Only choice (A), a prepared ad, is an example of public relations. Choices (B), (C), and (D) are examples of publicity, where the company has no control over what is said or shown. Even the press release may or may not be used in the manner in which the company wanted it presented.

5. **The correct answer is (C).** In addition to earning interest, money may yield other returns such as dividends and stock splits. Choice (A) is incorrect because the time value of money is a reason to invest in CDs, but that's not a definition of the time value of money, which is what the question is asking. Choices (B) and (D) are true about inflation, but not the answer to the question.

6. **The correct answer is (B).** Insider trading is buying or selling stock based on confidential information about a company and can directly harm investors, either by driving down the price of the stock through selling or driving up the price of the stock through buying, putting it out of the range of an average investor. The key word here is "directly." Insider trading may indirectly harm other employees, choice (A); customers, choice (C); and creditors, choice (D), if the stock price dives and investors and lenders lose confidence in the business. However, this represents indirect, not direct, damage.

7. **The correct answer is (A).** Sole proprietorships are the most common form of business ownership in the United States, making up about three quarters of U.S. businesses, but only about 5 percent of business revenue. Choice (D), corporations, make up about 20 percent of U.S. businesses. Choice (B), partnerships, and choice (C), limited liability partnerships, are also incorrect.

8. **The correct answer is (C).** The key word here is "value." Miss that word and you might select choice (A), distribution channel, which moves a product from raw materials to finished good. Choice (B) is incorrect because a quality improvement team operates within a single company to improve the quality of their processes and products. Choice (D) is incorrect because organi-

zational analysis is a review of strengths and weaknesses conducted within a single company.

9. **The correct answer is (C).** Step 1 is to identify the problem and step 2 is to generate alternatives, choice (C). This has to be done before evaluating alternative solutions, which is step 3 and choice (A). Step 4 is to choose one of those alternatives and implement it, choice (B). Step 5 is to evaluate how well the solution is working, choice (D).

10. **The correct answer is (A).** GDP stands for gross domestic product and is defined as the market value of all goods and services produced within a country during a year. Choice (B), GNP, stands for gross national product and includes the value of all goods and services produced by facilities owned by domestic companies, but located anywhere in the world. Choice (C), CPI, stands for consumer price index and refers to a market basket of goods and services that is monitored monthly for changes in their prices. Choice (D), PPI, is the producer price index and is the industrial equivalent of the CPI.

11. **The correct answer is (C).** Outsourcing means giving work that was handled internally to an outside company, typically a company based in another country, whereas offshoring, choice (D), is sending part of a company to another country. Choice (A) is incorrect because hiring a company in another country to provide customer service is not an indication that the company is not interested in offering good follow-up services to its customers post-purchase. Choice (B) is incorrect because the question states that the U.S. company is hiring another company; there is no mention of any kind of partnership arrangement.

12. **The correct answer is (B).** Cafeteria benefits plans are meant to reduce the cost to companies of employee benefits. Choice (A) is incorrect because benefits don't depend on performance. Choice (C) is incorrect; re-

duced price lunches are subsidized lunches. Choice (D) is incorrect because neither a profit-sharing plan nor a merit salary plan are matters of employee choice; both compensation programs are determined by company policy.

13. **The correct answer is (D).** eBay® enables consumers to sell to one another. Choices (A) and (C) are other types of e-commerce and so are incorrect. Choice (B) is incorrect.

14. **The correct answer is (B).** Direct marketing, or direct response marketing, is direct contact between the seller and the buyer. A department store is not an example of direct marketing, so choice (A) is incorrect. Choices (C) and (D) are incorrect because both are examples of direct selling, not direct marketing.

15. **The correct answer is (B).** Items I and II are both factors that affect demand, whereas item III is a factor that affects supply, so only items I and II are correct. The only answer choice that includes both of those items and only those items is choice (B).

16. **The correct answer is (C).** Outsourcing work to other countries or building plants in other countries is risky if the country has a history of political unrest or repressive government. Choice (A) is not a risk to a company moving production off shore, though it may be a possibility or even a certainty. Choice (B) is incorrect because products made by or for a home country company on foreign soil don't come under import regulations when the goods are being shipped to the company's home country; import quotas govern goods made by foreign companies with no affiliation to a home country company. Choice (D) is incorrect because a major reason that companies shift manufacturing offshore is the low cost of labor in other countries.

17. **The correct answer is (B).** A company's extranet is available to employees and to customers and vendors who are authorized

to gain access. Choice (A) is incorrect and describes public sites on the Internet. Choice (C) is too narrow an answer because it omits vendors. Choice (D) describes a company's intranet.

18. **The correct answer is (D).** An affiliative leader encourages goodwill and harmony among employees. A leader who is authoritarian uses a commanding style, choice (A). A visionary style, choice (B), inspires employees. Choice (C) describes a democratic style. The other leadership styles that have been identified are coaching (counselor, delegator), and pacesetting (micromanager, driven, and driver).

19. **The correct answer is (B).** Buying something because one's peers are buying it illustrates sociocultural influences on consumer behavior. Choice (A) is incorrect because a personal influence would be buying a cheap phone because the buyer is always losing phones. Choice (C) is incorrect because psychological influences refer to one's attitudes, motivations to buy or not to buy, and learning or experience. Choice (D), demographic, is a way to segment the market, not an influence on a consumer purchase.

20. **The correct answer is (B).** The high unemployment rate during and after the recession of 2007 to 2010 was a result of cyclical unemployment; the unemployed were willing and able to work, but businesses were not hiring because of economic conditions. Choice (A), seasonal unemployment, is unemployment tied to changes in season, such as construction workers who have no work in the winter and ski instructors who are unemployed in the summer. Choice (C), structural unemployment, is unemployment due to changes in an industry that may result from technological changes or changes in market demand, for example, the loss of jobs by typewriter repairers when computers replaced typewriters. Choice (D), frictional unemployment, is temporary unemployment that results from people changing jobs or careers or relocating.

answers diagnostic test

FOUNDATIONS OF BUSINESS

Every business produces a good or a service, or both. How it produces its product is determined by a number of factors, but before even those decisions are made, a businessperson needs to decide the type of business organization he or she wants to establish. Depending on the answer, the new business owner(s) will need to fill out government forms, pay taxes in a certain way, and obey rules and regulations pertinent to the business. Underpinning all this is the economics of conducting business.

Forms of Business Ownership

The basic forms of business ownership are (1) sole proprietorship, (2) partnership, and (3) corporation. There are also (4) co-operative and (5) nonprofit corporation types of businesses. Both partnerships and corporations have several different formats.

Sole Proprietorship

The sole proprietorship is the most common form of business ownership in the United States, accounting for almost three quarters of the business organizations in the country. Anyone who runs a business alone is a sole proprietor unless that person has incorporated the business. No paperwork or special reporting to the Internal Revenue Service is required of sole proprietorships. Sole proprietorships are run by one person, but that person may hire employees.

There are a number of advantages to the sole proprietorship form of business ownership: (1) lack of legal requirements for establishing and operating the business, (2) low start-up costs, (3) no separate tax filings so the owner gets all the benefit of any tax loss, (4) no need to divide any profits, and (5) no shared decision making. However, some of these benefits may also be a disadvantage. For example, without a partner, there is no one with whom to share losses.

The disadvantages to sole proprietorships are (1) unlimited liability, (2) difficulty in borrowing money, (3) responsibility for all losses, (4) no one to bounce ideas off in making decisions, and (5) the end of the business when the owner retires or dies. The major disadvantage is unlimited liability, that is, the sole proprietor is held responsible for all debts that the business incurs, as well as all liabilities. For example, if a plumber doesn't turn off the water before installing a new toilet and water floods the bathroom and leaks to the first floor, the homeowner could sue the plumber for damages. If the plumber is a sole proprietor and the homeowner wins, the homeowner could go after the plumber's savings and home to satisfy the judgment. A sole proprietor who employs others is responsible for them as well when it comes to liability. It is also difficult to borrow money to set up or expand a sole proprietorship because a bank will only lend based on the owner's assets.

Partnership

In forty-eight of the fifty states, a partnership must file information about the business under the federal Revised Uniform Limited Partnership Act. However, partnerships are similar to sole proprietorships in that (1) no separate business tax filings are required. However, an important advantage of a partnership over a sole proprietorship is that the former (2) will find it easier to borrow money for the business from banks. In a partnership, the business doesn't rest on the ability of just one person to make it grow. Other advantages include all partners share (3) in contributing to the start-up costs, (4) in any profits, and (5) in decision making.

The most important disadvantage to partnerships is unlimited liability. In a partnership, each partner is responsible for his or her own debts and actions in the course of conducting the business, but also for whatever the other partners incur in the course of doing business.

There are two types of partnerships: (1) general and (2) limited. The description so far of a partnership describes the general partnership arrangement. In a limited partnership, some partners are investors only and have no decision-making authority over the operations of the business. The liability of limited partners is equal only to the percentage of the business they own. A partnership that has limited partners must have at least one general, or active, partner. This person manages the business on a day-to-day basis and has unlimited liability.

All partnership agreements should establish at the beginning (1) the responsibilities of all partners and (2) the guidelines for the addition and departure of partners over time.

Co-operative

Another form of business ownership is the co-operative. A group of partnerships and/or sole proprietorships join together to benefit their individual businesses. As a group, they have more financial power than as individual businesses and, therefore, have greater bargaining power for things such as reduced rail rates for shipping goods. Co-operatives are more common in agriculture than in other industries.

Corporation

A corporation (1) is formed according to state laws; (2) is an entity that is separate from its owners, the stockholders; (3) thus has liability separate from its owners; (4) must file corporate tax returns annually; and (5) has certain legal rights, such as the ability to sue, and certain legal obligations, such as obedience to the law. Unlike the other forms of business ownership, a corporation raises capital by selling shares in its business. The liability of investors, or stockholders, in a corporation is limited; their liability extends only to the amount of their investment in the corporation.

In addition to (1) limited liability for investors, the advantages of a corporate form of business ownership are (2) ease of obtaining capital and (3) continuity of management. The future growth and management of a corporation doesn't depend on one person—unless the corporation is really a one-person operation formed for liability purposes. A major disadvantage of corporations is double taxation. The profits of a corporation are taxed as business income, and when they are paid out as dividends, stockholders must pay tax on them as personal income.

Corporations are owned by their investors, or stockholders. Overall governance falls to a board of directors, but day-to-day operations are overseen by the officers of the corporation, typically a chief executive officer (CEO) and a chief financial officer (CFO). Sometimes, the CEO is a chief operation officer (COO) instead.

There are six types of corporations:

1. *Privately or Closely Held:* The founding family, a group of investors, or the employees of the company may hold the shares. Outsiders cannot buy stock. Profits are taxed as corporate income and shareholders have limited liability.

2. *Public or Publicly Held, Also Known as a C Corp:* Any member of the public and employees can buy stock. Profits are taxed as corporate earnings, and shareholders have limited liability.

3. *Subchapter S, Commonly Called S Corp:* Shareholders pay personal income tax on their share of any profits that the business earns. S corps don't pay corporate taxes, but they must file tax returns annually. Shareholders have limited liability.

4. *Limited Liability (LLC):* Profits are taxed as personal income and shareholders enjoy limited liability.

5. *Professional:* These are formed by professionals such as lawyers and doctors and enjoy limited liability.

6. *Multinational or Transnational:* These corporations have operations in multiple countries and their stock is sold on multiple stock exchanges. Regulations, including taxes, vary from country to country.

Nonprofit Corporation

A nonprofit, or not-for-profit, is set up to support some social or educational mission. A not-for-profit, as the name implies, doesn't make a profit. Any revenue that it generates that isn't required for operations is used to further its mission. Nonprofits are tax-exempt if they qualify under federal regulations, but they must file a tax return and fulfill other reporting requirements for the federal government and for the states under which they operate.

Government and Business

Government influences the business climate in two ways: (1) through regulatory policy and (2) through economic policy. Governments—federal, state, and municipal—regulate what businesses can and cannot do. Through their tax policies, all three levels of government affect how much money businesses have to spend and can borrow, and the federal government also affects businesses through monetary policy.

Regulatory Policies

State and local governments have a variety of rules and regulations that affect businesses from requiring licenses for companies to do business to collecting city wage taxes on suburban commuters. These are statutory laws, which are made by state legislatures, and, therefore, vary from state to state. For example, some states require that companies of a certain size carry disability insurance on their employees, but other states do not. Some have right-to-work laws forbidding closed shops, and other states don't. However, when many think of "government," they think of the federal government and its regulatory reach. Every aspect of business is covered under some department or agency of the federal government. For example:

- *Department of Labor:* The Bureau of Labor Statistics compiles a number of economic indices to aid businesses and workers. The Occupational Safety and Health Administration (OSHA) is the main agency charged with setting and enforcing standards for the workplace and for workforce training and education. The Fair Labor Standards Act regulates the minimum wage.

- *Department of Agriculture (USDA):* In addition to overseeing farm subsidy programs, the USDA supports the Women, Infant, and Children (WIC) food assistance program, as well as other Child Nutrition Programs.

- *Department of Health and Human Services:* The Food and Drug Administration (FDA) oversees food safety programs and approves new drugs before they can be sold in the United States.

- *Department of Commerce:* According to its Web site, the U.S. Department of Commerce has "a wide range of responsibilities in the areas of trade, economic development, technology, entrepreneurship and business development, environmental stewardship, and statistical research and analysis." Commerce oversees patents and trademarks, imports and exports, and manufacturing standards.

- *Federal Trade Commission (FTC):* The FTC is a separate agency of the federal government, not affiliated with an executive branch-level department. The agency's mission includes consumer protection as well as the advancement of competition. Deceptive advertising practices come under its jurisdiction, as do the Telemarketing Sales Rule, the Pay-Per-Call Rule, and the Equal Credit Opportunity Act.

Other independent agencies related to business are the Consumer Product Safety Commission (CPSC), the Environmental Protection Agency (EPA), and the National Transportation Safety Board (NTSB).

Businesses, regardless of their size, are subject to a variety of laws:

- *Contract:* To be valid, a contract must (1) include a stated offer and acceptance, (2) have mutual consent, (3) include a consideration (exchange of item of value, such as a dollar), (4) be legal, and (5) be in the proper form depending on the amount and term of the contract.

- *Tort:* No contract exists: (1) intentional, (2) product liability, or (3) negligent

- *Property:* (1) intellectual, (2) tangible real, (3) tangible personal, or (4) intangible personal

- *Agency:* Governing those who act for another party

- *Commercial:* Uniform Commercial Code: contracts, warranties

- *Bankruptcy:* Federal law: (1) Chapter 7: liquidation and (2) Chapter 11: reorganization

Fiscal and Monetary Policies

One aspect of federal economic policy is the maintenance of a stable economic environment in which businesses can operate. As you will read below, economies go through fluctuations known as business cycles, and the federal government through fiscal and monetary policies seeks to smooth out these ups and downs in output, unemployment, and inflation.

Fiscal policy refers to taxes and government spending. With the exception of some fees, the federal government—like state and local governments—raises revenue through levying taxes on businesses and individuals. When inflation is rising, raising taxes can cool down the economy. The higher the taxes, the less money there is for consumers to buy goods and services and the slower the economy. When the economy is in a downturn, cutting taxes doesn't have the opposite effect. Some people will use the additional money for new spending as the government intends, but some will pay off old debts, and others will save the additional money. Another way to stimulate the economy in a downturn is to increase government spending. Rather than increase taxes, the government borrows money by selling Treasury bonds, notes, and bills for varying periods of time and at competitive market rates.

Monetary policy is the tool of the Federal Reserve System, commonly referred to as the Fed, which is an independent agency. The Fed is the nation's central bank, or banker's bank, and as such, (1) operates the twelve district banks of the Federal Reserve System, (2) oversees member banks in those districts, and (3) sets the nation's general money and credit policies. It has three tools that it can use:

1. *Discount Rate:* The rate charged to member banks to borrow money (the higher the discount rate, the less money banks will borrow, the less they will lend, and the slower the economy); a tool to keep inflation in check (the lower the discount rate, the more money banks will borrow, the more they will lend, and the more the economy will grow)

2. *Reserve Requirement:* The percentage of their deposits that member banks must hold as a reserve against their deposits (acts similarly to increases and decreases in the discount rate)

3. *Open-Market Operations:* Mechanism to buy or sell bonds and securities on the open market (buying puts money into the economy to stimulate it and selling takes money out of the economy to contract it)

Entrepreneurship

Ford didn't start out as a multinational corporation, nor did Apple®. They began with one or two individuals and an idea, and from that idea, the founders went on to produce a product and launch a business. They were entrepreneurs, individuals willing to take risks. Various characteristics are ascribed to entrepreneurs, such as being (1) innovative, (2) resourceful, (3) risk-takers, (4) flexible, (5) self-motivated, (6) able to work well with others, (7) good leaders, and (8) able to see the "big picture." The desire to be one's own boss also plays a role in entrepreneurship. Some entrepreneurs start their own businesses because they want to make a comfortable living, want more control over their lives, or want the flexibility that comes with owning their own business, whereas others start their businesses with the intention of making it as large and profitable as possible. The former are the owners of small businesses, the majority of U.S. companies, and the latter are the start-ups looking for sizable infusions of venture capital.

While many entrepreneurs start businesses based on their own idea, some choose instead to buy an existing business. (1) The risks are more or less known, (2) there is an existing base of customers and suppliers, and (3) there is a financial history to use as the basis for projections of future financial performance. For the same reasons, other entrepreneurs choose to buy franchises. The franchiser also provides (1) its expertise in helping the franchisee set up the business and (2) training and (3) marketing, including advertising materials. The downsides to a franchise are (1) the cost of buying the franchise license, (2) associated start-up costs, (3) the percentage that the franchisee pays the franchiser, (4) lack of creativity and control over the individual business, and (5) competition from similar national brands.

The first step for both types of entrepreneurs is creating a business plan that includes (1) goals and objectives, (2) a sales forecast, and (3) a financial plan indicating income, the break-even point, and a budget. Securing funding is the next big hurdle. Typically, a small business is funded with the owner's savings and loans or investments from family and friends. Other forms of funding include (1) venture capital companies, (2) small business investment companies (SBIC), (3) angel investors (individuals rather than companies), and (4) various programs of the Small Business Administration (SBA), including (1) 7(a) loans, (2) special purpose loans, (3) micro loans, and (4) the Certified Development Company (504) loan program.

Reasons for small business success include (1) competent management, (2) commitment to doing whatever it takes to succeed, (3) accurate reading of demand in the marketplace for the product or service, and (4) "being in the right place at the right time with the right product," in other words, good luck.

Some of the reasons for small business failures include (1) lack of planning upfront before the business is set up, (2) inexperienced or incompetent management, (3) lack of commitment to the business, (4) weak financial and inventory controls, and (5) lack of enough capital to support the business until it becomes profitable.

Economics of Business

Economics, as defined by Webster's dictionary, is "the science that deals with the production, distribution, and consumption of wealth and with the various related problems of labor, finance, taxation, etc." It almost sounds like a definition of business. Businesses try to accurately discern the needs, wants, and desires of the marketplace in order to produce and distribute the right mix of goods, or products, while dealing with labor, financial issues, competition, and the like.

A company may operate in any one of four types of economic systems:

1. *Traditional:* Rural, agrarian economy of which few still exist

2. *Planned:* Control by the government over what is produced, how, and for whom and at what price; complete control under a communist system and a lesser degree of control in a socialist system; in the latter, typically government-run social services and utilities

3. *Market:* Decisions about what to produce, how, for whom, and at what price made by businesses and individuals; free market, free enterprise, capitalist systems

4. *Mixed:* Combination of planned and market systems; economic decisions made by businesses and individuals with some government control and oversight; examples include the United States, Great Britain, and Germany

Regardless of the type of economic system, there are five factors of production in play: (1) labor, (2) natural resources, (3) capital, (4) entrepreneurs, and (5) technology. Capital is divided into real capital, meaning the equipment and facilities used to produce goods and services, and financial capital, the money needed to start up and operate a business.

Economics of Supply and Demand

In a market economy or mixed economy, such as the United States, market forces set prices through the laws of supply and demand. Demand is the willingness and ability of consumers to buy a good or service, and supply is the willingness and ability of producers to produce a good or service. The law of supply states that producers will offer more of a product/service as the price increases and less of a product/service as the price decreases. The law of demand works in reverse. Consumers will buy more of a product/service as the price decreases and less of a product/service as the price increases.

The point at which a balance between supply and demand is reached is called the equilibrium point or, in business terms, the market price.

Supply and demand are shown on supply curves and demand curves. A supply curve indicates the amount of goods or services offered at different price points, and a demand curve shows how many products or services will be bought at different price points. When there is more demand than supply, a shortage occurs. When there is more supply than demand, a surplus occurs.

A variety of factors can affect both supply and demand and thus the availability and price of goods and services. Factors affecting supply, positively or negatively, may be (1) changes in the price of raw materials, (2) forecasts of future prices—either up or down, (3) acceleration of technological change, (4) increase or decrease in the number of competitors, and (5) increase or decrease in the price of substitute goods. Demand may be changed positively or negatively by such factors as (1) increase or decrease in income distribution, (2) changes in consumer preferences, (3) changes in population age and distribution, and (4) increase or decrease in demand for substitute goods.

Competition

(1) Competition is one characteristic of market and mixed economies. The other three are (2) the right to own property, (3) freedom of choice in buying and selling goods and services and one's labor, and (4) profits. There are various degrees of competition from none to complete, or perfect, competition:

- *Monopoly:* Lack of competition; single supplier of a good or service, or one dominant supplier in an industry; controls pricing

- *Monopolistic:* Several producers making similar products that are perceived as slightly differentiated; no perfect substitute goods; each producer can set own price within certain limits of the marketplace; mix of large and small businesses competing for market share

- *Oligopoly:* Few producers, little differentiation of product, little difference in pricing; occurs in industries with high barriers to entrance, such as large initial investment costs, well-established firms, fierce competition

- *Perfect:* Many producers—large and small; no perceived differences by consumers among products; pricing set by the marketplace

Economic Indicators

To be successful, those who run businesses must be aware of the economic environment in which they operate. Aggregate output is the total amount of goods and services produced by an economy in a given period. There are a number of indicators that show how well or how poorly the economy is doing. Many of the reports are compiled and published by the federal government. Among the indicators are the following:

- *Gross Domestic Product (GDP):* Total value of all goods and services produced domestically in a given period; no goods and services produced outside the country are included.

- *Gross National Product (GNP):* Total value of all goods and services produced by a nation's companies regardless of where the facilities are located in a given period of time; considered a less accurate indicator of an economy's health than GDP

- *Consumer Price Index (CPI):* Based on a market basket of goods and services that doesn't vary from month to month in order to show a pattern of monthly expenses for the typical urban household; the eight categories are food, housing, clothing, transportation, medical care, recreation, education, and miscellaneous items, such as haircuts and cigarettes

- *Producer Price Index (PPI):* Measurement of selling prices received by domestic producers of goods and services for their products, includes prices for raw materials, component goods, and finished goods

- *Unemployment Rate:* Low rate can translate into difficulty finding qualified workers; high rate can indicate low consumer demand

- *Productivity:* Rate at which goods and services are produced in a given period; output per capita; the higher the productivity, the healthier the economy

Two other important numbers that affect a nation's economy are (1) the national debt and (2) the balance of trade. To raise money to pay its bills, the federal government sells bonds in addition to levying and collecting taxes. The more bonds the government sells, the more money it takes out of the general pool of investor dollars, which makes it more difficult for businesses—large and small—and individuals to borrow. The balance of trade may affect the economy positively or negatively. If a country sells more goods abroad than it imports, the balance of trade is positive. If the opposite is true, the balance of trade runs a trade deficit. The country owes more to other countries than it takes in from exports.

Over time, the economy goes through peaks and valleys—expansions and contractions—that are known as business cycles. Expansions are known as booms; severe contractions are called depressions and less severe contractions are called recessions. In addition, the economy can be affected by inflation, when price levels across the economy rise, and deflation, when price levels across the economy decline. The federal government through its fiscal and monetary tools attempts to even out these ups and down with stabilization policies. The aim of the polices is (1) to keep prices in check in order to slow inflation and (2) to expand demand in order to lower unemployment.

FUNCTIONS OF BUSINESS

What types of organization are used currently in companies? What makes a good manager? How are prices set? What financial controls should a company have? How do information systems make companies more efficient? This section answers these questions and more as it describes the varied functions of business.

Management

As Ebert and Griffin's *Business Essentials* defines management, it "is the process of planning, organizing, leading, and controlling an organization's financial, physical, human, and information resources to achieve its goals." Planning is an essential element of the role of management and includes setting the (1) goals, (2) strategies, and (3) tactics for the business. The function of control includes monitoring the business' performance and making adjustments as needed if goals are not being met.

Management is divided into three levels: (1) top managers who run the overall organization, (2) middle managers who see that the company's strategies are implemented and goals are being met, and (3) first-line managers who directly oversee employees. Organizations have a number of functional areas in common: (1) financial, (2) human resources, (3) information, (4) marketing, and (5) operations. Depending on the industry, an organization may have additional functional areas, such as research and development (R&D) or strategic alliances.

Managers need certain skills:

- *Technical:* The specialized skills required for a particular industry and series of jobs within that industry.

- *Interpersonal:* The ability to interact with and motivate employees. It's more than the ability to get along with people and includes the ability to communicate effectively and inspire confidence, loyalty, and good work.

- *Decision Making:* The ability to (1) identify problems, (2) gather and evaluate information, (3) develop alternative solutions, (4) evaluate alternatives, and (5) select the best one for the problem. The plan is then subjected (6) to further evaluation to determine if it met its goals.

- *Conceptual:* The ability to think in the abstract, to see the big picture; extremely useful in SWOT analysis (strengths, weaknesses, opportunities, threats; the first two are internal factors and the last two are external to the organization).

- *Time Management Skills:* Using time for one's self and one's subordinates most efficiently and effectively, includes (1) prioritizing paperwork, (2) establishing agendas for meetings, (3) setting aside a time for phone calls, and (4) organizing and prioritizing e-mails for response and filing.

In addition to these skills, many managers today will need to be able to manage in a global environment, which requires understanding of the global business environment and understanding of cultural differences with foreign nationals within their own companies and with strategic partners and competitors. The ability to conceptualize the use of technology for efficient operations and communication is also important.

Planning

Organizations develop five types of plans: (1) strategic, (2) tactical, (3) operational, (4) contingency, and (5) crisis. Contingency planning helps a company deal with unexpected changes, for example, a huge jump in gasoline prices that sends car buyers to smaller, more fuel-efficient foreign cars forced U.S. car makers to change their car designs and produce smaller, more fuel-efficient cars. Crisis management planning describes how an organization will continue to operate during an emergency such as 9/11 or the earthquake and tsunami that hit Japan in 2011.

An extremely important function of managers, especially top management, is strategic planning to set the future of the organization. Strategic planning encompasses (1) developing a vision statement, (2) developing a mission statement, (3) conducting a SWOT analysis, (4) establishing goals, (5) developing objectives, and (6) determining tactics to achieve the objectives and goals and ultimately create the vision.

An organization's goals typically fall into three categories: (1) long-range, (2) intermediate, and (3) short-range. Tactical planning is carried out by middle managers with the oversight of top managers and involves intermediate goals—from one to five years. Middle managers and first-line managers typically develop operational plans based on short-range goals—anywhere from daily to quarterly. Long-range goals refer to periods longer than five years.

Organizing

Organizing a company is determining how the company will be structured. Structure is determined by (1) specialization of tasks, (2) departmentalization of those specialties/tasks, and (3) distribution of decision making. Typically, large businesses have three levels of management: (1) top, (2) middle, and (3) first-line. This structure resembles a pyramid. Within this structure, there are three types of organizational frameworks possible, based on the distribution of authority: (1) vertical, or flat; (2) horizontal, or tall; and (3) network. The vertical structure flats out the pyramid. This type of structure decentralizes authority among various levels of management within the organization, including (1) line departments, (2) staff, and (3) committees and teams. The horizontal structure centralizes authority in top-line management.

Leading

Part of a manager's job is to motivate, encourage, and influence others. There are a variety of approaches to leadership as identified by researchers: (1) trait, (2) behavioral, (3) situational, (4) transformational, and (5) charismatic. Motivation may be (1) extrinsic or (2) intrinsic. There are three main theories about motivation:

1. *Maslow's Hierarchy of Needs:* From lowest to highest: physiological, safety, belonging, esteem, self-actualization

2. *Herzberg's Motivator-Hygiene Theory or Two Factor Theory:* Hygiene translates into basic features: pay and benefits, company policy and administration, relationships with coworkers, supervision, status, job security, working conditions, personal life; motivators include achievement, recognition, the work, responsibility, promotion, growth

3. *McClelland's Three Needs Theory:* Needs for achievement, affiliation, power

Controlling

Management establishes and oversees the controls necessary to ensure that the business is working toward and achieving its goals. The basic categories of controls are (1) bureaucratic, (2) market, and (3) clan, that is, the mutual sense of benefit that employees gain from working together.

Marketing

The concept of marketing has evolved through four stages since the earliest product marketing in the Industrial Revolution: (1) production, (2) sales, (3) marketing, and (4) relationship.

Marketing strategies have two components: (1) target market and (2) marking mix. Product, price, promotion, and place—the Four Ps of marketing—comprise the marketing mix. Place refers to distribution. An integrated marketing strategy merges the elements of the marketing mix so that the Four Ps are presented as a coherent whole to the marketplace.

Marketing Process

The first step in the marketing process may begin before there is even a product to sell; that step is (1) identifying a market need. (2) Market research helps identify the need and how to fulfill it and also (3) identifies the target market. (4) The next step is to develop a marketing plan that includes a SWOT analysis, the target market, the product, and how it will be produced, priced, promoted, and distributed. (5) The groundwork has been laid, so the fifth step is to implement the plan and then assess the effectiveness of the marketing plan.

Market segmentation is an important part of identifying a target market. Market segments may be (1) geographic, (2) demographic, (3) psychographic (lifestyles, personality traits, motives, and values), and (4) behavioral (benefits sought, volume use, brand loyalty, price sensitivity, and product end use).

Consumer and B2B Marketing

A variety of influences affect consumer behavior: (1) psychological, (2) personal, (3) social, (4) cultural, (5) situational, and (6) marketing mix. The process that consumers undertake in making buying decisions includes (1) need/problem recognition, (2) information search, (3) evaluation of alternatives, (4) purchase decision, and (5) post-purchase evaluation.

Business-to-business (B2B) marketing is different from marketing to consumers because (1) business buyers are trained professionals who specialize in purchasing, (2) business buyers are few in number compared to the millions of potential consumers in the nonbusiness marketplace, and (3) sellers and buyers in the B2B market develop close relationships over time that facilitate purchasing.

Consumer goods and services are classified as (1) convenience, (2) shopping, (3) specialty, and (4) unsought. B2B goods and services are categorized as (1) equipment; (2) maintenance, repair, and operating (MRO); (3) raw and processed materials; (4) component; and (5) professional services.

Product

Without products—goods or services or both—a company will have nothing to sell, and unless a company is a start-up or sells to a niche, a company will sell a group of products known as its product mix. A product mix is made up of a number of product lines, all the products, including peripherals, which serve a similar need for customers.

Consumer goods and services can be classified as (1) convenience such as milk and bread, (2) shopping (subject of some comparison shopping because of price), and (3) specialty such as a prom dress. Goods for the business-to-business market can be classified as (1) expense or component and (2) capital.

Products go through a life cycle: (1) introduction, (2) growth, (3) maturity, and (4) decline. During the growth phase of a product, competitors begin to introduce their own products to compete. During the maturity stage, the company may look upon the product as a cash cow, putting little money into new developments for the product in return for a higher profit. In doing this, a company is attempting to maximize profits and defend market share at the same time.

(1) Branding and (2) packaging are two important aspects of marketing a product. Branding is the use of a name, slogan, symbol, or design to differentiate a company and its products from its competitors. The intent of a company's branding activities is to generate (1) brand recognition, (2) brand

preference, and, ultimately, (3) brand insistence. There are several types of brands: (1) generic, (2) manufacturer's or national, (3) private, (4) family, (5) individual, (6) licensed, and (7) co-branding. Licensing takes place when a company or person sells the right to use its name or logo to another company for use on its products, such as the Italian designer Valentino's selling the right to use his name to a French fashion house. Co-branding occurs when two companies put both their names on the same product, such as the Intel logo on Lenovo computers.

Packaging is important because it (1) safeguards the product, (2) is meant to discourage stealing, (3) promotes the product/brand, (4) lists features and benefits, and (5) may add utility. Considering the emphasis on being "green" today, it should also be environmentally friendly to appeal to certain customers.

Price

Product pricing depends on the goal of the company, which may be to (1) maximize profits, (2) build market share, (3) build traffic, (4) maximize sales, and/or (5) foster an image, for example, low prices for value or high prices to denote quality. The major strategies for pricing are:

- *Cost-Based, or Cost-Plus:* Based on the cost of manufacturing/offering the product

- *Demand-Based, or Value-Based:* Based on the demand for or perceived value of the product in the marketplace

- *Competition-Based:* Pricing influenced by what the competition is charging

- *Price Skimming:* For new products; an initial high price to recoup costs associated with development and introduction of the product; high-profit margin

- *Penetration Pricing:* For new products; an initial low price to introduce a product to the market and begin to generate market share

Pricing is also affected by price adjustments like (1) discounts; (2) rebates; (3) product bundling (so that the combined price is lower than the single price of each item); (4) psychological, or fractional pricing, which prices items at less than a whole dollar ($1.99); and (5) loss leaders, which lower the price on one or more sale items to bring customers into the store.

Promotion

Promotion is all the techniques that companies use to get the message to the marketplace about their products. The promotional mix includes (1) advertising; (2) personal selling; (3) sales promotions like cents-off discount coupons, bounce-back coupons, and point-of-sale (POS) displays; and (4) publicity and public relations. To ensure a clear, coherent, and unified message for all contacts with customers, companies use an integrated marketing communication strategy.

Once a target market has been identified and objectives determined, a marketing manager or product manager (1) develops the product's "message," (2) determines the appropriate media mix to get the message out, (3) develops the budget, (4) launches the campaign, and (5) assesses the effectiveness of the campaign, revising as needed.

Place

Place is actually places; it's the distribution aspect of marketing. Distribution is made up of distribution channels that take products from raw materials to buyer. Distribution may involve intermediaries between the producer and end user: (1) wholesalers who buy from producers and resell to other intermediaries or to end users, (2) retailers who sell directly to end users, and (3) agents and brokers. Unlike wholesalers and retailers, agents and brokers do not purchase the products they sell; they act on behalf of the buyer or seller, depending on the type of agent or broker. Agents and brokers are paid a commission, rather than making a profit on their deals, and may be (1) manufacturer's agents, (2) selling agents, or (3) purchasing agents.

There are four distribution channels:

- *Channel 1:* Direct: producer to consumer or business

- *Channel 2:* Retail: producer to retailer to consumer or business

- *Channel 3:* Wholesale: producer to wholesaler to retailer to consumer or business

- *Channel 4:* Broker or agent: producer to broker or agent to consumer or business

There are a variety of retailers, with both physical and virtual presences:

- *Bricks-and-Mortar Retailers:* (1) department stores, (2) supermarkets, (3) specialty stores, (4) convenience stores, (5) discount/bargain stores, (6) wholesale/warehouse clubs, (7) factory outlets, (8) catalog showrooms

- *Direct Response Retailers:* (1) catalog mail order, (2) telemarketing

- *E-tailers:* (1) e-catalogs, (2) virtual storefronts

Finance

A company's financial management is responsible for the planning and budgeting of funding for both its short-term and long-term operations, including research and development and capital investments. Monitoring cash flow is an important part of the job of financial management. Having adequate cash flow ensures that creditors can be paid, but it also means that the company's invoices are being paid in a timely manner. Oversight of receivables and payables falls under the oversight of financial management.

To ensure that short-term needs are met, financial managers in collaboration with department heads prepare an operating budget for the organization. Long-term needs, including capital projects, for example, the purchase of new technologies or large-scale equipment, are provided for in a capital budget. Whereas operating expenses should be paid for out of revenue, capital expenditures may be financed by (1) borrowing money, (2) selling a new block of stock, or (3) issuing corporate bonds. Using the proceeds from the sale of stock is called equity financing.

Issuing bonds to raise capital is called debt financing. There are two types of bonds: (1) unsecured and (2) secured, also known as debenture bonds. An unsecured bond is backed only by the promise to repay the full value of the bond with interest at a stated time in the future.

Even short-term financial needs may require borrowing to balance cash out with cash in. Small businesses may be able to satisfy their needs with a bank line of credit or with a commercial loan;

corporations more typically sell unsecured commercial paper. A commercial loan may or may not be secured by a company's assets, which include any cash on hand, investments, equipment, and real estate. The creditworthiness of the business typically determines whether the borrower qualifies for an unsecured loan.

The gross profit margin determines the overall profitability of a company's production. It indicates the overall efficiency of the organization in using its resources—both human and material. Gross profit margin equals total revenue minus cost of goods sold divided by total revenue.

Accounting

Accounting is the recording, analysis, and reporting of a business' financial transactions, which includes all its income and expense activities—accounts receivable and accounts payable. There are different types of accounting:

- *Managerial:* Tracks the costs of doing business and the resulting income; monitors profitability of various business activities; develops budgets; audience is internal managers

- *Financial:* Prepares documents that show the financial performance of a company; the audience is those outside the company, such as stockholders

- *Auditing:* Reviews a company's financial documents to ensure their accuracy and reliability; may be internal accountants, but also reviewed by outside auditors

- *Tax:* Advises on tax strategies and prepares tax returns

The financial reports that accountants prepare for businesses typically consist of (1) balance sheets, (2) income statements, and (3) cash flow. Each contains different kinds of information about a company's financial health or lack thereof:

- *Balance Sheets:* (1) current assets, (2) fixed assets, (3) short-term liabilities, (4) long-term liabilities, and (5) owner's equity. Assets may also be intangible, like trademarks, patents, and goodwill.

- *Income Statements:* (1) revenues, (2) cost of goods sold, (3) gross profit, (4) operating expenses, (5) operating income, and (6) net income.

- *Cash Flow Statements:* cash from (1) operations, (2) investments, (3) and financing

Financing cash flow statements includes both inflows of cash from debt and equity financing, as well as outflows in the form of interest and dividend payments and repayment of principle borrowed.

Accountants must follow GAAP standards (generally acceptable accounting principles) in preparing and reviewing financial reports. All financial reporting starts with bookkeeping and is based on the accounting equation:

$$\text{Assets} = \text{Liabilities} + \text{Owner's Equity}$$

Owner's equity is what the business is worth if the owner chose to sell it. The owner would get whatever was left after the liabilities were deducted from the assets. Assets minus liabilities is the business' net worth.

Chapter 7: Introduction to Business

Production and Operations

Operations include all the activities that go into producing products; operations management is the control of those activities. Products may be tangible goods or intangible services. Services are also "unstorable"; you can't store the cheerful, helpful attention of a waiter in a restaurant. Production results in three types of utility, or value, for customers: (1) form (what customers need), (2) time (when customers need it), and (3) place (where customers need it).

There are a variety of processes that companies use to make goods and services and a variety of ways of classifying them. Three typical processes are (1) mass; (2) flexible, also known as custom; and (3) customer-driven. The first is the traditional assembly-line process instituted by Henry Ford at the beginning of the twentieth century. In a flexible system, a central computer operates a network of machines and can adjust product specifications and output as needed. The first two are typical make-to-stock operations and the last is a make-to-order operation. Service operations are classified as (1) low-contact or (2) high-contact, depending on the amount of involvement of the customer in the process.

Ford's assembly line was among the first uses of technology to speed and improve manufacturing. The most noticeable technology on the manufacturing floor today is the presence of (1) robots. They do many of the manufacturing processes that humans once did; humans still control the type and flow of work, however. Other processes that employ technology are (2) computer-aided design (CAD), (3) computer-aided manufacturing, and (4) computer-integrated manufacturing (CIM).

A number of factors need to be managed in order to establish smooth-running operations. These include determining (1) optimum number, size, and location of facilities; (2) optimum number of employees; (3) proximity of facilities to transportation networks, utility grids, and suppliers; and (4) design of the facility.

Once facilities are up and running, operations managers are responsible for the timely flow of materials through production to final goods and into the distribution channel, so part of the planning for smooth-running operations is (1) scheduling and (2) controls.

Controls on the operations side include (1) inventory control and (2) quality control. Inventory control consists of all the activities involved in receiving, storing, and tracking whatever the business uses to produce its goods—for example, raw materials—as well as the finished goods. Two popular methods of materials management among large corporations are (1) materials requirement planning (MRP) and (2) enterprise resource planning (ERP). Both use technology for planning/scheduling and inventory control, but ERP integrates them into the overall business. Two methods for tracking production processes are (1) PERT (Program Evaluation and Review Technique) charts and (2) Gantt charts (named after chart designer Henry Gantt).

A business' quality control methods and activities include (1) establishing what "quality" means in its environment and (2) monitoring goods and services to ensure that they provide that quality. It is not simply a matter of maintaining the same level of quality, but of improving that quality over time. With a process known as total quality management (TQM), companies attempt to infuse quality into the entire production process from the first design of a product to follow-up service after the product has been delivered to the customer. With TQM, ensuring quality becomes the mission of every employee in a company.

facebook.com/petersonspublishing

The International Organization for Standardization (ISO) establishes global standards for what constitutes quality. It has two programs worldwide: (1) ISO 9000 certification and (2) ISO 14000 certification. The latter certification attests to the company's development of an environmental management system.

Management Information Systems

Management information systems (MIS) is one part of the technology side of a business. Information technology (IT) is the overall umbrella label for a company's technology systems, and it is overseen by the chief information officer (CIO) in large corporations. The IT department designs and implements all computer-based information systems in a company, whereas MIS uses technology to (1) collect data, (2) analyze it, and (3) use the resulting information to inform decisions and solve problems. The shift from data to information occurs when the surveys, statistics, facts—whatever has been collected—is analyzed, arranged, and interpreted. The data that the business collects is stored in what is called a data warehouse. Analyzing the data to find trends and patterns is called data mining.

There are different kinds of information systems software: (1) decision support systems, (2) executive information systems, (3) knowledge information systems, and (4) business intelligence. Knowledge information systems software is used by knowledge workers to create new types of information based on manipulating data. The other three systems provide data and models to help various levels of management in different departments make informed decisions.

Companies face any number of threats to their information systems because of access to the Internet. Businesses may find themselves and their customers the victims of (1) hackers, (2) intellectual property theft, (3) identity theft, (4) spyware, (5) viruses, (6) Trojan horses, (7) worms, and (8) spam. (1) Firewalls, (2) encryption software that encodes e-mail, (3) spam-filtering software, (4) anti-virus protection, and (5) anti-spyware protection are ways to defend against hackers and malicious attacks on networks.

In addition to doing business over the Internet, large companies have (1) intranets that are closed to all but their own employees and (2) extranets that are available to employees, customers, and vendors who are authorized to gain access. Companies use social media to connect with customers. Some companies are also creating work and process groups on their own social media sites to exchange information.

Human Resources

The human resources department is a vital part of an organization, responsible for recruiting and training employees, developing compensation and benefits packages, and developing a system for evaluation employees. Many companies consider HR a strategic partner in planning the future goals and objectives for achieving those goals.

Recruiting and Hiring

HR is responsible for (1) job analysis within an organization and then creating (2) job descriptions and (3) job specifications for open positions. Recruiting to fill those jobs may be (1) external or (2) internal. External sources of candidates are (1) online job sites; (2) networking, both online and offline; (3) career fairs; (4) employing headhunters; (5) hiring employees away from competitors; (6) newspaper and trade journal ads; (7) employment agencies; and (8) referrals.

A number of federal laws regulate hiring practices. Title VII of Civil Rights Act of 1964 prohibits discrimination against the following protected classes: (1) race, (2) color, (3) national origin, (4) gender, (5) religion, and (6) retaliation ("for opposing unlawful employment practices, for filing a complaint, for testifying about violations or possible violations"). In addition, the Age Discrimination Act prohibits (7) age discrimination, that is, anyone over the age of 40, in companies with 20 or more employees. Discrimination against (8) those with disabilities is prohibited by the Americans with Disabilities Act, and discrimination against those who take a leave to serve in a state's National Guard is prohibited by the Uniformed Services Employment and Reemployment Rights Act. As more women have entered the workforce and many of them work in blue collar jobs, sexual harassment has become a more visible problem. Claims of discrimination are handled by the Equal Employment Opportunity Commission (EEOC).

A variety of issues have transformed the workplace in the last two decades. Hiring has been transformed to increase diversity in companies so that their workforce mirrors their markets. With each succeeding innovation from mainframes to desktops to laptops to smartphones, data has become increasingly important and along with this rise in the importance of data has emerged a new category of employees—knowledge workers. Beginning in the late 1980s, companies began turning to temp or contingent workers to save on salaries and benefits.

Training and Evaluation

The initial training that employees undergo is typically a half- or full-day orientation on a company's rules and regulations, history, and corporate culture. During the course of employment, workers also receive additional training—(1) on the job, (2) in an apprentice program, (3) at off-site sessions, or (4) through distance learning. Training programs deal with the here and now, whereas development programs take the long view and help employees learn skills that will help them grow in their jobs and the organization.

Performance appraisals assess how employees are doing their jobs. They include a (1) self-assessment by the employee as well as (2) an assessment of the employee by his or her managers. The assessment is conducted against a set of standards that includes the goals set by the employee and manager in the previous performance appraisal. Newer forms of employee assessment have reviews on an ongoing basis rather than once a year.

Compensation and Benefits

Wages are paid for hourly work, and salaries are paid for a specific job. Some employees, specifically salespeople, may work on commission only or on a combination of salary and bonus. Workers may be exempt or non-exempt, depending on how jobs are classified under the Fair Labor Standards Act. Employers of non-exempt workers must abide by the law. These workers must be paid the federal minimum wage and receive overtime pay for working more than a regular workweek, which is typically 40 hours.

Companies used to offer employees defined benefit pension plans for retirement, but many have changed in recent decades and now offer defined contribution pension plans. Other forms of retirement plans include (1) 401(k), (2) profit sharing, and (3) employee stock ownership plan (ESOP).

Companies must carry worker's compensation insurance by law, and many also carry disability insurance. Other benefits that companies may offer include (1) medical insurance, (2) health insurance, (3) paid vacation, (4) paid sick leave, (5) tuition reimbursement, (6) scholarships for children of employees, (7) child care, and (8) wellness programs. To reign in the cost of benefits, some companies have introduced a cafeteria benefits plan. With this plan, employees are provided with an amount of money they can use to select from a list of benefits.

With the entrance of more women into the workforce and the desire of men to spend more time with their families, companies have responded by creating more family-friendly work arrangements. In addition, computers, the Internet, and mobile devices make it possible to do many jobs from remote locations. Having fewer employees deskbound in company cubicles reduces facilities' costs for employers. Alternative work arrangements include (1) flextime, (2) flexplace or telecommuting, (3) shared jobs, (4) permanent part-time workers, and (5) compressed workweeks.

Termination

Perhaps the hardest job of an HR professional's job is terminating employees. Sometimes terminations occur because of poor performance, but other times it may be the result of an economic downturn for the company or for the economy as a whole. Employees who lose their jobs through no fault of their own are laid off rather than fired and typically given severance packages that may be based on one or two weeks for each year of employment. They are also eligible for unemployment compensation. Employees who are fired are not eligible for unemployment and do not receive severance.

Terminating an employee for cause requires following a process: a verbal warning and the opportunity to remedy the problem, written warning and the opportunity for remediation, and then termination if performance has not improved. Even though most workers fall under the category of "employment at will," the process is followed.

Labor Unions

Labor union contracts are built on the principle of collective bargaining. Management of a company sits down with representatives of the union and work through a set of compromises to come up with a contract. If agreement cannot be reached, there are several options: (1) work slowdown, (2) sickout, and (3) strike. A strike is accompanied by a picket line and sometimes by a boycott of the company's product by a sympathetic portion of the public. A company may bring in strikebreakers to take over the strikers' work. To end the impasse, the union and the company may agree to the use of a mediator or to binding or nonbinding arbitration.

CONTEMPORARY ISSUES

Companies—whether multinationals or sole proprietorships—face a number of issues in today's business environment. Among them are the role of e-commerce, business ethics and social responsibility, and the global business environment.

Role of E-Commerce

E-commerce is the business of buying and selling electronically. The customer may be another business, or it may be a direct sale to a consumer. The latter, known as e-tailing, is becoming an ever larger share of consumer sales, not only in the United States, but worldwide. E-tailing has several forms: (1) online auctions, (2) e-catalogs, (3) electronic storefronts (Web sites), (4) electronic or cyber malls (collection of sites), and (5) interactive marketing on e-tailer sites.

Like bricks-and-mortar sales, the e-tailing transaction involves one buyer and one seller, but in e-commerce, comparison shopping is easy and the product array is considerably larger than what is possible by going from store to store in a local area checking product features and prices. The consumer, therefore, has an advantage. However, the disadvantage is the inability to see and touch the actual product.

Business-to-business e-commerce is in many ways similar to business-to-business selling the traditional way. There are a few customers for a product, the orders are large, the transaction is formalized, and decisions are made by purchasing agents after internal consultations about product features and pricing among competitors.

With e-commerce, a company no longer has to warehouse goods. It can take orders, process them, and have them drop shipped from the manufacturer to the customer, saving on warehousing costs. The Internet also makes it possible to do business on a global basis without having a physical presence in other countries. It is not just manufacturing that can be moved offshore, but accounting and marketing functions as well.

With the ease of doing business over the Internet, however, comes a number of security risks. Even with what they consider secure sites, credit card companies, banks, and retailers have found their sites hacked and customers' personal information stolen. The result is identity theft and millions of dollars lost through the use of stolen information.

As companies turn more and more to doing business online—whether selling, buying, or exchanging information—their work processes are undergoing changes, known as business process reengineering.

Business Ethics and Social Responsibility

Ethics is a set of moral beliefs, a code of conduct based on what is considered right and wrong. Living an ethical life does not stop at the workplace door. Part of an organization's culture is its ethical stance on issues, which can be found in a company's code of ethics, mission statement, and legal compliance. Ethical behavior within a company includes doing right by fellow employees, customers, suppliers, and the organization itself. The organization in turn has a responsibility to treat employees, customers, suppliers, and other business partners ethically.

Social responsibility is the belief that organizations as well as individuals are obligated to act in such a way as to benefit the larger society. Corporate social responsibility (CSR) institutionalizes this belief on a company-wide basis. Areas of concentration for CSR activities include (1) human rights, (2) employees and other stakeholders including customers, (3) the larger community, (4) the environment, and (5) ethical business practices related to sourcing, producing, and marketing. The last includes recognizing consumer rights, disavowing deceptive advertising practices, and using fair pricing practices.

The benefits of CSR include:

- *Less government intervention into business practices* because the organization is obeying all applicable legislation and regulations

- *Better financial performance* as a result of efficient use of resources, including people and an enhanced perception in the marketplace

- *Fewer scandals* related to corruption and fewer accidents, thereby reducing the company's exposure to risk

- *Competitive edge with customers* by advertising CSR programs, including philanthropic endeavors

- *Easier recruitment of employees* because they embrace the company's CSR initiatives

- *Higher rate of employee retention* for the same reason

Some companies may adopt any one of four approaches to CSR, from embracing it wholeheartedly to doing as little as possible:

1. *Obstructionist Stance:* Do as little as possible to solve the problems that it creates, denies or hides any responsibility

2. *Defensive Stance:* Do what is legally required, admits mistakes, remedies the problem to the letter of the law only, defends the stance that the job of the company is to generate profits

3. *Accommodative Stance:* meets ethical obligations and legal requirements; participates in social programs, but does not seek them out

4. *Proactive Stance:* Seeks out opportunities to support social programs, perception as "citizens of society"

How well a company is living up to its CSR can be measured by taking a social audit in which the company's performance is measured against its goals. Some companies choose to make this information public. Another public expression of CSR is corporate philanthropy. Some corporations set up charitable foundations to donate money to worthy causes, thereby living up to their goals to support the larger community. A number of outside groups such as Boston College's Center for Corporate Citizenship and *Fortune* magazine also rate and rank corporations on their CSR programs.

Global Business Environment

Business ethics and CSR extend across borders when doing business. The globalization of the world's economies affects workers, consumers, businesses, unions, the environment, and national governments—and even state governments. Some states send trade representatives to other countries in an effort to encourage foreign companies to establish facilities in their states. The fat increase in the rate of globalization in the last two decades is a result of (1) changes in technology and (2) the lowering of trade barriers.

Globalization impacts both (1) markets and (2) production. A market for a company's products could be consumers in China as well as Chicago. With outsourcing of production, factories producing the components for smartphones could be spread across Asia. Cultural differences come into play in conducting market research and developing, advertising, and selling products in multiple markets. Cultural differences also affect the production process. In addition to (1) cultural differences, companies doing business across borders must deal with (2) economic, (3) legal, and (4) political environments that vary not only from their home country, but also from country to country worldwide.

A cultural difference that can lead to legal difficulties—and ethical ones—is the issue of bribery. Some nations consider it business as usual if a company wants to operate within their borders. However, the U.S. Foreign Corrupt Practices Act of 1977, the Anti-Bribery Convention of the Organization for Economic Cooperation and Development, and the UN Convention Against Corruption all prohibit bribery of foreign officials.

Trade Policies

Countries seek to have a favorable balance of trade, that is, having the value of exports be greater than the value of imports. This results in a favorable balance of payments, which is when a country takes in more than it pays out. When this occurs, the country has a trade surplus. The opposite is a trade deficit.

One issue that can constrain businesses is protectionist trade policies—their own countries' and that of countries they wish to do business with. A protectionist trade policy uses (1) quotas and (2) tariffs to protect domestic industries by making foreign goods more expensive to import. A home country may also use (3) subsidies as a way to protect domestic producers. Instead of limiting imports as a quota does or raising prices as a tariff does, a subsidy is a payment to domestic producers to enable them to keep their prices lower than those charged by importers of the same or similar goods.

Those in favor of protectionist trade policies use the following arguments to support their position:

- *Infant Industry:* Newly emerging domestic industries need to be protected from foreign competition

- *National Security:* Industries vital to the nation's security need to be protected so that foreign competitors do not undercut them on price or the nation will find itself dependent on the foreign companies

- *Cheap Foreign Labor:* Companies in developing nations will undercut domestic companies by using cheap labor to produce their goods

- *Bargaining Chip:* A tough trade policy can be used to negotiate with trading partners to get them to relax their trade policies

Dumping is selling goods abroad for less than they cost to make or are sold for domestically. Charges of dumping can be brought to the World Trade Organization for resolution.

Some countries have local content laws that require a product be made at least in part in the country where it will be sold.

Regional and International Organizations

There are a variety of organizations that promote free trade. Among them are the (1) World Trade Organization (WTO), (2) General Agreement on Tariffs and Trade (GATT), (3) European Union (EU), (4) North American Free Trade Agreement (NAFTA), (5) MERCOSUR (Brazil, Argentina, Paraguay, Uruguay), and (6) Association of Southeast Asian Nations (ASEAN).

Absolute and Comparative Advantage

A nation has an absolute advantage when it produces more of a product and, therefore, more cheaply than any other country. Comparative advantage occurs when a nation can produce a product more efficiently than any other country. Therefore, it should concentrate on producing that product and buying from other countries the products that they have comparative advantage in. Comparative advantage is competitive advantage.

Ways to Enter Foreign Markets

A company wishing to enter a foreign market has a variety of paths to choose from. It can simply (1) hire an import agent who deals with customs, tariffs, and selling the company's goods. A company can enter into a deal with a domestic company by selling a (2) franchise or (3) license. It can enter into a (4) joint venture or (5) strategic alliance, or, depending on the type of company, it can set up a (6) turnkey project for which it will be paid, but will have no ownership stake in when finished. Another arrangement for a manufacturing company is (7) contracting out its manufacturing to a company in the country it wishes to enter. Any type of company could set up (8) a wholly owned subsidiary.

POST-TEST ANSWER SHEET

1. Ⓐ Ⓑ Ⓒ Ⓓ	13. Ⓐ Ⓑ Ⓒ Ⓓ	25. Ⓐ Ⓑ Ⓒ Ⓓ	37. Ⓐ Ⓑ Ⓒ Ⓓ	49. Ⓐ Ⓑ Ⓒ Ⓓ
2. Ⓐ Ⓑ Ⓒ Ⓓ	14. Ⓐ Ⓑ Ⓒ Ⓓ	26. Ⓐ Ⓑ Ⓒ Ⓓ	38. Ⓐ Ⓑ Ⓒ Ⓓ	50. Ⓐ Ⓑ Ⓒ Ⓓ
3. Ⓐ Ⓑ Ⓒ Ⓓ	15. Ⓐ Ⓑ Ⓒ Ⓓ	27. Ⓐ Ⓑ Ⓒ Ⓓ	39. Ⓐ Ⓑ Ⓒ Ⓓ	51. Ⓐ Ⓑ Ⓒ Ⓓ
4. Ⓐ Ⓑ Ⓒ Ⓓ	16. Ⓐ Ⓑ Ⓒ Ⓓ	28. Ⓐ Ⓑ Ⓒ Ⓓ	40. Ⓐ Ⓑ Ⓒ Ⓓ	52. Ⓐ Ⓑ Ⓒ Ⓓ
5. Ⓐ Ⓑ Ⓒ Ⓓ	17. Ⓐ Ⓑ Ⓒ Ⓓ	29. Ⓐ Ⓑ Ⓒ Ⓓ	41. Ⓐ Ⓑ Ⓒ Ⓓ	53. Ⓐ Ⓑ Ⓒ Ⓓ
6. Ⓐ Ⓑ Ⓒ Ⓓ	18. Ⓐ Ⓑ Ⓒ Ⓓ	30. Ⓐ Ⓑ Ⓒ Ⓓ	42. Ⓐ Ⓑ Ⓒ Ⓓ	54. Ⓐ Ⓑ Ⓒ Ⓓ
7. Ⓐ Ⓑ Ⓒ Ⓓ	19. Ⓐ Ⓑ Ⓒ Ⓓ	31. Ⓐ Ⓑ Ⓒ Ⓓ	43. Ⓐ Ⓑ Ⓒ Ⓓ	55. Ⓐ Ⓑ Ⓒ Ⓓ
8. Ⓐ Ⓑ Ⓒ Ⓓ	20. Ⓐ Ⓑ Ⓒ Ⓓ	32. Ⓐ Ⓑ Ⓒ Ⓓ	44. Ⓐ Ⓑ Ⓒ Ⓓ	56. Ⓐ Ⓑ Ⓒ Ⓓ
9. Ⓐ Ⓑ Ⓒ Ⓓ	21. Ⓐ Ⓑ Ⓒ Ⓓ	33. Ⓐ Ⓑ Ⓒ Ⓓ	45. Ⓐ Ⓑ Ⓒ Ⓓ	57. Ⓐ Ⓑ Ⓒ Ⓓ
10. Ⓐ Ⓑ Ⓒ Ⓓ	22. Ⓐ Ⓑ Ⓒ Ⓓ	34. Ⓐ Ⓑ Ⓒ Ⓓ	46. Ⓐ Ⓑ Ⓒ Ⓓ	58. Ⓐ Ⓑ Ⓒ Ⓓ
11. Ⓐ Ⓑ Ⓒ Ⓓ	23. Ⓐ Ⓑ Ⓒ Ⓓ	35. Ⓐ Ⓑ Ⓒ Ⓓ	47. Ⓐ Ⓑ Ⓒ Ⓓ	59. Ⓐ Ⓑ Ⓒ Ⓓ
12. Ⓐ Ⓑ Ⓒ Ⓓ	24. Ⓐ Ⓑ Ⓒ Ⓓ	36. Ⓐ Ⓑ Ⓒ Ⓓ	48. Ⓐ Ⓑ Ⓒ Ⓓ	60. Ⓐ Ⓑ Ⓒ Ⓓ

answer sheet

POST-TEST

Directions: Carefully read each of the following 60 questions. Choose the best answer to each question, and darken its letter on your answer sheet. The Answer Key and Explanations can be found following this Post-Test.

1. Which of the following poses a question of social responsibility for a company?

   (A) Price fixing

   (B) Outsourcing

   (C) Harassing a whistleblower

   (D) Reporting inflated profits

2. Which of the following is an advantage to a business partnership over a sole proprietorship?

   (A) Limited liability

   (B) Greater ability than a sole proprietorship to borrow money to expand the business

   (C) Less paperwork than a sole proprietorship to start the business

   (D) Greater tax advantages to the owners than a sole proprietorship

3. A characteristic of business-to-business markets is

   (A) that purchasing decisions are made by individual agents.

   (B) the lack of personal relationships between sellers and buyers.

   (C) the small number of customers.

   (D) the informal nature of the seller-buyer process.

4. Businesses fail for which of the following reasons?

   I. Ineffective financial controls
   II. Lack of adequate capitalization
   III. Inexperienced management

   (A) I only

   (B) I and II only

   (C) II and III only

   (D) I, II, and III

5. The benefits that buyers receive from a product are categorized as what type(s) of utility?

   (A) Time, form, and place

   (B) Price, promotion, and place

   (C) Form, time, place, and ownership

   (D) Value

6. Which of the following type of information systems software allows users to create new types of information?

   (A) Decision support

   (B) Knowledge information

   (C) Business intelligence

   (D) Executive information

7. In which stage of a product's life cycle do competitors introduce rival products?

   (A) Introduction

   (B) Growth

   (C) Maturity

   (D) Decline

8. McDonald's® Big Mac® is a

   (A) family brand.

   (B) store brand.

   (C) brand licensing

   (D) national brand.

9. Which of the following is an accounting function in a company?

   (A) Preparing income statements

   (B) Investing a company's surplus funds

   (C) Providing input for budgeting

   (D) Determining whether to borrow money or issue stock to fund capital needs

10. A flat organizational structure is most often found in a/an

  (A) decentralized organization.

  (B) tall organization.

  (C) centralized organization.

  (D) autocratic organization.

11. Encryption software protects a company's e-mail by

  (A) filtering out spam.

  (B) identifying and removing spyware.

  (C) encoding messages so they can't be read without a passphrase to unscramble them.

  (D) erecting a barrier to block messages unless told to recognize the sender.

12. Which of the following is an example of dumping?

  (A) Manufactures sell goods in a foreign country for less than what it cost to manufacture them.

  (B) Clothing manufacturers cut up out-of-season clothes and trash them to clear inventory.

  (C) Stores sell goods for less than what they paid in order to clear inventory.

  (D) A foreign government offers a subsidy to domestic manufacturers that make and sell goods abroad to offset import duties.

13. Enterprise resource planning program (ERPP) software does which of the following?

  (A) Helps entrepreneurs predict the potential for success

  (B) Is an online performance appraisal system

  (C) Connects all functions of a business operation such as inventory control, scheduling, finance, marketing, and human resources

  (D) Is a tool for franchisees

14. The Smith Company wants to enter the German market with its product and decides to establish the business with a German company. They are setting up what kind of business?

  (A) Licensing

  (B) Joint venture

  (C) Strategic alliance

  (D) Contract manufacturing

15. The airline industry with few competitors could be characterized as

  (A) an oligopoly.

  (B) an industry with perfect competition.

  (C) having monopolistic competition.

  (D) a monopoly.

16. Which of the following is an example of a company's exercising its corporate social responsibility?

  (A) Returning an overpayment to a customer

  (B) Conducting an audit of working conditions in a foreign factory producing components for its smartphones

  (C) Turning over e-mails requested by a federal investigation into fraudulent dealings by a CFO

  (D) Labeling food packaging with nutrition information

17. Currency depreciation causes

  (A) imports to rise in price.

  (B) imports to become cheaper.

  (C) exports to rise in price.

  (D) ho effect on imports and exports.

18. According to the principles of financial management, which of the following should be paid for through the issuance of corporate bonds?

(A) Research and development

(B) Operating expenses

(C) Interest payments on loans

(D) Construction of new facilities

19. Which of the following is a conceptual skill that managers need to be effective?

(A) Empathy

(B) Ability to use situation analysis

(C) Ability to implement plans

(D) Ability to fact find

20. Entrepreneurship and technology are increasingly important

(A) capital requirements.

(B) elements in the product mix.

(C) operations units.

(D) factors of production.

21. Which of the following is an example of a shopping good?

(A) Computer tablet

(B) Wedding gown

(C) Doughnut and coffee

(D) Engagement ring

22. Which of the following is an internal environment that affects how companies do business?

(A) Cross-cultural environment

(B) Economic environment

(C) Corporate culture

(D) Political-legal environment

23. Net income is

(A) gross profit minus operating expenses and income taxes.

(B) gross profit minus operating expenses.

(C) assets minus liabilities.

(D) costs of materials used to produce goods during a given year.

24. How is B2B e-commerce similar to traditional B2B selling?

(A) The orders are small.

(B) The customer base for a product is small.

(C) There is decentralized purchasing.

(D) Little or no comparison shopping is done among competitors.

25. An organization would typically write an intermediate goal for something it wished to accomplish

(A) in less than one year.

(B) in one year.

(C) within one to three years.

(D) within one to five years.

26. A Gantt chart shows the

(A) structure of an organization.

(B) sequence of tasks that must be performed in order and the tasks that can be performed simultaneously with those tasks.

(C) steps in a project and time required to perform each step.

(D) products to be produced, their deadlines, and those who will be working on the projects.

27. Which of the following can be binding on both sides in a labor dispute?

(A) Mediation

(B) Arbitration

(C) Collective bargaining

(D) Check off

28. The ISO 9000 label indicates that a company's products

    (A) adhere to the highest quality.

    (B) are environmentally safe.

    (C) are manufactured in a socially responsible way.

    (D) are organic.

29. In determining where to locate a manufacturing facility, a company needs to consider

    (A) inventory management.

    (B) the size of the market.

    (C) the availability of workers with appropriate skills sets.

    (D) creating an efficient layout for the facility.

30. A nation has a comparative advantage in a certain good when that country

    (A) can produce the good at a lower cost than other countries.

    (B) was the earliest producer of the product.

    (C) can produce the good more efficiently than other nations.

    (D) can produce a higher quality of the good.

31. A small business selling craft materials and needing money to balance out cash flow would most likely

    (A) sell a debenture.

    (B) sell unsecured commercial paper.

    (C) issue stock.

    (D) apply for a bank line of credit.

32. The goal of U.S. monetary policy is to

    (A) issue government debt at a favorable market rate.

    (B) collect revenue for the purpose of operating the government.

    (C) stabilize the economy.

    (D) safeguard money kept in depository institutions.

33. Which of the following are reasons that motivate people to become entrepreneurs?

    I. Desire to control what they work at and how they do their work

    II. Desire for flexibility in their lives

    III. Desire to make more money

    (A) I and II

    (B) II only

    (C) I and III

    (D) I, II, and III

34. Employees who feel connected to the company and to their fellow employees most likely fall into which category in Maslow's hierarchy of needs?

    (A) Safety

    (B) Belonging

    (C) Esteem

    (D) Self-actualization

35. A balance sheet details a company's

    (A) profit and loss.

    (B) financial status.

    (C) receipts and payments.

    (D) assets, liabilities, and owner's equity.

36. Which of the following is an intrinsic motivator for employees?

    (A) Profit-sharing plan

    (B) Employee-of-the-month program

    (C) Sense of achievement

    (D) Promotion

37. Taking out a bank loan has an advantage over having an angel investor because

    (A) a bank will make a loan to a partnership, but angel investors typically prefer to invest in sole proprietorships.

    (B) a bank loan is paid off over time, whereas an angel investor is paid a share of the profits for as long as the business exists.

    (C) a bank will act in an advisory capacity to the entrepreneur, whereas an angel investor takes a hands-off role.

    (D) it means that the entrepreneur will still be eligible for a SBA loan.

38. Using an Internet job site is what type of recruiting for a new hire?

    (A) External

    (B) Prospecting

    (C) Internal

    (D) Headhunting

39. Which of the following is a contingent worker?

    (A) Call center employee

    (B) Lawyer on lease

    (C) Truck driver who owns and drives his own truck

    (D) Daughter employed as a sales agent for the family construction company

40. An organization that changes and adapts to its environment is referred to as a

    (A) continuous improvement organization.

    (B) TQM organization.

    (C) learning organization.

    (D) flexible organization.

41. Statutory law is law

    (A) established by administrative agencies.

    (B) passed by state legislatures.

    (C) developed from court decisions.

    (D) based on court precedents.

42. The amount of goods and services that will be bought at all price levels at a given point in time is

    (A) the equilibrium point.

    (B) aggregate output.

    (C) aggregate demand.

    (D) real growth rate.

43. Software that is designed to disrupt a computer's operation is

    (A) spyware.

    (B) malware.

    (C) spam.

    (D) cookies.

44. Total revenue minus cost of goods sold divided by revenue equals

    (A) operating expenses.

    (B) operating profit margin.

    (C) gross profit margin.

    (D) earning per share.

45. Jack's department is charged with analyzing data to find trends and patterns, which is known as

    (A) data mining.

    (B) data interpretation.

    (C) data collection.

    (D) data drilling.

46. Competition from goods manufactured in developing countries is used to support which of the following arguments for a protectionist trade policy?

    (A) Bargaining chip

    (B) Infant industry

    (C) Cheap foreign labor

    (D) National security

47. Which of the following is characteristic of a market economy?

    (A) Government control of some industries and competition in others

    (B) Central planning

    (C) Low barriers to entry into industries

    (D) The right to own property

48. To help new junior employees learn their jobs and adjust to the company culture, some companies

    (A) make them part of a work team.

    (B) enroll them in apprenticeships.

    (C) assign them a mentor.

    (D) give them an orientation program.

49. Price skimming is used in which stage of the product life cycle?

    (A) Introduction

    (B) Growth

    (C) Maturity

    (D) Decline

50. In backward scheduling, the operations department has to schedule

    (A) according to supplier availability.

    (B) based on input from the just-in-time inventory control system.

    (C) based on when raw materials are due to arrive.

    (D) based on when a product needs to be shipped.

51. In terms of assets, brand recognition and a company's reputation are classified as

    (A) intellectual property.

    (B) liquid assets.

    (C) goodwill.

    (D) tangible property.

52. Which of the following illustrates the concept of direct foreign investment?

    (A) Opening a sales office in a foreign city

    (B) Building a factory in a foreign country

    (C) Licensing the use of technology to a foreign company

    (D) Selling a business unit to a foreign company

53. Advertising, public relations, sales promotions, and personal selling are the components of which of the following?

    (A) Four Ps

    (B) Promotional mix

    (C) Media mix

    (D) Product differentiation

54. To calculate net income, an accountant would need what information?

    I.   Total revenue

    II. Total assets

    III. Total expenses

    (A) I only

    (B) I and II only

    (C) I and III only

    (D) I, II, and III

55. What is a disadvantage to e-tailing for consumers?

    (A) Comparison shopping is difficult.

    (B) The product array is limited.

    (C) The consumer cannot see and touch the product.

    (D) Prices are higher than in bricks-and-mortar stores.

56. Point-of-sale displays is an example of

(A) sales promotion.

(B) advertising.

(C) a distribution channel.

(D) an impulse buy.

57. The role of the World Bank in global development is to

(A) rescue failing banks that are too big for their own governments to help.

(B) fund programs to improve conditions and increase productivity in developing nations.

(C) provide advice and technical expertise to nations to avert financial crises.

(D) develop monetary policy to stabilize the economy.

58. Which of the following is a true statement about the minimum wage?

(A) All hourly jobs are covered by the minimum wage.

(B) The Federal Fair Labor Standards Act mandates those jobs that must be paid the minimum wage.

(C) Violations of the minimum wage are investigated by the Equal Opportunity Employment Act.

(D) Any job that is negotiated by collective bargaining is not covered by the minimum wage.

59. Which of the following is an example of corporate philanthropy?

(A) Sponsoring the Great American Cleanup

(B) Refusing to do business with a company that uses sweatshops

(C) Shifting to recycled packaging for a company's products

(D) A network's refusing to allow the product placement of cigarettes in a TV program

60. What is a major disadvantage of buying an existing business?

(A) Buying an existing business takes more time than setting up a new company.

(B) It can be easier to obtain financing for a start-up than to buy an existing business.

(C) There is little opportunity for creating a new look for the business or introducing new products.

(D) An existing business may have a poor reputation for customer service or product quality.

ANSWER KEY AND EXPLANATIONS

1. B	13. C	25. D	37. B	49. A
2. B	14. B	26. C	38. A	50. D
3. C	15. A	27. B	39. B	51. C
4. D	16. B	28. A	40. C	52. B
5. C	17. A	29. C	41. B	53. B
6. B	18. D	30. C	42. C	54. C
7. B	19. B	31. D	43. B	55. C
8. D	20. D	32. C	44. C	56. A
9. A	21. A	33. D	45. A	57. B
10. A	22. C	34. B	46. C	58. B
11. C	23. A	35. D	47. D	59. A
12. A	24. B	36. C	48. A	60. D

1. **The correct answer is (B).** Relocating jobs from the home country to another country because the other country has a lower wage scale involves a question of social responsibility if that means laying off workers and possibly closing a factory or offices in the home country, thereby taking income away from employees and suppliers of goods and services for both the company and the employees as consumers and depriving municipalities, states, and the federal government of revenue. Choice (A), price fixing; choice (C), harassing a whistleblower; and choice (D), reporting inflated profits, are not matters of social responsibility—they are illegal.

2. **The correct answer is (B).** Partnerships find it easier to borrow money because the business doesn't rest on one owner. Choice (A) is incorrect because neither sole proprietorships nor partnerships enjoy limited liability. Choice (C) is incorrect because partnerships require more paperwork to establish than do sole proprietorships. Choice

(D) is incorrect because sole proprietorships and partnerships have similar tax benefits; in both, owners pay taxes as personal income.

3. **The correct answer is (C).** In relation to the consumer market, the B2B is small. Choices (A), (B), and (D) more appropriately characterize the consumer market than the B2B market. In the latter, purchasing decisions are typically group decisions, making choice (A) incorrect. Buyers and sellers tend to develop personal relationships over time, making choice (B) incorrect. The buying process is highly formalized in B2B markets, making choice (D) incorrect.

4. **The correct answer is (D).** All three factors—ineffective financial controls, lack of adequate capitalization, and inexperienced management—can lead to the failure of a business. Only choice (D) includes all three items.

5. **The correct answer is (C).** The benefits of a product provide form, time, place, and ownership utility to buyers. Choice (A) is

incorrect because it omits ownership. Choice (B) is incorrect because price, promotion, and place are three of the Four Ps of marketing; the first is the product itself. Choice (D) is incorrect because the four types of utility create the value of a product.

6. **The correct answer is (B).** Choices (A), (C), and (D) are all systems software that enable managers at different levels in an organization to use data and models to make informed decisions about their departments.

7. **The correct answer is (B).** During a product's growth stage, competitors become aware of the product's surge in sales and market share and begin introducing products to compete with it. Choices (A), (C), and (D)—introduction, maturity, and decline—are incorrect.

8. **The correct answer is (D).** McDonald's® Big Mac® is made and sold across the country satisfying the characteristics of a national brand under one name. Choice (A) is incorrect because a family brand, also known as a brand extension, is the marketing of several different products under the same brand name, for example, the Big Mac and Happy Meals® are marketed under the McDonald's name. Choice (B) is incorrect because a store brand is the same as a private brand; a manufacturer, distributor, or store markets a product under its own name, for example, a department store creates a clothing line under its name. Choice (C) is incorrect because brand licensing is selling the right to use the brand name to a third party.

9. **The correct answer is (A).** The accounting department of a company prepares income statements and also budgets. However, choice (C) is incorrect because other departments provide input, which the accounting department then uses to develop budgets. Choices (B) and (D), investing surplus funds and determining capitalization strategies, are functions of financial managers, not accountants.

10. **The correct answer is (A).** A flat structure implies a decentralized organization. A tall structure, choice (B), implies a centralized organization, choice (C). An autocratic organization is not a recognized term, but autocratic management would come under the category of choice (D).

11. **The correct answer is (C).** Encryption software encodes messages so they can't be read without a key, which is "unlocked" with a passphrase. Choice (A) is incorrect because this describes spam-filtering software. Choice (B) is incorrect because it describes anti-spyware software. Choice (D) is incorrect because it describes a firewall.

12. **The correct answer is (A).** Selling goods abroad for less than what they cost to produce or less than their domestic price is dumping. Choice (B) is a practice some manufacturers use, but it is not dumping. Choice (C) defines a sale. Choice (D) is incorrect because it is the definition of a subsidy.

13. **The correct answer is (C).** All four answers may seem possible, but only choice (C) describes enterprise resource planning programs (ERPP). Choices (A), (B), and (D) are all incorrect because they don't relate to ERPP.

14. **The correct answer is (B).** Both companies will enjoy the benefit of shared resources and information. The downside is the potential for the loss of specialized knowledge and technology and the problems that may arise from sharing control. Choice (A) is incorrect because in licensing, one company sells the right to its name, product, or process to another and has no control over the resulting business, but it provides a quick entry into a foreign market. Choice (C) is incorrect because a strategic alliance is a working arrangement for a period of time and for some specific purpose; neither company cedes its independence or control to the other. Choice (D) is incorrect because in contract manufacturing, a company contracts with a

answers post-test

foreign company to manufacture its product for that foreign market; it provides quick, low-cost entry into the foreign marketplace.

15. **The correct answer is (A).** Unlike an oligopoly, which has few competitors, an industry that exhibits perfect competition is one with many sellers and buyers, almost no differentiation among products, and low barriers to entry. The airline industry doesn't fit either multiplicity of buyers nor low barriers to entry, so perfect competition doesn't characterize the airline industry. Choice (B) can be eliminated. Choice (C), monopolistic competition, characterizes an industry with many buyers and sellers, and buyers believe that there are differences among products, though in reality there aren't. The airline industry doesn't have many sellers, and buyers don't perceive much in the way of differences among those sellers, so eliminate choice (C). Choice (D), a monopoly, is incorrect because a monopoly has only one seller, and that doesn't describe the airline industry.

16. **The correct answer is (B).** Corporate social responsibility is a company's taking responsibility for the ways in which it affects the community—both internally, domestically, and globally. Choice (A) is incorrect because that is an example of ethical conduct. Choices (C) and (D) are incorrect because both are legal issues.

17. **The correct answer is (A).** A depreciating currency is declining in value, so imports cost more and exports cost less. Choice (B) is the opposite of the effect of currency depreciation on imports. Choice (C) is the opposite of what happens to exports when currency depreciates. Choice (D) is incorrect because currency depreciation causes imports to rise in price and exports to decline in price.

18. **The correct answer is (D).** Only capital expenditures such as the construction of new facilities are appropriate reasons for issuing corporate bonds. Choice (A), research and development, is paid for normally out of operating expenses, choice (B), and issuing corporate bonds to fund operating expenses is not appropriate. Nor is borrowing money to pay interest on borrowed money, choice (C).

19. **The correct answer is (B).** Situation analysis looks at the trends in a company's market and considers the customers, companies, and competitors, and considers opportunities. Even if you didn't know this term, you could determine the correct answer by the process of elimination. Choice (A) is an interpersonal ability, so it can be eliminated. Choices (C) and (D) are both steps in the decision-making process, so eliminate them.

20. **The correct answer is (D).** The five factors of production are labor, natural resources, capital, entrepreneurs, and technology. Choice (A) is incorrect because capital is either physical (facilities) or financial (money), and neither technology nor entrepreneurship fits this definition. Choice (B) is incorrect because a product mix is the products that a company sells. Choice (C) is incorrect because operations are the activities that produce a company's goods or services.

21. **The correct answer is (A).** A shopping good is one that is bought infrequently and for which a person does research and comparison shopping. Choices (B) and (D) are incorrect because a wedding gown and an engagement ring are classified as specialty goods. Choice (C) is incorrect because a doughnut and coffee are typically convenience purchases.

22. **The correct answer is (C).** The corporate culture is the shared beliefs, values, history, and norms that shape what an organization believes and does. Choice (A) is incorrect because cross-cultural environments are external and affect how businesses operate in countries other than their own. Choices

(B) and (D), economic and political-legal environments, are also external influences that affect companies both domestically and internationally.

23. **The correct answer is (A).** Choice (B) is incorrect because this is operating income. Choice (C) is incorrect because this is the owner's equity in a business. Choice (D) is incorrect because this is the cost of goods.

24. **The correct answer is (B).** In both e-commerce and traditional sales in the B2B marketplace, there are few customers for any given product. Choice (A) is incorrect because in both types of selling, orders are generally large. Choice (C) is incorrect because in both cases, purchasing is centralized in a purchasing department. Choice (D) is incorrect because comparison shopping to see what competitors offer is routine.

25. **The correct answer is (D).** Choices (A) and (B) describe short-term goals, so they are incorrect. Choice (C) is incorrect because intermediate goals are typically intended to be achieved within one to five years, not one to three years.

26. **The correct answer is (C).** Choice (A) is incorrect because this describes an organization chart. Choice (B) is incorrect because this describes a PERT chart. Choice (D) is incorrect because this describes a master production schedule.

27. **The correct answer is (B).** Arbitration may be binding or not, depending on whether the sides agreed to its being binding or whether they were ordered by a court to binding arbitration. Choice (A) is incorrect because mediation is a recommendation by a third party as to how to end a dispute between parties; it is not a mandatory resolution. Choice (C) is incorrect because collective bargaining is negotiations. Choice (D) is incorrect because a checkoff is a system in which an employer collects union dues from each worker's wages and pays the union.

28. **The correct answer is (A).** Choice (B) is incorrect because it is similar to the ISO 14000 certification that a company's products are manufactured in an environmentally friendly way. Choices (C) and (D) are incorrect descriptions of the ISO 9000 label.

29. **The correct answer is (C).** The question asks about locating a manufacturing facility, and only choice (C) describes a factor related to deciding where to place a new manufacturing facility. Choice (A), inventory management, is part of production management, but is not related to where to locate a new facility, although it may impact the size of the facility. Choice (B), the size of the market, is a marketing concern, and not one of the factors related to deciding where to locate a manufacturing facility. Choice (D) is part of laying out a facility, not locating it, so it is incorrect.

30. **The correct answer is (C).** Choices (A) and (D) both define absolute advantage, not comparative advantage. Whether a country is the earliest producer of a product, choice (B), is irrelevant.

31. **The correct answer is (D).** Of the choices given, a small business needing money for cash flow would most likely apply for a bank line of credit. It could also apply for a commercial loan, depending on the circumstances. Choice (A) is incorrect because a debenture is a bond and is a financial tool of large companies, as are choices (B) and (C).

32. **The correct answer is (C).** Choice (A) is the task of the U.S. Treasury Department and is part of fiscal policy, as is choice (B). Choice (D) is the job of the Federal Deposit Insurance Corporation, an independent agency of the federal government.

33. **The correct answer is (D).** All three items are motivators that push people toward becoming entrepreneurs. (Three additional reasons are the desire for financial independence, losing one's job, and the desire

to capitalize on a great idea.) Only choice (D) has all three items. Choice (A) is incorrect because it omits item III. Choice (B) is incorrect because it omits items I and III. Choice (C) is incorrect because it omits item II.

34. **The correct answer is (B).** Belonging is the third level of Maslow's hierarchy and satisfies the human need for social interaction and acceptance. Choice (A) is incorrect because safety is the second level and refers to feeling safe; while having a safe work environment is part of satisfying this need, the question refers to connectedness, which is more than just feeling safe. Choice (C), esteem, is the fourth level and refers to respect, which is more than feeling connected. Choice (D), self-actualization is the highest level and is not dependent on others.

35. **The correct answer is (D).** Choice (A) is incorrect because an income statement shows profit and loss. Choice (B) is not the best answer because it is not specific. Choice (C) is incorrect because a cash flow statement shows the receipts and payments.

36. **The correct answer is (C).** The sense of achievement at the end of the project comes from within the employee. Choices (A), (B), and (D) are extrinsic motivators.

37. **The correct answer is (B).** Choice (A) is incorrect. While it is true that it is easier for a partnership to get a bank loan, there is no support for the statement that angel investors prefer to invest in sole proprietorships. If part of an answer is incorrect, the entire answer is incorrect. Choice (C) is incorrect because it is unlikely that a bank will act as an advisor; it is more likely that an angel investor will adopt that role rather than take a hands-off approach. Choice (D) is irrelevant to a loan status.

38. **The correct answer is (A).** Choice (B) is not a recognized term. Choice (C) is incorrect; posting the job on the company Intranet

would be an internal method. Choice (D) is incorrect because using a headhunter is employing a company to do one-on-one recruiting for candidates.

39. **The correct answer is (B).** Part-time, temporary, and contract workers are contingent workers. While any of the workers listed in choices (A), (C), and (D) could be contingent employees depending on the circumstances, choice (B), a lawyer leased from a company that places lawyers in companies on contract, definitely refers to a contingent worker.

40. **The correct answer is (C).** Choice (A) may seem like a good choice, but continuous improvement refers to work process engineering. Choice (B) is incorrect because TQM stands for Total Quality Management, which is not the same as adaptability. Choice (D) may seem correct, but it is not a recognized term.

41. **The correct answer is (B).** Choice (A) is incorrect because regulatory law is established by administrative agencies, both state and federal. Choices (C) and (D) both describe common law.

42. **The correct answer is (C).** Choice (A) is incorrect because the equilibrium point is the point at which supply and demand are equal. Choice (B) is incorrect because aggregate output is the total amount of goods and services that an economy produces during a given period of time. Choice (D) is incorrect because the real growth rate is the gross domestic product adjusted for inflation and fluctuations in a country's currency.

43. **The correct answer is (B).** Malware can be a virus, worm, or Trojan horse. Choice (A) is incorrect because spyware transmits information such as passwords, contacts, and credit card numbers and transmits the data back to the sender of the spyware. Choice (C) is incorrect because spam is junk e-mail. Choice (D) is incorrect because cookies are bits of code left in computers when users

visit commercial sites that enable the sites to customize pages for viewers.

44. **The correct answer is (C).** The formula results in gross profit margin. Choice (A) is incorrect; operating expenses are the costs of doing businesses minus income taxes. Choice (B) is incorrect because operating profit margin is total revenue minus cost of goods sold minus operating expenses divided by total revenue. Choice (D) is incorrect because net income divided by number of outstanding shares equals earnings per share.

45. **The correct answer is (A).** Choice (B), data interpretation, may seem like a good answer, but the correct term is "data mining." Choice (C) is incorrect because the question doesn't ask about gathering the data, only analyzing it. Choice (D) is incorrect, but it may be confusing because it sounds like "drill down," which means "to look at data in increasingly more detailed levels."

46. **The correct answer is (C).** Choice (A) is incorrect because the bargaining chip argument contends that high tariffs can be useful in negotiating with a trading partner to reduce its tariffs in exchange for a reduction in comparable tariffs. Choice (B) is incorrect because the infant industry argument contends that a developing industry at home needs to be protected from foreign competition. The national security argument, choice (D), is incorrect because it claims that certain industries should be protected from foreign competition in the interests of their vital importance to the nation's defense.

47. **The correct answer is (D).** The right to own property is an essential characteristic of a market economy. Choice (A), some government control and some competition, describes an economy with some central planning, also known as socialism. Choice (B) is incorrect because central planning is a characteristic of communist and socialist

economies, not market economies. The barrier to entry, choice (C), is incorrect because the barrier in any industry may be high or low in a market economy. The answer is too narrow and is, therefore, incorrect.

48. **The correct answer is (A).** Choice (B) is incorrect because an apprenticeship is a specific type of training program for skilled workers; it would not include information on a company's culture. Choice (C) is incorrect because mentoring is typically a found on the managerial level, not on the junior employee level. Choice (D) is incorrect because an orientation program describes the company, but not a new employee's job.

49. **The correct answer is (A).** Price skimming might seem like a pricing strategy for the decline phase, but it's used at a product introduction in an attempt to recoup costs. Choices (B), (C), and (D)—growth, maturity, and decline—are incorrect. During choice (D), growth, penetrating pricing is used.

50. **The correct answer is (D).** Choices (A) and (B) are incorrect. Backward scheduling is used with a variety of inventory control systems; policy dictates whether forward or backward scheduling is used by a company. Choice (C) describes forward scheduling.

51. **The correct answer is (C).** Goodwill is a company's intangible assets. Choice (A) is incorrect because intellectual property describes a person's creative output. Choice (B) is incorrect because liquid assets are tangible things that can be easily converted to cash. Choice (D) is incorrect because brand recognition and a company's reputation are not physical things.

52. **The correct answer is (B).** There may be some investment in office equipment and supplies, but opening a sales office in a foreign city is not direct foreign investment, so eliminate choice (A). Choices (C) and (D) also aren't examples of direct foreign investment, so they are incorrect.

53. **The correct answer is (B).** The four Ps are product, price, promotion, and place, so choice (A) is incorrect. Choice (C) is incorrect because the media mix is the combination of medium used to advertise a product. Choice (D) is incorrect because product differentiation refers to the features of a product that distinguish it from its competitors.

54. **The correct answer is (C).** Net income is calculated on total revenue (item I) and operating expenses and income taxes (item III), so choice (C) is correct. Choice (A) is incorrect because item III is omitted. Choice (B) is incorrect because it contains item II and omits item III. Choice (D) is incorrect because it includes item II.

55. **The correct answer is (C).** Like catalog shopping, consumers can't see and touch the products they are interested in buying. Choices (A) and (B) are the opposite of what's true about e-tailing—comparison shopping is easier and product array is larger than a consumer would have in local stores. Choice (D) is incorrect because prices are comparable or even lower than bricks-and-mortar stores.

56. **The correct answer is (A).** Like bounce-back coupons and discount coupons, point-of-sale displays are sales promotion strategies. Advertising, choice (B), is not a sales promotion technique; product placement in a movie or TV show is an example of advertising a product. A distribution channel is a way to move goods from producer to consumer, so choice (C) is incorrect. Choice (D) is incorrect because while a point-of-sale display may prompt an impulse buy, it's not an impulse buy, but a sales promotion technique.

57. **The correct answer is (B).** Choice (A) is incorrect because it is not a policy of the World Bank. Choice (C) is incorrect because it describes a function of the International Monetary Fund. Choice (D) is incorrect because it is a function of the U.S. Federal Reserve System.

58. **The correct answer is (B).** Choice (A) is incorrect because choice (B) is correct. Choice (C) is incorrect because unless violations of the minimum wage would be related to job discrimination, the Equal Employment Opportunity Commission would not investigate. Choice (D) is incorrect; unions use collective bargaining to raise wages regardless of whether they are minimum wages or not.

59. **The correct answer is (A).** Corporate philanthropy involves donating some of a company's profits for charitable work, such as sponsoring civic projects like the Great American Cleanup. Choice (B), refusal to do business with sweatshops, is an example of CSR related to human rights, not corporate philanthropy. Choice (C) is incorrect because recycled packaging is an example of CSR related to environmental issues. Choice (D) is incorrect because refusing to allow cigarettes to be used in a program is an example of CSR related to marketing and health.

60. **The correct answer is (D).** Presumably a potential buyer will have done his or her homework ahead of time and discovered what the marketplace thinks about the business, but a poor reputation is a risk when buying an existing business, choice (D). Choice (A) is incorrect because buying an existing business takes less time than establishing a new business. Choice (B) is incorrect because the opposite is true; it is easier to get financing for an existing business than a start-up. Choice (C) is incorrect because this is a disadvantage for buying a new franchise, not an existing business. Once a person owns a non-franchise business, a person can do whatever he or she believes is necessary for the market.

SUMMING IT UP

- The basic forms of business ownership are (1) sole proprietorship, (2) partnership, and (3) corporation. There are also (4) co-operative and (5) nonprofit corporation forms of businesses.

- The sole proprietorship is the most common form of business ownership in the United States. Advantages include (1) lack of legal requirements for establishing and operating the business, (2) low start-up costs, (3) no separate tax filings, (4) no need to divide any profits, and (5) no shared decision making. The disadvantages are (1) unlimited liability, (2) difficulty in borrowing money, (3) responsibility for all losses, (4) no one to bounce ideas off, and (5) the end of the business when the owner retires or dies.

- With a partnership, (1) no separate business tax filings are required, (2) it is easier to borrow money from banks, (3) all partners contribute to start-up costs, and (4) all partners participate in decision making. A disadvantage is that any profits are divided as well, but the most important disadvantage is unlimited liability. Partnerships may be (1) general or (2) limited.

- In a co-operative, a group of partnerships and/or sole proprietorships join together to benefit their individual businesses.

- A corporation (1) is formed according to state laws; (2) is an entity that is separate from its owners, the stockholders; (3) has liability separate from its owners; (4) must file corporate tax returns annually: and (5) has certain legal rights.

- A nonprofit, or not-for-profit, is set up to support some social or educational mission.

- Government influences the business climate in two ways: (1) through regulatory policy and (2) through economic policy.

- Businesses are subject to a variety of laws: (1) contract, (2) tort, (3) property, (4) agency, (5) commercial, and (6) bankruptcy.

- One aspect of federal economic policy is the maintenance of a stable economic environment in which businesses can operate. This is the goal of the Federal Reserve System's monetary policy.

- People become entrepreneurs because they want to (1) be their own boss, (2) make a comfortable living, (3) have more control over their lives, or (4) have the flexibility that comes with owning their own business.

- Entrepreneurs may (1) start a business based on their own idea, (2) buy an existing business, or (3) buy a franchise.

- A franchiser provides (1) expertise, (2) training, and (3) marketing. The disadvantages are (1) the cost of buying the franchise, (2) start-up costs, (3) the percentage that the franchisee pays the franchiser, (4) lack of creativity and control over the business, and (5) competition from similar national brands.

- There are five factors of production: (1) labor, (2) natural resources, (3) capital (real and financial), (4) entrepreneurs, and (5) technology.

- In a market economy, or mixed economy, market forces set prices through the laws of supply and demand. Demand is the willingness and ability of consumers to buy a good or service, and supply is the willingness and ability of producers to produce a good or service.

- The law of supply states that producers will offer more of a product/service as the price increases and less of a product/service as the price decreases. The law of demand works in reverse.

- The characteristic of market and mixed economies are (1) competition, (2) private property rights, (3) freedom of choice in buying and selling goods and services, and (4) profits.

- Economic indicators are (1) gross domestic product (GDP), (2) gross national product (GNP), (3) consumer price index (CPI), (4) producer price index (PPI), (5) unemployment rate, and (6) productivity.

- Management plans, organizes, leads, and controls the financial, physical, human, and information resources of an organization.

- Planning is an essential element of management and includes setting the (1) goals, (2) strategies, and (3) tactics for the business.

- The function of control includes monitoring the business' performance and making adjustments as needed if goals are not being met.

- There are a variety of approaches to leadership as identified by researchers: (1) trait, (2) behavioral, (3) situational, (4) transformational, and (5) charismatic. Motivation may be (1) extrinsic or (2) intrinsic.

- Marketing strategies have two components: (1) target market and (2) marking mix. Product, price, promotion, and place—the Four Ps of marketing—comprise the marketing mix.

- Four Ps are presented as a coherent whole to the marketplace.

- The promotional mix includes (1) advertising, (2) personal selling, (3) sales promotions (4) publicity, and (5) public relations.

- A company's financial management is responsible for the planning and budgeting of funding for both its short-term and long-term operations.

- Accounting is the recording, analysis, and reporting of a business' financial transactions, which includes all its income and expense activities—accounts receivable and accounts payable.

- Operations include all the activities that go into producing products; operations management is the control of those activities. Products may be tangible goods or intangible services.

- Management information systems (MIS) use technology to (1) collect data and (2) analyze it and (3) use the resulting information to inform decisions and solve problems.

- The human resources department is responsible for (1) recruiting and (2) training employees, (3) developing compensation and benefits packages, and (4) developing a system for evaluation employees.

- E-commerce is the business of buying and selling electronically where the transaction may be between business and business or business and consumer.

- Ethics is a set of moral beliefs, a code of conduct based on what is considered right and wrong. Part of an organization's culture is its ethical stance on issues.

- Social responsibility is the belief that organizations as well as individuals are obligated to act in such a way as to benefit the larger society. Corporate social responsibility (CSR) institutionalizes this belief on a company-wide basis.

- Globalization impacts both (1) markets and (2) production.

- Some countries take a protectionist approach to their trade policies with the intent of protecting domestic industries from foreign competitors.

Here's to Your Health

The following chart outlines the sections and subsections in the Here's to Your Health test and offers a comparison between the percent of practice questions in this chapter and the actual DSST exam.

CONTENT OUTLINE: SECTIONS AND SUBSECTIONS	PERCENT OF EXAM DEVOTED TO EACH CONTENT AREA	NUMBER OF ITEMS IN THE DIAGNOSTIC TEST AND POST-TEST BY CONTENT AREA	PERCENT OF ITEMS IN THE DIAGNOSTIC TEST AND POST-TEST BY CONTENT AREA
I. Health, Wellness, and Mind/Body Connection	**20%**	**16**	**20%**
A. Responsible Health, Wellness and Lifestyles		6	37.5%
B. Mental Health Defined		2	12.5%
C. Psychological Disorders		3	18.75%
D. Stress Management and Coping Mechanisms		4	25%
E. Addictive Behaviors		1	6.25%
II. Human Development and Relationships	**20%**	**16**	**20%**
A. Reproduction		8	50%
B. Sexuality		1	6.25%
C. Intimate Relationships		3	18.75%
D. Healthy Aging		1	6.25%
E. Death and Bereavement		3	18.75%
III. Substance Use and Abuse	**10%**	**8**	**10%**
A. Alcohol		1	12.5%
B. Tobacco		2	25%
C. Other Drugs		4	50%
D. Substance-Use Behaviors		1	12.5%
IV. Fitness and Nutrition	**15%**	**12**	**15%**
A. Components of Physical Fitness		6	50%
B. Good Nutrition and Its Effects		6	50%
V. Risk Factors, Diseases, and Disease Prevention	**20%**	**16**	**20%**
A. Infectious Diseases, including Sexually Transmitted Diseases, Prevention and Control		4	25%

chapter 8

B. The Cardiovascular System		3	18.75%
C. Types of Cancer		4	25%
D. Immune Disorders		1	6.25%
E. Diabetes, Arthritis, and Genetic-Related Disorders		3	18.75%
F. Common Neurological Disorders		1	6.25%
VI. Safety, Consumer Awareness, and Environmental Concerns	**15%**	**12**	**15%**
A. Safety		2	16.6%
B. Intentional Injuries and Violence		2	16.6%
C. Consumer Awareness		4	33.4%
D. Environmental Concerns		4	33.4%
Grand Total	**100%**	**80**	**100%**

OVERVIEW

- **Diagnostic test**
- **Answer key and explanations**
- **Health, wellness, and mind/body connection**
- **Human development and relationships**
- **Substance use and abuse**
- **Fitness and nutrition**
- **Risk factors, diseases, and disease prevention**
- **Safety, consumer awareness, and environmental concerns**
- **Post-test**
- **Answer key and explanations**
- **Summing it up**

DIAGNOSTIC TEST

Directions: Carefully read each of the following 20 questions. Choose the best answer to each question and circle your answer choice. The Answer Key and Explanations can be found following this Diagnostic Test.

1. Which of the following is a hereditary condition that causes the body to produce sticky mucus that impairs the lungs and intestinal tract?
   - **(A)** Huntington's disease
   - **(B)** Achondroplasia
   - **(C)** Cystic fibrosis
   - **(D)** Hemophilia

2. The highest level in Maslow's Hierarchy of Needs is
   - **(A)** social.
   - **(B)** physiological needs.
   - **(C)** esteem.
   - **(D)** self-actualization.

3. An important concept of wellness that involves choosing to focus on only what you can control is
   - **(A)** holistic health.
   - **(B)** empowerment.
   - **(C)** spirituality.
   - **(D)** exercise.

4. Which of the following is a factor that favors fertility?
   - **(A)** Acidity of the vagina
   - **(B)** Alkalinity of the sperm
   - **(C)** Thick cervical mucus
   - **(D)** Small cervical opening

5. Which of the following drugs is classified as an opioid?
   - **(A)** Morphine
   - **(B)** Marijuana
   - **(C)** Phencyclidine
   - **(D)** Valium

6. Exercise in which the body supplies oxygen to all body parts is called
   - **(A)** anaerobic.
   - **(B)** isometric.
   - **(C)** aerobic.
   - **(D)** isokinetic.

7. Which of the following are the two forms of fiber?

   (A) Organic and inorganic

   (B) Synthetic and natural

   (C) Plant-derived and animal-derived

   (D) Soluble and insoluble

8. Which of the following is the first stage in grieving according to Kubler-Ross?

   (A) Depression

   (B) Anger

   (C) Denial

   (D) Acceptance

9. The hardening of arteries is called

   (A) arteriosclerosis.

   (B) arthritis.

   (C) atherosclerosis.

   (D) angina.

10. Which of the following is a characteristic of secondary depression?

   (A) Onset of depression for no apparent reason

   (B) Onset of depression clearly defined by a traumatic event

   (C) Depression attributed to brain chemistry

   (D) Depression related to insufficient exposure to sunlight

11. Hypertrophic obesity is defined as

   (A) the development of more fat cells in babies.

   (B) the body's preference to maintain current weight, making it difficult to lose weight.

   (C) obesity due to genetic factors.

   (D) the growth of fat cells to accommodate increased intake of food.

12. During the transition stage of birth,

   (A) the cervix dilates to about seven centimeters.

   (B) the "bloody show" discharges from vagina.

   (C) the cervix dilates from seven to ten centimeters.

   (D) the placenta is delivered.

13. Medical benefits based on financial need are provided by

   (A) Medicare.

   (B) Medicaid.

   (C) HMOs.

   (D) coinsurance.

14. Which type of cancer develops in connective tissue?

   (A) Leukemia

   (B) Melanoma

   (C) Sarcoma

   (D) Carcinoma

15. Which statement best describes the difference between barbiturates and tranquilizers?

   (A) Barbiturates are addictive, but tranquilizers are not.

   (B) Barbiturates cause sleep, and tranquilizers are used to cope during waking hours.

   (C) Barbiturates are safe, and tranquilizers are dangerous.

   (D) Barbiturates are no longer used, and tranquilizers are widely prescribed.

16. Which of the following is NOT one of the three stages of the GAS theory of stress?

   (A) Alarm reaction

   (B) Resistance

   (C) Distress

   (D) Exhaustion

17. Which energy source is most dense and provides stored energy for the body?

(A) Carbohydrates

(B) Vitamins

(C) Fats

(D) Proteins

18. The use of traditional free weights provides which form of exercise?

(A) Isometric

(B) Isotonic

(C) Isokinetic

(D) Aerobic

19. Which of the following can be detected by amniocentesis?

(A) Diabetes

(B) Cleft palate

(C) Down syndrome

(D) Hemochromatosis

20. Feces in water can be detected by the presence of

(A) coliform.

(B) campylobacter.

(C) *E. coli.*

(D) *Vibrio cholerae.*

ANSWER KEY AND EXPLANATIONS

1. C	5. A	9. A	13. B	17. C
2. D	6. C	10. B	14. C	18. B
3. B	7. D	11. D	15. B	19. C
4. B	8. C	12. C	16. C	20. A

1. **The correct answer is (C).** Cystic fibrosis is a hereditary and often fatal disease that is caused by a genetic mutation. The defective gene causes a deficiency in essential enzymes produced in the pancreas, so the body doesn't properly absorb nutrients. Thick mucus impairs the function of the lungs and intestinal tract. Choice (A) is incorrect because Huntington's disease involves a degeneration of brain cells in certain areas of the brain. Choice (B) is incorrect because achondroplasia is the term used for dwarfism. Choice (D) is incorrect because hemophilia is a genetic disorder in which individuals are missing the factor necessary for blood to clot.

2. **The correct answer is (D).** Self-actualization is the highest order according to Abraham Maslow's Hierarchy of Needs. He referred to people who reached this state as transcenders and Theory Z people. Self-actualization comes from the need for people to do what they were "meant" to do. Choice (A) is incorrect because social is the third level of Maslow's Hierarchy. Choice (B) is incorrect because physiological needs are the first level in the Hierarchy of Needs. Choice (C) is incorrect because esteem for self and others is the fourth level of the hierarchy.

3. **The correct answer is (B).** Empowerment is choosing to focus on controlling only that which you have power over. Choice (A) is incorrect because holistic health focuses on taking care of your physical, psychological, social, intellectual, and spiritual self. Choice (C) is incorrect because spirituality involves

focusing on your ability to understand the world and how you can serve others. Choice (D) is incorrect because exercise is only one aspect of life that you can control to promote overall wellness.

4. **The correct answer is (B).** Men's bodies produce a strong alkaline solution for the sperm that helps to offset the acidity of vaginal secretions. This helps the sperm survive in the woman's body. Choice (A) is incorrect because the acidity of the vagina can be harmful to sperm and decrease fertility. Choice (C) is incorrect because thick cervical mucus blocks sperm from entering the cervix and decreases fertility. Choice (D) is incorrect because the small size of the cervical opening is a factor that negatively affects fertilization.

5. **The correct answer is (A).** Narcotics such as opium, morphine, heroin, codeine, and methadone are classified as opioids. These drugs relieve pain, cause drowsiness, and induce euphoria. Choice (B) is incorrect because marijuana is derived from the plant cannabis and is not an opioid. Choice (C) is incorrect because phencyclidine is a dangerous hallucinogen also known as PCP or angel dust and is not an opioid. Choice (D) is incorrect because valium is classified as a tranquilizer.

6. **The correct answer is (C).** During aerobic exercise, the body can supply oxygen to all body parts. Choice (A) is incorrect because during anaerobic exercise, the body cannot be oxygenated fast enough to supply needed energy. Choice (B) is incorrect because

isometric refers to static exercises that focus on resistance. Choice (D) is incorrect because isokinetic exercise focuses on range of motion through mechanical devices used to provide resistance.

7. **The correct answer is (D).** Fiber is indigestible plant material, and there are two forms: (1) soluble and (2) insoluble fiber. Choice (A) is incorrect because all fiber comes from an organic source. Choice (B) is incorrect because fiber is derived from only a natural plant source. Choice (C) is incorrect because all fiber is derived from plant sources.

8. **The correct answer is (C).** According to Kubler-Ross, there are five stages in the process of coping with grief and tragedy. The first stage is denial, or refusal to accept the facts or any information about the situation. Choice (A) is incorrect because depression is the fourth step in grieving. Choice (B) is incorrect because anger is the second step. Choice (D) is incorrect because acceptance is the fifth stage of grieving.

9. **The correct answer is (A).** The buildup of plaque on inner walls of the arteries is known as arteriosclerosis. Choice (B) is incorrect because arthritis affects joints, not the heart. Choice (C) is incorrect because the buildup of plaque on inner walls of the heart muscle is called atherosclerosis. Choice (D) is incorrect because angina pectoris is a condition in which the heart doesn't receive enough oxygen.

10. **The correct answer is (B).** The onset of secondary depression can clearly be attributed to a traumatic event such as death or divorce. Choices (A) and (C) are incorrect because the onset of depression for no apparent reason that is often linked to brain chemistry is defined as primary depression. Choice (D) is incorrect because depression linked to the amount of sunlight an individual is exposed to is classified as Seasonal Affective Disorder (SAD).

11. **The correct answer is (D).** Adults typically take in more calories than they expend, causing fat cells to grow and accommodate the increased intake. This growth of fat cells is known as hypertrophic obesity. Choice (A) is incorrect because the development of more fat cells typically seen in babies who are overfed is known as hypercellular obesity. Choice (B) is incorrect because the idea that the body prefers to maintain its current weight is known as the set-point theory. Choice (C) is incorrect because obesity due to genetic factors usually relates to thyroid or endocrine issues, or metabolism.

12. **The correct answer is (C).** Transition occurs during the first stage of labor when the cervix dilates from seven to ten centimeters. This is the shortest and most strenuous part of labor. Choice (A) is incorrect because the cervix dilates from seven to ten centimeters during transition. Choice (B) is incorrect because the thick mucus discharge called the "bloody show" is apparent before transition. Choice (D) is incorrect because the placenta is delivered during the final stage of birth, not during transition.

13. **The correct answer is (B).** Medicaid is a benefit paid by the government based on financial need. Choice (A) is incorrect because Medicare is a federal program that pays benefits to those 65 and older (and some dependents under certain circumstances) who paid into the system when they worked. Choice (C) is incorrect because an HMO (Health Maintenance Organization) provides both health insurance and health care. Choice (D) is incorrect because coinsurance is the amount that the insured must pay for any prescription or procedure.

14. **The correct answer is (C).** A sarcoma is a cancer that develops in connective tissue. Choice (A) is incorrect because leukemia is cancer involving the blood cells. Choice (B) is incorrect because melanoma is skin cancer. Choice (D) is incorrect because a

answers diagnostic test

carcinoma can be in many types of body parts, but not in connective tissue.

15. **The correct answer is (B).** The major difference between barbiturates and tranquilizers is that barbiturates are designed to induce sleep, and tranquilizers are used to help cope during waking hours. Choice (A) is incorrect because both are addictive. Choice (C) is incorrect because when used properly, both drugs are safe. Choice (D) is incorrect because both drugs are still prescribed.

16. **The correct answer is (C).** There is no stage of distress in Selye's theory on stress known as General Adaptation Syndrome, or GAS, theory. Choice (A) is incorrect because the first stage of GAS is alarm reaction, which is a physical "fight or flight" response to stress caused by the surge of adrenaline. Choice (B) is incorrect because the stage of resistance is the second stage of GAS; it is the point at which the body reaches homeostasis with respect to adrenaline and energy levels. Choice (D) is incorrect because the stage of exhaustion is the third stage of the GAS theory. This is the point at which a stressed body becomes tired.

17. **The correct answer is (C).** Fats are an excellent energy source and are denser than carbohydrates. Fats store energy for long-term use. Choice (A) is incorrect because carbohydrates are also used for energy, but they provide a short-term energy source and are less dense than fats. Choice (B) is incorrect because vitamins are not a source of energy. Choice (D) is incorrect because proteins are not a readily accessible source of energy.

18. **The correct answer is (B).** Progressive resistance, or isotonic, exercises employ the use of traditional free weights to provide resistance. Choice (A) is incorrect because isometric exercise focuses solely on resistance. Choice (C) is incorrect because isokinetic resistance involves exercising through a range of motion. Choice (D) is incorrect because aerobic exercise has to do with the amount of blood supplied to muscles throughout the body.

19. **The correct answer is (C).** Down's syndrome, or trisomy 21, is a disorder in which there is an extra chromosome 21. This can be detected during pregnancy with amniocentesis. Choice (A) is incorrect because diabetes isn't detected by amniocentesis and usually doesn't develop in young babies. Choice (B) is incorrect because a cleft palate is a physical birth defect, not a genetic defect. Choice (D) is incorrect because hemochromatosis, or an abnormally high level of iron in the body, is not detected by amniocentesis.

20. **The correct answer is (A).** Coliform is a bacteria whose presence in water indicates the presence of feces. Choices (B) and (C) are incorrect because campylobacter and *E. coli* are generally bacteria found on raw meat. Choice (D) is incorrect because the strain of bacteria *Vibrio cholera* is best known to cause the disease cholera.

HEALTH, WELLNESS, AND MIND/BODY CONNECTION

Wellness is determined by overall health and vitality. Some aspects of health are not in our control; for example, age, gender, and genetic makeup are not things that we can control. However, wellness is determined in a large part by factors that we can control—such as diet, exercise, and relationships with others. Understanding that you can't control hereditary makeup, age, or gender helps achieve a feeling of empowerment, and empowerment is an important concept in overall wellness.

Responsible Health, Wellness, and Lifestyles

There are six dimensions to overall wellness: (1) physical, (2) emotional, (3) spiritual, (4) intellectual, (5) interpersonal, and (6) environmental. Each dimension is dependent on the others.

- *Physical wellness* includes not only the absence of disease, but also fitness level and the ability to care for oneself. Physical wellness is determined by coordination, strength, and the five senses (sight, hearing, taste, touch, and smell).

- *Emotional wellness* reflects the ability to understand and cope with feelings or emotions. This also includes identifying any obstacles or factors that may affect emotional stability.

- *Spiritual wellness* involves developing a set of guided beliefs, principles, or values that give meaning and purpose to life.

- *Intellectual wellness* involves constantly challenging the mind and keeping it active. Continued creativity, problem solving, and processing information is essential for wellness.

- *Interpersonal wellness* is defined by the ability to develop and maintain healthy, satisfying, and supportive relationships with others. This includes participating in society in a positive way.

- *Environmental wellness* involves support from one's environment. The overall livability of the environment affects wellness, so it is important to make the world a cleaner, safer place to live.

Lifestyle choices include (1) exercise, (2) diet, and the choice to use (3) alcohol or (4) tobacco. People can influence their own lives by the lifestyle choices they make, but these four lifestyle choices play a major role in the leading causes of death in the United States. Life expectancy has risen due to improvements in public health and public awareness in the twentieth and twenty-first centuries, but (1) tobacco, (2) obesity, and (3) alcohol consumption are still the top three contributors to deaths in this country.

The national Healthy People Initiative aims to improve the quality of life for Americans. Its two broad goals are (1) to increase the quality and years of healthy life for individuals and (2) to eliminate health disparities among population groups in the United States. Factors that contribute to generalized health differences are (1) gender, (2) ethnicity, (3) income, (4) education, (5) disability, (6) geographic location, and (7) sexual orientation.

A healthy lifestyle should focus on a holistic approach. Holistic health includes understanding the importance of all six dimensions of wellness. It also includes (1) good diet, (2) proper exercise, (3) adequate sleep, (4) preventative care, (5) moderation in alcohol consumption, and (6) no drug or tobacco use. Behavioral changes are also important in creating a healthy lifestyle. In order to build the motivation to make a change in lifestyle, the following steps are recommended: (1) examine the pros and cons of change, (2) boost self-efficacy, (3) identify the focus of control, (4) utilize visualization and self-talk, (5) utilize role models and supportive individuals, and (6) identify and overcome barriers.

The transtheoretical, or stages of change, model is an effective approach to lifestyle management. The stages of change include:

- *Precontemplation:* An individual doesn't think he or she has a problem and doesn't intend to change.

- *Contemplation:* An individual recognizes he or she has a problem and intends to change in six months.

- *Preparation:* An individual plans to take action to change a behavior within a month or has begun to make a change already.

- *Action:* An individual outwardly modifies his or her behavior.

- *Maintenance:* An individual has maintained a healthier lifestyle for at least six months.

- *Termination:* An individual has exited the cycle of change and is not tempted to lapse back into old behaviors.

A specific plan for change can be developed in the following way: (1) monitoring behavior by keeping a journal, (2) analyzing recorded data; (3) setting specific goals, (4) thinking of strategies for improving the environment, (5) rewarding one's self and involving others in the plan, and (6) making a personal contract.

Mental Health Defined

People who are mentally healthy are comfortable with who they are and feel confident that they can meet the demands of life. When mentally healthy people are faced with negative feelings of disappointment, anger, jealousy, or regret, they are able to deal with the feelings without succumbing to them.

A positive definition of mental health describes it as the presence of wellness. This definition encourages people to fulfill their potential, and a description of this ideal was presented by psychologist Abraham Maslow in the 1960s. He developed the Hierarchy of Needs, in which he suggests that most people are motivated to fulfill basic needs before moving on to more complex needs. The needs are arranged in a pyramid. As one progresses up the steps of the pyramid, the needs become more complex.

- The lowest level is made up of the most basic physiological needs, including food, shelter, sleep, clothing, and compensation.

- The next level displays the next level of needs: safety and security.

- Next is the need for social relationships, including family, friendship, and social interaction.

- Next is the need for esteem, including self-esteem, confidence, achievement, respect of others, and respect by others.

- The final stage is self-actualization, which is the point at which individuals are finally doing what they are meant to do. This level includes morality, creativity, spontaneity, problem solving, lack of prejudice, and acceptance of facts.

Self-actualized people are realistic; they accept themselves for who they are, and they have a positive self-concept, or self image. Psychologically healthy people are autonomous and inner-directed, meaning they find guidance from within. In contrast, other-directed people act in response to external pressure that they feel from others. Self-actualized individuals are also authentic and "real," and they can be intimate with others. Maslow calls self-actualized individuals transcenders, or Theory Z people.

Responses to challenges in life influence the personality and identity of individuals. Psychologist Erik Erikson proposed eight stages that extend throughout an individual's lifetime. Each stage is characterized by a turning point or a crisis. One must master a stage successfully before being able to progress to the next stage.

1. The first stage at birth to 1 year involves developing a trust that others will respond to your needs.

2. The second stage from 1 to 3 years involves learning self-control without losing the capacity for assertiveness.

3. From 3 to 6 years, individuals develop a conscience based on parental prohibitions.

4. From 6 to 12 years, individuals learn the value of accomplishment and perseverance without feeling inadequate.

5. In adolescence, individuals develop a stable sense of who they are based on needs, abilities, style, and values.

6. During young adulthood, individuals learn to live with and share intimately with others, often in a sexual relationship.

7. Middle adulthood includes doing things for others, such as parenting and becoming involved in civic activities.

8. Older adulthood includes affirming life's value and ideals.

Psychological Disorders

There are several types of psychological, or mental, disorders with varying degrees of severity: (1) anxiety, (2) mood, (3) schizophrenia, (4) dissociative, and (5) somatoform.

Anxiety disorders are based on fear. They cause physical symptoms such as rapid heartbeat and tenseness. There are several types of anxiety disorders.

*   *Simple phobia* is a fear of something definite, such as heights or closed spaces.

*   *Social phobia* is the fear of humiliation or embarrassment within a social setting. Shyness is associated with social phobia.

*   *Panic disorder* is the sudden and unexpected surge in anxiety and can lead to agoraphobia, which in its extreme is the fear of leaving home.

*   *Generalized anxiety disorder (GAD)* occurs when worries push out other thoughts and a person cannot banish these worrying thought.

- *Obsessive-compulsive disorder (OCD)* includes irrational thoughts and impulses and the compulsion to do things over and over again. People with OCD feel out of control and embarrassed.

- *Post-traumatic stress disorder (PSTD)* is a reaction to severely traumatic events, such as physical violence, natural disasters, and accidents.

Mood disorders create emotional disturbances that are intense enough to affect the normal functioning of an individual. Electroconvulsive therapy is effective for severe depression if no other treatments succeed. The two most common mood disorders are (1) depression and (2) bipolar disorder.

- *Depression* is the most common mood disorder and is an overwhelming feeling of worthlessness, despair, and sadness in such a way that reality is distorted.
  - o *Primary depression* seems to start for no apparent reason and is usually attributed to brain chemistry. The most successful treatment for primary depression is antidepressant medication.
  - o *Secondary depression,* also known as reactive depression, is brought about by a traumatic event. The most successful treatments for this type of depression include counseling and other therapies.

- *Bipolar disorders* are another type of mood disorder. People who experience mania are often restless, have a great deal of energy, need very little sleep, and talk incessantly. People that swing between a maniac state and a depressive state have a bipolar disorder. Medications such as the salt lithium carbonate can help prevent mood swings. Mood can also be stabilized with anticonvulsant drugs such as Tegretol and Lamictal, which are generally used to prevent seizures.

- *Seasonal affective disorder (SAD)* is directly related to the amount of sunlight an individual is exposed to. This disorder worsens during winter months, and phototherapy is an effective treatment.

Schizophrenia has a number of symptoms, including auditory hallucinations, delusions of grandeur, persecution, inappropriate emotions, disorganized thoughts, and deteriorating social and work function. About 1 in every 100 people has a schizophrenic episode at some point in his or her lifetime. Schizophrenia is likely caused by a combination of genetics and environmental factors during pregnancy. Being born to older fathers or prenatal exposure to certain infections or medications can make an individual more susceptible to schizophrenia. There are several types of schizophrenia: (1) disorganized types, (2) catatonic types, and (3) paranoid types.

Dissociative disorders cause a sudden, but temporary change in identity or consciousness of an individual. Psychogenic amnesia is the inability to recall a stressful event, and psychogenic fugue occurs when an individual moves to a new place and assumes a new identity after a stressful event.

Somatoform disorders are physical ailments without a medical condition to support them. Hypochondria is the belief that the person is sick when there is no medical evidence, and a conversion disorder is the unexplained loss of function of a body part.

Stress Management and Coping Mechanisms

Stress can refer to two different things: (1) the stressor and (2) the stress response. The situation that triggers physical or emotional reactions is called the stressor, and the physical and emotional reactions are called the stress response. Stress is the general term used to describe the physical and emotional state that is part of the stress response.

Two body systems control the physical response to a stressor: (1) the nervous system and (2) the endocrine system. The automatic nervous system consists of the parasympathetic division, which is in control when the body is relaxed, and the sympathetic division, which is activated during times of arousal. The sympathetic division triggers signals to tell the body to stop storing energy and to use it in response to crisis. This is carried out with the neurotransmitter norepinephrine. During times of stress, the sympathetic division of the nervous system triggers the endocrine system. The endocrine system releases hormones and other chemical signals into the bloodstream. This influences the body's metabolism and other processes. Some key hormones released in response to stress are cortisol and epinephrine.

Hans Selye developed a theory of stress called the General Adaptation Syndrome (GAS), which has three stages.

1. The first stage is the *alarm reaction* when the body encounters the initial stressor and initiates the fight or flight response, which is triggered by a surge of cortisol into the bloodstream. The physical changes during this response include (1) accelerated heart and respiration rates, (2) more acute hearing and vision, (3) release of sugar into bloodstream from the liver to increase energy, (4) perspiration to cool the skin, and (5) release of endorphins in the brain that block the sensation of pain.

2. The next stage of GAS is the *stage of resistance*. The body cannot maintain the levels of energy and adrenaline, so in this stage, the parasympathetic division of the nervous system takes over and restores a state of stability in terms of physiological functions. This state of stability is called homeostasis.

3. The third stage of GAS is *exhaustion*. The stressed body will be tired at this stage because the initial adrenaline surge and the return to homeostasis expend a large amount of energy. Depending on the stress response that was triggered, the body may have a weakened immune system or a strong need for rest. Stress triggered by a pleasant stressor is called eustress, and stress triggered by an unpleasant stressor is called distress.

Behavioral responses to stressors are controlled by the somatic nervous system. Personality types also play a role in how an individual deals with stress. Type A personalities have a high perceived stress level and usually have problems dealing with stress. Type B personalities are less frustrated by daily events and other people's behavior. Type C personalities have difficulty expressing emotion and suppress their anger. They have an exaggerated response to minor stressors.

The study of the relationship between stress and disease is called psychoneuroimmunology (PNI). This research involves the study of the (1) nervous system, (2) endocrine system, and (3) immune system. The basic concept is that stress triggers a response of the nervous system and endocrine system, and the actions of these systems can impair the immune system. Over time, stress can trigger (1) cardiovascular disease, (2) high blood pressure, (3) impaired immune function, (4) psychological problems, (5) accelerated aging, (6) digestive problems, and (7) headaches, among other problems. Sources of stress are (1) environmental (earthquakes and terrorism), (2) internal (pressure to reach personal goals), and (3) everyday hassles like losing keys, time pressures, and financial concerns.

Stress can be managed in a myriad of ways, including (1) having a good support system, (2) improving communication skills, (3) developing a healthy lifestyle, (4) improving time management, and (5) learning to identify and moderate individual stressors. (6) Spiritual wellness can also help individuals deal with stress and improve overall health. (7) Keeping a diary, (8) changing unhealthy thought patterns, and (9) using relaxation techniques that trigger a relaxation response are other ways to cope with stress.

A relaxation response is a physiological state that results in a slowing of breathing, heart rate, and metabolism; a decrease in blood pressure and oxygen; an increase in blood flow to the brain and skin; and a switch of brain waves to the relaxed alpha rhythm. Techniques include (1) visualization, (2) meditation, (3) yoga, and (4) tai chi. Creating a personal plan for managing stress includes (1) identifying stressors by keeping a stress journal, (2) designing a plan for reducing stress and creating a contract, and (3) getting help from friends, a support group, or therapy. Counterproductive strategies for coping with stress include alcohol and tobacco use, drug use, and unhealthy eating habits.

Addictive Behaviors

Addictive behaviors are habits that have become out of control and have a negative effect on a person's health. Typical addictions include (1) eating, (2) shopping, (3) alcohol, (4) drugs, (5) gambling, (6) television, (7) video games, (8) work, and (9) sex. There are several characteristics related to the formation of an addiction.

- Exposure and reinforcement of the activity

- Compulsion or craving in which an individual invests more and more time involved in the addictive behavior and everyday life and responsibilities become less and less important

- Loss of control in which behavior worsens and the individual cannot block the impulse to engage in the activity

- Escalation as more and more of the substance or activity is needed to get the desired effect

- Negative consequences in which the behavior continues despite serious negative results

A combination of factors leads to addictive behaviors. These factors include (1) personality, (2) lifestyle, (3) heredity, (4) social and physical environments, and (5) the nature of the activity or substance causing the addiction.

HUMAN DEVELOPMENT AND RELATIONSHIPS

Over the course of a lifetime, a person will meet many people, have a variety of relationships, and live to see some family and friends die before them. Healthy aging is the process of growing into a productive adult, coping with midlife issues, and facing mortality in a positive, healthy way.

Reproduction

Reproduction includes (1) fertility, (2) pregnancy, (3) birth, and (4) methods of birth control, or contraception.

The sex organs necessary for reproduction are different for women and men, but arise from the same structures and carry out similar functions. The gonads of females are called the ovaries, and the gonads of males are called the testes. The testes and ovaries produce sex hormones (androgens, estrogens, and progestins) that trigger the development and function of the reproductive system. Gonads produce germ cells (ova and sperm), which are the basic components of reproduction.

The external genitals of the female are the vulva, which is a rounded mass of fatty tissue over the pubic bone and the labia majora and the labia minora, which are two paired folds of skin. Inside these folds are (1) the clitoris, (2) the opening of the urethra, and (3) the opening of the vagina. The cervix projects into the upper part of the vagina, or the birth canal. The cervix is the opening to the uterus where a fertilized egg implants during pregnancy. The eggs descend into the uterus from the ovaries through channels called fallopian tubes.

The external genitals of the male are the penis and the scrotum. The scrotum contains the testes, which keeps the sperm at a temperature five degrees below normal body temperature. The urethra runs the entire length of the penis and carries semen to the opening at its tip. The sperm are produced and then travel to a storage tube called the epididymis on the surface of each testes. The sperm move from the epididymis to another tube called the vas deferens, and from there they move up toward the abdominal cavity through the prostate gland, which produces seminal fluid. The vas deferens tubes merge into a pair of seminal vesicles where nutrition for the semen is supplied. The sperm then flow into the ejaculatory duct, which joins to the urethra. The sperm pass through the urethra into the woman's vagina to possibly fertilize an ovum.

The biological sex of an individual is determined by the sperm that fertilizes an ovum at the time of conception. All ova carry an X-chromosome, and sperm carry either an X- or a Y-chromosome. Differences in the sexes become more apparent at puberty. In females, progesterone and estrogen cause breast development, rounding of hips, and the start of the menstrual cycle. Menarche, or the first menstrual period, begins on average at around age 12½. The menstrual cycle is divided into four phases: (1) menses (menstrual flow; 1 to 5 days), (2) the estrogenic phase (release of follicle-stimulating hormone [FSH] and luteinizing hormone [LH] and maturation of an ovarian follicle), (3) ovulation (release of ovum around day 14 of cycle), and (4) the progestational phase (increase in level of progesterone secreted; remains high until next menses). Maturation of the male reproductive system is about two years behind females. Testicular growth is the first sign of maturity. Body hair grows, the voice deepens, and height increases.

Conception and Infertility

Once individuals have reached sexual maturity, they are able to conceive a child. The process of conception involves the fertilization of an ovum inside a woman by the sperm of a man during sexual intercourse. Once an egg is fertilized by a sperm, it becomes a zygote. As soon as fertilization occurs, the zygote starts the process of cell division, and growth begins as the zygote moves through the fallopian tubes into the uterus. The cluster of growing cells forms a blastocyst that is implanted into the endometrial lining of the uterus. The blastocyst develops into a fetus, and around thirty-eight weeks after fertilization a fully developed baby is born.

Infertility is the inability to conceive a child after a year or longer. There are now many methods that can help treat infertility. Most cases of infertility are treated with conventional medical therapies: surgery to correct anatomical problems or fertility drugs to help women ovulate. If these treatments don't work, assisted reproductive technology (ART) may be used. ART methods include (1) intra-uterine insemination, (2) in vitro fertilization (IVF), (3) gamete intrafallopian transfer (GIFT), and (4) zygote intrafallopian transfer (ZIFT).

Pregnancy

Pregnancy is divided into trimesters of about three months each. The earliest signs of pregnancy include (1) a missed menstrual period, (2) slight bleeding after implantation, (3) nausea, (4) breast tenderness, (5) increased urination, (6) sleepiness, (7) fatigue, and (8) emotional upset. About four weeks after a missed period, a softening of the uterus above the cervix occurs. This is called Hegar's sign.

- *Mother:* During the first trimester, the uterus enlarges to about three times its nonpregnant size. Breasts enlarge and are sensitive, and the areola darken and broaden. Muscles and ligaments soften and stretch, and joints loosen and spread. During the start of the second trimester, the abdomen begins to protrude. The circulatory system and the lungs become more efficient. In the third trimester, the increased needs of the fetus put a strain on the woman's lungs, heart, and kidneys. Her body retains more water, and her back may ache from the extra weight. The average weight gain during pregnancy is about 27.5 pounds. Preliminary contractions called Braxton Hicks contractions start in the third trimester. In the ninth month, the baby settles in the pelvic region, and this stage of pregnancy is known as lightening.

- *Baby:* During the first trimester, the blastocyst implants in the uterus about four days after fertilization and continues to grow, eventually becoming an embryo at about the end of the second week after fertilization. At this point, the inner cells of the blastocyst are divided into three layers: (1) One layer becomes inner body parts such as the digestive and respiratory systems. (2) The middle layer of cells becomes muscle and bones, blood, kidneys, and sex glands. (3) The third layer of cells becomes skin, hair, and the nervous system. An outermost layer of cells becomes the placenta, the umbilical cord, and the amniotic sac.

These components provide nutrients and oxygen to the fetus. All major body parts are formed during the first trimester. During the second trimester, the fetus does a great deal of growing, and therefore, it needs large amounts of food, water, and oxygen, which are all supplied from the mother through the placenta. The mother can detect fetal movement during the fourth or fifth month. During the third trimester, the fetus gains most of its birth weight. A layer of fat tissue under the skin insulates the fetus and supplies it with energy. The fetus requires large doses of calcium, iron, and nitrogen from the mother.

Only about 3 percent of babies born have a major birth defect. The health and sex of a baby can be determined with several testing methods. These methods include (1) ultrasonography, (2) amniocentesis, (3) chrionic villus sampling, and (4) quadruple screen marker tests. Ultrasonography and amniocentesis are the most frequent methods used to detect fetal abnormalities. An ultrasound is done so that measurements of the developing fetus can be taken. A discrepancy in a fetal measurement can indicate an abnormality. Further detail can be obtained through amniocentesis. During amniocentesis, a needle is injected into the mother's abdomen to remove some of the amniotic fluid. The amniotic fluid contains all of the genetic material of the fetus, and so genetic, neural, and chromosomal abnormalities can be detected such as Down syndrome, Tay-Sachs syndrome, spina bifida, and cystic fibrosis. However, the severity of the problem is not known through amniocentesis. Fetal programming theory is a new area of study that focuses on how conditions in the womb may influence the risk of disease later in life.

Birth Process

The birth process occurs in three stages, and the whole process takes anywhere from about 2 to 36 hours. Labor begins when hormonal changes in the mother and the baby cause strong rhythmic contractions of the uterus. Contractions exert pressure on the cervix and cause it to thin (effacement) and open (dilation). The first stage of labor involves effacement and dilation of the cervix to 10 centimeters through contractions. The last part of the first stage is called transition and is characterized by stronger, more frequent contractions. During transition, the cervix opens completely. The second stage of labor begins when the cervix is completely dilated to 10 centimeters and ends with the delivery of the baby. The woman must push the baby down through the bones of the pelvic ring, past the cervix, into the vagina, and out through the stretched opening. During the third stage of labor, the uterus continues to contract until the placenta is delivered. During the postpartum period, the mother can begin breastfeeding and the mother's body begins to return to its pre-pregnancy state.

Birth Control

Contraceptives are devices, substances, or techniques that are used to prevent pregnancy by preventing the fertilization of an egg (ovum): (1) barrier method (condoms, cervical cones, diaphragms), (2) intrauterine device (creates an unstable environment in the uterus; IUD), (3) hormonal methods (birth control pills and skin patch), (4) natural methods (rhythm and withdrawal), and (5) surgical sterilization (tubal ligation or tubal sterilization in women and vasectomy in men).

Sexuality

The sexual response in humans follows a specific pattern of phases: (1) excitement, (2) plateau, (3) orgasmic, and (4) resolution. Two physiological responses explain the genital and bodily reactions caused by arousal and orgasm. These are (1) vascongestion (accumulation of blood in tissue) and (2) muscular tension.

Any type of disturbance in sexual desire, performance ability, or satisfaction is referred to as sexual dysfunction. Some common sexual dysfunctions in men are (1) erectile dysfunction, (2) premature ejaculation, and (3) retarded ejaculation. Female sexual dysfunction includes (1) the lack of desire to have sex, (2) failure to become aroused, and (3) failure to achieve orgasm.

Sexual health conditions that affect women are (1) vaginitis (inflammation of the vagina), which includes candida (yeast infection), trichomonas, and bacterial vaginosis (the overgrowth of bacteria); (2) endometriosis, (3) pelvic inflammatory disease (PID), and (4) ovarian cancer. Sexual health problems that affect men include (1) prostatitis (inflammation of prostate gland), (2) acute bacterial prostatitis, (3) chronic prostatitis, and (4) testicular cancer.

There are different sexual behaviors in which individuals engage. These behaviors include (1) fantasies and erotic dreams, (2) masturbation, (3) shared touching, (4) genital contact (foreplay), (5) oral-genital stimulation, and (6) intercourse. Sexual behavior is a result of many factors shaped by life experience and biological factors, and it is also influenced by gender identity.

When a person's gender traits don't match his or her gender identity, that person is considered transgender. Transgender includes (1) transsexuals (those whose gender does not match their gender identity), (2) transvestites (those who enjoy wearing the clothing of the opposite gender), and (3) intersexed, or androgynous, individuals (born without definitive sexual characteristics).

Most individuals engage in sexual intercourse as the ultimate sexual experience. Atypical sexual behaviors include (1) fetishism, (2) exhibitionism, (3) voyeurism, (4) sadism, (5) masochism, and (6) sadomasochism. Paraphilia is the term used to describe atypical sexual behaviors that cause harm to oneself or others. The use of force in a sexual relationship is a serious problem in human interaction. The most extreme forms of sexual coercion are rape, pedophilia, and sexual harassment.

Intimate Relationships

People involved in intimate relationships tend to believe in themselves and the people around them. An individual may have only one or two intimate relationships or several intimate friendships. To have a successful relationship, one must feel good about one's self. Our ways of relating to one another are rooted in our childhood and may be dependent on the style of attachment established during infancy.

The first relationships formed outside the family are friendships. Friendships include the following characteristics: (1) companionship, (2) respect, (3) acceptance, (4) help, (5) loyalty, (6) trust, (7) mutuality, and (8) reciprocity. Friendships require good communication skills, both verbal and non-verbal. Intimate partnerships are much like friendships, but these relationships include (1) sexual desire, (2) deeper levels of caring, and (3) a greater demand for exclusiveness.

There are several stages of attraction between individuals.

- The initial stage of a relationship is defined as *marketing,* when individuals "market" their best selves while finding new friends and acquaintances.

- The next stage is *sharing of common values and beliefs.* If there is enough compatibility then the relationship moves to the behavior stage.

- During the *behavior stage,* the relationship develops further into a friendship or a passionate love relationship.

- *Passionate love* is characterized by a temporary phase of intense feelings and attraction. This phase does not last very long and is often called infatuation or lust.

- Passionate love usually gives way to *companionate love,* which is a deep enduring attachment built on mutual support, empathy, and tolerance.

Friendship and marriage are based on many of the same characteristics of companionate love and the same level of deep commitment that strengthens over time. For most individuals, (1) love, (2) commitment, and (3) sex are important parts of an intimate relationship. Commitment represents a stable factor that is important in maintaining a healthy relationship, and sex intensifies the intimacy of a relationship.

Challenges that a relationship faces may include (1) being open and honest, (2) having unrealistic expectations, (3) competitiveness, (4) having unequal or premature commitment, (5) balancing time spent together, (6) jealousy, and (7) supportiveness. Unhealthy relationships are characterized by communication styles that include (1) criticism, (2) contempt, (3) defensiveness, and (4) withdrawal. Conflict is natural in an intimate relationship.

Dating and Marriage

Most people in the United States find a romantic partner through dating. Most people pair with someone who lives in the same region, is from a similar ethnic or cultural background, has a similar educational background, lives a similar lifestyle, and has the same ideas of physical attraction.

Living together, or cohabitation, is one of the most rapid social changes in our society. Today, by age 30, about 50 percent of all men and women have cohabitated. Living together does not give individuals the same legal protections, such as insurance benefits and property and inheritance rights, as marriage.

Sexual orientation in an intimate relationship refers to the gender that an individual is attracted to. There are three types of sexual orientation. (1) Heterosexuals are attracted to individuals of the opposite sex, or gender; (2) homosexuals are attracted to others of the same gender; and (3) bisexuals are attracted to both genders.

The majority of Americans marry at some point in their life. Today, people tend to marry for personal and emotional reasons rather than for more practical reasons, such as having children and economic security. Certain characteristics can predict whether a marriage will last, including (1) feeling good about each other's personalities, (2) having realistic expectations about the relationship, (3) communicating well, (4) agreeing on religious and ethical values, (5) devising effective ways to resolve conflict, (6) having an egalitarian role in the relationship, and (7) having a good balance between individual and joint interests. Approximately 50 to 55 percent of U.S. marriages end in divorce, a fact that is likely due to extremely high expectations of emotional fulfillment.

Starting a family can be stressful, but couples who keep their commitment strong after the arrival of a baby have three characteristics in common: (1) a strong relationship before having children, (2) planning their family and wanting children very much, and (3) communicating well about feelings and expectations. As individuals become parents, there are typically four general styles of parenting, which vary depending on the levels of demandingness and responsiveness of the parent. The four parenting styles include:

- *Authoritarian* (high demandingness, low responsiveness)
- *Authoritative* (high demandingness, high responsiveness)
- *Permissive* (low demandingness, high responsiveness)
- *Uninvolved* (low demandingness, low responsiveness).

Successful families share six major qualities: (1) commitment, (2) appreciation, (3) communication, (4) time together, (5) spiritual wellness, and (6) an ability to cope with stress and crisis.

Healthy Aging

Through good habits, individuals can delay, lessen, prevent, and sometimes reverse some changes associated with aging. Some of these good habits include:

- Challenging your mind
- Developing a physical fitness routine
- Establishing healthy eating habits

- Maintaining a healthy weight
- Controlling alcohol consumption and dependence on medication
- Refraining from smoking
- Maintaining a schedule of physical examinations for the detection of treatable diseases or conditions
- Recognizing and reducing stress

Midlife

In midlife, there is a general feeling of starting anew and coming to terms with mortality, although there is a slow decline of body function in terms of (1) loss of bone mass, (2) compression of vertebrae, (3) loss of lean body mass, (4) vision loss, (5) hearing loss, (6) fertility loss, and (7) decrease in sexual function. Women see a decline in their reproductive system during menopause. Women may also experience osteoporosis (loss of calcium in bones). Both men and women experience osteoarthritis due to wear of joint tissue.

There is a change in roles and relationships during middle age. Many people retire in middle age, and their children are grown and leave home. These changes can bring about increased leisure time and changes in economic status.

Later Life

During the final stages of life, a greater emphasis is put on maintaining physical function and independence. Some elderly people experience dementia or Alzheimer's disease, which is characterized by a progressive loss of mental function and memory due to loss of brain cells. It is possible to make lifestyle changes and commitments to help delay or prevent dementia. Since aging is associated with loss, there is a certain amount of grief associated with aging that individuals must learn how to deal with.

Life expectancy is the average length of time that an individual can expect to live. Life expectancy in developed countries like the United States has increased over time. It is possible that, in time, the average life span will be 100 to 120 years.

Health span refers to the length of time that one is generally healthy and free from serious disease. Family and community resources can often help older adults to stay active, involved, and independent. Rehabilitation is the return to normal functioning after an injury or illness. Remediation is the restoring of function through alternative methods. Government aid to elderly individuals includes (1) housing subsidies, (2) Medicare, (3) Medicaid, and (4) food stamps.

Death and Bereavement

Death and bereavement are a natural part of life and affect all individuals at one time or another. Death can challenge emotional and intellectual security. Death is the cessation of all body functions; the heart stops beating and breathing ceases. Life-support systems and respirators can sustain some body functions for a period of time, but if an individual does not regain independent breathing and heart functions, once life support is terminated, death occurs. According to medical standards, brain death has four characteristics: (1) lack of receptivity and response to external stimuli, (2) absence of spontaneous breathing and muscular movement, (3) absence of reflexes, and (4) absence of brain activity (measured by an electroencephalogram (EEG)). Clinical death is determined by the absence of a heartbeat and breathing. Cellular death is the gradual process that occurs after heartbeat, respiration, and brain activity have stopped.

According to Mark W. Speece and Sandor B. Brent who have studied concepts of death, especially those held by children, there are four components to death: (1) universality (all living things must die), (2) irreversibility, (3) nonfunctionality, and (4) causality (there is a biological explanation for death to occur).

Because death is inevitable, there are things that individuals can do to make it easier for their families to make decisions and deal with the end of one's life. People prepare wills and other legal documents to express their wishes and dispense their estate (property and possessions) after death. Some people also leave (1) instructions to donate their organs after their death, (2) living wills that specify the medical treatment preferred in the event the individual cannot communicate his or her wishes, and (3) orders not to resuscitate.

End-of-life care can be home care, hospital care, or hospice care, depending on the wishes of the individual. In some cases when a patient is in a persistent vegetative state (unconscious and nonfunctioning) and cannot maintain normal body functions without artificial life support, life support is discontinued so as not prolong life in a vegetative state. The practice of withholding medical treatment (such as feeding tubes and ventilators) that may prolong a life is called passive euthanasia. In physician-assisted suicide, the physician provides lethal drugs at the patient's request to end his or her life. Active euthanasia is the intentional act of ending the life of someone who suffers from an incurable and painful disease.

In dealing with death, a person will go through a process of bereavement. Dr. Avery Weisman, who with his team at Massachusetts General Hospital conducted clinical studies of dying patients, describes the process of learning how to accept and deal with death as middle knowledge. Patients and their families seek a balance between maintaining hope of survival and acknowledging reality.

Based on Kubler-Ross' five psychological states of bereavement (denial, anger, bargaining, depression, and acceptance), Charles A. Corr describes four main dimensions a person experiences while coping with a life-threatening illness: (1) physical, (2) psychological, (3) social, and (4) spiritual. Dr. Corr, professor emeritus of philosophical studies, has published extensively on the topic of death and dying, and life and living.

Grief is a natural reaction to death or loss, and grief is present during the bereavement process. Mourning refers to the process by which the bereaved adjust to a loss and incorporates this loss into their lifestyle. Psychologist William Worden has studied grief extensively and has posited the theory of tasks of grief. He identifies four tasks of the mourning process: (1) accepting reality, (2) working through pain, (3) adjusting to a changed environment without the presence of the deceased individual, and (4) emotionally relocating the deceased and continuing with life.

SUBSTANCE USE AND ABUSE

The use of drugs—either prescription drugs or illegal drugs—has become widespread. Addictive behaviors are habits (usually bad habits) that get out of control. Addictive behavior has negative effects on health and well being.

Alcohol

Alcohol, or ethyl alcohol (ethanol), is a form of a psychoactive drug. The concentration of alcohol in a particular drink is reflected in its proof value, which is twice the percentage of alcohol in the beverage. A standard alcoholic drink, referred to with the term one drink, is 0.6 ounces of alcohol. As an individual ingests alcohol, about 20 percent is rapidly absorbed from the stomach into the bloodstream. About 75 percent is absorbed through the upper part of the small intestine, and the remainder enters the bloodstream later and farther down in the intestinal tract. Once it enters the bloodstream, alcohol induces the feeling of intoxication. The rate of absorption can be affected by the type of drink or the presence of food in the intestine. Food slows down the absorption of alcohol into the bloodstream, but carbonation or artificial sweeteners in the drink increase the rate of absorption.

Alcohol is metabolized primarily in the liver. Most alcohol consumed is converted to acetaldehyde, which is converted to acetate. Acetate is burned as an energy source or converted to fat and stored. About 2 to 10 percent of alcohol consumed is not metabolized in the liver, but is excreted by the lungs, kidneys, and sweat glands. This excretion is what enables us to smell alcohol on the breath of someone who has been drinking. It is the basis of breath and urine tests that measures approximate alcohol levels in the bloodstream. Blood alcohol concentration (BAC) is determined by the volume of alcohol consumed over a given time period and by individual factors, including (1) body weight, (2) percent body fat, and (3) sex.

Alcohol crosses a restrictive layer of cells into the brain where it disrupts the function of neurotransmitters. This disruption creates many of the typical affects of drinking alcohol or drunkenness. With heavy alcohol consumption, these effects become permanent.

BAC is an important factor in determining the effect of alcohol on an individual. Drinking low concentrations of alcohol can lead to feelings of relaxation, joviality, and mild euphoria. Drinking in social settings can enhance conviviality or assertiveness. Higher concentrations of alcohol lead to feelings of anger, sedation, and drowsiness, and decreased internal body temperature. Small doses of alcohol may improve sexual function, but higher doses can impair sexual function. The effects of alcohol wear off slowly, and individuals often experience what is known as a hangover. It is most likely caused by the breakdown of alcohol, which produces toxins in the body, dehydration, and hormonal fluctuations.

Drinking large quantities of alcohol over a short period of time can rapidly increase BAC levels to a lethal range. This leads to alcohol poisoning, which can result in death. Drinking alcohol in combination with taking illegal drugs is the leading cause of drug-related deaths. Drinking excessive amounts of alcohol can also lead to serious injury or violence. Alcohol consumption (1) impairs judgment, (2) weakens sensory perception and motor coordination, (3) reduces inhibitions, and (4) increases aggressiveness.

Health problems related to chronic or excessive use of alcohol include diseases of the digestive and cardiovascular systems and cancers of the throat, mouth, esophagus, liver, and breast. Alcoholics can also develop a liver condition, known as cirrhosis, and a weakened heart muscle, known as cardiac myopathy. Many alcoholics also experience brain damage and shrinkage of the brain due to loss of grey and white matter, reduced blood flow, and slowed metabolic rates. During pregnancy, alcohol consumption presents health risks to both the mother and the developing fetus, and there is a strong chance of the baby developing fetal alcohol syndrome, an alcohol-related neurodevelopmental disorder.

Alcohol abuse includes recurrent alcohol use that has negative consequences. Alcoholism involves more severe problems with alcohol use and a dependence on alcohol. There are different patterns of alcohol dependence, which include (1) regular daily intake of large amounts of alcohol, (2) regular heavy drinking on weekends only, (3) long periods of sobriety interspersed with periods of heavy alcohol consumption lasting weeks or months, or (4) heavy alcohol consumption during times of stress. When an alcoholic stops drinking abruptly, he or she experiences withdrawal, the symptoms of which are (1) tremors, (2) rapid pulse, (3) accelerated breathing, (4) insomnia, (5) nightmares and anxiety, and (6) sometimes hallucinations and delirium tremens (DTs).

Tobacco

Smoking tobacco is the most preventable cause of poor health, disease, and death in the United States, but millions of Americans still smoke. Regular tobacco use causes a physical dependence on nicotine, which is characterized (1) by a loss of control (cannot stop smoking), (2) a buildup of tolerance to nicotine, and (3) withdrawal symptoms in the absence of nicotine. Smoking is associated with a low education level, low income, and the use of other drugs. People who smoke are often imitating others, such as a parent or sibling.

Tobacco smoke is made up of hundreds of chemicals, including toxic and poisonous chemicals such as acetone, ammonia, hexamine, toluene, arsenic, and hydrogen cyanide. When these particles are condensed, they form a brown sticky solid called cigarette tar. Cigarettes also contain at least forty-three carcinogens (cancer-causing agents). Nicotine, the key psychoactive ingredient in tobacco smoke, affects the nervous system and can act as a stimulant or a depressant. It also causes an increase in blood pressure and heart rate, which put an undue strain on the heart muscles. Cigarette smoke contains carbon monoxide, a deadly gas that depletes the body's supply of oxygen. In addition, menthol cigarettes contain added menthol, which is a bronchiodilator that opens the airways of the lungs to allow more nicotine into the bloodstream.

Nicotine stimulates the cerebral cortex of the brain, and it stimulates adrenal glands to release adrenaline. Nicotine (1) inhibits the formation of urine, (2) constricts blood vessels, (3) accelerates heart rate, and (4) elevates blood pressure. Other long-term effects of smoking are (1) cardiovascular disease, especially coronary heart disease (CHD); (2) lung cancer and other cancers; (3) respiratory diseases; (4) stroke; (5) aortic aneurysm; (6) chronic obstructive pulmonary disease (COPD); (7) emphysema; (8) chronic bronchitis; (9) ulcers, (10) impotence; (11) reproductive health problems; (12) dental (gum) disease; and (13) diminished senses, such as taste and smell. CHD is the most widespread cause of death among cigarette smokers and is often the result of atherosclerosis (plaque buildup in the walls of arteries).

Other forms of tobacco use, such spit tobacco, cigars, pipes, clove cigarettes, and bidis, also cause nicotine addiction and health issues. Oral tobacco use can lead to leukoplakia, the development of white leathery patches on gums, tongue, and inside of cheeks. This can be benign or a sign of cancer.

Second-hand, or environmental, tobacco smoke (ETS) contains high levels of toxic chemicals and poisons that cause headaches, sinus problems, eye irritation, and nasal irritation. Long-term exposure to ETS is linked to lung cancer and heart disease. Children and infants of parents who smoke are at greater risk of health issues. Smoking during pregnancy leads to an increase in the rate of (1) miscarriage, (2) stillbirth, (3) congenital abnormalities, (4) low birth weight, and (5) premature births. There are also (6) risks of SIDS and the development of behavioral problems and long-term impairments.

Other Drugs

Drug abuse is a harmful pattern of illegal or prescription drug use that persists in spite of negative consequences to health and psychological and social well-being. Dependence on drugs involves taking them compulsively despite any adverse effects that use might have. Studies show that the reasons for drug use are (1) curiosity; (2) rebellion; (3) escape from boredom; (4) the desire to alter one's mood; (5) relief of anxiety, depression, or other psychological problems; and (6) the lure of an illicit activity.

Psychoactive drugs affect the mind and body function by altering brain chemistry. The properties of the drug and how it is used affect how the body or brain reacts to it. The effect of these drugs also is dependent upon user factors, such as psychological and physiological factors, and social factors, such as the social and physical environment surrounding the drug user. Psychoactive drugs include (1) opioids, (2) central nervous system (CNS) stimulants and depressants, (3) marijuana, (4) hallucinogens, and (5) inhalants.

- *Opioids,* also called narcotics, are drugs used to relieve pain; they cause drowsiness and induce a state of euphoria. Opioids also reduce anxiety, produce feelings of lethargy and apathy, and affect the ability to concentrate. Some common opioids are opium, morphine, heroin, methadone, oxycodone, hydrocodone, methadone, and codeine. These drugs are typically injected or absorbed through snorting, sniffing, or smoking.

- *CNS depressants* slow down the activity of the nervous system. They reduce anxiety and also cause mood changes, impair muscular coordination, slur speech, and induce sleep or drowsiness. Results of use can vary from mild sedation to death. CNS depressants include alcohol, barbiturates, and anti-anxiety drugs, also called tranquilizers or sedatives. The latter includes valium, Xanax, methaqualone (Quaaludes) and gamma hydroxyl butyrate (GHB or liquid ecstasy). Tranquilizers help individuals cope during waking hours and are prescription medications. Barbiturates are used to help individuals calm down and sleep. They are used as an anesthesia and also for the treatment of anxiety, insomnia, and epilepsy. People are usually introduced to CNS depressants through a medical prescription or through peers.

- *CNS stimulants* speed up the activities of the nervous system and cause an accelerated heart rate, a rise in blood pressure, dilation of the pupils and bronchial tubes, and an increase in gastric and adrenal secretions. Examples of some common CNS stimulators include cocaine, nicotine, and amphetamines, which include dextroamphetamine, methamphetamine, crystal methamphetamine, ephedrine, and caffeine.

- *Marijuana* used in low doses causes euphoria and a relaxed attitude. Very high doses cause feelings of depersonalization and sensory distortion. The long-term effects of marijuana include chronic bronchitis and some cancers. Using marijuana during pregnancy can impair fetal growth.

- *Hallucinogens* alter perception, feelings, and thought and can also cause an altered sense of time, mood changes, and visual disturbances. Hallucinogens include LSD (lysergic acid diethylamide), mescaline, psilocybin, STP, DMT, MDMA, PCP, and ketamine.

- *Inhalants,* which are present in a number of common household products, can cause delirium, loss of consciousness, heart failure, suffocation, and death. Inhalants can be categorized as volatile solvents (paint thinner, glue, gasoline), aerosols (sprays containing propellants and solvents), nitrites (butyl nitrite and amyl nitrite), and anesthetics (nitrous oxide).

Treatment of drug addictions include medication, self-help groups, rehabilitation and drug treatment centers, peer counseling, and counseling for family members.

Substance-Use Behaviors

Addictive behaviors are habits that have gotten out of control and have a negative effect on health. The source or cause of an addiction can be the result of (1) hereditary factors, (2) personality, (3) lifestyle, or (4) environmental factors.

Drug addiction is defined as (1) the compulsive desire for a drug, (2) the need to increase drug dosage, (3) harmful effects to the addicted individual and those around them, and (4) psychological and physical dependence. Physical dependence is the most dangerous effect of drug use. A physical dependence means that the body relies on the drug for normal function. Removal of a drug from an individual who is physically dependent can produce significant withdrawal symptoms, including (1) irritability, (2) depression, (3) physical pain, and (4) death. Psychological dependence includes an intense desire to continue using a particular drug or drugs.

Drug habituation shares the same characteristics as drug addiction without the same level of compulsion or increased need of higher doses. Drug habituation is accompanied by psychological dependence, but not physical dependence.

Drug users can develop a tolerance to drugs so that they need an increased dosage to get the same effects. Cross tolerance relates to a tolerance of all drugs that are in the same family. The misuse of prescription medication is classified as substance misuse, whereas substance abuse is the use of any drug to a degree that is harmful to the individual.

FITNESS AND NUTRITION

Part of having a healthy lifestyle is being physically fit and eating well. Regular exercise and proper diet are important wellness factors.

Components of Physical Fitness

Exercise lowers the risk of cardiovascular disease by (1) lowering blood fat levels, (2) reducing high blood pressure, and (3) preventing arterial blockage. Exercise also (1) reduces the risk of some cancers, osteoporosis, and diabetes; (2) boosts the immune system; (3) improves psychological health; and (4) prevents injuries and lower back pain. The amount of exercise needed to maintain or improve a particular level of fitness is determined by the FITT principle. In the acronym FITT, "F" represents frequency (how often), "I" represents intensity (how hard), and "T" represents both time (how long) and type (what kind of activity).

There are two types of exercise: (1) aerobic and (2) anaerobic. During aerobic exercise, oxygen is supplied to all areas of the body. During anaerobic exercise, the body cannot be oxygenated fast enough to supply energy to muscles from oxygen alone. This type of exercise involves a high intensity of effort.

Endurance training is a form of aerobic activity. It improves the function of chemical systems in the body and enhances the body's ability to utilize food energy. It includes exercises with continuous rhythmic movements, such as walking, jogging, cycling, and aerobic dancing. An indicator of the level of aerobic activity performed is the calculation of one's target heart rate, which can be calculated by subtracting age from 220.

There are five components to physical fitness: (1) cardiorespiratory endurance, (2) muscular strength, (3) muscular endurance, (4) flexibility, and (5) body composition.

- *Cardiorespiratory endurance* is the ability to perform prolonged, large muscle, dynamic exercises at a moderate- to high-intensity level. It increases the strength of the heart and certain related physical functions: (1) the heart pumps more blood volume per heartbeat, (2) the resting heart rate and resting blood pressure decrease, (3) blood supply to tissue improves, and (4) the body is better able to cool itself. General guidelines recommend endurance exercise three to five times a week for 20 to 60 minutes. It is also recommended that resistance (strength) training be performed twice a week.

- *Muscular strength and endurance* involves exerting force against significant resistance (weight lifting). Strength training should be done about 2 nonconsecutive days a week and should involve 8 to 12 repetitions of 8 to 10 different exercises. Strength training improves physical fitness and increases muscle mass, which means the body will require more energy to sustain life. There are three ways to improve muscle strength:

  o *Isometric exercises* are static and focus only on resistance (for example: pushing against a wall). It is difficult to measure the effectiveness of an isometric exercise, so they are not used often.
  o *Progressive resistance exercises,* or isotonic exercises, are those that provide a fixed amount of resistance, such as the use of traditional free weights.
  o *Isokinetic exercises* are those that include a range of motion and resistance provided by a mechanical source. The development of muscular endurance includes the ability to keep a specific muscle group contracted for a long period of time or to continually contract the same muscle group for a long period of time.

- *Flexibility* is defined as the ability to move joints through a full range of motion. Flexibility depends on (1) the structure of a particular joint, (2) the length and elasticity of its connective tissue, and (3) nervous system activity surrounding the joint. Flexible pain-free joints are important for maintaining good health and well-being. Stretching can help to provide flexibility and should include exercises for all the major muscle groups and joints. One should do a series of active, static stretches at least two to three days per week. Muscle and joint injury can be treated with the R-I-C-E method: Rest, Ice, Compression, and Elevation.

- A healthy *body composition* includes a higher proportion of fat-free body mass than fat mass. The proportion of fat-free to fat mass varies by age and sex. A higher concentration of body fat, especially in the abdominal region, can lead to health issues, including (1) high blood pressure,

(2) heart disease, (3) stroke, (4) joint problems, (5) gall bladder disease, (6) back pain, (7) diabetes, and (8) cancer. Body composition can be altered by proper exercise and a healthy diet.

The ability to perform a particular activity is linked to six skill-related fitness criteria: (1) speed, (2) power, (3) agility, (4) balance, (5) coordination, and (6) reaction time. Increasing physical activity can be done (1) in an effort to improve overall health and wellness, (2) as a part of a weight management program, and (3) to manage or prevent the onset of disease. Regular exercise lowers the risk of cardiovascular diseases, cancer, osteoporosis, and Type II diabetes.

Obesity

Many people exercise as part of a regimen to overcome obesity. Obesity can (1) be caused by genetic factors or (2) be due to the set point theory, which maintains that the body prefers to stay at its current weight, making it difficult for a person to drop below that weight. People who were overweight as babies may develop more fat cells, a condition known as hypercellular obesity, and this may make them more susceptible to being fat as adults. People who eat more calories than they expend have hypertrophic obesity in which the fat cells expand to increase in volume and hold more fat tissue. People can remedy obesity through (1) diet modification, (2) physical intervention (appetite suppressants to control food intake), or (3) behavioral intervention (increased physical activity).

Good Nutrition and Its Effects

There are about forty-five essential nutrients that the body requires to maintain its maximum level of health and well-being. Food provides the essential nutrients and fuel that bodies require. The energy in foods is expressed in terms of kilocalories, commonly referred to as calories. Macronutrients include protein, fat, and carbohydrates, and each of these supply energy to the body in differing amounts. Fat provides nine calories (kilocalories) per gram, protein provides four calories per gram, and carbohydrates provide four calories per gram.

Proteins are composed of chains of amino acids folded into a complex three-dimensional structure. Proteins (1) form muscle and bone; (2) are required for the production of blood, enzymes hormones, and cell membranes; and (3) are found in various forms in every cell of the body. Food obtained from animal sources (meat, eggs) provides complete proteins, but food from plant sources provides incomplete proteins.

Fats are the best source of energy for the body and are stored in the body for long-term energy use. Fats also help to insulate the body and protect internal organs. Most fats are similar in structure: three fatty acids forming a triglyceride. Foods contain saturated or unsaturated fats or both. Saturated fats are solid at room temperature and generally found in animal products. Unsaturated fats generally come from a plant source and are liquid at room temperature. Trans fatty acids are unsaturated fats that have been altered so that their shape affects their behavior in the body.

Saturated and trans fats pose health risks, but some fats can be beneficial elements of a healthy diet. Omega-3 fatty acids are healthy polyunsaturated fats found in fish, nuts, and some plant-based foods like avocadoes. Omega-3 fatty acids (1) reduce the tendency to form blood clots, (2) inhibit inflammation, (3) decrease abnormal heart rhythms, and (4) help to reduce the risk of heart attacks, high blood pressure, and stroke in some people.

Carbohydrates supply energy to cells and are the exclusive supply of energy for the brain and other parts of the nervous system and red blood cells. Carbohydrates are either (1) simple or (2) complex. Simple carbohydrates include sucrose, fructose, maltose, and lactose; these provide sweetness to foods. Complex carbohydrates are found in starches and dietary fiber, nondigestible carbohydrates in many plants. Fiber can help manage diabetes and high cholesterol levels and improve intestinal health. Soluble fiber turns into a gel in the intestine, and binds to cholesterol to move it through the digestive tract. Insoluble fiber absorbs water and helps digestion. All carbohydrates break down into glucose, and cells take up glucose as an energy source. Foods that have a rapid effect on increasing glucose levels have a high glycemic index.

There are thirteen vitamins needed for proper nutrition and for proper maintenance of chemical and cellular processes. Four types of vitamins are fat-soluble (Vitamins A, D, E, and K) and nine are water-soluble (C and the eight B-complex vitamins: thiamin, riboflavin, niacin, B-6, folate, B-12, biotin, and pantothenic acid). Deficiencies in these essential vitamins can cause serious illness or death.

There are also seventeen essential minerals needed in a healthy diet. Minerals are inorganic substances such as calcium, phosphorous, sulfur, sodium, potassium, and magnesium that (1) regulate body functions, (2) help in growth and maintenance of body tissue such as teeth and muscles, and (3) help in the release of energy from foods eaten.

Water is required to (1) digest and absorb food, (2) transport substances to different areas of the body, (3) lubricate joints and organs, and (4) help maintain body temperature. Water is found in almost all food sources.

Dietary Reference Intakes (DRI) are recommended intakes for essential nutrients that meet the needs for overall health and well-being. The Dietary Guidelines for Americans address the prevention of diet-related diseases (cancer, diabetes, cardiovascular disease).

By law, almost all foods require labels that break down the composition of the food into fats, proteins, carbohydrates, fiber, and sodium. Serving sizes have been standardized, health claims of particular foods are regulated, and dietary supplements must also have food labels.

RISK FACTORS, DISEASES, AND DISEASE PREVENTION

Infectious Diseases, Including Sexually Transmitted Diseases, Prevention and Control

In order to contact an infectious disease, several components are required: (1) an agent, (2) an entry point, (3) a reservoir, and (4) an exit point. A disease-producing agent—a pathogen—can be bacterial, viral, or fungal. The entry point can be either (1) direct (bodily fluids, droplets, or fecal matter) or (2) indirect (inanimate objects or nonhuman organisms, for example, mosquitoes). For a disease agent to cause a full-blown infection, there needs to be a place in the body for it to "live"; this is the reservoir. An infectious disease needs an exit point so that it can leave its host and infect others (for example, mouth and nose for the common cold).

There are four basic stages of an infection:

1. *Incubation* is the silent stage where symptoms are not apparent, but an individual is capable of infecting others.

2. During the *prodromal stage,* the pathogen, or disease agent, multiplies rapidly. During this stage, the infected individual (host) will experience some symptoms and is more likely to infect others.

3. During the *peak*, or acme, stage, the symptoms are most intense; this is the most contagious phase of the disease.

4. The final stage is the *recovery stage* when the body begins to heal from the effects of the disease.

When a foreign organism infects the body, a complex system of responses is activated, two of which are (1) the inflammatory response and (2) the immune response. The immune system is the body's defense system against disease, and defense is carried out by different types of white blood cells, which are produced in bone marrow: (1) neutrophils (travel in blood stream to site of infection), (2) macrophages (devour pathogens and dead cells), (3) natural killer cells (directly destroy virus-infected cells or cancerous cells), (4) dendrite cells (eat pathogens and activate lymphocytes), and (5) lymphocytes (travel through the bloodstream and the lymphatic system).

Within the lymphatic system, lymph nodes filter bacteria and other substances from the lymph. When the lymph nodes are fighting off an infection, they fill with cells and become swollen. The location of the swollen nodes can alert doctors to the area of an infection. There are two types of lymphocytes in the lymphatic system: (1) T cells and (2) B cells. T cells come in several forms. (1) Helper T cells that are activated to send a message to killer T cells and B cells; B cells produce antibodies and killer T cells kill the antigens of the infecting agent. (2) Suppressor T cells and (3) memory T cells remember the immune system's response to a specific infecting agent to help prevent reinfection or to allow for a quick recovery if a reinfection occurs. The suppressor T cells also stop the antibody production of the B cells once the infection is overcome. If lymphocytes do not function properly and attack the body, the result is an autoimmune disease such as lupus and rheumatoid arthritis.

There are three types of immunity that can fight off an infection.

1. *Artificially Acquired Immunity (AAI):* Occurs when the body develops immunity from a vaccination or an infection

2. *Naturally Acquired Immunity (NAI):* Occurs when the body itself fights off an infection and develops a "memory" for the infection to prevent reinfection

3. *Passively Acquired Immunity (PAI):* Occurs when antibodies are used until the body develops a natural immunity against an infection.

Bacterial infections can be treated with the administration of antibiotics that can kill bacteria. Vaccines can be administered to manipulate the immune system and cause the body to develop immunity to a certain infectious disease.

There are seven sexually transmitted diseases (STDs) that pose a major health threat:

1. *AIDS (Acquired Immune Deficiency Syndrome):* Most serious and life-threatening sexually transmitted disease. AIDS is caused by the virus known as HIV (human immunodeficiency

virus), which compromises the immune system by attacking helper T cells (CD4 T cells). With a compromised immune system, individuals with HIV are more susceptible to viral, bacterial, and fungal infections. HIV is spread through bodily fluids such as blood, semen, and vaginal secretions, and it can pass from mother to baby. There is a great variation in the incubation time of HIV; from about 6 months to up to ten years. There is no cure for AIDS or HIV, but there are medicines available that can reduce the rate of destruction of helper T cells. AIDS is a preventable disease.

2. *Chlamydia:* Causes painful urination in both men and women. Most women with chlamydia are asymptomatic, but it can lead to pelvic inflammatory disease (PID) if left untreated. It increases a woman's risk of infertility and ectopic pregnancies and can lead to male infertility. It is the leading cause of epididymitis, an inflammation of the sperm-carrying ducts. It is the most widely spread bacterial STD in the United States.

3. *Gonorrhea:* Causes urinary discomfort in men and has a yellowish, green discharge. Most women infected with gonorrhea are asymptomatic, but some experience painful urination, vaginal discharge, and severe menstrual cramps. Gonorrhea can also infect the throat and rectum. It is treated with antibiotics.

4. *Human Papillomavirus (HPV):* Most common viral STD in the United States. About 6.2 million Americans are infected each year. Most people with HPV have no symptoms, and the virus can be cleared by the immune system without any treatment. However, if the infection persists, it can lead to genital warts (and common warts) and genital cancers, cervical cancers, penile cancers, and some forms of rectal and oropharyngeal cancers. Genital forms of HPV are spread through sexual activity. The spread of HPV can be decreased with the use of condoms, but condoms don't completely prevent the disease because viral particles are found in areas of sex organs that are not protected by a condom. Protection against HPV infection is now available in the form of a vaccine.

5. *Genital Herpes:* Infects about one in five adults in the United States, but most people don't know that they're infected. There are over 50 different herpes viruses, including chicken pox, shingles, and mononucleosis. There are two types of the herpes simplex virus: HSV-1 and HSV-2. HSV-1 generally causes cold sores, or oral-labial herpes. Most people are exposed to HSV-1 during childhood, and about 50 to 80 percent of adults have immunity to HSV-1. HSV-2 generally causes genital herpes, but may also cause oral-labial lesions. HSV-2 usually occurs between adolescence and early adulthood (ages 18 to 25). HSV can be transmitted through sexual activity, including oral sex, and HSV infections usually last a lifetime. The virus can lie dormant for long periods of time and reactivate at any time. An infected individual is always contagious. There is no cure for herpes, but antiviral drugs can shorten the time of an outbreak. A person on suppression therapy can still infect others.

6. *Hepatitis B:* Causes inflammation of the liver and can cause serious and sometimes permanent damage. Hepatitis B is found in most body fluids and can be transmitted sexually, through intravenous drug use, and during pregnancy and delivery. Hepatitis B is similar to HIV, but it can spread through both sexual and nonsexual contact. Hepatitis B can be fatal, and there is no cure, but there is an effective vaccine against hepatitis B. Infection can be prevented by avoiding

sexual contact that involves the exchange of body fluids, by using condoms, and by not sharing needles (including tattoo needles and tools used for body piercing).

7. *Syphilis:* Caused by bacteria and can therefore be treated with antibiotics. After infection, an individual may be asymptomatic for four to ninety days. During the primary stage of infection, a small ulcer called a chancre appears and heals within four to eight weeks. During the secondary phase, an infected person experiences a sore throat and loss of hair. In the late, or latent, stage, the disease is asymptomatic and can last fifteen to twenty-five years. During the late stage, the infection can reoccur and can cause permanent damage or even death. Although syphilis can be treated with antibiotics, damage of the late stage of infection can be irreversible.

Early diagnosis and treatment of STDs can help avoid complications and prevent the spread of STDs. Condom use is another effective way to help prevent the spread of some STDs.

The Cardiovascular System

The cardiovascular system consists of the heart and blood vessels. The heart pumps blood to the lungs through the pulmonary artery and to the body via the aorta. There are six major preventable risk factors for cardiovascular disease (CVD): (1) smoking, (2) high blood pressure, (3) unhealthy cholesterol levels, (4) inactive lifestyle, (5) obesity or being overweight, and (6) diabetes.

Risk factors of CVD that can be changed are (1) high triglyceride levels and (2) psychological and (3) social factors. Risk factors that cannot be avoided include (1) age over 65 years, (2) being male or (3) African American, and (4) having a family history of CVD. Some common CVDs include (1) atherosclerosis (hardening of arteries), (2) heart attacks, (3) stroke (ischemic and hemorrhagic stroke), (4) congestive heart failure, (5) peripheral arterial disease (PAD), (6) congenital heart disease, (7) rheumatic heart disease, and (8) heart valve problems.

Some ways to prevent CVD include (1) dietary changes, especially decreasing fat intake (saturated and trans fats) and increasing fiber intake; (2) regular exercise; (3) avoidance of tobacco; (4) managing blood pressure and cholesterol levels; and (5) developing effective ways of dealing with anger and stress.

Types of Cancer

Cancer is found in all areas of the body. Treatment options depend on where the cancer is located, what type of cancer it is, and how far the cancer has progressed. Most cancers take the form of a tumor, which is a mass of tissues that serves no physiological purpose. Tumors may be (1) benign (noncancerous) or (2) malignant (cancerous). The spreading of cancer cells from one part of the body to another is called metastasis. The extent or spread of a cancer can be categorized into one of five progressive stages (stages 0 to IV).

Malignant tumors are classified according to the type of cells the cancer is infecting.

- *Carcinomas* form from epithelial cells and account for 85 percent of all tumors. They can be on the skin, mouth, throat, intestinal tract, glands, nerves, breasts, genital structures, urinary tract, lungs, kidneys, and liver.

- *Sarcomas* are found in connective tissue such as bones, cartilage, and membranes that cover muscles and fat. Sarcomas account for about 2 percent of all cancers.

- *Melanoma* are skin cancers caused by prolonged sun exposure. (The American Cancer Society ABCD guidelines for determining if a mole may be melanoma are A = asymmetrical, B = border irregularity, C= color change, and D= diameter greater than six millimeters).

- *Lymphomas* are cancers of the lymph nodes or lymphatic system.

- *Leukemias* are cancers of blood-forming cells (bone marrow cells).

- *Neuroblastomas* generally affect children and start in the immature cells of the CNS.

- *Adenocarcinomas* are found in the endocrine glands.

- *Hepatomas* are found in liver cells.

Cancer is due to uncontrolled growth of cells because of (1) genetics, (2) exposure to mutagens, (3) viral infection, and (4) chemical substances in food and air. Dietary factors such as meat, certain types of fats, and alcohols can increase the risk of some cancers. Other risks include lack of exercise, obesity, certain types of infection, and exposure to chemicals and radiation.

Diets that include a large variety of fruits and vegetables are linked to lower cancer rates. Also, self-monitoring and regular screening tests are essential to early cancer detection. Early signs of detection can be remembered with the acronym CAUTION (C = change in bowel or bladder habits, A = a sore throat that does not heal, U = unusual bleeding or discharge, T = thickening or lump in breasts or elsewhere, I = indigestion or difficulty swallowing, O = obvious change in wart or mole, N = nagging cough or hoarseness).

Cancer treatment methods include (1) surgery, (2) chemotherapy, and (3) radiation. Lifestyle choices can greatly reduce the risk of cancer: (1) avoid smoking, (2) control diet and weight, (3) exercise, (4) protect skin, and (5) avoid environmental and occupational carcinogens.

Immune Disorders

Immune disorders occur when the body comes under attack by its own cells (as is the case in cancers). The immune system often is able to detect cells that have recently transformed to cancer cells and is capable of destroying these cells. However, if the immune system starts to break down because of (1) age, (2) immune disorders like HIV, or (3) chemotherapy, cells can grow out of control, often before the immune system can detect danger.

Another immune disorder occurs when a body confuses its own cells with foreign organisms. Some autoimmune disorders in which the immune system is too sensitive and attacks cells within the body include systemic lupus erythematosus and rheumatoid arthritis.

Diabetes, Arthritis, and Genetic-Related Disorders

Diabetes is a disease in which the pancreas does not produce insulin normally. Insulin is a necessary biological chemical that is used to process sugar in the body. There are three types of diabetes: (1) Type I diabetes, which usually occurs during childhood; (2) Type II diabetes, most often an adult disease; and (3) gestational diabetes, a temporary condition during pregnancy. An individual with Type I will spend a lifetime monitoring blood sugar levels and injecting insulin. Obesity is a risk factor for Type II diabetes and can often be controlled through diet and exercise.

Rheumatoid arthritis (RA) is an autoimmune response that occurs when the immune system attacks healthy joint tissue. Symptoms of RA include (1) stiffness, (2) joint pain, (3) swelling, (4) redness, (5) throbbing, (6) muscle atrophy, (7) joint deformity, and (8) limited mobility. Osteoarthritis is caused by the wear and tear on joints and is usually a problem in older people. There is no cure for arthritis, but pain management and therapy can help.

Genetic disorders are diseases inherited from biological parents. Some common genetic disorders include:

- *Hemophilia:* Passed from gene-carrying mothers to sons; the individual is missing factors needed for blood clotting

- *Retinitis Pigmentosa:* Eye disease that causes light sensitivity and the degeneration of the retina to eventual blindness

- *Color Blindness:* Affects the ability to discern colors

- *Cystic Fibrosis:* Fatal condition caused by a defective gene prompting the body to produce a sticky mucus in the lungs and elsewhere

- *Thalassemia:* Blood disorder that causes the body to produce less-than-normal levels of hemoglobin

- *Polydactyl:* Having extra fingers or toes; can be corrected by surgery

- *Achondroplasia:* Condition causing dwarfism

- *Adult Polycystic Kidney Disease:* Fluid-filled cysts that impact a kidney's function

Common Neurological Disorders

Two common neurological disorders are Rett syndrome and Huntington's disease. Rett syndrome affects brain development and is similar to autism. It is most common in girls. Development of affected individuals slows after 18 months, and children begin losing motor function.

Huntington's disease is characterized by the degeneration of brain cells in certain parts of the brain, causing loss of intellect, muscle control, and emotional control. A child of a parent with Huntington's disease has a 50/50 chance of inheriting the gene and developing the disease.

SAFETY, CONSUMER AWARENESS, AND ENVIRONMENTAL CONCERNS

In contemporary society, anxiety and even fear of random violence have become daily concerns for many. Learning simple safety procedures for the home and workplace can provide some sense of security. Being good health-care consumers and protecting the environment are other areas of interest to many.

Safety

Many injuries are caused by the interaction of humans with environmental factors. The chief areas of safety concern are (1) personal, (2) residential, (3) recreational, (4) motor vehicle, and (5) gun use.

To maintain personal safety, one must (1) think carefully, (2) be aware of one's surroundings, and (3) avoid atypical patterns.

Some common residential safety principles are (1) have a fire escape plan, (2) install a peep hole, (3) change locks when moving into a new home, and (4) ask strangers such as repair men for identification. The home can contain many (5) poisonous substances that should be kept safe and away from children and pets. Home fires can be prevented (6) by being safe about where smoking is done and (7) keeping cooking and heating equipment in good working order. Always be prepared for fire emergencies with a (8) fire escape route and (9) smoke detectors.

Many injuries during recreational activities are the result of (1) misuse of equipment, (2) lack of experience, (3) use of alcohol, or (4) failure to wear proper safety equipment, such as a bike helmet or seat belt.

Practicing motor vehicle safety includes (1) keeping a mechanical vehicle in good working order, (2) avoiding drinking and driving, (3) driving defensively, (4) giving pedestrians the right of way, and (5) keeping noise at a reasonable level.

The proper handling and storage of firearms can help prevent injuries. People should (1) know the gun laws in their state, (2) never point a gun at an unintended target, (3) keep fingers off the trigger, (4) educate children, and (5) keep guns locked away.

Intentional Injuries and Violence

Violence is defined as the intent to inflict harm on another person through the use of physical force. Factors that contribute to violence include (1) social factors, such as violence in the media, and (2) interpersonal factors, such as age, gender, ethnic background, and socioeconomic background. Alcohol and drug use also contribute to violence.

Battering and forms of child abuse occur at every socioeconomic level. The issue with this type of violence is the need for the abuser to control other people. Child sexual abuse most often results in serious trauma for the child because the abuser is usually a trusted adult.

Most rape victims are women, and most know their attackers. Date rape includes the problems of two individuals with different standards of appropriate sexual behavior and different perceptions of actions. Sexual harassment is defined as unwelcome sexual advances or other conduct of a sexual nature that has a negative effect on an individual or creates an intimidating or hostile environment.

Strategies for reducing violence include conflict resolution, social skills development, and education programs, especially ones that foster tolerance of diversity.

Consumer Awareness

In general, a person should seek the help of a health-care professional for symptoms that are severe, unusual, persistent, or recurrent. When new symptoms first occur, there are self-treatment options that may benefit some individuals and certain health issues. When using self-medication, it's important to follow some simple guidelines:

- Reading the label and following the directions carefully

- Not exceeding the recommended daily dose

- Using caution if taking other medications or supplements

- Selecting medications with only one active ingredient

- Buying generic drugs that have the same active ingredients as the brand-name product

- Never taking medication from an unlabeled container or in the dark where you cannot read the label

- Consulting a health-care professional before taking the medication if a woman is pregnant

- Using special caution with aspirin (it should not be given to children or adolescents who may have the flu or any other type of virus because of the risk of Reye's syndrome)

When seeking professional medical treatment, patients have the option of choosing conventional medical care or complementary and alternative medicine (CAM). CAM practices are not part of conventional or mainstream health care or medical practice taught in U.S. medical schools. CAM practices include (1) traditional Chinese medicine (TCM), (2) acupuncture, (3) energy therapies, (4) mind-body interventions, and (5) herbal remedies.

Conventional medicine, also called biomedicine or standard Western medicine, is based on the application of the scientific method. Professionals who practice conventional medicine include medical doctors, doctors of osteopathic medicine, podiatrists, optometrists, and dentists. Allied health-care providers include registered nurses (RN), licensed vocational nurses (LVN), physical therapists, social workers, registered dieticians (RD), physician assistants (PA), nurse practitioners (NP), and certified nurse midwives.

Health care in the United States is financed by a combination of private and public insurance plans. Medicare, Medicare Advantage, Medigap, and Medicaid account for 45 percent of patient coverage in the United States. There are several health insurance options for those covered by private insurance: (1) traditional fee-for-service, (2) health maintenance organizations (HMOs), (3) preferred provider organizations (PPOs), and (4) point-of-service plans (POS). A health savings account (HAS) is a tax-exempt personal savings account that can be used for certain qualified medical expenses.

Some important health-care terms are (1) deductible (amount an insured individual needs to pay before an insurance company covers costs), (2) coinsurance (sharing of costs between the patient and insurance, (3) exclusion (procedures not covered by an individual's health insurance), and (4) preexisting conditions (diseases or conditions that existed before a person bought insurance from a company and that will not be covered by the company).

Environmental Concerns

Environmental health began with the effort to control communicable diseases. It has since expanded to include concern for air quality, global warming, and various forms of pollution, all of which play a role in some infectious and chronic diseases. Increased amounts of air pollutants are especially dangerous for children, elderly adults, and those with chronic health conditions. Some of the gases that are causing damage to our atmosphere and contributing to air pollution are (1) carbon dioxide, (2) carbon monoxide, (3) chlorofluorocarbons (CFCs), (4) methane, and (5) nitrous oxide. Factors that contribute to poor air quality are (1) heavy motor vehicle traffic, (2) burning of fossil fuels, (3) hot weather, and (4) stagnant air.

The greenhouse effect occurs as thermal energy from the sun is trapped in the atmosphere by pollutants. This causes a rise in Earth's temperature that, in turn, causes droughts, ice melt, smog, and acid rain. In addition, the ozone layer that shields Earth's surface from the harmful UV rays of the sun is thinning and has developed holes in certain regions, including above Antarctica.

Concerns for water quality worldwide focus on (1) pathogenic organisms (bacterial, viral, or protozoan), (2) chemical and hazardous waste, and (3) water shortages, including shortages of clean drinking water. Water can become polluted by (1) human and animal wastes (the presence of the bacteria coliform is an indicator of feces in a water supply); (2) biological imbalance; (3) toxins, including pesticides; and (4) other chemical waste that is mutagenic (causes mutations), carcinogenic (causes cancer), or teratogenic (causes birth defects).

Land pollution is caused by landfills that release chemicals into the ground, pesticides, automobiles, accidental spills, radon gas, and nuclear reactors. Pollution also comes in the form of noise; loud and persistent noise can lead to hearing loss and stress.

POST-TEST ANSWER SHEET

1. Ⓐ Ⓑ Ⓒ Ⓓ	13. Ⓐ Ⓑ Ⓒ Ⓓ	25. Ⓐ Ⓑ Ⓒ Ⓓ	37. Ⓐ Ⓑ Ⓒ Ⓓ	49. Ⓐ Ⓑ Ⓒ Ⓓ
2. Ⓐ Ⓑ Ⓒ Ⓓ	14. Ⓐ Ⓑ Ⓒ Ⓓ	26. Ⓐ Ⓑ Ⓒ Ⓓ	38. Ⓐ Ⓑ Ⓒ Ⓓ	50. Ⓐ Ⓑ Ⓒ Ⓓ
3. Ⓐ Ⓑ Ⓒ Ⓓ	15. Ⓐ Ⓑ Ⓒ Ⓓ	27. Ⓐ Ⓑ Ⓒ Ⓓ	39. Ⓐ Ⓑ Ⓒ Ⓓ	51. Ⓐ Ⓑ Ⓒ Ⓓ
4. Ⓐ Ⓑ Ⓒ Ⓓ	16. Ⓐ Ⓑ Ⓒ Ⓓ	28. Ⓐ Ⓑ Ⓒ Ⓓ	40. Ⓐ Ⓑ Ⓒ Ⓓ	52. Ⓐ Ⓑ Ⓒ Ⓓ
5. Ⓐ Ⓑ Ⓒ Ⓓ	17. Ⓐ Ⓑ Ⓒ Ⓓ	29. Ⓐ Ⓑ Ⓒ Ⓓ	41. Ⓐ Ⓑ Ⓒ Ⓓ	53. Ⓐ Ⓑ Ⓒ Ⓓ
6. Ⓐ Ⓑ Ⓒ Ⓓ	18. Ⓐ Ⓑ Ⓒ Ⓓ	30. Ⓐ Ⓑ Ⓒ Ⓓ	42. Ⓐ Ⓑ Ⓒ Ⓓ	54. Ⓐ Ⓑ Ⓒ Ⓓ
7. Ⓐ Ⓑ Ⓒ Ⓓ	19. Ⓐ Ⓑ Ⓒ Ⓓ	31. Ⓐ Ⓑ Ⓒ Ⓓ	43. Ⓐ Ⓑ Ⓒ Ⓓ	55. Ⓐ Ⓑ Ⓒ Ⓓ
8. Ⓐ Ⓑ Ⓒ Ⓓ	20. Ⓐ Ⓑ Ⓒ Ⓓ	32. Ⓐ Ⓑ Ⓒ Ⓓ	44. Ⓐ Ⓑ Ⓒ Ⓓ	56. Ⓐ Ⓑ Ⓒ Ⓓ
9. Ⓐ Ⓑ Ⓒ Ⓓ	21. Ⓐ Ⓑ Ⓒ Ⓓ	33. Ⓐ Ⓑ Ⓒ Ⓓ	45. Ⓐ Ⓑ Ⓒ Ⓓ	57. Ⓐ Ⓑ Ⓒ Ⓓ
10. Ⓐ Ⓑ Ⓒ Ⓓ	22. Ⓐ Ⓑ Ⓒ Ⓓ	34. Ⓐ Ⓑ Ⓒ Ⓓ	46. Ⓐ Ⓑ Ⓒ Ⓓ	58. Ⓐ Ⓑ Ⓒ Ⓓ
11. Ⓐ Ⓑ Ⓒ Ⓓ	23. Ⓐ Ⓑ Ⓒ Ⓓ	35. Ⓐ Ⓑ Ⓒ Ⓓ	47. Ⓐ Ⓑ Ⓒ Ⓓ	59. Ⓐ Ⓑ Ⓒ Ⓓ
12. Ⓐ Ⓑ Ⓒ Ⓓ	24. Ⓐ Ⓑ Ⓒ Ⓓ	36. Ⓐ Ⓑ Ⓒ Ⓓ	48. Ⓐ Ⓑ Ⓒ Ⓓ	60. Ⓐ Ⓑ Ⓒ Ⓓ

answer sheet

POST-TEST

Directions: Carefully read each of the following 60 questions. Choose the best answer to each question, and darken its letter on your answer sheet. The Answer Key and Explanations can be found following this Post-Test.

1. Which type of psychological disorder is characterized as an affective disorder?
   - (A) Schizophrenia
   - (B) Stress
   - (C) Bipolar
   - (D) Anxiety

2. Which of the following is NOT a risk factor for heart disease that can be controlled?
   - (A) Weight
   - (B) Heredity
   - (C) Physical activity
   - (D) Hypertension

3. Which of the following are drugs derived from opium?
   - (A) Hallucinogens
   - (B) Tranquilizers
   - (C) Narcotic analgesics
   - (D) Barbiturates

4. Which of the following is an eating disorder caused by abstaining from eating food?
   - (A) Bulimia
   - (B) Obesity
   - (C) Dieting
   - (D) Anorexia

5. Which of the following lists three of the five chief areas of safety concern?
   - (A) Recreational, residential, personal
   - (B) Recreational, fire, violence
   - (C) Experience, personal, residential
   - (D) Recreational, physical, violence

6. What is the term used for people who reach the highest level in Maslow's Hierarchy of Needs?
   - (A) Achievers
   - (B) Needy
   - (C) Transcenders
   - (D) Champions

7. The primary stage of Selye's General Adaptation Syndrome (GAS) is
   - (A) resistance.
   - (B) compulsion.
   - (C) exhaustion.
   - (D) alarm.

8. Which condition is the result of too much tobacco use?
   - (A) Scar tissue
   - (B) Swollen lymph nodes
   - (C) Leukoplakia
   - (D) HIV

9. Which type of stress is "good stress" according to Dr. Selye?
   - (A) Distress
   - (B) Eustress
   - (C) Astress
   - (D) Stressors

10. Which type of nutrient is the most calorie-dense?
    - (A) Carbohydrates
    - (B) Fats
    - (C) Proteins
    - (D) Fiber

11. Which of the following are fat-soluble vitamins?

    (A) Calcium, magnesium, and iron

    (B) A, B, C, and D

    (C) A, D, E, and K

    (D) B, C, and iron

12. Which of the following is an atypical sexual behavior that causes harm to one's self or others?

    (A) Shared touching

    (B) Transsexualism

    (C) Paraphilia

    (D) Masturbation

13. When referring to checking for melanoma, what does ABCD stand for?

    (A) Abnormal, blending, color, description

    (B) Asymmetry, border, color variation, diameter

    (C) Asymmetry, big, color, deformed

    (D) Abnormal, big, color, depth

14. What are the two forms of dietary fiber?

    (A) Organic and inorganic

    (B) Vegetable and mineral

    (C) Soluble and insoluble

    (D) Carbohydrate and fat

15. A vaccine can instill which type of immunity?

    (A) Naturally acquired immunity

    (B) Passively acquired immunity

    (C) Artificially acquired immunity

    (D) Actively acquired immunity

16. In a developing fetus, which is the first major body system to develop?

    (A) Skeletal system

    (B) Circulatory system

    (C) Nervous system

    (D) Digestive system

17. What is the hormone cortisol secreted in response to?

    (A) Puberty

    (B) Release of ovum

    (C) Exhaustion

    (D) Stress

18. Which of the following is NOT a method of birth control relying on periodic abstinence?

    (A) Rhythm method

    (B) Basal body temperature

    (C) Annual review

    (D) Billings cervical mucus

19. Which of the following refers to hardening of the arteries?

    (A) Arteriosclerosis

    (B) Atherosclerosis

    (C) Angina pectoris

    (D) Hypertension

20. What does HIV stand for?

    (A) Human immune virus

    (B) Human immunodeficiency virus

    (C) Habitual immunodeficiency virus

    (D) Habitual immune virus

21. Which of the following is best categorized as a way in which to ensure personal safety?

    (A) Wear a bicycle helmet

    (B) Have a fire escape

    (C) Avoid atypical patterns

    (D) Drive defensively

22. Which type of depression is best controlled by medication?

    (A) Primary depression

    (B) Secondary depression

    (C) Seasonal affective disorder

    (D) Loneliness

23. Which neurological disorder has traits similar to autism?

    (A) Huntington's disease

    (B) Rett syndrome

    (C) Muscular dystrophy

    (D) Neurofibromatosis

24. An agent or particle that causes disease is known as a/an

    (A) vaccine.

    (B) antibody.

    (C) antagonist.

    (D) pathogen.

25. When a sperm is inserted into an ovum outside the women's body, this process is called

    (A) in vitro fertilization.

    (B) in vivo fertilization.

    (C) intracytoplasmic sperm injection.

    (D) gamete intrafallopian transfer.

26. Amniocentesis can detect which of the following abnormalities?

    (A) Diabetes

    (B) Cleft palate

    (C) Cystic fibrosis

    (D) Phocomelia

27. Which of the following types of cancer develops in connective tissue?

    (A) Melanoma

    (B) Sarcoma

    (C) Leukemia

    (D) Carcinoma

28. Which type of specialist would be considered part of CAM health care?

    (A) Dentist

    (B) Registered nurse

    (C) Herbalist

    (D) Midwife

29. The five stages of grieving according to Kubler-Ross are

    (A) denial, anger, bargaining, depression, acceptance.

    (B) denial, pleading, grief, rage, closure.

    (C) sadness, anger, grief, closure, moving on.

    (D) sadness, crying, anger, closure, moving on.

30. Sexual conduct that has a negative effect on an individual is defined as

    (A) sexism.

    (B) sexual harassment.

    (C) sexual misconduct.

    (D) rape.

31. Which of the following is an example of a remediation technique for an elderly person?

    (A) Teaching them to read

    (B) Physical therapy to learn to walk again after an accident

    (C) Providing a scooter for someone who has severe arthritis

    (D) Prescribing medication to treat an infection

32. Which of the following psychological disorders is linked to anxiety?

    (A) Phobias

    (B) Depression

    (C) Schizophrenia

    (D) Bipolar

33. Which dimension of health focuses on understanding self-purpose?

    (A) Physical

    (B) Intellectual

    (C) Emotional

    (D) Spiritual

34. Which is the most dangerous type of drug dependence?

    (A) Physical

    (B) Psychological

    (C) Emotional

    (D) Tolerance

35. What is the most basic level of need according to Maslow?

    (A) Love

    (B) Physiological

    (C) Esteem

    (D) Self-actualization

36. Which of the following lists the first three stages of addiction?

    (A) Habituation, compulsion, overuse

    (B) Reinforcement, compulsion, loss of control

    (C) Reinforcement, loss of control, negative consequences

    (D) Compulsion, escalation, loss of control

37. Which of the following is one of the goals of the National Healthy People Initiative?

    (A) Eliminate economic disparities among Americans

    (B) Eliminate health disparities among Americans

    (C) Focus on holistic health for all Americans

    (D) Focus on making alcohol and tobacco illegal

38. Which of the following is defined as an interpersonal factor that may contribute to violence and intentional injury?

    (A) Social factors

    (B) Gender

    (C) Violence in the media

    (D) Address

39. What percentage of marriages in the U.S. end in divorce?

    (A) 20 to 25 percent

    (B) 30 to 35 percent

    (C) 50 to 55 percent

    (D) 70 to 75 percent

40. Which of the following describes an authoritative parenting style?

    (A) High demandingness, low responsiveness

    (B) High demandingness, high responsiveness

    (C) Low demandingness, high responsiveness

    (D) Low demandingness, low responsiveness

41. Where is the primary site of alcohol metabolism in the body?

    (A) Intestines

    (B) Stomach

    (C) Liver

    (D) Kidneys

42. Which of the following is released during the estrogenic phase of the female menstrual cycle?

    (A) Ovum

    (B) Follicle stimulating hormone

    (C) Corpus luteum

    (D) Progesterone

43. Which of the following best describes anaerobic exercise?

    (A) Respiration of oxygen in the lungs

    (B) Insufficient oxygen supply to reach all muscles

    (C) Cardiorespiratory endurance

    (D) Continuous rhythmic movements

44. The belief that you are sick without any medical data to support this claim is a
    (A) dissociative disorder.
    (B) mood disorder.
    (C) somatoform disorder.
    (D) seasonal affective disorder.

45. During an infection, which type of cells fills the lymph nodes to fight off bacteria and other pathogens?
    (A) Antibodies
    (B) T cells
    (C) B cells
    (D) T cells and B cells

46. The initial stage of attraction between two individuals is
    (A) behavior.
    (B) sharing.
    (C) marketing.
    (D) mutual support.

47. Which of the following is NOT one of the four components of death?
    (A) Universality
    (B) Irreversibility
    (C) Nonfunctionality
    (D) Randomness

48. The R-I-C-E method of treating muscle and joint injury includes
    (A) rest, independence, compassion, and emotion.
    (B) regular, intervals, conditioning, and endurance.
    (C) rest, ice, conditioning, and endurance.
    (D) rest, ice, compression, and elevation.

49. The cluster of cells that implants into the endometrial lining of the uterus is called a
    (A) zygote.
    (B) fetus.
    (C) blastocyst.
    (D) ovum.

50. Which of the following is NOT a self-treatment option?
    (A) Watchful waiting
    (B) Exercise
    (C) Over-the-counter medication
    (D) Prescription medication

51. Synesthesia caused by hallucinogens is best described by which example?
    (A) Being able to interpret a poem
    (B) Identifying all the ingredients in a particular food by taste
    (C) Being able to taste a picture
    (D) Being able to describe how a flower smells

52. The most common viral STD in the United States is
    (A) AIDS.
    (B) HPV.
    (C) HSV-1.
    (D) HSV-2.

53. Which of the following best describes the greenhouse effect?
    (A) Thermal energy is trapped in Earth's atmosphere by air pollutants.
    (B) Sunlight is getting more powerful.
    (C) Holes in the ozone layer allow more heat from the sun in the atmosphere.
    (D) Many green plants are able to grow in certain regions of Earth.

54. Which of the following pollutes fresh water supplies?
    (A) Radon gas
    (B) Automobiles
    (C) Pesticides
    (D) Sewage

55. Which of the following is NOT a private health insurance option?
    (A) Health management organization
    (B) Medicare
    (C) Preferred provider organization
    (D) Point-of-service plan

56. What does the "U" stand for in the acronym CAUTION used to describe early detection of cancer?
    (A) Unusual growths
    (B) Unusual weight loss
    (C) Unusual bleeding or discharge
    (D) Unusual symptoms

57. Which of the following is NOT considered an environmental stressor?
    (A) Earthquake
    (B) Acts of violence
    (C) Financial concerns
    (D) Industrial accidents

58. During which stage of labor is the cervix opened completely?
    (A) First stage
    (B) Second stage
    (C) Third stage
    (D) Postpartum stage

59. The most widespread cause of death among cigarette smokers is
    (A) cancer.
    (B) cardiovascular disease.
    (C) bronchitis.
    (D) chronic obstructive pulmonary disease (COPD).

60. Progressive resistance exercises are called
    (A) isotonic.
    (B) isokinetic.
    (C) isometric.
    (D) stretching.

ANSWER KEY AND EXPLANATIONS

1. C	13. B	25. C	37. B	49. C
2. B	14. C	26. C	38. B	50. D
3. C	15. C	27. B	39. C	51. C
4. D	16. B	28. C	40. B	52. B
5. A	17. D	29. A	41. C	53. A
6. C	18. C	30. B	42. B	54. C
7. D	19. A	31. C	43. B	55. B
8. C	20. B	32. A	44. C	56. C
9. B	21. C	33. D	45. D	57. C
10. B	22. A	34. A	46. C	58. A
11. C	23. B	35. B	47. D	59. B
12. C	24. D	36. B	48. D	60. A

1. **The correct answer is (C).** Bipolar disorder is characterized as an affective disorder. Defective disorders are mental disorders in which an individual doesn't have the ability to express proper emotions. Choice (A) is incorrect because schizophrenic disorders are characterized by disorganized thought and distortions of reality. Choice (B) is incorrect because stress is a type of anxiety disorder. Choice (D) is incorrect because anxiety is a disorder that causes physical symptoms and is not characterized as an affective disorder.

2. **The correct answer is (B).** An individual is not capable of controlling inherited factors, and some hereditary factors put individuals at a higher risk for heart disease. Choice (A) is incorrect because weight can be controlled by diet and exercise. Choice (C) is incorrect because an individual has control over his or her level of physical activity. Choice (D) is incorrect because hypertension can be controlled with exercise, diet, and weight management.

3. **The correct answer is (C).** Drugs derived from opium are called narcotic analgesics. Choice (A) is incorrect because hallucinogens are either chemically synthesized or derived from mescaline (cactus). Choice (B) is incorrect because tranquilizers are sedatives produced synthetically. Choice (D) is incorrect because barbiturates are also produced by synthetic methods.

4. **The correct answer is (D).** Anorexia is an eating disorder in which individuals abstain from eating to a point of starvation. Choice (A) is incorrect because bulimia is an eating disorder in which individuals eat and then purge (vomit). Choice (B) is incorrect because obesity is a condition of being more than thirty pounds overweight. Choice (C) is incorrect because dieting can be used as a healthy way to control weight.

5. **The correct answer is (A).** Many injuries are caused by the interaction of humans with environmental factors, and the chief areas of safety concern are (1) personal, (2) residential, (3) recreational, (4) mo-

answers post-test

tor vehicle, and (5) gun use. Choice (B) is incorrect because fire and violence are not categories of individual safety. Choice (C) is incorrect because experience is not an area of safety concern, although lack of experience can be classified as a concern when operating motor vehicles. Choice (D) is incorrect because violence and physical concerns are not individual safety categories.

6. **The correct answer is (C).** People who reach self-actualization, the highest level of Maslow's Hierarchy of Needs, are called transcenders. Choice (A) is incorrect because Maslow doesn't define people who reach the highest level as achievers. Choice (B) is incorrect because people at the highest level are not needy. Choice (D) is incorrect because people at the highest level of Maslow's Hierarchy aren't champions.

7. **The correct answer is (D).** The first stage of Dr. Hans Selye's GAS theory is alarm, also known as the fight-or-flight stage. Choice (A) is incorrect because resistance is the second stage in the GAS theory. Choice (B) is incorrect because compulsion is not a stage of the GAS theory. Choice (C) is incorrect because exhaustion is the third stage of the GAS theory.

8. **The correct answer is (C).** Leukoplakia is a condition characterized by white patches on the tongue that aren't easily removed and are usually the result of excess oral tobacco use. Choice (A) is incorrect because scar tissue isn't a result of too much tobacco use. Choice (B) is incorrect because swollen lymph nodes are a symptom of an infection. Choice (D) is incorrect because HIV is a virus that can lead to the development of AIDS.

9. **The correct answer is (B).** The term "eustress" refers to good stress on the body, such as during exercise or stress induced by the desire to do well at something. Choice (A) is incorrect because distress is usually considered "bad stress." Choice (C) is incorrect because the term "astress" is not a psychological term. Choice (D) is incorrect because stressors are factors that can cause any type of stress.

10. **The correct answer is (B).** Fats are the most calorie-dense nutrients; there are nine calories per one gram of fat. Choices (A) and (C) are incorrect because carbohydrates and proteins both have seven calories per gram. Choice (D) is incorrect because fiber is a type of carbohydrate and has seven calories per gram.

11. **The correct answer is (C).** Fat-soluble vitamins include A, D, E, and K. Choice (A) is incorrect because calcium, magnesium, and iron are minerals, not vitamins. Choice (B) is incorrect because the B vitamins and vitamin C are water-soluble. Choice (D) is incorrect because iron is not a vitamin; it's a mineral.

12. **The correct answer is (C).** Paraphilia is any sexual act that causes harm to one's self or others. Choice (A) is incorrect because shared touching is usually done with mutual consent between two individuals. Choice (B) is incorrect because transsexualism refers to cases where an individual's gender doesn't match gender identity. Choice (D) is incorrect because masturbation is a form of self-stimulation and is generally not harmful.

13. **The correct answer is (B).** The ABCD test for melanoma refers to checking a mole for asymmetry, border irregularity, color variation, and a diameter larger than a quarter of an inch. Choices (A), (C), and (D) are incorrect because these aren't the criteria for checking for the properties of a melanoma.

14. **The correct answer is (C).** The two forms of dietary fiber are soluble and insoluble. Both are derived from indigestible plant material. Choice (A) is incorrect because all fiber is organic material. Choice (B) is incorrect because fiber is not a mineral. Choice (D) is incorrect because all fiber derived from plants is a source of carbohydrates and fats are not fiber.

15. **The correct answer is (C).** A vaccine is an injection of either an inactivated or a live virus that builds up immunity in the body. This is a form of artificially acquired immunity. Choice (A) is incorrect because naturally acquired immunity occurs when the body builds up immunity after being exposed to a disease. Choice (B) is incorrect because passively acquired immunity is the process of using antibodies to develop immunity. Choice (D) is incorrect because actively acquired immunity is not a type of immunity.

16. **The correct answer is (B).** The first major system to develop in the fetus is the circulatory system. Choices (A), (C), and (D) are incorrect because the circulatory system is fully developed before the skeletal, nervous, and digestive systems.

17. **The correct answer is (D).** Cortisol is a hormone that is released in conjunction with epinephrine in response to stress. Choice (A) is incorrect because cortisol is not a sex hormone that is elevated during puberty. Choice (B) is incorrect because estradiol and LSH are released during ovulation. Choice (C) is incorrect because cortisol is released as a response to stress, not exhaustion.

18. **The correct answer is (C).** Choices (A), (B), and (D) are true about methods of birth control relying on periodic abstinence, so they are incorrect answers to the question. Choice (A) is incorrect because the rhythm method of birth control involves keeping track of the phase of the menstrual cycle and abstaining from sexual activity during fertile periods. Choice (B) is incorrect because basal body temperature can be monitored to determine the time of ovulation, so this is a form of birth control. Choice (D) is incorrect because the release of the thickening of cervical mucus can be used as an indicator of ovulation. This leaves choice (C) as the correct answer because annual review is not a method of birth control.

19. **The correct answer is (A).** Choice (B) is incorrect because atherosclerosis refers to the buildup of plaque inside the walls of arteries. Choice (C) is incorrect because angina pectoris refers to chest pain caused by an insufficient amount of oxygen reaching the heart. Choice (D) is incorrect because hypertension refers to high blood pressure.

20. **The correct answer is (B).** HIV is a virus that attacks the immune system and is called human immunodeficiency virus. Choice (A) is incorrect because HIV is a virus that causes deficiencies in the immune system. Choice (C) is incorrect because the "H" stands for human, not habitual. Choice (D) is incorrect because HIV doesn't stand for habitual immune virus.

21. **The correct answer is (C).** Avoiding atypical patterns, especially after dark, is one way to ensure personal safety. Choice (A) is incorrect because wearing a bicycle helmet is best categorized as recreational safety. Choice (B) is incorrect because planning a fire escape route is a part of residential safety. Choice (D) is incorrect because driving defensively is categorized as motor vehicle safety.

22. **The correct answer is (A).** Antidepressants are most successful in the treatment of primary depression. Choice (B) is incorrect because secondary depression is linked to a traumatic event and best treated by therapy. Choice (C) is incorrect because seasonal affective disorder is related to the amount of sunlight a person receives and is treated with exposure to UV light. Choice (D) is incorrect because loneliness is not a form of depression.

23. **The correct answer is (B).** Rett syndrome is a neurological disorder, most common in girls, with traits similar to autism. Choice (A) is incorrect because Huntington's disease is a genetic disorder in which there is a degeneration of brain cells. Choice (C) is incorrect because muscular dystrophy is a genetic disorder in which there is a

degeneration of skeletal muscles. Choice (D) is incorrect because neurofibromatosis is a genetic disorder that causes tumors to grow in the nervous system.

24. **The correct answer is (D).** Choice (A) is incorrect because a vaccine is used to prevent infection. Choice (B) is incorrect because antibodies are used to fight against infection. Choice (C) is incorrect because an agent of infection is referred to as a pathogen, not an antagonist.

25. **The correct answer is (C).** Intracytoplasmic sperm injection is the process of inserting a single sperm into a single egg (ovum). Choice (A) is incorrect because in vitro fertilization is the process of fertilizing several eggs with sperm outside the woman's body and then reinserting them. Choice (B) is incorrect because in vivo fertilization is fertilization inside the woman's body. Choice (D) is incorrect because gamete intrafallopian transfer (GIFT) is removal of the egg from the ovary and mechanical insertion into the fallopian tube. Sperm is then added in hopes of fertilization.

26. **The correct answer is (C).** Cystic fibrosis, the fatal accumulation of too much mucous in the lungs, is the result of a genetic abnormality and can be detected through amniocentesis. Choice (A) is incorrect because diabetes isn't detected before birth. Choice (B) is incorrect because a cleft palate is a physical abnormality and isn't detected by amniocentesis. Choice (D) is incorrect because the short limbs associated with phocomelia are not detected by amniocentesis.

27. **The correct answer is (B).** Sarcoma is cancer that begins in connective tissue. Sarcomas are very rare and only account for 2 percent of all cancers. Choice (A) is incorrect because melanoma originates in the skin. Choice (C) is incorrect because leukemia is a cancer that originates in the blood. Choice (D) is incorrect because carcinoma doesn't originate in connective tissue.

28. **The correct answer is (C).** An herbalist would be considered a part of complementary and alternative medicine (CAM). Choices (A), (B), and (D) are incorrect because all of these professionals practice conventional medicine.

29. **The correct answer is (A).** According to the process of grieving outlined by Kubler-Ross, the five stages of grieving are denial, anger, bargaining, depression, and acceptance. Choices (B), (C), and (D) are incorrect because these aren't the five processes of grieving as outlined by Kubler-Ross.

30. **The correct answer is (B).** Sexual harassment is defined as unwelcome sexual advances or other conduct of a sexual nature that has a negative effect on an individual or creates an intimidating or hostile environment. Choice (A) is incorrect because sexism is discrimination against an individual based on his or her sex. Choice (C) is incorrect because sexual misconduct is a more general term, whereas sexual harassment is more specific to the actions and language that are unwelcome. Choice (D) is incorrect because rape involves the act of sexual intercourse against an individual's will.

31. **The correct answer is (C).** The remediation technique for elderly adults involves restoring function through alternative methods, such as providing a scooter or wheelchair for mobility. Choice (A) is incorrect because teaching someone to read is not remediation; it's literacy training. Choice (B) is incorrect because physical therapy is a type of rehabilitation, not remediation. Choice (D) is incorrect because prescribing medication to cure an infection is a medical treatment, not remediation.

32. **The correct answer is (A).** Phobias are a psychological disorder linked to anxiety. Choice (B) is incorrect because depression is an affective disorder. Choice (C) is incorrect because schizophrenia is a disorder linked to hallucinations and distortion. Choice (D)

is incorrect because bipolar is an affective disorder.

33. **The correct answer is (D).** Spiritual health focuses on the ability to understand one's purpose in the world and the ability to serve others. Choice (A) is incorrect because physical health focuses on physical wellness. Choice (B) is incorrect because intellectual health focuses on creativity and problem solving. Choice (C) is incorrect because emotional health focuses on the ability to deal with stress and conflict and to have emotionally appropriate response to external stimuli.

34. **The correct answer is (A).** Physical dependence is the most dangerous type of drug dependence; bodily functions become dependent on a drug. Choice (B) is incorrect because psychological dependence is a mental state and easier to overcome than physical dependence. Choice (C) is incorrect because emotional dependence falls into the category of psychological dependence. Choice (D) is incorrect because tolerance isn't a type of drug dependence.

35. **The correct answer is (B).** Physiological needs such as food and shelter are humans' most basic needs. Choice (A) is incorrect because according to Maslow, love falls under the third level of need. Choice (C) is incorrect because esteem is the fourth hierarchical level of need. Choice (D) is incorrect because self-actualization is actually the highest level of need.

36. **The correct answer is (B).** The first three stages of addiction include reinforcement of the behavior, a compulsion or craving to engage in the behavior, and loss of control. Choice (A) is incorrect because habituation and overuse aren't terms used to describe the stages of addiction. Choice (C) is incorrect because negative consequences are the fifth stage of addiction. Choice (D) is incorrect because escalation is the fourth stage of addiction.

37. **The correct answer is (B).** The National Healthy People Initiative has two broad goals: (1) to increase the quality and years of healthy life for all and (2) to eliminate health disparities among population groups in the United States. Choice (A) is incorrect because the Healthy People Initiative doesn't focus on economic measures. Choice (C) is incorrect because the Healthy People Initiative isn't limited to a holistic approach. Choice (D) is incorrect because the Healthy People Initiative isn't trying to eliminate tobacco and alcohol.

38. **The correct answer is (B).** There are several interpersonal factors that contribute to violence: gender, age, ethnic background, and socioeconomic background. Choice (A) is incorrect because social factors are different contributing factors to violence. Choice (C) is incorrect because violence in the media is considered a social factor that contributes to violence and intentional injury. Choice (D) is incorrect because one's address is a social, not an interpersonal factor.

39. **The correct answer is (C).** In the United States, approximately 50 to 55 percent of all marriages end in divorce. Choices (A), (B), and (D) are thus incorrect.

40. **The correct answer is (B).** An authoritative parenting style is one involving high demandingness and high responsiveness. Choice (A) is incorrect because high demandingness and low responsiveness is characteristic of an authoritarian style of parenting. Choice (C) is incorrect because low demandingness and high responsiveness is characteristic of a permissive parenting style. Choice (D) is incorrect because low demandingness and low responsiveness is characteristic of an uninvolved parenting style.

41. **The correct answer is (C).** Choices (A) and (B) are incorrect because most alcohol is metabolized in the liver, not in the intestines or the stomach. Choice (D) is incorrect because only about 2 percent of alcohol is

not metabolized in the liver and is excreted by the lungs, kidneys, and sweat glands.

42. **The correct answer is (B).** During the estrogenic phase of menstruation, there is a release of follicle stimulating hormone (FSH) and luteinizing hormone (LH). Choice (A) is incorrect because the ovum is released during the ovulation phase. Choice (C) is incorrect because the follicle changes into the corpus luteum during ovulation. Choice (D) is incorrect because progesterone levels are low during the estrogenic phase of the menstrual cycle.

43. **The correct answer is (B).** During anaerobic exercise, the body cannot be oxygenated fast enough to supply energy to muscles from oxygen alone. Choice (A) may seem like a good answer, but it doesn't relate to anaerobic exercise. Choices (C) and (D) are incorrect because they describe aerobic exercise.

44. **The correct answer is (C).** With a somatoform disorder, an individual presents physical ailments without any medical condition to support these ailments. Choice (A) is incorrect because dissociative disorders can cause a sudden, but temporary change in identity or consciousness. Choice (B) is incorrect because a mood disorder is itself a category of disorders. Choice (D) is incorrect because seasonal affective disorder is a form of depression.

45. **The correct answer is (D).** Both T cells and B cells fill lymph nodes to help fight off infection. Choice (A) is incorrect because antibodies are produced by B cells. Choices (B) and (C) are incorrect because each is only half the answer; both T cells and B cells fill lymph nodes during infection.

46. **The correct answer is (C).** There are several stages of attraction between two people, and the initial stage is defined as marketing, during which an individual will market his or her best self. Choice (A) is incorrect because the behavior stage of attraction is the third stage in which a relationship develops into friendship or passionate love. Choice (B) is incorrect because the sharing phase of attraction is the second stage. Choice (D) is incorrect because mutual support develops in the last stage of attraction.

47. **The correct answer is (D).** Randomness is not a component of death; all death has causality and there is a biological explanation for the occurrence of death. Choice (A) is incorrect because death is universal property; all living things must die. Choice (B) is incorrect because death is irreversible. Choice (C) is incorrect because death leaves an organism nonfunctional.

48. **The correct answer is (D).** Muscle and joint injuries can be treated with rest, ice, compression, and elevation. Choices (A), (B), and (C) are incorrect because they don't describe the components of the R-I-C-E method.

49. **The correct answer is (C).** The cluster of cells that grows after an egg has been fertilized and implants in the endometrial lining is called a blastocyst. Choice (A) is incorrect because once the egg is fertilized by a sperm, it becomes a zygote. Choice (B) is incorrect because after the blastocyst implants in the endometrial lining, it develops into a fetus. Choice (D) is incorrect because ova are unfertilized eggs.

50. **The correct answer is (D).** Prescription medication can only be prescribed by a medical doctor. Choices (A), (B), and (C) are incorrect because they are all methods of self-treatment.

51. **The correct answer is (C).** Being able to taste a picture is an example of synesthesia. Choice (A) is incorrect because interpreting poem requires language skills, not synesthesia, and it is a normal intellectual ability. Choice (B) is incorrect because a person with an educated sense of food tastes could identify food ingredients. Choice (D)

is incorrect because describing the smell of a flower is a normal sensory ability.

52. **The correct answer is (B).** The human papillomavirus (HPV) is the most common STD, infecting approximately 6.2 million Americans each year. Choice (A) is incorrect because although AIDS is an STD, it isn't the most commonly spread STD. Choice (C) is incorrect because herpes simplex virus I is not more common than HPV. Choice (D) is incorrect because herpes simplex virus 2 is not more common than HPV.

53. **The correct answer is (A).** The greenhouse effect occurs as thermal energy from the sun is trapped in the atmosphere by air pollutants, which causes Earth's temperature to rise. Choice (B) is incorrect because the sun's effects on Earth may be getting stronger, but the sun is not getting more powerful. Choice (C) is incorrect because holes in the ozone layer contribute to a rise in Earth's temperature, but it is air pollution that causes the greenhouse effect. Choice (D) is incorrect because it doesn't describe the greenhouse effect.

54. **The correct answer is (C).** Freshwater sources can be polluted by pesticides, which are often found in agricultural runoff. Choice (A) is incorrect because radon gas is an odorless, tasteless, invisible gas that can cause cancer. Choice (B) is incorrect because automobiles cause air pollution. Choice (D) is incorrect because sewage is treated, so it doesn't pollute fresh water supplies.

55. **The correct answer is (B).** Medicare is provided by the federal government. Choices (A), (C), and (D) are incorrect answers to the question because they are private insurance programs.

56. **The correct answer is (C).** The "U" in the CAUTION acronym stands for unusual bleeding or discharge, which is a possible sign of cancer. Choices (A), (B), and (D) are incorrect because they don't describe what the "U" stands for in CAUTION.

57. **The correct answer is (C).** Financial concerns are common sources of everyday stress, but they are not due to environmental factors. Choices (A), (B), and (D) are incorrect because these are all examples of environmental stress.

58. **The correct answer is (A).** During transition, the cervix dilates to ten centimeters and is fully open. Choice (B) is incorrect because during the second stage of labor, the mother pushes the baby out and the cervix is already fully dilated. Choice (C) is incorrect because the placenta is delivered in the third stage. Choice (D) is incorrect because during the postpartum phase, the body begins to return to its pre-pregnancy state.

59. **The correct answer is (B).** The most widespread cause of death among cigarette smokers is cardiovascular disease and in particular coronary heart disease. Choice (A) is incorrect because although cigarette smoking is a primary cause of lung cancer and can cause other cancers, cardiovascular disease is responsible for more deaths among cigarette smokers. Choice (C) is incorrect because bronchitis is a result of cigarette smoking, but it isn't a leading cause of death. Choice (D) is incorrect because COPD is a result of cigarette smoking, but not the leading cause of death among smokers.

60. **The correct answer is (A).** Isotonic exercises are progressive resistance exercises that provide a fixed amount of resistance. Choice (B) is incorrect because isokinetic exercises are those that include a range of motion and resistance from a mechanical source. Choice (C) is incorrect because isometric exercises are static. Choice (D) is incorrect because stretching is done to increase flexibility.

SUMMING IT UP

- There are six dimensions to overall wellness: (1) physical, (2) spiritual, (3) emotional, (4) intellectual, (5) interpersonal, and (6) environmental.

- Lifestyle choices include (1) exercise, (2) diet, and (3) the choice to avoid unhealthy habits.

- The transtheoretical model is an effective approach to lifestyle management that includes (1) pre-contemplation, (2) contemplation, (3) preparation, (3) action, (4) maintenance, and (5) termination.

- Psychologist Abraham Maslow developed a pyramid expressing the hierarchy of human needs. According to Maslow, (1) the most basic needs are physiological, (2) then safety and security, (3) social relationships, (4) self-esteem, and (5) the highest level of need, self-actualization. Those who achieve self-actualization Maslow called transcenders.

- Erik Erikson described eight stages of a human's lifespan: (1) birth to one year, (2) one to three years, (3) three to six years, (4) six to twelve years, (5) adolescence, (6) young adulthood, (7) middle adulthood, and (8) older adulthood.

- There are several types of psychological disorders, including (1) anxiety disorders, (2) mood disorders, (3) bipolar disorders, (4) schizophrenia, (5) dissociative disorders, and (6) somatoform disorders.

- Two body systems control the physical response to stress: (1) nervous system and (2) endocrine system.

- Seyle's theory on stress is the General Adaptation Syndrome (GAS), which has three stages: (1) alarm, (2) resistance, and (3) exhaustion. Behavioral responses to stressors are controlled by the somatic nervous system.

- Addictive behaviors involve habits that have become out of control. Factors leading to addictive behaviors include (1) personality, (2) lifestyle, (3) heredity, (4) social and physical environments, and (5) the nature of the activity or substance.

- Reproduction refers to fertility, pregnancy, and various methods of birth control. Human germ cells and sex hormones are key elements of reproduction. Fertilization starts the process of human development. Infertility can be overcome with several methods of treatment.

- Pregnancy is divided into three trimesters, each lasting about three months. The birth process takes place in three stages.

- The birth control methods that can be used to prevent unwanted pregnancies are (1) barrier method, (2) intrauterine device, (3) hormonal methods, (4) natural methods, and (5) surgical sterilization.

- Human sexual response goes through the following phases: (1) excitement, (2) plateau, (3) orgasmic, and (4) resolution. Two physical responses to arousal are vasocongestion and muscular tension.

- Common male sexual dysfunctions are (1) erectile dysfunction, (2) premature ejaculation, and (3) retarded ejaculation. Common female sexual dysfunction includes (1) lack of desire to have sex, (2) failure to become aroused, and (3) failure to achieve orgasm.

- There are several stages of attraction between individuals: (1) marketing, (2) sharing, (3) behavior, (4) passionate love, and (5) enduring attachment. Challenges that a relationship faces may include (1) being open and honest, (2) having unrealistic expectations, (3) competitiveness, (4) having unequal or premature commitment, (5) balancing time spent together, (6) jealousy, and (7) supportiveness.

- There are typically four general styles of parenting: (1) authoritarian, (2) authoritative, (3) permissive, and (4) uninvolved.

- Healthy aging is the process of (1) growing into a productive adult, (2) coping with midlife issues, and (3) facing mortality in a positive, healthy way.

- According to Mark Speece and Sandor Brent, there are four components of death: (1) universality, (2) irreversibility, (3) nonfunctionality, and (4) causality.

- Kubler-Ross proposed five psychological states of bereavement: (1) denial, (2) anger, (3) bargaining, (4) depression, and (5) acceptance.

- Alcohol, or ethyl alcohol (ethanol), is a form of a psychoactive drug. Blood alcohol concentration (BAC) is determined by the volume of alcohol consumed over a given time period and by individual factors, including body weight, percent body fat, and sex.

- Health problems related to chronic or excessive use of alcohol include diseases of the digestive and cardiovascular systems and some cancers.

- Nicotine is the key psychoactive ingredient in tobacco smoke. It affects the nervous system and can act as a stimulant or a depressant.

- Cardiovascular disease, especially coronary heart disease (CHD), is the most widespread cause of death among cigarette smokers. CHD is often the result of atherosclerosis.

- Cigarette smoke is the primary cause of lung cancer and is linked to other cancers.

- Psychoactive drugs affect the mind and body function by altering brain chemistry. Psychoactive drugs include (1) opioids, (2) central nervous system (CNS) stimulants and (3) depressants, (4) marijuana, (5) hallucinogens, and (6) inhalants.

- Drug addiction is defined as (1) the compulsive desire for a drug, (2) the need to increase drug dosage, (3) harmful effects to the addicted individual and those around him or her, and (4) psychological and (5) physical dependence.

- There are five components of physical fitness: (1) cardiorespiratory endurance, (2) muscular strength, (3) muscular endurance, (4) flexibility, and (5) body composition. The ability to perform a particular activity is linked to skill-related fitness criteria: (1) speed, (2) power, (3) agility, (4) balance, (5) coordination, and (6) reaction time.

- There are about forty-five essential nutrients that the body requires to maintain its maximum level of health and well-being. Macronutrients include protein, fat, and carbohydrates, and each of these supplies energy to the body in differing amounts. There are thirteen vitamins and seventeen minerals that are essential.

- Water is required to (1) digest and absorb food, (2) transport substances to different areas of the body, (3) lubricate joints and organs, and (4) help maintain body temperature.

- In order to contact an infectious disease, several components are required: an agent, an entry point, a reservoir, and an exit point. Disease begins as a pathogen, which is the disease-producing agent. An agent can be bacterial, viral, or fungal.

- There are four basic stages of an infection: (1) incubation, (2) prodromal, (3) peak, and (4) recovery. The immune system is the body's defense system against disease, and defense is carried out by different types of white blood cells that are produced in bone marrow.

- Within the lymphatic system, there are lymph nodes that filter bacteria and other substances from the lymph. When the lymph nodes are fighting off an infection, they fill with cells and become swollen. In the lymphatic system, there are two types of lymphocytes: (1) T cells and (2) B cells.

- There are seven sexually transmitted diseases (STDs) that pose a major health threat: (1) AIDS, (2) herpes, (3) hepatitis, (4) syphilis, (5) chlamydia, (6) gonorrhea, and (7) the human papillomavirus (HPV).

- There are six major preventable risk factors for cardiovascular disease (CVD), including (1) smoking, (2) high blood pressure, (3) unhealthy cholesterol levels, (4) inactive lifestyle, (5) overweight or obesity, and (6) diabetes.

- Cancer is due to uncontrolled growth of cells because of (1) genetics, (2) exposure to a mutagen, (3) viral infection, and (4) chemical substances in food and air.

- Immune disorders occur when the body comes under attack by its own cells.

- Diabetes is a disease in which the pancreas does not produce insulin normally. Insulin is a necessary biological chemical that is used to process sugar in the body. There are three types of diabetes: (1) Type I, (2) Type II, and (3) gestational diabetes.

- Rheumatoid arthritis (RA) is an autoimmune response where the immune system attacks healthy joint tissue.

- Genetic disorders are diseases that are inherited from biological parents.

- Safety issues include (1) personal safety, (2) residential safety, (3) recreational safety, (4) motor vehicle safety, and (5) gun safety. Violence is defined as the intent to inflict harm on another person through the use of physical force.

- When seeking professional medical treatment, patients have the option of choosing conventional medical care or complementary and alternative medicine (CAM).

- Environmental health includes concern for (1) air quality, (2) global warming, and (3) various forms of pollution, all of which play a role in some infectious and chronic diseases.

NOTES

NOTES

NOTES

NOTES